Managing Your School Counseling Program: K-12 Developmental Strategies Second Edition

by

Joe Wittmer

With Original Contributions by:

Gail Adorno   Ellen Amatea   James Archer

Bonnie Baker   Kim Bloss   Barbara Brown

Chari Campbell   Mary Ann Clark   Tom Clawson

Doris Coy   Marjorie Cuthbert   Diane Daniels

Harry Daniels   Marie Faubert   Mary Flynt

William Goodman   Gerardo Gonzalez   Tom Harrison

Mary Hermann   Linda Kobylarz   Don C. Locke

Larry Loesch   Phyllis McLeod   Leslie Martin-Rainey

Robert D. Myrick Beverly O'Bryant   Pam Paris

Nancy Perry   James Pitts   Theodore Remley

Russell Sabella   John Schmidt   Pat Schwallie-Giddis

Susan Sears   Beverly Snyder   Sondra Smith

Rex Stockton   Carolyn Stone   Paul Toth

JoAnna White   Nicholas Vacc

Publisher—
Educational Media Corporation®
PO Box 21311
Minneapolis, MN 55421-0311

(612) 781-0088

http://www.**educationalmedia**.com

Production editor—
Don L. Sorenson, Ph.D.

Graphic design—
Earl R. Sorenson

Dedication

This book is dedicated to the two very important women in my life; my wife Sue, a high school counselor, and to our daughter Diane, an elementary school counselor.

References and Acknowledgments:

A very special thanks to each of the writers who contributed to this book. A special thanks also to the American School Counselor Association (ASCA) for permission to quote from, and/or reprint, several of their publications.

Every effort has been made to give proper acknowledgment to all those who have contributed to this book. Any omissions or errors are regretted and, upon notification, will be corrected in subsequent editions.

The Author

Joe Wittmer, Ph.D., Distinguished Professor of Counselor Education at the University of Florida, Gainesville, has been a teacher and a school counselor. He often serves as a consultant to school systems desiring to implement developmental school counseling programs using the American School Counselors Association's *National Standards for School Counseling Programs*.

Dr. Wittmer has written more than 75 professional journal articles and has authored or co-authored 13 books. His four latest books are: (1) *Large Group Counseling: A K-12 Sourcebook* (1995), (2) *Classroom Guidance Activities: A Sourcebook for Elementary School Counselors* (1997), (3) *The Peace Train: A School-wide Violence Prevention Program* (1999), and (4) *RSVP: Responsible Steps toward Violence Prevention: A Family Intervention Strategy* (1999).

Preface

Although four new chapters have been added to update this book, the objectives of the second edition remain the same as that of the first edition—to provide the reader an overview and a general understanding of (a) the historical perspectives and current activities of K-12 developmental school counselors, (b) their role and function, (c) techniques and strategies utilized by effective developmental school counselors, (d) the organization and management of developmental counseling programs, and (e) additional topics of interest to school counselors and school counselors-to-be.

This book is intended as a basic graduate level text for counselor education students training to become school counselors. Additionally, practicing school counselors will find the book helpful since it aims at the implementation and the management of the major concepts and practices of contemporary, K-12 developmental school counselors.

Interest in the developmental approach to school counseling is increasing. Since the approach is still comparatively new, the book will also be useful in acquainting administrators, curriculum directors, teachers, and others with the scope of developmental counseling. Guidance supervisors who are interested in new approaches and strategies for implementing and managing a K-12 developmental school counseling program will also find the book helpful.

The book is divided into seven (7) sections. In the first section, I begin with a brief history of school counseling followed by the reconceptionalization of the school counseling movement. The training and the competencies needed by the developmental K-12 school counselor are also presented, including a description of the CACREP standards of training as related to school counselor preparation. In addition, guidelines for beginning the implementation of a comprehensive, developmental guidance program are given along with a model for changing an existing program into a comprehensive, developmental one, using the American School Counselor Association's National Standards for School Counseling Programs. Section I concludes with the role and function of a K-12 developmental school counselor as viewed by various school systems, state departments of education, practicing counselors, and experts in the counseling field.

Section II, written by school counseling practitioners and/or counselor educators, is concerned with managing a developmental counseling program. More specifically, the roles and the functions of the contemporary elementary, middle, and high school counselor are presented.

Section III is a continuation of the role of the developmental school counselor as it concerns individual and small group counseling, and large group guidance.

Section IV concerns the counselor's role in working with diversity issues, counseling with special needs students, student victims of abuse, and gay and lesbian students.

Section V focuses on the developmental counselor as consultant and as coordinator of the career, appraisal, and educational aspects of the counseling program. In addition, a chapter addressing the school counselor/consultant and the family is included in this section.

Section VI is devoted to strategies for involving peers, parents, teachers, and other professionals in the developmental school counseling programs.

Section VII, the final section of the book, focuses on special topics that are of concern to today's developmental school counselors. More specifically, original chapters concerning school counselor credentialing, ethical and legal issues, accountability, public relations, and the counselor's professional image are presented.

In the introduction to each section, I have attempted to briefly present the background for, and the theme of, that particular section. Each contributor to the book wrote his/her chapter(s) *specifically* for this book. This is to acknowledge my heartfelt thanks to all of the authors for revising and updating their respective contributions. Without them this book would not have been possible.

Joe Wittmer
February 2000

Educational Media Corporation®, Box 21311, Minneapolis, MN 55421-0311

Contents

Section I

Developmental School Counseling: History, Reconceptionalization, and Implementation Strategies

In the first section of this book, I begin with a brief history of school counseling followed by a description of the rather dramatic reconceptionalization movement that has occurred in school counseling during the past three decades. Next, the training and competencies needed by the developmental K-12 school counselor are presented along with a description of the CACREP standards that apply to school counselor training and preparation. In chapter 2, guidelines for implementing a comprehensive, developmental K-12 school counseling program are presented. Section I also includes the suggested role and function of a K-12 developmental school counselor as viewed by experts in the field. Following this, I present a workable, tested model for changing an existing school guidance program into a comprehensive, developmental one using the ASCA Standards for School Counseling Programs.

Joe Wittmer

Chapter 1

Developmental School Guidance and Counseling: Its History and Reconceptionalization

by
Joe Wittmer

A Brief History

Instructors teaching *Introduction to Counseling* courses usually cite Frank Parsons as the father of guidance. However, in actuality, the systematized approach to *school* guidance appeared first in 1889 when Jesse Davis made "guidance" a part of the school curriculum in a Detroit high school (Brewer, 1942). As school principal, Davis introduced "vocational and moral guidance" as a curricular component of each English course within his school.

Frank Parsons did found the Vocational Bureau of Boston in 1908 and also authored a text titled, *Choosing a Vocation* (1909). The Parsonian "counseling" method consisted of matching an individual's personal characteristics to the requirements of the occupation. However, his impact on the school guidance movement came much later. That is, his emphasis on testing and on stressing the measurement of individual aptitude and personality traits later influenced the role of the school counselor to a significant degree.

World War I and the Great Depression of the 1930s gave an even greater impetus to the testing of individuals. And, the term "counselor," rarely heard prior to the depression, was now in the vocabulary of all educators. Prior to this time, "guidance" was the term used by educators.

World War II and its aftermath created an even greater emphasis on "psychological testing" that directly affected school guidance (i.e., the use of the SAT and other tests to determine a student's admission to colleges and universities). During the 1950s, America's rapidly changing society created a need for more counseling and related services as crime, divorce, and so forth increased. Traditional values were being challenged. "Mental health" became important outside the school setting and "guidance counseling" became popular within the school, especially at the junior high and high school levels. The move was away from the technique of "testing" to one of "trait and factor," which later became known as "directive counseling."

Although his concepts did not "catch on" at that time, the first time that *developmental* guidance was written about, with schools in mind, can be credited to Robert Mathewson in 1949. Mathewson (1949) indicated that the school guidance process should move with the individual student in a "developmental sequence" up to the age of maturity. Mathewson (1962) later expanded and refined his notion of guidance as a process that aided student development. One book, *The Counselor in a Changing World,* by Gilbert Wrenn (1962) probably impacted school guidance more than any other publication. The central theme of Wrenn's book was that the primary emphasis in counseling students should be placed on their individual, developmental needs in contrast to the remedial needs and the crisis times in their lives. However, Wrenn's ideas were not incorporated in school counselor preparation until sometime later.

Both the American Psychological Association (APA) and the American Personnel and Guidance Association (APGA, later AACD, and now ACA) were formed during the 1950s. And, the client centered approach espoused by Carl Rogers made its impact on the counseling profession. His theoretical approach dominated the manner in which most counselors, including school counselors, were trained during the fifties, followed by more "directive" approaches in the early 1960s and back again to the "Rogerian" approach during the 1970s. The Rogerian approach to training school counselors is very much in vogue today, but is rapidly giving ground to brief counseling approaches.

The Impact of Rogerian Theory: On or Off Track for School Counselor Preparation?

As noted, Carl Rogers had a significant positive impact on the counseling profession and his theoretical approach dominated counselor preparation programs. However, it is my opinion that Rogers' almost total focus on the individual somehow took us off-track in school counselor preparation and may have contributed to the inappropriate training of many school counselors, especially during the late 1960s and '70s. That is, in too many training programs, the focus was too narrow as it was almost entirely on small group and individual counseling. Very little attention was being given to the co-equal emphasis on prevention and on environmental intervention techniques so desperately needed in schools. Little attention was being placed (in counselor education programs) on the consulting and the coordination roles needed by effective developmental school counselors.

As noted, school counselors did turn more toward the "directive" approach during the early sixties; an indirect result of Sputnik and of the passage of the National Defense Education Act (NDEA). However, this was a brief respite as the Rogerian model was the training approach of choice for counselor trainers from the mid-sixties through the seventies and into the eighties.

The Impact of Sputnik

Sputnik, the Russian spaceship, launched in 1957, also launched the rapid development of school counseling and guidance in America, especially at the middle and high school levels. Federal legislation, in particular the National Defense Education Act (NDEA) of 1958, brought middle and high school counselors to the forefront as huge amounts of funds for their training were provided with the passage of this law. And, school guidance definitely headed in a different direction as a result. In essence, the U.S. government, highly concerned, concluded that Russian students were obviously superior to America's students in math and science since Russia was able to launch a rocket first. It was decreed that this was directly related to the fact that there were too few school guidance counselors as well as other shortcomings in American education. The race to the moon was on and government funds specifically earmarked toward the training of school counselors poured into counselor education training programs. I remember the time well—those enrolled in the school counseling tracks within counselor education programs, as I was, were funded and funded well!

As noted, for a short time following the NDEA Act, school counselors turned away from the Rogerian approach (non-directive) in favor of the more "directive" approach. This most likely occurred because it was assumed that being more "directive" would somehow help recruit bright youth for college and head them toward math and science. Somehow, as if by magic, more rocket scientists would emerge as a result. Unfortunately, school counselors were neglecting non-college bound youth during these times.

While the NDEA Act brought about the tripling of secondary school counselors between 1958 and 1967 (Shertzer & Stone, 1971), appropriate school guidance and counseling services were actually diminishing. Between 15,000 and 20,000 secondary school counselor trainees were funded by the government and graduated from counselor training institutes between 1958 and 1965. According to Gibson and Mitchell (1998), their numbers increased from only 12,000 in 1958 to more than 30,000 in 1964. Yet, as Audrey (1982) indicated, the profession of school counseling was close to becoming anachronistic as too much emphasis was being placed on non-guidance activities such as "clerical and administrative duties." And, Drawer (1984) wrote that school counselors were an endangered species and were contributing to their own destruction. Some experts believe that high school counseling, as we know it, is still in serious jeopardy unless drastic changes are made as many school counselors are still conducting inappropriate duties. While conducting an in-service training program for a large southern city's system-wide school counseling program, the superintendent of schools bluntly lamented that school counselors, as a group, were the "most over-qualified but least effective" staff members in his schools. It is my opinion that this is still the direct result of the inappropriate, too brief training, which occurred during the 1960s and '70s. That is, a school counselor not adequately trained in small group counseling, for example, probably won't make small group counseling a part of his or her counseling program. Fortunately, time (retirements) will take care of this problem. However, the training of school counselors must stay "on track," toward the "developmental" approach if school counseling is to survive.

It is my opinion that counselor education programs were not prepared for the onslaught brought about by the NDEA passage. As noted, school counselors were trained too quickly and in a sub-par fashion. The training was simply too brief and inadequate; and school counselors were ineffective in the "real world"—the school. In addition, training models not conducive to counselor effectiveness in the schools were being followed. The result of this too brief and inappropriate training of school counselors set the profession back several years as school counselors turned toward mostly clerical and administrative duties. As noted, the impact is still being felt today, especially at the high school level. Also, as noted, school counseling was close to becoming obsolete. The reconceptionalization of school guidance—the developmental movement—was timely and much needed.

The Reconceptionalization of School Counseling

Fortunately, the guidance and counseling reform movement brought about the reconceptionalization of school counseling programs. That is, although still very important skills for the school counselor to possess, school counseling has moved from an ancillary, individual, small group, reactive, crisis oriented service to a more comprehensive, preventative, developmental approach. This reconceptionalization has resulted in a rather dramatic shift in training as well as in the role and function of today's school counselor. Not only are counselors being trained to provide crisis counseling, as well as to provide effective individual and small group services, they are also being trained as consultants, coordinators, and so forth. Unfortunately, *individual* counseling courses (technique oriented) *remain* extremely popular, and in my opinion, remain at the heart of too many school counselor education training programs.

The focus in the schools prior to the reform movement was almost totally "position" oriented. Somehow it was expected that the school counselor would simply "fix kids" or counsel them into the right university or into the right job, and then everything would be fine. School counselors possessed a "magic wand." Reconceptionalization toward the comprehensive, developmental approach has changed school counseling dramatically, and, for the betterment of students and society as a whole.

Other Players in the Reconceptionalization of School Counseling: ACES, CACREP, and NBCC

Various professional groups and organizations played major roles in the "paradigm shift" that occurred in school guidance over the past 35 years. However, changes have occurred slowly. For example, the Association of Counselor Education and Supervision (ACES) began pushing for the development of school counselor training standards in the late 1950s and developed and approved the first standards for the training of secondary school counselors in 1964. However, the first counselor preparation programs (four) were not accredited by the ACES Commission on Accreditation until 1979!

The ACES Commission on Accreditation subsequently became the Council for the Accreditation of Counseling and Related Education Programs (CACREP) in 1981 and began the regular accreditation of counselor education programs. CACREP further revised and upgraded the standards of training in school counseling. One such example concerned the CACREP minimum conditions for a program to qualify for an accreditation visit. Among several others, one of CACREP's "minimum conditions" required a two-year minimum training program (48 semester/72 quarter hours). Thus, the accreditation movement played a major role in the manner in which school counselors were trained, especially after the CACREP school counselor specialty standards were developed and adopted. These specialty standards moved the training programs more toward the "program approach" and away from the "position" of "counselor as counselor." In addition, and most importantly, school counselors began carrying out the roles for which they were trained.

In the early 1980s, the National Board for Certified Counselors (NBCC) began certifying individuals as National Certified Counselors (NCC's). Although the statistics are not clear, it is estimated that more than half of the original 17,000 National Certified Counselors (in 1982) were school counselors. Becoming a National Certified Counselor indicated to the public that these individuals (at least) met minimum standards that added immensely to their credibility. In addition, such a credential added to their own self-esteem and resulted in school counselors "carrying their heads a little higher" that ultimately added to their professionalization. And, in my opinion, improved their "on the job" performance. Then, in 1990, NBCC created the National Certified School Counselor (NCSC) specialty, the first such ever national credential for *any* professional educational group. Several other educational professions have initiated a national credential for their membership (i.e., school administrators). However, school counselors were the first. This activity has given, and continues to give, a tremendous boost to the "professionalization" of school counseling.

In sum, the basic reform in the school guidance movement was away from that of the counselor as simply a one-to-one, small group mental health service provider (as an individual in a counseling position), to that of becoming a coordinator, a consultant, and a programmer—an overall catalyst in the school counseling program.

Someone once described the new developmental school counselor as one who is upstream giving swimming lessons instead of downstream rescuing people that are drowning. However, as noted, this is only partially true. School counselors are also being trained and are effective in "rescuing" drowning individuals, those students in crisis, and should continue to be so trained. The question becomes, who does the most good? The school counselor who works with 25 children (using a large group guidance approach) in a six-week, one hour per week unit on improving self-concept, or the school counselor who spends six hours with one child in crisis? Although the latter is important (and may even be more fun for some), it is obvious that the school counselor using the former approach meets the needs of more students and does much more good in the long run.

The Emergence of the Elementary School Counselor

Historically, elementary teachers in their self-contained classrooms had been responsible for "counseling and guidance." Elementary counselors only appeared in schools some 30 years ago. Those professionals interested in training elementary school counselors worked at not repeating the mistakes incurred in training middle and high school counselors. One of the early leaders in the movement was Don Dinkmeyer, Sr. Also, Verne Faust (1968), a prime mover in the emergence of elementary school counselors, and one of his students, Robert D. Myrick, focused their approach on the developmental needs of the child and the use of the teacher and others in the school guidance process.

Don Dinkmeyer, Sr. was the first editor of the *Elementary School Guidance and Counseling Journal*, 1965 to 1972, and Robert D. Myrick was the second editor, 1972 to 1978. Both were pioneers in the training and research on elementary school counseling and remain so today. It should be acknowledged that Dinkmeyer's and Myrick's emphasis on the school counselor's competence and on accountability played a major role in school guidance reconceptionalization toward the developmental focus, not just at the elementary level, but at all levels. Both stressed that guidance programs be organized around the concept of a comprehensive guidance delivery system with a "true" guidance curriculum at its center. As noted, Wrenn (1962) also played a major role in this movement. In general, elementary school counselors tend to be much more involved in "guidance" and less in "non-guidance" activity than are their middle and high school counterparts.

At first, the value of placing counselors in the elementary schools was debated and questioned by educators and parents alike. For many, the words "school counselor" brought to mind someone they had seen a few times in high school to help them with their class schedules, testing, college applications, and discipline. This perception, in my opinion, resulted in the debate concerning the need for elementary school counselors back in the seventies when the movement to place them in schools first began (ASCA, 1997). However, as we begin this new century, more elementary counselors are being employed across America and there is a large "push" to add these specially trained professionals to school staffs. Educators and others seem to agree that more developmentally oriented elementary school counselors are necessary if we are to respond adequately and effectively to the needs of children today.

The New Approach: Developmental in Nature

As noted, the profession of school counseling has moved away from the individual, position-oriented, one-to-one, small group counseling approach to a more preventive, wellness oriented, pro-active one. The image of the school counselor sitting in his or her office waiting for a student client to drop by is passe. And, in those schools where a counselor simply manages a "miniature mental health clinic," priorities are out of sync and students fall "between the cracks."

The contemporary developmental school counselor is curriculum and program oriented, is available to all, and is knowledgeable and competent to teach life skills to every student in the school regardless of race, religion, gender, or creed.

The developmental school counselor has four basic publics: students, teachers/staff, administrators, and the parents/community. In an effective program, everyone in the school knows that "guidance" is everyone's business. Additionally, in an efficient counseling program, everyone in the school understands the needs of the students and how the counseling department is organized to meet these needs. In those schools where teachers, administrators, and staff appreciate and understand the role of the counselor, the more successful the school's counseling program will be. When teachers and administrators understand the counseling department's plan, they support the counselor(s) both in and out of the teachers' lounge.

As mentioned at the beginning of this chapter, no attempt was made herein to provide a comprehensive, historical overview of school guidance and counseling. For those interested, excellent accounts of school guidance history and its reconceptionalization are available elsewhere (Audrey, 1982; Gibson & Mitchell, 1998; Myrick, 1997; and Gysbers & Henderson, 1999).

Developmental School Counseling Defined and Delimited

Many definitions of a comprehensive developmental school guidance program have emerged. One of the most quoted authorities in the field of school counseling today is Robert D. Myrick. As noted, he is a well known, and highly respected professional and his 1997 book, *Developmental Guidance and Counseling: A Practical Approach*, is among the most used textbooks in school counselor preparation programs today. Myrick (1997) defined the developmental approach as follows:

The developmental approach is an attempt to identify certain skills and experiences that students need to have as part of their going to school and being successful. Learning behaviors and tasks are identified and clarified for students. Then, a guidance curriculum is planned which complements the academic curriculum. In addition, life skills are identified and these are emphasized as part of preparing students for adulthood.

In the developmental approach, students have an opportunity to learn more about themselves and others in advance of problem moments in their lives. They learn interpersonal skills before they have an interpersonal crisis. If a crisis situation does happen, they can draw upon their skills to work themselves out of the problem.

Myrick (1997) also postulated the following seven Principles of Developmental Guidance Programs:

1. Developmental guidance is for all students.
2. Developmental guidance has an organized and planned curriculum.
3. Developmental guidance is sequential and flexible.
4. Developmental guidance is an integrated part of the total educational process.
5. Developmental guidance involves all school personnel.
6. Developmental guidance helps students learn more effectively and efficiently.
7. Developmental guidance includes counselors who provide specialized counseling services and interventions.

Norman Gysbers has also been a pioneer in school counseling reconceptionalization. His model is being used in many school districts. He and his co-writer indicated that the major focus of a developmental program is to provide all students with experiences to help them grow and develop. School counseling programs are comprehensive in that a full range of activities and services such as assessment, information, consultation, counseling, referral, placement, follow-up, and follow-through are provided (Gysbers & Henderson, 1999).

Henderson and Gysbers further indicated that such a program is based on the assumption that *all* school staff are involved in the guidance program. It is understood in their model that the highly trained and professionally certified school counselor remains "central" to the program. In the model espoused by Gysbers and Henderson (1999), school counselors provide direct services to students as well as work in consultative and collaborative relations with other members of the guidance team—the total school staff. That is, the guidance team consists of members of the total school staff, parents, and the community.

A developmental school counselor cannot be effective standing alone; everyone's involvement in the school is needed, sought, and appreciated. Involving the administration, school staff, parents, and teachers provides needed support and backing. Interested, involved individuals will defend the program (and the counselor) and will play a vital role within the program.

The historical approaches to school counseling included crisis intervention (waiting and reacting to critical situations), the remedial approach, preventive guidance, and a combination of the three. The remedial approach assumes a proactive counselor role of anticipating problems prior to their occurrence. The comprehensive developmental approach of today is an attempt to identify certain skills and experiences that students need, both in school and across the life span, and *incorporates* the remedial, crisis, and preventive approaches. As written and implied throughout this book, a majority of the developmental school counselor's time is spent on the "program" and "guidance curriculum" portion of the overall guidance program.

Today's effective developmental school counselor is pro-active and strives for a flexible delivery system within his or her program. There are planned daily activities aimed at meeting the development needs of all students, not just those with problems. And, the program has a written philosophy statement, a written rationale, goals, objectives, and strategies and techniques for implementing the goals and objectives with the latter being targeted specifically for different grade levels (see Snyder, chapter 3). A comprehensive program has its beginning on the first day of school and ends on the last day of the academic year.

The program's curriculum implemented and conducted by the counselor consists of structured experiences presented in a systematic way to meet the developmental needs of all students. These are delivered via the classroom through large group activities, regular classroom structure, smaller groups, and so forth. The purpose of the curriculum is to provide students with competencies that they need for their personal, social, academic, and career development, and to assist them in gaining and using life skills (Dahir, Sheldon, & Valiga, 1998).

Developmental program priorities are set for the different services needed and there is always an accountability component. The administrative and clerical tasks will have been de-emphasized, and, although important, one-to-one counseling has also been de-emphasized. The developmental counselor knows when and how to refer a student to an outside the school agency counselor as needed.

Gysbers (1997), in his book, *Comprehensive Guidance Programs That Work,* indicated that the comprehensive school counseling program consists of structured developmental experiences presented through classroom and group activities Pre-K through Post-Secondary. The purpose of the program, according to Gysbers, is to provide all students at all grade levels with knowledge and assistance in acquiring and using life skills. Gysbers (1997) discussed the following as the main components of a comprehensive program:

Individual Planning: Consists of planned and counselor directed activities that help all students plan, monitor, and manage their own learning as well as their personal and career development.

Individual Appraisal: Counselors assist students in analyzing and evaluating students' abilities, interests, skills, and achievement.

Individual Advisement: Counselors assist students in establishing personal-social, educational and occupational goals, involving parents, students, and school.

Placement: Counselors assist students in making the transition from school to school, school to work and/or additional post secondary educational training.

Responsive Services: Consists of Activities to meet the immediate needs and concerns of students.

Consultation: Counselors consult with parents, teachers, other educators, and community agencies regarding strategies to help students.

Personal Counseling: Counseling is provided on a small group or individual basis for students.

Crisis Counseling: Counseling and support are provided to students and their families facing emergency situations.

Referral: Counselors use referral sources to deal with crises such as suicide, violence, abuse, and terminal illness.

System Support: Consists of management activities that establish, maintain, and enhance the total guidance program.

Staff and Community Relations: Counselors orient staff and the community to the comprehensive, developmental, standards based school counseling program.

Consultation with teachers: Counselors need to consult with teachers and other staff members to provide information, to support staff, and to receive feedback on the emerging needs of students.

Advisory Councils: Counselors support other programs through service on departmental curriculum committees, community committees, and so forth.

Community Outreach: Counselors participate in activities designed to help counselors become knowledgeable about community resources and referral agencies.

Program Management and Operations: Counselors coordinate planning and management tasks which support the activities of a comprehensive guidance and counseling program.

Research and Development: Counselors engage in and provide for program evaluation, data analysis, follow-up studies, and the continued development of updating learning activities and resources (Gysbers, 1997).

Gysbers (1997) indicated further that school counselors should continually monitor their professional development and be actively involved regularly in updating their professional knowledge and skills. And, in addition, counselors should support other school programs through service on school advisory councils, departmental curriculum committees, community committees, and so forth.

The American School Counselor Association's literature clearly indicated that a comprehensive school counseling program is developmental and systematic in nature, sequential, clearly defined, and accountable (ASCA, 1999). It is jointly founded upon developmental psychology, educational philosophy, and counseling methodology. The school counseling program is integral to the educational enterprise. The program is proactive and preventive in its focus. It assists students in acquiring and using lifelong learning skills. More specifically, effective school counseling programs employ strategies to enhance the academic, career, and personal/social development of all students. Writing on behalf of ASCA, Dahir, Sheldon and Valiga (1998) stated the differences between the "Traditional" and "Comprehensive/Developmental School Counseling" programs as follows:

Traditional Guidance	Comprehensive/Developmental
Reactive	Proactive
Process	Outcome
Deductive	Inductive
Services	Program
Subjective Evaluation	Objective Evaluation
Individual Counseling	Individual and Group
Students initiate	Counselors initiate
Generalists	Specialists

As noted elsewhere, the need for elementary school counselors was originally questioned by many educators and others. However, as we begin the new millennium, their numbers are growing rapidly in elementary schools across America. The American School Counselor Association advocates and supports the notion of comprehensive, developmental programs existing at all school levels, but especially at the elementary level (ASCA, 1999).

Elementary school is a time when students develop attitudes concerning school, self, peers, social groups, and family. It is a time when students develop decision making, communication, life training skills, and character values. Comprehensive developmental counseling is based on prevention, providing goals which are integrated into all aspects of children's' lives. Early identification and intervention of children's problems are essential to change some of the current statistics regarding self-destructive behaviors. If we wait until children are in middle or high school to address these problems, we lose the opportunity to help them achieve their potential as well as feelings of dignity and self-worth. For many children, the school counselor may be the one person who provides an atmosphere of safety, trust, and positive regard (ASCA, 1997). ASCA views the role of the elementary level developmental school counselor as follows:

Implement effective classroom guidance focusing on understanding of self and others; coping strategies; peer relationships and social skills; communication; problem solving; decision making; conflict resolution and study skills; career awareness and the world of work; substance education; and multicultural awareness.

Provide individual and small group counseling dealing with self-image and self-esteem; personal adjustment; family issues; interpersonal concerns; academic development and behavior modification; as well as peer facilitation and peer mediation.

Provide assessment by helping students identify their skills, abilities, achievements, and interests through counseling and guidance activities and interpretation of standardized tests.

Work with specialized populations and needs that require special attention, such as culturally diverse populations and students with varying abilities.

Develop students' career awareness as a lifelong process of forming basic values, attitudes, and interests regarding the world of work.

Coordinate school, community, and business resources; school-wide guidance-related activities; and extracurricular programs which promote students' personal growth and skill development.

Provide consultation with teachers, administrators, school psychologists, school social workers, and outside agencies and social services concerning the welfare of the students. Make appropriate referrals for special services for students and families within the school and community.

Communicate and exchange information with parents/guardians by way of conferences, parent education workshops, and by newsletters.

Participate as members of the school improvement and interdisciplinary teams and work as liaisons with PTA/PTSA/PTOs (ASCA, 1997).

In summary, ASCA leaders believe that elementary school counselors set the tone for developing the skills, knowledge and attitudes necessary for our children to become healthy, productive adults. With a comprehensive developmental counseling program, counselors work as a team with school, parents, and community to create a caring atmosphere whereby children's' needs are met through prevention, early identification and intervention (ASCA, 1997).

ASCA leaders believe that it is important to ensure that the school's "stakeholders," including the entire community in which the school is located, understands the important role school counseling programs play in the educational system. Professional school counselors therefore must become:

Facilitators of change, leaders in school improvement, partners in educational excellence, coordinators of collaborative community efforts, advocates for equity and excellence, and managers of student achievement of school counseling competencies (Dahir, Sheldon, & Valiga, 1998).

Dahir, Sheldon, and Valiga (1998), in their book concerning the implementation of the ASCA National Standards for School Counseling Programs (see chapter two), published by ASCA, indicated that if school counselors are going to change the perceptions and attitudes of school administrators, faculty, parents, and community members, they must get across the message that the school counseling program at all levels:

Helps students develop knowledge and skills that are needed in today's and tomorrow's world; is an integral component of the academic mission of the school; supports student success and assists in students' academic, career, and personal/social development; use for all students—not just those in crisis or those going to college, and is effective and accountable. (Dahir, Sheldon, & Valiga, 1998).

No doubt about it, much is expected from the "new millennium" developmental, K-12 school counselor. And, as in other helping professions, a school counselor's continued professional development is extremely important and expected by his or her "publics." When choosing an MD for our medical problems or concerns, we are always careful about our selection. We work at choosing the "best" and most "up-to-date" physician. The same applies to school counselors. *That is, your "publics" should have the confidence that you are indeed "up-dated" in your field.* As indicated elsewhere in this book, I believe that a developmental school counselor's professional development will be enhanced tremendously by becoming a National Certified Counselor (NCC) and subsequently, a National Certified School Counselor (NCSC). In addition, I believe that school counselors should, for many reasons, consider becoming licensed professional counselors in their state.

Have comprehensive, developmental counseling programs "caught on" in America? In an attempt to answer this question, Sink and MacDonald (1998) conducted a survey of all 50 State Departments of Education. They indicated that school counseling is in a period of renewal and revitalization where theory and practice have evolved from traditional organizational models to the widespread implementation of developmental comprehensive counseling programs. Sink and MacDonald (1998) concluded

that the movement in this direction is growing rapidly and that at the beginning of the new millennium some 35 States will have implemented developmental comprehensive school counseling programs.

The new millennium coincides with a time of unprecedented growth in America's K-12 school population with almost 54 million students enrolled in the year 2000. The new millennium also coincides with an unprecedented opportunity for the school counseling profession.

Along with the federal government, many related professions and organizations have "jumped" on our bandwagon and support school counseling currently as never before. Among these are the National Association of Secondary School Principals and the National Association of Elementary School Principals (Dahir, Sheldon, & Valiga, 1998). Another such organization is the National Education Association (NEA). The NEA passed a resolution in 1999 urging strongly that the school counselor/student ratio never be more than 1:250. The support is there and now is the time to implement developmental counseling programs in every preK-12 school in America. And, we must ensure that these programs are staffed by qualified and competent school counselors holding the appropriate professional credentials.

Summary

In this chapter I began with a brief history of school counseling followed by the reconceptionalization movement. The chapter concluded with a section focusing on the delimiting of, and several definitions of, developmental school counseling. Two figures concerning a description of the ASCA and CACREP standards of training as related to school counselor preparation are presented at the end of the chapter.

Figure 1.1
The Developmental School Counselor:
Training, Competencies, and Personal Characteristics as Viewed by ASCA

The American School Counselor Association (ASCA) has postulated several school counselor competencies deemed necessary. ASCA believes that school counselors must know various theories and concepts (knowledge competencies) and must be able to utilize a variety of skills (skill competencies). Further, school counselors, to be effective, must be competent professionals and effective persons with the appropriate caring and helping personality. The competencies needed by school counselors, as viewed by ASCA, are presented below:

Knowledge Competencies

School counselors need to know:
- Human development theories and concepts
- Individual counseling theories
- Consultation theories and techniques
- Family counseling theories and techniques
- Group counseling theories and techniques
- Career decision-making theories and techniques
- Learning theories
- Motivation theories
- The effect of culture on individual development and behavior
- Evaluation theories and processes
- Ethical and legal issues related to counseling
- Program development models

Skill Competencies

School counselors should be able
to demonstrate skills in:
- Diagnosing student needs
- Individual counseling
- Group counseling
- Consultation with staff, students, and parents
- Coordination of programs, educational testing, career development, substance abuse
- Career counseling
- Educational counseling
- Identifying and making appropriate referrals
- Administering and interpreting achievement, interest, aptitude, and personality tests
- Cross-cultural counseling
- Ethical decision making
- Building supportive climates for students and staff
- Removing and/or decreasing race and gender bias in school policy and curriculum
- Explaining, to the staff, community, and parents, the scope of practice and functions of a school counselor
- Planning and conducting in-service for staff
- Identifying resources and information related to helping clients
- Evaluating the effectiveness of counseling programs (ASCA, 1990)

Professional Competencies

School counselors should be able to:
- Conduct a self-evaluation to determine their strengths and areas needing improvement
- Develop a plan of personal and professional growth to enable them to participate in lifelong learning
- Advocate for appropriate state and national legislation
- Adopt a set of professional ethics to guide their practice and interactions with students, staff, community, parents, and peers (ASCA, 1990)

Personal Characteristics of Effective Counselors

The personal attributes or characteristics of school counselors are very important to their success. According to ASCA, effective counselors usually:
- Have a genuine interest in the welfare of others
- Are able to understand the perspective of others
- Believe individuals are capable of solving problems
- Are open to learning
- Are willing to take risks
- Have a strong sense of self-worth
- Are not afraid of making mistakes and attempt to learn from them
- Value continued growth as a person
- Are caring and warm
- Possess a keen sense of humor (ASCA, 1990)

As noted above, ASCA also maintains that today's school counselors should be familiar with the ASCA National Standards for School Counseling Programs and should begin their implementation at all levels (Dahir, Sheldon, & Valiga, 1998).

Figure 1.2
The Preparation of School Counselors:
ASCA and CACREP

The American School Counselor Association's (ASCA) leaders believe that school counselors are prepared for their work through the study of interpersonal relationships and behavioral sciences in graduate education courses in accredited colleges and universities. Preparation involves special training in counseling theory and skills related to school settings. Particular attention is given to personality and human development theories and research, including career and life-skills development; learning theories, the nature of change and the helping process; theories and approaches to appraisal, multi-cultural, and community awareness; educational environments; curriculum development; professional ethics; and, program planning, management, and evaluation.

ASCA indicates that counselors should be prepared to use the basic interventions in a school setting, with special emphasis on the study of helping relationships, facilitative skills, and brief counseling; group dynamics and group learning activities; family systems; peer helper programs; multi-cultural and cross-cultural helping approaches; and educational and community resources for special school populations.

ASCA leaders further indicate that school counselors are aware of their own professional competencies and responsibilities within the school setting. They know when and how to refer or involve other professionals. They are accountable for their actions and participate in appropriate studies and research related to their work (ASCA, 1990).

CACREP Standards of Training

The Council for the Accreditation of Counseling and Related Educational Programs (CACREP) developed and implemented the first specialty standards for the training of school counselors in 1985.

In essence, the most recent CACREP standards call for school counselors in training to experience certain curricular and supervised experiences. In addition, several curricular experiences and necessary, demonstrated knowledge domains specific to school counselors are given in the standards.

All counselor trainees in a CACREP accredited training program must have curricular experiences and demonstrated knowledge in each of the eight common-core areas that follow:

1. **Human Growth and Development**—studies that provide an understanding of the nature and needs of individuals at all developmental levels.

2. **Social and Cultural Foundations**—studies that provide an understanding of issues and trends in a multicultural and diverse society.

3. **Helping Relationships**—studies that provide an understanding of counseling and consultation processes.

4. **Groups**—studies that provide an understanding of group development, dynamics, counseling theories, and group counseling methods and skills.

5. **Career and Lifestyle Development**—studies that provide an understanding of career development and the interrelationships among work, family, and other life factors.

6. **Appraisal**—studies that provide an understanding of individual and group approaches to assessment and evaluation.

7. **Research and Program Evaluation**—studies that provide an understanding of types of research methods, basic statistics, and ethical and legal considerations in research.

8. **Professional Orientation**—studies that provide an understanding of all aspects of professional functioning including history, roles, organizational structures, ethics, standards, and credentialing (CACREP, 1994).

Each of the above **core** required curricular experiences are described in detail within the CACREP standards (CACREP, 1994).

As noted, the CACREP Standards also require certain supervised experiences including an on-campus clinical (laboratory) experience followed by a supervised practicum and an internship. The latter two are briefly described below:

An accredited CACREP program requires students to complete supervised practicum experiences that total a minimum of 100 clock hours. The practicum provides for the development of individual and group counseling skills under supervision.

An accredited CACREP program also requires students to complete a supervised internship of 600 clock hours that is begun after successful completion of the student's practicum. Consideration is given to selecting internship sites (must be in a school setting) that offer opportunities for students to engage in both individual and group counseling. The internship provides an opportunity for the student to perform under the supervision of a certified school counselor, all the activities that a regularly employed staff member in the setting would be expected to perform. A regularly employed staff member is defined as a person occupying the professional role to which the student is aspiring (CACREP, 1994).

Specialized Curricular Experiences for Accredited CACREP Programs in School Counseling

In addition to the common core curricular and supervised experiences listed above, specialized curricular experiences and demonstrated knowledge and skill competence in each of the areas below are required of all students in an accredited CACREP school program.

A. Foundations of School Counseling

Studies in this area include, but are not limited to, the following:

1. history, philosophy, and trends in school counseling;
2. role and function of the school counselor in conjunction with the roles of other professional and support personnel in the school;
3. knowledge of the appropriate school setting;
4. ethical standards of the American School Counselor Association; and
5. policies, laws, and legislation relevant to school counseling.

B. Contextual Dimensions of the Practice of School Counseling

Coordination—studies that provide an understanding of the coordination of counseling program components as they relate to the total school community.

1. referral of children and adolescents for specialized help;
2. coordination efforts with resource persons, specialists, businesses, and agencies outside the school to promote program objectives;
3. methods of integration of affective education in the total school curriculum;
4. promotion of the use of activities and of programs by the total school community to enhance a positive school climate; and
5. methods of planning and presenting educational programs for school personnel and for parents.

C. Knowledge and Skills for the Practice of School Counseling

1. **Program Development and Evaluation**—studies that provide an understanding of school counseling program development and evaluation.

Studies in this area include, but are not limited to the following:

a. use of surveys, interviews, and needs assessments; and

b. design implementation and evaluation of a comprehensive, developmental school counseling program.

2. **Counseling and Guidance**—studies that provide an understanding of specific approaches and strategies of counseling with children and adolescents and facilitation of related guidance activities.

Studies in this area include, but are not limited to, the following:

a. individual and group counseling and guidance approaches appropriate for the developmental stage and needs of children and adolescents;

b. large group guidance approaches that are systematically designed to assist children and adolescents with developmental tasks; and

c. approaches to peer helper programs.

3. **Consultation**—studies that provide an understanding of the theory and of the process of consultation within the school community.

Studies in this area include, but are not limited to, the following:

a. methods of enhancing teamwork within the school community; and

b. knowledge and skills in consulting with parents and teachers both individually and in small groups.

As of this writing, 113 counselor education school counselor preparation programs are CACREP accredited. Many more programs are expected to seek accreditation during the next several years.

The above brief descriptions of the CACREP Standards were taken from the CACREP Manual (1994) and will remain in force until 2001. For a thorough description of the Standards, write:

CACREP
American Counseling Association
5999 Stevenson Avenue
Alexandria, VA 22304

References

ASCA. (1990). *School counselor competencies.* Alexandria, VA: ASCA Press.

ASCA. (1997). *Why elementary school counselors?* Alexandria, VA: ASCA Press.

ASCA. (1999). *Role statement: The school counselor.* Alexandria, VA: ASCA Press.

Audrey, R.F. (1982). A house divided: Guidance and counseling in 20th century America. *Personnel and Guidance Journal, 61,* 198-204.

Brewer, J.M. (1942). *Education as guidance.* New York: Macmillan.

CACREP. (1994). *Accreditation procedures manual.* Alexandria, VA: CACREP.

Dahir, C., Sheldon, B., & Valiga, M. (1998). *Vision into action: Implementing the national standards for school counseling programs.* Alexandria, VA. American Counseling Association.

Drawer, S.S. (1984). Counselor survival in the 1980s. *School Counselor, 31,* 234-240.

Faust, V. (1968). *The counselor-consultant in the elementary school.* Boston, MA: Houghton Mifflin.

Gibson, L.G. , & Mitchell, M.H. (1998). *Introduction to counseling and guidance,* (3rd ed.). New York: Macmillan.

Gysbers, N.C. (1997). *Comprehensive guidance programs that work.* Greensboro, NC: ERIC Counseling and Personnel Services Clearinghouse.

Gysbers, N.C., & Henderson, P. (1999). *Developing and managing your school guidance program,* (3rd ed). Washington, DC: ACA.

Mathewson, R.H. (1949). *Guidance policy practice,* (1st ed.). New York: Harper & Bros.

Mathewson, R.H. (1962). *Guidance policy and practice.* New York: Harper & Bros.

Myrick, R.D. (1997). *Developmental guidance and counseling: A practical approach,* (3rd ed.). Minneapolis, MN: Educational Media Corporation.

Parsons, F. (1909). *Choosing a vocation.* Boston: Houghton Mifflin.

Shertzer, B., & Stone, S.C. (1971). *Fundamentals of counseling.* Boston, MA: Houghton Mifflin.

Sink, A., & MacDonald, G. (1998). The status of comprehensive guidance and counseling in the united states. *ASCA: Professional School Counseling, 2,* 88-94.

Why elementary school counselors? American School Counselor Association. *www.schoolcounselor.org* (1999).

Wrenn, C.G. (1962). *The counselor in a changing world.* Alexandria, VA: ACA Press.

Chapter 2

Implementing a Comprehensive Developmental School Counseling Program

by
Joe Wittmer

Implementation Strategies

Administrative Understanding and Support

It is important that the school administration understand and support a developmental school counseling program—its priorities, its demands on the staff and the counselors' time, the cost of an effective program, the facilities and materials needed, and so forth. The place to begin, then, is with the school principal. It is important that the principal has an *in-depth* understanding of a comprehensive program and that you as the school counselor, have his or her support for such a program prior to initiating one. Otherwise, it is doomed to failure.

School administrators will make decisions and establish policies and procedures in light of their understanding (or lack of it) of developmental counseling. For example, since access to students is necessary for an effective developmental program to be initiated, an administrator who understands and supports such a program will develop student schedules that allow maximum flexibility in students' accessibility. It is vitally important that the school principal understand the developmental counselor's role in the overall program (i.e., what such a program *does* and *does not* entail). And, only the school counselor can bring about this understanding on the part of the principal.

It is suggested that the counselor's role and function be placed in writing, shared, and discussed with the principal, and his or her approval and support gained. When possible, also have the statement approved by the central administration and/or school board. Discussion and understanding of the time commitment needed from teachers, staff, the administration, and others to the program should be made clear. Overall, it is important for the principal to understand and support the conditions required for effective program implementation, including

the proper facilities needed, overall work environment, and an adequate budget. When your school principal truly understands, he or she will realize that a developmental counseling program will make your school a better place for all, a more productive staff, and a school more conducive to overall student learning.

Selecting a School Guidance Advisory Committee

In the four chapters that follow (Section II), the focus is on managing a comprehensive program and on the roles played by the effective developmental school counselor at the elementary, middle, and secondary levels, respectively. Each of the writers emphasizes the selection and the utilization of a School Counseling Advisory Committee as a necessary prerequisite to initiating any effective developmental school counseling program. Members of the school guidance committee almost always include teachers, administrators, parents, and when appropriate, students. Some school counseling departments also have a school board member on their advisory committees while others also have a well-known local business leader as a member. An advisory committee's membership should depict and provide a link with the schools' various publics (Wittmer & Thompson, 1995).

The effective developmental K-12 school counselor coordinates the advisory committee meetings, its functions, and keeps the school administration informed of all deliberations, of meetings, and of the plans of the committee. One high school counselor has organized his advisory committee by electing a chair, a vice-chair, and a secretary. The secretary records the minutes of each meeting that are subsequently shared with the school's administrators, staff, and teachers. No doubt about it, an effective advisory committee is essential if a developmental counseling program is to be effective (Wittmer, Thompson, & Loesch, 1997).

Developing and Writing a Philosophy Statement

One of the advisory committee's first duties should be to develop and to write a program philosophy statement that is locally appropriate for the school in question and developmental in nature. This does not need to be an elaborate, lengthy, or scholarly statement, but simply written along the lines of, "This we believe..." where students, education, learning, and so forth are concerned. The written philosophy statement, sometimes referred to as a "mission" statement, should lead directly into the development of goals and objectives based on the identified needs gathered from students, teachers, staff, parents, and other publics most appropriately reflecting the local school. As noted, it should be written simply and in a straight forward manner.

Developing and writing a philosophical statement is extremely important. A strong, well-written, philosophy statement will become the corner stone upon which the total counseling program is developed and built. It should be written in clear terms to coincide and be compatible with the overall school philosophy, and where appropriate, with the state and district-wide philosophies as well. It is advantageous for the counselor to have the school's overall written philosophy statement available (and, if it is in writing, also have available the one from the district-wide school system) prior to having the advisory committee initiating the development and the writing of the specific school's counseling program's philosophical statement. As mentioned before, a school counseling program is an indisputable, integral part of the overall instructional program. Thus, the philosophy statement should reflect the values and beliefs of the total school faculty and staff, the local publics, and provide the basis from which this contribution will be made.

Needs Surveys

Experts differ on which should occur first—the appointment of the advisory committee or a needs survey of the school's publics. However, I suggest the selection of the advisory committee first. Then, the committee, coordinated by the counselor, writes the philosophy statement and develops and administers specific needs surveys to the entire student population, the staff, the faculty, and parents.

Analyzing the survey results should next occur. This will clarify the guidance and the counseling needs of the students, teachers, parents, and so forth from their viewpoints—the needs of *your* consumers! Accurately assessing and identifying the needs of the various publics the counselor serves may well be the most important component within a developmental counselor's role. For students and for parents, this should be done with a formal written needs assessment survey. Surveys can be developed quite easily. Simply ask questions or give checklists that you believe will help you obtain the most accurate and viable data. In addition to paper and pencil surveys, a simple, structured interview of the administration and the faculty may provide similar results. Most school counselors agree, it is best to use paper and pencil surveys for all publics.

Aside from the two sample needs surveys given at the conclusion of this chapter (Figures 2.1, 2.2, and Chapter 25), excellent sample school guidance philosophy statements, rationale statements, and sample needs surveys are available elsewhere. For example, Rye and Sparks (1998) provided several ideal (written) school philosophy statements and needs surveys. Rye and Sparks permit the copying of their surveys by any school counselor desiring to use them in the development and/or strengthening of their specific school's counseling program.

Developing and Writing a Program Rationale

Following the writing of the philosophy statement and the development, administering, and analyses of the needs surveys, it is important for the Counseling Program Advisory Committee to develop and write a program rationale statement. Such a rationale statement clearly states the societally based reasons for having a comprehensive, developmental counseling program in place and is based on the results of the needs surveys. Each school district is unique and the rationale (the reasons for having a developmental program) should "fit" with the specific "needs" of your school; it should be "locally appropriate." That is, the rationale statement should specifically state the rationale and how the developmental guidance program benefits the students, the faculty, the parents, and the specific community being served. The rationale statement should clearly imply and support the notion that school counseling services are a vital part of the overall educational process—an integral part of the overall school curriculum. Such a rationale statement (the most significant reasons for having a developmental program) should also emphasize how the developmental counseling program coincides and is coordinated with the philosophy and overall curricular aspects of the school.

Why have a comprehensive developmental counseling program? If somehow, by magic, the problems students have today suddenly disappeared, there would be no need, no rationale, no significant reasons for having a guidance program. Would it not be great if the President of the United States, as he or she began the new term, January, 2005, called for a press conference (on national TV), and stated:

"My fellow Americans. I bring you fantastic news as we begin this new year—2005. Our American society has progressed beyond our wildest dreams during the past few years. As you know, the standard of living has increased dramatically, medical advances have eliminated or reduced almost all communicable diseases including AIDS, technology and computers have changed the way we communicate, travel, do business, educate our children, and so forth. But most importantly, due to the excellent work of our school counselors, the social problems as we knew them, have been eliminated." The following are just a few examples the President would speak of:

- **Teen pregnancy.** *"Our sex education through the schools' counseling programs have been 100% successful. All of our youth are either abstaining from sexual activity or using birth control. As far as is known, as I speak, there are no pregnant teens in America!"*

- **Alcohol and drug abuse.** *"Again, our alcohol and drug abuse prevention programs, under the auspices of the school counseling office, have made our youth so aware of the dangers of drugs that they rarely even experiment with them anymore. We have nipped their curiosity in the bud."*

- **Dropouts.** *"Currently in this country we can boast of a 100% high school graduation rate. Our educational and career counseling programs in the schools appear flawless. Our students are completely invested in their education. Again, thanks to the school counselors and comprehensive, developmental counseling programs."*

- **Violence.** *"Thanks to the great work of our school counselors and others, we have not had a single incidence of school violence in the new millennium."*

- **Suicide.** *"We have found a surefire method to help our adolescents through this difficult period in their lives. Our school counselors have taught them coping skills that allow them to work through their problems successfully. We have seen a 100% reduction in teen suicides."*

The President continues: *"My aides inform me that, beginning in elementary school, the American children now have tremendous support systems which include intact, supportive families, a strong sense of community, and schools with adequate staffing and unlimited funding. By the time they reach adulthood they are so well-informed and well-educated that they become fully productive members of society. Therefore, we believe our current school counseling programs are meeting the needs of all our students. And, further...."*

Unfortunately, the above scenario is, of course, a fictitious dream impossible to achieve in America. It is total fantasy; in actuality, the problems mentioned are on the increase. As we begin the twenty-first century, our complex culture is characterized by diverse and ever-changing values in the home, in the community, and in the school. Societal problems are reflected in dramatic increases in substance abuse, suicide, child abuse, teen pregnancy, truancy, school drop out, and random acts of violence.

As we begin the new century, school violence is but one of many serious problems facing America's school aged youth (Wittmer, Thompson, & Sheperis, 1999). However, because of the recent school shootings, school violence continues to receive the most "press" and attention from the public at large. School violence claimed the lives of 251 Americans between the 1992-93 (173 between 1994 and 1998) and 1998-99 school years, according to the National School Safety Center. During this time, California had 56 deaths, followed by Colorado with 15 killed in school violence. All of Colorado's deaths came at Columbine High School in Littleton on April 20, 1999. On that unforgettable day, two young gunman killed 12 fellow students, a teacher, and finally themselves (Ciabattari, 1999). A 1999 survey conducted by *Time Magazine* (1999) reported that 50% of children ages 9 to 17 are worried about dying young and that 31% of children aged 12 to 17 know someone their age who carries a gun!

In addition to youth violence, other current trends in youth related issues are cause for deep concern and give impetus to the need for developmentally oriented school counselors at all grade levels. In addition to youth violence, *The Center for 4th and 5th R's* (1999) has provided the following as "troubling trends" among our youth:

1. Increasing dishonesty (lying, cheating, and stealing)

2. Growing disrespect for parents, teachers, and other legitimate authority figures

3. Increasing peer cruelty

4. A rise in prejudice and hate crimes

5. A decline in the work ethic

6. Declining personal and civic responsibility

7. Increasing self-destructive behaviors such as premature sexual activity, substance abuse, and suicide

8. Growing ethical illiteracy, including ignorance of moral knowledge as basic as the Golden Rule and the tendency to engage in destructive behavior without thinking it wrong (The Center for 4th and 5th R's, 1999)

The Center for 4th and 5th R's (1999) provided the following statistical examples representative of the above trends:

- According to FBI statistics, arrests of 13- and 14-year-olds for rape nearly doubled during the past decade.

- In a 1994 survey cited by the Boston Globe, more than half of ninth-graders in an affluent suburb said they saw nothing wrong with stealing a compact disc or keeping money found in a lost wallet.

- In a study of more than 6,000 college students by Rutgers University professor Douglas McCabe, more than 2/3 said they had cheated on a test or major assignment during college.

- Almost six of ten high school students say they have used illegal drugs, not counting alcohol, according to a federal study.

- According to a Centers for Disease Control study, 40% of American ninth-graders say they have already had sexual intercourse; a United Nations report finds that U.S. teens have the highest abortion rate in the developed world.

- Rising levels of hate-inspired youth violence promoted the organization Research for Better Schools to publish a handbook on dealing with hate crime in schools (Center for 4th and 5th R's, 1999).

In late 1999 the annual National Household Survey on Drug Abuse reported that illicit drug use by 12– 17-year-olds declined slightly from 1997 to 1998. That was the good news and provides a glimmer of hope. The bad news is that the same survey results indicated that illicit drug use among this age group (12–17-year-olds) had doubled since 1992!

We also know that between 5,000 and 6,000 adolescents take their lives each year and another 500,000 teens make unsuccessful attempts. Today, suicide ranks as the second or third leading cause of death among adolescents. According to a recent study, there has been a 300% increase in teen suicide since the 1960s and a 1000% increase in depression among children since the 1960s (Cloud, 1999). We also know that daily, approximately 3000 children witness the divorce of their parents. And, about every 50 seconds a child is abused or neglected in America. And, approximately every 10 seconds of every school day a child drops out of school and every 30 seconds or so a child runs away from home.

According to the Children's Defense Fund's "Everyday in America," (1998), Every day in the United States: 3 children and youths under 25 die from HIV infection. 6 children and youths under 20 commit suicide. 13 children and youths are homicide victims. 16 children and youths are killed by firearms. 316 children under 18 are arrested for violent crimes. 1,420 babies are born to teen mothers. 2,556 babies are born into poverty. 3,356 students drop out each school day. 5,702 children under 18 are arrested. 13,076 public school students are suspended each school day.

Many more statistics about our youth problems and concerns could be given here. It is obvious that the problems are immense and are on the increase. The question also appears obvious; what can we do to prevent these terrible things from happening to our youth?

It is my opinion that, in our "heart of hearts" we all know that the most viable "answer" to the above problems are "prevention" programs for all children beginning in preschool. Of course, such programs should involve parents and/or guardians as needed. And, yes, we also all know that prevention programs are expensive and a "hard sell." The results of the time, effort and money we put into prevention programs are long term and not immediately evident. Thus, we tend to continue to focus on the "problem" after it occurs, to respond to a crisis, instead of being proactive and trying to prevent it from occurring. We know that real prevention is much harder. It means addressing the underlying causes of the problem. But, we also know how important it is to do something and to do it soon! For, as a very wise man once said; "Children make up only about 25% of our current population, but 100% of our future!"

So, the question becomes, why don't we address the underlying causes? Real prevention is much harder; as noted, it means addressing the underlying causes. In my opinion, those in power, such as politicians, find it much more popular (and vote-getting) to allocate more money to focus on the problem after it occurs than the underlying causes. For example, politicians will willingly fund the building of more prison cells but often balk at funding prevention programs that most experts agree would keep many, if not most, from breaking the laws that lead to prison. As we begin the twentieth century, approximately 1.8 million of our fellow citizens are held in US prisons at a staggering cost of $22,000, on average, per year per inmate! These billions of dollars would fund many "prevention" programs.

These disturbing trends among our youth clearly reflect the need for highly trained counselors working in comprehensive, developmental school counseling programs that focus on prevention at all school levels (Wittmer, Thompson and Loesch, 1999).

The results of a national teacher opinion poll raised doubts about the progress being made with the above listed problems and concerns. The 1,007 public school teachers in the survey were questioned twice: in July, prior to beginning their first school year as a teacher, and again in the spring upon completing their first academic year.

Sixty-five percent of the teachers initially agreed that (in their opinion) many children appear in school with so many personal problems that it's very difficult for them to be effective learners. Unfortunately, following a year of teaching, *89%* held that view! In addition, *58%* responded (after a year of classroom teaching) that even the best teachers will find it difficult to educate more than two-thirds of their pupils, compared with 45 percent who said so before their first classroom jobs.

An identical *89%* replied both times that their students would benefit "If I do my job well." These teachers felt strongly that they would need assistance from other professionals in the school in order to "Do my job well." The surveyors concluded that school counselors are obviously among these "professionals" sought out by teachers for assistance with troubled students incapable of learning because of "personal" situations that impede learning.

More and more teachers are calling on school counselors (the perceived and hopefully true experts in human relations, student motivation, learning, etc.) for assistance with all their students. They have come to realize that a child bringing a problem to school that "gets in the way of learning" (and *89%* do, according to the teachers in the above mentioned survey) needs special professional help. They are realizing that all the "yelling" and "nagging" in the world won't make the problems that impede learning disappear—in many cases professional help is needed.

Children affected by problems who are unable to achieve their academic potential may drop out of school and out of society. The school counselor's primary task is to assist each in becoming better, more effective learners by providing the appropriate programs and services to enhance current educational endeavors and learning across the life span. This is where a developmental school counselor enters the picture.

We know that growing up in today's world is difficult, resulting in students of all ages having many common concerns—substance abuse, violence in the home, divorce, and so forth. Developmental school counselors know that intensive one-on-one counseling is important, is needed, and will work; but the counselor also realizes that it is the least satisfactory school counseling model. It is a fact: in those schools where the basic, responsive, counselor interaction is one-on-one counseling, the needs of most students are not being met! In addition, effective school counselors know that *all* students need counseling services and are in need of assistance in their "normal" every day development. Thus, the basic rationale for

having a comprehensive developmental counseling program is because it is well-known that:

- All students need counseling related services.
- Self-esteem and self-confidence are strong predictors of a child's academic success.
- Important aspects of child and adolescent development can be effectively addressed through a structured, developmentally oriented counseling curriculum.
- Intensive one-on-one and small group counseling is needed, but it is the least satisfactory model for school counseling and most students do not need "therapy."
- Most schools are large and complex and services can be best delivered to large groups of students with common needs.
- Most students, K-12, are simply growing up and in need of assistance in "normal" developmental tasks (i.e., assistance with their every day concerns so that effective classroom "learning" can occur).

You may wish to incorporate some, or all, of the above concerns into your program rationale statement. However, every attempt should be made to incorporate specific, locally appropriate concerns into the statement based on your own needs survey results.

Setting Goals, Objectives, and Developing Strategies for Implementation

Developing a plan as to how the program can best, and most efficiently, meet the needs (gathered through needs surveys) is the next step in implementing a developmental school counseling program. This is best accomplished by developing a set of goals and objectives, followed by strategies and techniques for achieving each. Of course, these should coincide, and be representative of, the philosophy and rationale statements previously discussed.

Where appropriate, such goals and objectives should be the goals of the entire district, or even stateside system, and be similar for preschool through twelfth grade levels. There is obvious strength inherent in having common program goals and objectives across schools (district-wide and/or statewide) where possible. This permits counselors to work together as a unit; to pool "targeted" student and other evaluation data, and so forth. For example, one school system has written counseling program *goals* for grades K-12 that are in place in each elementary, middle, and secondary school within the district as follows:

To assist *all* students in:

1. community pride and involvement
2. career development and educational planning
3. school success skills
4. interpersonal communication skills development
5. decision-making and problem-solving skills
6. understanding attitudes and behaviors
7. understanding of self and others, and
8. understanding the school environment

Following the development of written goals for its particular school publics, the next task of the advisory committee is to develop and to write *objectives* revealing specifically how each goal will be reached. For example, again referring to the above mentioned school system, under goal number 8 above (*Understanding the school environment*), the district-wide *objectives* for grade six in *every* elementary school are:

1. Students will demonstrate knowledge of the physical layout of their school.
2. Students will demonstrate knowledge of the school code of conduct.
3. Students will demonstrate knowledge of extracurricular activities, special programs, and services.
4. Students will demonstrate knowledge of school personnel and their roles.

This large system has developed a set of objectives for *each* of the *eight* goals (listed above) for *each* specific *grade* level across the entire school system. These were developed with the different levels of student developmental stages in mind and differ from grade to grade.

After the goals and objectives have been written, the next step is to develop and to place into writing, those strategies and techniques to be utilized by the guidance department in carrying out and in fulfilling each of the objectives. A more detailed description of this process is given in Chapter Three.

Accountability: A Continuous Process

The effective developmental school counselor is accountable. Counselors simply "doing their job" without documentation of their effectiveness is passe. School counselors cannot simply believe and verbally contend that what they are doing "is good;" they must prove it with *hard* data through continuous evaluation. That is, the entire program should be evaluated in an ongoing, continuous process. Each aspect, each phase of the program should be evaluated for its effectiveness as well as each

activity used to carry out the structure of the program. An ongoing evaluation process will reveal the strengths and limitations of the program, thereby permitting appropriate adjustments where and when they are called for. For detailed strategies on program evaluation and school counselor accountability, see John Schmidt's article (Chapter 25).

The Developmental School Counselor: Appropriate Role and Function

As indicated throughout the first two chapters, most experts agree that to be effective, a developmental school counselor needs a written role and function statement approved by their respective principal, system-wide guidance supervisor, and so forth. I have studied many such role and function statements and have found them to be highly similar from school to school and even from state to state where effective developmental programs exist.

Many experts, counseling organizations, state departments of education, and various others have developed appropriate role and function statements for counselors. Among these is the American School Counselor Association (ASCA). ASCA leaders indicate that a school counselor is a certified professional educator who assists students, teachers, parents, and administrators. According to ASCA, the three generally recognized helping processes used by the school counselor are *counseling, consulting* and *coordinating.*

ASCA recently (October 1999) released a statement describing the role of the professional school counselor for the new millennium. They state clearly that the school counselor is a professional educator who addresses the needs of students comprehensively through the implementation of a K-12 developmental school counseling program.

According to ASCA, the developmental school counselor's work is differentiated by attention to age-specific developmental stages of student growth and the needs, tasks, and student interests related to those stages. And further, ASCA indicates that school counselors work with all students, including those who are considered "at-risk" and those with special needs. They are specialists in human behavior and relationships and provide assistance to students through four primary interventions: *counseling (individual and group); large group guidance; consultation; and coordination.* ASCA defines these four counselor interventions as follows:

Counseling is a confidential relationship in which the counselor meets with students individually and in small groups to help them resolve or cope constructively with their problems and developmental concerns.

Large Group Guidance is a planned, developmental, program of guidance activities designed to foster students academic, career, and personal/social development. It is provided for all students through a collaborative effort by counselors and teachers.

Consultation is a collaborative partnership in which the counselor works with parents, teachers, administrators, school psychologists, social workers, visiting teachers, medical professionals, and community health personnel in order to plan and implement strategies to help students be successful in the education system.

Coordination is a leadership process in which the counselor helps organize, manages, and evaluates the school counseling program. The counselor assists parents in obtaining needed services for their children through a referral and follow-up process and serves as liaison between the school and community agencies so that they may collaborate in efforts to help students (ASCA, 1999).

According to ASCA, school counselors are experts in student learning and motivation and are responsible for developing comprehensive school counseling programs that promote and enhance student learning at all levels.

By providing direct interventions within a comprehensive program, ASCA states that school counselors focus their skills, time, and energies on direct services to students, staff, and families.

ASCA recommends that professional school counselors spend at least 70% of their time in direct services to students as described above. ASCA considers a realistic counselor student ratio for effective program delivery to be a maximum of 1:250.

Above all, according to ASCA:

School counselors are student advocates who work cooperatively with other individuals and organizations to promote the development of children, youth, and families in their communities. School counselors, as members of the educational team, consult and collaborate with teachers, administrators, and families to assist students to be successful academically, vocationally, and personally. They work on behalf of students and their families to insure that all school programs facilitate the educational process and offer the opportunity for school success for each student. School counselors are an integral part of all school

efforts to insure a safe learning environment for all members of the school community (ASCA, 1999).

ASCA indicates that professional school counselors must meet the state certification/licensure standards and abide by the laws of the states in which they are employed. To assure high quality practice, school counselors are committed to continued professional growth and personal development. They are proactively involved in professional organizations which foster and promote school counseling at the local, state, and national levels. They uphold the ethical and professional standards of these associations and promote the development of the school counseling profession (ASCA, 1999).

American School Counselor Association (ASCA) National Standards for School Counseling Programs

As stated previously, in the fall of 1997 the American School Counselor Association (ASCA) published the *National Standards for School Counseling Programs*. ASCA's National Standards for School Counseling Programs, long overdue, provide the organizational basis for developing quality comprehensive, developmental school counseling programs that promote educational success and meet the developmental needs *of all students*. By creating this document, ASCA has not only provided a framework for school based school counseling programs, but a comprehensive outline of the developmental needs of school children of all ages. In my opinion, every school in the nation should take the necessary steps to implement these very important standards as soon as possible. *And, ASCA stands ready and available to assist any individual school or school district with the implementation of these very important standards* (see below).

Development of the National Standards for School Counseling Programs

Standards and credentialing in the counseling profession are not a new concept. For example, standards for ethical practices for school counselors were developed by ASCA several years ago and a national specialty certification for school counselors (NCSC) was developed by the National Board for Certified Counselors (NBCC) in 1986. Preparation standards for school counselor training programs were developed by CACREP in 1981. The 1997 ASCA National Standards for School Counseling Programs were established to advocate quality professional school counseling practice and training (ASCA, 1998).

In July 1994, ASCA accepted the challenge of the national standards movement within education and began the process of developing the voluntary national standards for school counseling programs. This process required an examination of theory, research and practice to ensure that all aspects of school counseling were considered. The American College Testing Program (ACT) personnel served as research consultants. In addition, ACT served as the coordinator for the collection of survey information and donated personnel and resources to ensure that the survey design, distribution, and analyses followed universally accepted research practices. Three distinct but integrated components were the basis of the foundation for developing the National Standards: (a) ASCA membership survey data; (b) school counseling research and literature; and (c) field reviews of a draft document by ASCA members. These research components played an important role in designing the comprehensive National Standards for School Counseling Programs that contribute to designing a K-12 school counseling program that focuses on the developmental needs of all students (Campbell & Dahir, 1997).

Results of the ASCA Research

The research conducted by ASCA underlying the development of the National Standards for School Counseling Programs revealed conclusively that a comprehensive school counseling program is developmental and systematic in nature, sequential, clearly defined and accountable. And further, that quality school counseling programs are founded upon developmental psychology, educational philosophy, and counseling methodology. More specifically, the research confirmed that effective school counseling programs should enhance academics, career awareness, basic work skills, self-awareness, interpersonal communication skills and life success skills for all students. According to ASCA, the design of a comprehensive, developmental school counseling program is developed by focusing on needs, interests and issues related to the various stages of student growth. In general, there is a commitment to accept individual uniqueness and to maximize development in three major areas: (a) academic, (b) career, and (c) personal/social development (Campbell & Dahir, 1997).

Organization of the National Standards for School Counseling Programs*

The National School Standards for School Counseling Programs are divided into three broad areas: (1) Academic Development, (2) Career Development, and (3) Personal/Social Development. The standards for each content area are designed to furnish guidance and direction for States, school systems and individual schools to develop effective school counseling programs that encourage academic, personal/social and career success for all students. There are three standards found within each of the three content areas followed by several student competencies suggested as guidelines only, that enumerate desired student learning outcomes. The student competencies define the specific knowledge, attitudes and skills that students should obtain or demonstrate as a result of participating in a comprehensive school counseling program. In other words, the student competencies list the developmental needs of kindergarten through twelfth grade students. The competencies offer a foundation for that which a comprehensive developmental school counseling program should address and deliver, as well as a basis to develop measurable indicators of student performance and success (Campbell & Dahir, 1997). However, ASCA has clearly indicated that the student competencies given under the nine standards described below are suggested as "guidelines" only. That is, the student competencies for each standard *must be adapted to reflect the particular needs of the student population and the academic mission of the school using the ASCA Standards for School Counseling Programs.*

Academic Developmental Needs

The content standards for academic development found in the ASCA National Standards for School Counseling Programs are to be used as a guide for implementing strategies and activities to support and maximize student learning within the school counseling program. Academic development pertains to obtaining the skills, attitudes, and knowledge necessary for effective learning in school and across the lifespan; employing strategies to achieve success in school; and understanding the relationship of academics to vocational choice, and to life at home and in the community. ASCA leaders believe that when students' academic developmental needs are met, they are more likely to achieve in school (Campbell & Dahir, 1997). The three academic development standards along with some sample student competencies are listed next:

Standard A: Students will acquire the attitudes, knowledge, aptitudes, and skills that contribute to effective learning in school and across the life span. Students will (following are two of the many examples of student competencies as given under Standard A in the ASCA Standards):

- *Use communication skills to know when and how to ask for help when needed*

- *Achieve their full academic potential (Campbell & Dahir, 1997).*

Standard B: Students will complete school with the academic preparation essential to choose from a wide range of substantial post-secondary options, including college. Students will (again, two examples of the many given in the ASCA Standards):

- *Establish realistic academic goals in elementary, middle/junior high, and high school*

- *Use problem solving and decision making skills to assess progress towards educational goals (Campbell & Dahir, 1997).*

Standard C: Students will understand the relationship of academics to the world of work, and to life at home and in the community. Students will (two examples of the many given under Standard C):

- *Understand the relationship between learning and work*

- *Demonstrate an understanding of the value of life long learning as essential to seeking, obtaining, and maintaining life goals (Campbell & Dahir, 1997).*

Note: Many additional student competencies (not listed here) are listed in the booklet provided by ASCA under each of the three specific standards related to Academic Development described above. As noted above, ASCA indicated that student competencies must be adapted to reflect the particular needs of a school's student population and those found above are guidelines only.

Career Developmental Needs

Standards found in the career development section of the ASCA Standards provide the foundation for skill, attitude and knowledge acquisition that enable students (K-12) to make a successful transition from school to the world of work, and from job to job across the life career span. Career development includes using strategies that enhance future career success and job satisfaction as well as assisting understanding of the association between personal qualities, education and training, and a career choice. The recommendations of the Secretary's

Commission on Achieving Necessary Skills (SCANS) and the content of the National Career Development Guidelines are also reflected in the career content area standards and competencies listed below (Campbell & Dahir, 1997).

Standard A: Students will acquire the skills to investigate the world of work in relation to knowledge of self and to make appropriate career decisions. Students will (two examples as found in the ASCA Standards):

- *Develop an awareness of personal abilities, skills, interests and motivations*

- *Identify the balance between work and leisure time (Campbell & Dahir, 1997).*

Standard B: Students will employ strategies to achieve future career goals with success and satisfaction. Students will (two examples of the many given under Standard B):

- *Apply decision making skills to career planning and career transitions*

- *Learn to use the Internet to access career planning information (Campbell & Dahir, 1997).*

Standard C: Students will understand the relationship between personal qualities, education, training and the world of work. Students will (two examples follow):

- *Demonstrate how personal qualities relate to achieving personal, social, education and career goals*

- *Understand that work is an important and satisfying means of personal expression (Campbell & Dahir, 1997).*

Note: Again, many additional student competencies (not listed here) are listed in the booklet provided by ASCA under each of the three specific standards related to Career Development described above. I have provided only a few examples of the student competencies as developed by ASCA as guidelines only.

Personal/Social Developmental Needs

As students progress through school and into adulthood, ASCA believes they need to acquire a firm foundation for personal and social growth. Implementing activities and strategies related to the content standards for personal/social development provide students with this foundation and contribute to academic and career success. Personal/social development includes skills, attitudes and knowledge which assist students in respecting and understanding others, acquiring effective interpersonal skills, understanding safety and survival skills and developing into contributing members of society. The standards and sample competencies for personal/social development are given below (Campbell & Dahir, 1997).

Standard A: Students will acquire the knowledge, attitudes and interpersonal skills to help them understand and respect self and others. Students will (two examples follow below):

- *Respect alternative points of view*

- *Learn how to make and keep friends (Campbell & Dahir, 1997).*

Standard B: Students will make decisions, set goals and take action. Students will (three examples):

- *Learn to use a decision-making and problem-solving model*

- *Develop effective coping skills for dealing with problems*

- *Learn when, where and how to seek help for solving problems and making decisions (Campbell & Dahir, 1997).*

Standard C: Students will understand safety and survival skills. Students will (2 examples of the many student competencies given):

- *Demonstrate knowledge of personal information (i.e., telephone number, home address, and emergency contact)*

- *Learn coping skills for managing life events (Campbell & Dahir, 1997).*

Note: As noted previously, many additional student competencies (not listed here) are listed in the booklet provided by ASCA under each of the three specific standards related to Personal/Social Development described above. I have provided only a few examples of these very important student competencies as developed by ASCA (Campbell & Dahir, 1997). Again, the student competencies listed here, and others found under the nine standards given above, are guidelines only and may not apply to your particular student population. The student competencies must be developed, written and adapted to reflect the particular needs of the students and the academic mission of the school. That is, they must be "locally relevant."

Why National Standards?

As a school counselor, or as a school counselor to be, you realize that schools and students have changed and will continue to change and it up to you to remain abreast of these changes. The ASCA Standards provide school counselors with the frame work with which to plan their school programs to keep up with the fast paced changes taking place in our society today. Therefore as noted, every school counselor should begin the process of implementing ASCA's National Standards for School Counseling Programs. These Standards provide developmental school counselors with a direction and a pathway to respond to the needs of students, at all levels (Dahir, Sheldon, & Valiga, 1998).

The National Standards support involvement in and commitment to increasing student achievement. The standards clearly connect school counseling to the current educational reform initiatives and to the educational mission of schools. A National Standards-based program requires school counselors to work collaboratively with classroom teachers to improve student learning and to document success. The standards provide a focal point and offer organizational structure to school counseling programs. They define a quality school counseling program and offer methods to be used to measure its effectiveness once put in place (Dahir, Sheldon, & Valiga, 1998).

Implementing a National Standards-based program requires school counselors to challenge their belief systems and to provide the advocacy and leadership to improve school success for all students. As educators who are student advocates, school counselors support equity in educational opportunities for all students and nurture dreams and aspirations (Dahir, Sheldon, & Valiga, 1998).

The National Standards define the vision and goals for the 21st century school counseling programs. The nine National Standards shift the focus from the school counselor to the school counseling program. As noted above, the standards:

1. Create a framework for a national model for school counseling programs;

2. Establish school counseling as an integral component of the academic mission of school;

3. Encourage equitable access to school counseling services for all students;

4. Identify the key components of a developmental school counseling program;

5. Identify the attitude, knowledge and skills that all students should acquire as a result of the K-12 school counseling program; and

6. Ensure that school counseling programs are comprehensive in design and delivered in a systematic fashion for all students (Dahir, Sheldon, & Valiga, 1998).

Implementation of the National Standards

Within the booklet describing the National Standards for School Counseling Programs, ASCA addresses the need for a systematic method for implementing the National Standards (Dahir, Sheldon, & Valiga, 1998). ASCA indicates that implementation does not "just happen" because the school system has adopted a model program with standards, but that in-depth discussions, planning, designing, implementation and evaluation must occur. During the discussion and planning stages of implementation, ASCA stresses the importance of understanding students' needs and how they relate to the mission of the school. ASCA suggests that a student need assessment be conducted to acquire information regarding the skills students in each school need as they progress through school. Then designing and implementing a school counseling program that encompasses the needed skills outlined in the National Standards that ensure a successful transition throughout the school experience and on to life after high school should follow (Dahir, Sheldon, & Valiga, 1998).

*Note: The American School Counselor Association has granted permission for Dr. Joe Wittmer to reproduce the nine national standards, and the descriptive information presented above to use for educational purposes only.

A copy of the National Standards for School Counseling Programs and the book on implementing the Standards: *Visions into Action: Implementing the Nationals Standards for School Counseling Programs* (1998), can be purchased from ASCA Publications, P.O. Box 960, Herndon VA 20172-0960. (Telephone: 800-401-2404)

More on the School Counselor's Role

Robert Myrick (1997) listed the following as the developmental school counselor's role:

- to assume leadership of organizing and developing a comprehensive developmental guidance and counseling program.
- to provide individual counseling services to students.
- to provide small group counseling services to students.

- to organize and lead large group guidance units, sessions, and activities.
- to train and coordinate peer facilitators.
- to consult with parents, teachers, and administrators regarding special concerns and needs of students.
- to consult with teachers and administrators about guidance and counseling interventions for students.
- to develop guidance units that evolve from students needs.
- to help develop and coordinate a teachers as advisors program (TAP).
- to co-lead, on occasion, a guidance unit or session with a teacher, perhaps during Teachers as Advisors Program (TAP).
- to serve as a professional resource to teacher-advisors about brief counseling and behavior change.
- to help identify students who have special needs or problems and to help find alternative education or guidance services for them.
- to coordinate faculty and staff development programs related to guidance.
- to coordinate other guidance related services (student assessment, advisement, community resources, special education, and placement). (Myrick 1997)

In addition to the above five interventions suggested by ASCA, Myrick (1997) added a sixth under the "indirect services" category; as *trainer/coordinator* of peer facilitator programs and projects. Myrick (1997) provided the following *weekly* time commitment scheduling plan for K-12 counselors: four to six individual counseling sessions with high priority students *(2 to 6 hours per week)*; 4 to 5 small groups *(4 to 10 hours per week)*; 2 to 3 large groups *(2 to 3 hours per week)*; peer facilitator training/coordination *(1 to 5 hours per week)*; consultation and coordination activities *(variable as needed)* (Myrick, 1997).

Hannaford (1991) suggested that the counselor's delivery program include three basic services; *coordinating, counseling,* and *consulting.* She described these services as follows:

1. **Coordinating Services:** These services relate to testing, placement, and post-secondary planning at all levels.

2. **Counseling (academic, career, and preventive/developmental)** Academic counseling is provided through classroom planning and motivational group dynamics. On the high school level the Four-Year Plan begins in the ninth grade and continues through graduation.

Career counseling begins in kindergarten with exposure to basic job awareness and the self understanding and decision making skills necessary to implement lifelong decisions. This activity continues through seventh grade and ends in the spring of a student's eighth grade. This includes an Interest Planning Program that involves all eighth grade students, a night for parents, and involvement with teachers. Through these formative years, emphasis on job awareness is planned for each school year (Hannaford, 1991).

She further indicated that as a part of career counseling, the ninth grade counselor begins individual student planning toward a definite direction. Postsecondary preparation is emphasized during the junior and senior year along with vocational school opportunities and other post-secondary chances. Hannaford strongly supported the notion of providing career centers in high schools.

In addition to academic and career counseling, Hannaford added *Preventive/Developmental Counseling* as a counselor function. She stated that the major goal of an elementary and middle school counselor is preventive/developmental while the high school counselor works with students in this area on *request*. This dimension is developed as part of the basic program. According to Hannaford, in an effective program, students are taught basic coping skills, interpersonal relations, communication skills, decision making and problem solving techniques.

3. **Consulting.** According to Hannaford, it is the task of the counselor to provide consultative services to the adults surrounding the student in order that reinforcement can be strengthened (pp. 66-67).

In addition to the above, Hannaford stated that K-12 counselors should lead parent workshops and teacher staff development (credit or non-credit). Hannaford (1991) considered it to be very important that counselors teach counseling skills to a large number of people in order to meet the heavy demands.

Summary

In this chapter, the following guidelines for beginning the implementation of a comprehensive developmental guidance program were suggested:

1. Gain the support and approval of the school's administration for an appropriate role and function statement.

2. Appoint a School Counseling Advisory Committee.

3. Develop and place into writing a philosophy and/or mission statement for the guidance program.

4. Develop, administrate, and analyze the needs surveys of students, parents, and other appropriate school counselor publics.

5. Write a locally appropriate program rationale statement—why a comprehensive program is needed in the school.

6. Write realistic goals and objectives for the program.

7. Develop strategies for implementation and for delivery of the goals.

8. Develop an accountability system that is ongoing and continuous.

The chapter concluded with the role and function of a developmental school counselor as written by ASCA and others. Of three figures, one concerned strategies for changing an existing school counseling program into one based on the 1997 ASCA Standards for School Counselling Programs, and two are examples of needs surveys.

As noted throughout the first two chapters, students need specific information and counseling to address the societal problems they bring to school. Early exposure to a comprehensive school counseling program builds an emotionally healthy foundation for children and results in improved academic achievement.

Also, as noted, we must all take responsibility for our children as their future is our future. Teachers and parents look to counselors to respond to the academic, social, emotional, and career development needs of all students. Counselors should be prepared for their challenge.

In developing policies and programs to address the problems our young people face, we must make the best use of all our resources. School counselors are often the only mental health professionals to whom students will have access and they are the professionals who bridge the academic, career, and affective domain in students' lives.

Together, counselors, teachers, parents, and policy makers create a powerful force in the fight to enhance the lives of our young people. Through their collaborative efforts, children will achieve their maximum potential.

Figure 2.1
Sample High School Student Needs Assessment

Instruction to Students:

Please read the following items CAREFULLY and CHECK any category that applies to you. Please answer this survey seriously!! Checking a category will NOT automatically place you in a group—this is just a survey, not a sign up sheet. At the end of each area there is a *blank line* which can be used to make suggestions as to activities you'd like to see offered, but are not listed here. The purpose of this survey is to help the Guidance Office determine what type of activities/groups students want offered during the next school year. We will review the categories most often checked by students and will try to offer those activities for you. Thanks for your cooperation.

Career Concerns

❑ I need help in choosing a career; I don't know what I want to do after I graduate; I'm confused as to what type of work would really suit my personality, abilities, and interests.

(CAREER VALUES)

❑ I know what I want to do but need more specific information on a particular career; I'd really like to talk with someone in the career field I've chosen.

(CAREER CLUSTER EXPLORATION)

❑ I would like more information on the right way to apply for a job; I'm somewhat nervous about going on a job interview.

(JOB INTERVIEW SKILLS)

❑ I need someone to help me find a job; I'd like to or need to work part-time and don't know where to apply.

(JOB PLACEMENT SERVICES)

Other Career Concerns: _____

Health Concerns

❑ I would like help to lose weight; I would like to improve my physical appearance and condition; I'd like to learn more about exercising.

(WEIGHT CONTROL GROUP)

❑ I'd like to generally improve my physical appearance/health; I would like to know more about nutrition; how to care for my skin/hair.

(GENERAL HEALTH CONCERNS)

❑ I'd like to learn more about drug/alcohol use and abuse; I have a friend whose really into drugs and I'm worried; what drugs are really dangerous; someone in my family is an alcoholic and I don't know how to handle it.

(DRUG ABUSE)

❑ I would like to talk to someone individually about a health-related problem (nurse, counselor, etc.).

(INDIVIDUAL CONFERENCES)

Other Health Concerns: _____

Home/Family Concerns

❏ I'd like to learn how to cope with my parents' separation or divorce; I'm having difficulty accepting a new stepparent, stepsister, or stepbrother.

(DIVORCE/SEPARATION)

❏ My parents don't understand or trust me, we seem to disagree all the time; I can't talk to them about a lot of my problems—I'm treated as a child! I need help to try to get along better with my parents.

(FAMILY CONFLICT GROUP)

Other Home/Family Concerns: _____

Personal/Social Concerns

❏ I lose my temper easily, lack of self-control, I always seem to feel nervous in the classroom and/or with other people. I worry a lot, I need to learn to relax.

(STRESS/ANXIETY MANAGEMENT)

❏ I'd like to discover more about myself and others, better understanding of my feelings and personality; I'd like to be able to discuss my values, fears, and needs with other people my age; learn how to get along better with others.

(SELF-AWARENESS ACTIVITIES)

❏ I would like to discuss dating, relationships (male/female), marriage and family with others; how do I really know if I'm in love; I feel shy with the opposite sex.

(MALE-FEMALE RELATIONSHIPS)

❏ I'd like to be able to talk to a counselor privately about a personal problem.

Other Personal/Social Concerns: _____

Educational Concerns

❏ I have trouble taking tests; I'm not good at studying; I Don't really know how to take notes or do research properly; I can't seem to manage my study time properly; I'm usually worried about my grades.

❏ I need help in choosing a college; I need to know more about financial aid; how do I apply to a college; what tests (SAT/ACT) do I need to take to go to college and what are those tests like; what classes should I take in high school to prepare for college.

(COLLEGE WORKSHOP)

Other Educational Concerns: _____

Adapted from Zephyrhills High School Guidance Department, Zephyrhills, Florida

Figure 2.2
Sample Middle School Student Needs Assessment

Student directions:

This survey is anonymous. PLEASE DO NOT WRITE YOUR NAME ON THIS PAGE OR ON THE ANSWER SHEET. Read the list slowly. After reading, please rank order the five (5) concerns important to you (in order of importance to you). Number one (1) is the greatest concern you have, number 2 is the second greatest concern, and so forth, down to number 5 in descending order. Place your ranking in the blank to the left of the items. Thanks.

_____ Poor complexion or skin trouble

_____ Want more information about alcohol/drugs

_____ Overweight

_____ Worried about death or dying

_____ Often tense or uptight (stressful feelings)

_____ Don't know how to study

_____ Afraid of failing in school work

_____ Not getting along with a teacher

_____ Afraid to speak up in class

_____ Parents separated, divorced, or fighting

_____ Parents not understanding me

_____ Deciding what courses to take in high school

_____ Want to know more about careers/career options

_____ Dating

_____ Slow in making friends

_____ Wanting a more pleasing personality

_____ Losing my temper

_____ Getting into trouble

_____ Lacking in self-confidence

Other Concerns I Have (not listed above):

1. _____
2. _____
3. _____
4. _____

Adapted from Gulf Middle School Guidance Department, Pasco County, Florida

Figure 2.3
Implementing the ASCA Standards: One School District's Approach

(Much of Figure 2.3 first appeared in *The ASCA Counselor,* the newspaper of the American School Counselor Association, Summer 1999. Appreciation is extended to Robert Kuhn for his assistance with writing Figure 2.3.)

The newly elected superintendent of a small school district in Florida outlined an agenda of his initiatives for changes within the school system. His number one initiative was to increase the district's graduation rate as it had been a dismal 50% the previous year. The superintendent believed strongly that one of the necessary first steps was to focus on the school counseling program and wanted to begin by conducting a top to bottom review/revision of his school system's K-12 school counseling program. It was at this point that I, the editor of this book, was asked to serve as a consultant to the small district in this important process.

In my first meeting with the superintendent, I briefly presented an overview of the process I would use to evaluate the then K-12 school counseling program, how I would go about revising the program, etc. Following a discussion of the ASCA Standards, *it was agreed that the district would work toward the implementation of these K-12 standards* in a "locally relevant" manner. We further agreed that the place to begin was with the current counselors and then to involve representatives from all constituents, all of the district's publics (from School Board members to students) in the development, implementation and subsequent evaluation of the revised program. At this meeting, timelines and a structure for revision were put into place.

In sum, the recommended steps agreed to with the superintendent were:

1. The superintendent would call for a meeting with all of the district's K-12 school counselors to seek their commitment, to explain the process, etc. Each of the 19 counselors was present at this meeting conducted by the superintendent. It was obvious that the counselors were eager but yet anxious about the upcoming process and what it would mean for them and their school. However, the superintendent put them at ease and both he and the counselors came to the conclusion that the district's K-12 school counseling program was in need of major revision. At one point during that meeting, the superintendent put on a T-shirt with the following written on the front: *"I'm a School Counselor"* with a picture of a school bus leading the way toward: *"Destination Graduation"* and: *"School Counselors Make all the Difference."* He also showed the counselors a T-shirt he had specially made for the occasion with a picture of a person with the head of a chicken and the following words appearing under it: *"I'm Satisfied with a 50% Graduation Rate!"* On the back of this same T-shirt were pictures of counselors (characterizations) meeting in a group. The counselors were making statements such as: *"I'm too busy,"* and *"It's School Policy,"* etc. At that same meeting *The superintendent informed the counselors that no one would be losing their counseling position (unless that was their choice) but that changes in role and function would be necessary and that in-service professional development would be made available to all counselors needing, or wanting it, once the program was revised and ready to be put in place within their respective schools.* Of course, the counselors had many questions. One question on everyone's mind was: "What about my school principal's commitment to the revised program?" *The superintendent made it clear to the counselors that all school principals would be required to implement the revised program at their school and would be held accountable for it's evaluation at the end of each school year.*

2. That the superintendent would meet with K-12 school principals, other administrators and staff and seek their commitment to the revision. It is obvious that a committed superintendent will greatly "assist" with the principals' implementation of the revised program at his/her school, respectively.

3. That the process would take *a year or more* to complete and that, when the final revision was completed and the "new" counselor role and function statement written as based on the ASCA National Standards for School Counseling Programs, The superintendent would be present in support of the revised program when the counselors presented the new program to the *School Board for approval and endorsement.* It is very important that the school counselors (by level-elementary, middle, and high school) present the revised "ASCA Standards" program to the School Board followed by the superintendent's public endorsement of the "new" school counseling program. This is needed for system wide implementation to occur.

4. That when the revised school counseling program was approved by the School Board, each K-12 school in the district would elect or appoint a Student Development Committee, consisting of building level counselor(s), teachers, parents, administrators, and students. *The major role of this committee would be to implement and evaluate (annually) the revised program and to report back to the district's school board on an annual basis.*

A Workshop Approach

Many methods and procedures have proven effective in changing/revising an existing school counseling program. The method selected was to convene all concerned school publics for an all day long workshop addressed specifically to the existing guidance programs at the elementary, middle and high school levels. That is, *three such day long meetings* were scheduled; one focusing on the elementary level, one on the middle school program and a third focusing on the high school guidance program.

Since the superintendent, his administrative staff and school board members were invited to attend each of the three day-long meetings, all meetings were held at the district's main, administrative office complex. Meeting at the "downtown" administrative complex gives the process immediate credibility and clearly demonstrates the commitment of the superintendent and his or her staff.

As noted, the first day-long meeting was held with representatives from the 9 elementary schools in the district. The superintendent formally invited each of the counselors to the main office complex for the day-long meeting and requested they each bring their *building principal and/or assistant principal, their curriculum director and/or equivalent administrator, two teachers, and a minimum of two parents to this first meeting.*

One week later similar "invitations" were sent to the five middle schools (6 counselors) for their meeting at the downtown school system's administrative office complex. And, subsequently, the same meeting was set for the five high schools (8 counselors). In addition to bringing parents and teachers to the meeting, each of the middle and high school counselors was asked to bring a cross section of 4-5 students from their respective school to participate in the day-long workshops. **Note:** A meeting room with movable chairs and tables on which to write is a "must" when conducting such a workshop.

It important to set an "openness" tone and clearly state the objectives to those present: (1) "to take a good 'look' at the current guidance program at each educational level; (2) to seek assistance from you who are here today in strengthening it, and, (3) to ask that you be willing to revise any and all aspects of the current counseling program needed to bring it into compliance with the ASCA Standards." I also asked the participants to be open, honest and forthright concerning the process and subsequent activities that were about to occur during this day-long workshop.

Again, encouragement from the top administrator for openness and requested assistance from the participants by him/her is crucial when conducting such a workshop. The presenters, with the presence and vocal support of the "head" administrator, set the tone for whether the workshop will be productive and have the desired outcomes.

The following (positive) participant guidelines were presented at the beginning of each of the 3 day-long workshops: (1) "We are here to honestly, and in an open manner, share our ideas, thoughts, and feelings regarding the school counseling program without getting into personal names or particular school counseling programs, and (2) To listen and work at hearing each others thoughts, ideas and feelings without judgment, untimely advice or evaluation."

The Three Workshops

Following are the steps that were followed in conducting each of the three separate (elementary, middle and high school) workshops. Again, the purpose of each was to evaluate the current district's K-12 school counseling programs and to revise them as needed to coincide with the ASCA Standards. *(I strongly suggest a district wide approach to a revision of the entire K-12 school counseling program be undertaken as opposed to an individual school only).*

The following steps are written for "would be" workshop presenter(s) wishing to revise an existing program into one using the ASCA Standards.

Step One:

Following the "head" administrator's opening comments, state the objectives and guidelines for participation (see above, but keep them "locally relevant") for the day-long workshop. With the middle and high schools groups, spend some extra time assuring the students present that you want them to be as open as possible. Stress to them that they will not be evaluated nor will there be any retribution against anyone present or not present.

Divide the participants into *homogeneous* groups of five-six each. That is, if 30 teachers are in attendance, divide them into six groups of five each (at 5 tables). If 15 parents have been invited (and this is an appropriate number if 30 teachers are present) there would be 3 tables of five parents each. And, if 15 students are in attendance you would have 3 tables of 5 students each, and so forth. There will probably be one table for the school superintendent and staff/administration, one for the school board, and one for the counselors.

Step Two:

Provide each homogeneous group with a piece of 3 x 4 newsprint and a black felt tip pen. Request that they take a few minutes to become acquainted at their respective tables and to then appoint a recorder and presenter for their table. Then, ask them to think about an ideal guidance program for a school that coincides with their school level - elementary, middle, or high school, racial mix, rural, urban, and so forth. Suggest they not think about their specific school's guidance program, but to think instead of the ideal program and what such an ideal program would "look like." That is, ask each group (use an overhead transparency) to *"List 10 to 12 aspects, components, or characteristics of the ideal (elementary or middle or high school) school guidance program. That is, what would such a program look like? What type services and to whom would they be provided? What would the components be?"* Ask the table recorders to use the *black* felt tip pen when writing on the newsprint, abbreviate if necessary, and suggest the printing be large enough (2 inches in height) so all can see it when the newsprint is later taped to the wall.

Encourage each table's participants to use the democratic process in deciding which 10 to 12 characteristics/components/aspects of an ideal program to place on their respective papers. Allow 25-30 minutes for this exercise. Encourage them to be creative and give support where needed. Especially provide support to the student and parent groups if deemed appropriate. It has been found that both parents and students will need your encouragement to proceed with the assignment. Let them know that their ideas are equally as important as any other group in the room. Each table should identify themselves (their group) on their respective newsprint papers—students, teachers, and so forth and to choose a presenter for the next exercise below (Step Three).

Step Three:

Using masking tape (it won't peel off the wall paint!), have each homogeneous table tape their newsprint to the room wall and provide a 15-20 minute discussion on those characteristics appearing on the different papers. Some discussion might ensue concerning the meaning of certain statements found on the papers, etc. Be especially concerned that those "characteristics" listed by the students and parent groups are understood by all present. Teachers and administrators generally have little difficulty with this assignment. You will probably be surprised at some of the "ideal" components generated by the various groups, especially by the students. Use your best "facilitative" skills when leading this discussion.

Step Five:

Next, divide the participants equally and as *heterogeneous* as possible. That is, have at least one administrator at each table as well as some parents, students, teachers, and non-instructional staff. One method of accomplishing this is to simply have the participants at each homogenous table count off to the desired number of heterogeneous tables you want. If desired, the heterogeneous groups could be somewhat larger, perhaps seven or eight participants at each table. Again, each table group should appoint a recorder and a presenter and take a few minutes to become acquainted.

Leave the first newsprint's (Step One) taped to the wall and give each group a new piece of newsprint and ask them to study (carefully) the papers now on the wall (developed by the previous homogeneous groups) and to take from them any ideas they like, or come up with *new* ones, and to again; *"Develop the ideal guidance and counseling program for a school system of your size and nature"* (i.e., if you are in a rural setting and at the elementary level, your assignment given might be to: *"Develop and list 8 to 10 characteristics of the ideal counseling and guidance program for an elementary program in a rural setting."*) Again, request that they not focus on their particular school's guidance program. Allow 25 minutes or more for this exercise. Remind them that the democratic process should be used at each table. Make certain that each participant, especially the students, parents and non-instructional staff at each table, realizes that his or her vote, ideas, are equally important as anyone else's at their particular table (including the principle, teachers, etc.). That is, take the appropriate measures to insure that the students are not intimidated into not participating at the heterogeneous tables. Their input is vital. **Note:** Selected, upper level, elementary students (5th and/or 6th graders) might also participate in such a workshop approach.

Step Five:

Prior to having these particular papers (the heterogeneous tables) taped to the wall, pick up each *black* felt tip pen and provide each table's recorder with a *red* felt tip pen. Next, ask each table to evaluate their overall school district's guidance program (the overall program as they know it—elementary or middle or high school level!) against each of the points of the ideal program described on their respective papers *(This evaluation, to be effective, must be a complete surprise to the participants). Participates knowing in advance that it will occur sabotages the process).* That is, request that they rate the school systems' overall school counseling program against each ideal component on their newsprint using 0 to 5 as a rating scale with 5 being absolutely ideal; the highest possible rating for that particular characteristic/component. The bottom line goal is to objectively evaluate the school systems' current guidance program against each of the ideal characteristics (one at a time) appearing on their respective papers, 0 to 5. Remind them that they are not to evaluate one particular school's guidance and counseling program.

This is not a time for the school counselor, the administration, or anyone else present to be thin-skinned, defensive, or overly sensitive regarding the current guidance program. Make it clear that you want the participants to give their honest evaluation of what they know about the district's current guidance program. If some indicate that they lack specific knowledge regarding certain aspects, ask them to be general in their evaluations.

Each table group should be requested to evaluate each characteristic on their respective paper concluding with a "table consensus" for each listed component. That is, each of the characteristics on their paper should be evaluated with either a 0,1,2, 3, 4, or 5 or a fractional combination of these numbers. Some table groups may desire to use a closed ballot for their (vote) evaluations. However, most will simply vote by a show of hands. But, again, there should be a general consensus; a number (O to 5) in *red*, should appear beside each characteristic on the ideal list when compared to the school systems' current guidance program at that particular level.

This can be somewhat of a tense moment for the participants, especially the counselors present. No one likes a "public evaluation." Again, encouragement from the upper level administration and the counselor(s) to carry out this task in an honest and forthright manner will expedite the process and lower the emotions of the moment. Individual group newsprint should (must) remain as anonymous as possible. However, if certain groups insist on identifying their particular paper, do not discourage them. However, it has been my experience that the evaluation process works much better if no attempt is made to tie a certain newsprint paper to a particular table group.

Step Six:

Ask that each heterogeneous table group again tape their respective papers to the wall and have the presenter for each table lead a brief discussion concerning the content and evaluations found on their respective papers. Again, this is not the time to be defensive about anything written on the paper or concerning any evaluation appearing on the respective papers. There is no doubt that some evaluations for particular components found on the pa-

pers will be negative, or below average (3 or below). Thus, take what you see, go from there, and "take your gains later." If you've asked the participants to be open and honest, praise them for being so.

Remind the participants, that up to this point in the workshop, the ideal guidance program characteristics have come from the participants and they in turn have evaluated their school counseling program against the ideal. And, let them know that a next step will be for them to "fix" the current program as needed. At this point in time, it is appropriate to hold an open discussion with the entire group or, if there are several counselors available to serve as facilitators, in smaller groups. Make certain individual students and parents are permitted to present their views; that they are heard regarding their evaluations.

An excellent discussion method for a large group such as this is to bring specific groups into the center ring, a "fishbowl" approach. Perhaps, a group of teachers, then parents, then students, etc. could appear in the fishbowl. This is an effective method for holding an open discussion of the newsprint papers and subsequent evaluations as they appear on the wall.

Following this discussion, conduct a quick survey of the evaluations appearing on the papers. A hand-held calculator will come in handy at this point. The limitations, strengths, weaknesses and where improvements are needed in the guidance program will be immediately obvious. *Any "3" or below evaluations are definite signs of limitations. Look for consistencies across the papers. Generally, the limitations of the systems' current guidance program at the elementary, middle or high school level will appear similarly on most newsprint.*

Step Seven:

Following the break, point out the obvious strengths and limitations of the current guidance and counseling program at this level (elementary/middle/high) program and hold an open and frank discussion of the evaluations. Use your best large group counseling skills while facilitating this discussion. Many large group approaches could be used to facilitate this discussion, i.e., to continue the "fishbowl" approach or use others. This is not the time for talking about what could have been, but instead, what is. Allow the amount of time needed to fully discuss these issues.

Step Eight:

Have each of the heterogeneous table group's work on (solve/fix) two or three of the problem areas (those evaluated three or below). Request they list specific methods, strategies, and actions needed that will improve the guidance program in this area and to develop a plan of action toward a specific solution. Ask them to discuss their solutions among themselves—brainstorm, but to be realistic! If the superintendent has not agreed to "new dollars" including the following guideline to the table' participants: *"What can be done to accomplish the part of the guidance program you're working on at your table without more money or more personnel."* Request that their brainstorming solutions be placed in writing and then each group should report (to the entire group of participants) their suggestions or solutions for improving the guidance program. Involve the superintendent in this part of the workshop by having him/her comment (positively) on the different solutions brought forward by each table group. *You will find that the solutions are always in line with an ASCA Standard and this is the best time to introduce the ASCA Standards to the non-counseling participants.*

Step Nine:

Introduce the ASCA Standards to the participants. Some well-designed overheads, or a power point presentation, are excellent methods to use to accomplish this task. Let participants know that you and the Superintendent (or other high level administrator) believe that incorporating the ASCA Standards in each school within the system will go a long way toward solving the problems *"We've been discussing today."* You will find that the participants are excited about the ASCA Standards. Be prepared for many questions about how they might be implemented.

Have the participants return to their original homogeneous table groups to conduct a quick paper and pencil evaluation of the workshop, and then have each group elect *two* persons from their respective table to become representative members of the follow-up, very important *"District Wide ASCA Standards Steering Committee."* This should result in having teachers, parents, administrators, counselors and two non-instructional personnel as Steering Committee members (students are optional since they may not be able to give the time needed to serve on the steering committee). I suggest electing three Steering Committees, one for each grade level (elementary, middle and high school). The job of each Steering Committee is to work with the district's student services administrator toward an implementation of the ASCA Standards at their educational level, respectively. They are asked to keep everyone at their school informed of the progress.

It is important to save all newsprint, written solutions, and so forth and to meet regularly with this steering committee during the year as needed. This is an important, time consuming committee assignment and released time to serve *must* be given to the school personnel selected if the revision begun with the day-long workshops described above is to be successful.

Step Ten:

Have the district wide, elected Steering Committees meet periodically with the district guidance director (and others as deemed appropriate) to study the materials from the workshop; the heterogeneous papers, the homogeneous papers, implementation of the ASCA Standards, and so forth.

The main objective assigned to the Steering Committees should be to identify national ASCA competencies pertinent to local student needs and to design and carry out an action plan detailing strategies to achieve the ASCA competencies identified at their educational level. The committees should be instructed to establish the desired program outcomes by assessing student, teacher and community needs in a paper and pencil needs survey.

The three Steering Committees where this workshop occurred were instructed by the Superintendent to design the guidance program so that the counselors at all three levels would be working jointly with classroom teachers, media specialists, students, parents and community personnel to address the needs of students in each ASCA competency selected. That is, to develop an appropriate guidance delivery system for the development of the "total student" that would include the appropriate school and community personnel as needed to be effective.

The committees were instructed to write action plans that would include priority objectives, based on the ASCA Standards, with appropriate activities and strategies designed to fulfill the objectives. The action plan at the elementary level includes such things as: suggested materials and activities to be incorporated into the regular classroom curricular, use of career interest surveys, activities to involve parents and community volunteers in academic, personal/social and career development activities, a peer helper program in each school, and so forth.

At the middle and high school level, the action plans include peer mediation programs at each school, new units focusing on peer pressure, conflict resolution, career planning, academic planning, personal decision making among others. Of course, ongoing individual and group counseling will be the norm at each school.

More specifically, each of the three Steering Committees in this particular Florida school district were given the charge to develop an action plan as follows:

1. Identify the competencies under each specific ASCA Standard as locally relevant in each of the three areas (Academic, Career and Person/Social Development),

2. Develop a strategy for the implementation of each competency and,

3. Identify the personnel in the school responsible for carrying a specific strategy to completion. For example, under the ASCA area of Academic Development, Standard C, one competency identified by the Elementary level Steering Committee is: Relate School to Life Experiences. The committee has identified 3 specific Strategies for assisting K-5 students to become "competent" in this area and have identified the personnel responsible for assisting the school counselor in carrying out each of the three specific strategies.

4. Develop a locally appropriate, developmental guidance program at each educational level that will involve all "stake-holders" in a program designed for all students.

5. Develop an evaluation/accountability plan to be conducted annually.

6. With these five objectives in mind, write a job description for guidance counselors at each educational level to be endorsed and approved by the Superintendent and School Board.

The Committees met once a month for the entire academic school (1998-99) year and finished their assignments on time as scheduled. The work and commitment involved in meeting the above 6 objectives was tremendous.

The counselors at each of the three educational levels presented the revised school counseling program to the Superintendent and School Board and received unanimous endorsement and approval. The district K-12 counselors are excited about their "new" role and function as based on the *ASCA Standards for School Counseling Programs*.

References

ASCA. (1999). *Role statement: The school counselor.* Alexandria, VA: ASCA Press.

ASCA (1990). *School counselor competencies.* Alexandria, VA: ASCA Press.

Campbell, C.A., & Dahir, C. (1997). *Sharing the vision: The national standards for school counseling programs.* Alexandria, VA: ASCA Press.

Character education. The Center for the 4th and 5th R's. www.character.org (1999).

Ciabattari, J. (1999). Blackboards and bullets. *Parade Magazine,* July, 25, 1999, p.10.

Cloud, J. (1999). What can schools do? *Time Magazine.* May 3, 1999. Author.

Dahir, C., Sheldon, B. & Valiga, M. (1998). *Vision into action: Implementing the national standards for school counseling programs.* Alexandria, VA: ASCA Press.

Gysbers, N.C. (1997). *Comprehensive guidance programs that work.* Greensboro, NC: ERIC Counseling and Personnel Services Clearinghouse.

Hannaford, M.J. (1991). *Counselors under construction.* Marietta, GA: Active Parenting, Inc.

Myrick, R.D. (1997). *Developmental guidance and counseling: A practical approach,* (3rd ed.). Minneapolis, MN: Education Media Corporation.

Rye, D.R., & Sparks, R. (1998). *Strengthening K-12 school counseling programs: A support system approach.* Muncie, IN: Accelerated Development.

Sink, A. & MacDonald, G. (1998). The status of comprehensive guidance and counseling in the united states. *ASCA: Professional School Counseling, 2,* 88-94.

Time Magazine. (1999). *Numbers.* May 17, 1999. Author.

Why elementary school counselors? American School Counselor Association. www.schoolcounselor.org (1999).

Wittmer, J. & Thompson, D. (1995) *Large group counseling: A k-12 sourcebook..* Minneapolis, MN: Educational Media Corporation.

Wittmer, J., Thompson, D., & Loesch, L. (1997). *Classroom guidance activities: A sourcebook for elementary school counselors.* Minneapolis, MN: Educational Media Corporation.

Wittmer, J., Thompson, D. & Sheperis, C. (1999). *The peace train: A school-wide violence prevention program.* Minneapolis, MN: Educational Media Corporation.

Section II

The Counselor's Role in Managing the Program

As noted in Chapter 2, school developmental guidance and counseling programs are designed to help *all* students (K-12) develop their educational, social, career, and personal strengths. In addition, effective developmental school counselors assist students to become responsible and productive individuals. What is the role of developmental school counselors and how do they effectively manage comprehensive counseling programs? That is the focus of this section.

The appropriate roles of developmentally oriented elementary, middle, and high school counselors, along with management strategies, are described and delineated. The writers of the chapters concerning the three school levels (elementary, middle, and high school) clearly indicate that the developmental approach focuses on the *normal* processes students encounter while growing up in our complex society. And, as noted several times throughout these next three chapters, the school counselor's function includes *creating*, *organizing*, and *managing* comprehensive developmental guidance and counseling programs which includes providing appropriate counselor interventions as needed. Developmental counseling programs, at all three school levels, are integral parts of a school's total educational program.

In Chapter 3, Dr. Beverly Snyder writes: *In an effective program, the school administration, faculty, students, parents, and community combine efforts to provide an all-encompassing, comprehensive guidance program for all students.*

Dr. Snyder does an excellent job of providing the organizational structure needed for a successful developmentally oriented counseling program at the elementary level. In addition, she discusses implementation strategies and describes the role and function of an effective elementary school counselor. As noted, management strategies needed to succeed as an elementary counselor are also presented.

In discussing the role and function of a developmental middle school counselor (Chapter 4), Dr. Bonnie Baker writes: *The often used phrase 'caught in the middle' could easily serve as a motto for the middle school counselor of the new millennium for several reasons. First, the unique population of middle school students are 'caught in the middle' between childhood and adolescence in a developmental stage known as 'transescence' This difficult developmental period accounts for many of the counseling issues middle school counselors must address each and every school day.* Dr. Baker does an excellent job in delineating workable strategies for today's developmentally oriented middle school counselor. Her section on effective "time management" strategies is especially appropriate for the busy middle school counselor.

Drs. Doris Coy and Susan Sears (Chapter 5) have written an excellent chapter concerning the developmentally oriented high school counselor's role and function. They state that the effective high school developmental counseling program is "*driven by student needs and results in student outcomes for which counselors are accountable.*" Coy and Sears also remind us that high school counselors must carefully choose how they spend their time and energy, something that has not been the case in too many high schools. In addition, they've provided (Figure 5.1) a crisis management policy that applies to schools at all levels.

Chapter 6 is a new chapter and concerns the school counselor as a mental health provider. Drs. Smith and Archer have written an excellent chapter on this concept.

Drs. Mary Ann Clark and Carolyn Stone write concerning the developmental school counselor as educational leader in the final chapter of Section II. They urge counselors to look for opportunities to develop and implement their special leadership skills in their respective schools.

School counselors must be able to effectively and succinctly articulate their role and function to "self" and "others." If not (and unfortunately this is too often the case) someone else, usually the school principal, does it for them, and too often, in an inappropriate manner.

Joe Wittmer

Chapter 3

Managing an Elementary School Developmental Counseling Program: The Role of the Counselor

by

Beverly A. Snyder

Beverly Snyder, EdD, NCC, is an Associate Professor at the University of Colorado at Colorado Springs, School of Education, Counseling and Human Services Program. She held the position of district Instructional Support Counselor in Orange County, Florida during the time the elementary counseling program described here was being developed and when this chapter first was written.

Introduction

Many researchers and school counseling experts (Gysbers, 1997; Myrick, 1997) believe that the learning, personal/social, and career development needs of students can be more effectively met with a kindergarten through twelfth grade guidance program that systematically and comprehensively addresses developmental stages that students experience as they progress through the school. Such developmentally-based school counseling programs are structured so as to systematically parallel the identifiable developmental stages through which children progress. Modern day developmental programs, such as the one described in this chapter, have advanced from a reactive, crisis model to a proactive approach.

As stated by Wittmer in Chapter 1, the concept that guidance and counseling services should be for all students is a fundamental tenet of the developmental approach described in this chapter. This approach also embraces several other ideas that found their beginnings in the school restructuring/reform movement. They include the following: (1) The elementary school developmental guidance program should have a curriculum-based approach responsive to the needs of the population it serves; (2) Activities conducted through classroom guidance, small groups, and so forth should be based on overall goals and objectives that are applicable to this age level (Gysbers & Henderson, 1999; Myrick, 1997; Wittmer & Thompson, 1995); and (3) Developmental guidance programs are proactive and based on educating today's youngsters rather than simply being reactive to the multiple concerns that invariably appear in their lives (Myrick, 1997).

Program Description

Orange County, Florida's comprehensive elementary level developmental guidance program was founded on the belief that each student is unique and singular, possessing intrinsic and specific rights. In the Orange County system, developmental guidance counselors attempt to identify certain skills and experiences that elementary age students need to experience as part of their being successful in school and in other aspects of their lives. As noted, the skill building component in the developmental approach is related directly to children's developmental stages, tasks, and learning conditions. The comprehensive developmental approach to elementary school guidance described in this chapter focuses on the needs common to all students and is based, in large part, on the often quoted and still relevant Havighurst (1972) model given below:

Developmental Stages/Tasks

Infancy and Early Childhood (Ages 0-5)

1. Learning to walk
2. Learning to take solid foods
3. Learning to talk
4. Learning to control elimination of body wastes
5. Learning sex differences and sexual modesty
6. Forming concepts and learning language to describe social and physical reality
7. Learning to relate emotionally to parents and siblings; identifying relationships
8. Getting ready to read
9. Learning to distinguish right and wrong and beginning to develop a conscience

Middle Childhood (Ages 6-11)

1. Learning physical skills necessary for ordinary games
2. Building wholesome attitudes toward oneself and sense of self-concept
3. Learning to get along with age mates—moving from the circle to groups outside the home
4. Learning the skills of tolerance and patience
5. Learning appropriate masculine or feminine social roles
6. Developing fundamental skills in reading, writing, and calculating
7. Developing concepts necessary for everyday living
8. Developing conscience, morality, and a scale of values
9. Achieving personal independence
10. Developing attitudes toward social groups and institutions, through experiences and imitation

A comprehensive developmental guidance program is an integral part of the total elementary school program with the *counselor* being responsible for providing the leadership for its success. In an effective program, the school administration, faculty, students, parents, and community combine their efforts to provide an all-encompassing, comprehensive guidance program. Such a team approach to guidance and counseling is crucial to the success of any elementary school counseling.

I believe that the comprehensive, developmental counseling and guidance program described here results in the academic, career, and personal social development of elementary aged children as given in the ASCA National Standards for School Counseling Programs (Dahir, Sheldon, & Valiga, 1998). And, I urge all elementary schools to begin the implementation of these very important standards in their respective schools as Wittmer discusses in chapter two of this book.

Program Overview

In order to conceptualize Orange County's elementary guidance program more easily, a chart was developed showing the basis of the program, the structure used to achieve goals, and the functions assumed in implementing the program's components. This conceptualization of an elementary level guidance program may be unique to Orange County. However, acknowledgment is given to the work of Norman Gysbers and Robert D. Myrick, pioneers in the field. A program overview is presented in Figure 3.1.

Basis of the Program

Student goals and Myrick's (1997) principles of developmental counseling provide the basis of Orange County's elementary guidance program. The structure of the program includes outlines of the system-wide philosophy and identifies the expected student outcomes. In addition, this structure provides an objective method for evaluating the effectiveness of the comprehensive developmental approach by measuring parent and student perceptions according to the goals. Further, administrators', counselors', and teachers' perceptions of the program's effectiveness can be measured by correlating their perceptions with the *principles* of the program. In order to be effective, the foundation of an elementary guidance program must also provide the means by which it can be evaluated. This is the age of counselor "accountability," regardless of the school level (Schmidt, 1999).

Myrick (1997) identified eight goals for school guidance programs which Orange County adopted for use with its K-12 programs. These goals, the same for each grade level, are:

1. understanding the school environment
2. understanding self and others
3. understanding attitudes and behavior
4. decision making and problem solving
5. interpersonal and communication skills
6. school success skills
7. career awareness and educational planning
8. community pride and involvement

Objectives for each of the above goals were created. These objectives are developmentally appropriate for each grade level and the activities to achieve the objectives are age specific.

Knowing your objectives, having them approved by your administration and adhered to by the rest of your school's staff is essential to an effective elementary school guidance program. Place your goals and objectives in writing, have them approved by the school's administration, and then share them with all school faculty and staff members.

As Wittmer stated in Chapter 1, "A developmental counseling program serves all students." This is the main foundation of the elementary guidance program in Orange County schools. In addition, developmental guidance includes counselors who provide specialized counseling services and interventions. These specialized components are described next.

Program Components

Orange County's program structure provides the means to achieve student goals and is referred to as "Program Components." The program components are divided into the two categories of *direct* and *indirect* services. The direct category includes all activities conducted with students in order to provide necessary and needed services. This category includes, for example, large and small group guidance, counseling individuals, setting up and working with the peer helpers' program, consultation, parenting classes, and so forth. The indirect category includes those activities required to support the provision of the above direct services to students and others, and includes the coordination and administrative functions, facilitation of the career education program, and professional development activities.

Large Group Guidance

The large group guidance component in the Orange County elementary program provides delivery of services to the largest number of students possible (at one time) and is based on their age level developmental needs. The large group guidance lessons are arranged by goal (listed previously) with lessons for both primary and intermediate objectives for each goal.

In addition to the lessons written by Orange County educators, elementary counselors use Pumsy (Anderson, 1987) with all primary grade levels and DUSO (Dinkmeyer & Dinkmeyer, 1990) with all elementary grade levels. Many of these classroom guidance activities are conducted by others in the school (i.e., teachers who use the "Cooperative Discipline" program) (Albert, 1996). However, all such activities are coordinated by the counselor. Various groups and members of the community also provide large group guidance lessons on a variety of topics. Among some of these groups are The Women's Junior League, several psychiatric hospitals, private organizations who conduct meaningful puppet shows for children, the Florida Extension Service, Orange County Mental Health Services, and many other state licensed mental health providers. There are also county-wide programs such as "Developing Capable People," "Conflict Resolution," and the "Student Assistance Program." Such groups' efforts are coordinated by the counselor to best meet the previously described goals of the counseling program. Conducting effective classroom guidance presentations must be a team effort and cannot rest with the counselor alone. It is best to incorporate *all* who work with children in your school. The team approach is the best and most effective approach in achieving the goals and objectives of a developmental program (Wittmer & Thompson, 1995).

Small Group Guidance

Small group guidance is defined by Myrick (1997) as "a unique educational experience in which students can work together to explore their ideas, attitudes, feelings, and behaviors, especially as related to personal development and progress in school" (p. 187).

An Orange County writing team developed a "Curriculum for Small Group Counseling" by focusing on problem-centered, growth-centered, and crisis-centered groups as described by Myrick (1997). The curriculum was revised to include additional sessions for groups on "Divorce" and "Appreciating Cultural Differences."

As mentioned previously, accountability is vital for the elementary school counselor. Thus, counselors in Orange County conduct regular evaluations of their small and large group counseling units.

Counseling Individual Students

Professional elementary school counselors can guide students toward more productive actions at school and home and can assist students in solving problems that often occur unexpectedly.

Individual counseling is popular in schools for many reasons. First, most school based organizations are structured around classes and individual classroom teachers. Orange County teachers seem more inclined to release one student at a time from classes since, to them, it is less disruptive to classroom routines. Individual counseling is easier to schedule than other interventions and may seem more practical (Myrick, 1997) to a counselor's non-counseling colleagues. While it is the most frequently used counselor intervention (Schmidt, 1999), elementary counselors are gradually reducing the time spent with individuals because it is less efficient than working with large numbers of children (Wittmer, Thompson, & Loesch, 1997).

In the first four years of implementation of the comprehensive developmental guidance program in Orange County, the elementary level counselors have reduced their time with individual students from 25% to 12%.

Too much time with individual students may cause you to be perceived as a "therapist" and will probably shortchange most of the student body. You simply do not have the time; know when to refer a troubled student!

Problems appropriately addressed by individual counseling include peer-related difficulties, academic problems, and assistance in dealing with parents or community agencies. Individual counseling priorities in Orange County include facilitating behavior change, increasing coping skills, improving decision making and problem solving, improving peer relationships, and facilitating client potential. An additional goal, targeted for exceptional education students, is normalization. This is a process in which exceptional students are helped to acquire skills that allow for integration into the *regular* classroom. Again, Orange County's individual counseling component is based on the previously described goals.

With the advent of the Student Assistance Program (SAP), more help is available to children and families in crisis. The Student Assistance Program is an outgrowth of the national effort to reduce the number of children who are at risk for drug and/or other substance abuse and is funded with *"Drug Free Schools"* money available through the Federal government. This provides each school counselor in Orlando with a SAP team who can be of immediate assistance when crisis intervention is needed. The SAP team members are considered to exist under the "umbrella of services" offered by the school counselor. Such a structure is imperative if the program is to be effective. Otherwise, some students will fall between the cracks. This allows the counselor to continue implementing the regularly scheduled program (i.e., classroom guidance, small groups, consultation, peer helpers) while the individuals requiring crisis intervention also receive needed services from the SAP team personnel. Again, these services are coordinated by the school counselor.

Individual counseling is a respected and valued intervention; it is a luxury in elementary schools where the student/counselor ratio may be 1,000 to 1. Counseling students in groups provides more services to more students more efficiently. Thus, as indicated in Figure 3.2, Orange County counselors are encouraged to do *no* more than *5 hours* of individual counseling with students each week.

Peer Helpers

Several terms are used interchangeably to describe peer helpers in Orange County. They include Peer Facilitators, Peer Counselors, Pals, and Helping Hands.

The process of peer helping refers to students who use helping skills and concepts to assist other students—and sometimes adults—to think about ideas and feelings, to explore alternatives to situations, to lead the conflict mediation program, and to help others make responsible decisions. These programs have grown in size and number until today there are programs throughout the Orange County School System.

Many peer programs have become successful because of their well developed and well organized systematic procedures for teaching interpersonal skills and preparing facilitators for different roles. In Orange County counselors have also identified helping projects in which the peers can put their skills to use while being supervised.

Systematic training programs for peer helpers makes a positive difference, not the least of which is the professional and personal reward experienced by the peer trainer. Orange County peer helping programs have enhanced the developmental guidance program by extending more services to more people, developing leadership skills among students, and empowering students to learn more about themselves and each other. Peer helping is a program that "works" at the elementary level. Peers can be excellent helpers for the elementary counselor in various important areas and topics of interest to elementary level students. One of these very important and current, timely areas is in violence prevention programs where specially trained fifth grade peer mediators give invaluable assistance to the elementary school counselor (Wittmer, Tompson, & Sheperis, 1999).

Consultation

The counselor's consultant role includes working with teachers, parents, administrators, and other educational specialists on matters that involve student understanding and management. The America School Counselor Association (ASCA) defines consultation as a cooperative process in which the school counselor/consultant assists others to think through problems and to develop skills that make them more effective in working with students (ASCA, 1999). Noting that consulting is a relatively new function, Schmidt (1999) stated that "consulting is a relationship in which two or more people identify a purpose, establish a goal, plan strategies to meet that goal, and assign responsibilities to carry out these strategies" (p. 85).

There is a distinct difference between consultation and collaboration, which counselors may also engage in periodically. Collaboration occurs when the consultant agrees to be part of the plan. In doing so, the consultant loses some objectivity and increases the personal investment in seeing that the plan works. In collaboration, planning and implementing are a joint effort. It is an important distinction for elementary level counselors to be aware of when making professional judgments about entering counseling, consultation, or collaboration with a person who has requested their assistance. Each function requires a different perspective and involves the counselor in varying degrees. Orange County elementary counselors agree that consultation is an important component of their comprehensive guidance programs.

When the perceptions of counselors, teachers, and administrators were examined regarding the perceived level of function and effectiveness of counselors in Orange County, counselors' professional colleagues viewed them as being more effective than did parents or students. And, it is important to note that all constituent groups perceived consultation, counseling, and coordinating as being important and appropriate methods for guidance service delivery, but suggested that counselors spend more time providing consultant services to teachers, parents, and administrators.

Orange County school authorities investigated the effectiveness of computer-assisted school consultation in situations where the teacher found it difficult to manage a particular student. Teachers found that the computer-generated suggestions of how to work with the problem students were accurate and helpful. After learning of the computer strategies, the teachers were then willing to implement the suggestions. When the computer suggestions were put into practice with the students, there was significant improvement in the quality of work, the amount of work, and the amount of effort that the student put into schoolwork. Unfortunately, however, there was no significant improvement in the overall student teacher relationship, suggesting that computers cannot take the place of one to one interaction between teachers and students.

To be an effective and accountable counselor of the new millennium, one would be wise to search for innovative ways to infuse the use of technology into the elementary guidance program. The above description of computer-assisted consultation is one example of that effort being made in Orange County, Florida.

Parenting Classes

Orange County, Florida, like other parts of the country, has witnessed the advent of inexpensive personal computers, an increase in convenience foods, electronic games, and laser technology, among other things. It appears that many families' lifestyles revolve around a chase for better jobs, different housing, and the latest sports equipment, while others deal with the impact of abuse, neglect, poverty, and many varieties of dysfunctionalities. Each of these changes has its impact on the lives of our children and families. The changing face of the American lifestyle has affected all ages of children from preschoolers who lack security and stability to latchkey elementary aged students who have little supervision or little quality time with parents. These children, with their high energy levels, often lack guidance from the adults in their lives to cope with the fast-paced change surrounding them. Chaos often prevails in neighborhoods where little direction is provided on how to get through the growing years. Elementary school counselors play a major role in assisting both students and their families to effectively manage this fast pace.

Based on the work of Capuzzi and Gross (1995) involving at-risk children and youth, Orange County counselors recognize they must involve the parents in a proactive guidance program. Rather than a psychotherapeutic approach, Orange County has focused on a psycho-educational model entailing instruction for parents and families on a problem-solving method of handling stress and children's inappropriate behaviors. Elementary school counselors *teach* parents that interventions should be responsive to the factors that put children and families at risk, rather than just focusing on the behaviors themselves.

Experience indicates that if parents don't know how to be effective models for their children, they can and need to be taught. I believe this is the best (and maybe only) way to interrupt the cycle of unmet needs. To meet this goal, counselor-led parenting programs have been established in each Orange County elementary school.

Many counselors use the *Systematic Training for Effective Parenting (STEP)* materials or have developed their own sessions based on their personal experience of "what works." The Student Assistance Program (SAP described previously) also offers parenting classes at *all* adult education school settings in Orange County. This program provides child-care at the same location with certified teachers and with aides who work with the children, while their parents attend parenting classes. Orange County also has a Parent Resource Center. Personnel work closely with school counselors and others in community agencies to provide multiple programs in an attempt to meet the diverse needs of a multi-cultural population.

Coordination: An Indirect Service

While coordinating is not always highly visible as one of the indirect services offered to students, it is a routine part of an elementary counselor's role and function. Coordination as a counselor intervention is the process of managing *indirect* guidance services to students, including special events and general procedures. It often involves collecting data and information, allocating materials and resources, arranging and organizing meetings, developing and operating special programs, supervising and monitoring others, and providing leadership (Myrick, 1997).

As we move further into the new millennium, more and more coordinating challenges will arise that need to be managed by the school-based elementary level counselor. These include the Peer Helper Program, Student Assistance Program, the psychiatric hospital and drug rehabilitation center groups that are conducted at the schools, the rise of full-service schools that house a comprehensive battery of services provided by many agencies in the community, the various Partners-in-Education businesses that most schools have, parent volunteers, and the many community groups who have programs designed to meet students' *affective* needs. Orange County visualizes the counselor as the hub of this wheel, holding together (by coordination) the many spokes that complete the team effort required of a comprehensive developmental guidance program.

Administrative Functions: Indirect Services

This component of indirect services includes the behind-the-scenes activities that need to occur to support the direct services of any effective school guidance program. Coordinating administrative functions includes records management, supervision of clerical support, and other guidance-related administrative duties. Since many schools have a very high transient ratio (some in excess of 80% in Orange County), it is an important part of the counselor's function to monitor the incoming and outgoing cumulative folders to assure as smooth a transition as possible for the students. Counselors frequently have the guidance paraprofessionals (whom they have trained) check student folders for the necessary documentation to enter school. And then, the paraprofessionals pass them on to the counselor for perusal and subsequent action. This is especially so for exceptional student education records and any court ordered documents.

All elementary schools in Orange County have been provided with a halftime Student Services clerical allocation. It is the school principal's decision as to how that allocation is to be used. In those schools where counselors are proactive, clerical services are allocated to the guidance department for one to four hours per day and in some instances, provide support to the counselor for the entire day. This takes action on the counselor's part—those who "sell" their principals on the need for these services obtain the services. The district guidance office also provides annual training for the paraprofessionals in the areas of communication skills, records management, computer utilization, multi-cultural awareness, ethics, and exceptional education paperwork.

Other guidance related administrative functions include assisting the district-wide assessment coordinator with the process of arranging the test schedule, occasionally monitoring the test-taking rooms, and most importantly, interpreting the test results to students and their parents. Most often, test results are conveyed to students and parents in group settings. However, counselors do consult with parents individually if they have specific concerns or make a special request for further interpretation or follow-up concerning their child.

Career Education

Career Education includes coordinating the exploration and the acquisition of skills and attitudes necessary for students to be successful in a high-tech world. In Orange County there is an articulated plan for all grade levels. Its aim is to help students acquire and utilize the knowledge, skills, and attitudes necessary to make work meaningful, productive, and satisfying. The plan begins in kindergarten and extends throughout school, and hopefully, throughout one's working life, linking basic subjects together and relating them to the contemporary "real" world.

The elementary career education program assists children by developing career awareness. It helps them to know themselves, their interests, talents, and abilities; to know about available careers; to develop wholesome attitudes toward work and society; and to develop awareness of the decision-making process. The program also assists parents in becoming more involved in their child's decision-making process and to become more knowledgeable of occupations and labor trends.

Professional Development

A counselor's continued professional development is imperative. This includes attending the monthly meetings held for all counselors district-wide, local ACA meetings if available, state ACA conventions, making presentations, being aware of which legislation affects counselors, and in general, staying abreast of the latest developments in the counseling field. The elementary school counselor's role will continue to change rapidly. The best way to "stay abreast" is through professional development activities. The non-involved counselor often "burns out."

Program Implementation Strategies

Figure 3.3 depicts the process of implementing a developmental guidance program in Orange County, Florida. Beginning with a needs assessment, the process then moves to the selection of specific goals and objectives by the school based guidance committee. Following the selection of annual priorities, the plan is developed and made available to the principal, faculty, and the county-level program specialist for guidance. As can be seen (and described throughout this chapter), the delivery of specific activities is conducted by teachers, administrators, counselors, and other specialists and parents. The plan is evaluated near the end of the school year to determine program effectiveness and to demonstrate accountability for having met student needs.

The Guidance Committee

As Wittmer mentioned previously, it is important to establish, early on, a guidance committee, as every school with an effective guidance program has one. The committee helps identify student needs and recommends different kinds of guidance programs and activities throughout the year. It serves as a funnel through which information can be processed by both counselors and teachers. The committee meets regularly to search for ways that all school personnel can work together more efficiently in the delivery of guidance services.

The guidance committee may elicit support from faculty before initiating certain guidance and counseling procedures. In Orange County this committee is composed of the counselor and one teacher representative from each grade level, from exceptional education, an elective teacher, and parents, with input from the administration.

These committees can be initial sounding boards for new ideas and programs that are being considered. The committee might: (1) review guidance materials and activities; (2) recommend strategies and interventions; (3) examine student data to identify target populations that need guidance and counseling services; (4) help evaluate the guidance program; (5) discuss ideas before they are presented to the total faculty; and (6) serve as a resource group to the counselor.

In Orange County, each elementary counselor develops an annual guidance plan; this is the guidance department's proposal for meeting the goals and objectives targeted by the guidance committee. The plan specifies the approximate dates for delivering the various guidance components such as classroom guidance sessions, small groups, and so forth, and includes activities provided by other resources beyond the counselor. The plan also contains procedures pertaining to program evaluation.

The Annual Guidance Plan is most effective if developed in coordination with the principal and the guidance committee. When completed, all school staff should be aware of and have access to the written plan. A copy of the plan should also be provided to the district administrator. The elementary level, comprehensive, developmental annual guidance plan is a team effort by administrators, teachers, counselors, other support personnel, the parents, and other community members representing the guidance committee.

Principal's Role

The elementary school principal, as chief administrator, is ultimately responsible for the success of a developmental guidance and counseling program. He or she must *understand* and *appreciate* the counselor's role and function. Only the counselor can obtain this understanding from the principal. Such support includes the provision of adequate facilities, materials, clerical help, and permitting the counselor to use his or her special training and competencies in an effective manner. Principals should also be encouraged by the counselor to provide input for program development. In addition, encouragement by the principal to support the participation of all school personnel in implementing the comprehensive developmental guidance program is needed. Of course, the school principal facilitates program improvement by providing a school climate conducive to innovation in guidance and counseling. Without such administrative support, chances for success are slim.

Teachers Roles

Teachers play a vital role in the planning and implementation of an elementary level comprehensive developmental guidance program. As the professionals who have the most daily contact with students, teachers are in the best position to recognize and help provide for the developmental needs of students. Through appropriate communication and referrals, teachers facilitate the interaction between the students and the counselor. Teachers demonstrate their support for the program by providing adequate opportunities for counselor-student contact. Teachers can contribute directly by helping the counselor deliver programs that facilitate the emotional and social development and well being of students. Their support is needed to be effective. With their support, input, and expertise, teachers make it possible for guidance and counseling to become an integral part of the elementary child's educational experience.

Summary

When elementary level school personnel understand the purposes of a comprehensive developmental guidance and counseling program, they realize the goals of education and the goals of guidance and counseling are congruent. Principals, counselors, and teachers are most effective in promoting the cognitive, emotional, and social development of students when they are sensitive to both the distinct and the common elements of their roles. Mutual respect for and understanding of the professional competencies and contributions that each brings to the school setting will enable principals, counselors, and teachers to implement a comprehensive, elementary school, developmental guidance program that will become an essential element of the total school program.

The effectiveness of an elementary school counseling program in the new millennium clearly depends on the elementary school counselors' ability to deliver services as part of a team, with emphasis on learner outcomes and consideration for all aspects of a child's development.

Figure 3.1
Program Overview: Orange County Public Schools

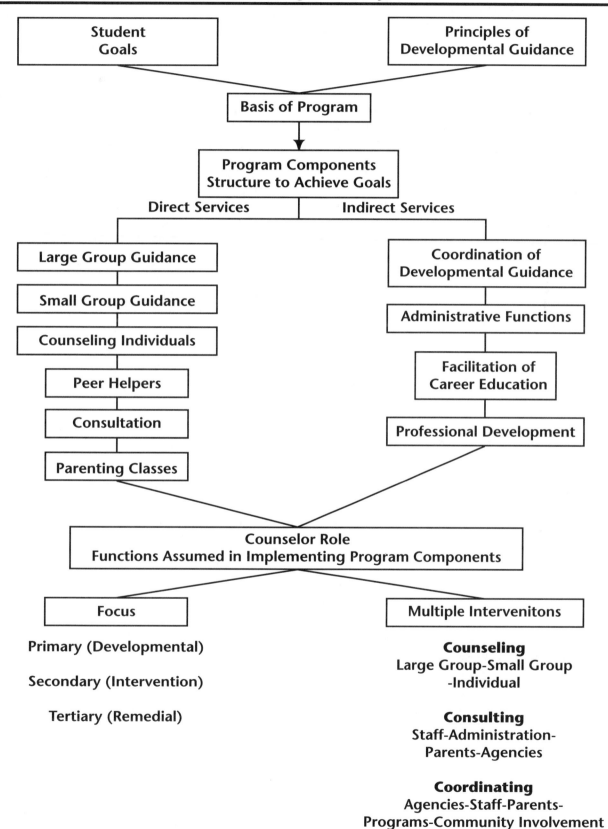

Figure 3.2
Elementary Comprehensive, Developmental Guidance Program Checklist

	Ideal	Acceptable	Unacceptable
*1. **Classroom Guidance** career education, orientation, 8th grade development and coordination, involvement	6-8 sessions/week	4-6 sessions/week	0-3 sessions/week
*2. **Group Counseling** by counselors (scheduled, on-going)	4-6 sessions/week	2-3 sessions/week	0-1 sessions/week
*3. **Counseling Individuals** Scheduled Unscheduled	2-5 hours/week 2-3 hours/week	2-5 hours/week 2-3 hours/week	> 5 hours/week > 5 hours/week
*4. **Consultation** (parents, faculty, etc.)	Scheduled time daily (1-2 hours) - Attends school administrative meetings. Responds to requests in timely and appropriate fashion.	Consultation occurs, but in an unplanned way.	No scheduled time for consultation. No school administrative meetings attended.
5. **Teaching the Peer Helpers' Class**	Regular basis; either semester or year long. Both training and projects.	Training only; no projects (partial program).	No class.
*6. **Coordinating Developmental Guidance**	Written plan; all students have access; program planned, implemented and evaluated; community oriented.	Written plan; all students have access; program planned, implemented and evaluated.	No developmental guidance program.
*7. **Administrative Functions**	Counselors supervise clerical assistance; review incoming/outgoing records; responsive to student needs; attends cluster meetings.	Clerk not directly supervised by counselor; records reviewed and processed; responds to student needs.	Clerk used for non-guidance activities.
8. **Career Education Program**	Provides classroom presentations, special career projects. Helps teachers to infuse curriculum.	Same as ideal.	No involvement with career education.
*9. **Coordinating Exceptional Education Program**	Timely and appropriate meetings conducted; clerk prepares letters and forms.	Program is managed with limited clerical support.	No program or only reactive program management evident.
*10. **Testing and Development**	Coordinates standardized testing; interprets test results.	Same as ideal.	Clerical aspects of managing the testing program evident.
11. **Professional Development Activities**	Attends and is involved at all levels: local, state, and national associations; participates in all staff development activities.	Maintains memberships; attends district in-service activities.	No activities.
*12. **Advisory Program**	Participates regularly; provides materials; serves as consultant.	Participates in advisory, but on an irregular basis.	No participation.

* Indicates a critical component

Figure 3.3
Program Implementation

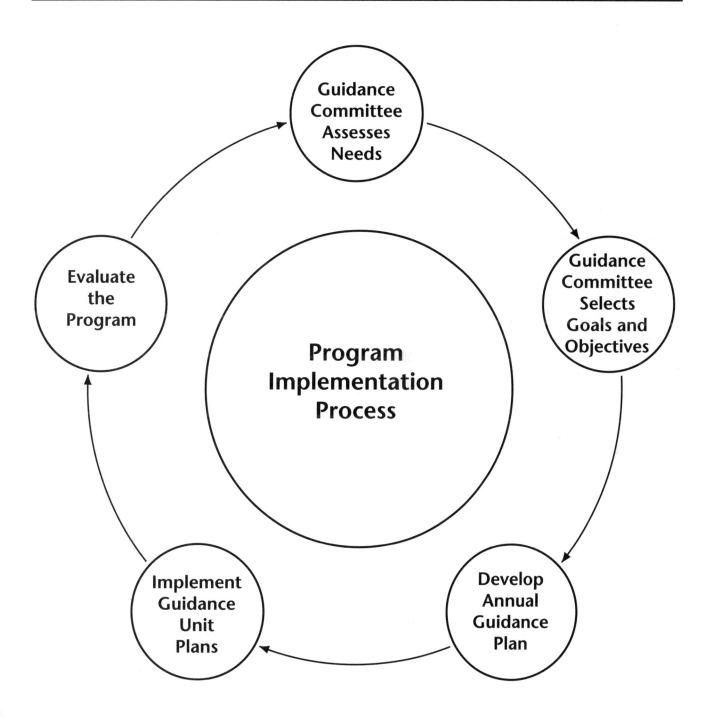

This diagram depicts the process of a developmental guidance program. Beginning with a needs assessment, the process moves to the selection of specific goals and objectives by the school based guidance committee; after selection of priorities, the annual plan is developed and made available to the principal, program consultant for guidance, and faculty. The delivery of specific activities is conducted by teachers, administrators, counselors, and other specialists and parents. The plan is evaluated near the end of the school year to determine program effectiveness and to demonstrate accountability for meeting student needs.

References

Albert, L. (1996). *Cooperative discipline.* Circle Pines, MN: American Guidance Service.

Anderson, J. (1987). *Pumsy in pursuit of excellence.* Eugene, OR: Timberline Press, Inc.

ASCA. (1999). *Role statement: The school counselor.* Alexandria, VA: ASCA Press.

Capuzzi, D., & Gross, D.R. (1995). *Youth at risk: A resource for counselors, teachers, and parents.* Alexandria, VA: American Counseling Association.

Dahir, C., Sheldon, S., & Valiga, M. (1998). *Implementing the national standards for school counseling programs..* Alexandria, VA: American School Counselor Association.

Dinkmeyer, D., Sr., & Dinkmeyer, D., Jr. (1990). *Developing understanding of self and others.* Circle Pines, MN: American Guidance Service.

Gysbers, N.C. (Ed.). (1997). *Comprehensive guidance programs that work.* Ann Arbor, MI: ERIC Counseling and Personnel Services Clearinghouse.

Gysbers, N.C., & Henderson, P. (1999). *Developing and managing your school counseling program.* Alexandria, VA: American Counseling Association.

Havighurst, R.J. (1972). *Developmental tasks in education.* New York: Longmans.

Myrick, R.D. (1997). *Developmental guidance and counseling: A practical approach* (3rd ed.). Minneapolis, MN: Educational Media Corporation.

Schmidt, J.J. (1999). *Counseling in schools: Essential services and comprehensive programs.* Needham Heights, MA: Allyn & Bacon.

Wittmer, J., & Thompson, D. (1995). *Large group counseling: A k-12 sourcebook.* Minneapolis, MN: Educational Media Corporation.

Wittmer, J., Thompson, D., & Loesch, L. (1997). *Classroom guidance activities: A sourcebook for elementary school counselors.* Minneapolis, MN: Educational Media Corporation.

Wittmer, J., Thompson, D., & Sheperis, C. (1999). *The peace train: A school-wide violence prevention program.* Minneapolis, MN: Educational Media Corporation.

Chapter 4
Middle School Counseling in the New Millennium:
A Practitioner's Perspective

by

Bonnie B. Baker

Dr. Bonnie Baker, PhD, NCC, is a Past-President of the Florida School Counselor Association and is currently employed as a middle school counselor in Gainesville, Florida. Dr. Baker is also licensed as a mental health counselor and maintains a part-time private practice.

Introduction

The often used phrase "caught in the middle" could easily serve as a motto for the middle school counselor of the new millennium for several reasons. First, the unique population of middle school students are "caught in the middle" between childhood and adolescence in a developmental stage known as "transescence." This difficult developmental period accounts for many of the counseling issues a middle school counselor must address each and every school day.

Secondly, the middle school institution itself is "caught in the middle" between elementary and secondary school. As a result, middle school counselors must be knowledgeable of both elementary and secondary school programs and spend a considerable amount of time and energy in transition-related activities such as orientation, registration, and so forth.

Additionally, in performing their many roles and responsibilities, middle school counselors are frequently "caught in the middle" between various segments of their school communities, such as between students and parents, students and teachers, students and administrators, parents and teachers, and teachers and teacher. In short, middle school counselors may find themselves "caught in the middle" of most school-based relationships. This happens most often for those middle school counselors who view their "student advocacy role," as I do, as crucial. The goal of this chapter is to familiarize you with varied aspects of middle school counseling from the personal perspective of a middle school counselor who has been "caught in the middle" for over two decades, but who has, and continues to, enjoy each and every working day with this unique age group of students.

Program Development

The trend toward creating comprehensive, developmental guidance and counseling programs that began in the '70s, '80s, and '90s will continue in the new millennium.

Middle school counselors play a key role in developing and coordinating the school guidance program. However, the entire school staff must participate in guidance-related activities in order to successfully implement a comprehensive, *developmental* guidance program.

An effective first step in developing a middle school guidance program is to form a school guidance committee. The function of this committee is to assist the counselor in developing and implementing the guidance program. The committee also serves as an ongoing advisory group and communication link between the guidance department and the school community. Committee members should include school counselors, teachers, parents, administrators, and students.

Initially, the school guidance committee is helpful in identifying and prioritizing student, teacher, and parent needs. An efficient method for collecting this type of information is the use of a needs assessment instrument. The committee then analyzes the collected data and assists the counselor in formulating a written program to meet the identified needs. Support for the program will increase because of the widespread participation in its development. Committee members, who served as program developers, will also be valuable in interpreting and promoting guidance program activities.

Ongoing school guidance committee meetings and projects should continue throughout the school year. A prepared agenda, minutes of meetings, and frequent reports to the entire school community about committee activities will produce a positive image for the guidance department. In addition to the development of the guidance program, suggested projects for the guidance committee include the following:

- Preview and selection of guidance material

- Research projects

- National School Counseling Week activities

- Career awareness programs

- Public relations project such as newsletter, bulletin boards, or newspaper articles

- Sponsorship of parent education programs

A year-end program evaluation is an appropriate concluding activity for the school guidance committee. And, showing your appreciation and recognition of individual committee member's participation at the end of the year is important. The benefits of an actively functioning school guidance committee are well worth the busy middle school counselor's time and effort.

Counseling

The core of the middle school developmental guidance program is counseling. This unique function sets the school counselor apart from all other professional staff members. As societal problems grow in complexity, the need for social and emotional counseling increases. The middle school counselors of the future will need an extensive knowledge of counseling theory and methods. Expertise in counseling special populations will be required to assist students in understanding and resolving issues new to their generation. For instance, "crack cocaine babies" and the AIDS epidemic will impact many students and their families during this decade. Beginning, as well as veteran, school counselors need to learn about the characteristics of these and other special populations and need to discover counseling strategies to respond to their unique needs.

The middle school counselor is increasingly viewed as the school-based mental health professional and is called upon to work collaboratively with community based mental health care providers to develop treatment plans and to provide therapeutic interventions for students with mental disorders. School counselor trainees would benefit by becoming familiar with diagnostic criteria to understand and facilitate the collaboration process.

Crisis Counseling

Middle school counselors must be able to effectively intervene in crisis situations. Those who work in large schools face crises on a daily basis and need to develop skills for immediate intervention. The following is a sampling of the types of crisis situations encountered by this author in a single school year.

- Divorce
- Death of student
- Death of parents, grandparents, and siblings
- Peer rejection and conflict
- Family violence
- Homelessness
- Chronic transience
- Child abuse and neglect
- Abandonment
- Sexual molestation—familial and non-familial
- Runaways
- Drug and alcohol abuse—student and family
- Academic failure
- Teen pregnancy
- Miscarriage
- Truancy
- School phobia
- Discipline problems
- Incarceration of parents
- Incarceration of students
- Crime victimizations—assault and battery, larceny, rape
- Gang violence
- Poverty-related crisis—lack of food, clothing, and shelter
- Chronic medical problems and terminal illness of students and family

Due to the sudden onset of many crisis situations, individual counseling is the most immediate type of intervention. Group counseling can also be effective in assisting students experiencing crisis situations. Middle schoolers, in particular, desire peer group acceptance and support. Knowing that others are experiencing similar circumstances can be therapeutic. Individual screening sessions *should* (required by ACA Ethical Standards) be held before placing students in a crisis-oriented group, or in any group for that matter.

In some instances, additional resources may be needed to assist large numbers of students in crisis. For example, a natural disaster or the death of a student or a faculty member may disrupt the entire school. Crisis management plans and personnel should be available on short notice for such emergency situations. District-wide crisis teams composed of school counselors, psychologists, district staff, and community mental health personnel frequently serve on emergency crisis teams. It is important to become familiar with the school system's plan (e.g., telephone networking, etc.) prior to a crisis situation occurring. Volunteering to become a part of the school crisis team can be a rewarding experience.

Group Counseling

Group counseling is an efficient method of delivering counseling services in the middle school. Besides allowing middle school counselors to serve more students, group counseling is especially suited to peer-conscious middle school students. Group participation is preferable to individual counseling for many students. The camaraderie of group membership and of positive peer interaction assists the counselor in achieving group goals.

Developmental as well as problem-centered issues can be addressed in small group counseling sessions. Problem areas that can be treated in small group counseling include family issues such as divorce, academic failure, peer conflict, and behavioral problems. Developmental group topics that interest middle schoolers include study skills, friendship, career exploration, decision making, and interpersonal relationships.

Scheduling group counseling sessions can be tricky in a middle school. Scheduling problems can be avoided by informing classroom teachers about the purpose of the group, group membership, and group time schedules well in advance. Teacher referrals for group membership help to increase support for this activity. One method of scheduling recommended for middle schools is to schedule sessions on a rotating class basis throughout the school day. Teachers are more supportive if students miss their class only once or twice during the course of the group. Also, notifying the teachers of the group schedule helps them plan for student absences. Most teachers will require students to make up work missed while attending group sessions. And if this is the school policy, it should be supported.

Classroom Guidance

Classroom guidance units provide school counselors with the greatest opportunity to impact large numbers of students. Topics selected for these units should have relevance for all students and, when possible, be infused into appropriate places in the regular school curriculum. For instance, a drug education unit might best be offered in a science class that is studying the human body. The affective guidance curriculum compliments the academic aspects of the same topic. Whenever possible, classroom guidance units should be inserted into related classes (Wittmer, Thompson, and Loesch, 1997).

Consultation

Consultation is a process in which a human services professional assists a consultee with a work-related (or caretaking-related) problem within the client system, with the goal of helping both the consultee and the client system in some specified way (Dougherty, 1990).

A considerable amount of a middle school counselor's time is devoted to consulting with teachers, parents, administrators, and referral agency personnel. Through effective use of consultation, the counselor can impact greater numbers of students than would be possible through solitary efforts. Discussions and models of consultation appear frequently in the school counseling literature (e.g., Dougherty, 1990; Myrick, 1997; and Schmidt, 1999).

Consultation with Administrators

Middle school administrators and school counselors must work together to develop appropriate and effective programs and services for students. Frequent communication, however, is often difficult due to the many demands placed on the administrator's and counselor's time. One technique to resolve this dilemma is to schedule a regular weekly counselor-administrator meeting. The agenda for this consultation and planning session might include the following components:

- Program planning, such as faculty in-service or parent workshops you are planning to conduct, or that the administrator might want done

- Curriculum planning, such as Advisor-Advisee program activities

- Discussions and intervention planning for students experiencing academic or behavioral difficulties

- Individual administrator or counselor work-related concerns

Consultation with Teachers

Most middle schools have adopted some form of team approach to assigning teachers to work with particular groups of students. Discussions and decisions about student concerns are frequently made during regularly scheduled team meetings. By participating in these team meetings, the middle school counselor provides consultation services on an ongoing basis.

More formal methods of teacher consultation, such as in-service programs, are well-received when presented in a timely and succinct manner. Examples of topics that have been found to be of interest to middle school teachers include the following:

- child abuse identification and reporting procedures

- classroom management techniques

- affective classroom activities
- identification and interventions for exceptional education students
- career education activities
- standardized testing procedures and preparation activities
- sex education activities
- drug education activities

In addition to in-service programs, individual and small group consultation services are frequently requested of the middle school counselor. For instance, a teacher may be having a difficult time controlling a certain class and needs assistance in developing appropriate classroom management strategies. You might observe the class, make recommendations, or suggest resources that may help this particular teacher.

Consultation with Parents

The "storm and stress" of the middle school years frequently results in equally distressing "storm and stress" for parents. An important role of the middle school counselor is that of consultant to parents who must guide their children through this difficult developmental stage. Talking to parents and providing information about "normal" middle school behavior will assist them in understanding and in responding appropriately to their children. Both individual and group consultation are needed. Program presentations at parent orientation and at organization meetings (PTA) are beneficial in meeting this need. Some counselors may choose to offer parenting classes or support groups to help prepare parents for the challenge of raising today's teenagers.

Consultation with Referral Agency Personnel

Representatives from public and private agencies, such as mental health centers, commonly request consultation with middle school counselors. Either the agency personnel or the school counselor may initiate the discussion. Prior to any discussion or written communication, the school counselor must be certain that all ethical and legal guidelines regarding confidentiality have been observed. Occasionally subpoenas for court appearances will be issued to school counselors. When this occurs it is, generally, a good idea to consult with the principal and the school attorney in preparing for testimony. Depending on the type of hearing, the counselor's records could also be subpoenaed.

Coordination

Program and services coordination is another major responsibility of the middle school counselor. Parents, teachers, and students rely on the counselor's leadership in planning and coordinating numerous special services and programs. The effectiveness of such programs and/or services often depends on the skills of the coordinator. In fact, poor coordination can ruin an otherwise excellent program. Some examples of coordinating activities a middle school counselor may be required to spearhead in a typical year are listed, here, in chronological order.

September	New student orientation program (Students and parents) Child abuse awareness program (Faculty in-service)
October:	Drug awareness program (Students and parents)
November:	Sex education programs (Students and parents)
December:	Peer facilitator training program (Students)
January:	Career interest survey (Students)
February:	Career Day (Students)
March:	High school registration/orientation (Students and parents)
April:	Standardized testing program (Faculty in-service and students)
May:	Fifth grade registration/orientation (Students and parents)
June:	Student recognition programs (Students and parents)

Additional coordination activities occur on an ongoing basis throughout the school year. They include the coordination of the following:

- referrals for community services
- referrals for psychological testing
- registration of new students
- peer facilitator program and special projects
- student records—maintenance and transfer

Tips for Successful Coordination of Guidance Program Activities

1. Start planning early to allow ample time to thoroughly prepare for the program or activity.

2. Involve others in the planning stage of program development to offer suggestions for strengthening the program.

3. Attend to details in planning and coordinating activities. Written communication is helpful when coordinating a major activity such as a standardized testing program. All those involved should be kept well informed about program goals, objectives, and procedures for implementation. If necessary, a briefing session should be conducted to make certain that everyone involved understands what is being planned.

4. Evaluate the program immediately following its conclusion, prepare a written summary, and save it for future planning sessions.

Time Management

Time is a precious commodity for today's middle school counselor. Finding ample time to develop and implement a comprehensive, developmental guidance program is difficult, particularly in schools with high counselor-to-student ratios. Counselors who are recognized as being helpful will soon find themselves inundated with requests for counseling, coordination, and consultation services. Not surprisingly, successfully responding to such requests generates even more. Quite often, the harder the counselor works, the more that is requested. A tee shirt purchased at a counselor convention proclaiming "I'M COUNSELING AS FAST AS I CAN!!" best sums up how many middle school counselors feel by the end of the first semester each year.

Effective time management is one of the greatest challenges facing the middle school counselor. The following are offered as ways to avert becoming overwhelmed by the myriad of roles and responsibilities assumed in the middle school setting.

1. **First, accept the reality that as a middle school counselor you cannot be all things to all people.** This is a difficult concept for school counselors because, by nature, we are helpers and dislike saying "NO" to requests for help.

2. **Your parameters for professional responsibilities should be clearly set.** This can be accomplished by developing and presenting a written guidance program and a role description to the administration, faculty, and parent community. Defining roles and responsibilities enables you to delineate essential activities and set limits on inappropriate requests. The program should be evaluated and revised annually to ensure that all functions are being performed as stipulated in your role and function statement.

3. **Develop good organizational skills.** A tremendous amount of your time can be saved by being well organized. Counseling material, counseling notes, calendars, and time schedules should be kept current and be maintained in an easily accessible system. Being able to quickly retrieve information can save you untold hours of searching for or recreating lost material.

4. **Avoid time wasters.** Unnecessarily lengthy telephone conversations, excessive socialization in the teacher's lounge, visitors, procrastination, lengthy meetings, and cluttered work spaces can reduce your efficiency and lessen the effectiveness of your guidance program.

5. **Be prepared for the unexpected.** Events that demand immediate attention will occur on a random basis throughout the school year. For example, crisis situations such as child abuse, death, accidents, and medical emergencies will inevitably occur. Prior to their happening, plans should be developed to allow you to quickly respond and resolve the situation with a minimal amount of disruption to scheduled activities.

6. **Differential staffing.** This technique saves time for middle school guidance departments with more than one counselor. Responsibilities are divided among department members in order to reduce the quantity of functions each counselor must assume. For instance, one counselor could be responsible for coordinating the standardized testing program and high school registration activities while another counselor organizes the fifth grade registration, career day, and the drug awareness program.

Ingredients for Success

I am frequently asked how I have successfully managed to survive working as a middle school counselor for twenty years. Reflecting on this question has turned up a "baker's dozen" of what I consider to be essential ingredients for success as a middle school counselor. In concluding this chapter, I offer these suggestions to colleagues and future colleagues:

1. **Genuine enjoyment in working with the middle school-aged student.** Genuinely liking and appreciating this age group is essential. Understanding and tolerance of the "storm and stress" experienced by the early adolescent is needed for survival in the middle school. Students quickly identify those adults who lack understanding of their behavior and turn away from their guidance. You can't play at being genuine with this age group.

2. **Tolerance for chaotic days.** Days rarely go as planned in the middle school, particularly in larger schools. Because of the high counselor-student ratios in most areas of the country, learn to anticipate some type of crisis or unexpected event to occur daily. The successful counselor must be able to adjust to change quickly. At times, multiple unexpected events happen simultaneously. Your ability to juggle activities will be put to a test on a daily basis.

3. **Flexibility.** The ability to change directions at a moment's notice is needed in middle school counseling. Within an hour's time, you may be called upon to participate in a parent-teacher conference, comfort a crying student, answer three phone calls, and consult with the school nurse. Successful counselors have developed skills in focusing on the task at hand and being able to quickly focus on completely different issues within a matter of minutes. This is a skill seldom taught in graduate school, but is one you can teach yourself "on the job."

4. **Crisis management skills.** Middle school counselors must have the ability to intervene quickly and competently in crisis situations. Middle school aged students are easily aroused emotionally during crisis events and require immediate counseling services. They are often inconsistent, but *you* must be consistent or their trust will be lost. Successful middle school counselors have crisis management plans in effect to handle unusual circumstances.

5. **Time management skills.** The many demands made on the middle school counselor's time makes this an essential ingredient for success. Specific suggestions for effective utilization of time have been previously discussed in this chapter.

6. **Communication skills.** The ability to effectively communicate with students, teachers, administrators, parents, and the public is vital to success as a middle school counselor. The use of active listening and appropriate feedback will assist in relating to such varied groups. Verbal as well as written communication skills are needed. Frequently middle school counselors are asked to speak or write about counseling issues or activities. You must be able to clearly articulate information about program objectives and strategies to students, parents, and professional colleagues.

7. **Organizational skills.** Middle school counselors are always coordinating or organizing something. Whether it be a standardized testing program, orientation program, or career education activity, the well organized counselor will achieve far greater success. The many details, time constraints, and paperwork associated with the middle school counselor's coordinator role makes this an essential skill. The well-organized middle school counselor will enjoy greater cooperation and support of the faculty and staff.

8. **Team player.** Cooperative relationships with school administrators and faculty members are essential for middle school counselors. Regular attendance and participation at team and faculty meetings will ensure colleagues that you are an integral member of the team. Demonstrations of support and appreciation for the efforts of other staff members and participation in non-counseling school activities, such as the science fair or band concert, will remind others that you are concerned about the entire school program. Staff members will reciprocate when you request their participation in guidance-related activities and will make access to students much easier.

9. **Ability to manage stress.** Stress management skills are needed in most professional positions. The level of stress in a typical middle school counseling office is especially high. This is due to the characteristics of the population served and the demands placed upon the counselor in fulfilling the numerous roles and responsibilities of the job. Unless preventive measures are

taken, the middle school counselor could begin to feel "burnt-out." By attending to their personal emotional, physical, and spiritual well-being, middle school counselors will strengthen their performance at work and longevity in the profession.

10. **Personal support system**. Middle school counselors spend much of their professional energy nurturing their students and others. Although this is quite fulfilling professionally and personally, you, as a counselor, have similar needs for nurturing that *must* be met in order to continue helping others. The successful middle school counselor is aware of this need and receives such nurturing from family and/or friends on a regular basis. Allowing time for personally supportive relationships is needed for your personal growth as a school counselor.

11. **Professional support system**. Strong professional support systems help middle school counselors achieve success. The support of the school principal is essential and is best gained by frequent communication. The quality of this relationship can "make or break" the guidance program. Frequently you will need the principal's support and encouragement in handling difficult cases.

Support of the faculty can be gained by implementing the previously discussed school guidance committee and staying involved in school activities. Once you are viewed as a team player, you will discover tremendous support from teachers.

Joining a support group of other middle school counselors can also be beneficial. Processing difficult cases, planning district-wide programs, and sharing materials and strategies are ways that professional support group members can assist each other.

12. **Continued professional development**. Successful middle school counselors keep informed of the latest developments in the counseling field and continuously strive to improve their professional skills. The best way to accomplish this is by becoming involved in professional development activities. Joining professional organizations, reading journals, and attending conferences are ways to revitalize your counseling practices. Professional development activities help to strengthen weak areas and allow counselors to benefit from successful ideas shared by their peers.

13. **Sense of humor**. Last, but certainly not least in importance, is the ability to maintain a sense of humor. Students as well as co-workers appreciate school counselors who can laugh and enjoy their work. Using humor in your counseling sessions and classroom presentations often relieves tension and allows students to work on counseling issues with greater comfort.

References

Dougherty, A.M. (1990). *Consultation: Practice and perspectives*. Pacific Grove, CA: Brooks/Cole.

Myrick, R.D. (1997). *Developmental guidance and counseling: A practical approach* (3rd ed.). Minneapolis, MN: Educational Media Corporation.

Schmidt, J. (1999). *Counseling in schools: Essential services and comprehensive programs* (3rd ed.). Nedham, MA: Allyn & Bacon.

Wittmer, J., Thompson, D., & Loesch, L. (1997). *Classroom guidance activities: A sourcebook for elementary school counselors*. Minneapolis, MN: Educational Media Corporation.

Chapter 5
The Scope of Practice of the High School Counselor
by
Doris Coy and Susan Sears

Doris Rhea Coy is an Assistant Professor of Counselor Education at the University of North Texas. She has served as President of the American School Counselor Association and has been a teacher and school counselor. She is a National Certified Counselor, National Certified School Counselor, and a Licensed Professional Counselor.

Susan Jones Sears, PhD, is an Associate Professor in Counselor Education at The Ohio State University, Columbus, and a former high school, junior high, and elementary school counselor. She is a Licensed Professional Clinical Counselor and has written extensively in the areas of school counseling and career development.

Introduction

Adolescents encounter many very real dangers as they grow up in our complex and ever changing society. The possibility of contracting sexually transmitted diseases, the availability of alcohol and other drugs, growing economic pressures on them and their families, and lack of clear family and community values to guide them make young people's adolescence years both confusing and challenging. As indicated by the data presented by Wittmer in Chapter 2 of this book, there are many personal and social problems confronting our youth as we begin the new millennium.

Helping adolescents deal with these personal and social challenges, as well as helping them make effective educational and career decisions, have long been the stated goals of secondary school counselors. A look at the past and current role of the secondary school counselor is the focus of this chapter.

Secondary School Counseling: The Past

As Wittmer noted in Chapter 1 of this book, secondary school counseling and guidance really began in the early 1900s when the primary emphasis of counseling was on guidance activities. An early distinction was made between guidance and counseling in which *guidance* focused on helping students make important choices, whereas *counseling* focused more on helping individuals make behavioral changes (Gladding, 1999). Early guidance work often occurred in schools with adults helping students make vocational decisions. Aubrey (1979) contended that the spread of public education, advancement in testing and psychometrics, and increasing diversity in the student population influenced the growth of guidance in schools. As guidance theory and practice became more clinically oriented, the focus shifted to counseling for personal and social adjustment. As stated previously in this book, in the late 1970s and 1980s, experts in school counseling encouraged counselors to develop "comprehensive programs" organized around student needs rather than simply offering a series of guidance services (Gysbers, 1997). The information and advice-giving that is called "guidance" is still a component of most high school counseling programs. However, it should be acknowledged that other components such as individual and group counseling, parent consultation, staff consultation, community consultation, and coordination have taken on much greater importance.

Secondary school counselors, more than counselors at either elementary or middle school, have performed (and too many continue to do so) clerical and quasi-administrative duties such as entering scheduling data into computers, checking the number of credits students have accumulated, pasting test scores into cumulative folders, organizing the senior prom, and so forth. In fact, to a large extent, the roles of high school counselors have been defined by the administrators with whom they work. Most counselors help students schedule; some counsel individually and in groups; while others complete clerical or administrative tasks their respective principals view as needing to be done. Thus, the tasks high school counselors perform in one school might have little similarity to the those performed in another school. The lack of clearly defined roles is a result of several circumstances. First, since guidance was more process than content and counselor qualifications were not described as unique competencies, counselors have been, and still are, vulnerable both to criticism and to the assignment of inappropriate duties and tasks (Gibson & Mitchell, 1998). Secondly, early guidance began in secondary schools. And, since the organization of secondary schools is departmentalized and rather rigid, counselors tended to form departments similarly to the way secondary teachers are organized. Departmental organization resulted in an isolation that only seemed to heighten the confusion about what high school counselors did and continue to do. Thirdly, it was difficult to evaluate the effectiveness of the counselor. Evaluation became a numbers game (how many students were seen, how many parents were contacted, i.e., a head count) and a laundry list (what activities had been completed, how many letters of recommendation had been written, etc.). Without an appropriately defined content, without the appropriate professional qualifications, and without effective evaluation, it is not surprising that many high school counselors were, and still are, viewed as autonomous professionals without a road map.

During the last two decades, the accountability movement has gained greater and greater strength in education, and especially in school counseling. National studies criticize schools and teachers for graduating students unprepared for the "information age" and the increasingly technological workplace. Schools and educators are being forced to reconsider outdated techniques and curricula. Legislative mandates dealing with curricula and assessment of student progress are common. Education and schools are changing. School counselors, especially high school counselors, must also change.

Past roles played by counselors in schools have been characterized by diversity and sometimes confusion. During the last fifty years, secondary school guidance programs have reflected different educational trends. Vocational guidance, educational guidance, testing, pupil mental health, group guidance, guidance for the gifted, guidance for the disadvantaged and cultural minorities, and career guidance have all been emphasized at one time or another (Gibson & Mitchell, 1998).

The Role of the Secondary School Counselor: Developmental in Nature

Out of the various emphases given above, several important services performed by the secondary school counselor have emerged. They are: individual counseling, group guidance, group counseling, career development and information services, placement, coordination of testing services, and consultation. These services are important in any comprehensive, developmentally oriented high school counseling program and are briefly described below:

Individual Counseling

With so many students experiencing serious social and emotional concerns, counselors at all levels find themselves dealing with more and more complex problems. Substance abuse, teen pregnancy, threats of suicide, and physical and sexual abuse are common concerns of too many of today's youth. Because of the seriousness of these problems, more time is required to deal with them. Consequently, in individual counseling, counselors actually work only with a minority, rather than a majority, of students. Individual counseling is really more remedial than preventative. And most high school counselors are using brief approaches (because of the lack of time) and making referrals when long term counseling is needed by a student.

Group Guidance

Providing educational and career information to classroom size groups is an important function of school counselors. In high school, students need accurate educational information to assist them in scheduling appropriate courses. Other important educational information includes post-secondary and financial aid options. Relationship building and conflict resolutions skills can also be taught to students using a group guidance format. Many high schools have even added "guidance periods" to the curriculum to ensure that counselors have time to provide these services (Wittmer & Thompson, 1995).

Group Counseling

Small group counseling gives the secondary school counselor the opportunity to work with more students who may have similar or related problems. Small groups can focus on a range of topics from adjusting to a new school (new students) to dealing with alcoholic parents. Groups can be offered during lunch hours, before and after school, and during study halls.

Career Development and Information Services

Helping students make appropriate career choices has long been a function of high school counselors. This function includes providing opportunities for students to have interest inventories and achievement tests interpreted to them as they attempt to develop post-secondary career options. With both career inventories and information on computers, counselors can drastically improve their career services.

Placement

The traditional concept of placement (placement in an occupation) has been broadened in high schools to include placement of students in colleges, technical schools, jobs, and even in appropriate high school classes (scheduling) or extracurricular activities. While placement is important, most high school counselors maintain that far too much attention is given to scheduling students into classes.

Consultation

Over the years, high school counselors have increased the amount of time spent in consultation with others. This service enables school counselors to share their knowledge and skills with others such as teachers, administrators, parents, and community agencies. The consultative role was formally acknowledged for the first time in 1966 when the American School Counselor Association (ASCA) and the Association for Counselor Education and Supervision (ACES) specified that counseling, coordination, and consultation should be the three primary role responsibilities of elementary school counselors. As indicated, this function is an increasingly important one for high school counselors as well.

Coordination

Coordination is the process of managing various indirect services which benefit students and may include being a liaison between school and community agencies (ASCA, 1999). Coordinating the testing program or the substance abuse program would be examples of instances in which counselors would perform this function. Coordinating gives counselors many opportunities to demonstrate leadership within and outside their school setting. The above described services or functions are used by effective high school counselors. However, more importantly, how do these services reflect student needs?

As summarized in Chapter 2 of this book, in 1997 the American School Counseling Association (ASCA) published the *National Standards for School Counseling Programs* (Campbell and Dahir, 1997). These National Standards provide the organizational basis for developing quality comprehensive, developmental school counseling programs that promote the academic, personal/social and career development for all students at all levels. By creating this document, ASCA has not only provided a framework for the development of excellent school counseling programs, but a comprehensive outline of the developmental needs of school children of all ages. *In our opinion, every secondary school in the nation should take the necessary steps to implement these very important ASCA standards as soon as possible.*

Developmental High School Counseling Reflects Student Needs

Developmental-oriented high school counselors are not merely "doing more of the same" but rather they are "charting new courses." The major "new course," developmental in nature, is driven by student needs and results in student outcomes for which counselors are accountable.

As mentioned in previous chapters of this book, the work of developmental school counselors at the various levels (elementary, middle/junior high, and senior high) is largely differentiated by attention to age-specific developmental stages of student growth (ASCA, 1999). Today's "new" secondary school counselors realize that they work with young persons who are experiencing adolescence—a unique developmental stage which includes biological, cognitive, and socioemotional aspects. They also realize that "special approaches" are needed to be effective as counselors with this age group. Biologically, adolescence is characterized by significant amounts of physical growth. Height and weight increase dramatically, especially during a growth spurt that takes place in early adolescence for girls and mid-adolescence for boys. This is accompanied by greater strength and stamina. The release of hormones is responsible for the physical changes as well as for the emergence of primary and secondary sexual characteristics. Effective high school counselors are cognizant of these changes and reflect them in their approach to working with high school students.

A Skills-Based Approach

Cognitively, adolescents attain the highest level of thought with the onset of formal operational thought (Piaget, 1952). Reasoning at this stage is characterized by a new form of logic and the quality of thought becomes more abstract and hypothetical since young people are not capable of imagining possibilities and combinations that they have not actually experienced or seen. In addition, they can become more efficient learners because they are capable of screening out distractions. Guidance activities should reflect these developmental aspects of adolescence.

Experts indicate that, socioemotionally, adolescents struggle to achieve a mature identity. According to Havighurst (1972), achieving the following eight developmental tasks will help young people prepare for young adulthood:

1. Achieving new and more mature relationships with peers.

2. Achieving a masculine or feminine social role (or sex-role identity).

3. Accepting one's physique and using the body effectively.

4. Achieving emotional independence of parents and other adults.

5. Preparing for marriage and family life.

6. Preparing for an economic career.

7. Acquiring a set of values and an ethical system as a guide to behavior.

8. Desiring and achieving socially responsible behavior.

Using adolescent developmental tasks as a foundation for building school counseling programs and giving direction to the role of school counselors makes good sense and is not a new idea. Employing this approach, today's developmental school counselors spend much of their time helping students develop skills in understanding themselves, developing effective relationships with others, resolving conflicts, setting educational and career goals, managing stress, valuing diversity, and making effective decisions. Thus, the role of the developmental school counselor, rather than vague and administrator-driven, is *student-driven and measurable*. Student needs become the content of a proactive and developmentally oriented high school counseling program. That is, these well-documented needs give direction to the day-to-day functions of school counselors.

In order to focus on students' needs and facilitate the development of student skills, it is important that counselors move from a services-oriented approach only (career development and information services, group guidance services, counseling services, placement services, consultation, and coordination services) to a developmental, comprehensive skills-based program approach. We believe strongly that counselors must be clear about their "scope of practice"—the responsibilities for which they are trained—and *not* allow themselves to become assistant principals, attendance officers, substitute teachers, and clerks. (No one doubts that the school needs someone to complete the tasks mentioned above, but they should not be within the role of the school counselor.)

If student needs and student skills (understanding self, developing effective relationships, setting educational and career goals, etc.) are the content of the counseling program, what functions do high school counselors need to perform to carry out or implement this skills-based approach? The responsibilities and specific functions of a developmental school counselor (with examples of appropriate activities) are given below:

1. A major responsibility of high school counselors is to develop the content of the skills-based program. Gysbers (1997) referred to the content of the school counseling program as a "guidance curriculum." As suggested above, the content of the program is designed to help students gain specific life skills that they will accomplish upon graduation from high school. Deciding which life skills will be emphasized in your counseling program is the first step. Using adolescent developmental tasks as a foundation, suggested earlier in the chapter, provides for a developmental counseling program based on solid human development theories and concepts. Examples of life skills that would be appropriate in a high school counseling program include the following:

   • Understand themselves.

   • Analyze their personal skills, interests, and strengths.

   • Set appropriate educational and career goals.

   • Develop effective relationships with others.

   • Control and direct their feelings/emotions.

   • Resolve conflicts effectively.

   • Value diversity.

   • Practice strategies for resisting alcohol and other drugs.

   • Manage stress effectively.

   • Students will value learning.

   • Students will make effective decisions.

If each high school counselor was responsible for roughly one hundred students, all of the life skills mentioned above could be included in the counseling program. However, in most high schools counselors are responsible for many more students (350 to 800). Therefore, it is more realistic to focus on three, four, or five skills per year, choosing those that reflect the greatest needs in the school at the present time (conducting needs assessments as described in Chapters 2 and 25 of this book can guide the counselor's choices).

Once you've chosen the life skills upon which you plan to develop the content of the counseling program, then divide the life skills into manageable parts or tasks that students will need to master. By mastering these tasks (or subskills), students will accomplish the general skill. For example, if, as a high school counselor, you wanted to ensure that students learn how "to make effective decisions," then we suggest you divide that skill into the following:

Students will:

- Learn a decision-making process that includes generating alternatives and assessing the consequences of each before making decisions.

- Discuss how decisions made today affect decisions of tomorrow.

- Apply decision-making processes to their own educational planning and career choosing.

- Evaluate their skills in setting goals, gathering information, and assessing the consequences of decisions.

- Take responsibility for their own decisions.

  These tasks are simply the building blocks for the general skill of decision making. The tasks give counselors ideas for activities and experiences they can design to help their students achieve the skills. Such specific, locally appropriate tasks also make evaluation of the program easier. Another advantage of emphasizing the skills-based approach is that counselors are seen as contributing to the growth of all students and not just working with those "in trouble."

2. Counselors are directly involved in the *delivery* of the skills-based program content they have developed. Therefore, counselors will have to allocate significant amounts of time to facilitate or team-teach activities designed to help students master skills. Given the structure of schools, much of the counselor's time should be spent in individual classrooms (This represents a major change for many high school counselors; many of whom rarely conduct classroom guidance activities). In addition to facilitation of classroom activities, as noted, developmental counselors deliver their program content in small group sessions. Large group or classroom sessions may be appropriate for information about and discussion of post-secondary or vocational education options and financial aid while small groups may be more appropriate for interest or aptitude test interpretations. Also, a major role of the developmental counselor is to in-service teachers enabling them to assist in the facilitation of the activities. Clearly, counselors must convince administrators and teachers that what they want to do with students makes as much or more sense than the so-called academic curriculum does. While some will be less accepting than others, many administrators and teachers will be supportive of a life skills approach, particularly if they have been consulted and their input valued as the program is being designed and developed.

3. As noted previously, the role of the developmental high school counselor includes counseling students both individually and in small groups. Effective school counselors do not forget their unique training in counseling skills. While schools are not appropriate sites for large "caseloads of clients," counselors must always allot time for counseling students with personal-social problems and allot time to engage in crisis counseling when needed (see Figure 5.1). In order to be as effective as possible in a limited number of sessions, counselors should utilize newer theoretical approaches such as brief therapy (a focused, structured approach with a limited number of sessions). Some school counselors have not continued to improve their counseling skills and openly admit to not being skilled in counseling. In the opinion of the authors, such neglect is indefensible. Individuals who call themselves school counselors have an ethical and legal obligation to be able to perform the individual and small group counseling duties they have been certified to perform. If they do not feel competent as counselors, they should either seek additional training or switch to a different job.

High school counselors must be prepared to see students before school, during lunch hours, and after school. Finding enough time to talk to counselors is a problem for students. Thus, effective high school counselors are as flexible as possible. Obviously, counselors' caseloads do not allow for more than five or six sessions with a student. Students with more chronic problems should be referred to appropriately credentialed mental health care providers in the community.

4. As noted, consulting with parents and other is an important function of the developmental high school counselor. Consultation is a cooperative process in which the counselor-consultant assists others to think through problems and to develop skills that make them more effective in working with children/students (ASCA, 1999). As a result of the parent consultation function, counselors should be prepared to assist parents by:

   - Disseminating educational information including information about courses offered.

   - Providing periodic workshops on parenting skills needed to work with adolescents and workshops on post-secondary options and financial aid opportunities.

   - Disseminating testing/appraisal information to help them better understand their adolescents.

   - Facilitating parent/teacher conferences. Newsletters, video tapes, radio, TV, and so forth, can be used effectively to disseminate information to as many parents as possible.

5. Consulting with various community agencies to help students deal with more serious personal and educational problems is another important aspect of the counselor/consultant role. Interventions may include (1) referral of students and families to community agencies, and (2) the development of collaborative programs designed to assist students and their families. While counselor referral of students to social agencies in the community is not new, high school counselors have not collaborated with mental health counselors or social workers as much as is needed to offer family counseling or parenting workshops. Developmental counselors create ongoing, not just occasional, links between the schools and the community's social agencies.

6. Training school staff to facilitate their personal and professional development is a primary function of today's high school counselor. School counselors possess many skills that teachers need such as skills in communication (e.g., listening, demonstrating empathy, being non-judgmental, problem solving, conflict management, stress management, and group processing). By conducting regular in-service sessions with staff, counselors can train staff, especially teachers, so they can master these communication and relationship building skills needed to work with students effectively. Not only will such training be helpful to teachers (and therefore students), but it will also enable counselors to be seen as leaders within the educational team.

7. Coordinating or collaborating with others who may be offering mental health-oriented assistance in the school (e.g., community substance abuse agencies working within the school) is a coordinating function developmental counselors play. High school counselors report that more and more community-based programs are operating in the schools. Effective school counselors coordinate the efforts of these programs and collaborate in their delivery. Separate and disparate efforts by outside agencies attempting to impact students in the school have little success if coordination with the school counselor is lacking.

   In addition, counselors coordinate programs within schools such as the testing program. In these days of accountability, you will want to be careful not to permit this counselor responsibility to consume too much time. As a counselor you should understand thoroughly all relevant interest, aptitude, and achievement tests and should be able to in-service teachers on their interpretation and use. Spending time in direct administration of tests is not the most effective use of your valuable time.

8. Managing the school counseling program is a critical function of high school counselors since system-wide directors of guidance are a dying breed. Many counselors find themselves supervised by individuals who have more responsibilities than they can handle and have little direct knowledge of counselors and the services they provide. Effective counselors take charge of their own programs and encourage interaction and regular meetings of the counselors in their district in order to assure program progress. If more than one counselor is employed in your high school, one of you should consider taking a lead role in the management process. Rotating leaders (on a yearly basis) is often an effective management system. Managing a school counseling program includes developing an active *staff/community* public relations program. Counselors should orient staff and community to the counseling program through newsletters, local media, and school and community presentations. As mentioned in previous chapters, assembling advisory committees of parents and community members to provide input regarding the needs of students is another task that falls within the management function of the counselor.

9. Evaluating the counseling program including counselor efforts with students, staff, and community is an especially important function of today's high school counselor. The best and most effective way to evaluate a counseling program is to determine whether program activities are effective in achieving program outcomes. As suggested earlier in this chapter, ad-

equate program outcomes describe desired changes in student behaviors. Also, a well designed program incorporates short-term, intermediate, and long-term objectives. As noted, in a skills-based approach to counseling the desired student outcome (i.e., students will make effective decisions) is divided into manageable parts called tasks or subskills. These tasks are the short-term and intermediate objectives of the program while the desired student outcome is the long-term objective. The more specific these tasks or subskills are the easier they are to evaluate.

Gathering good evaluation data takes time. Teacher and student rating scales and short surveys to determine what students gained from the guidance activities are two techniques that can be used to evaluate whether or not student outcomes are being achieved. Standardized tests and performance-based assessments can also be used when appropriate (again, the focus is on student outcomes).

Counselors may want to gather some general evaluation data also. Examples of "general evaluation" data includes (1) the number of students seen in individual or crisis counseling, (2) the number of small group counseling sessions held, (3) the number of large group information sessions conducted, (4) the number of conferences with parents, and (5) the number of phone calls to parents and community agencies. While this kind of general evaluation does not speak to student outcomes, it does provide the school board and administration information about the scope or breadth of the counseling program.

Evaluation of "counselors as professionals" is included in the "evaluating" function. Obviously counselors need to evaluate themselves. Effective professionals must be willing to closely scrutinize their practices. Unfortunately, counselors have been content to let administrators who know little about counseling evaluate them using "teacher" evaluation forms. Effective counselors take the lead in designing and gaining approval of evaluation instruments developed to evaluate counselors specifically. Even though administrators are designated as the school district evaluators, counselors should advocate for peer evaluations also. By involving peers (other counselors) in evaluation efforts, counselors can receive feedback relative to their unique counseling functions (for specific details on counselor accountability, see Chapter 25).

Summary

We have presented several daunting challenges facing the secondary school counselor as we begin the new millennium and how the challenges and demands on their time will continue to grow. We have also discussed how the profession of school counseling is changing rapidly and how very important it is for school counselors to "stay abreast" and to keep up with these changes. There are many organizations such as the American School Counselor Association that stand ready to assist you in keeping up with your fast changing profession. Among others, one such entity is *The Adjunct ERIC Clearinghouse for School Services* located on the campus of the University of North Texas. This is a clearinghouse for the latest documents, articles etc. regarding the school counseling profession (To learn more about the Clearinghouse, contact the senior author via e-mail at: coy@coefs.coe.unt.edu).

If secondary school counselors are to chart a new course in the new millennium, then they need to design and deliver a student-oriented, developmental-in-nature, counseling program with measurable student outcomes. This new century will either bring an "ending" or a "new beginning" for high school counselors. It is up to "the secondary school counselor to be" and to those now practicing, to ensure that it is a "beginning."

Figure 5.1
A Crisis Management Intervention School Policy and Program

It is extremely difficult for an elementary, middle, or high school and its guidance department to respond in an effective manner to a crisis situation if a crisis management/intervention policy and program is not in place when the crisis occurs.

It is probably only a matter of time before your school will be confronted with a crisis. Any counselor who has been greeted with, *"A student in our school has died,"* for example, knows the value of having a crisis plan in place. Attempting to respond to such a traumatic event without a prior plan almost always exacerbates the problem. In addition to having a plan in place, school counselors will be expected to be experts in how the crisis will impact students initially, its long term effects, grieving behaviors, etc. How the counselor(s) responds to a crisis will have a significant influence on students, staff, and faculty grieving (if a death occurs), overall school togetherness, and so forth. Such a policy should be adopted and approved by the school principal and, if appropriate, by the local board of education.

We have designed herein a program to assist the school counselor, as coordinator of the crisis team, and the other members of the team in developing a policy and program that will best meet the needs of the school population in time of crisis.

The purpose of a policy and program is to aid the educational institution beset by trauma due to a crisis minimize disruption of educational activities. Preparation for a crisis mollifies the overall impact and disruption to the educational process. As noted, a school without a crisis policy in place will experience great difficulty coping and responding effectively when a crisis does occur.

An effective education and preventive program should include a proactive as well as reactive plan and approach to crises situations. The plan should have a broad base of community involvement and support. Information concerning various types of crises that might arise should be included as a part of the plan.

Crisis as used in this brief essay is defined as any sudden death or other traumatic event that directly impacts an entire school population.

The policy should be developed by those individuals who will implement the policy. The crisis team should include, but not be limited to, the school counselor(s), school nurse, school psychologist, school social worker, administrators, and other qualified mental health caregivers from the community who volunteer to be members of the team. The inclusion of nonteaching school staff can also be beneficial. A secretary, cook, custodian, or bus driver is often more aware than others of the mood of the total school population, especially of the students, and their expertise should not be overlooked. As noted, it is our belief that one of the guidance department counselors should be the coordinator of such a team.

When developing a school crisis policy and/or action plan, the following questions should be addressed and answered specifically:

1. In the event of a crisis who is the first person to be contacted?

2. If the first person or organization is unavailable, who becomes the second and third main contact?

3. Who verifies what happened? How will the information be verified for accuracy and consistency?

4. How will the procedures the school will use to deal with the crisis be shared with the family, or families directly affected by the crisis?

5. Who notifies members of the crisis management/ intervention team?

6. How and when is the school staff informed and by whom?

7. How and when is the student body informed?

8. Is a phone tree in place?

9. When and where does the crisis management/ intervention team meet?

10. What specific information will be shared with the teachers and staff concerning the tragedy? Suggested faculty guidelines (i.e., how to identify students in distress, appropriate classroom discussions regarding the crisis, dealing with student reactions regarding loss and death, etc.) should be in place.

11. What specific information concerning the tragedy will be shared with the students?

12. How will the involved family's privacy be protected by the school?

13. What information will be released by the media and who will be the spokesperson for the school?

14. If teachers/staff are contacted by the media, will they have been briefed or told what to say? Who will brief them?

15. If a student or school staff member is killed or dies unexpectedly, how will the personal possessions of the deceased be handled?

16. Who will follow the schedule of the individual and explain or answer questions concerning the tragedy?

17. Will a crisis center (safe room) be available for students, faculty, and non-instructional staff members?

18. Where will the crisis center be set up?

19. Who will be responsible for covering the crisis center? What hours?

20. How will individuals be identified to come to the crisis center? Will teachers have been given guidelines to assist them in identifying students in distress?

21. For what length of time will the crisis center exist?

22. How will qualified community resources be identified and utilized?

23. What action will be taken on the first day? How will those students directly involved with the incident be dealt with? By whom?

24. If a death occurs, what policy will be followed on the day of the funeral?

In sum, each school should have formulated a detailed disaster/crisis plan which includes plans for the immediate reaction to the crisis, immediate steps for crisis control, as well as on-going and long-term intervention plans. As noted, such a plan should always include steps to help individuals, support for peer groups (teachers and students) and guidance for the entire student body.

It is extremely important to realize that a policy and program cannot cover every aspect of a crisis. Flexibility within a policy and program provides the ability to adjust to the unexpected needs created by the crisis. However, the policy and program should provide a clear directive to the crisis management/intervention team and present clear guidelines for delivering the crisis intervention service to the school's population.

Once the policy has been written, it should be reviewed by a school board attorney prior to school or school board adoption. In addition, the policy should be reviewed to ascertain that the policy follows and/or is not in conflict with any appropriate ethical standards (i.e., those of the American Counseling Association, state guidelines, others).

The individual counselor designated as responsible for the crisis management/intervention program should develop the team membership early in the school year. Team members should be educated concerning the adopted school policy and drills on implementing the crisis program should occur on a regular basis. Key players on the team should be identified and major responsibilities assigned and practiced. In-service opportunities in crisis intervention and management should be made available throughout the school year to team members as well as for faculty and staff. This provides the opportunity for individuals to be informed regarding the appropriate response to various crises and will assist in keeping their crisis management/intervention skills sharpened.

The policy and program should be evaluated on an annual basis. By reviewing the policy and program, additions, deletions, and modifications can be made and the policy and program strengthened. The counselor coordinator of the program should update the school board on the strengths and weaknesses of the revised policy and program.

Figure 5.2
Warning Signs of Adolescent Suicide By Joe Wittmer

Situational Clues

Recent loss of a loved one

Survivor of suicide attempt

Anniversary of death or loss—especially suicide

Loss of prestige, loss of face

Serious illness

Exhaustion of resources real or imagined

Family history of suicide

Close friend commits suicide

Behavioral Clues

Talking or writing about suicide

Giving away personal possessions

Change in behaviors—eating and sleeping habits

Ending close relationships

Preparing for death—talking about funeral arrangements

Crying frequently

Buying weapons, pills, etc.

Reading a lot regarding suicide

Emotional Clues

Sense of personal failure

Continual or constant sadness

General lack of interest

Expressing feelings of helplessness

Guilt

Withdrawal/isolation

Feels like a burden to others

Sudden lifting of depression

Verbal Clues

"I can't go on."

"I have nothing to live for."

"No one cares."

"There's nothing left to do."

"What's the use."

"They won't have me to kick around anymore."

"I'm at my rope's end."

"They're better off without me."

"I just want to stop the pain once and for all."

What to Do

Listen:

Take feelings seriously

Avoid criticism or advice

Don't be judgmental or moralistic

Offer genuine concern, not sympathy or pity

Maintain contact

Inquire About Suicidal Plan:

Is a specific plan formulated?

How lethal is the chosen method? Is it easily accessible?

What outcome is expected? Anticipated reaction of others?

Were previous attempts made?

If so, when, how serious, response of others?

Remove any lethal methods

Explore Resources:

Personal strengths and abilities

Willingness to consider alternatives

Ability to ask for help

Significant others—friends, family, clergy, teacher, etc.

Community resources—local suicide prevention center, professional

Counseling, community mental health center.

Figure 5.3
Myths About Suicide

Myths and fallacies tend to arise and circulate about the subjects our society has deemed taboo. Suicide is one of those subjects. Present knowledge refutes the following myths.

Suicidal adolescents just want to die.

FACT: Most of the time suicidal people are torn between wanting to die and wanting to live. Most suicidal individuals don't want death: they just want the pain to stop.

Adolescents who commit suicide do not warn others.

FACT: Out of 10 people who kill themselves, eight give definite clues to their intentions. They leave numerous clues and warnings to others, although clues may be non-verbal or difficult to detect.

Teens who talk about suicide are only trying to get attention. They won't really do it.

FACT: WRONG! Few commit suicide without first letting someone else know how they feel Those who are considering suicide give clues and warnings as a cry for help. In fact, most seek out someone to rescue him or her. Over 70% who do threaten to commit suicide either make an attempt or complete the act

After a person has attempted suicide, it is unlikely they will try again.

FACT: People who have attempted suicide are very likely to try again: 80% of people who commit suicide have made **at least one previous attempt:**

Suicide only happens to "crazy" people:

FACT: Suicide among adolescents knows no boundaries. Gifted and homosexual teens are more likely to show suicidal behaviors and attempts but it can happen to any family anywhere.

Don't mention suicide to someone who's showing signs of severe depression: It will plant the idea in their minds and they will act on it.

FACT: Many depressed youth have already considered suicide as an option. Discussing it openly helps them sort through the problems and generally provides a sense of relief and understanding. It is one of the most helpful things you can do. However, the danger is still there.

More males attempt suicide than females:

FACT: Gender differences in the suicidal behavior of adolescents do exist. More adolescent females do attempt suicide than males. However, more males are successful. This may be that males tend to choose more violent and lethal methods.

Sexual orientation does not play a role in adolescent suicide.

FACT: Attempted suicide rates among both gay and lesbian adolescent populations are two to six times greater than suicide rates within the general population. Most experts attribute this to lack of support systems, societal homophobia, parental and peer rejection, feelings of isolation, etc.

Race is not a factor in suicide:

FACT: Suicide rates among African-American populations have been found to be somewhat lower than for White Euro-Americans. The evidence concerning other sub-populations is not available.

References

ASCA (1999). *Role statement: The school counselor.* Alexandria, VA: Author. ASCA Press.

Aubrey, R.F. (1979). Relationship of guidance and counseling to the established and emerging school curriculum. *The School Counselor 26,* 150–162.

Campbell, C., & Dahir, C. (1997). *Sharing the vision: The national standards for school counseling programs.* Alexandria, VA: ASCA Press.

Coy, D. (1999). The role and trainig of the school counselor: Background and purpose. *NASP Bulletin, 83,* 2-8.

Gibson, R.L., & Mitchell, M.H. (1998). *Introduction to counseling and guidance* (3rd ed.). New York: Macmillan.

Gladding, S.T. (1999). *Counseling: A comprehensive profession* (4th ed.). Columbus, OH: Merrill.

Gysbers, N.C. (1997) *Comprehensive guidance programs that work.* Greensboro, NC: ERIC Counseling and Personnel Services Clearinghouse.

Havighurst, R.J. (1972). *Developmental tasks and education.* New York: McKay.

Hughes, F.P., & Noppe, L.D. (1991). *Human development: Across the life span* (2nd ed.). New York: West Publishing Company.

Piaget, J. (1952). *The origins of intelligence in children.* New York: Norton.

Sears, S., & Coy, D. (1991). The scope of practice of the secondary school counselor. *ERIC Digest.* Ann Arbor, MI: ERIC Counseling and Personnel Services Clearinghouse.

Sears, S. (1999). Transforming school counseling: Making a difference for students. *NASP Bullitin, 83,* 47-53.

Wittmer, J., & Thompson, D. (1995). *Large group counseling: A k-12 sourcebook.* Minneapolis, MN: Educational Media Corporation.

Chapter 6
The Developmental School Counselor and Mental Health Counseling

by

Sondra L. Smith and James Archer

Sondra L. Smith is an Assistant Professor in the Department of Counselor Education at the University of Florida in Gainesville. Her research interests include delinquency prevention and counseling at-risk youth and their families. She has prior work experience teaching and counseling special needs children and adolescents in schools, agencies, and residential treatment settings.

James Archer is a Professor in the Departments of Counselor Education and Psychology at the University of Florida in Gainesville. He was director of the University Counseling Center prior to moving to Counselor Education. He is a fellow of Division 17 of the American Psychological Association and holds a diplomate in Counseling Psychology from the American Board of Professional Psychology. His most recent book is titled, Counseling and Mental Health Services on Campus.

Introduction

In today's school age populations, serious emotional and behavioral problems have been growing dramatically, concomitant with the growth of such social problems as dysfunctional families, pregnancies, poverty, homelessness, violence, gangs, suicide, divorce, child abuse, and substance abuse (Baker, 1996; Carlson & Lewis, 1998; Collins & Collins, 1994). According to several recent reports, there is a growing population of students whose social-emotional needs interfere with the learning process.

- Though 15% to 22% of children and adolescents have mental health problems, fewer than 20% receive mental health services (National Advisory Mental Health Council, 1990; see Costello, 1990; Lockhart & Keys, 1998; Tuma, 1989; Zill & Schoenborn, 1990).

- From 3 to 6 million children suffer from clinical depression and are at risk for suicide (American Psychiatric Association, 1992).

- Each day, 6 children commit suicide (Sears, 1993).

- The number of children admitted to psychiatric hospitals increased from 17,000 to 43,000 between 1980 and 1986 (Darnton, 1989)

- Between 3% and 29% of children are diagnosed with ADHD (Erk, 1995).

- In 1992, 22% of children were living in homes with incomes below the poverty line (Dryfoos, 1994).

- Each day, 3000 children see their parent's marriage end in divorce (Sears, 1993).

- Sixty thousand to 100,000 children are homeless (Bassuk, 1991; Carroll, 1993).

- Each day 2,796 adolescents become pregnant and 1,106 have abortions (Sears, 1993).

- Each day 1,512 adolescents drop out of school (Sears, 1993).

Before students can learn effectively, the personal and social challenges that interfere with their learning must be addressed. Schools throughout the United States have been faced with the challenges of today's complex and often troubled society. School counselors are the designated personnel within the school environment specifically trained to deal with students' social-emotional needs and their impact on the learning process (Ballard & Murgatroyd, 1999; Sears, 1993).

As Wittmer indicates in chapter one of this book, the role and function of the school counselor has been debated throughout the history of the school counseling profession. The role of the school counselor has evolved from providing guidance and career information to addressing the developmental needs of students including their personal, social, educational and career needs (Bailey, Henderson, Krueger, & Williams, 1998). It has been suggested that the evolution and sometimes confusion about the school counselor's role is reflective of changing forces in society and the demands that are placed upon schools to meet the needs of increasingly diverse student populations (Murray, 1995). Recently, discussion related to the role of the school counselor has emerged regarding their role as either a developmental specialist and/or as a mental health provider in the schools. Central to the debate is whether or not school counselors do "real counseling," and to what extent, given their already exhaustive list of tasks and responsibilities, they have time for the provision of mental health services (Paisley & Borders, 1995). In this chapter, we take the philosophical approach that school counselors are both developmental specialists and mental health providers in the schools. Current models of school counseling and mental health counseling are reviewed and recent literature regarding the mental health role of school counselors will be summarized.

The chapter is organized into three parts. In part one, we present an overview of mental health counseling. Next, we detail the status of school counselors as mental health providers according to school counseling organizations. In part three, we outline a suggested approach for strengthening the mental health counseling role of school counselors to meet the needs of at-risk and special needs students.

Some Fundamentals of Mental Health Counseling

"Mental health counseling" is not unlike "school counseling" in its professional roles and functions. For example, proposed paradigm shifts in both mental health and school counseling center around the de-emphasis of long-term psychotherapeutic techniques for working with individuals in favor of preventive strategies for handling groups or managing broad programs, and briefer, targeted counseling interventions. Much like school counseling, the mental health counseling model focuses on the development and well being of the whole person, promotes wellness in clients as well as assisting clients in preventing or treating mental disorders. Specific ways in which clients are served in all of these areas is dependent on the skills of the counselors and the needs of their populations (Gladding, 1997). Following is a brief overview of principles related to mental health counseling which illustrate the philosophical similarities between mental health and school counseling. In the mental health counseling model,

1. Primary prevention is characterized by having a "before the fact quality," intentional, and group-level counseling process, rather than individually oriented process.

2. Counselors in mental health settings "are actively involved in primary prevention types of programs through collaboration with the schools, colleges, churches, community health centers, and public and private agencies" (Baker & Shaw, 1987, p.2; Gladding, 1997).

3. Counseling delivery services also are characterized by secondary prevention (i.e., controlling problems that have already surfaced but are not severe) and tertiary prevention (i.e., controlling serious problems such as mental disorders, to keep them from becoming chronic or life threatening) (Gladding, 1997).

4. Mental health counseling is interdisciplinary in its history, practice settings, skills/knowledge, and roles performed. Though the profession has evolved and changed in its role and function throughout its history in the literature related to mental health counseling, two foci emerge: (a) the prevention and the promotion of mental health and (b) the treatment of disorders and dysfunctions (Gladding, 1997; Spruill & Fong; 1990).

5. Mental health counseling considers the cultural contexts in which people relate and communicate. Ecological considerations in counseling practice are fundamental (p. 221, Lewis, Lewis, Daniels, and D'Andrea, 1998). Ecosystemic thinking is "thinking that recognizes the indivisible interconnectedness of individual, family, and sociocultural content" (Sherrard & Amatea, 1994, p.5).

6. In addition to serving a wide range of clients, mental health counselors consult and at times perform administrative duties (Hosie, West, & Mackey, 1988).

Newer theories of mental health counseling, such as solution focused and narrative therapy stress a non-pathological, constructivist approach to clients and their problems. An emphasis is placed upon attending to the client's reality and upon helping the clients form solutions and rewrite the narratives of their lives (Eron & Lund, 1999; O'Hanlon & Beadle, 1997). These modern approaches fit very well with more traditional, growth-oriented approaches to counseling that have been at the heart of the traditional developmental guidance model. The postmodern mental health approaches provide a useful addition to contemporary school counseling in that they offer brief, effective interventions that can help the school counselor provide brief and focused interventions that can be both preventive and remedial and that can be directed toward problems and issues that interfere with school performance and disturbance to the school environment.

Current Trends in School Counseling: School Counselors as Mental Health Professionals

The primary role of the school counselor is to facilitate the mission of schools, that is, to help children to learn. According to Paisley and Borders (1995), "the appropriate focus for school counseling is considered to be comprehensive and developmental programs. Such programs include individual, small-group, and large-group counseling as well as consultation and coordination. These programs still offer certain types of responsive services related to remediation and crisis intervention, but they now emphasize primary prevention and the promotion of healthy development for all students" (p.150). The role statement of the professional school counselor recently adopted by The American School Counseling Association (ASCA) includes the following statement: "School counselors work with all students, including those who are considered "at risk" and those with special needs" (ASCA, 1999). ASCA also recently has developed standards for school counseling which articulate the goals of school counseling programs as "to promote school success through a focus on academic achievement, prevention and intervention activities, advocacy, and social/emotional and career development" (ASCA, 1999). These two statements taken together emphasize the importance of school counselors having the skills and knowledge to work with both the developmental concerns of students as well as those who have special mental health needs. ASCA has adopted a stance that does not limit the school counselor from providing mental health counseling services in the schools, but neither the role statement nor the national standards clearly articulate the extent to which they are to provide direct counseling services to students with special mental health needs.

The recent research conducted by The Education Trust, however, does specifically state that school counselors should focus more on academic achievement than on counseling students with serious emotional problems. The Education Trust received a grant from the DeWitt Wallace-Reader's Digest Fund to start an initiative to transform school counseling. In 1996, the team developed a list of problems faced by many school counselors:

- School counselors focus too much on counseling students with serious emotional and social problems while denying students sufficient academic guidance and direction.

- There is little connection between how counselors are being trained in universities and colleges and the services they need to provide to students.

- School counselors are trained in isolation from teachers, administrators, and other school personnel-all of who must collaborate to support success for each student.

- Current counselor training programs offer a core of generic counseling courses that do not provide counselors with the specific knowledge and skills needed to be effective in schools. For example, the vast majority of counselor preparation programs emphasize a mental health model with few connections to student achievement as an important indicator of student success.

The proposed solutions to these problems included:

- Focus on the relations and interactions between students and their school environments.

- Foster conditions that insure educational equity, access and academic success for all students K-12.

- Be assertive advocates who create opportunities for all students to define, nurture, and accomplish high aspirations.

- Serve as leaders, team members, and consultants working with students, teachers, principals, parents, guardians, and the community to create the pathways needed for students to succeed. (*Counseling Today*, February 1998).

The Mental Health Counseling Role of School Counselors

Authors advocating for the strengthening of the mental health counseling role for school counselors cite the shortcomings of the developmental model as it relates to children at risk (Keys, Bemak, & Lockhart, 1998). According to these authors, the primary prevention focus of traditional developmental guidance and counseling programs may be too broad to meet the mental health needs of students in today's society. According to Keys, Bemak, & Lockhart (1998), it is naïve to think that all students respond similarly to the same intervention. Many students require more focused and intensive counseling services to prevent the further development of an existing problem. These intensive counseling services often are not provided without the intervention of the school counselor. Community mental health services are isolated from schools, are inaccessible to students and families, and are declining in number (Lockhart & Keys, 1998; Wylie, 1992). Though the delivery of counseling interventions targeted toward students' mental health needs may rely on the school counselor, it has further been suggested that they often are not equipped with the training needed to provide these more intensive counseling services (Coll & Freeman, 1996). The following limitations of the developmental guidance and counseling model in meeting the mental health needs of students are cited by Keys, Bemak, and Lockhart (1998):

1. Primary prevention may be too broad and less sensitive to the needs of at-risk youth.

2. Strategies school counselors use in their primary prevention efforts have not been shown to be effective in the long-term with at-risk youth and are often limited in scope and duration, are poorly implemented, fail to account for contextual factors, and are seldom integrated with other school-and community-based programs (Dryfoos, 1990; Webster, 1993; Weissberg, Caplan, & Harwood, 1991).

3. An emphasis on individual change through school-based strategies rather than an emphasis on systems-based intervention that include intervention with family, peers, world of work, school, and community (Dryfoos, 1990; Hamburg, 1992) are less effective with at-risk youth (Dryfoos, 1990; Lerner, 1995).

4. School counseling programs are linked to the broader educational program instead of linking with community services and are thus, unable to meet the diverse services needed to help at-risk youth (Hobbs & Collison, 1995; Keys & Bemak, 1997).

5. Predetermined student competencies, rather than mental health needs, are the focus of program planning rather than assessing the mental health needs of the school, the students and the larger community.

6. "Guidance" as a term diminishes the role and identity of the school counselor as a counseling professional. "School counseling" has been suggested as a term more descriptive of the counseling and consultation services provided by counselors (Schmidt, 1996). Also, the term "counseling" should be defined broadly to include a variety of services, not just remedial or one-to-one relationships.

Keys, Bemak, and Lockhart (1998) proposed a "transformed model" for school counseling which includes program organization and planning, and suggestions for changing school counselors' role and function, and their skills and expertise.

Program organization and planning. School personnel are discovering the importance of collaboration with service providers in the community in meeting the mental health needs of their students (Dryfoos, 1994). Keys, Bemak, and Lockhart suggested that in a transformed model of school counseling, "the school counselor provides leadership within the school for an alliance with school-based mental health professionals and helps to establish school-based mechanisms to support a variety of collaborative efforts (pp. 383-384)." Their suggestions for school-based, mental health collaborative mechanisms which school counselors will establish and coordinate follow:

1. "School-family-community mental health teams" are designed to join school personnel, family members, representatives from service institutions (i.e., social services, health and mental health agencies, juvenile justice, and law enforcement) and helping institutions (i.e., churches, parks and recreation, and libraries) (Keys & Bemak, 1997). The team meets on a regular basis to ensure the quality and continuity of services provided throughout the community. Though this model is not inconsistent with the "guidance advisory committee" suggested by Wittmer in chapter two in this book, it is suggested by us that it is more comprehensive in scope and function.

2. "Program development groups" are comprised of a subcommittee designed to extend the goals of the school-family-community mental health team by developing new community outreach programs and activities for the larger team's consideration. Several program development groups may exist at the same time, focusing on different mental health needs (Adelman & Taylor, 1993).

3. "Case management teams" also are a subcommittee of the school-family-community mental health team though it may include other members such as a school administrator, the school counselor, or school psychologist. The goal of the case management team is to provide multidisciplinary planning and intervention for individual students.

Role and function of the school counselor. The "transformed model" extends the coordination, consultation, and counseling functions of the school counselor in the following ways:

1. "Coordination" becomes the primary function of the school counselor, but it is expanded to include the service integration provided by the school-family-community mental health teams, program development groups, and case management teams.

2. "Consultation" as traditionally defined as a "counselor as expert" model is extended to include collaborative consultation. "Collaborative consultation is an interactive, interdependent process in which all members of the collaborative group (e.g., school-family-community mental health team; case management team) exchange expertise and roles, engage in joint problem-solving, and share responsibility for outcomes (Dettmer, Dyck, & Thurston 1996; Keys, Bemak, & Lockhart, 1998; Keys, Bemak, Carpenter, & King-Sears, 1998).

3. "Counseling" services provided by school counselors in the "transformed model" prioritize "therapeutically focused group counseling (Keys, Bemak, & Lockhart, p. 385)," short-term models of intervention (i.e., systematic problem-solving and solution-focused counseling) (Myrick, 1997; Walter & Peller, 1992), crisis intervention teams, and family counseling (Hinkle, 1993). Concerning brief therapy in schools, Paisley and Borders suggest,

"Although we do not want to gloss over the frequent need to refer students for long-term therapeutic work, recent literature on brief counseling has much relevance for school counselors. Brief counseling models are not only a reactive response to those situations in which a counselor has only six to eight sessions with a student or client. (The limited number of sessions is now common across settings.) Brief models also are built on research indicating that a counselor's most effective work may be accomplished in the first eight sessions. Several writers have proposed ways to apply brief models in the school setting. Thus, training in brief models may offer one critical avenue to helping school counselors more effectively provide individual counseling to their students (p. 152)."

4. "Classroom-based instruction" is suggested as an integral part of the school counselor's program, though it must provide "more in-depth skill development on an on-going basis, need(s) to be relevant to the issues students face and the problems identified by teachers, need(s) to integrate real-life problem situations in the curricula's content, and need(s) to be connected with other school- and community-based programs (p. 386)" than traditional classroom guidance models.

Skills and expertise. Recommended new knowledge and skills which school counselors' should acquire to implement a "transformed model" of school counseling included the following (Keys, Bemak, & Lockhart, 1998; Lockhart & Keys, 1998):

1. Recognize students who are functioning outside of the range of normal development and coordinate services. Knowledge of the *Diagnostic and Statistical Manual of Mental Disorders* (4th ed.) is recommended.

2. Understand and apply the principles of systems theory related to families and community organizations (i.e., social service programs, juvenile justice, and managed care).

3. Increase skills in multicultural counseling techniques critical to the counselor's success in forming effective relationships with students, families, and the community.

It should be noted here that the "transformed" model of school counseling does not contradict the traditional school counseling and guidance models. There is an artificial dichotomy between school counseling and mental health counseling in the discussion concerning the role of the school counselor as a mental health provider. The integration of developmental school counseling and mental health counseling is imminent though some efforts in the current context of school counseling seem in opposition.

In our view the artificial dichotomy between "developmental guidance" and "mental health" models of school counseling is archaic and does not provide a useful foundation for school counseling in the twentieth century. It seems clear to us that school counselors must provide what has traditionally been called developmental guidance, focusing on the larger student body, the school environment and academic success, and they must also serve as mental health consultants and counselors for their schools. The recent round of shootings in schools in various parts of the nation underscore the need for counselors to stay in touch with students who are alienated and who have serious psychological problems. Certainly the typical school counselor does not have the time to provide extensive mental health counseling for students, but he or she will be called upon to facilitate and spearhead a team approach to providing mental health services in collaboration with community resources. School counselors cannot serve in this role unless they have mental health training and a broader scope than the role apparently suggested by the Educational Trust study team. We agree that the goal of school counseling programs should be academic success for all students. However, we maintain that this goal cannot be met if the school counselor's role in providing brief, targeted, mental health services is diminished in importance.

References

Adelman, H. S., & Taylor, L. (1993). School-based mental health: Toward a comprehensive approach. *The Journal of Mental Health Administration, 20,* 32-45.

American Psychiatric Association. (1992). *Childhood disorders* (Brochure). Washington, DC: Author.

American School Counselor Association. (1999). *The role of the professional school counselor.* Alexandria, VA: ASCA Press.

American School Counselor Association. (1999). *National standards for school counseling programs.* Alexandria, VA: ASCA Press.

Bailey, M., Henderson, P., Krueger, D., & Williams, L. A. (1998). A visit to a comprehensive guidance program that works. Greensboro, NC: ERIC-CASS.

Baker, S. B. (1996). *School counseling for the twenty-first century.* Englewood Cliffs, NJ: Prentice-Hall.

Baker, S. B., & Shaw, M. C. (1987). *Improving counseling through primary prevention.* Columbus, OH: Merrill.

Ballard, M. B., & Murgatroyd, W. (1999). Defending a vital program: School counselors define their roles. *NASSP Bulletin, January NEED VOLUME NUMBER,* 19-26.

Bassuk, E. L. (1991). Homeless families. *Scientific American, 265,* 66-74.

Carlson, J., & Lewis, J. (1998). *Counseling the adolescent: Individual, family, and school interventions, 3rd. ed.* Denver, CO: Love Publishing.

Carroll, B. W. (1993). Perceived roles and preparation experiences of elementary counselors: Suggestions for change. *Elementary School Guidance and Counseling, 27,* 216-225.

Coll, K., & Freeman, B. (1997). Role conflict among elementary school counselors: A national comparison with middle and secondary school counselors. *Elementary School Guidance and Counseling, 31,* 251-261.

Collins, B. G., & Collins, T. M. (1994). Child and adolescent mental health: Building a system of care. *Journal of Counseling and Development, 72,* 239-243.

Costello, E. J. (1990). Child psychiatric epidemiology: Implications for clinical research and practice. In B. B. Lahey & A. E. Kazdin (Eds.). *Advances in clinical child psychology, 13,* pp. 53-90. New York: Plenum Press.

Darnton, N. (1989). Committed youth. *Newsweek, 114,* 66-68.

Dettmer, P. A., Dyck, N. T., & Thurston, L. P. (1996). *Consultation, collaboration, and teamwork for students with special needs.* Boston, MA: Allyn & Bacon.

Dryfoos, J. (1994). *Full-service schools*. San Francisco: Jossey-Bass.

Dryfoos, J. (1990). *Adolescents at risk: Prevalence and prevention*. New York: Oxford University Press.

Erk, R. R. (1995). The evolution of attention deficit disorders in terminology. *Elementary School Guidance and Counseling, 29*, 243-248.

Eron, J. B., & Lund, T. W. (1999). *Narrative solutions in brief therapy*. New York: Norton.

Gladding, S. T. (1997). Mental health, addiction, and employee assistance counseling. In *Community and Agency Counseling*, pp 229-249. Upper Saddle River, NJ: Prentice-Hall.

Guerra, P. (1998). Revamping school counselor education: The DeWitt Wallace-Readers Digest Fund. *Counseling Today, February 1998*. ACA: Author.

Hamburg, D. A. (1992). *Today's children: Creating a future for a generation in crisis*. New York: Times Books.

Hinkle, J. S. (1993). Training school counselors to do family counseling. *The School Counselor, 27*, 252-257.

Hobbs, B. B., & Collison, B. B. (1995). School-community collaboration: Implications for the school counselor. *The School Counselor, 43*, 58-65.

Hosie, T. W., West, J. D., & Mackey, J. A. (1988). Employment and roles of mental health counselors in substance-abuse centers. *Journal of Counseling and Development, 10*, 188-198.

Keys, S. G., Bemak, F., Carpenter, S., & King-Sears, M. (1998). Collaborative consultant: A new role for counselors serving at-risk youths. *Journal of Counseling and Development, 76*, 123-133.

Keys, S. G., Bemak, F., & Lockhart, E. J. (1998). Transforming school counseling to serve the mental health needs of at-risk youth. *Journal of Counseling and Development, 76*, 381-388.

Keys, S. G., & Bemak, F. (1997). School-family-community linked services: A school counseling role for changing times. *The School Counselor, 44*, 255-263.

Lerner, R. M. (1995). *America's youth in crisis, challenges and opportunities for programs and policies*. Thousand Oaks, CA: Sage.

Lockhart, E. J., & Keys, S. G. (1998). The mental health counseling role of school counselors. *Professional School Counseling, 1:4*, 3-6.

Murray, B. A. (1995). Validating the role of the school counselor. *The School Counselor, 43*, 5-9.

Myrick, R. D. (1997). *Developmental guidance and counseling: A practical approach (3rd ed.)*. Minneapolis, MN: Educational Media.

National Advisory Mental Health Council. (1990). *National plan for research on child and adolescent mental disorders*. Washington, DC: National Institute of Mental Health.

O'Hanlon, B., & Beadle, S. (1997). *Guide to possibility land: Fifty-one methods for doing brief, respectful therapy*. New York: Norton.

Paisley, P. O., & Borders, L. D. (1995). School counseling: An evolving specialty. *Journal of Counseling and Development, 74*, 150-153.

Schmidt, J. (1999). *Counseling in schools 2nd edition*. Needham Heights, MA: Allyn & Bacon.

Sears, S. J. (1993). The changing scope of practice of the secondary school counselor. *The School Counselor, 36*, 384-388.

Sherrard, P. A. D., & Amatea, E. S. (1994). Through the looking glass: A preview. *Journal of Mental Health Counseling, 16*, 3-5.

Spruill, D. A., & Fong, M. L. (1990). Defining the domain of mental health counseling: From identity confusion to consensus. *Journal of Mental Health Counseling, 12*, 12-23.

Tuma, J. M. (1989). Mental health services for children: The state of the art. *American Psychologist, 4*, pp.188-199.

Walter, J. L., & Peller, J. E. (1992). *Becoming solution-focused in brief therapy*. New York: Brunner/Mazel.

Webster, D. (1993). The unconvincing case for school-based conflict resolution programs for adolescents. *Health Affairs, 12*, 126-141.

Weissberg, R. P., Caplan, M., & Harwood, R. L. (1991). Promoting competent young people in competence-enhancing environments: A systems-based perspective on primary prevention. *Journal of Consulting and Clinical Psychology, 59*, 830-841.

Wylie, M. S. (1992). Revising the dream. *Networker, 16*, 11-23.

Zill, N., & Schoenborn, C. A. (1990). Developmental, learning, and emotional problems: Health in our nation's children. United States, 1988. *Advanced data from vital and health statistics*. Hyattsville, MD: National Center for Health Statistics.

Chapter 7
The Developmental School Counselor as Educational Leader

by

Mary Ann Clark
and Carolyn Stone

Mary Ann Clark, PhD, NCC, is an Assistant Professor in the Department of Educational Leadership and Counseling at Old Dominion University in Norfolk, Virginia. Dr. Clark was a school counselor at the elementary, middle and high school levels as well as a school administrator for twenty years, working in both stateside and overseas school districts.

Carolyn B. Stone, EdD, is an Assistant Professor in Counselor Education at the University of North Florida in Jacksonville, Florida. Dr. Stone spent 22 years with the Duval County public school system in Jacksonvillle as teacher, counselor, and Supervisor of Guidance. As a counselor educator, she has written a number of articles and has conducted workshops in the areas of legal and ethical issues for student service personnel as well as school counseling program development.

Introduction

As we embrace the new millennium, many educators are taking stock of where we stand currently and where we are headed in the future with regard to student academic achievement. Statistics concerning at risk youth, increasing violence in the schools, and American students' underachievement academically have become urgent issues as cross-cultural comparisons have caused us to question our country's ability to compete on a global scale. Leadership is becoming an increasingly valued and shared phenomenon at the school level but for the school counselor it has not been duly explored and emphasized in either practice or in school counseling preparation programs. Thus, even when counselors play leadership roles, they are not necessarily given credit for such professional activities. And, unfortunately, many counselors do not see themselves as educational leaders.

School counselors specifically, as part of an educational team in the schools, have a vital role to play as proactive leaders, social change agents, and advocates for student success (Lee & Walz, 1998; Capuzzi, 1998; House and Martin, 1998). The mission and climate of the school, student advocacy, school effectiveness in delivering academic success, staff development, the change process, and institutional decision making are all areas that school counselors can, and should, positively impact through a leadership role. Further, by assuming the challenge of such a role, counselors can expand their services and increase their resources. In the process counselors can empower themselves to do so by seeking new and creative ways to benefit students and schools (Worzby & Zook, 1992). In this chapter we explore and highlight what we view as the evolving leadership role of the school counselor. In addition, we validate and promote the ongoing leadership efforts made by school counselors throughout the nation.

Educational reform efforts, learning, and student achievement are at the heart of every educator's job; each has an important contribution to make. Rather than becoming a quasi-administrator, the school counselor has many unique opportunities to assert leadership in his/her own right. The counselor's role is involving increased collaboration and consultation interventions with those significant people in the lives of students; teachers, administrators, family members and people in the community (Cooper & Sheffield, 1994). Instead of being isolated in their offices, to increase their effectiveness, counselors need to play an integral role in the total educational process (Myrick, 1997; Kaplan & Evans, 1999; Tollerud & Nejedlo, 1999). The past model of school counselors serving in a passive role waiting for students and parents to come to them for assistance is no longer meeting the needs of the school population. Taking a stand on important educational issues and being perceived as a strong leader and an advocate for change and continuous improvement has become essential to the effectiveness of the school counselor. "Counselors need to be role models and change agents which is more easily accomplished when they are seen in a leadership role in the schools. The more they are in the classrooms and working with teachers, parents, and administrators, the more credible they become" (Guerra, 1998).

Voices in the profession are calling for a shift in the role of the school counselor from service provider to that of leader and advocate for removing barriers which impede students' academic success, thus promoting optimal achievement for all students (The Educational Trust, 1997; Dedmond, 1998; House & Martin, 1998). As team builders, counselors can enlist the support of teachers, parents, administrators, and the community to help visions become reality (Worzbyt & Zook, 1992). To this end, The American School Association (ASCA) has published a work titled *National Standards for School Counseling Programs* (ASCA, 1998) which is a framework for school counselors focusing on basic principles of a developmental counseling approach. The emphasis is on making the school counseling program an integral part of the total school program with the school counselors as leaders in implementing these standards.

Specific Ways Counselors Can Demonstrate Leadership

Professional Image

Developing and maintaining a professional image is essential to the perception of the school counselor as an educational leader. A counselor who is perceived as assertive, credible, hardworking, dependable, responsible, open and honest about beliefs, and is a skilled facilitator and communicator will stand out in the eyes of many as a true leader. Moreover, heading up school groups/teams, and taking a stand on important issues will further a leadership image and will empower the counselor in the school. More general areas of leadership related to image and visibility also include involvement with extracurricular activities and student organizations, serving as guest speaker for parent and community organizations, and coaching sports which involve a cross section of the student body.

Organizational Roles

Specific organizational roles that a counselor may choose to play can include participation and leadership in school and district committees on school improvement, student assessment, enrichment programs, management advisory committees, curriculum committees, and parent-teacher organizations. Such involvement can increase visibility and infuse counselor input into a number of vital school functions.

Staff Development

Staff development is another avenue for demonstrating leadership potential among school counselors (Dedmond, 1998). Conducting inservice training for teachers and parents in such important areas as educational planning, motivation, student appraisal and achievement, identification of and interventions for special needs students, and issues of student diversity and related attitudes is an example of where counselors can play a unique role in fostering understanding and cooperation among the school community. Other examples of counselor facilitated staff development can include medical issues for school age children, learning styles and strategies, student leadership training, school improvement plans, cooperative discipline and classroom management, study skills, and college admissions procedures. Although school counselors are knowledgeable and skillful in many of these areas, their role in staff development may involve the organization and planning of such inservices to include obtaining outside resources as well as being presenters themselves. An ultimate goal is to provide support to teachers through information, intervention, modeling, and encouragement (Cooper & Sheffield, 1994).

One middle school counselor decided to address some student behavioral issues that frequently frustrated parents and teachers by organizing a Parent/Teacher Forum in her school. She conducted a needs assessment and identified the most frequently occurring problems and concerns of educators and parents in her school such as Attention Deficit Hyperactivity Disorder (ADHD), lack of study skills, underachievement, aggressive/defiant behavior, and substance abuse. She then organized and hosted a one night fair at the school in which parents and teachers were able to choose three different presentations to attend. Speakers were obtained from various community agencies to provide information and facilitate discussions on the topics of interest. The physical education coaches assisted in the endeavor by providing clinics in the multipurpose room for children ages 6 – 16 while the adults were attending the workshops.

Staff development took a different twist for the counselor of a large elementary school when she decided to address the stress level of her faculty following a particularly grueling spring testing schedule. During a teacher planning day she set up wellness workshops in which teachers could attend lectures on nutrition, receive a massage, listen to a chiropractor, and participate in a healthy, low-calorie lunch. Evaluations indicated that these workshops were well received and contributed to an increase in faculty morale during a difficult period of the school year.

Large Group Guidance

A traditional school counselor intervention, that of large group guidance, can be updated to incorporate more direct advocacy for student success. Test preparation, study skills, educational and future planning, career development, and the use of specific data to further such topics can be used to encourage a positive "mindset" for achievement and success for all students. For example, sharing statistics with students for how education affects lifetime salaries is appropriate information for them to have and may encourage a higher degree of motivation and understanding of course relevancy than just presenting course sign up sheets to students to complete. Specific up to date information on what jobs and accompanying skills/ training will be required in our future society is very important data for students as well as for their parents to possess. Additionally, the use of technology to access such information should be an integral part of the counselor-as-leader repertoire. As well as facilitating the large group

sessions themselves, counselors can serve as consultants and resources for Teacher Advisor Programs (Myrick, 1997) which can disseminate similar types of information to students in an organized program with a planned curriculum.

One large urban school district has implemented large group guidance using closed circuit television and teachers as the purveyors of guidance lessons. Just prior to the school district's career and college fair, counselors trained teachers in delivering a simple lesson to encourage high schoolers to attend the fair and to instruct the students in how to get the most from the experience. The lessons were easy to follow and took only 30 minutes of the teachers' time. Additionally, the counselors of the district delivered daily 10 minute messages on closed-circuit television for six days preceding the college and career fair resulting in a significant increase in attendance.

Coordinating Counselor Leadership Roles

In schools where there is more than one counselor, counseling departments should coordinate their leadership efforts in order to utilize and maximize their various personalities, strengths and interests. Counselor leadership is a fluid role that involves ongoing growth and development. Emphases and participation on committees as well as topics for staff development can change from year to year. One person can not effectively carry out all of the mentioned functions by oneself all of the time. Sharing of such leadership roles can make them more workable for individual counselors and more effective for the department as a whole. Counselors should be encouraged to find a "niche" with regard to leadership which would capitalize not only on their personal strengths but on the specific needs of the school and system for which they work. Such strategies as initiating planning and problem solving groups, expanding the use of parent and community volunteers, delegating appropriate tasks, and building political connections can strengthen the guidance and counseling program as well as heighten its visibility (Worzybt & Zook, 1992). All of these aspects should be a part of a comprehensive, developmental counseling program.

Advocacy as Leadership

The *Random House Dictionary* defines advocacy as "active espousal: recommending and supporting" (Humphrey & Myer, 1994). Helping to create alternatives and opportunities for people is one of the action steps that counselors can take. All people, particularly those who have been marginalized in society need more life choices (Lee & Walz, 1998). Counselors can advocate in numerous ways for students, particularly with regard to motivation, achievement, and future planning. To be seen as an advocate for "all students" is particularly important with regard to the perception of the counselor as an educational leader (House & Martin, 1998). There are a number of specific areas in which counselors can demonstrate such advocacy.

School Reform

Developmentally oriented school counselors can play an advocacy role by forming partnerships with school staff and by promoting the change process in school reform. Although school counselors have traditionally been left out of the school reform literature (House & Martin, 1998), they are in a unique position to exert a powerful influence on reform. As part of leadership teams as well as being trained facilitators, counselors can provide technical and staff support to facilitate change efforts and team building within a school and community thus promoting ongoing school improvement (Sheldon, 1998). Further, with their specialized knowledge and skills in collaboration, coordination, cooperation, resource brokering, and assessment and evaluation, counselors can be leaders in policy and process changes that can affect education and student achievement (Dedmond, 1998). Institutions do not change unless leaders within them initiate and implement change. Counselors are in a strategic position to do so.

More specifically, the developmental school counselor as leader establishes a vision and belief in the development of high aspirations in every child. The developmentally oriented school counselor who believes that all children should be supported to be successful in rigorous academic coursework, behaves in ways that demonstrate that belief. "The leader must live the vision. He or she must not only believe in it but must be seen to believe in it.... To be real it has to come from the deepest parts of you, from an inner system of belief" (Handy, 1987, p. 11). Further, school counselors as human relations experts can impact the beliefs and attitudes of teachers and administrators regarding educating all students to achieve high standards. Their training in communication, interpersonal relationships, problem solving and conflict resolution give them a vantage point in promoting collaboration among colleagues to promote such achievement (West & Idol, 1993).

The partnership between the counselors and the school administration is particularly crucial. Although the two departments may have separate and specific roles and responsibilities to carry out, there is overlap with regard to accomplishing common goals for the school and its students. Close communication and the coordination of efforts to improve and ensure student success are vital. Ideally, school administrators and counselors should be seen as a partnership who work closely together. Cooper and Sheffield (1994) write of a collaborative management model where the principals' and counselors' roles are interchangeable allowing them to work together to improve instruction and provide support in the classroom. Although this model is not implemented in many school settings, the principle of collaboration between school administrators and counselors is being seen as increasingly necessary to the operation of an effective instructional program.

An example of helping students develop high aspirations can be found in one large school district who has made a commitment to inform students earlier in their high school careers than in the past as to available financial aid and scholarship opportunities. The school counselors in this district annually train approximately 100 volunteers who then deliver individual advising sessions to high schoolers about how to access financial aid and scholarships for postsecondary education. Plans are underway to move this program to the middle schools.

A school district who recently implemented a policy in which all students must pass algebra to obtain a high school diploma has mobilized the counselors to help change the attitudes and beliefs of teachers about the policy. Armed with data about the success of similar programs in other school districts, these counselors were able to show how the percentage of students enrolling in and passing algebra had skyrocketed.

Multicultural Awareness

Our public schools continue to reflect the increasingly diverse population that makes up our society. By most population projections, the changing demographics of the United States are transforming the country into one in which a majority of its citizens are members of a variety of minority groups. Because of their training, visibility and positions of leadership, it is essential that school counselors and administrators work as a team to embrace cultural diversity for students, teachers, parents, and members of the community (Harris, 1999).

Collaboration and consultation on the part of the counselor with teachers, administrators, and parents to help individual students and classroom groups communicate regarding gender and racial/ethnic equity, multicultural awareness and understanding, as well as prejudice reduction is an essential role in today's rapidly changing society. Specifically, being willing to champion such causes and confront and challenge intolerance are roles for the counselor as leader and advocate for all students (Ponterotto, 1991; Ponterotto & Pedersen, 1993; Grieger & Ponterotto, 1998). Action should also include promoting student interest in careers in which students of culturally diverse groups have been underrepresented (Lee, 1995). School counselors as educational leaders can promote the concept of equitable access to job opportunities and can work to keep potential employers and other personnel from restricting such access based on stereotypes (Herring, 1998). Career Fairs which include speakers and representatives of a variety of cultural groups can help promote the concept of equitable access to job opportunities as well as to help dispel stereotypes about ethnicity and gender with

regard to employment. One developmental school counselor we know held a Career Day for middle school students featuring the parents as guest speakers. The counselor made a point of inviting people who were in nontraditional occupations. For example, a male nurse and a female police officer were among the participants. A variety of ethnic and racial groups were involved in the presentations as well.

School counselors can play a central role in the multicultural training and development of other educators as well as students (Pedersen & Carey, 1993). Counselors can help others recognize what teaching a diverse population involves, encourage them to become more knowledgeable about other cultures, and assist them in examining their own beliefs, values and prejudices (Lee, 1995). Further, by teaching communication skills and emphasizing the valuing of differences, they can work with teachers to help children learn to convey caring and respect for one another. The school counselor, serving as a consultant and collaborator with teachers, parents, administrators and community members can be in a pivotal position to teach and promote such skills (Ponterotto & Pedersen, 1993; Lee, 1995, Harris, 1999).

Child Study Committee

Leadership by the school counselor in the Child Study Committee which is used for special education referrals, processing and placement can be a means to advocate for needed services for special students. Additionally, counselors can be instrumental in modifying programs and ending special services for students when that option is most appropriate. They can help teachers, school psychologists, and other resource personnel collaborate to identify and resolve student problems by designing the most appropriate and innovative program or instructional modifications. Their collaboration and facilitative skills as well as their unique perspective of the total school program make them natural leaders in coordinating such team efforts (Kaplan, 1994).

Leadership in child study committee provides the school counselor the opportunity to help team members explore options for students with learning difficulties who may not qualify for special education services. A number of elementary schools in one school district initiated a prescreening team called "The Care Team" for the purpose of implementing alternative interventions to address learning problems. One Care Team established a reading lab using computers and organized the Rotary Club to man the lab. This lab became a very effective intervention for this school and even reduced the number of special education placements.

Mentoring Programs

All students need the positive influence of a significant adult(s) in their lives. Unfortunately, with the many changes occurring in society and the family, many students miss out on these special relationships. The number of single parent families has increased as has the number of dual career families often limiting the amount of time that parents spend with their children. More students are spending their after-school hours alone or unsupervised (Myrick, 1997). Initiating mentoring programs in the community is an important way to link students with adults who can have an important impact on the outcome of their lives. There are a growing number of community projects springing up around the country to facilitate the education and development of our "at risk" youth (Campbell-Whatley, Algozzine, & Obiakor, 1997). These mentoring programs are being developed in order to establish relationships with young people and to offer assistance and incentives encouraging them to set and achieve short as well as long term goals (Schnurnberger, 1997). Educational literature cites the importance of resilience and the role of significant adults in the successful development of young people considered to be at risk (Barbarin, 1993; Connell, Spencer & Aber, 1994, Lee & Cramond, 1999).

Counselors can play a vital role in helping create linkages between such programs and students who need them. Specific ways in which counselors can contribute to successful mentoring projects include: identifying the students who would most benefit from having a mentor, leading, designing and developing programs that would best meet the needs of students, clarifying the focus of mentoring relationships, helping define the role of mentors, and enhancing parent and community involvement. Critical to the successful mentoring of students in the schools is the leadership and facilitation skills of the professional school counselor (Henderson, 1994).

Student Leadership

Counselors are in an advantageous position to recognize and encourage leadership potential in students. They have student data as well as observations and individual and group interaction on which to base such opinions. Positive student leadership can be a very powerful force in a school and can facilitate a school climate conducive to personal and academic growth and achievement as well as perceived needed changes in the school environment.

Several school counselors in one school system along with high school administrators and district office personnel, combined talents to conduct leadership training for sophomores and juniors who had been referred by teachers as having leadership potential. A weekend retreat was held where 50 students participated in small and large group activities designed to teach and foster communication and leadership skills. Various community organizations contributed food and supplies as well as providing some speakers for the event.

Political Involvement

Counselors can also exert leadership through political involvement, either at the school and district level regarding school policies and procedures or through professional organizations. The American Counseling Association (ACA), the American School Counselor Association (ASCA) as well as state and local branches of these organizations are involved at a political level to promote policies to support the well being of students and their positive growth and development. There is a growing amount of federal legislation that promotes and supports the expansion of school counseling programs. It is becoming increasingly clear that ongoing political action is necessary to obtain funding for vital programs and counseling positions in the schools.

Accountability and Leadership

Counselors can increase their visibility and empower their positions as leaders by demonstrating accountability and sharing pertinent data with students, teachers, parents, administrators and the community (Myrick, 1997). Keeping records of students' educational and career decisions after high school graduation, tracking drop out rates and enrollment and retention in higher education, and sharing such information with the current school population can enhance the counselors' position as a credible resource and leader. Other examples of data to be collected and shared are school climate information, needs assessments, outcomes from various guidance and counseling interventions, and case studies.

Such information can be publicized through articles in local newspapers and school and community newsletters as well as speaking to student, parent and community groups. Further, messages can be placed on an automatic dialer of the school telephone system. Counselors in a school system can create a website with a number of informational links of interest to students, parents and citizens in the community or they can have a link to the homepage of the local school district. If counselors systematically gather and analyze results of their work, ask for ideas for program improvement, and use this information to modify their services as appropriate, they will gain support, understanding and advocacy for their work (Humphrey & Myer, 1994).

Conclusion

The time has come for school counselors to assume and exert leadership within their schools and communities. Educational reform and numerous societal changes have both contributed to the need for a shift in the role of the school counselor as an educational leader who establishes a vision and belief in the development of high aspirations for every child. Opportunities for leadership through social action and collaboration through increased community involvement and improved communication are natural roles for the counselor serving at the hub of a wheel in a school. Many counselors are involved in a variety of the activities and strategies described in this chapter. What remains is for counselors to view themselves as natural educational leaders and to look for opportunities to develop and implement their special leadership skills in order to maximize their effectiveness in the promotion of success for all students.

References

American School Counselor Association. (1998). *The national standards for school counseling programs.* Alexandria, VA: ASCA Press.

Barbarin, O.A. (1993). Emotional and social development of African American children. *Journal of Black Psychology, 19,* (4), 381-390.

Campbell-Whately, G.D., Algozzine, B., & Obiakor, F. (1997). Using mentoring to improve academic programming for African American male youths with mild disabilities. *The School Counselor, 44,* (5), 362-367.

Capuzzi, D. (1998). Addressing the needs of at-risk youth: Early prevention and systemic intervention. In C.C. Lee & G.R. Walz (Eds.), *Social action: A mandate for counselors* (pp.99-116). Alexandria, VA: American Counseling Association.

Connell, J.P., Spencer, M.B., & Aber, J.L. (1994). Educational risk and resilience in African-American youth: Context, self, action and outcomes in school. *Child Development, 65,* 493-506.

Cooper, D.E., & Sheffield, S.B. (1994). The principal-counselor relationship in a quality high school. In D.G. Burgess & R.M. Dedmond (Eds.), *Quality leadership and the professional school counselor* (pp. 101-114). Alexandria, VA: American Counseling Association.

Dedmond, R.M. (1998). Total quality leadership and school counseling. In J.M. Allen (Ed.). *School counseling: new perspectives & practices.* (pp. 133-137). Greensboro, NC: ERIC Clearinghouse on Counseling and Student Services.

Grieger, I., & Ponterotto, J.G. (1998). Challenging intolerance. In C.C. Lee & G.R. Walz (Eds.), *Social action: a mandate for counselors* (pp.17-50). Alexandria, VA: American Counseling Association.

Guerra, P. (1998, April). Reaction to DeWitt Wallace grant overwhelming. *Counseling Today, 40* (10).

Handy, C. (1987). The language of leadership. Paper presented to the Irish Management Institute, 34th National Management Conference.

Harris, H.L. (1999). School counselors and administrators: Collaboratively promoting cultural diversity. *NASSP Bulletin, 83,* (603), 54-61.

Henderson, P.G. (1994). Mentoring programs. In D.G. Burgess & R.M. Dedmond (Eds.), *Quality leadership and the professional school counselor* (pp. 259-278). Alexandria, VA: American Counseling Association.

Herring, R.D. (1998). *Career counseling in schools: Multicultural and developmental perspectives.* Alexandria, VA: American Counseling Association.

House, R.M., & Martin, P.J. (1998). Advocating for better futures for all students: A new vision for school counselors. *Education, 119,* 284-291.

Humphrey, R.S., & Myer, J. A. (1994). Telling and selling customer satisfaction: Advocacy. In D. G. Burgess & R. M. Dedmond (Eds.), *Quality leadership and the professional school counselor* (pp. 279-287). Alexandria, VA: American Counseling Association.

Kaplan, L.S. (1994). School-based assistance teams. In D.G. Burgess & R. M. Dedmond (Eds.), *Quality leadership and the professional school counselor* (pp. 193-216). Alexandria, VA: American Counseling Association.

Kaplan, L.S., & Evans, M.W. (1999). Hiring the best school counseling candidates to promote students' achievement. *NASSP Bulletin, 83,* (603), 34-39.

Lee, C. (Ed.). (1995). Counseling for diversity: A guide for school counselors and related professionals. Needham Heights, MA: Allyn & Bacon.

Lee, C.C. (1998). Counselors as agents of social change. In C.C. Lee & G.R. Walz (Eds.), *Social action: A mandate for counselors* (pp. 3-14).

Lee, J., & Cramond, B. (1999). The positive effects of mentoring economically disadvantaged students. *Professional School Counseling, 2* (3), 172-178.

Myrick, R.D. (1997). *Developmental guidance and counseling: A practical approach* (3rd ed.). Minneapolis, MN: Educational Media Corporation.

Pedersen, P., & Carey, J. (Eds.). (1993). *Multicultural counseling in schools: a practical approach.* Needham Heights, MA: Allyn & Bacon.

Ponterotto, J.G. (1991). The nature of prejudice revisited: Implications for counseling interventions. *Journal of Counseling and Development, 70,* 216-224.

Ponterotto, J.G., & Pedersen, P.B. (1993). *Preventing prejudice: A guide for counselors and educators.* Newbury Park, CA: Sage.

Schnurnberger, L. (1997). When donors become mentors. *The American benefactor.* Summer, 1997, 48-53.

Sheldon, C.B. (1998). School counselor as change agent in education reform. In J.M. Allen (Ed.). *School counseling: New perspectives & practices.* (pp. 61-65). Greensboro, NC: ERIC Clearinghouse on Counseling and Student Services.

The Education Trust (1997, February). *The national guidance and counseling reform program.* Washington, DC: Author.

Tollerud, T.R., & Nejedlo, R. (1999). Designing a developmental counseling curriculum. In A. Vernon (Ed.). *Counseling children and adolescents* (2nd ed.), pp.333-362). Denver, CO: Love Publishing Company.

West, J.F., & Idol, L. (1993). The counselor as consultant in the collaborative school. *Journal of Counseling and Development, 71,* 678-682.

Worzbyt, Z.C. & Zook, T. (1992). Counselors who make a difference: Small schools and rural settings. *The School Counselor, 39,* 344-350.

Section III

Individual, Small, and Large Group Counseling

This section begins with a chapter by Dr. Tom Harrison focusing on individual counseling in the school setting. As noted throughout this book, the successful developmental school counselor's role includes one-on-one individual counseling. However, the counselor seldom has the time to conduct intensive, in-depth individual "therapy" with lots of students. In addition, the counselor knows when, and how, to refer students to outside agencies. However, individual counseling (responsive, crisis) is important (sometimes in-depth) and is an important role of school counselors. But, as Harrison states; *Due to a school counselor's numerous duties, individual counseling approaches used need to be flexible, and in many situations, brief.*

Dr. Harrison presents three brief individual counseling approaches; the *Systematic Problem-Solving Model,* the *Structured Problem-Solving Model,* and *Solution-Focused Counseling.* Each can be effectively used by school counselors in K-12 counseling programs. All three approaches focus upon specific student client behaviors, are action-oriented, and use step-by-step, easily applied procedures. The three approaches are discussed in detail and practical examples are included for each.

In Chapter nine I also write about the school counselor as "personal" counselor with individual student clients. My approach is somewhat different than the one espoused by Dr. Harrison in Chapter 8.

In Chapter 10, Drs. Rex Stockton and Paul Toth focus on the counselor and small group counseling as a function in the school setting. They have written regarding the importance of pre-planning for the small group experience, the training of group leaders, making interventions appropriate to the developmental age of the group members, the stages of development through which the group can progress, and so forth. They also stress the importance of structure and goal setting in organizing counseling and support groups. However, Stockton and Toth state: *While structure is very important, it is critical not to be so set in your plans and notions about how to conduct the group that you lose sight of the desirability for flexibility and being able to respond to the needs of the moment.* Stockton and Toth also present several excellent strategies for "how to get started" in leading groups, setting the climate, confidentiality concerns, and guidelines for group participants.

Delivering large group developmental guidance is an important dimension of a K-12 developmental school counselor's role. As Dr. Marjorie Cuthbert states (Chapter 11): *The large group format allows counselors to interact with many students and to impact on their development in a preventative way. They can reach large groups of students with developmental issues or timely topics that need addressing, and, can create units to meet specific needs of their populations.*

Large group guidance is one aspect of the total curriculum which helps counselors know many students. Dr. Cuthbert indicates that while working with students in large groups, counselors are often able to identify those who might need more individualized attention, either through the small group format or through one-on-one counseling. Cuthbert also makes the point that presenting large group guidance units allows counselors to serve as "teaching" role models for classroom teachers and other professionals who see them managing large groups of students with successful classroom techniques and behavioral interventions. She presents several excellent strategies for the K-12 counselor desiring to deliver large group guidance and provides an excellent example of a planned, six week unit for elementary students concerning individual uniqueness.

Joe Wittmer

Chapter 8

Brief Counseling in the K-12 Developmental Counseling Program

by

Tom Harrison

Tom Harrison, PhD, an Associate Professor in the Department of Counseling and Educational Psychology at the University of Nevada, Reno, also serves as a consultant for Nevada's comprehensive school guidance program. He has authored several articles on school counseling.

Introduction

Counseling, consultation, and making referrals constitutes the "Responsive Services" element of K-12 developmental guidance programs. Due to the numerous duties assigned to school counselors, time for responsive services is limited. However, in spite of the limited time available, a review of the literature on school counseling outcome research (Whiston & Sexton, 1998) reveals that there is a high interest in school counseling activities which are remedial rather than preventive or developmental in focus. Therefore, the counseling approaches used need to help counselors function effectively given time constraints. Individual counseling approaches also need to be flexible in order to address the variety of student client concerns.

Brief counseling approaches can help address both counselor time constraints and concerns regarding effectiveness. Moreover, brief approaches can be implemented in preventative, developmental, and crisis situations thus making them ideal for the K-12 school setting. A review of the literature on brief counseling indicated several characteristics of successful approaches: Brief approaches tend to be action-oriented and geared towards problem-solving. They are logical, structured and are usually step-wise. Most often they are structured while being flexible enough to allow for their application to a variety of student clients' concerns. Effective approaches usually emphasize specificity and detailed clarification of the problem or issue of concern. They structure steps for the development of action plans. Finally, brief approaches are interactive in that they require counselors to be active, quickly helpful, expert, but yet non-judgmental and permitting the counselor's demonstration of the core conditions of warmth, empathy, respect, and genuineness.

In this chapter, I present three brief counseling approaches; the *Systematic Problem-Solving Model,* the *Structural Problem-Solving Model,* and *Solution-Focused Counseling.* Each can be effectively used by school counselors in K-12 guidance programs. All three approaches focus upon specific student client behaviors, are action-oriented, and use step-wise procedures. Each approach is discussed in detail and examples are included for each approach.

The Systematic Problem-Solving Model

The Systematic Problem-Solving Model is based upon the works of Myrick (1997). The approach is a logical sequence of questions designed to guide student clients through the thought processes involved in solving a personal problem. While helping student clients resolve current problems, the Systematic Model is also a teaching model enabling student clients to generalize their problem-solving successes to other problematic concerns. Responsibility for successful resolution rests with the student client. However, counselors may choose to increase their involvement, especially in the action phase of the model.

One can often hear school counselors lament how no two days are alike and how they need to be flexible in order to meet the needs of the students as well as the administration's demands placed on them. The Systematic Problem-Solving Model lends itself to this type of atmosphere. The model is flexible so that counselors can utilize the approach with a variety of counseling orientations. It is as useful for the 20-minute session as it is for those situations requiring more time. Additionally, counselors will need to be flexible while relying upon their skill and judgment in assessing how long each question needs their and the student client's attention. For example, an emotionally charged situation might leave the student client needing more time to process his or her emotions than a situation carrying less emotional intensity. Counselors need to be attuned to this need and act appropriately. It is useful for school counselors to remember that even while exploring emotions, problems are being clarified and prioritized. Therefore, no time is lost. In fact, if emotions are ignored, just the opposite will occur: Valuable time can be lost. The Systematic Problem-Solving Model is action-based and uses four open ended "trigger" questions to structure the process. The four questions are: **1)** *What is the problem or situation?* **2)** *What have you tried?* **3)** *What else could you do?* and **4)** *What is your next step?* Each question represents a distinct paradigm shift in the problem-solving process. The first two questions essentially serve to collapse the problem and clarify it. The third and fourth questions set the course of action. By asking these four open-ended questions, student clients can explore their personal situation in terms of their own emotions, cognitions, and behaviors.

What is the problem or situation?

By asking the student client to describe the problem or situation and then using selective attention and high facilitative responses to clarify the problem, the counselor is really attempting to accomplish several goals. One, of course, is for the counselor to understand the student client's situation so that needed help can be given. Another goal is for student clients to gain a different understanding of the problem situation. In describing their personal situations to their counselors, student clients may have a chance to hear themselves describe the problem in ways they have not done heretofore. This new awareness can often lead to increased ownership of the problem and motivation to solve it. Another goal of clarifying at this stage of the process is to help identify exactly what is the problem. As any experienced counselor realizes, in many cases the presenting issue, while an appropriate starting place for counseling, is not really the student client's central concern.

For example, 10-year-old Aaron transferred schools in the middle of March because his mother took a new job which required her to be away from home frequently. Although the travel was temporary, Aaron's aunt and uncle were taking care of him for the remainder of the school year. Aaron's fourth grade teacher had referred him to the school counselor because it had come to the teacher's attention that Aaron had been lying to the teacher and classmates about his background and current situation.

At first, Aaron was unable to, or did not want to, tell the counselor what the problem was. So, the counselor, aware of the teacher's concern, asked Aaron to go over in detail the conversation he had with his teacher that had lead to Aaron's being sent to see the counselor. What did his teacher say? Where did this conversation take place? Who else was around? What did Aaron say back to the teacher? As the dialogue progressed, the counselor listened for themes and attended selectively to those areas of student client concern. The counselor's use of high facilitative responses (tuning in to feelings, clarifying content, etc.) prompted Aaron to continue talking, and soon it became apparent that much was happening in Aaron's life. His parents had just divorced and were fighting over custody of Aaron and his sixteen-year-old brother. Aaron had left a lot of friends and a good support system at his previous elementary school. Because both his aunt and uncle worked outside the home during the day, it was very difficult for Aaron to get a ride over to see his old friends. Alone, confused, and hurt, the "bottom line" was: *Aaron was finding it difficult to make new friends.* He believed that exaggerating the truth would make him more appealing to others and they would befriend him. Although his lying was of concern, the counselor, by using the model, helped Aaron clarify *his* concern as really "feeling afraid of making new friends." His home situation would need attention and warranted the need for consultation with his mother and perhaps father as well as a possible referral for family therapy. However, the immediate concern of the counselor ("What is the problem or situation?") was helping Aaron to take steps to make some new friends at school.

What has been tried?

Once the problem was clarified by both the student client and the counselor, attention was turned to identifying what Aaron had tried to do to solve the problem. As with the first question, there are several goals in exploring, "What has been tried?" This line of inquiry allows the counselor to demonstrate respect and a non-judgmental attitude, thus strengthening the relationship. The counselor's exploration of what has been tried by the student client also helps set the stage for appropriate counselor suggestions for possible solutions to the problem. Mutual exploration of what has been tried also allows the counselor to focus upon the student client's feelings. Identifying pleasant and unpleasant feelings puts student clients more in touch with their own personal process while clearing the way for action. Continuing with the example of Aaron, it was found that Aaron felt anxious and scared a great deal of the time. Making friends was an unpleasant experience for him. Through the use of paraphrases and clarifications, both Aaron and the counselor found that his fears of rejection were impeding his desire to make new friends. Aaron soon understood how trying to solve the problem by lying to his teacher and friends had distanced others rather than bringing them closer. That is, what he had tried, simply had not worked to this point. He truly needed the counselor's help in learning how to make friends.

What else can be done or tried?

After clarifying what has been tried, counselors can encourage student clients to explore alternative ways of behaving. It is important that student clients initially generate this list. Counselors can ask questions such as, "What can you try?" or "What else can you try?" and, "Does anything else come to mind?" This reinforces the student clients' abilities in solving their own problems. Counselors can then add to the list. Using brainstorming techniques to generate a list of alternatives is effective. When brainstorming with the student client, the goal is to generate a list first and then go through the list and

evaluate each alternative. Thus, the model is most effective if the counselor keeps the student clients focused upon generating a list while at first ignoring the feasibility of each alternative. Additionally, it is important that alternatives be clarified. This process allows for a more clear understanding of how each alternative will impact the solution.

Once the counselor and student client have generated a list of alternatives (other things to try in solving the problem or situation), it is now time for the counselor to guide the process into the valuation stage. That is, it is now time to employ values clarification to see which behaviors would be most effective in achieving the goal for the individual student client. Which solution best fits the student client? Counselors can use open-ended questioning (what, how, when or where) and feeling-focused responses to aid in this process. For example, Aaron's goal was to make friends and his list included among other things sitting with classmates at lunch, calling one of his classmates after school, getting to the bus stop 10 or 15 minutes earlier each day so he would have more time to talk, calling one of his old friends to see if they could get together, and asking his aunt and uncle if he could have a friend over to spend the night. Aaron felt frightened to ask his aunt and uncle about a friend staying over. He felt hesitant to call anyone after school. The counselor helped Aaron see how his fears kept him from making friends. However, the next step in the problem-solving model was to deal effectively with his inability to make new friends.

What is the next step?

In this phase, a plan of action is specified and agreed upon. Counselors need to help student clients organize a step-by-step plan which should include what will be done, when will it be done, how will it be done, what are possible barriers that might come up and hinder the process, and ways to overcome potential barriers. The plan does not need to be elaborate. However, it needs to be specific, and the steps need to be organized in such a manner as to increase the probability of success. And, helping a student client to clarify, and agree to take, the next step is one of the more important parts of the process. Some counselors have found it most effective if the student client places "the next step" into writing.

Because of Aaron's fears and anxieties about calling or asking his aunt and uncle, the counselor helped Aaron develop an initial plan whereby he would get himself to the bus stop early. Getting there early posed no problem because Aaron's aunt and uncle were up early and would feed him breakfast in plenty of time for him to walk the two blocks to the bus stop. The favorite activity at the bus stop was throwing rocks to see who could come closest to a big tree that was growing in the ravine. The plan was for Aaron to become involved in throwing rocks but to not say anything to others. He would do that for three days. Then, on the fourth and fifth day while at the bus stop, he was to throw rocks, sit in a seat on the bus close to someone he liked but not say anything. The following Monday, he was to repeat this sequence and add a new behavior: He was to sit close to someone and ask them one or two questions. Any type question would be okay. After that, Aaron and the counselor were to meet again to review how things were going and to make additional plans.

The follow-up is important. It can be very brief and conducted in the halls if need be. Touching base serves to reinforce the relationship and to provide an opportunity to adjust plans.

Naturally, the counselor was confident that even though Aaron was shy, nervous, and frightened about making friends, the plan of action almost guaranteed that someone would talk to him in spite of his self-imposed silence. The "win-win" approach would be effective because if Aaron followed what had been agreed upon and not talk, then he would have successfully followed his plan. If he altered the plan and spoke, he would still be meeting his goal of making friends.

The counselor's use of the four "trigger" questions helped Aaron make significant headway in making new friends because the model follows the sequential process that individuals go through when solving problems. In this fashion, a counselor's work is established. A challenge for counselors is to refine their skills in determining *when* to move on to the next "trigger" question.

Effective use of high facilitative responses is another challenge for counselors using this model. When exploring the student client's issue and what has been tried previously, using high facilitative responses helps put "chips in the bank" in the relationship with the student client. (Wittmer & Myrick, 1989). Strengthening the relationship during the initial phase of problem exploration and what has been tried, allows the action phase, questions three and four, to move along quickly. Finally, a counselor's demonstration of respect, empathy, genuineness, and being non-judgmental helps ensure student client success.

Aaron's problem may seem to some as being insignificant in the scheme of things. However, it was very important to Aaron and was obviously causing him problems at school, impeding his learning. Regardless of how insignificant or trivial it may seem, a student client with this type problem will take much precious counselor time unless dealt with appropriately. The problem-solving model is a quick, effective, yet facilitative method for dealing with problems such as Aaron's.

One middle school counselor has effectively used the model in homework assignments, especially with those students who seem to have "chronic" problems or situations and "must see you" everyday. She has written the four steps on an 8 1/2 X 11 sheet of paper with appropriate space available for the student client to fill in under each trigger question. She reports that many students, using this homework approach, report back that they've "solved" their own problem. The benefits incurred to the student client solving his/her own problem is obvious.

Structural Problem Solving

Another brief counseling approach found effective in school situations is called, *Structural Problem Solving*. It is based upon the social learning work of Bandura (1997). The structural approach borrows from the cognitive aspects of Bandura's ideas and works well with student clients because it follows the natural thinking sequence leading to increased awareness, increased motivation, and problem resolution. Focus is upon the identification of behaviors and student client beliefs surrounding the behaviors.

According to Bandura (1997) and Sutton and Fall (1995), self-efficacy beliefs are based on an individual's expectations that he or she possesses certain knowledge and skills and the ability to take the action necessary to solve problems. Self-efficacy expectations result from the individual reflecting on and appraising the strength of these three components. Student clients who *believe* they cannot perform the behaviors necessary to resolve a problem will exhibit less motivation toward problem resolution. When student clients increase their self-efficacy beliefs, motivation increases.

Beliefs also play an important role in student clients' understanding of how a specific behavior will impact the goal. This is known as the outcome expectancy (Bandura, 1997; Sutton & Fall, 1995). If one does not believe a behavior has a significant impact upon the outcome, motivation to perform that behavior will decrease. For example, a student who had received a poor test grade might "realize" that memorizing information for a test did not help, complaining that other students studied less and performed better. Hence, the student who did not do as well may not spend time memorizing for the next test because it is believed that memorization has little impact upon earning a good grade. The Structural Problem-Solving approach focuses on student clients' beliefs about the impact specific behaviors have upon a desired goal and on student clients' beliefs concerning their abilities to perform those specific behaviors.

The Structural Problem-Solving model utilizes a rating system to specify behaviors and one's beliefs regarding those behaviors. By assigning numbers indicating strength of beliefs, student clients actually operationalize their belief system. This method of specification allows student clients a more clear understanding of the problem, an increased understanding of the behaviors involved in problem resolution, insight into their motivation, and increased awareness of self-efficacy beliefs.

Structural Problem-Solving can be a paper-and-pencil exercise, can be strictly a verbal exchange between counselors and student clients, or a combination of mediums can be used. Additionally, the model is flexible in that, as in the Problem-Solving Model previously described, it can be used as homework for student clients. For example, student clients can be given written directions guiding them through the process and asked to complete the assignment before meeting with the counselor to go over the worksheet. In this manner, valuable face-to-face counseling time can be diminished.

The structural problem-solving approach also works well with student clients in a group setting. Moreover, it can be employed in classroom guidance activities where the counselor would lead the class through this process and make appointments for those students who need additional attention. This approach also works well both with clients who are self-referred and those who are referred by teachers or other school personnel. Finally, a structural approach is most effective with middle (sixth grade on) and high school students. While it could be adapted to K-5 students, their cognitive development might preclude their ability to use a rating system. Therefore, elementary school counselors might employ this strategy omitting the use of numbers.

The Structural Problem-Solving Model involves seven basic steps and the counselor's use of high facilitative responses. The steps are:

1. Identification and clarification of the goal or outcome.

2. Generating a written list of *all* behaviors that are involved in attaining the desired goal or outcome.

3. Rating the impact *each* behavior has upon the goal or outcome using a scale of 1 to 30 (1 being "low impact upon the goal").

4. Prioritizing the behaviors from "most impactful upon the goal" to "least impactful upon the goal."

5. Rating clients' beliefs about their ability to perform each of those behaviors on a scale of 1 to 30 (1 being the belief they have "little ability to perform the behavior").

6. Examining student client's beliefs about their abilities to perform the important behaviors.

7. Helping clients develop a plan of action.

Identification of the Goal

Identification and clarification of the student client's goal is a natural and logical place to begin. Clarification ensures counselors that they are working on the correct problem. Asking the student client to become more specific also lays a solid foundation upon which action plans can be built. For example, Debbie was struggling in her geometry class and sought help from her counselor. Debbie was aware that she wanted to do well on the exam but was confused as to why she couldn't seem to motivate herself to study. Debbie's school record indicated she had the ability to accomplish her goal. However, her awareness of the problem and her recognition that she wanted to do well were not sufficient in motivating her to study. Debbie's procrastination compounded the problem since she now had to deal with increased feelings of pressure, inadequacy, and guilt.

The counselor hypothesized that a part of Debbie's problem was that she had not clearly identified her goal. The ambiguity would likely account for her apparent lack of motivation to study. The counselor spent time clarifying what Debbie meant by "doing well" on the exam. Did doing well mean she wanted a perfect score of 100? Did it mean getting 90%? If she was getting mostly C's and B's in her class, did doing well mean getting another B? Through the counselor's use of facilitative responses such as open-ended questions, clarifications, and summaries, Debbie revealed that doing well for her actually translated into a range of scores falling between a perfect score of 100 and a high B. This range of scores allowed her to have "wiggle room" and helped to decrease her anxiety.

Generating a List of All Behaviors Involved

When the goal has been clearly identified, the next step is to focus upon identifying *all* the behaviors involved in accomplishing the goal. More often than not, counselors will find that student clients are aware of only a few of the more obvious and necessary behaviors. Therefore, once student clients have exhausted their list, counselors can add to it. It is crucial to generate the list prior to assessing the impact of each behavior upon the outcome. Premature assessment will defocus the process and will usually result in the development of an incomplete list.

Continuing with the example, Debbie and her counselor jointly developed a list of behaviors involved in getting an A or a high B on her geometry test. Her initial list included typical behaviors of reading, going over class notes, memorizing postulates and corollaries, and practicing proving theorems. The counselor helped Debbie add to the list by identifying other behaviors such as going to class, paying attention in class, asking questions in class

when confused, each day going over the material covered in class, having a quiet place to study, having some time to just relax and watch her favorite television show or to be able to telephone a friend, getting other class assignments done in advance to afford time for studying, and rearranging her after school work schedule. Debbie was surprised at all of the behaviors involved, and her insight prompted her to remark, "Wow, I never realized how much went into one stupid test!" No wonder I'm not studying. I don't have time!"

Rating the Impact of Each Behavior Upon the Goal

Once the goal has been clearly identified and a list is made of all the behaviors impacting the goal, the next step is to invite student clients to examine the specific impact of each behavior upon the goal. This can be done with the use of a Likert-type scale. For example, counselors might ask, "To what extent do you think each of these behaviors impact your goal?" Going over the list of behaviors, student clients are asked to assign a number from 1 to 30 (1 = very little; 30 = very much) reflecting the extent to which they believe the behavior impacts their goal. It is important that all of the behaviors be rated. The same rating can be assigned to different behaviors.

Debbie assigned high numbers, indicating a strong impact upon the goal, to asking questions when confused (27), rearranging her after school work schedule (29), going over material each day (27), practicing proving theorems (29), and spending time with a girlfriend (22). Lower numbers were assigned to such behaviors as relaxing watching television (7), getting other class assignments done in advance (12), reading (16), and having a quiet place to study (10).

Prioritizing the Behaviors

Prioritizing the behaviors impacting the goal is now appropriate. Using the numbers indicating the impact upon the goal, behaviors are ranked beginning with "most impactful" to "least impactful." This can be accomplished verbally or by actually having the student client write them down. Debbie's prioritized list included "rearranging her work schedule" (29) at the top and finished with "finding a quiet place to study" (10) at the bottom.

Rating Beliefs About Abilities to Perform Behaviors

Once the student clients have rated the impact of each behavior upon the outcome, they are asked to identify the extent to which they believe they can successfully *perform* each behavior. Similar to rating the impact of behaviors, student clients are asked to assign a number ranging from 1 to 30 (1 = low belief in ability) to *each* behavior. This number will reflect student clients' self-efficacy beliefs or specific beliefs regarding their abilities to perform the behavior. The counselor might ask, "Okay, we have looked at how each behavior impacts your goal. Now, to what extent do you think you can actually perform each of those behaviors?"

A note of caution. Student clients will have a tendency to assign self-efficacy numbers based upon how the behavior impacts the goal. Beliefs about the impact of behaviors upon a goal and beliefs about one's abilities to perform the behavior can be quite different! Therefore, counselors will need to help student clients remain focused upon rating their beliefs about their *abilities* to perform the behavior *regardless* of the impact of that behavior upon the stated goal or outcome. (If the Structured Problem-Solving Model is used for homework, counselors will need to remember and focus upon the validity of self-efficacy ratings).

When Debbie was asked to rate her beliefs about her abilities to perform each behavior, she became very surprised upon noticing that many of the behaviors which had a strong impact upon her goal (those having high numbers) were the same behaviors she believed were the most difficult for her to perform. "Rearranging the work schedule" was perceived as significantly impacting her test score (29), however, Debbie did not believe she could accomplish this and rated it a "2." She rated "Asking questions when confused" as having a high impact (27) upon her goal. Yet, she assigned a "6" indicating little belief in her ability to get her confusion clarified. Similar patterns were found throughout Debbie's list.

Examining the Student Client's Beliefs

It is now appropriate to examine the student client's beliefs about their abilities in performing the tasks necessary to accomplish their goal. The use of high facilitative responses is important during this process. As noted, high facilitative responses include open ended questions, paraphrases, clarifications, summaries, and feeling-focused responses. Open-ended questions such as, "What do you mean when you say you believe you can't do anything about it?" and "How is it that you know you cannot do that (specific behavior)?" Frequent use of clarifications and summaries allows student clients greater insight, will often increase their self-efficacy beliefs, and will usually positively impact motivation to perform the behavior. Additionally, the use of feeling-focused responses can facilitate student client's understanding of the problem as well as point out their resistances to problem resolution.

In Debbie's case, the counselor noticed that she linked rearranging her work schedule to many of the other behaviors. Focusing upon Debbie's work schedule was thus seen as the key to resolving the problem and would act to clarify her self-efficacy beliefs surrounding the other problematic behaviors such as having time to practice proving theorems, having time to go over the material each day, and having free time to attend the teacher's special help periods.

Focusing upon her beliefs about her work schedule, the counselor soon discovered that Debbie was afraid to ask for a different work schedule fearing her boss would refuse and think of her as not caring about her work. The counselor spent time focusing upon Debbie's feelings of fear and rejection. This examination served to lessen her anxieties and increase her beliefs that she could solve the problem by asking her boss for a different schedule.

Developing a Plan of Action

The stage is now set for action planning. A detailed plan of action would include what would be involved in the task, how student clients will go about accomplishing the task, when they will accomplish the task, and predicting personal resistances. The counselor might say, "You have identified some behaviors that are important in reaching your goal and some of your beliefs about your abilities to perform those behaviors. Let's now plan how you can begin to get started and carry out those behaviors."

How could Debbie go about asking her boss for a different schedule? What would she need to do in order to increase the probability of a favorable response from her boss? When would she take the risk and ask her boss? What might keep Debbie from asking him?

By working together, Debbie and her counselor agreed it would be good to arrange someone to switch shifts prior to asking her boss for a schedule change. She worked at a fast food chain, and there were times when business was fast. So, they agreed that Debbie would ask her boss during a slow time. For Debbie, the sooner she asked the better. Finally, the counselor remarked that Debbie might become nervous right before asking and that would be okay. She could feel nervous and ask anyway.

A follow-up meeting with the school counselor was scheduled with Debbie to see how the conversation went with her boss.

Solution-Focused Counseling

The time constraints facing school counselors can be greatly compounded when faced with student clients who are referred by school personnel and who are reluctant or resistant to change. Working with referred and reluctant student clients is a "double-whammy" and likely a source of significant frustration for many school counselors. While counselors are trained to deal effectively with reluctant student clients, little has been done in training counselors to work quickly with reluctance. Based upon the works of de Shazer (1988, 1994) and Miller, Hubble, and Duncan (1996), the solution-focused counseling approach (Downing & Harrison, 1992) addressed both time constraints and resistant student clients and works well for K-12 students. Solution-focused counseling can be employed with a variety of student clients and a host of student client concerns. The model is especially effective in working with "reluctant" student clients.

Students who are referred by teachers and other school personnel for counseling likely see themselves as flawed or having something wrong with them as people. Often, the students believe they have been "wronged" or are totally blameless. The resulting reluctance to change can be a formidable challenge to counselors.

The reason this approach is effective with the reluctant/resistant student client is that the focus is upon minimizing student client resistance to the counselor and to the overall counseling process. This goal is accomplished by 1) focusing upon "what is right" as opposed to "what is wrong" with student clients; 2) accepting student clients' perceptions that "there is no problem;" 3) reframing student clients' experiences so they can accept that a problem does exist; 4) focusing upon the thoughts, feelings, and behaviors already employed by student clients, and 5) aiding student clients in the identification of their own strengths and past or current successes.

Solution-focused counseling is a step-wise process which emphasizes client strengths, helps to reinforce student clients' self-esteem, and focuses upon solutions. This approach involves five steps, and like the two approaches previously described in this chapter, requires the effective use of high facilitative responses such as open-ended questions, paraphrases, reframings, clarifications, summaries, and feeling-focused responses. The five steps include:

1. Helping the student clients identify the issue or problem to be addressed.

2. Helping the student clients identify the desired change or coping goals related to the problem.

3. Encouraging the student clients to actively search and recall times when they have been successful in solving similar or other problems.

4. Encouraging the student client to identify and focus upon their strengths or "what worked" in that situation.

5. Helping the student client develop and carry out a plan of action.

Key to using this approach is the concept of stability and change which is a central concept in many family and other type counseling approaches. Briefly, this concept accentuates the idea that in order to change, student clients must have a sense of control over their environment. Without that stabilizing feeling and perception, change becomes too chaotic, too threatening. The stabilizing effect of the student client's environment is achieved by the counselor focusing upon what student client is *already* doing. In essence, no new behaviors, thoughts, or feelings are introduced. Student client awareness that nothing (or very little) new will be required of them for change acts as a stabilizing force giving way to feelings of increased self-control. The stability created by requiring little or nothing new in the way of student client behaviors also increases the rapport between the student client and counselor while decreasing student client resistance.

Another central concept in solution-focused counseling is that of identifying "rules" and "exceptions to the rules." The "rule" is the student client's perception of the problem. Often, student clients will likely see the problem as unmanageable and see little hope for change. This rigidity of perceptions acts as a rule which serves to govern student client behaviors and can actually help reinforce the problem and will serve to limit student client perceptions of options available to them. "Exceptions to the rule" are essentially student client success stories in which they have had positive experiences in solving similar or other concerns. That is, the "exceptions" are those instances in which the rules were "broken" and success was experienced. With reluctant student clients, identifying previous successes may be challenging for the counselor. However, it is important for counselors to remember that everyone has experienced success. By believing this and behaving with resolve, counselors can help student clients recall times when problems seemed more manageable and times when student clients were effective in changing themselves and their environment. As a result, student client's strengths and self-concept will be positively reinforced thus giving way to positive change.

Gary: A Reluctant Teenager

Gary was referred to the school counselor by his eighth grade social studies teacher because of a "poor attitude." Mrs. Fisher, the school counselor, made an effort to talk with Gary's social studies teacher during the teacher's planning period. Mr. D'Andrea told the counselor of his repeated attempts to reach Gary, but says he "had given up" on Gary when the behavior persisted following spring break. Although Mrs. Fisher had seen Gary for class scheduling, that was the extent of their interaction. Still, from observing Gary during the counselor's hall duty, Mrs. Fisher was aware that he got along with his peers.

When the counselor called Gary out of his third period class, he arrived sullen and withdrawn. An explanation of the reasons for the visit did little to warm him up. To deal with this resistance, the counselor reframed the problem by explaining that Mr. D'Andrea expected her to be able to "fix" Gary, and asked Gary to help her solve this problem. She told Gary that it would be difficult for her to "fix" him because Gary saw nothing wrong, but that still left her feeling the need to satisfy Mr. D'Andrea. How could Gary help? Gary then began suggesting ways to get Mr. D'Andrea "off her back" which included telling him to "cool it," saying nothing and letting Mr. D'Andrea deal with it, telling him nothing was wrong, and telling him it was his problem. The counselor used the high facilitative responses of open-ended questions and clarifications during this exchange which was aimed at building rapport and decreasing resistance. She acknowledged his suggestions and assisted Gary in agreeing that the problem was indeed a challenging one. The counselor asked Gary, "When have you had a similar problem to mine where someone expected you to do something that appeared quite impossible?" Gary responded, "All the time." This was followed by the counselor asking, "What do you mean?" Now the focus began shifting more toward Gary. He disclosed, "Life stinks."

The use of paraphrasing and clarifications along with feeling-focused responses allowed the counselor to help identify that Gary had found out two weeks prior to spring break that his girlfriend had begun dating his best friend while still claiming to be in love with Gary. Gary said that his girlfriend did not know he knew, but that she had become confused and angry with him for his abrupt change in behavior. Gary said he had tried to forget about the incident and pretend that nothing was wrong, but that had not helped. He agreed he needed to talk to her about his concerns, but was afraid he would lose control. The counselor asked Gary which of the two problems would he like to discuss, the counselor's problem with Mr. D'Andrea or Gary's problem with his girlfriend? Gary said that if they could work on his first, he would be willing to help her figure out what to do with Mr. D'Andrea.

The counselor explored the ways in which Gary was dealing with his anger, hurt, and disappointment. She asked him how he would like things to be between him and his girlfriend, and Gary said that he would like things to be the way they were before she began dating his best friend. The counselor clarified what Gary meant by this. He wanted things back to normal where they would talk, laugh, and go out. Gary was asked what would need to be different in order to achieve this goal. At first he said she would need to never mess up again but finally agreed that he had little control over what she did or did not do. He said he would need to talk with her without losing control. The "rule" or problem was defined as Gary's perception that he was unable to talk about his feelings of anger without exploding into a rage. The counselor inquired when there had been a time that Gary had been hurt and angry and had been able to talk it out. Together, the counselor and Gary identified occasions in the past where Gary had been successful. The counselor encouraged a detailed exploration of how Gary had managed to be successful in those situations. She focused her facilitative responses upon Gary's strengths. Finally, she asked him to identify how he could use his past successes to help him out now, and a plan of action was set.

Summary

When used appropriately, brief counseling approaches have been shown to be quite successful in the schools. The three approaches described in this chapter are geared toward quick, yet empathic, problem resolution. However, this is not to be confused with their being superficial. While effective for use with a variety of student clients and student client concerns, it is important to remember that not all student clients or issues will lend themselves to brief approaches. Some student client concerns will require counselors to use a more long-term approach, to consult with parents, teachers and staff, or to refer out to community services.

A few reminders are helpful. Faced with severe time constraints, counselors can be tempted to rush through the counseling process in attempting to "fix" problems. It is important that counselors initially take time building rapport with the student client. The effectiveness of brief approaches relies upon a solid counselor/student client relationship. Moreover, the counselor must spend time getting specific about the issue of concern. The action phases of brief approaches are greatly expedited when the problem is sufficiently clarified. Another reminder concerns helping student clients own their own problems. Counselors, in attempting to resolve issues quickly, might assume too much responsibility for the problem thus forgetting the basic tenet of any counseling approach which is that student clients need to *own* their *own* problem. Regardless of which approach is utilized, counselors must remember to use high facilitative responses. Open-ended questions, paraphrases, summaries, clarifications, and feeling-focused responses are basic to the counseling process and to successful problem solving. It is up to the expertise of school counselors to determine the appropriateness of brief counseling. The approaches will not work for every student client. Some students need in-depth counseling. Finally, counselors need to ensure they follow-up with the student client even if it is for only a few minutes in the hall. A simple, "How are things going with the action plan?" may be all that is necessary. Not only will student clients greatly appreciate your efforts, but a follow-up helps counselors assess their effectiveness and make adjustments when and where needed.

References

Bandura, A. (1997). *The exercise of control.* New York: N.W. Norton.

de Shazer, S. (1988). *Clues: Investigating solutions in brief therapy.* New York: Norton.

de Shazer, S. (1994). *Words were originally magic.* New York: Norton.

Downing, C.J., & Harrison, T.C. (1992). Solutions and school counseling. *The School Counselor, 39*(5), 327-332.

Miller, S., Hubble, M., & Duncan, B. (1996*). Handbook of solution-focused brief therapy.* San Francisco: Jossey-Bass.

Myrick, R.D. (1997). *Developmental guidance and counseling: A practical approach* (3rd ed.). Minneapolis: Educational Media Corporation.

Sutton, J. M., & Fall, M. (1995). The relationship of school climate factors to counselor self-efficacy. *Journal of Counseling and Development, 73*, 331-336.

Whiston, S. C., & Sexton, T. L. (1998). A review of school counseling outcome research: Implications for practice. *Journal of Counseling and Development, 76*, 412-426.

Wittmer, J., & Myrick, R.D. (1989). *Teacher as facilitator.* Minneapolis: Educational Media Corporation.

Chapter 9
Counseling the Individual Student Client

by

Joe Wittmer

Introduction

This chapter is about the school counselor as "individual" counselor. As noted throughout this book, personal, individual counseling with students is just one of the several interventions used by the effective school counselor working in a developmental counseling program. That is, there are many roles played, and various student interventions used, by the effective school counselor working in a developmental school counseling program. However, being effective as a "personal" counselor with individual student clients may be one of the most important of all interventions used by the school counselor.

The Counselor as a Person

Because it has been difficult to empirically identify "effective" or "ineffective" methods of counseling, some experts have suggested that the effective counselor is an "artist" who is uniquely skillful in bringing about the desired results through a personal helping relationship. That is, these experts believe that counselors who are effective in their individual counseling with clients find ways of using themselves, their talents, and their surroundings to assist their clients in making the changes in their lives as needed to be more mentally healthy and productive persons.

Considerable research has been conducted in an attempt to discover more about the counselor as a person and his/her impact upon the counseling process. Researchers have compared the beliefs held by effective and ineffective counselors about people in general. Studies indicate that effective counselors, regardless of the settings in which they work, possess an internal rather than external frame of reference. The effective counselor is also more concerned with perceptual experiences rather than objective events. Moreover, effective counselors perceive others as having the capacity to look at their own problems, and, in most cases, have the capacity to solve their own problems with direct and/or indirect assistance from the counselor.

Personally, I believe that, regardless of the settings in which they work, effective counselors view themselves as *catalysts* in helping others to change by *empowering* them to do so. Effective counselors are also *"trusted experts"* who have the ability to "help" those who come to them seeking their assistance. And, in general, students and others seek counseling because, at that time in their lives, they feel "helpless" and thus seek "help" from an expert! A "trusted expert" is a professional who is *predictable and consistent.* Predictable and consistent helpers quickly gain the trust of their clients and are more effective personal counselors.

Effective counselors in any setting also view others with dignity and worth and as non-threatening individuals capable of enhancing their own personal growth. The effective counselor also has the skill to understand another person's "worldview" without any evaluation or interpretation of that worldview. That is, they have the unique ability to "enter" the other person's frame of reference, the way they view their current reality, without evaluation or judgement. This does not mean that they condone inappropriate behavior on the part of their clients. Effective counselors work at accepting and understanding the person and his/her frame of reference regardless of the behavior shown. Effective counselors know that there are as many views of "reality" as there are persons. *They are not deluded into thinking that their "reality" is the only "reality." They also understand that they may expose, but never impose, their values on their student clients.*

Research further indicates that effective counselors are sensitive to others and see themselves as *adequate, trustworthy, and able to help others.* Finally, effective counselors tend to see their purpose in counseling as one *of freeing rather than of controlling* their clients. Effective counselors also tend to be personally involved in the counseling situation and are concerned with the process as much as they are in achieving goals and outcomes.

In my opinion, everything written above applies to those school counselors who are effective in their work with individual student clients.

The School Counselor as an "Enhancer" of Personal Growth

Within the last two decades we have learned a great deal about human behavior, about the counselor as a person, and about effective counseling relationships in general. Much of what we now know has come through careful analysis of helping relationships found in counseling and related fields. We have learned that to be successful as a counselor takes more than being an expert in the field of psychology; it is more than providing information and helpful insights; and, it is more than being thoroughly trained in counseling theory, techniques and procedures.

There was a time when we thought that lack of progress in counseling was probably because of some deep-seated problem that a student client was unable to discuss. Often those type students are referred to by the counselor as "resistant." The term "resistant clients" may be a misnomer. That is, perhaps ineffective counselors have coined this term. One thing we do know, if you refer to a student client as "resistant" to your counseling efforts, he/she now has at least two problems!

In the past, if a student client didn't function any better personally or academically as a result of counseling, it was certainly a loss and a disappointment, but the student probably was no worse off than before. Unfortunately, it now appears that these naive assumptions can no longer be accepted. We now know that counseling can be for better or for worse! That is, our counseling efforts make a "difference;" one way or another; we are almost never neutral. In some cases student clients may actually deteriorate into a routine that is detrimental to their overall personal growth and development. *The idea is frightening, but clients actually can be harmed in situations that are theoretically designed to enhance their growth.*

Closer examination suggests that counselors can differ in approach, theoretical rationale, training, sex, personal values, and experience; but there seem to be some essential "conditions" or core dimensions present in all successful counseling situations. When student clients experience these conditions, they tend to solve their problems quicker and become more fully functioning individuals. In general, these conditions are; *understanding, nonpossessive warmth, interest in others, genuineness, respectfulness, unconditional positive regard, caring, and acceptance.* And, as mentioned above, the effective school counselor is also a trustworthy and knowledgeable individual. I discuss some of these in greater detail below.

By now, as reader, you probably have the impression that I believe that a student client must experience a relationship that reduces defensiveness and opens the avenues for communication in a warm, close, non-threatening setting for personal counseling to be successful. Generally speaking, clients in any setting who show the most therapeutic change, as measured by various indices, perceive more of the helping conditions in their relationship with the counselor than those who show less change. Thus, regardless of the theoretical orientation of the counselor, his/her clients "get better" if the above "conditions" are present. That is, it doesn't seem to make much difference whether the effective counselor was trained as a "Rogerian" or an "Adlerian," or in any other type theoretical orientation for that matter; it is when these core conditions are present that effective outcomes result.

As noted, counseling can be for better or for worse. We can no longer assume that if a student client does not benefit from a counselor there will be a negligible effect. In reality, it is possible that some students can actually suffer and become worse when the helping conditions are not present.

Although there is more to effective counseling than just a personal relationship with the client, I believe that school counselors who are effective in individual counseling situations are those who have the above described characteristics and the ability to reflect or create the essential core dimensions given above. These highly functioning individuals have a positive effect on their student clients. A truly person-centered approach to counseling nourishes these conditions. They are at the center of the counselor's success.

How do effective counselors create these core conditions? What do they need to do when counseling with student clients to bring them about? What things must be considered when developing a treatment plan that leads to resolving a student client's personal problem?

In this brief overview, I attempt to address these issues. But first, let's look at some personal characteristics of effective counselors.

Characteristics of an Effective Counselor

There are probably many school counselors who have one or more of the characteristics which describe effective counselors. "Now there is an effective personal counselor," people might say. Some people describe effective counselors as "outstanding," "empowering," and "wonderful." Yet, they may not be certain as to what characteristics they possess that make them so effective as counselors.

As mentioned above, there are several conditions necessary for effective counseling outcome to occur. In addition, there are various selected, personal characteristics frequently used to identify counselors who are high facilitators of personal growth and who are recognized as most effective by students, their colleagues and others. In general, effective counselors are:

1. Attentive
2. Genuine
3. Understanding
4. Respectful
5. Knowledgeable of culture
6. Skilled in Counseling Techniques

Let's look at each of these characteristics/skills in more detail.

The Effective Counselor is Attentive

Problems in personal counseling often result from non-attentiveness and ineffective listening on the part of the counselor. Although it seems like a simple thing to do, and we often take it for granted, being attentive is an effort that requires skills and practice. Fortunately, those skills can be taught and learned.

Being truly "attended to" and having an opportunity to talk about a matter that is personal for us is usually a pleasurable and relieving experience. It makes us feel better about the problem or situation we are discussing. This is especially true when the "helper" has the listening skills and other characteristics discussed above. For instance, when you feel that an objective and trustworthy person has really taken time to listen to you, and that what you are saying has been received with understanding, you probably feel better than before sharing it. In addition, there is usually a sense of our feeling closer emotionally to the person who has truly been listening to us. Data indicates that your student clients have the same feelings regarding your "attending" to them during personal counseling.

Unfortunately, the vast majority of people are not effective listeners. Except from among your trained counseling colleagues, you may not encounter very many during your lifetime. Sometimes, people seek out counselors for the simple reason of having a chance to talk to an objective, caring listener who will hear them without judgment or evaluation. How often do people in your life really listen to your words and feelings? How do you know if they have really heard you?

The next time that you are with a group of people at a party, note how well each attends and responds to you and the others present. Unless it is an unusual group, the conversation will jump quickly from one person to another, with little communication (i.e. two-way) being exhibited.

One person might start by expressing a concern about resistant students. The usual response from someone who is "listening" is to relate that particular idea to their own experience, without responding directly to the speaker. For example, "You know, I've been thinking of the same thing....And I've decided...." At this point the focus moves to a new talker leaving the original talker to wait another turn. We usually agree or disagree, almost immediately, with the talker as opposed to truly tuning into him/her and listening for understanding.

As we examine everyday listening experiences and habits, and perhaps take note of our own behaviors, we recognize that many times a listener is simply waiting for a speaker to stop talking so that person can say something. Subsequently, many listeners hear only the first few words spoken, and then their minds rush rapidly ahead to their own concerns and reactions. In most cases, the periods of silence while listeners are waiting a turn to speak, represents a period of tolerance more than a period of attentive listening.

Motivations and feelings affect listening. These change, of course, even as the conversation moves along because listening is a shifting process. Attentive counselors know how to stay focused on their student clients and to absorb what is being said before jumping to conclusions or offering a quick reaction or solution.

Effective school counselors want to know more about their student clients. They want to know what the student is thinking and feeling. They know how to "tune in" and to listen with the "third ear." They know how to be effective. Subsequently, they have a powerful influence on the way in which helping relationships, as well as the flow of the conversations, are formed with their student clients.

Effective counselors are also aware that when they are unable to focus their full attention on their student client, they may be reacting to some of their own hidden feelings or motives. This preoccupation with our own interests and thoughts can communicate that we do not care what is being said. Sadly, the student talking might feel rejected or dismissed as unimportant.

Attending might be described as the process of acknowledging particular stimuli from an environment. Thus, listening is a selective process in which we choose from the things around us that most fit our needs, purposes, and desires. Sometimes we select a stimulus because of its suddenness, intensity, or contrast to what we have been experiencing. At other times there might be sounds (stimuli) that we hear automatically because of habit. We focus upon things to which we have learned to attend. This is often referred to as "selective listening" or hearing what we want to, or expect to hear. That may be true in everyday conversation. However, the effective counselor has learned the skill of "attentiveness" and possesses true, active listening skills.

If a counselor prejudges and expects to hear some expressed anger from his/her student client, for example, there is a higher probability that that student will be perceived as being angry. That is, our presuppositions control our perceptions, which determine how we will behave in that situation. The effects of such "mind sets" are significant. They can be detrimental to effective counseling, especially if the counselor jumps to conclusions and is unwilling to hear the student tell all of the "story". Unfortunately, we are not always aware of our mindsets and they are at times difficult to control. Listening habits that help us go beyond what we expect in a situation can be valuable and are imperative as a skill for effective counselors.

Attentive and careful listening on the part of the effective counselor also involves hearing "deeper levels" of communication. Effective counselors not only attend literally to words, but they also make a special effort to understand the personal meanings of the client's words. They have the ability to make "hunches" or "hypotheses" about what is really "going on" with their student clients. Effective counselors tune in to the feelings, thoughts and attitudes that are "behind" the content of the words. In summary, the counselor who wants to be an effective facilitator of change hears the words of the student client, but more importantly, hears and understands the feelings that add special meaning to what is being said.

Attentive, Active Listening Counselors:

1. Have the ability to understand another person's ideas, thoughts and feelings without evaluation or interpretation.

2. Accept that feelings are always legitimate ones; a student client's feelings are never right or wrong. However, acceptance does not mean letting the student continue to "pull the wool" over his/her eyes as well as yours! Effective counselors also know how to give effective, helpful feedback as needed.

3. Are sensitive to the student client's feelings and let him/her know they are sensitive and not denying or ignoring any of their feelings (Going well beyond the student client's expressed feelings provides the student with a major new view of the emotions he/she is experiencing).

4. Notice the attitudes and feelings involved in the message given and respond appropriately.

5. Hypothesize (stating a hunch without interpretation or advice) back to the student client as precisely as they can regarding what they are hearing them say in terms of the attitudes, ideas, thoughts and feelings.

6. Always use words different (fresh words) from what the student client is using without changing their meanings (Credit for being a good listener is given only for short, precise statements).

7. Do not add or subtract from the student client's message. They deal only with the feelings they are hearing instead of with the facts surrounding the event the student is discussing. That is, when responding, they always "go to the student as a person" first before the event. For example, if a student client is talking about the impending divorce of her best friend's parents, effective counselors first focus on her *feelings* regarding the divorce; not the friends or the divorce, per se.

8. Do not respond with their own message and do not immediately agree or disagree with the student client. Examples: evaluating, sympathizing, giving opinions, using logic or persuasion, analyzing, untimely advising, ordering, probing or closed questioning.

How Does Active Listening Help?

1. Helps free student clients of troublesome feelings when permitted to express them openly in the presence of a trusting person (burdens are usually lighter when shared with an objective other).

2. Helps student clients become less afraid of their negative thoughts and feelings and to label and understand how they (negative feelings and thoughts) often lead to negative behavior with unwanted consequences.

3. Helps promote a feeling of understanding between the counselor and the student.

4. Helps to facilitate problem solving through personal insight and ownership of the problem.

Some Guidelines for Effective Listening:

1. Look directly at the student client. Effective eye contact suggests that you are attending to what is being said.

2. Avoid being preoccupied with your own thoughts. Don't rush ahead with your own ideas; rather, give attention to the way things are being said, the tone of the voice, the particular words or expressions being used, and bodily gestures. *Listen with the intent to "hear" and to "understand" and not with the intent to reply!*

3. Listen for feelings. A student client's feelings are the most important part of counseling. Feelings precede the way they will perceive the event, their problem or situation, and usually determine how they will respond in that particular situation or to that problem.

4. Say something to the student client that shows that you are listening carefully. This encourages (facilitates) the student to talk more about the subject. It enhances and invites the student client to continue talking.

5. Always respond in a non-evaluative manner and be sensitive and aware of the student client as a person who possesses both personal dignity and worth.

Some Attending Skills:

1. Bodily and squarely face the student client

Facing the student you are counseling squarely is the basic posture that will reveal your interest and involvement. This says, "I'm available to you." Turning to the side, for example, lessens your involvement and receptivity.

2. Maintain eye contact

This lets the student know that he or she has your attention. Don't stare, but do look directly into a student's eyes when possible.

3. Maintain "open" posture

Facing the student client is a sign that you are open to what the student has to say and interested in communicating in an open manner. It is a non-defensive position. Crossed arms and crossed legs are often at least minimal signs of lessened involvement.

4. Lean forward

When both of you are seated and you lean forward toward him/her, it says to the student that you are interested and/or involved.

5. Smile, with a relaxed, open expression

This is important in order for you to be perceived as a warm, open, receptive, caring and respectful person. Be aware of the impact of your facial expression as you listen to your student client.

6. Simple acknowledgment

Smile, nodding, and "uh-huhing," "thanks for sharing that," "OK," etc. encourages your student client to continue talking and shows that you are interested in him/her as a person and that you are following what is being said. Acknowledge all client responses.

The Effective Counselor is Genuine

Effective listening and understanding in the counseling process inevitably depend upon a counselor's genuine interest. However, unlike listening and attentiveness, genuineness is not really a skill to be learned. Are you genuinely concerned about how your student client thinks and feels? One thing is certain; your own authenticity will bring out the authenticity in your student clients. You may wonder how you can be genuine and yet practice and work at learning all the things discussed above. There is considerable evidence that if one continues to "try out" a new or different technique, role or skill in a sincere manner, genuineness will follow. That is, it will become spontaneous, natural and a "way of life" for you as a counselor.

"Tell it like it is" is still a popular expression. Children are especially suspicious of adults who talk one way and live another. Young people deplore hypocrisy. They want people to be trustful, honest, and genuine with them. Genuineness implies authenticity. You cannot be genuine if you are playing a role. Rather, genuineness denotes being in tune with yourself and acting in a way that reveals congruence. It is extremely difficult to feel one thing and communicate another, as the truth will always win out. However, genuineness does not mean that we should say exactly what we think at all times; to let it "all hang out."

Counselors who "say what they think" often hurt their clients emotionally. Genuine counselors can be themselves, but they are their "polite" selves and do not hurt student clients in the name of genuineness!

The counselor's genuineness could be the most important characteristic in a helping relationship. It sometimes makes "helpers" out of certain people simply because student clients realize quickly that they can depend on them for honest responses. On the other hand, some counselors, even though they have studied under the best instructors and know many counseling techniques, still play at being a helper. If you play a role that is not characteristic of yourself, then your ability as a personal counselor may be limited.

There is no real alternative to genuineness in a counseling relationship. As noted, even if we are shrewd and very skilled counselors, it is still doubtful that we could hide our real feelings from student clients. When we pretend to care, pretend to respect, or pretend to be open to experiences, we fool only ourselves.

The Effective Counselor is Understanding

Being genuine is important. However, it does not mean necessarily that a person will understand another. As we listen to and discover our student clients' perceptions of their world, we begin to understand those students. Being genuine and listening attentively helps us to be empathic. The effective counselor also has the ability to understand the "worldview" of their student clients without evaluation of that worldview; or telling them how they should be acting in, or toward their "world."

True empathy means fully understanding another person, at both cognitive and emotional levels. It involves going beyond the mere expression of words and intellectual ideas to a deeper level of communication. Empathy means coming to know, to value, and to respect another person from that person's own frame of reference.

You have probably heard the expression, "Put yourself in the other person's shoes." This does not mean you must try to be that other person. Rather, when you have empathic understanding with a student client, you have an awareness of that student's internal frame of reference. However, you do not need to abandon, or change your own frame of reference or give up your values. Counselors who abandoned their values in counseling are vulnerable to change in a direction in which they may not wish to go. Empathic understanding means that, for a few moments at least, you are united with the student and the two of you have an overlap of perceptions, a commonality of meaning. You're "reading" and are "with" that student client without your evaluation entering in to the picture.

Your attempts to perceive and respond to clients' feelings, more than anything else, tells them that you are trying to understand. Moreover, they respect and appreciate these attempts even when you are not always accurate. The more accurate the empathy, the more credit you get. However, even the attempt at being empathic puts a "chip in the bank" towards the development of a non-threatening, effective relationship with the student client. A few "chips in the bank" statements can help create the counselor/student bond that is needed for effective individual counseling.

Student clients come to know themselves and their feelings better through empathic understanding on the part of the school counselor. Letting them know that we are trying to understand also provides opportunities for self-initiated change. There is, unfortunately, considerable evidence that empathic understanding is not a characteristic of the general population. However, it is an interpersonal skill which can be learned. "Tuning-in" to our student client's feelings in an empathic manner is a skill that can be acquired, but it takes practice.

The Effective Counselor is Respectful and Accepting

Respect for, and acceptance of, student clients means recognizing and accepting their experiences as important influences on their lives, regardless of their ages. All people have the human potential for joy, depression, success, and failure. It is not easy to be perfect and few accomplish such a lofty goal. In addition, it is an illusive goal that is not easy to define. Yet, we often judge students by some mysterious set of standards that reflect a desire for perfection. This perception on the part of the counselor will always lead to ineffective counseling outcomes.

True counselor respect indicates a concern for the student client as a special person with unique feelings and experiences. This encourages counselors to search for the real person rather than rushing in to approve, disapprove or to "fix them" which takes time. A 12-year-old who has a problem with authority, for example, took 12 years "to get that way" and cannot be "fixed" overnight. We live in a microwave-like, fast changing, fast paced society and students may expect quick results from our counseling. However, effective counseling still takes time.

Respect does not mean agreement with student clients or to "choose up sides" with them. To respect another person as a human being implies that we value that person's feelings and worth. It does not mean that we must agree with or condone their actions or approve of their behaviors.

Respect goes beyond optimism or simple reassurance. It is the communication of deep interest and concern. A high positive regard for your student clients emphasizes that their dignity is valued, their feelings are accepted, and that they are not being judged as good or bad. The degree to which a counselor communicates respect for student clients helps define the counseling relationship. If we feel and show positive regard for students, then they feel more positive toward us and are more willing to explore ideas and behaviors with us during counseling. Mutual respect opens the doors to effective counseling outcome.

Some students may come to you for counseling because they have low self-respect and their every day functioning is impaired; they have little or no personal regard for themselves. In many cases it is because their feelings and behaviors were not (are not) accepted or valued by self or others. As these students begin to experience your unconditional respect, they may stop "defending" themselves long enough to examine new patterns of living and thinking.

Knowledgeable of the Student Client's Culture

Thus far I have given primary attention to what some call the "affective domain" of counseling. Effective counselors are also thoroughly familiar with the theories on which their techniques are based and know how to be of "expert" assistance to students in need. Effective counselors know that love, caring, respect, empathy, etc. are very important in counseling, but never enough! They know when not to offer "untimely advice" and when to offer "timely advice" to their students. Effective school counselors are also knowledgeable regarding the different cultures represented by the students in their respective schools.

As noted above, effective counselors are viewed by those students needing personal help as "trusted experts." In general, students seek out a school counselor because they feel "helpless" and thus expect to be "helped" by the "trusted expert." This applies especially when counseling with a student dissimilar in culture from the school counselor. Effective counseling with a student client dissimilar in culture takes the entire above discussed counselor skills and characteristics along with a thorough knowledge of that particular culture.

Surveys of school counselors in the United States suggest that most represent "white, middle class" America. And, many believe that this fact gives "white middle class" students an unfair advantage. Several publications describe how school counselors have suffered when they were forced to work in a situation that calls for cognitive knowledge of the culturally different. That is, in addition to knowledge of theory and knowledge of communication skills, there is a need for school counselors to know the cultural background and environmental situations of their student clients. Culturally competent and informed school counselors are knowledgeable about the various cultures represented by the students in their respective schools. They also know that "mental health" and or "psychological wellness" is culturally defined and that knowledge of their student clients' culture is imperative.

In today's diverse world, school counselors will, most likely, have many students who represent many different cultural backgrounds, religious beliefs, race, etc. It would be foolhardy to ignore these differences and assume that all students approach personal counseling with the same values and attitudes. In addition, to ignore student backgrounds and experiences is to ignore valuable resources and opportunities for counseling.

A large percent of America's total population lives in cities of 100,000 or more today, or in areas which lead into these large cities. This concentration greatly intensifies social and economic problems that could conceivably destroy the structure of society. In addition, intercultural conflicts, which are discouragingly high, could increase.

Effective school counselors are keenly aware of these issues and their affect on their roles as personal counselors.

A basic reason for the lack of such understanding of other cultures is the prescriptions concerning American behavior, standards of conduct, and morality. That is, middle and upper class college graduates determined these. A middle-class, Anglo European American may be caught up in the notion of *assumed similarity*. That is, they may feel that everyone is like them, or should be; therefore, communication is one-way and distorted. School counselors with a sound knowledge of a student client's culture and environment will more likely understand the source and reasons for some student behaviors that appear odd or peculiar. That is, they know that a student's thinking, dreams, feelings and behaviors are culturally based. A thorough knowledge regarding participants from a different culture also helps overcome the "negative assumptions" sometimes held regarding participants from a culture different from ours.

When counseling the culturally different, or those students from environmental situations of which you may not be familiar (i.e. poor children, children from violent homes), it is important to preserve the self-respect and dignity of the student. The best way to do this is to learn all you can about the cultures represented in your school. The salesman in Meredith Wilson's *Music Man* lamented the fact that the new salesman would be ineffective because he was not familiar with his clientele to whom he was supposed to sell a certain product. Thus, his advice to the new salesmen was; "You gotta know the territory." *School counselor, know your territory!* Take a field trip through the communities where your students live! Learn as much as you possibly can about their values, mores and methods they use to cope in "their world."

Informed and Culturally Skilled School Counselors Know that:

1. Culture is the predominant force in shaping behaviors, values and institutions.

2. The dignity of the student client cannot be preserved unless the dignity of his/her culture is preserved.

3. When the student client and counselor come from different cultures, there is a strong likelihood that sooner or later they will miscommunicate by misinterpreting or misjudging the behavior of the other.

4. They, most likely, have been trained in the traditional theories and models that are European and male based.

5. Traditional psychological and counseling theories and approaches have limited applicability when working with diverse client populations.

6. Not taking into consideration the cultural backgrounds of the student clients with whom they work results in their failure with those students.

7. Western values may be in direct contrast to the non-western worldviews of the student clients with whom they work on a day to day basis.

8. The objectives for the culturally different student client cannot be a reflection of Western perspectives.

9. Most Western cultures strongly encourage looking out for number one, which may be in direct contrast to the values held by some of their minority student clients.

10. There are many psychological similarities among participants from different cultures, but, that,

11. Cultural factors do significantly affect a student's psychological development.

Can attitudes concerning other cultures be changed and new ones taught? Yes, but, as Milton Bennett stated, where intercultural sensitivity is concerned, it isn't easy!

Intercultural sensitivity is not natural. It is not part of our primate past, nor has it characterized most of human history. Cross-cultural contact often has been accompanied by bloodshed, oppression, or genocide. Clearly this pattern cannot continue. Today, the failure to exercise intercultural sensitivity is not simply bad business or bad morality —it is self-destructive. So we face a choice: overcome the legacy of our history, or lose history itself for all time.

Milton Bennett

The School Counselor's Theoretical Orientation

As Harrison indicated in the previous chapter, time for long term counseling with individual student clients is limited for the busy school counselor. Thus, brief individual counseling approaches can help address both the counselor's time constraints and concerns regarding counseling effectiveness. Considering the setting, it is my opinion that using brief counseling approaches with individual student clients is the most appropriate.

One such approach being used by many school counselors today is the solution-focused approach. Not only is it a brief counseling approach, most agree that it may be the most "culture free" approach available today. It is viewed as "culture free" because the school counselor focuses on the solution, not the client or the problem presented.

The solution focused approach:

1. Begins with a collaborative versus authoritative role in setting goals with the student clients.

2. Collaborates with the student in a joint effort to explore areas of concern and interest. This strengthens the student client's sense of empowerment and ownership in the counseling process.

3. Does not impose his or her values when using this approach as it should be used.

4. Helps students solve their problems while not converting them to the counselor's worldview and/or culture.

5. Builds on the pre-existing adaptive strengths of all students, including those who are ethnically diverse.

6. Looks at how student clients construct their world and act on it, not how the counselor thinks they should act on it!

7. Respects and accommodates what student clients bring to counseling. That is, the student client's culture and resources is central to the solution-focused approach.

8. De-emphasizes the past history and underlying pathology and moves away from focusing on problems to focusing on the solution.

9. Adapts the counseling process to student clients instead of expecting them to adapt to the counseling process.

10. Respects and utilizes that which the student client brings to the counseling session. This concept lies at the heart of the solution-focused approach.

The solution focused approach seems to be a good "fit" for today's developmental school counselor because it is practical and efficient, shifts the focus from what's wrong to what's working or will work, and works in a short period of time. Counselors skilled in this approach know that, instead of trying to push, pull or resist the student client, it is more effective and efficient to go "with the flow." That is, the counselor skilled in this approach to counseling works with, rather than against, a student client's position. Student clients become a consultant to the counselor in how to best solve their own problems. The emphasis is on looking at what has worked in the problem solving process in the past for the student and what might work in the future. It also tends to work well when even slight improvement is beginning to show. Again, as noted previously, using the solution focused approach, or any other for that matter, does not negate the importance of the core counseling conditions described above.

Facilitative and Not-so-Facilitative Counselor Responses

This section is about various verbal responses used by the counselor in the counseling relationship. More specifically, it is about counselor "talk" and how it influences the counseling relationship as well as the perceptions and subsequent behaviors of student clients. And, ultimately, how certain responses affect counseling outcome.

Current research indicates that some verbal responses used by counselors and other helping professionals tend to be perceived by clients as more empathic, caring, warm, and person-centered than do other responses. These responses have a higher probability of creating a more effective counseling relationship than others create and, once learned, are essential keys toward becoming an effective counselor. It is my belief that such responses are more likely to enhance the degree of counseling effectiveness and bring about the desired outcome a school counselor is seeking. There is no doubt that their use will greatly assist the counselor in postulating the "core dimensions" of an effective counseling relationship described above.

These responses have emerged from studies of verbal behavior in counseling and are categorized below from the most to the least in the degree to which they enhance a counselor's effectiveness. These are:

1. **Focusing on feelings**

2. **Clarifying and summarizing**

3. **Questioning (open-ended)**

4. **Reassuring and supporting**

5. **Analyzing and interpreting**

6. **Advising and evaluating**

While all of the above responses might be used by an effective counselor at one time or another (i.e. timely advise can be effective with certain student clients), they are ranked as above because of their probable effect in building a more helping, enhancing and facilitative relationship with student clients. Again, the point being made here is that the higher ranked verbal responses above will lead to more positive counseling outcomes. And I believe this to be so regardless of the techniques used and/or the theoretical counseling orientation espoused by the counselor.

Focusing on Feelings: A feeling-focused response conveys to students with whom we are counseling that we are "reading" or attempting to read what they are experiencing. It is a reflection of understanding of their message, their "story." It communicates that we are working at becoming aware of how they are feeling about themselves at this time. For example:

You're disappointed, Jane, with your father's behavior and confused about what's causing it.

The reflection or understanding of feeling statement can be a difficult response to learn. It demands that we be empathic listeners (listening beyond mere words) who are sensitive to not only the words and behaviors being expressed, but also the feelings behind them. It calls for us to reflect, to mirror, these feelings back to the student client in a non-threatening and facilitative manner. An effective, aware, sensitive counselor knows that the feelings concerning a problem or situation affecting us almost always predetermine how we will behave in that situation and/or in respond to a particular problem.

Effective counselors often verbalize what they think their student clients are feeling. This involves more than a restatement of words and should not be confused with other responses that focus on the general ideas that are being expressed. Nor should it be confused with an interpretation, which tends to explain why a person might be doing something. Rather, it gives priority to feelings that go with the words and behaviors that are being seen and heard.

To begin a sentence with "You feel..." does not necessarily mean that you will focus on someone's feelings. For example, "I feel that you would make an effective teacher" is not a feeling-focused response. It is an opinion. Effective counselors go beyond the words to the feeling within the speaker. Sometimes it can be helpful to ask yourself: How would I feel if I were to say something like that? Or, how would I have to feel to do something like that? After answering these questions, you may have some insight into the student's feeling. If this seems to be accurate or compatible with what you are sensing from the student, then this feeling could be appropriately stated and would be helpful to the student.

Effective counselors are aware that they can easily distort what a student client is saying. That is, their own value systems and perceptions, at times, can prevent them from being sensitive and accurately empathic to their clients' feelings.

It is almost impossible for us to talk, or to be silent for that matter, without showing feelings of some sort. That is, we humans cannot, **not** communicate feelings. All of us feel something at all times. Both verbal and nonverbal cues tell us how a person feels.

For our purposes, feelings can be categorized into 1) *pleasant* feelings or 2) *unpleasant* feelings. Sometimes we hear *both* kinds of feelings when a student client is talking. When listening to a student talk, we might ask ourselves: Do I hear unpleasant feelings or pleasant feelings, or both, at the moment? Think about the feeling words that might best describe what is heard or sensed from a student. If we hear pleasant feelings, then we might say something like:

You're excited about how your relationship is now changing.

You were feeling confident before that happened.

You're delighted with the idea that you might be switching math teachers soon.

On the other hand, if we hear some unpleasantness, we might say:

It was a painful experience for you.

You're really angry with him right now.

The results disappointed you.

Maybe we are hearing both pleasant and unpleasant feelings. Or, perhaps some ambivalence. We might then say something like:

Getting to know her better is challenging to you and it is awkward just starting.

The first experience disappointed you, but you're encouraged now about the new possibilities.

You're excited about the new baby brother, but a little bit afraid of what's going to happen to you.

You're proud, yet skeptical.

You are interested in taking that course, but afraid you'll fail.

After responding to feelings, try not to rush in with other statements. Let the responses you made to the student have its impact; its full effect. Let them "soak." Pause a little, giving the student client an opportunity to experience your interest and understanding. More often than not, if you are reasonably accurate, the student will unconsciously nod (as if to say, "Yes, that's right" or "Thanks for hearing me" or almost an "ah ha" experience.) and talk some more. It is a pleasant experience for both counselor and student. I referred to this previously as putting a chip in the bank. But, again, pause and let the response "soak in" with the client before moving on.

It should be noted that when you respond to a student client's feelings, your statement could be rejected. Sometimes it's difficult for students to acknowledge their feelings, especially negative ones. They may even deny them. However, it is important that your response be made because it says you are trying to understand what the student is experiencing. Feeling focused responses communicate that you are not only listening to words, but that you are listening to that special part of the student client which makes up those words. A reflection of feeling is almost always effective because the student will usually gently correct you if you have misunderstood. That is, even the attempt at understanding puts another "chip in the bank" toward building that necessary facilitative counseling relationship.

Counseling in an attempt to tune in on a person's feelings and reflect them accurately takes practice, practice, and more practice! It does not come easily to most of us because we have not had many adult models to learn from while we were children, or even now as adults.

Clarifying and Summarizing Responses

Any counselor response that is an attempt to acknowledge the content of what a client has said, or to identify the most significant ideas that seem to have been stated, can be termed a clarifying or summarizing response. Such a statement is helpful when there is some doubt as to whether you're really following the student's thinking and feeling. In this case, a clarification statement is a simple way of checking out what has been heard. In other situations, the clarifying or summarizing response is deliberately used to help student clients "hear back" what they have just stated. It also lets them know you "heard" them. Students, and others for that matter, like to be "heard." It gives us a feeling of affirmation and often brings about personal insight.

When there is a lot of talk in a spontaneous and fast conversation, you cannot expect to understand or grasp everything the student client is saying. Yet, an attempt to let students know that you are interested in following what is being said can help facilitate the type of communication needed to facilitate effectively counseling outcome.

The clarification statement involves "fresh" (or new) words. That is, we should not "parrot" what the student is saying. That is of no value whatsoever and often turns students off. A true clarification response is an attempt to simplify, restate, reframe or refocus what has been said while using new words. Clarifying. reframing, restating, refocusing, repeating or summarizing statements focus on the ideas or content of the discussion. This emphasis tends to separate these responses from feeling-focused responses. Clarifying or summarizing responses can give you some "wiggle room" so that you do not appear interpretative or evaluative. Consider the following:

If I hear you correctly, you are telling me that....

You seem to be saying that....

If I am following you, you're saying....

The above responses could also be used in providing a student feedback as needed. For example, "Stop me if I'm wrong, but last session you were saying that your difficult relationship with your parents is causing you all this stress. However, today you seem to be saying something else. Help me to understand this difference." That type statement is much more effective and counseling appropriate (and won't cash in any chips!) than would be, "You're really inconsistent in what you're saying." Or worse yet, "You're a real phony." Yet, I believe the student will get the message just as quickly when you use the first, more facilitative response than the latter responses. Effective school counselors use clarifying or summarizing statements when they want to check out a student's thoughts and ideas. These statements have a way of reassuring students that they are being listened to and heard but not necessarily being agreed with. Notice that none of these responses imply a reason for the student's behavior or why they did what they did. A "why" or a "because" becomes an interpretative response. Other examples include:

I think you're telling me that this has happened before.

Let me see now, you're saying that cheating on a test, as long as you don't get caught, is okay.

Let's see, you said... and... and....

Using "Wiggle Room" Responses to Avoid Interpretation

To understand the thoughts, feelings, emotions, and behaviors of their student clients, effective, facilitative counselors attempt to enter their phenomenal field. That is, their personal frame of reference. Effective counselors have the ability to let their clients know that they understand how they (student clients) interact with their world without judgment, evaluation or interpretation. Think of it as "wearing their shoes" and/or understanding "their worldview" without imposing your values in any way shape or form. Work at being "with" them and/or "reading" them. This is when appropriately worded clarification of content and/or reflection of feelings statements can be very helpful and facilitative. Such understanding statements on your part will, as mentioned above, put a "chip in the bank" with your student clients. Then, should you "miss" with your reflection or clarification response, the student will still be willing to fill you in on "how you missed" and another chip still goes in the bank! If you remember to go first to your student (as a person) with your reflection or clarification response, and then to the "*event*" about which he/she is speaking, you'll be on your way to effective counseling outcomes.

Counselors need not be concerned about stating their "hypotheses or guesses" at what is going on with a student client. However, effective counselors make their "guess" or "hypothesis" statements without any form of interpretation or analysis. That is, they do not tell him/her why they think, feel and or behave in a certain ways; they simply state their hypothesis. However, they do give the client room to disagree without being defensive by using "wiggle room" phrases.

Below are some "wiggle room" phrases that may be useful when you trust that your perceptions are accurate and that a student client will be receptive to your hypothesis or guess as to what is "going on" with him/her:

Stop me if I'm wrong, but I sense a real...

From your point of view it almost seems that...

Your experience seems to be telling you...

I may be way off base here, but from where I stand...

If I'm with you on this...

It's almost as if you think she...

What about the possibility that...

I'm wondering if when...

I'm not sure if I'm with you, but...

What I guess I'm hearing is...

Correct me if I'm wrong, but...

From where I stand you seem...

This is what I think I hear you saying, you...

You appear to be...

It appears you...

Perhaps you're...

I somehow sense that maybe you...

Maybe I'm out to lunch with this one, but...

This may be a long shot, but

As I try to hear what you're saying, it seems...

I almost get the impression that.....

Let me see if I'm following you, you seem.....

Some other phrases you may find helpful are:

You seem to believe...

What I hear you saying...

You're...(identify the feeling; but you need not use the redundant word "feeling")

I'm picking up that you...

I hear you saying that...

Where you're coming from...

You figure...

Questioning Responses

The art and skill of questioning has often been thought of as the central part of the counseling process. A lot has been written about how to ask questions, how to probe, etc. Counseling textbooks almost always include chapters with a series of "good" questions for counselors to use with their clients.

There is no doubt that questions are a valuable tool in the counseling process. However, many times counselors tend to ask too many questions. A question can be used to obtain information, stimulate further discussion, or to query an individual student client regarding a particular matter. Counselors assume that clients will benefit by answering a question and developing a point of view. Questions may also open up new areas for discussion. Effective questions encourage the sharing of information by *inviting* the client to *share thoughts, ideas and feelings.* Open questions also reveal your *interest* in hearing more about what the student is saying, an invitation for the client to continue to share.

Some counselors see cross-examination procedures or probing as an essential part of their trade. It is assumed that questioning procedures will be productive and that probing questions lead to problem solving and in-depth counseling. However, clients are also led to believe, concurrently, that whoever is asking the questions also has the answers.

If a student has a problem and a school counselor asks a lot of questions there may be the expectation that, since the counselor now has the information, the counselor should solve the problem or make the decision for him/her. Students reason that if counselors cannot solve the problem then why do they ask all the questions? This may be perfectly acceptable in cases where cognitive counseling is based upon confirmed information and facts. But, it can lead to a dead end street when there is no easy answer or correct response.

The open-ended question encourages student clients to develop their answers and responses further. The closed question, on the other hand, is structured for only a shrug of the shoulders or a yes or no response. It tends not to elicit an in-depth response and certainly isn't inviting the student to continue with their current line of thought. Look at the following examples:

Do you like school? (closed)

What do you like or not like about school? (open and inviting)

Did you like reading this section? (closed)

How did you feel about this section? (open and inviting)

Are you ready to try out this homework assignment? (closed)

What can I do to get you better prepared to carry out this homework assignment? (open and inviting)

As you read the above questions, did you "feel" the difference between the open and the closed questions? Did you find the open questions more "inviting"?

Our research indicates that the open-ended question invites clients to answer from their own perceptual fields. That is, they feel as if the counselor is truly interested in hearing more from them; more about the problem or situation they are dealing with in counseling. A closed question is narrow and forces student clients to answer in terms of the counselor's perceptual field. The open question solicits a wide range of thoughts and feelings. The closed question tends to seek cold facts. Consider the following questions, some of which seem to be open but are not.

You don't like this classroom activity, do you? (closed)

What is it that you don't like about this classroom activity? (open)

Is this the part that's confusing to you? (closed)

What part is confusing to you? (open)

Of all possible questions a counselor could ask, I believe that open-ended ones are the most effective for client growth. While closed questions might be used at times to gain specific information that will help clarify a situation; open-ended questions give student clients the most room to discover their innermost feelings and thoughts about a matter. However, it should be acknowledged, the effective counselor realizes that if he/she can ask a student a question, they might make a more appropriate and effective, non-question type response instead. That is, instead of asking a question, the effective counselor works at making a verbal response that is even more facilitating for the client such as a feeling focused and/or clarification statement as described above.

The "why" question is a type of closed question that deserves special attention. Most students, or anyone else for that matter, really do not know why they do the things they do. Do people who are abusing drugs really know why they started? A "Why are you sick" question will seldom get you any relevant information. Do individuals know why they are sick? Do persons who tell dirty jokes know why it is fun to tell them? Do children know why they have the friends they have? Why questions often have a negative connotation in our society left over from childhood, i.e. "Why don't you cut your hair?" "Why don't you study harder?" "Why don't you date someone more suitable for you?"

While there is probably an explanation behind most behavior, it is doubtful that a "why" question will help discover it. These questions have a way of making students uneasy. They require student clients to explain themselves, to be accountable, to come up with a reasonable link or connection. Effective counselors have learned to be cautious in the use of "why" questions. When such questions are posed, individuals tend to become defensive and feel pressure to "explain away" their behaviors, without seeking changes. When we ask a why question, student clients often get the feeling that we have the answer before asking the question, or at least think we do. In addition, students feel that they have to give us a "reason" for their behaviors, feelings or thoughts.

The Least Effective Counselor Responses

As stated several times above, some verbal responses tend to be perceived by student clients as more empathic, caring, warm, and person-centered than do certain others. They have a higher probability of facilitating students to think more about their ideas, thoughts and feelings and to be willing to share them with the counselor. They provide a tone, which fosters a helping relationship, eliciting the conditions of warmth, understanding, respect, regard, and so forth. As noted, regardless of the counselor's theoretical orientation or techniques being used, skill in the use of these responses is the key to becoming an effective counselor.

The talking that takes place in counseling is important since every response makes some kind of impact on clients. And, as stated previously, counseling, whether in school situations or in other settings is for better or worse! Our responses invariably affect general perceptions, attitudes, and degree of comfort. Impressions are formed which, in turn, influence other responses, choice of topics, and what the student client will share with the counselor.

Thus far we have examined three of the more facilitative counseling responses, now let's look briefly at some others that are not used, at least not used as frequently, by the effective school counselor. Unfortunately, if used at the **"wrong" time**, these responses are considered practically non-effective in the counseling process. That is, their use offers the counselor a lower probability of effectiveness in personal counseling situations. They are; *reassuring and supporting, analyzing and interpreting and advising and evaluating*

Reassuring and Supporting

Reassurance or support involves statements which are intended to tell student clients that the counselor believes in them, in their ability to meet situations, and their potential for solving their own problems. Such statements are meant to instill confidence that they will be successful. It is supposed to be a pat on the back, intended to empower them to keep going. Unfortunately, instead of empowerment, reassuring or supporting responses imply that students need *not feel* as they do. That is, there is a tendency by the counselor to dismiss their feelings as being normal or common and the student client is told, in so many words, not to be concerned, or worse yet, not to talk any more about these feelings at this point in time. For example:

Don't worry, everyone feels worthless on occasion.

You don't have to feel that way because everything's going to turn out okay. His behavior isn't that bad.

You know, in that respect you're not much different from other children I've worked with.

Oh, all good friends are like that.

Things always look bad at this time of the year, but it will turn out okay.

Data indicates that the reassuring or supportive type statement is the second most popular response used by counselors. However, data also reveals that they are not very effective in bringing about positive change on the part of student clients. Only advice and evaluation are used more frequently. Many counselors believe that a support-

ive statement can encourage a student with whom they are working to do better. "I am building the student's self-confidence," is a common rationalization for this statement. But, it doesn't usually strike the student client this way. Despite efforts to reduce the apparent anxiety or intense feelings, the message comes through telling the student not to feel as he/she does. It denies feelings. It does not communicate acceptance, respect, or understanding. As a matter of fact, as mentioned above, it will often keep students from continuing to talk about those feelings or the situation involved. The message they hear is…"The counselor really does not want to hear more about the feelings I'm talking about." In other words, the message the student client hears is; don't feel that way. In every day situations this is understandable. That is, as a society, we tend not to like or to facilitative the negative feelings of others and often use reassurance or support to make them "go away." However, the effective school counselor realizes that the facilitation of negative feelings on the part of the student client is a must for individual counseling to be effective.

Sometimes supporting and reassuring statements create a negative effect because they come from a seemingly superior position. When we give reassurance or support, it frequently implies that we can see into the future and that our positive estimations will be correct. They can depend on us. Creating dependency on the part of the student client is seldom effective.

Analyzing and Interpreting

Some counselors think that they can be helpful by analyzing (and subsequently "explaining") a student's situation to the student. Perhaps this response gained its popularity from the theory that there is always a logical reason why people do things. Look at these responses:

Don't you see, you see your teacher being like your father. They both are authority figures and both trigger rebellion in you.

Your unhappiness stems from all your problems at home.

In each of these examples, the intent is to explain, analyze, or interpret the student's behavior. Sometimes an effort is made to connect one event to another in the hope that this will give the student client some insight. Analyzing or interpreting responses try to give meaning to a counseling situation but they usually end up telling clients what they might or ought to think, why they did what they did, etc.

Remind yourself of how you feel when someone tries to analyze or interpret your behavior, i.e. "Oh I know why you did that, its because...." or, "I know why you wore that dress, its because..." Chances are you don't like it, especially if the interpretation is correct. Most of us dislike the idea that another person seems to know more about ourselves than we do and we will often "avoid" that person when possible.

One danger in making an interpretation to a student client is that we may, inadvertently, project our own attitudes, values, and feelings onto him or her. Such a response often emphasizes our personal interpretation of the world rather than the student client's perception of their world. Fortunately, effective counselors no longer rely heavily on these types of statements in an attempt to facilitate personal growth

Advising and Evaluating

School counselors are often viewed by students as the one adult in their school who has the answers to their problems. Since counselors have probably studied more human behavior, and usually have more experience than most of their students have in the mental health area, they are sometimes prone to think they are in a position to evaluate, make judgments, and give untimely advice to their students. When counselors dispense untimely advice to student clients, their probability of counseling success goes down. Moreover, if that is their usual method of counseling, they are prone to use more of the less facilitative responses given here, and in my opinion, will be less effective as counselors.

As noted above, effective counselors are more concerned with what the student client is thinking and feeling than simply giving information and advice. Advising or evaluating are responses that indicate a judgment of relative effectiveness, appropriateness or rightness within the counselor's own value structure. An advising or evaluating response somehow implies what the student might or ought to do. Here are some examples:

Don't let him get to you like that. Stand up to him!

Instead of arguing, try to see your mother's point of view.

If you'd be better at getting your homework in, your teachers wouldn't be so upset with you.

Unfortunately, while most counselors are trying to give helpful advice, there is the likelihood the advice is a projection of the counselor's needs, problems, or cultural values. This can be easily seen in the statement, "If I were you...." Students might even follow the advice and find that it was not valid for them. Students who experience this approach from their counselor seldom continue to see their problem (if they ever did) as one they "own." Instead, ownership of the problem being discussed has now shifted from the student to the counselor. The student becomes the "subject" and the counselor becomes the "expert" operator with all the answers! Giving untimely advice to a student client is sort of like moving a neighbor's furniture around without their permission. They move it back as soon as you leave their house! That is, students may smile and acknowledge your untimely advice, but will forget it as soon as the session if over!

When advice is relevant, timely, logical, and practical, it can be very helpful to a student client. This is particularly true if it is offered at an appropriate time; a time when it is viewed as a suggestion, or as leading their thinking, rather than as a command (i.e. "Have you given thought to maybe going to a community college or...").

School counselors can fall into the trap of giving advice when a student continually seeks their advice. However, students are often defensive once the advice is dispensed and may no longer be receptive to anything the counselor has to say. They might even argue more in order to maintain their individuality following untimely advice. They may begin to play "Yea, but..." games with the counselor (who may respond in kind) and "counseling" per se, is now nonexistent. That is, neither one is hearing the other!

The effective counselor doesn't get caught up in the societal concept that implies that everything must be done in a hurry. That is, they do not "rush in and fix" students with an evaluation and then give quick, untimely advice on what the student client should do to "get better."

Using the High Facilitative Responses

In summary, three counseling responses that have a higher probability of resulting in success for the counselor have been emphasized in this chapter. These three responses (feeling-focused, clarifying and summarizing, and open-ended questions) can be effectively used with most any counseling orientation, technique or intervention the school counselor chooses to use. Most importantly, their use will result in better, more facilitative counseling relationships with student clients and more positive counseling outcomes.

If an open, facilitative counseling relationship is not present, then student clients will, most likely, pull back into their proverbial "shells." They behave like a tortoise who, when threatened, will not stick it's head out. That is, student clients in a non-facilitative counseling relationship will not take the "risks" that might result in positive changes for them. They stop sticking their "necks out" for fear of even more rejection. Words never penetrate their hard shells or enter into their perceptual fields. As student clients experience a relatively nonthreatening relationship with their counselor, they are more apt to "stick their necks out and risk more." They are more likely to consider the alternative suggestions and methods that the counselor offers in an attempt at helping them.

Chapter 10
Small Group Counseling in School Settings

by

Rex Stockton and Paul Toth*

Rex Stockton, EdD, a former high school counselor, a Professor of Counseling and Educational Psychology at Indiana University, has long been active as a researcher, writer, and teacher in the area of group work. He recently produced a video tape series on the training of group leaders released through the American Counseling Association.

Paul L. Toth, PhD, is a Psychologist in the Student Health Center at Indiana University, Bloomington. His doctoral studies focused on group counseling and the training of group leaders. He has had a career of active involvement in youth work through public school teaching and YMCA work.

*A special thanks to the following school counselors who shared their group work expertise with the authors: Sherry Basile, Peggy Hines, Maureen Killila, Christine Sawyer, and Sandra McGinn.

Introduction

Take a minute or two and think about the influence of groups in your life. As you think about how groups have impacted your life, the prevalence of groups and human beings' attraction to groups, probably becomes quite clear. Most people live in some type of group, we work in groups and we play in groups. In many ways groups make life easier and there is no doubt that "groups" are an integral part of any society.

Groups are an integral part of any type of educational institution. The very organization of schools relies on the organization of groups (Tyler, 1992). Task oriented group work is essential to both the administrative organization of the school and the educational experience of the students. Much of the day to day work of the institution is done through group work. Moreover, students are purposefully involved in groups in order to design yearbooks, plan a debate strategy, complete a class project, engage opponents in an athletic contest, and many other activities and undertakings.

Schools have employed the use of small groups indirectly for the purposes of social skill education for a very long while. One way our nation coped with the economic and social changes born of the turn of the century industrial era was to teach a turn-of-the-century version of human and social relation skills to children. The schools saw as one of their duties, in the midst of radical social change, the transformation of naive children into socially astute adults who could make their way in a world of business. Perhaps even more importantly, schools took on the responsibility of teaching students skills which would help them get along in a world of strangers. A primary vehicle for this social education was the small group (Wiebe, 1969).

Of course, group work in these early years was not as we know it today. The first groups were clearly task-oriented; they were not the psychoeducational or counseling groups that school counselors employ today. Teachers worked with students, and students worked with one another on various projects and problems in order to, not only solve the problem, but also to gain experience in working with peers and strangers.

Since these early beginnings, the impact of small groups within the educational setting has continued to grow. As the decades progressed, educators began to gain a more clear understanding of the importance of the student's emotional health and well-being in the educational process and the role small groups could play in the construction of a healthy and well-functioning person. Over 30 years ago Clarence Mahler (1969) wrote:

If young people are to have a real choice, both personally and professionally, in planning their futures, they must have help in learning how to better understand themselves, learning how to make wise decisions and solve problems, and integrating their own personal growth with the increasing complexity of present-day society... A good group experience provides strong support for people to clarify their attitudes and strengthen their individuality (pp. 5-7, italics added by the authors).

Helping students clarify their attitudes and working with them to come to understand their sense of self continues to be the challenge for counselors in the schools today. Small group work continues to provide an important means to meet this challenge.

Cole (1987) identified a number of trends over a two-decade period which effect school counselors. These trends include: "increasing the emphasis on work with parents and other family members, substance abuse prevention activities, consultation and coordination, and public awareness on the topics of suicide, eating disorders, and separation and loss." Herring (1997) underscored the difficulties that schools are facing when, "Many youths in this nation are socialized within the context of alcoholic, drug-dominated, and abusive familial environments." He went on to emphasize that multicultural issues will be even more important as American culture continues to become a melting pot of cultures and types of individuals. Moreover, in 1992 the *Indianapolis News* reported a Student Assistance Program's survey conducted at a local high school which identified these major concerns of students: how to deal with depression, gang activities, physical and emotional abuse, and divorce or family breakup. In this same article one educator stated that every day there are students who face drug abuse, pregnancy, depression, peer pressure, grief, divorced parents and physical and sexual abuse. And still, they "...are told by some adults, 'Enjoy these years. They are the best times of your life'" (Hess, 1992).

Even though we can identify a shift from Mahler's concerns about the student's self-awareness and actualization, to Cole's list of problems with which school counselors are confronted, to the current reports of social issues that reflect problems concerning today's counselors, (including the recent school shootings that have so profoundly affected today's youth), all of these problems are often dealt with in a group setting. From Mahler to Cole to current struggles, we can find a common therapeutic agent in group work. It should be remembered, however, that major social problems are not a necessary starting point for group work in schools. Many counseling groups are arranged around such topics as new student support groups, raising self-esteem, peer relationships, anger management, social skills, study skills, dealing with parents and other significant individuals, and assertiveness training.

Groups: A Definition

Small groups are a microcosm of the larger society. They are made up of a variety of people from various backgrounds with differing values and points of view and pathologies. Each member brings his or her own agenda. Like social groups, counseling groups have a definite *beginning, middle,* and *end.* Groups are the place for the activities of life to be experienced and explored: people meet, they share their lives, they learn about rules for membership, they learn to trust and confront one another, they share a variety of feelings, and they are faced with saying good-bye. Groups provide the forum in which members are able to learn authentic ways of relating.

The Association for Specialists in Group Work defined group work as a

...broad professional practice that refers to the giving of help or the accomplishment of tasks in a group setting. It involves the application of group theory and process by a capable professional practitioner or to assist an interdependent collection of people to reach their mutual goals, which may be personal, interpersonal, or task-related in nature (1992, ASGW).

School counselors have both the challenge and the opportunity to continue forward with various types of group interventions that assist people to clarify their attitudes and meet their personal goals.

Training Group Leaders

There are many models for training group workers which have been examined by leaders in the field. In commenting on these models, Stockton (1980), the senior author of this chapter, noted there are four general areas of competency called for: (a) didactic knowledge; (b) individual clinical skills; (c) knowledge of group dynamics; and (d) achieving a healthy personality oneself. Standards for training group leaders are provided by the Association for Specialists in Group Work (ASGW), a division of the American Counseling Association (ACA). Current ASGW training guidelines reflecting generic and specialty skills are specifically outlined, ranging from that expertise required for basic task oriented groups through various gradations of personal growth groups to psychotherapy groups concerned with the reconstruction of personality. The preamble of the ASGW professional training standards stated:

> All counselors should possess a set of core competencies in general group work. These basic knowledge and skills, provide a foundation which specialty training can extend. Mastery of the core competencies does not qualify one to independently practice any group work specialty (ASGW, 1992).

Because some of the areas in which counselors find themselves leading groups these days requires specialized skills, it may be necessary for those lacking training to further develop their knowledge and skill levels through additional professional development. It would be quite helpful, and perhaps necessary, to enroll in group counseling or group dynamics courses at a local university or take part in one of the many workshops offered by professional organizations like ASGW. Especially important is taking advantage of opportunities for supervised group leadership.

Leading Groups

Have you been a group leader? If yes, do you remember leading your first group? Think about how you felt before you began? What was your biggest fear? Perhaps you have not yet led a group; think, then, of how you might feel about leading your first group. Even counselors who are well read in the area of group theory and well trained in group intervention are usually anxious about the prospect of leading their first group. The senior author has found that beginning group leaders who have all the didactic knowledge and experiential training needed to begin a group, are still often frozen by anxiety and feelings of inefficacy at the prospect of beginning their own group. When asked what it is they fear most when embarking upon their first group leadership endeavor, school counselors at workshops led by the authors usually respond with the following fears: they fear the group will confront them with silence; they fear one or more members will breach the contract of confidentiality, or the teachers who referred the groups members will expect the leader to share confidential material with them; they fear they might perform the wrong intervention; they fear an inability to keep the group on task; they fear someone in the group, or even the whole group, will become confrontational in a way that challenges the leader's authority--that is, they fear they will lose control of the group. In short, group leaders are people who fear failing. These fears are very common among, not only novice group leaders, but more experienced counselors as well.

Getting started brings out feelings of anxiety and uncertainty. Knowledge, training and practice, however, will lessen the counselor's fear. As one gains a sense of self-efficacy in his or her group counseling ability, anxiety dissipates and the counselor feels more at ease in the situation.

Pregroup Planning: Involving Teachers and Administrators

Before a school counselor actually begins the group, a great deal of reflection and planning should take place. Proper understanding of what needs to take place before the group ever begins includes necessary approvals (of parents, administration, and teachers), recruitment and *screening* of members, contact with teachers and administration, and scheduling appropriate times and comfortable facilities. In the authors' experiences, without proper attention to detailed planning before the group begins, leaders are likely to find themselves caught up in a variety of problems which may well hinder the progress of the group.

It is important to involve teachers in the group planning process (i.e., how many times, and when, will students be called out of class?) Some counselors have found it effective, at the middle or high school level to schedule the group during different class periods each meeting time so as not to have a student miss the same class time over and over again. Figure 10.1 reveals how one elementary school counselor effectively involves teachers in the planning process. Figure 10.2 is a proven method employed by a high school counselor for "signing up" students for small group counseling.

When planning a group it is important to consider the needs and characteristics of the population which you wish to serve. Gazda (1989) presented a compelling case for the counselor's consideration of the developmental level of children. He outlines developmental tasks, or stages, and suggests appropriate coping behaviors for various areas of human development. This provides a useful perspective for those planning a group for children or youth. For example, knowing the developmental level of a preadolescent (9 to 13 years old) means understanding that they form natural groups of the same sex. Therefore, in keeping with their developmental stage it is usually better to have single sex groups in this age range. This would contrast with adolescent groups where mixed sex groups would be more appropriate (Gazda, 1989). Grade level placement is the public school's way to maintain developmental homogeneity. Carroll (1996) suggested that it is best to form groups according to grade level when working in a school setting. The child's developmental level is also a useful guide to help determine maximum group size. Generally, younger children profit from a smaller group. Carroll reminded us that young children, immature adolescents, and those with special needs usually have a short attention span. Thus, she suggested that when working with very young children, the size of the group should be no more than three or four members.

Corey and Corey (1996) suggested developing a proposal as a part of the group planning. They recommend that this proposal include five major areas: (1) rationale, (2) objectives, (3) practical considerations such as meeting time and durations of group, (4) procedures, and (5) evaluation. Marianne Schneider Corey, in writing about her experiences in doing group work in the public schools, recommended building trust with the teachers and administration as a first step. She suggested meeting with them to describe the group's rationale and objectives prior to the involvement of children or adolescents in the group (Corey & Corey, 1996).

In his school counseling days, the senior author found it helpful to consult with central administration staff, as well as teachers and principals, who then became supportive of a group program for potential school dropouts he co-developed. It was also found helpful to have support for the program already in place before the program began in order to head off any questions or confusion on the part of an uninformed administration. As Dansby (1996) has noted, communication with relevant parties concerning the use of groups, including teachers and parents is essential. With support in place, any questions could be diverted away from the program and toward the proper administrators who understood and supported the group counseling effort.

Morganett (1995) had a very well-developed pregroup plan. Her book, *Skills for Living,* included a plethora of helpful techniques for group work with young adolescents. Although her work is specifically geared for young adolescents, the principles therein remain intact for older teens and younger children as well. According to Morganett, the process of getting a group counseling effort moving includes the following steps: (1) conduct a needs assessment; (2) develop a written proposal; (3) advertise the group; (4) obtain informed consent from parent/guardians; (5) conduct a pregroup interview; (6) select group members; (7) administer a pretest; (8) conduct the sessions; (9) administer a post-test; (10) conduct postgroup follow-up and evaluation.

In addition to the authors' personal experiences and our review of literature in the area of group counseling in schools, we have had the opportunity to lead and interact with panels of school counselors who were either conducting their own groups or wished to learn more about group work. The panelists concurred with the authors' personal observations and understanding of the literature concerning the importance of continued contact with teachers and administrators in order to forestall potential problems. From time to time throughout the remainder of this chapter, the authors refer to this panel as a useful source of information from those counselors currently in practice in K-12 school settings.

Beginning a Group: Establishing the Climate, Norms, Goal-Setting, and Feedback

The way one begins a group sets in motion the tone and tenor, and begins to establish the ground rules, which last the duration of the sessions. Perhaps most counselors have a sense for the importance of the first few sessions of the group and this is one reason why they experience anxiety at the start. There are some activities, however, in which you can engage the group members, and there are behaviors you can model for your members, which will serve to set a therapeutic tone as your group gets going.

It is important to have in mind a fairly concrete outline of activity for the first meeting. This outline can always be used or abandoned at the leader's discretion, but having such an outline in place will lessen the leader's opening session jitters. The outline can be very simple and can include things like the introduction of the leader(s), norms, and special considerations and activities that you choose to use to break the ice. Since silence is one of the fears mentioned most often by beginning group leaders, it is very helpful to have a couple of activities that can be effectively used to help get the group talking. It is also important to remember that you, as the group leader, are not the only person in the room feeling a little anxious.

The members have many questions and concerns as the group commences: "Will I be accepted by the others?" They are also asking: "Am I on the inside or the outside?" "Am I going to have to talk about something that embarrasses me?" "What's an appropriate level of self-disclosure?" "Can others be trusted?" "How am I supposed to act in here?" "What are the group norms and rules?" These are all common concerns of students in the group setting. Therefore, a planned, structured opening activity will serve to bring reticent members into the group's social interaction from its inception and set the stage to begin to answer the students' concerns as well as reduce the counselor's "opening night" anxiety.

The first stage in group development is the *beginning* stage. One of the developmental tasks of this stage is for the members to get to know one another. One way to accomplish this task is to simply go around the group asking each member to say his or her first name and whatever else they want the group to know about them. You may, or may not, give the members some guidelines or suggestions as to what they might talk about, such as: "Tell us something about what brought you to this group"; or, "Make sure to include in your statement what you hope to get out of this group"; or, "What is your greatest fear as you enter this group" (Corey, et al., 1992). One counselor uses music as an icebreaker. She might play familiar tunes or ask the children their favorite music in order to begin to

get them talking together. Another activity to break the ice, which works well with younger members, is to have them describe an animal which they imagine they are like and tell why they are like this animal. As each member introduces him or herself they repeat the first name of the people before them (this may be too difficult for younger children) and say anything about any of them that has especially captured their attention. This little exercise facilitates introductions, begins the process of group interaction and encourages the members to participate in giving feedback to one another which is a strategy vital to group work. Another recommendation is to break the group up into dyads and have them carry on an activity similar to those mentioned above with just one other person. After time in the dyads each member introduces the other to the group. Though this activity is probably suitable only for older teens, the dyad exercise offers the members the security of one-to-one communication when they might not be quite ready to speak before the entire group. The authors find that people are much less reluctant to speak when speaking to just one other person. We also recommend that the leader(s) gets involved in the dyad introduction activity. Matter of fact, we suggest that you involve yourself in all activities where appropriate.

The major point of structuring the group is to create a safe environment for the members where they feel free to interact with others and reveal information about themselves. Focus, then, is not so much on the counseling techniques, but on the goal of providing a safe place for members to explore themselves.

One useful generalization is that the younger the group member, the more *concrete* the opening activity needs to be. Gazda (1989) advocated heavy use of play and action oriented techniques for young (ages 5 to 9) children. One counselor who attended our workshop and works with very young children suggested using various materials such as paper, crayons, scissors, glue, and such, to help the children express their initial thoughts and feelings about being in a group.

Adolescents are very peer-conscious and self-conscious. Beginning a group with adolescents offers unique challenges and opportunities. They are experiencing life in the "here-and-now." Relationships appear very immediate. A crucial question for the adolescent is; "Am I accepted by the group, *today*?" Tomorrow may seem one hundred years away. One workshop participant with extensive experience with junior and senior high school level youth reported that she begins her groups by demystifying the process. "I make it very clear to them what I am going to do. When they know that what we do is not some mysterious ritual, they are more apt to participate."

Every group requires social interaction and whenever there is social interaction in a new situation it is very important to know the "rules of the game." Norms are the rules by which the group operates. Group norms provide structure; they help members feel secure and comfortable. Influencing and helping to set positive norms is an essential leader behavior. Norms are not always acknowledged—but they are always there. What is sanctioned in terms of language, attendance, confidentiality, degree of self-disclosure, punctuality, are all examples of norms. The most important benefit of therapeutic norms is their capacity to empower members to be able to share their life situations with others and to learn from the experience.

Group counselors need to be clear about the norms that have the greatest impact upon the success or failure of their group, and be sure to discuss these norms early on. With this in mind, it is important to remember that norms are an expression of the group, not any single member (including the leader). However, group counselors can and do have an important influence upon norm development. One useful way to involve the members with norm development is to list on newsprint or a blackboard "what works..." in the group, and "what doesn't work...." This usually brings up enough discussion to involve everyone in the decision making. The younger the child, the more concrete and structured the counselor needs to be. One school counselor indicated that she begins all groups with the following, positively stated, simple guidelines: (1) "We are here to listen to one another" (as opposed to; "You should not interrupt one another"); (2) "We will be sharing our ideas, thoughts, and feelings"; and (3) "We may pass a turn when we want."

Confidentiality is universally seen as an essential group norm. One counselor explored this norm with her group by asking the members if they have ever told a secret to another who, in turn, has reported that secret to those for whom it was not intended. Feelings around secret telling are explored and members begin to understand the impact of this norm; members begin to discuss the importance of confidentiality (**Note:** It must be remembered that there are certain situations where confidentiality legally must be broken. For example, when child abuse is reported most jurisdictions require that the counselor notify the proper authorities. Any exceptions to the confidentiality rule *must* be discussed at the very beginning of the group. Some panel members reported using contracts with students in order to impress upon members the seriousness of confidentiality. Others pointed out that teachers, who often wish to be kept abreast of a child's progress, should have the importance of confidentiality explained to them before the group begins so that they understand when you, the counselor, cannot talk to them in specifics about any given student. It is also important to remember that when the group is over the group members will, most likely, continue to see one another in the class rooms and around the halls of the school. Therefore, it is important to be clear from the beginning that when the group ends, the *rule of confidentiality continues.* However, as one school counselor indicated, maintaining confidentiality in a group, especially with younger children, is difficult. Thus, among his group guidelines he always states: "If you feel you must share with another person regarding something that happened in any of our group meetings, it must concern *only* something that happened to you within our group. That is, you should not share *anything* about any other person in this group." This counselor feels this provides younger children a little leeway on the important notion of group confidentiality.

Group members also have the opportunity to learn important information about themselves through interpersonal feedback. As noted by Morran, Stockton, Cline, and Teed (1998), "interpersonal feedback represents one of the most direct avenues for group members to interact and learn from one another" (p. 258). In order to be most effective it is important for feedback to be linked to member's experiences. Leaders have an important role in facilitating member's recognition that the feedback that they have received is relevant to their individual goals, how they behave in the group, and what they say about their actions outside the group. This connection can be important to insight into themselves and their personal growth within and outside the group.

Along with the social process of getting started—learning the norms and asking, "How do I behave?" It is also very important for group members to talk about why they are there and what they need to do to get better. A very helpful way to do this is to have the members set goals for themselves. It is important for leaders to help members clarify their goals and make them concrete and realistic. Even though this is a difficult exercise for some, it is a very useful thing to work on. As members are helped to set goals, they are also establishing norms; as the leaders model appropriate behaviors they help the group process move along. Paraphrasing the member's goal and narrowing it's focus is a helpful way for the leader to operationalize the member's desired change. If the group member's goal is rambling and not focused (this can be quite common) the leader should say something like, "What you say, Rachel, is very important; could you say it again using fewer words?"

Establishing group norms, discussing individual goals, and facilitating feedback sets the tone for a therapeutic group.

Moving Through Conflict and Transition to the Working Stage

It is important to realize that conflict is a very normal part of a therapeutic group experience. How conflict is dealt with will determine the degree to which the group can become a trusting working entity where members are free to examine their values and concerns. It must be remembered that conflict does not have to be like a violent storm. Conflict is often manifest as relatively mild interpersonal disagreements. One does not have to be in a fight in order to be in conflict. In psychoeducational groups, conflict is usually not dramatic. However, if a group is not experiencing at least some conflict at some level, the leader needs to examine why this might be. Is the leader too authoritarian to allow dissension? Are the members not trusting one another to the point that they can risk sharing emotions such as anger or grief? If feelings of disappointment or differences of opinion are not openly aired the leader would want to examine why this might be.

For any kind of group, the ability to resolve troubling issues is quite liberating. Once group members are able to work through their differences in a way that honors each person, they are more willing to take risks and become vulnerable. This leads to a greater degree of trust and creativity among members.

Leaders are especially able to help resolve *conflict* in two ways: 1) When a member is in conflict with him or her, the leader can model conflict resolution for the group by accepting the member's feelings in a non-defensive and non-judgmental manner; and 2) When two members are in conflict with each other, the leader can help the two process (and facilitates) their disagreement utilizing a structure that allows for safety as well as honest feedback; members will learn much from watching conflict being resolved. These appropriate leader behaviors model for the members a process for such resolution. This permits the members to risk greater involvement in the group and, therefore, enhances the potential for positive change. There are many facilitative techniques a leader can use which help the group move through conflict.

One helpful technique in working through *conflict* is the "go-around." The go-around is a very simple, yet important, group work skill. It can be used for a variety of purposes, but essentially it works to bring every member into some (if modest) level of participation. The leader simply asks the group to do a go-around by saying something like: "I'm wondering how the rest of the group is feeling about Bill not wanting to talk to Casey? Let's go around the group and each of us respond briefly to Bill." The group then proceeds, one at a time, to give Bill appropriate feedback. Go-arounds can consist of brief comments, one word responses, phrases that come to mind around significant words or conflicts, or some other concern that will stimulate a response or elicit feedback from members. The go-around both defuses and objectifies the conflict which frees members to gain a broader perspective.

Another example of good *conflict* resolution is making use of "I-messages." I-messages express the feelings of the speaker very personally and concretely, directing the message directly to the recipient. I-messages begin with "I" statements. For example, "I really feel hurt when I hear you say...." Stating an I-message is a nonthreatening way to confront another with how the speaker is feeling. It helps the speaker to take responsibility for the feelings and the statement as well as inform the person to whom the message is intended as to how they are being perceived. The counselor can not only model I-messages for his or her group members, but he or she can also instruct the members in this form of communication with relative ease.

When conflicts are successfully resolved it is possible for the group to move into the *working* stage. The working stage of the group is more difficult to explain theoretically, than it is to see in practice. One of our panelists pointed out that she knows when her groups are working; it's when the group members are telling their friends that they ought to be in a group.

The *working* stage of the group is characterized by a greater proportion of member to member communication and less member to leader communication. Members become less defensive and begin to self-disclose at more frequent intervals and at deeper levels. There is also an increased frequency of more appropriate member to member feedback. Interactions have much more personal depth and a wide range of emotions is seen. Leaders can take a less active role, using more process statements and fewer norm-setting statements.

A particular useful leader intervention during the group's *working* stage is the use of *process illumination* statements. Using this approach, the leader clarifies the group dynamics which are occurring at that particular moment, or have previously occurred. Process statements are often made about observed behavior, or what takes place in the group as a result of this behavior. One example of process illumination is a statement which ties (links) together past and present behavior: The counselor says, "It seems that the group has been working very hard and has been very helpful to Mary today. Having worked through much of our conflict over the past two weeks has allowed us to be more helpful to one another." *Process illumination* statements can be made at any time in the group's development and can encompass any kind of group behavior but are especially helpful in moving the group along in the working stage.

Termination

In our experience we have found that beginning group leaders need to spend more time than they had anticipated in planning for the beginning and ending of their group, and less time than they had anticipated in planning for the actual working stage. Just as with other parts of the group experience, it is important to give serious thought as to how you are going to end your group. It is important to help people make sense out of the experience, to take what they learned about themselves in the group and transfer that learning to the wider world. This is fine for all group members, but especially so for elementary aged children.

An important leader behavior is to remind the group throughout the meetings as to how much *longer* the group will continue. This reminder works to help keep the group on task and focused. This is particularly important with younger children. One of our panelists who works with very young children reminds the children every week of the number of sessions until conclusion. She has the children hold up their fingers, concretely illustrating the number of weeks left.

It is hard for people to say good-bye. This is as true for groups terminating (or perhaps even more true for groups) as it is in our social sphere. It is important for the members of a group to recognize the reality of termination and process related thoughts and feelings. Members may well hesitate to say good-bye and get sidetracked by less significant interaction. Again, proper use of structure on the leader's part can help the group accomplish its task. One useful approach is to have the group do a go-around where the members voice their appreciations for what they have taken from the group experience and regrets about what they were not able to accomplish.

The single most important task in termination is to help the members *transfer* their newly acquired understandings, skills and behaviors to the world outside the group. The process of evaluating the group experience can include a group discussion, and thoughtful probing on the leader's part, as to how the members might use what they have learned from the group in a different setting.

When members have had the chance to sum up experiences in a personally meaningful way, mourn the loss of the group, consider how to implement their new skills and attitudes in a wider context, they will then have successfully experienced termination.

Summary

In this chapter we have written about the importance of planning, making interventions appropriate to the developmental age of the group members, and the stages of development through which the group can progress. We have stressed the use of structure in organizing counseling and support groups. While these are all very important, it is critical not to be so set in your plans and notions about how to conduct the group that you lose sight of the desirability for flexibility and being able to respond to the needs of the moment.

For those wanting to know more, there are many resources available. We have referenced a number of authors and books in the field and, of course, there are many others. Publishers also have begun to develop helpful materials which stimulate group discussion and interpersonal learning, particularly at the lower grade levels. We have found that State Departments of Education and state professional counseling associations often collect and circulate helpful ideas for group leaders.

We cannot, in one short chapter, include more than an introduction to group counseling with students. We hope that you have been stimulated to learn more about this process through further reading, course work, attending workshops, and supervised practice in leading groups. More importantly, we hope that, if you currently aren't, that you will incorporate group work in your school counseling program.

Figure 10.1
Involving Elementary Teachers in the Small Group Process

Memorandum

To: Third, Fourth, and Fifth Grade Teachers
From: (Counselor's Name)
Re: SMALL GROUP COUNSELING (5 or 6 weekly sessions)

I need your input so we can begin small group counseling. Below are listed some suggested timely topics for student groups which I feel we need to offer this Fall semester. You may have other topics in mind. *Please share them with me.* The purpose of each group, and some suggestions as to the type of student you may want to include are:

TITLE	PURPOSE	POSSIBLE TYPES OF STUDENTS
RETENTION	To encourage retained students to utilize their retention in a positive way and to help them feel success rather than failure.	Student who repeated a grade this year.
SELF-CONCEPT	Encourage a better understanding of each individual's strengths and weaknesses.	Insecure, unrealistically confident, low self-esteem.
COMMUNICATION	Strengthening listening and communication skills.	Inappropriately verbal, non-verbal. Inappropriate affect.
DIVORCE	To help students deal with family situations involving divorce, separations, etc.	Students having difficulty adjusting to divorce situations.
SELF-CONTROL	Developing responsibility and an understanding of one's own behavior.	Combustible, lacking in self-discipline.

Please list any of your students who you think would benefit from being in one of the above listed groups. I will then talk to you and to each student before I begin any of the groups.

Retention	Self-Concept	Communication	Divorce	Self-Control

Joe Wittmer, PhD

Figure 10.2
High School Group Sign Up Sheet

(In packet outside the guidance office with sign indicating: "Take One")

Dear Student:

If you would like to participate in a small group experience, please indicate by checking the line next to the topic in which you are interested; also check your second choice. Groups will meet weekly for six weeks.

Groups will begin in about two weeks. Please complete your class schedule so we know where to find you as one of us will talk to you individually prior to the beginning of the group meetings. Each group will be limited to seven individuals. If you have questions, please stop in the Guidance Office.

_____1. Weight Control - being smart about staying in shape

_____2. Looking Good - clothes, make-up, hair

_____3. The Dating Game - the opposite sex

_____4. Temper-Temper - how to be in control and not lose your cool

_____5. Career and life span planning - your future

_____6. Divorce - how to cope with your changing family

_____7. Managing Stress - staying cool during stressful times

_____8. Study Skills - how to become a better student

_____9. Peer Pressure - how to manage it

_____10. Interpersonal skills - becoming a better communicator

Student Name_____ Date_____

Schedule

Period	Subject	Room Number	Teacher
1.	_____	_____	_____
2.	_____	_____	_____
3.	_____	_____	_____
4.	_____	_____	_____
5.	_____	_____	_____
6.	_____	_____	_____
7.	_____	_____	_____
Homeroom	_____	_____	_____

References

Association for Specialists in Group Work. (1992). Association for specialists in group work: Professional standards for the training of group workers. *Journal for Specialists in Group Work, 17*, 12-19.

Carroll, M.R. (1996). *Elements of group counseling,* (2nd ed.). Denver, CO: Love.

Cole, C. (1987). *The school counselor: Image and impact, counselor role and function—1960s to 1980s and beyond.* Alexandria, VA: Paper presented at the ERIC/CAPS 20/20 Conference.

Corey, M.S., & Corey, G. (1996). *Groups: process and practice,* (5th ed.). Pacific Grove, CA: Brooks/Cole.

Corey, G., Corey, M.S., Callahan, P., & Russell, J.M. (1992). *Group techniques.* Pacific Grove, CA: Brooks/Cole.

Dansby, V.S. (1996). Group work within the school system: Survey of Implementation and leadership role issue. *The Journal for Specialists in Group Work, 21*(4), 232-242.

Gazda, G.M. (1989). *Group counseling: A developmental approach* (3rd ed.). Newton, MA: Allyn and Bacon.

Herring, R.D. (1997). *Multicultural counseling in schools.* Alexandria, VA: American Counseling Association.

Hess, S. (1992). Perry program helps in coping. *Indianapolis News,* October 3, p. 3.

Mahler, C.A. (1969). *Group counseling in the schools.* Boston: Houghton Mifflin.

Morganett, R.S. (1995). *Skills for living.* Champaign, IL: Research Press.

Morran, K.D., Stockton, R., Cline, R.J., & Teed, C. (1998). Facilitating feedback exchange in groups: Leader Interventions. *The Journal for Specialists in Group Work, 23*(3), 257-268.

Stockton, R. (1980). The education of group leaders: A review of the literature with suggestions for the future. *Journal for Specialists in Group Work, 5*, 55-62.

Tyler, M. (1992). *Group activities in school settings: An explanation of common categories.* An unpublished manuscript.

Wiebe, R.H. (1969). The social functions of public education *American Quarterly, 21*, 147-164.

Chapter 11

Large Group Developmental Guidance

by
Marjorie I. Cuthbert

Marjorie I. Cuthbert, PhD, NCC, is Project Director, The Academy for Educational Development, Washington, DC. She is the former Supervisor of Guidance and School Support Services for Alachua County Schools in Gainesville, Florida.

Introduction

Large group developmental guidance, often referred to as developmental classroom guidance, is the systematic delivery of age-appropriate preventative guidance concepts and units to groups of students which usually contain more than 10 to 15 members. Counselors would differ on what they define as a large group; however, most would certainly agree that a classroom size (25 to 30 students) fits the description of large group guidance. As with the management of any classroom-size group around chosen curriculum or a specific program, selected techniques to enhance the delivery are used to help facilitate discussion, processing and learning (Wittmer & Thompson, 1995).

Large Group Developmental Guidance sessions provide unlimited opportunities for counselors to get to know significant numbers of students at any age or grade level. In addition, it permits the counselor to capitalize on the energy that the larger group naturally provides by the diversities of the backgrounds and experiences of the group members. Even though all students may not get a chance to present their own thoughts or feelings about a topic each session, they are exposed to a broad array of others' ideas. The large grouping allows those students who are really shy and have not yet developed the skills to speak out in the groups, to be exposed to their peers' perceptions on various topics. The large group format also allows those who choose not to participate to be in a group setting which, by its design, allows them to be a part of a peer grouping without the pressure of having to perform.

From leading the large group, the counselor learns quickly which students have difficulties managing their behavior in large group settings. These students can later be considered for inclusion in small groups or individual counseling to address specific behavioral needs where skills can be introduced and practiced. When the students have practiced chosen skills in the smaller group, the real test comes when they return to the large group setting. Often this test comes for the regular classroom teachers, but it is particularly effective if the counselor can monitor the targeted behaviors in the classroom when delivering large group guidance lessons.

Not only do large groupings of students for guidance units allow the counselors to know many students, this delivery system also allows counselors to be seen as "teachers of curriculum" in the perceptions of their colleagues. This will improve your image with those who are in the classrooms every day managing large groups of students. It helps dispel the misconception that some educators have, that counselors are teachers who no longer can, or want to manage large groups of students. It helps also dispel the misconceptions that counselors, particularly at the high school level, do mostly paperwork and do not interact much with the students. It helps counselors be seen as persons to whom others can go for suggestions on classroom management, especially when the counselor demonstrates effective techniques for classroom management during the large group guidance sessions. It is beneficial for classroom teachers to remain in the room when units are being delivered so they can do follow-up exercises; and it is an optimum time for the counselor to utilize skills and model techniques that work effectively with all kinds of student populations. Because of this exposure, it becomes a major responsibility of counselors to develop sound units which are age-appropriate and to know how to deliver them using large group behavioral skills. Counselors in these settings are powerful agents of change for both teachers and students.

Effectiveness of Large Group Guidance Lessons

Large group classroom guidance units are an accepted delivery model today and have been found as an effective and efficient vehicle to use with students of all ages. Many studies involving different age levels and varied content have shown positive changes in outcome variables as evaluated by both students and teachers. There are many methods and instruments available to evaluate units. It is useful to write parallel statements to which both the teacher and students respond so comparisons to each other can be made, as well as outcome measures rated.

For example, a study involving fourth-grade students indicated that there were positive changes and significant differences in school attitude for both low and high students after their participation in six classroom guidance units (Myrick, 1997). Cuthbert (1987) concluded that developmental guidance units designed for counselors to teach school success skills to third graders, using modeling and coaching techniques, can influence student attitudes about school situations. There is thus substantial support in the literature to show that developmental guidance units delivered to large groups of students are effective in teaching students ideas and skills (Wittmer, Thompson, & Loesch, 1997).

Many different topics can be delivered to large groups. School counselors at all levels create units to meet objectives which often include ideas of understanding one's self and others, getting along with peers, dealing with peer pressure, accepting limitations, capitalizing on strengths, recognizing differences, using conflict resolution techniques, learning communication and interpersonal skills, exploring careers, etc. Any of the topics could be easily put into systematic units for delivery, keeping in mind the age to which they would be delivered so that appropriate developmental concepts can be included and age appropriate activities chosen.

Counselors, in addition to creating units around general topics mentioned above, teach units to any or all levels on subjects which include:

- Emotional, physical, and sexual abuse
- Safety from strangers
- Assertive skills
- Conflict resolution skills
- School success skills
- Drug education awareness
- Human growth and development (puberty/changes)
- Career planning
- Grade level transitions
- Death issues
- Crisis management techniques
- Choosing colleges and financial aid
- Sexual harassment
- Sexually transmitted diseases/AIDS
- Awareness of physical disabilities
- Multicultural Awareness

Once you establish a workable format for a guidance unit that feels comfortable for you, you can create a viable set of lessons around any topic area. For example, teachers might request that the counselor come in for several sessions and work with the students on name-calling, or handling student-to-student "putdowns." Even though the counselors might not have sessions and activities readily available on the exact topic being requested, they can develop specific objectives and fulfill them through activities adapted from any other units.

Counselors at all levels are often asked to create units around very serious issues. For example, during the Persian Gulf and Balkan Wars, many school counselors in large group guidance sessions gave information, processed feelings, and responded to needs of students who were affected by it both directly and indirectly. They were able to reach large numbers of students. Certainly, some students needed more personalized attention when they were adversely affected by some aspects of the wars, and were seen individually for further processing. The death of a teacher or classmate often affects the entire school. The counselor goes in perhaps only once to help students gain correct information and begin processing the tragedy, but may end up designing units for subsequent sessions as a tragedy often elicits other fears of death, separation, or world catastrophes.

High school counselors meet success with large group guidance units dealing with registration procedures and issues that arise when students are transitioning from grade level to grade level. The middle school counselors also deliver large group guidance lessons to their eighth graders as they move from middle school to high school. They address some specific procedures, but also attend to all the social and emotional changes that accompany these level changes. Addressing similar developmental changes and concerns, developmentally oriented elementary counselors deliver large group units to fifth graders as part of the orientation process for middle school.

High school counselors also meet with large groups of students to discuss results from interest surveys and career counseling instruments. They group college bound students to counsel with them about writing resumes and application essays, and to make them aware of general ways to look at colleges to meet personal needs and financial realities.

Middle school counselors help large groups work on career plans that cut across all the high school years which might include college, vocational opportunities, or general areas of study. Along this same topic, elementary counselors deliver units on career awareness which serve as the starting points for the other levels to build upon. As can be observed from the flow of an effective K-12 career education program, counselors often deal with the same topic at different levels and adjust the information given and its processing to the developmental level of the students.

Elementary guidance counselors deliver classroom guidance lessons on most of the topics listed above. Most local, district, or county guidance programs list goals and objectives for the different grade levels. Elementary counselors can best realize these objectives through 20 to 30 minute sessions in individual classroom settings, usually conducted once or twice a week for a total of four to six sessions depending on the content of the unit being delivered.

Designing a Large Group Developmental Guidance Unit

By now it should appear clear to you that any topic or subject can become the theme of large group guidance sessions and be effectively delivered to students. However, such units must be developed appropriately and delivered through activities which reflect developmental levels. Creating sessions that comprise a large group developmental guidance unit with developmental levels in mind is not always an easy task.

There are some excellent resources available from educational companies for counselors to use on many specific large group topic areas. Often times these materials contain activities which can be utilized to comprise a systematic series of lessons to make a unit. These materials can frequently be used just as they come from the companies. However, there are times when counselors want to design their own units to reflect timely local topics or to realize their goals differently from the way someone else has marketed the activities. Activities from commercial units can often be incorporated into individually designed units. A workable format helps organize materials and sharpen the focus. A well designed developmental guidance unit is one that has an identified *purpose; age-appropriate activities for students to experience; coordination over sessions* (usually 4 to 10, depending on the topic and available time); *a processing component;* and *closure* or *summary.*

Myrick (1997), in the Florida Classroom Guidance Project, presented a logical workable format that consisted of six thirty-minute sessions, each of which was divided into four sections of Introduction, Activity I, Activity II, and Closure. Vernon (1989) utilized a user friendly approach in designing the individual sessions in her K-12 emotional education curriculum based on Rational-Emotive Therapy. Each session lists an *Objective, Materials, Procedure,* and *Discussion.* Since the sessions are designed for others to use, another section, *"To the Leader,"* was also included. This would be helpful for all counselors to include when creating large group units, since so many effective units are passed between counselors informally within systems or at conventions.

I have found several different formats helpful in organizing material. The first begins with the stated Purpose of the session, followed by the *Introduction, Activity One, Activity Two, Processing, Summary,* and for certain topics, an *Assignment* due by the next session. Along the same basic progression, a somewhat simpler format, which includes the *Goal; Objectives; Activity and*

Processing; and *Closure* is very logical and useful in designing developmental guidance units.

Perhaps it would help you most at this point to show briefly how an original unit is developed from an idea into a systematic set of activities which comprise a large group developmental guidance unit. Keep in mind that effective units can, and should, also be evaluated. In this day and age of tight budgets and emphasis on accountability, it becomes imperative that counselors be able to show that their units are making positive changes for the students who participate in them. There are many ways to evaluate the units (e.g., a decrease in behavioral referrals, increased participation in classroom discussions, changes in self-perception ratings and/or teacher ratings from pre and post administrations of instruments, etc.). The particulars of evaluation and specifics of research designs are beyond the scope of this chapter, but counselors need to be aware of sound research practices. There are excellent books available for further study on research procedures. Many straightforward methods are available and easily implemented even in busy, day-to-day counselor schedules.

For the purpose of example, I will present here the idea of building positive self-concepts or raising self-esteem for the theme of a developmental guidance unit. There are many references available that support the importance of students perceiving themselves positively for success in school and life, and many that show those who have low self-esteem to be achieving less and more likely to drop out of school. I like to find studies and ideas from other sources to add strength and support to the unit being created.

A major emphasis of this unit became the use of activities which could foster the growth and identification of self-accomplishments. Additionally, the unit was developed in order to aid students in developing a belief system based on self-accomplishment and realistic self-assessment so that resulting beliefs could have corresponding values which were positive. This goal was then implemented through chosen activities. The activities were chosen so that each could be adapted for any level (K-12) based on the stated goals.

A second goal was incorporated into the unit to assist students in understanding, communicating, and appropriately responding to their own feelings; and, in understanding the feelings of others. Learning how to express feelings about one's self is a growth-producing experience which can raise self-perception. This goal then could be made operational through objectives that state what students will experience. These could include the following objectives: (1) Students will increase their awareness of personal feelings, (2) Students will develop a vocabulary to describe their feelings, (3) Students will become aware of how feelings can impact on behaviors, and (4) Students will learn appropriate ways of responding to personal feelings. All goals included could be similarly supported by statements or research findings from other professionals. All the objectives presented could be developed into sessions which include activities and comprise a unit for any age level.

To illustrate the process of writing a complete developmental guidance unit which moves from choosing a theme and documenting supporting findings (as illustrated above), to making goal statements which become operational through objectives, identifying the grade level to which it will be given, choosing age-appropriate activities to be included, and finally compiling all information into a usable format. The following unit is included (see Figure 11.1) as a completed model for your use. I chose to call the unit *"Each of Us is Special"* and designed it for delivery in the second grade. Remember, by changing the activities and method of processing, the unit could be adapted for any grade level.

As mentioned before, the effectiveness of any large group unit needs to be measured for outcome effectiveness. This unit was evaluated by students' self-perception on a pictorial rating scale which was given to them prior to experiencing the unit and again following the sixth (final) session. The results revealed that the guidance unit was effective in changing at least some aspects of children's ratings regarding several aspects of school and self.

The development of the large group unit was presented to illustrate how any developmental unit can be created to meet the needs of students, and modified if results of evaluation show that it is not making a positive difference for students. Once the unit is developed, the delivery becomes the next important stage.

Implementing the Developmental Guidance Unit

When and how to deliver developmental guidance units is an important topic. Many counselors work closely with a guidance committee in their schools to plan out a yearly calendar which includes time for the counselors to work with large groups of students. In crowded curricula, it is very important for counselors to be included in master planning, so that time to work with students is given with everyone's knowledge of how guidance services enhance the school environment for students. Elementary counselors plan with the guidance committee or grade level chairpersons to schedule blocks of time which allow for delivery of classroom guidance units of about 30 minutes for six sessions in every classroom. Of course, with counselor to pupil ratios often exceeding 1:600, it becomes difficult to meet this standard and sessions are cut down in number, or several classes are grouped together for a very large group delivery. This latter method works well for some topics, but can become impersonal if used too much for topics that demand more individualized discussions.

Middle and high school counselors often arrange to deliver career planning or college planning guidance units during chosen classes (e.g., all English classes or all math classes). When they are able to do this, they know they have reached the majority of their students. Many middle and high schools have designated a block of time at the beginning of each day where teachers give out necessary information about scheduling and planning. They also help deliver chosen guidance objectives which are consistent with the goals and objectives of the developmental plan. These blocks of time where teachers are delivering guidance components are often referred to as Teacher Advisor Programs (see Chapter 19 in this book). Guidance counselors often assist classroom teachers with information for these units and suggest ways to process with students. The counselors often rotate through these designated times to discuss timely topics such as sexual abuse awareness, and sexual harassment policies, and so forth.

It is crucial that all counselors work closely with their faculties to plan times when they can deliver their large group guidance units. Meet with teachers and find out timely issues they feel would be important to include in units. Knowing how to build a strong unit and creating it is exciting, but its actual delivery is the key to knowing how it really affects students. In crowded and limited daily schedules, it is imperative that counselors and their large group guidance units be seen as part of the total curriculum so that they (counselors) do not have to constantly fight for time. That is, your large group units are scheduled at the outset because of the recognized *importance* of what you do with and for students.

Delivering the
Large Group Guidance Unit

Actually, teaching the guidance lesson is an exciting and rewarding experience. It is so important to be enthusiastic about being there in the classroom and excited about what you have to teach, since you see the students in this setting perhaps only 4 to 6 times for unit delivery, or much less if presenting on a timely topic. Each lesson can begin with charged energy if you are there on time, have planned ahead and have your content well prepared.

Successful teachers are knowledgeable about their subject matter, understand it in depth, and are also able to deliver the ideas to students in ways that they can understand it, experience it, and process it. By the same token, successful, effective school counselors create theoretically sound large group guidance units with exciting age-appropriate activities and present them in ways that the students can understand and benefit from them. Knowledge of subject matter and effective planning cannot be over emphasized. Counselors at all levels need to be aware of large group dynamics and become excellent behavioral managers when they are delivering units. Counselors are often working with established groups or intact classrooms where teachers have already created certain learning climates. Teachers also have evaluative power over students which can help with classroom management. Counselors come into these existing environments and must adapt to them, but also must make them workable situations for their own curriculum delivery. Because counselors do not have to evaluate students when working in the classrooms, students may respond more freely. However, students may also realize that they can act out more since the counselor does not contribute to the grades given. This is why the counselor needs to be aware of large group dynamics and aware of behavioral techniques that are effective in working with large groups.

Over the years, I have been asked to help beginning counselors prepare for delivery of classroom guidance units and to help teachers know better how to manage large groups. From these requests, *"Cuthbert Cues"* evolved. It is a series of "c" words that help me remember different parameters to consider when ensuring all has been attended to in order to assure optimum success. The word "cues" is used as a signal to me or to the user to make certain all bases are covered when working with large groups of students or adults. The *"Cuthbert Cues"* include the following dimensions of large group management: (a) *Cohesion,* (b) *Cooperation* (c) *Communication,* (d) *Coaching,* (e) *Contribution,* (f) *Control,* (g) *Configuration,* (h) *Closure,* and depending on the topic being discussed, (i)

Confidentiality. Let us look briefly at each category to trigger more thinking about how you might want to make yourself aware of all the parameters and dynamics that go into an effective large group guidance unit.

Cohesion can be built in any group, one that is already in existence or a new one you may be forming. Begin to establish it quickly by saying, *"We work together"* and *"We will plan how we will use our time,"* and so forth. Use go-arounds in early sessions, where everyone in the group will get to share something about himself or herself, even though it is a large group. Obviously, this cannot be done every time by everyone, because of time constraints. When you know you will be coming back to this particular classroom for more sessions, have a symbol to leave with the group that you can add onto each week (e.g., the school mascot cut out and laminated works well to post in each room so that a sticky dot can be added to it each week upon the successful completion of a guidance session). Brightly colored folders seem to work well for older students or adults. This reminds them that those who have these folders are all working on the same project. This helps to build group cohesion.

Cooperation is explained and modeled by the counselor in groups. You teach group skills to the group about taking turns; listening to others as they will be asked to listen to you; respecting risk-taking and knowing that you will not be laughed at by anyone; and learning skills for how to disagree, agreeably. These skills can be practiced and learned, if part of your large group guidance lesson includes a time when the group is divided into smaller groups. When the smaller groups are brought back to one large group, you can process how things went in terms of both the groupings and how well cooperation was achieved in both.

Communication is the key element to success for counselors and teachers. Choose a system of communication and practice the suggested skills so that delivering content and eliciting feelings from large groups becomes natural and very rewarding. Myrick (1997) and Wittmer, Thompson, & Sheperis (1999) suggested a continuum of skills that moves from least facilitative responses to those most successful in keeping good communication flowing. They would suggest using open-ended questions, clarification techniques, and responding with feeling-focused statements which let those to whom you are responding know that you have heard, not only the content of their words, but also have picked up on the underlying feelings. Other techniques suggested by Myrick (1997) are also very useful in maintaining communication flow in large groups. The *"simple acknowledgment"* statement guides you to say "Thanks" to a group member for giving out ideas by actually saying the word "Thanks" or something like, "Okay, that's a unique idea" or, "Thanks for sharing that," and then moving on to the next member. Counselors effective as large group leaders will also *"pair"* ideas and link them with other members' ideas. This communication skill contributes heavily to group cohesion.

Coaching is a technique for instilling new behavior by direct instruction and practice with shaping by observers. The group leader or group members help other students by encouraging them to "try out" the presented skills and reinforcing their performance. Large groups work well when counselors teach students that no one fails in the group because all other members "coach" each other for success. Students also learn how to give facilitative, helpful feedback to each other which makes participation valuable to members.

Contribution refers to everyone in the group feeling that they have valuable opinions, ideas or something to give the class. Everyone likes to feel that their presence in the lesson is important. You may need to teach volunteering skills to those who are not able to raise their hands, take risks about sharing ideas, and so forth. They may need some added work on deep breathing techniques, positive self-talk, to name a few. Invite students to help with handing out papers, choosing whether to write on the board or newsprint, or any kind of managerial skills that you as the counselor do not need to own.

Control refers to your leadership style in large groups. Are you autocratic, facilitative, permissive? Know yourself and what you can tolerate and what is acceptable to you in terms of the behaviors of the group members. When counselors go into all the different classrooms in their schools, they see all the extremes of leadership styles. It is very important for you to know what works for you and quickly let the group know your style, since they will be already have been members in the teachers' systems. Control has to do with not only leadership style, but with classroom techniques such as pacing, varying formats of activities, and being sensitive to ever changing individual behaviors and group behaviors. This permits control techniques to be applied which match the presenting situations. Counselors who present some ideas didactically and then have students role-play, break into smaller discussions, or demonstrate ideas with other students as models, etc. find that these varied activities help control the group and often alleviates the need for disciplinary procedures.

Configuration has to do with room arrangement. Many times because of time constraints of multiple groups using classrooms in the middle and high schools, or elementary teachers not wanting their own room design varied too much, counselors are asked to work in rooms where the placement of the students' desks, and so forth, may not be conducive to the most effective delivery of the guidance unit. Planning ahead with classroom teachers can sometimes help remedy the situation. Since the time the counselor is in the room is so limited, teachers ask their students to put the room into the configuration the counselor has requested just before the scheduled time for delivery of the unit. This is ideal as lesson time does not have to be devoted to moving desks, charts, and so forth. Time to put the room back for the classroom teacher should be built into each lesson so that the courtesy is reciprocated. There are many excellent books available on room configuration with attention given to placements for hard to manage students and how your configuration enhances learning. How the room is set up and where you place yourself as the group's leader is important to consider as you get ready to deliver large group guidance units (Wittmer, Thompson, & Loesch, 1997).

Closure means giving a summary of what you have learned within the lesson. This is particularly important in that counselors may not see the same group until the following week or even longer. The closure from a previous lesson serves as review in the next session and helps bring continuity to lessons that are often separated by long periods of time. In the closure section you give the summary and outline plans for next time. This helps insure that the students participating in the large groups look forward to your next lesson.

Confidentiality or keeping ideas contained within the group most often comes up in small groups. However, it helps the counselor in large group settings to be aware of the concept and the possibility that the issue might need to be discussed. When counselors create caring, comfortable atmospheres, and discuss issues that conjure up personal experiences, anything can happen in large groups. Students begin to self-disclose very personal perceptions and counselors must attend to the protection of students by addressing confidentiality issues with the other students. In peer counseling classes in the high schools and peer training classes in the middle schools, confidentiality issues are dealt with in large group sessions.

As you can observe from the above, working with students in large group guidance lessons demands a lot of thought about many concepts, and much energy goes into actual delivery of the units. Managing large group guidance involves not only attending to the content of the units but to the classroom dynamics which are there and ever-changing. Using effective managerial skills when working with large groups adds to the success of such units. There is nothing more exciting than presenting a good classroom guidance unit to students who feel the cohesiveness of the group, cooperate with each other, communicate freely as they coach each other, contribute without fear of being ostracized or repeated, and who are in working configurations where control is shared between leader and group. It is an exhilarating experience that is beneficial to the counselor, to many students and can be an excellent learning experience for the participating teacher as well.

Summary

In summary, delivering large group developmental guidance is an important dimension of counselors' roles. This format allows counselors to interact with many students and to impact on their development in a preventative way. They can reach large groups of students with developmental issues or timely topics that need addressing. They can create units to meet specific needs of their populations. Large group guidance is one aspect of the total curriculum which helps counselors know many students. In working with them in large groups, counselors are often able to identify students who might need more individualized attention, either through the small group format or through one-on-one counseling. Presenting large group guidance units also allows counselors to serve as role models for teachers and other professionals who see them managing large groups of students with successful classroom techniques and behavioral interventions. This role strengthens the consultative aspect of the counselor's role, as teachers feel that the counselor is in touch with how to manage students with varying presenting behaviors and will seek consultation for strategies that will assist them in becoming more effective in their own teaching. In tight budget times, delivering developmental guidance units is also an efficient and effective way for students to receive direct services from their counselors and at the same time experience success while participating in a group of their peers.

Figure 11.1
Each of Us is Special:
A Large Group Classroom Guidance Unit for Second Graders

Session I
We are Alike and Different

Goal:

To assist students in developing positive and realistic self-concepts.

Objectives:

1. Students will increase their understanding of the ways in which people are similar and different.

2. Students will become aware of personal strengths and limitations.

Activity and Processing:

Begin the session by having the students describe "Glenna Springs," the school doll. Have the students compare her to the counselor (likes and differences). Lead the group in generating ways in which people are alike and different by having a student volunteer to come up and stand with counselor for comparison. The list might reflect the following ways that people are alike or different in their (1) thinking, (2) feelings, (3) actions, (4) physical appearance, (5) family size, and (6) choice of sports, and so forth.

Discuss the fun of having differences and likenesses and the importance of respecting these uniqueness in each other.

Closure:

Summarize how people are alike and different. Tell how the class will make a *"This is Me"* poster in the next session.

Session II
The Real Me

Goal:

To assist students in developing positive and realistic self-concepts.

Objectives:

1. Students will increase their understanding of how being different is valuable.

2. Students will gain an appreciation for the unique qualities of each individual.

Activity and Processing:

Review ways people are alike and different (skills, bodies, ideas, etc.). Make a *"This is Me"* poster where the students will draw or list five positive unique things about themselves.

Each individual student will be asked to share one special thing about himself or herself. The counselor will encourage each, but students may pass if they cannot share. They will be reinforced for listening nicely to others so that all may have a positive experience.

Closure:

Summarize the session by restating that each of us is unique and important to school, home, and society.

Session III
My Feeling—Your Feelings

Goal:

To assist students in understanding, communicating and appropriately responding to their own feelings and to understand and appropriately respond to the feelings of others.

Objectives:

1. Students will increase their awareness of personal feelings.

2. Students will develop vocabulary to describe their feelings.

3. Students will become aware of how feelings can impact on behaviors.

Activity and Processing:

Categorize feelings into *pleasant* and *unpleasant*. Generate a list on the board of feelings words. Demonstrate how feelings are affected by words, tones of voice, body language, and facial expressions. As time permits have the students share times that they felt certain ways.

Closure:

Summarize about listening to see if someone's feelings are *pleasant* or *unpleasant*. Highlight the fact that we are all special and can feel all the ways that were listed.

Session IV
Dial-up a Feeling

Goal:

To assist students in understanding, communicating and appropriately responding to their own feelings and to understand and appropriately respond to the feelings of others.

Objectives:

1. Students will increase their awareness of personal feelings.

2. Students will learn appropriate ways of responding to personal feelings of others.

Activity and Processing:

Review the feelings categories and list at least six *pleasant* and *unpleasant* feelings the board. Make feelings wheels. Have students choose three *pleasant* feelings and three *unpleasant* ways that they sometimes feel so that they can print these words on their wheels. Have them put their wheels together. With time permitting have volunteers dial-up a feeling on their wheels and share them with the class (self-disclosure).

Closure:

We all have unique feelings. We can feel different from others but also understand and respect how they might feel because each of us is unique and special.

Session V
The Proud Clubs

Goal:

To assist students in understanding personal values, attitudes, beliefs, and rights in understanding, recognizing and respecting these in others.

Objectives:

1. Students will gain awareness of personal attitudes, values, and beliefs.

2. Students will become aware of similarities and differences in attitudes, values, and beliefs of self and others.

Activity and Processing:

Use the *"Proud Whip"* activity (Canfield & Wells, 1995) for value clarification. The counselor "whips" around the room calling upon students in order. Students respond with 1) I am proud of , or 2) I'm proud that. The following questions could be used to begin the "whip": 1) What are you proud of that has to do with you in school?, 2) What are you proud of in relation to your family? and 3) What are you proud of about yourself?

The counselor records all who are able to share in the different categories by making a tally on the board. As each is tallied the students are told that they have joined the School Club, the Family Club, or the Self Club. The momentum is kept going by whipping around and asking who else would like to join one of the clubs.

Closure:

Reiterate that we are all alike, yet uniquely different. We all have our own looks, feelings, and beliefs. We all learn to respect each other for our special qualities.

Session VI
Giving and Receiving

Goal:

To assist students in developing positive and realistic self-concepts.

Objectives:

1. Students will experience the "cool seat" or positive strength bombardment.

2. Students will experience giving and receiving positive statements to classmates.

Activity and Processing:

Review how we learned that people are alike and different and unique in the ways they look, act, and feel inside. People have their own beliefs and values too. Today we will tell each other the things we admire in each other. (Only positive statements are allowed). Verbal praise is given to the sender of the message and to the receiver of the feedback.

Closure:

Each of us is very special. We have all heard others tell us special things about ourselves today. We have also told others the things about them that make them special too. Let's remember to respect the special things about our classmates and about all others that we come into contact with in our activities at school and at home. (An award is given to every student at the conclusion of the session).

References

Canfield, J., & Wells, H. (1995). *100 Ways to enhance self-esteem in the classroom.* Englewood Cliffs, NJ: Prentice-Hall.

Cuthbert, M.I. (1987). *Developmental guidance for school success skills: A comparison of modeling and coaching.* Unpublished doctoral dissertation, University of Florida, Gainesville.

Myrick, R.D. (1997). *Developmental guidance and counseling: A practical approach* (3rd ed.). Minneapolis, MN: Educational Media Corporation.

Wittmer, J., & Thompson, D. (1995). *Large group counseling: A k-12 sourcebook.* Minneapolis, MN: Educational Media Corporation.

Wittmer, J., Thompson, D., & Loesch, L. (1997). *Classroom guidance activities: A sourcebook for elementary school counselors.* Minneapolis, MN: Educational Media Corporation.

Wittmer, J., Thompson, D., & Sheperis, C. (1999). *The peace train: A school-wide violence prevention program.* Minneapolis, MN: Educational Media Corporation.

Section IV

The Counselor and Special Student Populations: The Culturally Different, Victims of Abuse, Gay and Lesbian, and Those with Special Needs

Section III concluded with a chapter which dealt with the "how-to" of large group guidance. Section IV begins with an excellent example incorporating the large group approach in teaching K-12 students about an important but often neglected concept—the valuing of cultural diversity. More specifically, in Chapter 12, Dr. Marie Faubert, Dr. Don Locke, and Ms. Phyllis McLeod present a structured model for teaching students to value cultural diversity via large group, classroom activities at the elementary, middle, and high school levels, respectively. They present developmentally appropriate, creative strategies for delivering large group guidance activities. The three, six-week long, large group guidance units presented by Faubert, Locke, and McLeod were written with the school counselor as coordinator/director of the activities and the classroom teacher as co-facilitator.

In Chapter 13, Dr. JoAnna White and Ms. Mary Flynt focus on K-12 counselors and their important work with student victims of abuse. As a school counselor, it is important to remember that each student you counsel may be the ongoing victim of abuse, or may be carrying the secret of abuse alone. Contemporary school counselors are currently grappling with the difficult issues abuse raises with their students. White and Flynt present several excellent workable strategies and programs for school counselors struggling with the tragedy of student victimization.

Next, Ms. Gail Adorno and Dr. Paris write (Chapter 14) concerning counseling with students who are "victims" of a different kind—gay and lesbian youth. These youth are the least "visible" of any minority group in the school and often need the assistance of a skilled counselor. Several strategies for working with these youth are provided by Adorno and Paris.

Federal and state legislation have changed the role of the school counselor where "exceptional" students are concerned. Dr. Beverly Snyder, in Chapter 15, insists that developmentally-oriented school counselors hold the keys which assure that special needs students in their schools will achieve and succeed. She writes: *Counselors, being child development specialists, play pivotal roles in their work with special needs students. No other educator is better equipped to assist the exceptional students, their families, or their teachers to reach greater understanding of the nature of being a special needs student. It is through using the skills of both counseling and consulting that counselors reach out to all who work with this unique population.* They provide many excellent strategies, program ideas, and tips that "work" with special needs students.

Joe Wittmer

Chapter 12
The Counselor's Role in Teaching Students to Value Cultural Diversity

by
Marie Faubert, Don C. Locke, and Phyllis W. McLeod

Marie Faubert, CSJ, EdD, is Associate Professor and Director of the Counselor Education Program at the University of Saint Thomas (UST) in Houston, Texas. The UST Counselor Education Program concentrates on preparing culturally competent and confident professional school counselors and licensed professional counselors. She is past president of the Texas Association for Multicultural Counseling and Development and is active as a presenter of workshops on cultural competence in the Texas Counseling Association, the Houston Counseling Association, and in school districts around Houston. Her publications focus on the preparation of culturally competent counselors and activities for professional school counselors.

Don C. Locke, EdD, is Professor and Director of the North Carolina State University (NCSU) Doctoral Program in Adult and Community College Education at the Asheville Graduate Center. Before this appointment he was Head of the Department of Counselor Education at NCSU in Raleigh. He is an internationally known authority on issues of culture and diversity and has had active leadership positions in the American Counseling Association (ACA), the Association for Counselor Education and Supervision (ACES), the Southern Association for Counselor Education and Supervision (SACES), and Chi Sigma Iota, the international honor society for professional counselors.

Phyllis W. McCleod, MA, is Dean of Students at Fuquay-Varina High School, Fuquay-Varina, North Carolina. She has been named outstanding counselor of the year for Wake County Schools, North Carolina and has presented at numerous county, state, and national conferences.

Introduction

The population of the United States is changing significantly. People from Nigeria, Ghana, Ethiopia, the Caribbean, Bosnia, and Herzegovina are present in significant numbers in some cities. Albanians from Kosovo, people from Iran, Iraq, Pakistan, India, and Cambodia are only some of the new immigrants. The presence of newly immigrated Latin Americans from Mexico and Central and South America result in Spanish becoming a significant language in many cities of the United States, especially in the South West and large cities like Miami, Los Angeles, Chicago, and New York. These Latin Americans join those who have been in what is now the United States for centuries.

Many new immigrants are coming with religions rare in the United States just a few years ago. At the University of Saint Thomas, a liberal arts, Catholic university located in Houston, Texas, there were no Buddhist or Islamic students in 1989. In 1998, the most recent year for which figures are available, 2% of the students were Buddhist and 2.6% Islamic. These are still small percentages, but they have steadily risen each year during the decade.

During the same time frame, the Asian-Pacific student population at the University of Saint Thomas has grown from 6% to 9%; the African-American student population from 5% to 7%; and the Latin-American student population from 13% to 22%. During the same decade, the European-American student population has fallen from 68% to 52%.

These figures correlate well with the predictions made by the United States Bureau of the Census (1998). According to these records, the percent distribution of populations in 2000 is expected to be 11.4% Hispanic, 71.8% Non-Hispanic White, 12.2% Non-Hispanic Black, 0. 7% Non-Hispanic American Indian, Eskimo, Aleut, and 3.9% Non-Hispanic Asian, Pacific Islander. By the year 2050 it is predicted that the United States population will change to 24.5% Hispanic, an increase of 13.1%; 52.8% Non-Hispanic White, a decrease of 19.0%; 13.6% Non-Hispanic Black, an increase of 1.4%; 0.9% Non-Hispanic American Indian, Eskimo, Aleut, an increase of 0.2%; and 8.2% Non-Hispanic Asian, Pacific Islander, an increase of 4.3%.

Even more significant for educators is the age distribution in each sector of the population by 2025: 16.1% of the Hispanic population, 14.6% of the Non-Hispanic, Black population, 15.6% of the Non-Hispanic, American Indian, Eskimo, Aleut population, 13.4% of the Non-Hispanic Asian, Pacific Islander population, and 10. 2% of the Non-Hispanic White population will be between 5 and 13 years old. In the first three cases, this represents the largest in-group percentages. For Non-Hispanic Asian, Pacific Islanders the largest percentage (15.0%) is for those between the ages of 25 to 34, and for the Non-Hispanic, White population the largest percentage (12.7%) is for those between 65 and 74. Obviously, as soon as 2025, the major population of the schools of the United States will be children of color.

At the same time that new immigrants are finding homes in the United States, United States citizens who have been here for many generations are faced with racism and prejudice, discrimination and alienation, and even threats to personal safety. On June 28, 1999 ABC 's Night Line documented racism against Asian Americans. It was pointed out that, although one out every six physicians in the United States is Asian, there is not one Asian actor playing a doctor on *L.A. Doctors, ER,* or *Chicago Hope,* popular TV shows. Recently, there have been heinous hate crimes perpetrated against African Americans in North Carolina, Texas, Illinois, and Indiana.

During the last decade there have been successful interventions used to enhance appreciation for one's cultural self (Faubert, 1992, Faubert, Locke, 1993; Faubert, Locke, Sprinthall, & Howland, 1996). The importance of infusing a school curriculum with activities which reinforce an appreciation of self is well documented (Hilliard, Payton-Stewart, and Williams, 1990). While differing groups are provided with environments which can enhance their appreciation of self,

simultaneously, we need curricula which will enhance appreciation of diversity. Although we are always more alike that we are different, our differences are real and must be valued. In fact, only those citizens of the United States comfortable with difference will be able to influence policy and bring about growth in the next century. Professional school counselors are a key to students' learning to value diversity. Counselors have a unique responsibility and opportunity to prepare students to value difference. The valuing of diversity is an important component of achieving a well functioning society. It is developed in the schools with a comprehensive, developmental guidance and counseling program (Texas Education Agency, 1998), and the professional school counselor plays a major role in this regard.

Developmental Perspectives for Enhancing the Value of Difference

Did you ever watch a 5-year-old, a 10-year-old, and a 15-year-old play a game on a personal computer with a mouse? What is it about the interfacing between the 5-year-old, the 10-year-old, the 15-year-old, and the personal computer that is so intriguing? The answer lies in the understanding of the stages of human development. The personal computer was designed by those who had a clear understanding of how human development occurs.

The earliest learning takes place between birth and two years old. Even in the delivery room infants have been known to grab whatever is there to grasp. Early learning is a touching/feeling learning. Appropriate to their level of development, toddlers snatch impulsively whatever is in view and reach. A primary task of the toddler is to learn that *I* is different from *you*. The concepts of *same* and *difference* are rudimentary indeed.

By the time children enter elementary school, grasping is well coordinated. Children are developing at a rapid pace because they are able to process mental images and use symbols (Sprinthall & Mosher, 1978). The development of language permits elementary school students to more clearly understand *same* and *difference*. Since their perception of the world is intuitive, they relish magical stories which provide opportunities to exercise their imaginations. Elementary school students can understand opposites. For example, first grade teachers teach *over* and *under*, *before* and *after*, and *up* and *down*. Elementary school is an ideal and opportune place to begin to teach the concepts of *same* and *difference*.

In middle school, students' language becomes less self-centered; they are better able to take the perspective of others, to see and understand another's perception of the world. However, their perspective is appropriately self-protective, concrete, and absolute. Middle school students tend to be *either/or* people; they do not deal with ambiguity or uncertainty well. They expect the adults in their lives to be consistent, but they are inconsistent. The development of an understanding of *same* and *difference* is in the context of concrete, absolute experiences. Because of the characteristics of middle school students, drama is one of several effective mediums for developing the concepts of *same* and *difference*.

Adolescence also brings on many psychological and physical changes. High school is a time for honing abstract thinking including symbolic meaning. Adolescents can draw abstractions from personal experiences and apply these abstractions to unfamiliar situations. High school aged students perceive personal gain as being connected with the advancement of the group that is most like them. With the development of trust, adolescents venture out from the protection of the peer group with whom they identify and explore those whom they may perceive as *different*. Counselors have the opportunity to enhance adolescent growth from being "rejecting of difference" to being that of "accepting of difference". Counselors can become the catalysts in helping adolescents begin the lifelong journey toward valuing difference and being able to feel comfortable with ambiguity and uncertainty.

Human development is complex. Although we've mentioned only a few stages in the previous section, school counselors, one of whose tasks is to provide an environment in which students will learn to appreciate cultural differences, can be effective if they plan their strategies from a perspective of human development stages. The following six-week long large group guidance units have been developed for elementary, middle, and high school students with the same developmental stages in mind that were used by the designers of personal computers and summarized briefly above.

Establishing the Environment

For most of the activities herein suggested, principles of large group guidance are recommended. Where possible, it is suggested that the students be seated in a circle with the counselor and teacher sitting in the circle with the students. It is recommended that the counselor and teacher do not sit side-by-side. The purpose of the presence of the teacher is to enhance the probability that the values developed in the large group guidance sessions will be further reinforced in the daily experiences of the classroom. The importance of seating arrangements when working with students in large groups is well documented.

In addition, it is obvious that sufficient lighting, adequate ventilation, and a comfortable temperature are contributing factors to effective large group guidance sessions. It is imperative that appropriate space for large group guidance activities to occur be provided. The large group sessions which follow are written with the school counselor as coordinator/director of activities with the classroom teacher as co-facilitator. We suggest that the classroom teacher continue the theme throughout the week or school term if appropriate. Handouts for the teacher may also be appropriate.

Developing an Appreciation for Cultural Difference

Elementary School Students

Introduction

During the elementary school years, students move from being spontaneous and magical to becoming more concrete and absolute. With this in mind, the following guidance unit was designed to enhance an understanding of *same* and *different*. Each of the six sessions was planned to last approximately 20 to 30 minutes, an appropriate attention span expectation for elementary school students, and were designed for groups of approximately 25 students.

The purpose of the first large group guidance session is to provide a concrete, simple experience of *same* and *different* in order to introduce the ideas in a manner that will best encourage the students to want to continue. The objective of the second session (one week later) is to furnish the students with something potentially creative, something "hands on" in order for them to talk about *same* and *different* comfortably during the following week. The purpose of the third session is to bring the concepts of *same* and *different* nearer to them personally and at the same time provide the shelter of the telephone. Only with the fourth session is the concept of *same* and *different* brought to the *here and now* experience of the students. The purpose of the fifth session is to have the students consider their personal school experiences of *same* and *different* as it relates to others. In the sixth session the counselor will want to summarize the confidence that students have developed around the concepts of *same* and *different* as applied to individuals and groups of people who might be different from themselves.

Session 1:

Begin the first session by agreeing on the guidelines for speaking and listening. We suggest simple guidelines stated in the positive: 1) We listen to and respect one another's thoughts, ideas, and feelings; 2) We share, when comfortable, our own ideas, thoughts and feelings; and 3) Anyone can pass a turn if they wish (i.e., you will not force participation).

Elementary school students appreciate knowing concretely the rules by which they are expected to play. At the beginning of each subsequent session it is helpful if the counselor and/or teacher request students to remind one another of the guidelines for behavior as noted.

The *materials* needed for this session are three clear, glass containers, some flour, table salt, yellow corn meal, chalkboard or flip chart, chalk and/or magic markers.

Place the three glass containers on a table. Put a substantial amount of flour in the first, table salt in the second, and yellow corn meal in the third. Do not tell the students the contents of the containers.

We suggest you say something like this to the students: *"Tell me how the substance in the first bowl looks. If I could not see it, how would you describe it to me?"* (Repeat this activity for bowls two and three.)

Place the words *same* and *different* on a chalkboard or a flip chart. Ask the students how the contents of the bowls are the same and how they are different. Write the descriptive words given to you by the students on the board or flip chart in the corresponding column under the words *same* or *different*.

It is acceptable if some of the words are not in the reading vocabulary of the students. They are in their speaking vocabulary; therefore, it is appropriate to place them in their visual range. Early elementary school students might give some magical answers. Older elementary school students will probably provide more concrete description of the bowls' contents.

Ask the students to come forward in turn to place their hands in each of the bowls and to *feel* the contents. Have them describe how the contents of the bowls feel; how they feel the *same* and how they feel *differently* from one another. Add their responses to the corresponding columns marked *same* and *different*.

Summarize with the students how the substances in the three bowls are the same and how they are different. Ask the students what other things that they know about are the same or different. Suggest to the students that they think of things that are the same and things that are different during the following week.

Session 2

The *material* needed for this session is enough plasticine (play putty or play dough) of different colors for each child to have approximately equal amounts.

Have the students report what they remember about the first session and facilitate the discussion so as to "link" or "pair" student's responses where possible. That is, tie their responses together. This brings about more comfort and cohesiveness on the part of the large group. Encourage the students to share what things they have thought of during the week that were the *same* and that were *different*. At the end of the introduction, ask each student to tell, to restate, to clarify, back to one other student in the group what that student just shared. This helps increase their listening skills and will result in their "tuning in to" other students.

Give each student plasticine (play putty or play dough) of approximately the same amount but of different colors, if possible. Suggest to them that they shape it into something that they like. Encourage the students to verbally share with the group what they have made. In turn, ask the students to tell how what they have made is unique but yet the *same* and *different* from what one other student in the room has made.

Summarize or clarify to the students how they seemed to feel about sharing sameness and difference with one another. Where possible, reflect their feelings, thoughts, and ideas. Help the students to understand that everything is the *same* in some ways and yet *different* in other ways. Finish this session by helping the students to understand that the sharing of sameness and difference can make them feel good and an important part of the group.

Session 3

The *materials* needed for this session are two play, or real, telephones, two empty tables, and two additional chairs; one at each table.

Have the students review what they have learned about *same* and *different* to this point. And, during the discussion, have students "tune in to" or "summarize the content," of what other students have shared. Introduce them to the idea that people are the *same* as one another and also *different* from one another. Ask them how people are the *same* as one another and how they are *different* from one another.

Place one play telephone on one of the tables (with an empty chair) and place another play telephone on another table (a short distance away). Tell the students that in this activity they are going to *pretend* that a new boy (if they be a boy) or a new girl (if they be a girl) *different* from themselves is in their classroom for the first time. Ask them to pretend that it is after school and they are calling one of their best friends (on the telephone) to tell them about a "pretend" new classmate of theirs.

Have one student pretend to be the caller and another student pretend to be the friend called. After five or six pairs of students have had a turn, process and facilitate the content of the conversations. Encourage the students to talk about the kinds of things that they said about the new classmate. Summarize how the *sameness* or *difference* of the new classmate might influence how they described the new person to their friend.

Session 4

No special materials are needed for this session.

Review briefly what the students remember of the previous sessions.

For this fourth week's activity the students will concentrate more directly on themselves. Ask each student to share three adjectives (descriptions) about themselves. For example, "I am tall; I like to read; I have a big sister." After each student has spoken, have students pair up and to tell each other one thing that they heard that is the *same* as they and one thing they heard that is *different* from that person with whom they are paired.

Summarize by reflecting to the students how they feel about having some things about themselves that are the *same* as other students and some things that are *different* from other students. Provide a supportive environment so that the students will leave the session feeling good about being like other students while also feeling good about being different from others as the case may be.

Session 5

No special materials are needed for this session.

First, review briefly what the students remember about the previous four sessions. You may wish to review the guidelines previously established.

Reflect to the students a positive, or pleasant feeling that they, as a group seem to have in relation to their remembrances. Be specific; it will be helpful if counselors name the students about whom they are speaking (i.e., "Joe, you felt *encouraged* to learn....") Encourage the students to talk about times when they were with people that were the *same* as they or were *different* from themselves. Stimulate the students to talk about how they get along with other students whom they see as the *same* and other students whom they see as *different* in class, at the mall, on the playground, or wherever. Again, facilitate the discussion by having students "tune in to" one another (i.e., to clarify another students thoughts, ideas and/or feelings).

Have the students tell how they are going to work to appreciate those students whom they see as *different* from themselves and their friends, one or two things they will *personally* do during the next month. They may resolve to listen better or more closely to a student whom they perceive as *different*; to provide a warm welcome to a student whom they perceive as *different* into a game that they may be playing with their friends; or invite a student whom they perceive as *different* into a task that they have to perform in a group in the classroom, and so forth.

Session 6

No special materials are needed for this session.

Begin with a discussion on what they remember from the previous sessions. Then tell the students that this is the last time they will be discussing this unit for now but their teacher may, from time to time, focus on *"sameness"* and *"differences"* throughout the rest of the school year. Process their feelings about what they have learned about sameness and difference. Use the student's own stories to summarize what they have learned and have them rephrase, repeat, or restate what others have learned. Stimulate them to provide examples of things they can think of that are the *same* and *different* (e.g., trees are the *same* and *different;* houses are the *same* and *different;* cars are the *same* and *different;* and, most importantly, people are the *same* and *different).* Lead a discussion on the latter.

Encourage them to talk about how people are the *same* but *different.* What does this mean to them? Help them to understand that *sameness* and *difference* are part of life, that it is not only acceptable, but desirable. And finally, help them to appreciate that things and people are the *same* as one another and also *different* from one another; and that in our diversity, we have strength as a society.

Conclusion

As the designers of personal computers are successful in producing a user friendly instrument by applying human development attributes, counselors of elementary school students can be successful in developing an appreciation of *same* and *difference* among themselves if they keep the developmental tasks of students in mind when preparing their guidance sessions. Counselors have a plethora of data to support the notion that it is vitally important to teach students to value diversity and differences—that the future of our society depends on it!

As noted, elementary school students can be spontaneous, magical, concrete and absolute. When these attributes of elementary school students are taken into consideration, successful interventions can be designed to develop an appreciation for *same* and *difference.* Effective counselors use the lived experiences that the students share during the planned sessions as the fabric, the raw material and substance for teaching awareness, respect, and appreciation for *same* and *difference.*

Middle School Students

Introduction

During the middle school years, students move from being concrete and absolute to being able to think more abstractly. With this in mind, the following six large group sessions are designed for enhancing an understanding of *same* and *difference* for middle school aged students. Each of these sessions is planned to last approximately 30 to 40 minutes, an appropriate attention span expectation for middle school students. The sessions are designed for classes of 20 or more students. If school counselors are working with more or fewer students, they can modify the activity to the class size. Again, we urge the classroom teacher to remain in the room during these activities so as to better conduct follow-up activities concerning the material being presented.

Middle school students are very creative. They enjoy performing. Because they are physically active, they appreciate the opportunity to *do* as well as to *think.* The structures for concrete *either/or* thinking are well developed, and students of this age like to solve problems. From becoming overly logical and concrete, middle school students begin to consider new factors and change their minds. Middle school students are prepubescent or early pubescent. They are moving from being appropriately self-protective to being appropriately conformist.

Since middle school students are comfortable with guidelines for behavior that are applied to all in the same way, begin the first session by discussing and agreeing upon the policies to which the class will adhere during the sessions. Middle school students will appreciate having been part of the policy making and will help enforce equal adherence to the guidelines. The agreed upon guidelines can be posted. The counselor can refer to them whenever it is appropriate. We suggest the guidelines be stated in the positive (i.e., "We listen to one another" as opposed to "We don't interrupt one another," etc.).

Session 1

The *materials* needed for this session are newsprint, magic markers, and masking tape.

Give each student one piece of newsprint and one magic marker. Have each write at least five words to describe themselves on the newsprint under their names. When finished, have them tape their newsprint sheet on the classroom wall or chalkboard. Always use masking tape, it won't peel off the paint.

Observe with the students which words are repeated from person to person and which words are unique. Reflect with the students that there are characteristics that some have in common and characteristics that are unique to them as individuals. Again, facilitate the discussion so as to have students "tune in to" one another's thoughts, ideas and/or feelings. Also, where possible, involve the teacher in the discussion.

Encourage the students to explore what happens in the classroom when a student is perceived as *different* by the other students. Have them discuss concrete examples of when they saw students who were perceived as different isolated, ignored, or censured. List the characteristics that rejected students might have. Encourage the students to provide concrete examples. Encourage the students to express their feelings about rejection. Facilitate their feelings and stay on your toes; middle school students may say anything. Be prepared to use your best group counseling skills. Provide a lot of support; this can be a discordance producing activity. Dissonance is required for growth, but be prepared to handle it with reassurance, encouragement, and gentle facilitation.

Stimulate the students to think of solutions to the problems that arise as a result of some students' being rejected or ridiculed by other students because they are thought of as *different*. Prompt students to provide concrete examples of how they can include others who are *different* in their study, play groups, or trips to the mall. Students at this age like to solve problems. Help the students to see that the difficulties that result from issues of *difference* can be thought of as opportunities to solve problems.

Assist the students in summarizing concretely some of the ideas and suggestions of the session. Ask them to make statements revealing their understanding of what others in the class have said (i.e., "Bill, as you listened to Jane talk, what did you hear? Summarize what she said for the rest of us".) Emphasize that they are to think about what has transpired in the session for fifteen minutes each day between this session and the next session (one week hence). Request that they write their reflections each day and bring their reflections to the next session. Indicate that some may want to share their reflections with their classroom teacher during the week.

Session 2

The *materials* needed for this session are the written reflections that the students were assigned in the previous session.

Have the students share what they remember from the previous discussion. Ask them to share some of their written reflections. Reflect and clarify back to them their feelings in an accepting manner. Collect their written reflections. (Read the reflections before the next session. Write encouraging remarks on them. Return them individually to the students between sessions.)

Discuss different places in the students' lives where difference might be a problem. Develop some concrete ideas around experiences in their neighborhoods, churches, classrooms, playgrounds, and so forth which involve differences of culture, economics, life style, and so forth. Brain storm. Keep the students concrete. Include specific examples of solutions to problems.

Tell the students that they are going to dramatize an example of difference where it has become a problem with people working or playing together. Inform the students that the drama they develop must include *solutions* to the problem that they are illustrating.

Discuss how the ideas they shared might be used to plan a dramatization. Detail some examples with the students. Be specific.

Session 3

Materials needed for this session are chalkboard or flip chart, chalk or magic markers.

Review with the students and place on the chalkboard or flip chart some of the ideas that were generated in the previous session. Be concrete and specific. Accept all responses without comment. To use complimentary responses implies the permission to use critical reactions. Genuine acceptance of students' proposals without commentary will be interpreted as affirmation and result in more student openness.

Next, divide the members of the class into groups of five each and assign them to plan a dramatization illustrating a problem caused by *difference* and its solution. Give the student groups ten minutes to decide on their topic. Encourage them to be creative. Remind them that when they plan their topic they must include *solutions* to problems. Allow all but the last five minutes to plan their dramatizations.

Assuming their are 25 students in the class, assign Group 1 and Group 2 to Session 4 (next week), Group 3 and Group 4 to Session 5 (the week after next), and Group 5 to Session 6 (the last session in this unit). If the classroom numbers are different, make workable adjustments.

Session 4

The students will need props for their dramatizations. It will be helpful if the counselor and teacher persuade the students to take responsibility for acquiring their props. Encouragement will help ensure effective dramatizations.

Have Group 1 and Group 2 present their dramatizations of students solving problems resulting from issues of *difference*. Influence students to make their problem and its solution concrete and clear. Be affirming of the creative expressions of the students.

Discuss the two dramas with the class. Find meaningful ideas in both dramas. Be careful not to concentrate on one group more than the other. Encourage the students to share their feelings. Reflect their feelings and ask them to tune in to other students' feelings, concerns, and so forth. Stimulate the students to tell when they have felt *different* in similar situations as those dramatized in the skit.

Have the student leaders in each of the two groups summarize one or two things it would be helpful for the class to remember regarding their drama presentation. Have some students who were *not* in the dramatizations share what they appreciated in a special way about one of the dramatizations. Make sure both dramatizations are affirmed by students, by yourself and by the teacher.

The counselor closes the session with a summary and expression of appreciation to the students for their contributions to the class. Group 3 and Group 4 are reminded that they are responsible for the dramatizations concerning *differences and solutions* the next session.

Session 5

Repeat the activities of Session 4 with Group 3 and Group 4 conducting the drama presentations. At the end of the session, the counselor reminds Group 5 that they are responsible for the dramatization in the next and last session. Remind them again that solutions must accompany the story of the problem. Encourage them to be original and creative.

Session 6

Repeat the activities of Session 4 with Group 5.

Encourage the students to share their feelings. Influence the students to report when they have felt different in similar situations as those dramatized in the skit.

Tell the students that this is the last time that the class will meet about this issue for now. Assign the students to write as much as they want to tell you how they feel about the past six sessions. Ask them to do this in their free time and to bring it by the counselor's office. Write personal encouraging remarks on these student journals and return the papers to each student personally (perhaps at lunch the following week).

Conclusion

Middle grade students are energetic. They benefit from expressing their thoughts concretely. Drama provides middle grade students with the opportunity to dynamically express their thoughts. They can use their performances to problem solve, an especially beneficial activity.

Middle grade students recognize clearly when they, or specific classmates, are not accepted by other students. A setting in which an appreciation of difference is the goal is a wonderful opportunity to empower middle grade students to think about their role in accepting or rejecting other students and to enable them to effectively intervene to make the school a place where difference is valued.

Counselors affirm students by accepting what they have to say without judgment. When counselors actively listen to students and encourage students to actively listen to one another, students are accepted, affirmed, and valued. Counselors can model empathy, genuineness, and reflection; students will mirror counselor behavior.

The substitution of active listening skills and other counseling procedures for overt praise helps students move from depending on others for approval to the internalizing of approval. Middle grade students who experience genuine acceptance of their expressed thoughts and points of view develop the ability to appreciate the points of view of others even when those points of view differ from theirs.

High School Students

Introduction

High school students are moving from conforming to their peers and feeling unreasonable guilt for nonconforming behavior to being able to evaluate their own behavior somewhat more objectively. They are beginning to turn inward and develop an interior life. This interior life is directly related to their new abilities to think abstractly. In general, high school students are developing the capability to think logically and rationally.

It is the responsibility of the school counselor, where possible, to enhance these developing powers. The interventions reported here are planned to encourage and stimulate the new potency of high school students. Being comfortable with difference is one way that adolescents mature. Adolescents require assistance to grow in their capacity to use their new abilities to appreciate difference and thereby be prepared to effectively contribute as a citizen in a culturally diverse society.

High school students are beginning to be able to set goals for themselves. They are beginning to learn how to take the perspective of others without judgment when encouraged to do so. Older high school students can be encouraged to see life as complex, not simple, as *both/and* rather than *either/or.*

One of the most important roles of high school counselors is to help high school students make meaning of their school, home, and community experiences and to use these experiences as opportunities for maturation. This is especially true when helping high school students to understand their own prejudices and the consequences to them and to others in their lives. Furthermore, when dealing with diversity with high school students the issues of prejudice, bigotry, and racism must be addressed directly.

Counselors have the responsibility to be aware of and to manage their own prejudices before they can effectively deal with the those of their students and the institutional racism of the school. The issues of diversity cannot be dealt with effectively unless the issues of prejudice, bigotry, and racism are dealt with openly and honestly.

The following six large group guidance sessions are planned for a class of 20 or more high school students in a full 50 minute class period. There is a great difference in maturity between ninth and twelfth grades. These activities can be modified to address the specific needs of each of the four high school years. Each session begins with a stimulating activity the purpose of which is to focus the group and to contribute to the cohesion of the group.

Session 1

Each student needs a piece of paper and a pen.

Have the students place the name by which they like to be called in the middle of a piece of paper (a 5 by 7 card). In the upper left hand corner, have them write the place where they were born; in the upper right hand corner, a place they have visited in the past year; in the lower right hand corner, one thing that they would like everyone to know about them; and in the lower left hand corner one thing they do not want people to know about them.

Have each student share what they have written in only one of the corners of the paper with the other members of the group. Have each member of the class tell *one* person what they remember about what that student shared. *These responses must be without any judgment words. Ask them to clarify and/or reflect one another's thoughts and feelings. They must be straightforward evidence that one student heard the other student without judgment or evaluation.* You will want to demonstrate such responses before students begin their interactions.

Talk about how they chose the corner of the paper that they shared with the group. List the responses in columns under headings (1) where I was born, (2) where I have visited, (3) what I want to share, (4) what I do not want to share. Count the numbers of responses in each column. Make a generalization about the kinds of things that they were willing to share with one another. Have students share feelings about the written corners that might have made them different from others in the group (e.g., maybe one person was born outside the country or state; perhaps another had not visited any place outside the neighborhood in the past year). Infer how *difference* can, at times, make us feel uncomfortable. Sometimes the person who feels different feels uncomfortable; sometimes people feel uncomfortable around others whom they perceive as different. Conclude by discussing how we handle difference in the home, community, and school settings.

Session 2

Materials needed for this session are both a Mercator projection and a Peters projection of the world map.

Almost every American high school classroom has a Mercator projection of the world map. Place this map where the students can see it clearly. Next to it place a Peters projection of the world map.

Use the information on the Peters projection to point out the differences between the two maps: Explain as follows:

The traditional map portrays the world to the advantage of European colonial powers. The land mass of the northern hemisphere, in actual fact, is half as large as the land mass of the southern hemisphere but appears on the Mercator maps to be much larger.

The traditional map was devised by Mercator in 1569 in Germany. It shows Europe larger than South America, which is almost double the size of Europe. It places Germany in the middle, even though it is in the northernmost quarter of the earth.

The traditional map distorts not only Europe in relation to the rest of the world. The American continents also are shown in false proportions: Alaska appears about three times as large as Mexico, though in reality Mexico is larger.

The traditional map is skewed to the advantage of the northern hemisphere where whites have traditionally lived. Africa is made to look smaller than some land masses of the northern hemisphere when in actual fact it is much larger.

The traditional map exaggerates the northernmost areas; as a result, southern areas seem small by comparison. Greenland appears to be larger than China, thought China is actually four times as large.

The traditional map distorts the world to the advantage of the countries in which white people predominate. Though Scandinavia appears to be larger than India, India is actually about three times larger.

The traditional map is not compatible with objectivity, which is required in a scientific age. Two-thirds of the map is taken up to represent the northern hemisphere, while the southern hemisphere is compressed in the remaining one-third (World Map, 1983).

Explain to the class that a culture that teaches that big is better encourages distortions detrimental to high school students' developing a realistic view of the world. The purpose of using this comparison of the Mercator and Peters projections in this session is to begin the development of an understanding of point of view and the influence of one's point of view on the development of one's attitudes toward one's place in the culturally diverse world.

Conclude by having the students share their feelings about these two maps. It has been experienced that this exercise stimulates high school students to think and share their feelings about the curricula to which they are being, and have been exposed. Counselors have the opportunity to help students think analytically about exclusive curricula and its limitations and the need for inclusive curricula. Counselors can help students think about how they can influence the things they learn in school by choosing inclusive topics when researching assignments, by reading related literature with differing points of view from that which they are studying, and by asking informed questions in class.

Session 3

Choose an historical event related to the content of the student's study in their classes (e.g., the voyages of Columbus, the Middle Passage, or Westward Expansion). Have the students review the facts about this event briefly. Then have the students look at the event from the point of view of each of the groups of people who were impacted by the event. For example, the voyages of Columbus impacted the experiences of Native Americans, Africans, and Europeans. The Middle Passage impacted the lives of Africans, Europeans, and United States Americans of European and African heritage. Westward expansion was *Manifest Destiny* from the point of view of the United States government and European American settlers but a series of massacres from the point of view of Native American peoples. Hold a discussion on how a Native American might describe the "Winning of the West?" How Hispanic Americans would describe the "Battle of the Alamo?" How African American might describe "Plymouth Rock?" "How an Anglo would describe the historical significance of Selma, Alabama?" Ask the students to share other similar concepts.

High school students will follow this consideration with reflections of their own related to their personal experiences. The content of this discussion will differ a great deal depending upon the ethnic and lived experiences of the students present. The counselor will want to move the students to understand how their personal perspective on historical events is related to their own experiences of diversity in their respective high school, community, churches, and homes. The counselor will need to use attending skills, empathic responding, and encouragement in order to stimulate higher order thinking on the part of the students regarding how the differing perspectives of the people involved in an historical event is related to the way they think and behave around diversity in their lives.

Session 4

Put the words *prejudice, bigotry,* and *racism* on the chalkboard or flip chart. Have the students, in turn, share with the group their meanings of each of these words. Encourage the students to give examples. Point out that prejudice and bigotry are personal, and racism is prejudice plus the power to enforce the prejudice.

Now write the phrase *institutional racism*. Tell the students how racism can be systemic and systematic, pervasive and deliberate. Give examples, and encourage the students to give examples.

Tell the students the story of the Lomboko Slave Fortress in Sierra Leone, the Portuguese Slave Ship Tekora, and the Spanish Slave Ship La Amistad. Show the students the video tape of that part of Steven Spielberg's Amistad when Anthony Hopkins playing John Quincy Adams presents the case of Cinque played by Djimon Hounsou and the other Africans in the Amistad case before the Supreme Court of the United States in 1839.

Concentrate on two issues: (1) the reasons that the students were not taught about La Amistad in their United States history courses, and (2) the words of John Quincy Adams when he said to the Supreme Court, which was made up of seven holders of people in slavery out of nine members:

Cinque, would you stand up if you would; so everyone can see you. This man is Black, we can all see that, but can we all see as easily that which is equally true that he is the only true hero in this room?

Now if he were white, he wouldn't be standing before this Court fighting for his life. If he were white and his enslavers were British, he wouldn't be able to stand, so heavy the weight of the medals and honors we would bestow upon him. Songs would be written about him. The great authors of our times would fill books about him. His story would be told and retold in our classrooms. Our children, because we would make sure of it, would know his name as well as they know Patrick Henry's....

Talk with the students about institutional racism. Dialogue with them about overt racism and more subtle forms of racism. Encourage them to talk openly about times when they have experienced racism or have seen racism.

Close by letting the students journal for about five or ten minutes. Collect their journal papers; write encouraging remarks on them; return them to the students personally during the week. Remind the students that there is only one more session for now.

Steven Spielberg's film Amistad can provide the counselor with the information to tell the La Amistad story. There is a great deal of violence and some nudity, both in an historical context and appropriately handled, in this film. Hence, it is not recommended that the counselor require that the students see this film in its entirety.

Session 5

You will need newsprint, magic markers, and masking tape for this activity.

Have at least as many stories or current events from the recent news regarding racial or ethnic relations in the United States as you will have groups of students in this activity. Review the facts of the cases.

Divide the students into groups of five or another convenient grouping depending upon the size of the class. You can randomly assign groups or let the students choose their groups. The groups can be racially mixed or racially the same. The dynamics will be different depending upon how the groups are assigned and the make up of the groups. However, both can be fruitful experiences. Both can be opportunities for teachable moments.

Invite the students of each group to analyze the case that they have from the point of view of all those involved and from the point of view of each member of the group. Have the students generalize from what they learned in the last four sessions about prejudice, bigotry, and racism to the contents of the current even that they are analyzing.

After about 20 minutes, have the students write three sentences on newsprint that summarizes what they have learned as a group. Have the students hang these papers on the wall. Return the students to the large group and invite them to read their sentences to the class.

Close by summarizing what has happened in the session. Pay particular attention to ways in which points of view were different or the same. Let the students know that you are aware of the effort that this exercise took. Thank the students for their hard work and commitment to growth.

Session 6

Inform the students that this is the last time they will meet about this issue at this time, but that their teacher will, from time to time, continue the discussion. Have students review their experiences over the last five weeks and apply them to their experiences in school, community, and home. The role of the counselor is to provide the students with an opportunity to express their real feelings without evaluation or judgment. Students, with the counselor's assistance, can use the session to understand one another's points of view. From common issues about which students might disagree, consensus building might be done with the help of the counselor and the teacher. Students can be asked to personally Agree, Disagree, or be Undecided concerning the topic at hand.

Encourage the students to discuss the issues of prejudice, bigotry, and racism that are part of their lived experience. European-American students may have been aware of times when they have been privileged by their race. For example, they may have been approached by a salesperson before a person of color even when the person of color had been waiting longer than they. Ask that such experienced be shared with the group.

Counselors do have to be careful that blatant racism does not go unchallenged. This can be done by letting the students know that racism is learned, that there is no evidence to support racist points of view, and that we are certainly more alike than we are different. At the same time, there are ways in which we are different, and the valuing of difference can be enriching for all.

Close by having the students share what they personally will do to work for an inclusive home, school, and community. Have them put into writing (they keep it) one thing that they will do to help bring about the valuing of diversity at school — a personal contract. Then, as you encounter these students in the coming weeks, ask if they've "carried out" that personal contract.

Conclusion

Very often high school students in a supportive setting that addresses the issues related to diversity will share experiences that they have had in class or in the school that they need to personally understand better. For example, African American students will tell of being ignored in class, being sanctioned in class for reasons they do not understand, and being singled out for behavior that they see not being sanctioned in non-African American students.

Summary

Counselors have the opportunity to provide these students with tools for feeling empowered. Adolescents need to feel in control of their lives. They are moving from childhood where someone else controlled their lives to adulthood where they will make serious decisions about their lives and begin to rationally think about the consequences of their behaviors. Very often, adolescents act out when they feel powerless in the face of situations that they know are not just.

European American students may feel free to overtly express their feelings of racism against the African American students. They may not understand their feelings in relation to African American, Hispanic, or Asian Pacific Islander students, and so forth. Counselors have the opportunity to support their expressions of feelings while at the same time helping them to change their understandings and behaviors concerning others who are different.

Educators are preparing the citizens for a significantly different United States and world. Myriad data can be provided to support the conclusion that the United States of America is becoming more and more culturally diverse. In addition, the nations of the world, not even studied in United States schools just a generation ago, are impacting on the lives of United States citizens in new and disparate ways.

If counselors use developmentally appropriate, creative strategies such as those described herein, they can contribute to the empowering of students at all levels to assess difference, appreciate difference, and esteem difference. When students feel empowered, then they can be encouraged to operationalize these skills and use the very difference to grow personally and to make the institutions of the home, church, school, and civic community more nearly whole and healthy.

Counselors are part of the educational system which has the responsibility to prepare students for culturally diverse societies. Those who are effective in the coming generations will of necessity have to be able to be comfortable with diversity and be able to contribute among diverse peoples, languages, and points of view. All students have the right to participate successfully in a culturally diverse society. Counselors can provide students with the opportunity to develop, evolve, and mature in ways in which they will become competent to exercise that right effectively.

References

Faubert, M. (1992). *Cognitive and ego development of successful African American rural youth: Deliberate psychological education.* Unpublished doctoral dissertation, North Carolina State University, Raleigh.

Faubert, M., & Locke, D.C. (1993). Getting on the right track: A program for African-American high school students. *The School Counselor, 41,* 129-133.

Faubert, M., Locke, D.C., Sprinthall, N.A., & Howland, W.H. (1996). Promoting cognitive and ego development of African-American rural youth: A program of deliberate psychological education. *Journal of Adolescence, 19,* 533-543.

Hilliard, A.G., Payton-Stewart, L., & Williams, L.0. (Ens.). (1990). *Infusion of African and African American content in the school curriculum: Proceedings of the first national conference October, 1989.* Morristown, NJ: Aaron.

Locke, D.C. (1998). *Increasing multicultural understanding: A comprehensive model* (2nd ed.). Thousand Oaks, CA: Sage.

Sprinthall, N.A., & Mosher, R.L. (Eds.). (1978). *Value development as the aim of education.* Schenectady, NY: Character Research.

Texas Education Agency. (1998). *A model developmental guidance and counseling program for Texas public schools: A guide for program development pre-k-12th grade.* Austin, TX: Author.

U.S. Bureau of the Census. (1988). *Statistical abstract of the United States* (31st ed.). Washington, DC: Author.

World map in equal presentation: Peters projection. (1983). Cincinnati, OH: Friendship.

Chapter 13

The School Counselor's Role in Prevention and Remediation of Child Abuse

by

**JoAnna White
and Mary Flynt**

JoAnna White, EdD., a Professor in the Department of Counseling and Psychological Services at Georgia State University, is a former school counselor and coordinator of the school counseling program at Georgia State University. She has many years of experience in counseling abused children and consulting with their families.

Mary Flynt, EdS., a school counselor at Nesbit Elementary School in the Gwinnett County School System near Atlanta, has worked extensively with students and school personnel In the areas of behavioral diagnosis and remediation. She is also an adjunct instructor at Georgia State University.

Introduction

School counselors are called upon to provide a variety of services to students, teachers, parents, and administrators and have become their school's number one expert on affective education. In order to ensure that students are emotionally prepared to learn, the school counselor must assure that all students are provided a place where they feel safe and valued. Of the variety of children and adolescents seen by the school counselor, no student is more in need of an adult who will listen, understand, and advocate for them than the one who has been abused.

With the dramatic increase in the number of reported cases of child abuse in the United States and the increase of violence in the schools as well as in homes, school counselors are increasingly called upon to report cases of child abuse, coordinate counseling services for abused students, and develop child abuse prevention programs for the schools in which they are employed. In this chapter the writers describe types of abuse and the role of the school counselor in employing remediation and prevention efforts to deal with child abuse issues.

Child abuse and children's rights are relatively new concepts when one considers that legal rights for adults, and not children, are documented throughout history. In fact, the history of child rearing, until the mid-twentieth century, appears to be synonymous with the history of child abuse. Attitudes toward children have traditionally been ones of ownership and indifference in which child abuse of all kinds was the norm. Alice Miller (1990) called this attitude toward children "poisonous pedagogy." This attitude is driven by the mistaken belief that we must retaliate against children for their own good; in other words "spare the rod and spoil the child."

Throughout history one can read accounts where children have been wrapped in swaddling clothes, sexually molested, tortured, killed to fulfill religious rites, abandoned, sent away to monasteries, ignored, starved, and generally emotionally abused and neglected. Not until 1974 did Congress pass the Child Abuse and Prevention and Treatment Act (Paisley, 1987). This act required each state to develop a policy for reporting and investigating child abuse. Today, each state and the District of Columbia have passed this type of legislation (Paisley, 1987). It is legally mandated, as well as ethically correct, that school counselors *must report any and all cases of suspected child abuse.*

In spite of the fact that each state recognizes that child abuse is illegal and society is becoming more aware of the realities of child abuse, in 1998 there were still 1,200 child abuse related deaths in the United States. This was a five percent increase over child fatalities of the previous year. This translates into three victims of fatal child abuse each day (Georgia Council on Child Abuse, 1999). The Georgia Council on Child Abuse (1999) also reported that in 1997 an estimated 3.19 million children were reported to have been abused. Every 4 to 7 seconds a child is abused or neglected (Glosoff & Kiprowicz, cited in Thompson & Rudolph, 1992).

Abusive detachment from children is evident in our society wherever one chooses to look. Adults are often obsessed with the attainment of wealth and status. They are stressed with their "getter" life-style and unavailable to their children. There is little time for play with their child. Even on vacations, many families plan to go to a place where they can engage in adult fun (golf, tennis) and their children are put in structured activities away from them.

On the other end of the continuum, parents are struggling with the inability to make a living, lack of adequate child care, and stress related issues such as drug or alcohol abuse. These societal stressors are precursors to abusive situations, ranging from emotional detachment to violence and sexual abuse.

Ethical and Legal Issues

School personnel have learned to rely on their counselors when confronted with procedural and legal concerns regarding the subject of abuse. In order to fulfill the requirements of efficient crisis intervention, counselors must have a clear understanding of the existing legal parameters. School administrators are increasingly utilizing a counselor's expertise and special training as a source of leadership and responsibility for identifying and reporting cases of child abuse to the investigative agency, sometimes titled the Department of Family and Children Services (DFACS), Health and Rehabilitation Services (HRS) and so forth. Throughout this chapter the writers refer to this service as DFACS.

School districts are required to offer their support by providing a written policy for counselors and other employees of the district to follow when abuse is suspected. As an example, in the Gwinnett County Schools in Georgia, as well as all others, school personnel who fail to report their suspicions to the school designed may be prosecuted under state law. Typically, school counselors and school personnel are also granted immunity from liability because they are presumed to be acting in good faith. To further ensure clear application of the law, DFACS representatives in Gwinnett County and a specialist in school law serve as consultants at yearly staff development offerings for all county counselors. This information is then shared with local school staff through special meetings led by the school counselor.

Gwinnett County, Georgia Child Protective Services is no exception to the case overloads experienced by similar agencies throughout the country. This situation creates delays and breakdowns in the system. As cited by Sandberg, Crabbs, and Crabbs (1988), one way in which school counselors can help to expedite the investigative process is to cultivate a professional working relationship with the state appointed protective service worker. Counselors' busy schedules should be interrupted if necessary to allow for visits and or calls from DFACS personnel. Communication with DFACS workers should facilitate the acquisition of helpful case related information and provide a supportive atmosphere in which the serious and painful reality of abuse can be treated. The child further benefits from this cooperative approach by the familiar and reassuring presence of the school counselor during the investigation conducted by the DFACS worker.

The existence of a school team composed of three or four school members to handle abuse cases enhances the accuracy of the abuse report by clarifying any discrepancies existing among other professional educators before the report is filed by the counselor (Howell-Nigrelli, 1988). The involvement of several school members necessitates the clear awareness on the part of the counselor of the issue of responsibilities to the student as outlined in the Ethical Standards of the American Counseling Association (ACA) and the 1998 Ethical Standards for School Counselors of the American School Counselor Association.

As a counselor, you will want to make the abused student aware of the steps and procedures to be followed prior to any action taken with his/her particular case. The distrust and sense of hopelessness associated with the experience of abuse are considerably lowered (toward the professionals involved in the reporting aspect of the case) when the child is cognizant of the future steps that will be taken in his or her behalf. The assurance of confidentiality and knowledge of the procedures encourages the victim to disclose in an accurate and confident manner. In reference to record keeping, counselors should note the dates of interventions in abbreviated form. This note taking is for the school counselor's knowledge rather than documentation for other agencies.

The 1999 ASCA Position Statement accentuated the importance of the issue of confidentiality and reestablishing the trust of the child after the report of abuse is made. It is the opinion of the writers that your relationship with the child must remain intact so that ongoing counseling services can continue after the crisis is over and/or referred to appropriate community agencies. Your role as a child advocate is at the heart of the issue of efficient and successful solutions to child abuse. Your utilization of up-to-date information and skillful ethical practices will produce positive outcomes for children and parents involved in the tragedy of family violence. (ASCA, 1999).

Types of Child Abuse

Neglect

Neglect has been defined as the failure by the parents to provide those things needed for the child's healthy growth and development. This concept implies that harm may come to the child as a result of the parents unreliability as providers (McFadden, 1987). Indicators include:

- Abandonment
- Lack of supervision
- Lack of adequate clothing and good hygiene
- Lack of medical or dental care
- Lack of adequate education
- Lack of adequate nutrition
- Lack of adequate shelter

The ASCA position statement adds "exploitation" and "overworking of children" to the previously cited characteristics of neglect. It is often extremely difficult to obtain decisive action from investigative agencies when cases of neglect are reported by the school counselor. This is usually because of the lack of concrete evidence. This sad state of affairs, however, should not be a deterrent to the reporting process. ASCA (1993) emphasized that it is the legal responsibility of the school counselor to report suspected child abuse, not to be responsible for conducting the investigation.

Behavioral signs of neglect need to be constantly monitored by the school counselor in order to ensure affirmative action during the investigative process. They are as follows:

- The child begs or steals food.
- The child attends school in an erratic manner.
- The child is addicted to alcohol or other drugs.
- The child engages in delinquent acts such as vandalism or theft.
- The child states that there is no one to take care of or look after him or her.
- The child constantly falls asleep at school.
- The child comes to school very early and leaves very late (Crosson Tower, 1984).

When dealing with cases of suspected neglect the school counselor must actively work to have daily and/or weekly involvement with the child. Even though the counselor's role only requires reporting the neglect, a substantial amount of information gathered (i.e., dates of absences, duration of illnesses, etc.) creates a much stronger case. Such counselor initiated documentation enables the DFACS worker to proceed in a more decisive and swift manner.

Statistics given by a national study of reported child maltreatment shows that neglect causes more deaths than physical abuse in children. The American Humane Association (cited in McFadden, 1990) indicated that 4% of the population of children studied experienced major physical injury, while 60% experienced a type of physical neglect. Neglect was associated with 56% of child deaths. In view of these data, counselors have an ethical and humane responsibility to engage in the painstaking and often times frustrating labor of tracking suspicions of neglect.

As counselors become involved with the child within the context of the family, it becomes important to be able to identify common characteristics of the neglectful caretaker. These parents/guardians may have a chaotic home life, may live in unsafe conditions, may be mentally retarded, may abuse drugs or alcohol, may be impulsive individuals, may be employed but unable to afford child care, have experienced little or no success in life, have little motivation or skill to create changes in their lives, and tend to be passive.

One important consideration to investigate is whether the resulting conditions of maltreatment are present because of poverty or neglectful parental behaviors. Through effective, non-judgmental parent consultation, the school counselor can obtain a clear assessment of the situation and offer referral sources, such as free medical services or mental health services that in many instances may improve the situation at home. These successful exchanges foster positive and open relations between home and school. In many instances the child's situation will improve as the parent becomes connected with a caring professional such as the school counselor.

Individual counseling and small group counseling are preferred interventions to use with the abused child. Encouragement, problem solving skills, coping skills related to latchkey issues, the use of play tools in counseling are all important components that address the low self-esteem and the sense of helplessness often felt by the neglected child.

Emotional Abuse

Emotional abuse or neglect implies a consistent indifference to the child's needs and covers a range of behaviors. It is an underlining consequence present in all forms of abuse and one of the hardest conditions to prove in court. It can be observed in the following examples:

- Parent who never speaks to the child

- Psychotic parent unable to acknowledge the reality of the child's world

- Parent who actively rejects the child through verbal abuse and excessive punishment (McFadden, 1990).

School counselors caseloads are flooded by emotional abuse and neglect. Garbarino, Guttrnan, and Seeley (1986) described five types of psychological maltreatment: rejecting, isolating, terrorizing, ignoring, and corrupting. They also accentuate the importance of prevention and intervention techniques utilized with families and the community at-large. The counseling channels suggested are marital counseling, family therapy, parent/child intervention methods for working with socially isolated families, and educating the public. The three latter suggestions can be included in the school counselor delivery systems such as PTA meetings, parent study groups, individual consultation and follow-up with parents. Efforts in emotional abuse prevention are especially important because it is difficult to show concrete evidence to the investigative agency. The difficulty in showing proof of abuse often leaves the school personnel as the only advocates for this child. Crosson Tower (1984) identified certain behavioral indicators as follows:

- Habit disorders (bed wetting, sucking, hitting, rocking)

- Conduct disorders (withdrawal and antisocial behavior; destructiveness, cruelty, stealing)

- Neurotic traits (sleep disorders, inhibited play)

- Psychoneurotic reactions (hysteria, obsession, phobias, hypochondria)

- Behavior extremes (passive-aggressive, very demanding or compliant)

- Overly adaptive behaviors (parenting other children or infantile behavior)

- Lags in emotional and intellectual behavior

- Attempted suicide

The lines that exist between faulty parenting skills and actually damaging interactions are difficult to define. School counselors must rely on their psycho-educational skills to provide a support system within the school setting. The appropriate school placement, taking into consideration the psychological as well as the developmental needs of this child, must be the result of counselor coordinated efforts that involves teacher consultation and staff development on psychological maltreatment. Healthy adult role models in the schools might be the only opportunity available to children to learn how to value themselves and others.

Sometimes school personnel themselves are perpetrators of emotional abuse of students. Krugman and Krugman (cited in Neese, 1989) found, after investigating third and fourth grade classrooms, psychologically abusive teacher behaviors that included labeling, screaming at children, allowing some children to harass others, and setting unrealistic academic goals. School counselors must be leaders in adjusting and changing the climate in schools where teachers and peers may be among the perpetrators of emotional abuse.

In Alachua County, Florida reports of sexual harassment were made by several students in that school system to the Board of Education. Reports of students being sexually molested by other students in the school restrooms were reported along with some parents' emotional pleas for a school policy to prevent this from happening again. One middle school student stated that when she reported being molested to some teachers and female counselors, they told her that she had brought the attacks on herself (Silva, 1992). These mixed messages of who is responsible for abuse and violence are confusing ones to children and youth. The Alachua County Florida School System now has a sexual harassment policy in place, and, any such harassment, at any grade level, is not tolerated.

The counseling utilized in dealing with the emotionally maltreated child needs to allow the child to proceed at his or her own pace. That is, where the tools of communication are controlled by the child, whether they may be drawings, puppets, playing with a doll house, storytelling, and so forth. The sensitive counselor can sometimes break through the wall of secrecy created by parental threats or excessive loyalty to the family and bring a change to this child's life by reporting the pertinent information to the authorities and/or forming a bond of trust and respect with the child (McFadden, 1990).

Physical Abuse

Physical abuse of children involves non-accidental physical injury. Indicators include:

- Unexplained bruises or welts
- Unexplained burns
- Unexplained fractures
- Unexplained lacerations or abrasions
- Ünexplained death

Physical abuse may occur through hitting, beating, kicking, pinching, or falls that are a result of aggression from an adult. Even though accidents do happen to children it is the counselor's duty to thoroughly investigate the incident, especially with children who have repeated injuries. In many instances children are threatened not to tell, so they cover up the incident by stating that it was an accident. It is important for counselors to be aware of the probability of this happening and continue to follow through (McFadden, 1987).

As a school counselor, you will want to be aware of the behavioral indicators of physical abuse in order to identify and help these children. White and Allers (1994) conducted a literature review of the play behaviors of abused children. They found that these children are often developmentally immature, oppositional and aggressive, withdrawn and passive, self-deprecating/self-destructive, and hypervigilant. They further contended that abused children exhibit literal play themes that tend to be repetitive and compulsive in nature. Elementary school counselors should have a heightened awareness of these issues as they work with children in individual play counseling and in play groups.

Adolescent physical abuse does occur, but it is often incorrectly identified. Unfortunately, adults often have the attitude that adolescents can take care of themselves. Signs of adolescent abuse may be:

- Rebelliousness/problems with authority figures
- Drug and alcohol abuse
- Running away
- Change in grades and academic attitudes
- Withdrawing
- General lack of self esteem
- Unusual compliance toward adults

In addition, children's and adolescent's artwork will often serve as a metaphor for the child's and teen's abusive situation. Drawings may display violence, threatening figures, and large adult figures in relation to small child figures who appear powerless (McFadden, 1987). The child's use of colors and the intensity with which they draw are also indicators of their emotionality related to the physical abuse. The use of blacks, brown, and other dark colors along with heavy strokes could possibly indicate anger and violence, while faint lines using pencils or other light colors could indicate evasiveness and low self-esteem.

Sexual Abuse

Sexual abuse is the exploitation of a child for sexual gratification of an adult or an older child (Georgia Council on Child Abuse, 1999). Sexual abuse includes exhibitionism, the exposure of children to pornographic material, the use of children in pornographic materials, fondling, and intercourse. Often sexual abuse involves an incestuous relationship. Vanderbilt (1992) described incest as, "any sexual abuse of a child by a relative or other person in a position of authority over the child." Vanderbilt estimates that one in three persons are the victims of incest before the age of 18. Incest involves a second traumatizing dynamic for the child because he or she cannot run home for help. The abuser is usually in the home.

Because sexual abuse is not as evident as the signs of physical abuse, it is even more important that the school counselor be aware of the signs of sexual abuse. They are often subtle and more difficult to detect than are signs of physical abuse.

Signs of sexual abuse may include:

- Sleep disorders
- Enuresis or fecal retention
- Fear of being alone with an adult
- Low self-esteem
- Eating disorders
- Inappropriate sexual behaviors toward adults or other children
- Masturbation in public
- Poor peer relationships
- Withdrawal
- Dissociation

- Sudden drop in school performance
- Difficulty in walking or sitting
- Urinary tract infections, yeast infections, pain or itching in genital area
- Suicide attempts (especially in adolescents)
- Chronic runaway (adolescents)
- Anorexia (adolescents)
- Early pregnancies (adolescents)

In their literature review, White and Allers (1994) indicated that in addition to the typical play behaviors of physically abused children, sexually abused children often exhibit play behaviors that are sexually beyond their developmental age. They are often hypervigilant or protective of themselves from any perceived danger. In addition, they often exhibit a behavior known as dissociation in which they appear to go off to another place. For example, one child expressed that she was "in the wall" when her counselor asked what she was thinking. Dissociation is a way for the child to escape from the reality of sexual abuse.

Several experts suggested that the use of art materials is an appropriate counseling technique for sexually abused victims (Hackbarth, Murphy, & McQuary, 1991; Riordan & Verdel, 1991; Sadowski, & Loesch) 1993). Drawing provides a safe way for these children and adolescents to ventilate their feelings and show the counselor what they are dealing with. Pelcovitz (cited in Hackbarth, et al., 1991) stated that school personnel often join in the denial system surrounding sexual abuse. They fail to pick up clues, possibly because it is too emotional for them (Roscoe, cited in Hackboarth, et al., 1991). Art activities may be an answer to missing cues from abused children and adolescents.

The artwork for sexually abused children and adolescents may include many of the themes described previously for physically abused children. In addition, there may be more themes of violence, sexuality, or aggression. Children and adolescents may draw people with no eyes or no mouth. If there are eyes present, they may be just dots that no one could see out of. There may also be people in the drawings who have a marked division between the upper body and the lower body such as emphasis on the waist or a line drawn across the neck. Further, the child or adolescent may draw people with just heads and no bodies.

Abuse Prevention

The concept of prevention is an integral component of a developmental school guidance and counseling program. Paisley (1987) described the early involvement of school counselors centered around the tasks of identification and intervention "after the fact" for abused and neglected children. The importance of these roles is not to be discounted; however, the child advocacy movement has precipitated the effort of addressing the issues of abuse prior to its occurrence. There are a variety of prevention programs in use at the present time. The most comprehensive plan for schools is the one that would include a variety of publics by targeting parents, school personnel, teachers, and students. Researchers have met little success in evaluating prevention programs. Gerler (1988) recommended that school counselors who are involved with abuse cases in a direct manner need to continue to work towards the development of effective treatment programs as well as the implementation of promising programs of child abuse prevention. It is important to note that no one program can reach out to all the publics you have as a school counselor. A variety of program strategies can best address the multiple objectives of a comprehensive abuse prevention curriculum. The following is a skeletal outline of abuse prevention programming.

Preventive

Target Population	Strategies	Outcomes

Students	Classroom guidance And Small Groups
	1. Sequential
	2. Age appropriate
	3. Variety of techniques
	   A. Role play
	   B. Puppets
	   C. Discussion
	   D. Open-ended stories
	   E. Information giving
		1. Develop assertive skills
		2. Develop problem-solving skills
		3. Increased self-esteem
		4. Increased awareness of their rights

Parents	1. Individual Consultation 2. PTA program 3. Material preview night 4. Parent education classes	1. Parenting skills 2. Improved communication skills with their child 3. Increased knowledge of community resources 4. Increased trust in school personnel
Teachers	1. Individual consultation 2. Staff development (faculty meetings, teacher groups, written handouts)	1. Improved skills for Identification of abuses 2. Increased knowledge concerning reporting process 3. Ability to communicate more effectively with the abused student.

A review of the literature, Allsopp and Prosen (1988), Vernon and Hay (1988), the Curriculum for Prevention of Child Sexual Abuse written by Bridgework Theater Inc. (cited in, Shewmaker, 1988), Thompson and Rudolph (1992), and Tenant (1988), revealed certain educational objectives must be present in order to ensure the effectiveness of sexual abuse prevention programs. They are as follows:

- Sexual abuse may be inflicted by someone known by the child.

- Identify who can offer help.

- If the adult does not believe the child try, other adults until someone does.

- Sexual abuse occurs in many ways other than just touching.

- Differentiate between good touches, bad touches, and confusing touches.

- Sexual abuse is never the child's fault.

- The importance of verbalizing feelings connected with the abuse.

- Secrets are not OK unless they are about something positive.

- It is important to tell so the abuser can get help and no one else will be victimized.

- People can get into difficult situations but that does not mean that they are bad people.

- When to trust and when to be cautious.

- Not all adults are to be obeyed, how to tell the difference.

- Teach the child to say "no" to inappropriate abuse behavior.

Thompson and Rudolph (1992) pointed out that because of children's developing cognition, and in order to soften the anxiety connected with sexual abuse, most programs utilize a variety of activities such as role play, coloring books, films, and puppets. Prevention programs are delivered to adolescents within the context of human sexuality programs, dating issues and communication skills training. Freeman and Hart-Rossi (cited in Hollander, 1989) summed up the concept of prevention by pointing out that children who are empowered by knowing what steps to take concerning the prevention and handling of abuse are less likely to be victimized.

Abuse Remediatlon

Play counseling can be an effective technique for elementary school counselors to use with children who are suspected of being abused. Because children cannot engage in "talk therapy" due to their developmental level, play provides a comfortable environment in which they can express and explore interpersonal conflicts through the use of toys and art materials. Experts agree that children need play in order to learn and develop, yet abused children often do not or cannot play due to malnutrition, neglect, overwhelming anxieties, unrealistic adult expectations, or perfectionism (McFadden, 1987).

White and Allers (1994) stated that even though there is little empirical research on the relationship of play therapy to abuse issues of children, most of the anecdotal literature suggests that it is effective. In addition, this process affords the counselor the opportunity to observe patterns of play that may indicate abuse. As previously mentioned in this chapter, these patterns revolve around literal, compulsive, repetitive play in which the child has difficulty being creative or imaginative.

Through the use of individual play counseling or small group play, the school counselor can help children work through fears and anxieties, learn how to play freely, and increase self-esteem. The school counselor can help children and adolescents create a safe distance from the abuse through age appropriate toys, artwork, puppetry, dramatic play, and expressive, movement play.

Remediation in the school should incorporate three major phases: identifying, reporting, and follow-up. This process cannot end after the physical signs have healed and the abuser has been relieved of the custody of the child. In many instances the child continues to live in the same abusive environment, which creates a mandate to remain involved with the child. Thompson and Rudolph (1992) pointed out that the violation of the victims' trust level influences their ability to verbalize and benefit from traditional counseling methods. McFadden (1987) stressed that in view of the mistrust and pain experienced by abused children, the counselor needs to provide a safe place and a safe relationship within which the child may experiment with new adaptation to a safer world. The awareness of the normal developmental process of children and ways in which this step by step process becomes altered are important concepts to consider in working with maltreated children.

The following is a remedial sequence for school counselors to follow and two case studies to illustrate the comprehensive nature of this process.

Remedial

I. Identification

    A. Teacher referral

    B. Student self referral

    C. Family referral

    D. DFACS referral

II. Reporting process

    A. Referral to principal or principal designate (School Counselor)

    B. Student interview by School Counselor

    C. DFACS contacted by School Counselor

    D. School Counselor available for DFACS visitation to school (Ideally the school counselor should be present for child/DFACS interview) (In some states the professional first suspicious of abuse is required to make the phone call to DFACS).

III. Counseling

    A. Follow-up with child and teacher

    B. Further consultation may take place with DFACS and police officer in case of student removal from the home.

    C. Provide counseling (individual, small group)

    D. Possible parent consultation, parent volunteer, and peer helper

Case Study 1: Elementary Child

Identification Process

Danielle was a six-year-old kindergarten student who transferred to School X during the seventh month of the school year. She lived in an apartment housing complex with her mother and mother's boyfriend. There was a great-aunt who lived nearby and baby-sat with the child on a daily basis. Danielle exhibited a variety of characteristics that concerned the classroom teacher, such as: tardiness, excessive sleeping at school, unkempt appearance and daydreaming. The teacher, Mrs. B., consulted with the counselor describing Danielle as a compliant child who utilized her vivid imagination when asked about her family. The teacher added that she had been unable to establish contact with the mother.

The counselor saw the child for play sessions twice and excellent rapport was established through play media.

Reporting Process

One early morning Danielle's great-aunt, Rose, reported to the counselor that Danielle had been beaten and terrorized by the mother's boyfriend. After reassuring Rose and answering her questions concerning the reporting process, the counselor interviewed the child. She related that her "dad" had thrown her against the wall and hit her with his belt because she could not find her shoes. She was still very sore from the injuries on her back and leg.

After actively listening to Danielle's story, the counselor proceeded to tell her that what happened was not her fault and beating her in such a manner was wrong. The counselor also told her about the reporting process, as follows: "There are some people I know whose job it is to help children and their families. They also make sure that children are safe from harm." The counselor then asked:

"How would you feel more comfortable showing me the marks. Would you like to do it in my office or maybe in the office's bathroom." She chose the office's bathroom. There were purple lacerations on the buttocks and on the back of both legs. The counselor clarified further the reporting process and reinforced the child for telling about the abuse.

The counselor called DFACS and the worker visited the school that afternoon. A report was filed and mother was contacted directly at work from the counselors office.

Danielle's mom tried to conceal the incident and to protect the boyfriend by saying he was out of town. As a result the DFACS worker decided to remove the child from her home. Danielle was allowed to spend the night with Rose and on the following day she was visited at school by a female police officer and the DFACS worker. That seemed to ease the tension. Danielle was taken from the school that afternoon by DFACS and the police.

Counseling/Follow-Up

Danielle returned to school a week later. Aunt Rose brought her back and stopped by the counselor's office. She explained that the judge had given her unlimited access to the child, and mother's boyfriend had been ordered to obtain help for his drinking problem. Rose felt good about Danielle's safety at the present time.

The counselor began play sessions with the child. This time her storytelling was more closely related with the abuse and violence among family members. After four sessions she began to incorporate problem resolution to the hitting and fighting among family members. Danielle's appearance had greatly improved and her energy level was more in tune with other students in her class.

Community and School Resources

The counselor coordinated with a parent volunteer to spend time with Danielle to help and support her with academic tasks. A fifth grader, a trained peer helper, came everyday at playground time to facilitate cooperative play between Danielle and her classmates.

Case Study 2: Middle School Child

The following case study is one in which many school personnel were involved as opposed to just the school counselor. Jimmy was a sixth grader in a middle school in an upperclass neighborhood. He lived with both biological parents and his third grade sister. Jimmy exhibited a variety of aggressive behaviors such as: verbal arguing, name calling, physical outbursts towards other students, and refusal to do work and cooperate in the classroom (at times). His student record indicated that he was in a self-contained emotionally handicapped (E.H.) classroom prior to entering sixth grade at his new school. In sixth grade he was placed in a regular classroom due to parent pressure. He received some resource help in the area of E. H. Jimmy's academic potential was above average, but his performance was below his ability level. Often he appeared sullen and detached.

Identification Process

Jimmy's special education teacher consulted with the school counselor relating his lack of progress in spite of a variety of interventions and classroom modifications. She was concerned about his despondency toward life in general and possible suicidal tendencies. She was also very concerned that he had violated school rules several times (fighting) resulting in disciplinary actions from the principal. It was agreed by the counselor, special education teacher, and assistant principal that parent consultation would be a helpful step to take.

At the parent conference all three professionals agreed that the parents were very much into denial concerning Jimmy's special needs. It was also noted that the family exhibited poor communication skills and some behaviors that led the counselor to the suspicion of alcoholism in the family.

Counseling began with Jimmy and the school counselor. About two weeks later, he came to school with a bruise on his eye and a cut on his cheek. That morning he shared with his special education teacher that his mother had hit him in anger and used a knife to cut him. The teacher immediately reported this to the school counselor.

The school counselor, the teacher, and Jimmy then talked about the abuse, and he confirmed it. The counselor explained to the child the procedure that she would be following in reporting this abuse. She then called the Department of Family and Children Services (DFACS) to report the incident. The DFACS worker related that they had a thick file already compiled on this family.

The DFACS worker called the school counselor back the next morning to tell her that the father had been given the choice of hospitalizing his wife for alcoholism or the children would be removed from the home. He further indicated that the father had hospitalized the mother, and that he (the DFACS worker) felt encouraged by the father's reaction and attitude toward the family's recovery. The school counselor then shared this information with the special education teacher, the principal, and Jimmy's other classroom teachers.

That same day the counselor met with Jimmy and plans were made for him to join the Children of Alcoholics group at school, and individual counseling was to be continued. Even though this may seem farfetched, the counselor found Jimmy smiling with friends in the lunchroom only two days later. As of this writing his progress continues, especially in the area of academics. Jimmy continues to struggle with activities that involve structured interactions with others since the trusting of others is so difficult for him at this time in his life.

Summary

School counselors are responsible for a variety of functions related to the identification of abused students and for providing various services for them. In addition to reporting the abuse and working cooperatively with protective services, it is important that school counselors be prepared to provide counseling for the student on an individual basis, in small group, and through family consultation. Finally, counselors should be prepared to train teachers and other school personnel concerning the issues of abuse and how to help abused students at school.

In addition to remediation, the school counselor has primary responsibility for abuse prevention in the schools. This is best accomplished through classroom guidance, small targeted groups, parent education, and teacher workshops. Many times adults (even administrators and teachers) would rather not deal with the issues surrounding abuse. This fear may lead to denial of the problem even when a child is communicating the abuse clearly. The school counselor is the key to insuring that all abused children are heard and properly assisted.

References

Allsopp, A., & Prosen, 5. (1988). Teacher reactions to a child abuse training program. *Elementary School Guidance and Counseling, 22,* 299-305.

American School Counselor Association. (1999). *The school counselor and child abuse & neglect prevention.* Alexandria, VA: ASCA Press.

Crosson Tower, C. (1984). *Child abuse and neglect: A teachers handbook for detection, reporting and classroom management.* Washington, DC: National Education Association.

Garbarino, J., Guttman, E., & Seely, J. (1986). *The psychologically battered child.* San Francisco, CA: Josey-Bass.

Georgia Council on Child Abuse. (1999). *The problems of child abuse.* Atlanta, GA: Author.

Gerler, E.R. (1988). Recent research on child abuse: A brief review. *Elementary School Guidance and Counseling, 22,* 325-327.

Gil, E. (1991). *The healing power of play.* New York: Guilford Press.

Hackbarth, S.G., Murphy, H.D., & McQuary, J.P. (1991). Identifying sexually abused children by using kinetic family drawings. *Elementary School Guidance and Counseling, 25,* 255-260.

Hollander, S.K. (1989). Coping with child sexual abuse through children's books. *Elementary School Guidance and Counseling, 23,* 183-193.

Hollander, S.K. (1992). Making young children aware of sexual abuse. *Elementary School Guidance and Counseling, 26,* 305-316.

Howell-Nigrelli, I. (1988). Shared responsibility for reporting child abuse cases: A reaction to Spiegel. *Elementary School Guidance & Counseling, 22,* 275-283.

Landreth, G.L. (1991). *Play therapy: The art of the relationship.* Muncie, IN: Accelerated Development.

McFadden, E.J. (1987). *Counseling abused children.* Ann Arbor, MI: ERIC Counseling and Personnel Services Clearinghouse, The University of Michigan.

McFadden, E.J. (1990). *ERIC/CAPS digest.* Ann Arbor, MI: ERIC Counseling and Personnel Services Clearinghouse, The University of Michigan.

Miller, A. (1990). *For your own good.* New York: The Noonday Press.

Nesse, L. (1989). Psychological maltreatment in schools: Emerging issues for counselors. *Elementary School Guidance and Counseling, 23,* 194-200.

Paisley, P.O. (1987). Prevention of child abuse and neglect: A legislative response. *The School Counselor, 34,* 226-228.

Riordan, R.J., & Verdel, A.C. (1991). Evidence of sexual abuse in children's art products. *The School Counselor, 39,* 116-121.

Sadowski, P.M., & Loesch, L.C. (1993). Using children's drawings to detect potential child sexual abuse. *Elementary School Guidance & Counseling, 28,* 115-123.

Sandberg, D.N., Crabbs, S.K., & Crabbs, M.A. (1988). Legal issues in child abuse: Question and answers for counselors. *Elementary School Guidance & Counseling, 22,* 268-2 74.

Shewmaker, D. (1988). Child abuse prevention program and referral procedure. *Elementary School Guidance and Counseling, 22,* 31 7-318.

Silva, T. (1992, May 6). Students tell board of sexual harassment. *The Gainesville Press,* p. 2A.

Tenant, C. (1988). Preventive sexual abuse programs: Problems and possibilities. *Elementary School Counseling and Guidance, 23,* 48-53.

Thompson, C.L., & Rudolph, LB. (1992). *Counseling children.* Pacific Grove, CA: Brooks/Cole.

Vanderbilt, H. (1992, February). Incest: A chilling report. *Lear's,* pp. 49-77.

Vernon, A., & Hay, J. (1988). A preventive approach to child sexual abuse. *Elementary School Guidance and Counseling, 22,* 306-31 2.

White, J., & Allers, C.T. (1994). Play therapy with abused children: A review of the literature. *Journal for Counseling and Development, 48,* 324-329.

Wilder, P. (1991). A counselor's contribution to the child abuse referral network. *The School Counselor, 38,* 203-214.

Chapter 14
Counseling Gay and Lesbian Students
by
Gail Adorno and Pam Paris

Gail Adorno, LCSW, ACSW is currently employed at Shands Teaching Hospital at the University of Florida, Gainesville. Ms. Adorno has made presentations to different professional groups on various issues regarding gays and lesbians.

Pam Paris, PhD, is a licensed mental health counselor and completed her doctoral dissertation in 1998 with a focus on domestic violence. Dr. Paris worked in a variety of mental health agencies before transitioning to the private sector where she works as a project manager for a medical software company in Gainesville, Florida.

In the previous chapter, White and Flynn discussed the very serious social, ethical and legal problems school counselors face when a student becomes a victim of abuse. In general, these are visible victims; and as a school counselor, you know when they need your assistance. However, there are many students facing an issue which is seldom visible, a silent minority struggling with their sexual identity. And, sadly, if they do bring this situation to the awareness of others, they face discrimination and frequently violence. Many school counselors are not capable, because of their own biased views and beliefs, or lack of training, to be of effective assistance to gay, lesbian or bisexual students.

In 1973, after much heated discourse, the American Psychiatric Association eliminated "homosexuality" as a category within the Diagnostic and Statistic Manual widely used by mental health professionals in the diagnosis of mental illness. In addition, the gay and lesbian civil rights movement in the 1970s opened the door to dramatic, positive, attitude changes in general by society, gays and lesbians themselves, and helping professionals. Never before have there been so many positive images of gays and lesbians in film, television and literature. As a result,

gay youth are coming "out" to their peers, teachers and family in growing numbers and will continue to do so despite the polarization of attitudes that currently exists in our society about sexual minorities. Although many gains have been made in the past 30 years, there still exists a deep and pervasive current of discrimination, prejudice and even hatred in society for gays, lesbians and bisexuals. These negative attitudes continue to exist even among some helping professionals. A major concern is that counselors may be inexperienced and lack an understanding and comfort level with gay and lesbian issues, thus, making intervention ineffective or even harmful. As gay youth choose to come "out," they open themselves to visibility with a price that includes the potential for harassment, discrimination and even violence. As school counselors, you have a responsibility to explore ways you can work effectively with this population.

What role should school counselors play in eliminating the discrimination and violence against sexual minority students? It is doubtful that you have had, or will have, a college level course devoted specifically to these issues. More often, courses offer a perfunctory section about diversity with a focus on ethnicity and culture. Lacking is a full exploration of the salient issues that have led sexual minority youth to claim a spot in the 1999 U.S. Surgeon General David Satcher's document, The Surgeon General's Call to Action to Prevent Suicide, as a group defined by its increased risk of suicide, particularly for males. Counselors must be proactive in pursuing continuing education and research to learn the issues that concern gay youth and to become effective advocates for change in individuals and society as a whole. Awareness of your own attitudes, beliefs and feelings is a beginning step for counselors towards understanding and helping this diverse group.

Do you have any gay or lesbian friends? How do you feel being seen alone in public with them? What is your reaction to two men or two women kissing? Do you feel revulsion? Does something inside your head say this is "wrong?" What do your religious beliefs tell you? These are but a few of the questions asked by inventories available for persons to gauge their level of homophobia, which is commonly defined as an irrational fear or abnormal fear of homosexuality. An honest exploration of your own attitudes, beliefs and feelings including comfort with your own sexuality whether gay, straight or bisexual, is the basic foundation for learning more about gay youth.

This is indeed a daunting task because our society remains a heterosexist culture where same-gender affection is not legitimized, but often vilified. The attitude that being heterosexual is inherently better and morally superior to being gay, lesbian or bisexual is encoded in our governmental statutes and institutional policies and practices. Although many universities and private companies are including domestic partner benefits for their employees (e.g., IBM, Microsoft, American Airlines), the majority of adult gay and lesbian couples lack the legal safeguards taken for granted by the heterosexual population. Further, heterosexist views are encoded in assessment forms, interview questions and how we communicate with each other.

One way you, as a school counselor, can initiate an accepting environment is a review of your intake forms and other questionnaires to incorporate inclusive language. When speaking with a parent, do you ask, "Are you *married*?" A better way to phrase that is "Do you have a *partner*?" or "Who do you include in your *family*?" These statements imply "acceptance and awareness" on the part of the speaker. Gay youth pick up on this kind of language. They also watch you and know from your past behavior in situations with gay and minority issues, or other unpopular causes, whether or not you are trustworthy.

Keeping items in your office such as a rainbow flag or pink triangle symbolizing gay pride or advocating for curriculum inclusion of gay and lesbian history may be other ways to signal to gay youth that you have done your own work in understanding their issues, validates their experience and identifies you as an advocate.

Gay youth are a varied heterogeneous group much like adult gays, lesbians and bisexuals. Their commonality lies in their same-gender affectional orientation and having to live with society's attitudes toward them including discrimination, hatred and violence. Stereotypes abound when discussing gay youth. They are often referred to as troubled kids with higher rates of drug abuse and truancy who frequently run away. And, indeed, many gay youth may cope with their confusion and the stigma, rejection and isolation imposed by society through risk-taking behaviors such as alcohol and drug abuse, multiple sexual partners, and unprotected sex; thus, increasing their exposure to HIV. While this may be true for many gay youth, often overlooked are gay and lesbian adolescents that

don't fit the classic gay stereotypes, such as, a class president who busies himself with activities to the exclusion of dating, or the high school quarterback, or a popular cheerleader. Some teens choose to have multiple opposite-gender sexual partners. Some lesbian teens may deliberately pursue pregnancy. These kinds of behaviors are sometimes the result of efforts to change, to "fit" and conceal a budding awareness of same-gender sexual identity.

Gender differences also exist among gay, lesbian and bisexual youth (Saewyc, Bearinger, Heinz, Blum, & Resnick, 1998). Males may come to an awareness of their sexual identity partly through sexual experiences with other males while females more so develop their awareness through affectional ties with other females prior to sexual contact. Gay males are particularly prone to violence and taunting from peers, especially other males, whether they have actually "come out" or if they simply do not adhere to traditional notions of masculinity. This is not to negate the experience of prejudice faced by lesbian teens; rather, this point emphasizes our society's particular abhorrence of male-male affection.

Historically, research efforts have neglected female experience and generalized results from male population samples to girls and women. The study of lesbian youth is no exception. Much still needs to be learned about their particular issues.

As school counselors, your focus should *not* be on attempting to change the teen's identification as gay, lesbian or bisexual. In a position statement on psychiatric treatment and sexual orientation (September 1998), the American Psychiatric Association's Committee on Gay, Lesbian and Bisexual Issues listed the potential risks of attempting to change a person's sexual orientation (also known as reparative or conversion therapy) and explained the APA position on this issue as follows:

The potential risks of "reparative therapy" are great; including depression, anxiety and self-destructive behavior, since therapist alignment with societal prejudices against homosexuality may reinforce self-hatred already experienced by the patient. Many patients who have undergone "reparative therapy" relate that they were inaccurately told that homosexuals are lonely, unhappy individuals who never achieve acceptance or satisfaction. The possibility that the person might achieve happiness and satisfying interpersonal relationships as a gay man or lesbian is not presented, nor are alternative approaches to dealing with the effects of societal stigmatization discussed. The American Psychiatric Association recognizes that in the course of ongoing psychiatric treatment, there may be appropriate clinical indications for attempting to change sexual behaviors.

Several major professional organizations including the American Psychological Association, the National Association of Social Workers and the American Academy of Pediatrics have all made statements against "reparative therapy" because of concerns for the harm caused to patients. The American Psychiatric Association has already taken clear stands against discrimination, prejudice and unethical treatment on a variety of issues including discrimination on the basis of sexual orientation.

Therefore, the American Psychiatric Association opposes any psychiatric treatment, such as "reparative" or "conversion" therapy which is based upon the assumption that homosexuality per se is a mental disorder or based upon the a priori assumption that the patient should change his/her homosexual orientation. (APA Position Statement on Psychiatric Treatment and Sexual Orientation, September, 1998).

Rather than attempting to change a teen's identification as gay, lesbian, or bisexual, the school counselor's focus should be on transforming the environment's negative impact on gay youth to one of acceptance and empowering gay youth to develop skills to cope with society's attitudes towards them. One example of counselor advocacy at work can be seen in the American Counseling Association's (ACA) response to ads that appeared in 1998 in the Washington Post, New York Times and USA Today which suggested gay and lesbian persons can and should be "converted" to heterosexuality. The following is a draft of the letter that was sent to many organizations inquiring about ACA's position (from *www.counseling.org* website):

September 1, 1998

Dear

The American Counseling Association (ACA) shares your concern over the recent series of newspaper advertisements which suggested that lesbian, gay, and bisexual persons are mentally ill and should be "converted" to heterosexuality.

The American Counseling Association, a nonprofit membership organization that represents more than 50,000 professional counselors employed in educational, career development, rehabilitation, mental health, and community settings, formally opposes

discrimination based on sexual orientation. This policy has been subsequently reaffirmed and further elucidated through a series of resolutions that have been adopted for nearly thirty years.

Most recently, on March 27, 1998, the Governing Council of the American Counseling Association passed the following resolution with respect to sexual orientation and mental health:

"The American Counseling Association opposes portrayals of lesbian, gay, and bisexual youth and adults as mentally ill due to their sexual orientation; and supports the dissemination of accurate information about sexual orientation, mental health, and appropriate interventions in order to counteract bias that is based in ignorance or unfounded beliefs about same-gender sexual orientation."

We believe that the information that was disseminated through these advertisements was wrong. Please feel free to disseminate our recent resolution to your members, allies, and the general public. I also hope that you will call upon ACA to assist you in your continuing efforts to provide more accurate information to the public concerning sexual orientation and mental health. For additional information about this matter, you may contact Mr. Richard Yep, ACA Interim Executive Director, at (703) 823-9800 x210.

An additional resource that may be valuable to you in your efforts is the Association for Gay, Lesbian, and Bisexual Issues in Counseling (AGLBIC), a division of the American Counseling Association. The mission of AGLBIC includes educating professional counselors on issues related to gay, lesbian, and bisexual clients, fostering sensitivity to the unique needs of client identity development, and creating a nonthreatening counseling environment by aiding the reduction of stereotypical thinking and prejudice based on sexual orientation. Please feel free to contact Dr. Colleen Logan, President of AGLBIC, by mail at 7900 Westheimer, Apt. 214, Houston, TX 77063, by email at clogan6987@aol.com, or by telephone at (713) 975-6061.

Sincerely,

Loretta Bradley, Ph.D.

President

As counselors, it is important to be aware of the context in which gay teens live. Is your school located in a rural tradition-bound community or is it located in a metropolitan or suburban area with progressive resources and outreach programs? Are the teen's parents religiously conservative? What other minority issues affect the teen (e.g., race, religion, and disability)? Does this teen already live in a chaotic home situation? What coping skills, adaptive or maladaptive, has this teen already developed to navigate life's challenges? What is the climate in your particular school district surrounding gay and lesbian issues? Are topics of sexuality allowed in the classroom? Questions such as these will help frame the environment, both internally and externally, in which gay youth "come out."

The Gay, Lesbian, and Straight Education Network (GLSEN) is a national organization, founded in 1994 and based in New York City, dedicated to addressing anti-gay bias in public, private, and parochial schools. According to GLSEN reports, gay students hear anti-gay remarks 26 times per day, which breaks down to about once every 14 minutes during the average school day (Bart, 1998).

GLSEN recommends the following 10 steps as starting points to creating a safe and welcoming school for gays and straights alike (Bart, 1998):

1. Adopt a mission or policy statement that makes it clear that yours is an open and affirming school where differences are respected and honored.

2. Adopt policies against any form of harassment based on sexual orientation as part of the school's general anti-harassment policies. Be clear that intolerance is unacceptable.

3. Promote the sharing of information about sexual orientation and inclusiveness in school publications, at school assemblies, and at other student forums.

4. Provide training for all faculty and staff, and offer it each year for new employees.

5. Provide workshops and forums for school leaders, governing boards, and parents.

6. Provide support for gay, lesbian, and bisexual adults in the community, including employees and parents, making it safe for anyone to be open about his or her sexual orientation.

7. Provide support for gay, lesbian, and bisexual students through appropriate student groups, such as gay/straight alliances.

8. Ensure that your library has accurate resources dealing with gay issues.

9. Address the school's curriculum so that it includes gay issues and acknowledgment of the contributions of gays and lesbians in areas ranging from history and literature to science and the arts.

10. Establish an oversight or coordinating committee charged with recommending goals and monitoring progress.

"Hush-hush" attitudes about sexuality, especially about being gay, lesbian or bisexual, breeds isolation, loneliness and fear. A teen becoming aware of their same-gender sexual identity within a context of hatred, fear, shame and secrecy with few to no resources for understanding and support, is at risk for depression and other psychosocial difficulties when hiding one's true self becomes a daily challenge. Gay youth face the real possibility of rejection and violence by peers and family when they come out (Hunter, 1990). They often lack adult role models and must negotiate relationships during a period of tremendous developmental change without guidance and support. According to the 1999 U.S. Surgeon General's Report, gay youth have been considered two to three times more likely to attempt or commit suicide than their heterosexual peers. This is cause enough for school counselors and the school system as a whole to develop strategies for these teenagers to cope with their development and provide a supportive, safe environment for exploring their awareness and concerns. This kind of environment must exist before gay and lesbian teenagers can learn to *celebrate* their differences.

Glimpse the world of gay youth through the following excerpts:

I was a lucky one—I had a friend to talk to, and I found a support group. Most gay teens do not have these luxuries. We grow up hating ourselves like society teaches us to. I would not be here today if I had succeeded in my suicide attempt.

If someone would have been "out" at my school—if the teachers wouldn't have been afraid to stop the fag and dyke jokes, if my human sexuality class had even mentioned homosexuality (especially in a positive light), if the school counselors would have been more open to discussion of gay and lesbian issues, perhaps I wouldn't have grown up hating what I was and perhaps I wouldn't have attempted suicide. (19-year-old female)

Fag was very commonly used, though never to my face. I remember sitting in class and quickly looking down at papers every time someone said "gay" or "fag" because I was afraid people would see the expression of surprise or pain on my face and figure it out. At that point, of course, life would be over. (18-year-old male) (Grace, 1999)

The public schools have been viewed as the agency most essential in bringing about appreciation for diversity and respect for the rights of all. Some local school districts and communities have developed special schools (e.g. the Harvey Milk School in New York City, the EAGLE Center in Los Angeles) and programs of positive education and counseling about sexuality including sexual minority issues (e.g. Project 10 in Los Angeles, Project 10 East in Massachusetts, The Triangle Program in Toronto). These programs have been designed with the participation of parents, teachers and representatives of the gay and lesbian community. Relatedly, school counselors are uniquely positioned to facilitate positive changes in students and school environments. In 1995, the American School Counselor Association (ASCA) adopted a position regarding the school counselor and sexual minority youth. The position of ASCA includes the commitment to:

Facilitating and promoting the fullest possible development of each individual by reducing the barriers of misinformation, myth, ignorance, hatred, and discrimination which prevent sexual orientation minorities from achieving individual potential, healthy esteem, and equal status. School counselors are in a field committed to human development and need to be sensitive to the use of inclusive language and positive modeling of sexual orientation minority equity. ASCA is committed to equal opportunity regardless of sexual orientation. (The School Counselor & Sexual Minority Youth, Adopted by ASCA, 1995)

In the same document, ASCA also provides a framework for the school counselor's role:

The school counselor uses inclusive and non-presumptive language with equitable expectations toward sexual orientation minority individuals, being especially sensitive to those aspects of communication and social structures/institutions which provide accurate working models of acceptance of sexual orientation minority identities and equality.

Counselors must become vigilant to the pervasive negative effects of stereotyping and rubricating individuals into rigid expressions of gender roles and sexual identities.

The professional school counselor is sensitive to ways in which attitudes and behavior negatively affect the individual. School counselors are called to provide constructive feedback on the negative use of exclusive and presumptive language and inequitable expectations toward sexual orientation minorities. The school counselor places emphasis on a person's behavioral choices and not on their unalterable identity and uniqueness.

Demonstrations of sexual orientation minority equity also includes fair and accurate representation of sexual identities in visible leadership positions as well as other role positions.

. . . School counselors should be challenged to follow the example set by ASCA in support of conscious raising among school counselors and increased modeling of inclusive language, advocacy and equal opportunity for participation among sexual orientation minorities' identities. This is done in order to break through individual, social and institutional behaviors and expectations, which limit the development of human potential in all populations. (The School Counselor & Sexual Minority Youth, Adopted by ASCA, 1995)

Counselors and other educators committed to justice and human rights need to continue to examine their own responsibilities concerning students who are struggling with their sexual identity. There are children in every classroom that will at some time in their lives recognize themselves to be gay or lesbian. They need your counsel, your support and protection, along with the opportunity to mature into sensitive, confident, productive adults. Every classroom also has children with a first-generation relative (e.g. mother, father, sibling) or extended family member (e.g. grandmother, aunt, cousin) who is gay or lesbian. For these reasons, it is timely and appropriate for educators to introduce sexual minority issues (e.g., gay, lesbian, bisexual, transgender) into the school curricula.

In recognition of the need for understanding and for appropriate services to all students, the Representative Assembly of the National Education Association adopted the following resolution in July, 1997.

NEA Resolution

C-29—Student Sexual Orientation

The National Education Association believes that all persons, regardless of sexual orientation, should be afforded equal opportunity within the public education system. The Association further believes that, for students who are struggling with their sexual/gender orientation, every school district and educational institution should provide counseling services and programs by trained personnel that deal with high suicide and dropout rates and the high incidence of teen prostitution. (NEA Resolution, July, 1997)

Is this important NEA resolution being followed at your school? As a school counselor, or counselor-to-be, are you qualified, both personally and professionally, to counsel with students facing these concerns? Again, it begins with you — awareness is the key along with total acceptance on your part; unconditional positive, genuine regard is a prerequisite. Are you willing to take a stand, a personal, courageous commitment on behalf of these students?

In addition to creating a more positive environment for teenagers, counselors must become aware of the unique personal pressures facing gay and lesbian teenagers. As previously mentioned, it is often during early adolescence (a period of critical development) that gay/lesbian youth come into self-awareness regarding their same-gender attractions. While the majority of gay and lesbian adolescents eventually develop a positive and healthy identity into adulthood, most find living with a stigmatized sexual identity stressful and a significant number of lesbian and gay youth are unable to cope with this stress without appropriate resources and support. Can you, if you are heterosexual, imagine the stress faced by a gay adolescent who realizes his or her sense of being different? Counselors know that adolescence is a time of conforming. How do you conform, if gay or lesbian, when your environment lacks appropriate gay and lesbian role models to mirror development? Can you imagine, as a youth, suddenly realizing that you are attracted to a member of the same gender and hearing from an early age that this is "forbidden" and "shameful" according to our society? Since many gay/lesbian students fear being discovered, they may begin isolating themselves as much as possible. Some may become chronic school truants while others may drop out completely. They learn to hide their true feelings and behave in ways to "fit in" in order to protect themselves or risk physical harm and/or rejection. School can be a source of great stress for these youth, many of whom will choose to either suppress their sexual feelings or deny their true sexual orientation. However, there will be those teens who decide to begin the process of accepting their same-gender orientation (i.e., "coming out.")

Those gay/lesbian youth who do decide to come out may face immediate rejection from their peers. Rejection by one's peers is always difficult, but this type of rejection can be devastating. Gay and lesbian youth who come out may be rejected by their own family. Sadly, such blatant, overt, nonacceptance by family and peers can lead to alienation, abandonment and even physical abuse by family members (Hunter, 1990). Counselors know that feelings of alienation among youth frequently plays a role in attempted or completed suicide. Unfortunately, few solid research studies on the possible relationship between sexual orientation among youth and suicide have been conducted to this date (Muehrer, 1995). Sampling difficulties and methodological limitations have impeded drawing accurate conclusions about suicide among gay youth. What is clear is the need for continued research to identify accurate links among sexual minorities in general, particularly gay youth and suicide.

Can gay and lesbian teenagers get help in their schools? As noted, very few counselors have been appropriately trained and courses that confront attitudes and beliefs about homosexuality are still almost nonexistent in counselor education programs. Does your school have a policy prohibiting discrimination on the basis of sexual orientation? Very few schools have such a policy in place. A counselor who decides to take a stand and advocate for change on behalf of gay and lesbians students will need much personal courage because the kind of rejection faced by these students may also be experienced by those who try to help. In addition, if you are a proactive counselor, most of your school colleagues, parents, and students may assume you are gay/lesbian. Are you willing to take that risk?

We believe that school counselors are the professionals being counted on most for positive action on this issue. After convincing your principal of the need for programs concerning sexual orientation, the place to begin is with the teachers in your school. The Institute for Sexual Inclusiveness through Training and Education (INSITE) suggests specific guidelines for teachers.

Providing in-service education for your teachers concerning these strategies (given below) may be the place to begin.

1. Address negative school-based incidents on the spot, with special attention to targeted harassment put-downs (whether or not targeted to individuals), anti-gay jokes, graffiti, and labeling. Treat them the same way you would if they were directed at a racial group.

2. Change language that assumes everyone is or should be heterosexual (use "partner" rather than girl/boyfriend, "permanent relationship" rather than marriage).

3. Change human relations and personnel policies to protect students and staff from discrimination on the basis of sexual orientation; train school personnel to follow up such violations with appropriate discipline.

4. Identify gay/lesbian contributions throughout the curriculum (history, literature, art, science, religion, etc.).

5. Provide history of oppression (such as Holocaust, origin of the word "faggot," etc.).

6. Submit requests to improve library holdings (both fiction and nonfiction) related to sexual diversity/orientation.

7. Include issues for gay/lesbian students and staff in coverage in school newspaper.

8. Bring openly lesbian/gay adults as resources in classes and assemblies.

9. Include gay/lesbian concerns in all prevention programs (suicide, dropout, pregnancy, etc.) and in training of peer leaders, student government, and so forth.

Mary Bart, a former editor of *Counseling Today,* told the story of Justin Smith in an article, *Creating a safer school for gay students* (*Counseling Today,* Sept. 1998):

Justin Smith, a 17-year-old openly gay student in Memphis, Tennessee, offers school counselors a very simple piece of advice: "Be accepting of anyone who talks to you." Shortly after he came out to his mom, Smith went to a favorite teacher to tell her and talk things out. Unlike some of the counselors in his school—who he's heard give gay or questioning students who are seeking help the phone number to an organization that "straightens out" gays - his Latin teacher was very supportive and asked him if he knew about Memphis Area Gay Youth (MAGY), a support group for gay teens which he has become active in during the past two years.

"She helped me sort things out in my mind," said Smith. "It was a very good experience that I wish every [gay] youth could have. Counselors need to be supportive and not try to further mix up an already confused teenage mind."

Smith came out just after his 15th birthday. He started to notice his attraction to the same sex at around age 12, but fought the feelings. Being an only child and the only grandchild in his family only made it worse as he knew the expectations his family had for him to marry and have children. His parents divorced when he was seven.

"It was difficult to accept my feelings just to myself," he said. "I denied my feelings for years and hid them as best I could. I harassed homosexuals and just tried my hardest to deny that I was one myself."

Eventually, he accepted the fact that he is gay and started coming out to his friends. His friends had mixed reactions, but most soon realized he was the same person they've always known. His best friend didn't take it so well and wouldn't talk to him for a few months, but now he and his girlfriend double date with Smith and his boyfriend.

"When I told my mom she was shocked, but took it well," Smith said. "She told me it was all right and she still loves me. Then she went through a period of being upset about it, went into denial, and wouldn't let me be around certain people. Now she's fine with it. I haven't told my dad."

Smith said that one of the hardest things for him now is relationships.

"It's hard to find someone else who's gay, and then to find someone who's gay that you connect with," he said. "Then, once you are in a relationship, you can't publicly display affection like all the straight people do."

Smith, who is just beginning his senior year, said he believed his experiences as a gay teen are pretty similar to those of other gay youth around the country, except that he probably has had an easier time of it than some.

"My mom is accepting, my friends are accepting, and I've had support," he said. "I hear many stories about teens losing friends, being estranged from their families, or who are just too afraid to be themselves."

Tips on Counseling Students Questioning Their Sexual Identity

Can you, if "straight" imagine being asked: "When did you first decide you were heterosexual?" Can you imagine, if gay/lesbian, being told: "Your sexuality doesn't offend me as long as you don't flaunt it?" Can you imagine, as a heterosexual, someone asking you not to hold hands with your spouse because "We don't want our kids to observe such behavior?" Can you imagine being hated simply for who you are? One young gay person indicated to a counselor educator that being a heterosexual male obviously means "you hate your same sex." During a valuing diversity college level retreat that the same counselor educator facilitated, an 18-year-old gay who had recently come out told the participants, "I think I know what it felt like to be a Jew trying to pass in Nazi Germany."

The "Tips" given below for school counselors were developed by Darren Covar and presented at a Florida School Counselors Conference. They are summarized here with his permission.

1. First, look to yourself as a person and understand your true feelings regarding homosexuality. This is the most important tip you can receive and incorporate when counseling anyone "different" from yourself. If you feel that homosexuality is "wrong," "wicked" or "immoral," the gay/lesbian student will immediately be aware of these biased feelings; and you will be ineffective. If you hold these beliefs, or if you feel pity, repulsion, and so forth; you must refer the student to another counselor.

Covar indicates that there are many ways you can tell if you are homophobic. For example, would you perform the following activities? And, if yes, how would you feel while performing the activities?

   a. Consider doing a presentation on Gay and Lesbian issues at your school, in your community, at your state convention, and so forth.

   b. Go into a crowded bookstore and ask the person behind the counter for a book on "coming out."

   c. Read a book about being gay/lesbian in a public place where people can walk by and read the cover. Watch their reactions.

   d. Join PFLAG (Parents and Friends of Lesbians and Gays).

Covar indicates that if you would feel awkward performing these activities, you should ask yourself why? Most likely the answer is because others will assume you are gay or lesbian and you would find this embarrassing. Think about what you are saying and revealing about yourself by being afraid of being labeled gay/lesbian. What is it about being gay/lesbian that you find negative? How would these beliefs (if you hold them) affect the way you, as a school counselor, would deal with students questioning their sexual identity? It is important that you acknowledge and challenge these beliefs if you are to work effectively with these youth.

2. Understand that gays and lesbians are aware of their orientation at a young age, just as heterosexuals are, even if they have never had a sexual experience. Understand also that gay/lesbian students have very few (visible) positive role models, especially couples. Unlike other minority students in your school, gay/lesbian role models simply are not available, at least publicly.

3. Become involved in local gay and lesbian organizations. This will help break down any stereotypes you might have and will help you develop friendships with gay and lesbian individuals. It will also help you learn about available resources for these students. It is also a great opportunity to ask questions and learn. Become familiar with those groups that are available in your community.

4. Know where your school administration, especially your principal, stands on this issue. Once you know your administrator's stance regarding gay and lesbian students, talk with him or her about the depth of education allowable (i.e., in-service for teachers concerning different sexual orientations, gay/lesbian student clubs, etc.). Then, you will know you can go at least that far each time the situation arises. Depending on the school district and principal, this can be a very touchy issue, and sadly, keeps many counselors from being of full service to these students. Counselors would not hesitate to recommend a community group for children coping with loss, but few counselors would feel comfortable referring a lesbian/gay student to a support group. Why? Some fears that prevent school counselors from feeling comfortable with this subject are that

they do not now how their principal will respond. Would your principal support you in case a parent calls and is angry that you implied that it was okay to be a gay, lesbian, or bisexual? No member of a school staff, including a counselor, likes being "hung out on a limb" without the support of the principal. Thus, have a heart to heart talk with your school principal and find out where he or she stands on the issue. Use gentle facilitation to assist the administrator to permit you to do what you know is ethically best for these students, the teachers, and the school in general. When you know where your principal stands, next time you will be comfortable providing the best services since you know you have his or her support.

5. When trying to help a student deal with their feelings regarding homosexuality, it is important that you not invalidate their family or church beliefs. For example, if their religion dictates that homosexuals are sinners, avoid imposing your opinion by saying, "You don't need to attend a church like that, there are plenty of gay-affirming churches you can attend." Instead, focus on their feelings.

6. Reduce the "us" and "them" in your speech and actions. One middle school counselor said, during a large group guidance session on AIDS, "It's not just homosexuals, it could happen to us too." This would immediately alienate any students in the audience facing the question of their own sexuality. Would you, if a student in that situation, open up to that counselor? Probably not.

7. Assume every student is somewhere along the continuum of sexual orientation. Don't immediately assume every student is "straight." This puts the student in the position of lying and causes them to feel uncomfortable, incongruent, and so forth. Asking a female student new to your school if she has met any boys she likes would make her feel very uncomfortable if she were a lesbian. Instead (if you feel the need to ask such a question), try to leave her sexual orientation neutral by asking if she has found anyone special.

8. Be aware of what the research says about changing one's sexual orientation. Most knowledgeable researchers consider it unethical and ineffective to make such an attempt. Also, learning some of the theories about the origins of homosexuality can be of help when you work with gay/lesbian students.

9. Have visible, appropriate resources in your school counseling office concerning homosexuality. This gives students the idea that you can be trusted and that it is okay to come out to you.

10. Have empathy for your gay/lesbian student clients, not sympathy or pity. The latter emotions imply to students that there is something terribly "wrong" with being gay/lesbian, which is something they've most likely heard, overtly or covertly, over and over again.

11. If you don't understand the feelings of the student, don't be afraid to ask. Asking (without probing) if you don't understand something is usually taken as a sign of interest and caring. And, if you (for some reason) do offend the student, simply recover by apologizing and then follow with more genuine questions.

12. Seek consultation from an adult who is gay or lesbian. Friends or fellow counselors who are gay or lesbian will provide you with valuable insight and many helpful hints for counseling gay/lesbian youth. Do not rely on the gay or lesbian student as your sole source of information.

13. Do not personally label the student lesbian or gay. The research indicates that over 50% of the population have had some type of same-gender sexual experience. Labeling should be left to the individual student. That is, if they wish to label themselves, fine; but, as counselor, do not label them.

14. Coming out should be left entirely to the student. This is a very important, and most likely, a risky step for them to take. They should decide when and who to come out to. No one else can do it for them. You can, and should, help them realize the possible personal "costs" and "benefits," but allow the student to maintain control over the coming out process.

15. Refer the gay/lesbian student to reputable community groups. Throughout their life they may have felt different and alone. There is only so much you as a counselor can do to assist the student, especially if you are straight. And, even if you are gay or lesbian (which would probably be very helpful to the student), you are still older and, most likely, in a very different, personal situation. They will still feel isolated and alone with regard to peers. Referring them to groups with fellow, understanding students helps them discuss issues with others their age who are experiencing the same things they are currently experiencing. Most cities have resources available to gay and lesbian students. Your local information and referral hotline will also have these

resources available for you. The Internet also has a wealth of resources and on-line groups of gay youth.

16. Help students, where possible, to develop a new network of friends before they come out. A seventeen-year-old recently related how he was ostracized from his church and family when he came out. Try to imagine (at age 17) your parents turning against you, refusing to talk to you, and the church you have attended all your life suddenly having written you off. The seventeen-year-old's whole world came crashing down around him. Luckily, he made immediate contacts with other gay and lesbian students and received needed support from his high school counselor. Otherwise, he might have become a suicide statistic.

17. Understand the possible implications of coming out in your school, community, to his or her parents, and review them with the student prior to his or her coming out. To do otherwise is unethical and perhaps dangerous physically and emotionally for your student client. And, as noted, the decision must be their decision to make.

18. Parents feel a loss when they are told their offspring is gay/lesbian and often need counseling. They may also seek you out, especially if their child came out to you. Be prepared, some may blame themselves. Being aware of the current literature regarding the etiology of homosexuality can be very helpful when these parents come to your office. Many parents, especially if it is their only child, will question their own identity as future grandparents. Some will be in a state of profound shock, and others will reveal overwhelming grief. One young gay male said that the first thing his parents proclaimed was, "But we wanted grandchildren!"

We believe that statements as above correlating gay and lesbian with childlessness are archaic and being transformed as we begin the new millennium and as more and more gay and lesbian couples in committed, long-term relationships give birth to or adopt children to create new meanings of family.

Summary

Schools can have a negative or positive affect on gay and lesbian students. The school climate will influence gay youth to repress and/or suppress their true feelings regarding their sexual orientation, or, lead to a process of trust and true expression. Creating a safe climate for an authentic self should be our goal as school counselors. What is the climate in your school? Is it open to such free expression? School counselors have the opportunity and the responsibility to respond positively to the needs of the lesbian and gay students in their respective schools.

Resource List

Books

Cantwell, M.A. (1998). *Homosexuality: The secret a child dare not tell.* Rafael Press. 1998. ISBN: 0-964-98299-4.

Chandler, K. (1997). *Passages of pride: True stories of lesbian and gay teenagers.* Alyson Publications. ISBN: 1-555-83417-5.

Griffin, C.W., Wirth, M.J., & Wirth, A.G. (1986). *Beyond acceptance: Parents of lesbians & gays talk about their experience.* St. Martin's. ISBN: 0-312-16781-4.

Harris, M.B. (ed.). (1998). School experiences of gay and lesbian youth: The invisible minority. Haworth. 1998. ISBN: 1-560-23109-2.

Organizations

The Human Rights Campaign
1101 14th Street, NW, Suite 200
Washington, DC 20005

National Coming Out Project
1-800-866-6263
http://www.hrc.org

Parents, Families and Friends of Lesbians and Gays (PFLAG)
1101 14th Street, NW
Washington, DC 20009
202-332-6483
http://www.pflag.org

The National Gay and Lesbian Task Force
2320 17th Street, NW
Washington, DC 20009
202-332-6483
http://www.ngltf.org

Religious Organizations

Emergence International
P.O. Box 6061-423
Sherman Oaks, CA 91413

Interfaith Working Group
P.O. Box 1170
Philadelphia, PA 19101

Dignity/USA (Catholic)
1500 Massachusetts Avenue, NW
Washington, DC 20005
800-877-8797
http://www.dignityusa.org

Integrity (Episcopal)
http://www.integrityusa.org

Affirmation: United Methodist for Lesbian, Gay and Bisexual Concerns
http://www.concentric.net/Umaffirm/

World Congress of Gay and Lesbian Jewish Organizations
P.O. Box 233
Washington, DC 20026-3379
http://www.wcglijo.org

The Association of Welcoming & Affirming Baptists
P.O. Box 2596
Attleboro Falls, MA 02763-0894
http://members.aol.com/wabaptists/index.html

The United Methodist Church
The Reconciling Congregation Program
3801 N. Keeler Avenue
Chicago, IL 60641
http://www.rcp.org

Interweave: Unitarian Universalists for Lesbian, Gay, Bisexual, and Transgender Concerns
25 Beacon Street
Boston, MA 02108
http://www.qrd.org/qrd/orgs/UUA/interweave.txt

Universal Fellowship of Metropolitan Community Churches
8704 Santa Monica Boulevard, Second Floor
West Hollywood, CA 90069
http://www.ufmcc.com

References

ASCA. (1995). *Role statement: The professional school counselor and sexual minority youth.* Alexandria, VA: ASCA Press.

Bart, M. (1998). Creating a safer school for gay students. *Counseling Today*, September, 1998.

Gray, M. (1999). *In your face: Stories from the lives of queer youth.* New York: Harrington Park.

Hunter, J. (1990). Violence against lesbian and gay male youths. *Journal of Interpersonal Violence, 5*, 295-300.

Saewyc, E.M., Bearing, L.H., Heinz, P.A., Blum, R., & Resnick, M. (1998). Gender differences in health and risk behaviors among bisexual and homosexual adolescents. *Journal of Adolescent Health, 23*, 181-188.

Chapter 15
School Counselors and Special Needs Students

by

Beverly Snyder

Beverly Snyder, EdD, is an Associate Professor of Counselor Education at the University of Colorado at Colorado Springs. She formerly served as Resource Counselor for Orange County Public Schools, Orlando, Florida.

Introduction

School counselors often feel overwhelmed by the many hats they find themselves wearing during the course of a school day. But, most likely, counselors find that working with exceptional education students is one of the most rewarding and enlightening parts of their busy day. School counselors can often be heard saying that working with Exceptional Student Education (ESE) provides them with more satisfaction than any other facet of their work as counselors. However, it must be acknowledged that, if working with special needs students becomes (or is) a part of your role as a school counselor, you will find yourself being a lawyer, a public relations expert, an advocate, a teacher, sometimes a lobbyist, and often a mediator.

While you are, or will become, a "counselor" in the true sense of the word for all your students, nowhere is it more important than with the exceptional student and his or her family. We believe that our role as school counselors is to promote these students' rights to have and to fulfill their dreams of a better education, and ultimately, a better life. School counselors hold the keys which assure that these special needs students will achieve and succeed "just like everyone else" in the school.

Special Needs Students and the Law

The Federal Education for All Handicapped Act of 1975 changed the role of the school counselor by providing equal opportunity for all students classified as "handicapped." Counselors had always provided services for the gifted and highly talented, but the 1975 act increased their participation in the lives of special needs children. This participation takes the form of coordinating the Exceptional Student Education (ESE) Program and managing the flow of paperwork required to document the various phases of placement.

The federal legislation, *Individuals with Disabilities Education Act* (IDEA), requires that anyone with a perceived handicapping condition (i.e., asthma, obesity, abnormally short for age) must receive accommodations in the learning environment to equalize his or her educational opportunities. These students are not necessarily staffed into an ESE program, but are eligible to receive appropriate interventions so that they may participate equally in learning experiences. In the Orange County, Florida schools, as in many other systems, counselors are directly responsible for coordinating these specially designed interventions.

Students with "special needs" with whom counselors work can either be described as "ESE" or as "regular" education students. In either case, documented interventions required by federal law must be noted in the student's permanent cumulative folder to establish that the school recognizes that a special need exists and has been, and is, being considered when planning that child's education.

The Exceptional Education program is regulated by Federal laws and guidelines as to documentation, procedures, processes, and approaches that must be followed when working with special students. An ESE student will have an easily recognizable folder inside his or her cumulative folder in which records are kept that relate to placement in an exceptional education program. "Regular" special needs students do not usually have such a special folder; therefore, documentation for their interventions are kept in chronological order with other records inside the cumulative folder.

Federal and state statutes for exceptional education students require students to receive the *"least restrictive environment"* possible. This means that all school personnel must utilize the regular school facilities and adapt them to the needs of the exceptional student. This ensures that ESE students are not isolated from regular students any more than is absolutely necessary. The law further stated that no segregation should occur unless it is proven necessary by the student's behaviors which indicate an inability to benefit from a regular classroom. Thus, all students, including the ESE students, begin their school careers in the regular classroom. Placement in a more restrictive environment follows only after many interventions have been attempted, conferences with parents and teachers held, vision and hearing screenings conducted, and most often, after psycho-educational testing has been completed. Each district and state has its own approaches to Exceptional Student Education, and counselors are encouraged to become familiar with them. The process of placing a student in an exceptional program is a complicated one that requires constant referral to a policy and procedures manual.

The Process of Exceptional Student Education

The ESE process usually begins with a teacher or parent raising a question regarding the special nature of a student (i.e., an inability to stay on task, to complete assignments, hyperactivity, sleeping in class, or a host of other concerns). An Educational Planning Team (EPT) meeting is scheduled (usually by a counselor, who also functions as staffing chairperson or staffing coordinator). In Orange County, Florida, this meeting is usually attended by whomever has insight as to the nature of the child's problem(s). This includes parents, classroom and elective teachers (especially a PE coach), administrators, the counselor, and a Curriculum Resource Teacher (CRT). Depending on the nature of the problem, the school psychologist and/or social worker might also be invited to attend.

In some Orange County schools, this team meets for 15 or 20 minutes prior to the parents' arrival to ensure that all information is available and meeting goals are understood by all school personnel. The counselor, in the role of chairperson, keeps the team on task and creates a "safe" place for the entire team to be heard. The counselor also has the responsibility for making sure the parents feel welcome and a vital part of the meeting. The teacher(s) discuss the specific *academic* issues and specific *behaviors* they have observed which have created their concerns. It is important that the child's *behaviors* and *problems* are discussed, not his or her *personality*. In Orange County, counselors document the meeting on an EPT form, noting interventions, who is responsible for what, follow-up meetings to be held, and so forth. Everyone present signs the document and the parents receive a copy.

In Florida, as well as all other states, parents have particular rights concerning their child. Thus, if the EPT recommends testing, parental permission must be obtained. All testing, regardless of the type, requires written permission from the parents. Since parents are the child's "case managers," they have the right to refuse any and all evaluations, and some do. (In extreme cases, when parents withhold permission to test, the School Board, acting "in loco parentis," can request the court order the tests be done.) Once permission is obtained, the evaluation process can begin.

Each exceptionality has its own procedures for placement and the paperwork varies from district to district. The typical range of programs usually includes: Specific Learning Disabilities (SLD), Emotionally Handicapped (EH), Educable Mentally Handicapped (EMH), Trainable Mentally Handicapped (TMH), Physically Impaired (PI), Visually Impaired (VI), Hearing Impaired, (HI), Speech and Language (S/L), Autistic or Profoundly

Mentally Handicapped (PMH). There can be other classifications as well, such as Gifted, Highly Gifted, or Learning/Language Disabled. The list of acronyms grows longer each year. School counselors *must* remain abreast of the language so as to effectively manage the maze of program requirements and procedures.

In addition to the above noted acronyms, "mainstreaming" is a concept that counselors need to also be familiar with as they facilitate the appropriate placement of students. The process in which students are placed in regular classrooms with regular students "as much as possible" is called "mainstreaming." Research reveals that ESE students consistently achieve higher when they are with regular students in regular classrooms. In addition, every effort should be made to avoid placing "labels" on students by referring to them as "EH" or "LD." Labeling only restricts the view of a student's capabilities and does nothing to assist (it may cause harm) the learning process. It is important that students are not described as "handicapped students," but rather, as "students with handicaps."

The process leading to placement continues with collecting evidence which suggests that the child needs an exceptional education program in order to achieve at his or her optimal level in school. As noted above, the process differs among the exceptionalities. As noted, counselors are encouraged to refer to the school district's *Staffing Handbook* or an *ESE Manual* for information relative to each program. In Orange County, once documentation has been assembled, an Educational Planning Conference (EPC) is scheduled by the counselor.

Various members of the original EPT meeting group are invited to the EPC, and others, as dictated by the specific program under consideration, are also invited to participate. At the meeting, to which parents *must* be invited, the documentation is discussed and a team decision is made by those involved as to whether or not the student should be staffed into a particular special program.

Since parental permission must be obtained for placement to occur, it becomes apparent how important parental involvement is throughout the process. Their agreement with placement is much more likely if they understand the situation thoroughly and that their child is not a "problem," but rather a "student who has a learning problem." When an EPC results in a student being placed into an ESE program, it is referred to as a "staffing." At that time, an Individual Education Plan (IEP) is developed by the parents and the exceptional education teacher(s). Counselors' involvement in the IEP is crucial, and they are viewed as "learning experts."

For the counselor, the process does not end here. An EPC can be held at any time a program modification on behalf of the student needs to be considered. There are annual reviews required to determine eligibility for continued placement in a program, and three year reevaluations as well. All meetings involve the counselor, who as chairperson, facilitates the smooth flow of interpersonal interactions and the appropriate paperwork. If, as counselor you are in charge of Exceptional Education at your school, you will be called upon to use all your counseling, consulting, coordinating, and mediation skills.

Important Considerations

Orange County counselors are encouraged to develop an intellectual framework in which they can operate as they facilitate the success of their special needs students. The conceptual framework begins with an understanding of what "exceptional" means. Webster defines it as "exclusive, extraordinary, important, particular, remarkable, and unusual." Reflecting on this definition provides an excellent basis on which to work. With this focus, it is possible to reframe your approach from working with "handicapped" students to working with students with "special needs." The counselor is the child advocate in your school for all students, but those who need the support the most are probably those with special needs. Think of these special needs as "extraordinary" or "remarkable" or even "exclusive," not just as a handicap or a disability.

I believe there are three major considerations which require understanding by counselors to be effective in working with the ESE population in their schools. These include: *1) working with the special needs students, 2) working with their families,* and, *3) working with the faculty.*

Working with Special Needs Students

Once a student has been identified and labeled with an exceptionality, the basic role of the counselor is to assist with the adjustment process. Some students will be relieved to know they have been diagnosed in a specific way; others will feel that something is "wrong" with them. Many feel they must be "stupid." Some will be open and excited about the new path and eager to get started in their new environment, most often an exceptional education setting. Some will be extremely frightened about the change and will need your close attention and counsel. Others are so accustomed to failure and the frustration that coincides with their special condition, that to them, the new diagnosis, the new possibility, is just another road to personal disaster. Whatever the case, it is extremely important that counselors are sensitive to their individual needs, meet them where they are, and understand their unique worldview, their way of seeing things, without evaluation.

It is important to reinforce students who indicate that moving to exceptional education has given them new hope. They usually recognize that their "old" academic life just wasn't working for them. And now, after being placed in exceptional education programs, they have found a different educational approach that, hopefully, will work for them.

An effective way to explain this to just staffed ESE students is to sincerely inform them that they will be receiving the *same* information as any other child in school, just in a different way. They will experience the same information at a *different* pace—*their* pace—and it will be presented to them at *their* level. In the long run, they will gain and learn as much as anyone else in their grade level. Above all, counselors should facilitate the school's personnel to remove the harmful labels where possible. These students know who they are (i.e., there is no need to have a room labeled "Special Education.")

When students are assigned to exceptional education, counselors should work hard at having them leave their offices to enter an ESE class feeling as positive and confident as possible. It may be best to go with them that first day in order to help them feel the support, safety and encouragement needed to succeed. The first few weeks are crucial and may require some close monitoring by the counselor. They will need and cherish the special attention only a professional counselor can provide.

ESE students have the same wants and needs as other children: to be successful, to experience some measure of control over their lives, to be liked, and so forth. Urge teachers to focus on their good habits and any strengths that emerge (all do have strengths!) and how these strengths can add to their ability to succeed at school and in life. That is, encourage teachers to use each child's special strengths to the advantage of both the student and the teacher. This tends to reinforce appropriate classroom behavior and raise self-esteem.

It is most effective to remain calm when talking and working with these students. Being calm and consistent seems to work best. However, like any other students, they sometimes misbehave to gain attention since it has worked for them in the past. Their exceptionality has probably been their lifelong approach for getting attention. However, it is best not to demand a rational explanation when they do misbehave (to do so requires an intellectual answer, and individuals who misbehave from an *emotional* point of view, as these students do, will be unable to supply cognitive reasons). Instead, try to understand what's happening *behind* the unacceptable behavior. Try to identify the emotion causing the behavior.

Counselors are encouraged to provide teachers with methods of dealing with the behavior instead of "labeling" the child because of acting out (i.e., "brat," or even worse). Generally speaking, special needs students will have little trouble correcting their "misbehavior" if teachers are specific enough when attempting to help them change.

There are some behavioral symptoms that counselors and other educators should be aware of concerning these children. Many tend to give up easily, some withdraw quickly and others act out. Some complain about others and are quick to blame others for their own problems. It is common for ESE students to associate with others who are not good influences. Special needs children tend to seek out peers who will accept them, problems and all. Counselors will want to use their counseling skills to intervene in these cases.

The Counselors Role

Schmidt (1999) outlined specific services counselors can be expected to provide for special needs students; these services generally include the following:

1. Participating in school-based meetings to determine appropriate services and programs for exceptional students.

2. Assisting with the development of the Individual Education Plan (IEP) required for every student who has an identified exceptionally.

3. Providing direct counseling services for students.

4. Counseling and consulting with parents.

5. Consulting with classroom and special education teachers.

6. Planning, coordinating, and presenting in-service programs for teachers.

7. Planning extracurricular involvement for special education students.

8. Keeping appropriate records of services for students.

The American School Counselor Association (ASCA) developed position statements concerning various special needs students (ASCA, 1994). For example, ASCA states the following regarding the school counselor's role in working with Attention Deficit Disorder (ADD) students:

ASCA encourages its members to participate in the implementation of the following counseling activities: (1) serve on the school's multidisciplinary team actively involved in the multimodal or multifaceted delivery of interventions or services to the ADD child/adolescent; (2) serve as a consultant and resource to the parents, staff, and other school personnel on the characteristics and problems of ADD students; (3) serve in the capacity of providing regular feedback on the social and academic performance of the ADD child to the members of the multidisciplinary treatment team; (4) help staff design appropriate programs for ADD children which include opportunities for ADD children to learn more appropriate social skills and self-management skills; (5) provide ADD children activities to improve their self-esteem, self-concept and encourage children to practice transferring the content of individual counseling sessions to external settings; (6) promote ADD workshops for staff and support groups for parents and families with an ADD child; and (7) serve as an advocate for ADD children in the community (ASCA, 1994).

A Note on Working with the Gifted

It may surprise some counselors to learn that gifted and talented students also need their services. As a matter of fact, oftentimes more than the "average" student as they have their own set of unique concerns and problems. Many gifted students have poor self-esteem and are "stressed" by the pressure, both real, and imagined, to succeed and excel academically. Hitchner and Tifft-Hitchner (1987) indicated that the gifted student and their parents need counseling services as much, or more, than others. They provide a list of unique and common problems faced by these youngsters. Their list, in part, includes:

- A loss in enthusiasm for learning.

- Doing poorly—or even failing—for the first time in their lives.

- Being shunned for life by family and friends if he or she doesn't go to a "good" college.

- A super-accelerated freshman's feelings about being kidded about his diminutive size as he sits with juniors in an honors math class.

- Being too focused on the academics, and not enough on the non-academics. Here you can warmly—but candidly—bring reality to bear, and share with your counselee the real world of college admission.

- Reaching out and leveling with parents who may have unrealistic expectations. Not only might a youngster be misplaced in a particular course, he or she might be misplaced in a particular school.

- Helping a student sort through his or her priorities to keep things in perspective.

- Counseling a high achiever who looks on cheating as a practical, not an ethical issue.

- Helping a counselee deal with the pressure to get into a "hot" college, which he or she views as a ticket to a "hot" career.

- Helping gifted and talented students through the bureaucracy as they search to satisfy a special objective.

- Counseling a gifted and talented youngster who feels he or she has dishonored the family name and is contemplating suicide.

Being gifted and talented isn't easy. Then again, being exceptional in any way isn't easy.

The American School Counselor Association (ASCA) believes that the counselor has a role to play in the gifted program and suggests the following:

1. To assist in the identification of gifted students through the use of a multiple criterion system that uses at least the following:

   A. General intellectual ability

   B. Specific academic ability

   C. Visual and performing arts ability

   D. Practical arts ability

   E. Psycho-social ability

   F. Creative thinking ability

2. To advocate that the personal, social, emotional and vocational needs of the gifted are included in the program.

3. To act as an advocate for gifted students in all matters involving the school.

4. To act as a consultant to the school administration in curricular concerns and the school's involvement with the parents.

5. To provide leadership in the establishment of training and sensitivity programs concerning the gifted to staff, parents, and administrators.

6. To recommend material and resources for gifted programs.

7. To provide group and individual guidance and counseling to all gifted students.

8. To continue to upgrade knowledge and skills in the area of the gifted and talented (ASCA, 1999).

Working with the Families of Special Needs Students

Families with special needs children are like any other family. They are units connected emotionally, physically, intellectually and spiritually. When any part of the unit becomes disconnected, imbalance is created in the unit and disruption occurs. Therefore, when a child is classified by the educational system as needing "exceptional" services, the family is deeply affected.

There are various ways that a family might discover that their child is exceptional. Sometimes a neighbor, friend or family member raises the question. Sometimes it is the school, either through a teacher, administrator, or counselor. Occasionally a family is strong enough to bring their special child's needs to your attention. Regardless of how the exceptionality is discovered, you will find that it is important that consideration and nurturing be provided to the family. School counselors should be available to the family when it learns of its child's exceptionality as they most likely will need your assistance and counsel during this stressful time. You will learn that you, as counselor, will usually be the first one in the school to whom they turn.

Various Family Styles

Families react differently when they learn their child has been diagnosed as having special needs. The *supportive* families are usually better educated and accept what the school can do for their child. They are more aware of options and alternatives and are willing to embrace new methods which might enhance their special child's learning. These families are the school counselor's allies. They function well as a unit and family members usually have high self-esteem. Suggestions and assistance do not threaten them, and you will find that they appreciate the services being offered to their child. If you approach them as team members, you can learn many things from them that will help you (and the school) be more successful with their special child.

The more educated, supportive type of family desires to learn all they can about the particular needs of their child. It is best to be open, honest, and as knowledgeable as possible about their child's special needs. They will expect it. This type family will quickly inform you if there is something you or the school should become more familiar with concerning their child. Their expectations are high and they reveal an awareness of their child's interests and show the same pleasure and pride in his or her achievements that other parents do. No matter how small or trivial it may seem to others, they truly value the accomplishments of their special needs child. Most of all, the supportive family accepts and respects its child for what he or she "is" and "is not."

Within the supportive type families there are some who are less well educated. They are supportive in that they accept their special child and what "education" can and is doing. They have the same dreams as other parents have, but there is a difference in their knowledge and understanding of their child's exceptionality. They often do not understand the limitations their child has, sometimes creating impossible expectations. However, because of their supportive nature, they will be open to the counselor's suggestions. They are interested in working with the school counselor, but they need constant support, and above all, a counselor's expertise concerning the nature of their child's exceptionality.

A third family type is one that has intellectual ability but has very little to give to the special child emotionally. This type family often finds it difficult to accept the fact that their child is "exceptional" or that they have the personal resources capable of coping with him or her. Such families have great difficulty in getting through the "denial stage" and will need the counselor's assistance to do so. Their own self-esteem becomes involved and they may attempt to cover up the special needs their child has, as well as the overall reality of the situation. They will often use every resource available to prove the counselor wrong and/or get someone else (usually an authority) to prove the counselor or the school wrong!

Fear is a big factor with this type family—they are fearful that their child will never be successful in the "real world." They also fear rejection, discrimination and often have a defeatist attitude. They need patience and honest, open, facilitative feedback concerning their child. Provide them with information as factually as possible and make certain they understand their alternatives and rights. Be aware that the expectations they place on their child may create problems for the counselor and others in the school. These students may spend many hours in counseling simply because of the impossible, unrealistic demands placed on them. Many counselors have found it most effective to provide family counseling in these situations.

Another family type is the uneducated family who is also unable to provide emotional support for their child. Even though they sometimes reject their own child because the child is "different," counselors must continue to work with this student. No other child in the school needs support more than does the special needs student whose family is under-educated and unable (for whatever reason) to provide the emotional support needed by their special child. The school must provide the many missing ingredients their families cannot share with their own special needs child. Seek consultation with professional colleagues when encountering this type of family to discover other ways of reaching out to them and their child. Also look for the support services in your community available to work with such families. One may also need collegial support for one's own personal wellness when working with such difficult situations.

Working with the Faculty

Working with the faculty as they work with ESE students will test a counselor's facilitative skills, his or her public relations skills, and every other counseling skill he or she possesses! Remember that these are colleagues, educational peers, and that most have a strong desire "to fully educate" the students in their classroom. However, when working with ESE students, they often become frustrated and their patience grows thin.

Special needs students can disrupt dreams, goals, desires, and the best laid plans that the teacher has for his or her classes. And, these students often create overwhelming frustration, especially among untrained teachers. Most teachers are not adequately prepared to teach exceptional children and many say it is unfair that a special child is "mainstreamed" into their class. Others feel inadequate, helpless, and confused when encountering the various exceptionalities. Even though teachers work hard to instill a love of learning in their students, ESE students often appear uninterested in learning, as if they do not care. This combination is sufficient to deprive teachers of the feedback they need to feel effective.

Sometimes it is difficult for a teacher to realize the difference they make in an exceptional child's life is not necessarily in the academic area. Often it is not. Your role as counselor is to care for, support, and give assistance to teachers who work with special needs students. Become as knowledgeable as possible about the many exceptionalities that teachers find in their classrooms, and be assertive about your availability to help. Some counselors send out a *confidential* memo at the beginning of each school year informing teachers of the special needs students in their respective classrooms. The confidential memo details the special needs each student has and provides suggestions (when appropriate) on how best to teach this student. Too many teachers never know which students in their classes are ESE students, nor do they know what the disabilities are. Teachers appreciate knowing these things and will value suggestions or tips on how best to teach such students.

You will find that teachers desire more strategies, techniques, and assistance when it comes to teaching these children than when working with non-special needs students. Find out what the teachers already know (perhaps a needs survey) and then assist them in learning more about the various exceptionalities. The school counselor can provide a real service to children by helping teachers become more skilled in understanding and applying how special needs students learn as well as how to motivate them.

One of the critical concepts counselors can help teachers develop is that special needs students must feel that "no student has more worth and dignity" than any other. If teachers understand that logic often tends to work best with certain special needs students, it makes it easier for them to understand how to apply discipline, and so forth. Some teachers need to be reminded that certain students require more time for written work, test taking and so forth. Some need special assignments, preferred seating, peer tutors and other types of assistance.

As a counselor, you can provide workshops for regular teachers on how to work effectively with ESE students who have been mainstreamed into their classes. And finally, gently inform teachers that to embarrass a special needs student in front of peers almost always fails to achieve the desired results. Encourage teachers to correct these students in private when needed. ESE students, like most others, simply don't hear us when we yell.

Summary

Counselors, being child development specialists, play pivotal roles in their work with special needs students. No other educator is better equipped to assist the exceptional students themselves, their families, or their teachers to reach greater understanding of the nature of being a special needs student. It is through using the skills of both counseling and consulting that counselors reach out to all who work with this unique population. The special needs students are some of the most challenging, and at the same time, the most rewarding students you will work with.

Finally, I offer the following ten "tips" to lessen your and their stress when working with special needs students:

1. Show genuine affection at all times.

2. Find opportunities to build their self esteem where and when possible.

3. Give them your undivided attention when working with them.

4. Be available to talk to them about their problems when they are ready to talk.

5. Use humor and empathy, not sympathy.

6. Try to understand their stressors—wear their shoes.

7. Provide them with safety and security.

8. Most enjoy having fun, so have fun with them.

9. Provide them with love, patience, and understanding.

10. Generally enjoy them.

References

ASCA. (1994). *Role statement: The school counselor and attention deficit disorder.* Alexandria, VA. American School Counselor Association. Author.

ASCA. (1999). *Role statement: The school counselor and the gifted student.* Alexandria, VA. American School Counselor Association. Author.

Hitchner, K., & Tifft-Hitchner, A. (1996). *Counseling today's secondary students: Practical strategies, techniques, and materials for the school counselor.* West Nyack, NY: The Center for Applied Research in Education.

Schmidt, J.J. (1999). *Counseling in schools: Essential services and comprehensive programs.* Needham Heights, MA: Allyn & Bacon.

Section V

The Counselor as Consultant and Coordinator: The Family, Appraisal, Career, and Educational Counseling Programs

This section begins with a chapter written by Dr. Tom Harrison concerning the developmental school counselor's role as consultant and coordinator. Dr. Harrison provides some excellent "real life" examples of consultative roles faced by the school counselor of the new millennium and presents an easy-to-follow model for effectively working through several consultative situations. In addition, several consultant models are presented that a school counselor will find extremely helpful. The counselor/coordinator function is also described in detail.

The school counselor and strategies for working with families as a counselor and consultant is a topic that has seldom appeared in school counseling books. However, it is a role that is becoming increasingly important to school counselors. In fact, the results of a counselor work behaviors study, conducted by the National Board for Certified Counselors (NBCC), revealed that randomly selected counselors, including school counselors, placed "working with families" as one of their five main functions. Dr. Ellen Amatea and Ms. Barbara Brown (Chapter 17) indicate that: *Families often report feeling trapped, coerced, and criticized in their interactions with school counselors and others about their child's school problems. And, school professionals often feel misunderstood and unappreciated in their efforts to work with students' families.* What can be done to improve this situation? Amatea and Brown suggest that often what is missing is an analysis of, and an effective method of, intervening in the larger school/family *ecosystem* that is formed when the family and school come together to create ways of relating that either facilitate or impede a child's problem resolution and development. They address this issue by: a) considering the ways in which schools and families become engaged with or disengaged from one another in a system of interaction, b) proposing a model which school counselors can use in assessing and intervening in the ecosystem comprised of the family and school, and c) illustrating its use by means of actual student cases with which they have been involved.

Next, Dr. Larry Loesch and Mr. William Goodman detail the appraisal function K-12 school counselors fulfill in a developmentally oriented counseling program. They describe the coordination role the counselor plays in the appraisal program and emphasize the importance of appropriate consultation with teachers, parents, and others concerning results of appraisals given in schools. Concerning the latter Loesch and Goodman write: *When school counselors help other school personnel understand appraisal results effectively, these school personnel can then provide the best educational services to students.* Loesch and Goodman also offer some excellent strategies for interpreting appraisal results to students, teachers, parents and others.

Dr. Pat Schwallie-Giddis and Ms. Linda Kobylarz offer several innovative career development concepts and practices for the K-12 school counselor in Chapter 19. They write: *It is clear that the workplace of tomorrow will be very different from the workplace of today. The emphasis in the future will be on change, flexibility, multiple career paths and lifelong learning.* The writers also suggest various strategies for school counselors to use in implementing and managing a comprehensive K-12 career development program. They challenge K-12 school counselors to *reenergize our schools and help all our students succeed in a dynamic and demanding workplace.* Schwallie-Giddis and Kobylarz indicate that school counselors are uniquely positioned to promote movement toward a truly comprehensive approach to career development through their coordination activities.

In Chapter 20, Dr. Jim Pitts focuses on the educational counseling and educational guidance roles of the K-1 developmental school counselor. Pitts defines the two concepts as follows: *Educational counseling refers to counselors' efforts to help students develop self concepts which keep their educational options open. Educational guidance refers to counselors' interventions aimed at assisting students to make the best use of the options available.*

Helping students realize that they have educational and career options, helping them keep their options open, and assisting them to make the best use of those options are important school counselor tasks. School counselors can make a difference in students' lives by finding ways to do these things effectively. Pitts writes: *Effective educational counseling and guidance is highly important and should be a high priority for all developmental K-12 school counselors.*

As stated repeatedly throughout this book, consultation and coordination are two very important functions of the K-12 developmental school counselor.

Joe Wittmer

Chapter 16
The School Counselor as Consultant/Coordinator

by

Thomas C. Harrison

Tom Harrison, PhD, is Associate Professor in the Department of Counseling and Educational Psychology at the University of Nevada, Reno. He teaches courses in counseling and consultation and is a consultant to school counselors throughout the state as well as a consultant to the district's K-12 comprehensive career guidance program.

Introduction

The school counselor may have the toughest job in the educational profession. The student population itself is challenging enough, but what makes the counselor's job so challenging is the variety of roles assumed in their respective schools. As noted throughout this book, these roles include: counselor, advocate, confidant, leader, collaborator, human relations expert, teacher, administrator, consultant, and coordinator. The latter functions, consultant and coordinator, are two important roles for the counselor and are addressed in this chapter. When utilized effectively in a comprehensive guidance program, these two important counselor functions can help in shaping the direction of the entire school in different and exciting ways.

In this chapter the author addresses the role that consultation and coordination play in the comprehensive school guidance and counseling program. A definition and discussion of consultation is followed by several examples depicting consulting issues in the schools. The role of school counselor as coordinator is also presented. The goal of this chapter is to help those training to become school counselors better understand the implications of a consulting and coordinating role in the school setting. In addition, practicing school counselors hoping to do their job as consultant/coordinator more effectively, should find the chapter very helpful.

Promoting the Guidance Program through a Consulting Role

Consultation Defined

Consultation became a widely accepted form of service delivery for school personnel during the 1970s (Schmidt, 1999). Simply stated, consultation is a process whereby the first party (consultant) assists a second party (consultee) in finding a solution to a problem that concerns a third party (client). In schools, consultation is considered an *indirect* service to students through *direct involvement* with teachers, administrators, and parents. That is, students are the central focus and counselors working directly with teachers, administrators, and parents serve to benefit the student population. Consultation, when put into practice by professional educators, can be a key element in helping to design effective learning environments for the twenty-first century (Dettmer, Dyck, & Thurston, 1999).

Counselors can be consultants to individual professionals such as teachers, other counselors, administrators, and so forth. In addition, they often consult with parents as well as to groups and various systems throughout the community. The interventions can be *developmental, educational, preventative,* or *crisis-oriented*. For example, a developmental guidance program is designed to be proactive and preventative and counselors work with individual teachers, administrators, and parents in implementing the developmentally oriented program. Within the domains of the program itself, counselors can help individual students assess career goals which are developmental issues. Counselors can also help teachers and others deal with crises situations and may aim their efforts toward the prevention of similar crises in the future. In addition, counselors often work with groups of teachers on learning ways to better manage their respective classrooms, which is considered educational consultation.

In order to meet the challenges of a consulting role, school counselors-in-training, and those now employed as counselors, need to be equipped with *knowledge* and *skills*. Knowledge of the consulting process is requisite as is the knowledge of consultant characteristics, needed skills and behaviors. Moreover, knowledge of Schein's (1988) *process consultation model*, Caplan and Caplan's (1993) mental health consultation and collaboration model, and Myrick's (1997) *systematic consultation model* can be of help to the counselor assuming a consulting role.

In the following section, I describe pertinent stages for consulting in the schools and consultant characteristics and behaviors. Relevant information from the three consulting models mentioned above are presented briefly. For a detailed analysis of the consultation models, you are urged to refer to the works of Caplan and Caplan (1993) and Myrick (1997).

Consultation Stages

In general, the stages of consulting include *entry, initiation of a relationship, assessment, problem definition and goal setting, strategy selection and implementation, evaluation,* and *termination* (Brown, Pryzwansky, & Schulte, 1998). These stages are of particular importance for an "outside" consultant (one who is hired for a specific purpose). However, when applied to the school setting, some consulting stages are seen as having unique implications for the counselor/consultant. In particular, the *entry stage* and *relationship initiation* stages are of special significance. And, it is important for a school counselor to understand the implications.

School counselors are considered "internal consultants" because they are employed members of the organization in which they consult. Thus, the school counselor's "entry" into the system is unique because administrators are likely to be familiar with the consultant (school counselor), although in another role. If you are a beginning school counselor, your entry into a school setting is even more unique and contains important issues needing to be addressed. For example, administrators will be familiar with the counselor(s) already practicing in their respective school. As a new "internal consultant," you may be cast into the same role(s) as is the established counselor(s), one which you may not desire. Therefore, it is to the beginning school counselor's advantage to discuss his or her anticipated role with the administrator (and new counseling colleagues) and have that role clarified and agreed upon as soon as possible.

A request for a formal introduction to the school faculty, parents, and others, describing the counselor's role as consultant can be very helpful. This introduction will serve to diminish "role ambiguity" which occurs when the counselor/consultant becomes unsure of his or her role. This uncertainty can lead to problems when implementing the guidance program's objective and goals. For example, a counselor unsure of the consulting role may perpetuate the perception that he or she will eventually take responsibility for someone else's problem(s) by providing counseling to a student who is having a personality conflict with a teacher. In a consulting role, the counselor would help the teacher and student solve *their* problem and never "owns" the problem, per se.

Also during the entry stage, the new school counselor will want to anticipate confidentiality issues involved in the consultant role and relate his or her concerns and orientations of confidentiality to the school administrators, faculty, and staff. Without this discussion and understanding, the counselor new to the school can be placed in uncomfortable situations or in situations where there is a possible conflict of interest. Attending to this concern early in the entry and relationship-building stage presents an opportunity to deal with confidentiality before critical situations arise (Brown, Pryzwansky, & Schulte, 1998).

Developing good relationships requires the school counselor to gather *informal or "working" knowledge* of how their respective school operates. Informal knowledge refers to having information about the particular idiosyncrasies of the school. Without this "working" knowledge, new counselors can likely find themselves quickly overwhelmed with resistances from administration and staff. For example, historically, many school personnel have considered counseling an ancillary service. Therefore, knowledge of how counseling and current counselors are viewed by the school's administration and staff can help the beginning counselor avoid pitfalls which may hinder the implementation of the guidance program's objectives.

In building relationships in a consulting role, effective school counselors understand that consultation is not a process whereby one person (consultant) *imposes* upon another individual (consultee or client). They do—and are expected to—*expose* their values and beliefs. However, consultation is always a *collaborative effort* and the importance of this cannot be understated. Collaboration is an approach in which one professional (consultant) is helping another professional (teacher, administrator, or parent) and requires the establishment of a "*coordinate relationship.*" Each "professional" has his or her own areas of expertise. A problem for the counselor can arise if he or she is remiss in demonstrating a collaborative approach. For example, it is not uncommon for the counselor to be asked by the principal to work with a particular teacher who is "unaware of any problem" or who has a history of reluctance to work through issues. Unless the counselor can focus efforts in a collaborative manner by demonstrating understanding of *both* sides (principal and teacher), the risk of alienating the teacher increases dramatically and may impede the consultative process.

Fortunately, counselors find collaboration and the "coordinate relationship" to be a familiar approach because it is also used in counseling situations. Moreover, the school administration and parents also understand and expect this approach. Both collaboration and the "coordinate relationship" is covered in greater detail later in this chapter.

With the knowledge of consulting stages and, in particular, the importance of the entry and relationship-building phases, the counselor is prepared to initiate a consulting role in the schools. When initiating this process, awareness of the characteristics of successful consultants can help.

Consultant Characteristics

Counselors wishing to work in a consulting role in the comprehensive guidance program will likely find that the characteristics needed for a successful consulting experience are essentially the same characteristics as those needed for effective counseling. Core conditions so important to effective counseling outcomes need to be demonstrated as does an ability to 1) *assess problems*, 2) *explore alternatives*, and 3) *choose appropriate courses of action*. Likewise, the use of open questions, clarifications, restatements, and summaries can be especially enhancing to the consulting process.

It should be acknowledged, however, that consultation does require a need to focus upon specific attitudes, values, knowledge, and skills that are somewhat different than those of counseling. For example, in a consulting role, counselors will need "*structural integrity*." This refers to the counselor's abilities to maintain the *perception* of themselves as consultants in the face of adversity or other challenges within the system. A counselor taking on the role of consultant will also need to set *parameters* or *boundaries* upon his or her role and upon the activities undertaken. Establishing parameters or "boundaries" refers to a counselor's willingness to communicate to school personnel activities that are appropriate, and those inappropriate to her or his role. Coordinating an activity such as an intramural softball game between the school's seniors and sophomores, while sounding like fun, will consume valuable counse-

lor time and might be more appropriately coordinated through the physical education department. Finally, counselors need to be *patient* and mindful that system change requires some discomfort, anxiety, preparation time, work up-front, and much attention to establishing collaborative relationships with teachers, administrators, and parents.

Consultation Models

Equipped with informal knowledge, counselors can then utilize more formal knowledge of group leadership styles and group processes to assist them in consultative situations. Specifically, counselors need to be especially knowledgeable in *diagnosing* group dynamics and the ways in which groups arrive at solutions to problems. This is required in part because of the many people involved and the variety of decisions needing to be made.

Schein's (1988) *process consultation model* addressed the dynamics of group problem-solving and group decision-making styles (i.e., "plop method," authority rule, minority rule, majority rule, unanimity, and consensus). Awareness of how the decisions are made can help the counselor plan for teacher and administrator's resistances as well as helping the counselor see potential ways to reduce resistances. Consensus occurs when communication is open to the point that a formal vote does not need to be taken, yet all have a "sense of the meeting" and of the decision (Schein, 1988). For example, all meetings in which guidance issues are discussed will be regulated by the group's decision-making style. A decision on a course of action made by consensus is more difficult to achieve, but drastically increases the group's cohesion and performance (Schein, 1988). Cohesion can then enhance commitment to the guidance program and it's objectives since "all have a sense" of the program's goals. Subsequent behaviors by those in the group will likely reflect this supportive commitment to the program.

In addition to awareness of group process, knowledge of Caplan and Caplan's (1993) mental health consultation and collaboration model can be helpful to the counselor/consultant. Useful principles of Caplan and Caplan's model include the *consultant as collaborator* with an emphasis upon establishing a "*coordinate relationship*" with consultees and clients, and his diagnostic categories identified in "consultee-centered" case consultation.

In the guidance program, *collaboration* occurs when the consultant (school counselor) engages one or more individuals in working upon the same problem. For example, the counselor has learned of a problem occurring in the classroom between a teacher and a student. Using a collaborative approach, the counselor works with the teacher (consultee) on learning new methods of interacting and reinforcing student behaviors while at the same time provides individual consultation (perhaps using specific counseling strategies) to the student (client) on how he or she can help themselves be more successful by controlling their behaviors in the classroom. To help the student, both teacher and counselor need to successfully execute their "part of the deal." In this case, the teacher benefits and can generalize his or her new knowledge to other situations involving students; the student benefits by learning new ways to feel more in control in the classroom; and the school system benefits as a result because the student's other teachers can now experience more classroom compliance with this student.

Caplan and Caplan's advocation of a *"coordinate relationship"* implies that school counselors will be most effective as consultants when they approach teachers, administrators, and parents "on the same level." That simply means that the counselor demonstrates *respect* for everyone's expertise and knowledge. Therefore, using a "coordinate relationship" approach when consulting through collaborating takes on the idea of two or more professionals working on the same problem together. The concepts of collaboration and "coordinate relationships" also help with the counselor's "mental set" or role orientation.

Collaboration and the establishment of "coordinate relationships" ought not to be problematic for the school counselor. Collaboration is a skill with which all counselors have some familiarity upon graduating from a counselor preparation program. However, ease in establishing "coordinate relationships" could prove more problematic and does require practice and experience. While most school personnel and parents will anticipate being respected for their knowledge, the school counselor just beginning the consultant role should move slowly and deliberately in assuring that this "coordinate relationship" is established and maintained.

Differentiating four diagnostic areas of consultee-centered case consultation into a *lack of knowledge, lack of skill, lack of confidence,* or *lack of objectivity* have also proven useful to Caplan in his professional work and can prove to be of equal value to the school counselor/consultant. Counselors using this perceptual framework can more effectively assess problems and determine

appropriate courses of action to help teachers, administrators, and parents. For example, in working with a teacher having a problem communicating with an administrator, one counselor noted a close parallel between the teacher's problems with the administrator and the teacher's well-known problems with his spouse. The counselor determined that the problem was one of a *lack of objectivity* on the part of the teacher. This "diagnosis" guided the counselor's consultive intervention. Simply having told the teacher what to do or trying to educate him on how to behave differently (lack of skill or knowledge) would likely have been unsuccessful.

Effective diagnosis of problem areas through the use of Caplan and Caplan's (1993) categories require time and practice in which to become skillful. However, it can help the counselor to understand that these categories closely parallel the assessment processes used in normal counseling situations and therefore should present little challenge in the incorporation of these concepts.

While the consulting models of Schein (1988) and Caplan and Caplan (1993) can help orient the counselor to the consulting role, Myrick's (1997) *systematic consultation* model is a "how to" model and puts consultation into action. When combined with the works of Schein and Caplan and Caplan, the systematic consultation model provides the counselor with an explicit consulting paradigm. The systematic consultation model is a step-wise model which includes: *1) identifying the issue, 2) clarifying the problem, 3) identifying the goal, 4) observing the behaviors (when indicated), 5) developing a plan, 6) initiating the plan,* and *7) following-up.* Emphasis is upon the consultant's facilitative skills and the willingness to become involved.

School counselors can readily use this model because it falls well within the range of what school personnel expect from a school counselor. The use of core conditions and facilitative responses such as those used in counseling have particular value in this consulting model.

What follows are examples that demonstrate an integration of the models and behaviors given above. These examples are presented because they will likely be experienced in one form or another by all school counselors. The step-wise procedures outlined in *"The Action Phase"* section of each example are specific. However, you are urged to adapt the methods and steps used to your styles and situations.

Case Example: Consulting with an Administrator

"Would you Please do me a favor?"

Administrators, like the rest of the school staff, are busy and appreciate it when other school personnel can help. However, the request for help can be a two-edged sword, and the counselor/consultant will want to be aware of both edges. On the one hand, consulting with administrators can increase the probability that the counselor is seen as trustworthy, competent, and a team player. On the other hand, such assistance can sometimes jeopardize the long term goals of the program. Sometimes the counselor/consultant will inadvertently create mistrust with one contingency while attempting to build rapport with another. Mistrust of the counselor/consultant will create serious problems for the counselor and the comprehensive guidance program. If the long-range goals of the program are to have counselors be of more help to students, parents, and staff, then the counselor/consultant will want to attend to building trust among *all* of the personnel including parents.

Situation: Your principal has learned that a teacher is having some problems in the classroom and asks you to help by "checking-up" on the situation.

Assessing the Situation and Planning for Action

It is important for the counselor/consultant in this situation to fully understand the ramifications of accepting such an assignment. Of primary importance is the fact that helping in this fashion could quickly change the role (or at least the perception) of the counselor from consultant to "enforcer," an inappropriate and punitive role. Be aware of this pitfall. Such a role change will also most probably leave you being perceived by teachers as pro-administration and anti-staff. The effective counselor/consultant is perceived as advocates for *both* the administration and staff!

Second, a report of such counselor activities, as described above, will likely be passed along to others in the teachers' lounge before the end of the day. The result can be teachers beginning to mistrust the counselor's intentions and decrease their requests for help with students, and so forth. Moreover, acting upon the request can hinder the communication lines between teachers, counselors, and staff, thereby creating more problems and the need for more counselor intervention time.

Third, counselors need to remain aware of "who owns the problem." If consultation is effective the administrator will learn that the problem delineated above is his or her problem, not the counselor's. However, this does not mean that you do not consult with the principal in this situation. You might suggest to the administrator that he/she approach the teacher directly. However, if not accepted, you may want to take a different consultative approach with the principal, perhaps Myrick's (1977) approach previously described.

The Action Phase

1. Let the administrator know that you will honor the request after having a chance to discuss some of your concerns with him or her. This is an opportunity for the counselor to "gently" educate the administration about short and long term implications of such a request. A counselor can help the administrator see that such a request, if not dealt with appropriately, can jeopardize future counselor relationships with other teachers. It can be helpful to point out how the short-term solution might create long-term problems for the counselor/consultant and the overall guidance program. Or,

2. Utilize Myrick's (1997) Systematic Consultation Model and help the administrator brainstorm other solutions. And,

3. Follow-up.

Case Example:
Consulting with a Teacher

"This student is a pain; you fix it."

Teachers often need a counselor's consultation skills in dealing objectively with troublesome students. The demands of teaching everyday can be overwhelming at times, and teachers may "give up" on a problematic student while asking you to provide a quick remedy to the problem. In many cases, the problem in the classroom is the result of dynamic but inappropriate interaction between the teacher and student. Therefore, the responsibility for the problem is actually shared by both the teacher and student. However, some teachers will only focus upon the student's behavior. The student needs "fixing" or "remediation", but as teacher, "I'm not a part of the problem." By doing so, teachers with this approach to troublesome students essentially deprive themselves of feelings of empowerment and can make the consulting process challenging for the counselor.

Situation: A teacher believes a student is unmanageable and sends the student to you. The teacher's expectation is that you will provide a quick solution and will not allow the student back in the classroom until you give the okay.

Assessing the Situation and Planning for Action

The teacher has asked for your expert assistance. Begin by asking yourself: is it a lack of skill, confidence, knowledge, or objectivity on the part of the teacher? The more upset and rigid the teacher, the more likely the key to the solution resides in the teacher. Think of a collaborative effort. Think of how you can help the teacher clarify the problem. Think of how you can "gently" avoid being placed in the role of "fixer-upper." Once the word spreads that you can solve problems by seeing only the student, you will have a difficult time restructuring assistance in the future to include working with other teachers. A "magic wand" approach on the part of the counselor/consultant is short lived, and if a future situation requires teacher involvement, he or she might feel singled out or might experience feelings of failure because they suddenly are being asked to participate in the solution. As a result, teacher resistance to your suggestions might increase, adding to your already busy schedule.

Be aware that three dimensions of the school system are operating in the above situation: an adult teacher, a student, and you—an adult counselor. This situation often involves "saving face" for the teacher.

The teacher has made a decision to remove the student and for the counselor to countermand that decision will leave the teacher in an awkward position—having lost power to a student as well as to a peer/colleague. You may need to "go in the back door" by discreetly citing examples of how similar past problems with other students have been successfully handled. It has been my experience that getting the student back in the class quickly so that academic performance is not inversely impacted is most important.

Finally, remember that when seeing the student, your role as a consultant is: helping a second party solve a problem or concern with a third party. The problem certainly involves the student, but the successful solution will likely result from the collaborative input of teacher, student, and counselor/consultant.

Planning for Action

One approach might be to:

1. Avoid triangulation by accepting the teacher referral directly.

2. Consider talking to the teacher prior to seeing the student. Therefore, you might schedule the student to see you later in the day and mention to the teacher that an appointment has been scheduled.

3. Utilize a "coordinate relationship" strategy by demonstrating understanding and acceptance of the teacher's view of the student and the problem. Demonstrate a willingness to help while sharing your concern about the student's performance.

4. Assess the extent of the teacher's concerns in terms of lack of knowledge, skill, confidence, or objectivity. Lack of knowledge or skills can be addressed directly with information or skill-building after a relationship has been established. Lack of confidence or objectivity will require more of a "counseling" orientation on your part.

5. Work on a plan with the teacher to get the student back in the classroom as quickly as possible so achievement will not be seriously impaired. If academic achievement is impaired, this will only complicate the problem. The student now has two problems! You may want to have the teacher prioritize the student's aberrant behaviors. Take the first behavior on the prioritized list and affirm that your central concern is getting the student back in the classroom and that your objective priority is to act upon the behavior identified as first on the list.

6. Follow-up.

Case Example: Consulting with a Parent

"Not my child!"

Parents want their children to succeed in school. They want them to exhibit positive behavior at all times, to respect teachers, and so forth. Counselors can assist parents by teaching parents effective ways of promoting such behaviors in their child by consulting with them individually or in groups.

One of the more unpleasant tasks falling upon counselors is the dreaded phone conversation with a parent whose child has been disciplined by the teacher and/or administration. The counselor will usually be aware of the problem, but may not have had much involvement in the decision making nor in the disciplinary action. Nevertheless, it is often the counselor who receives the phone call from the parent wanting to know, "What happened?"

Situation: A student has been asked to leave the classroom for repeatedly creating a disturbance. The teacher will not allow the student back into the class until some intervention is undertaken. The parent calls you complaining that the teacher is being unfair, too harsh, and is a larger part of the problem than is their child.

Assessing the Situation and Planning for Action

Remember that the parent has much emotional investment in their child and will likely be reacting strongly to the teacher out of a sense of protection. This is not a time to be overly objective with the parent. Subjectivity on your part may be needed. It is likely the parent is responding to some perceived failure on his or her part as parent. Anger and resentment may be masking feelings of guilt and helplessness. It can be useful to remember that anger is also comprised of hurt and fear; resentment usually accompanies feelings of guilt.

Use the information provided in how the parent is responding as a means of understanding his or her child's behaviors. Students acting out in the classroom often have learned how to do so in their homes.

In some cases, the counselor might actually be in agreement with the parents' assessment of the teacher's abilities. However, agreeing with the parent will usually lead to triangulation, and the counselor will experience the unwanted consequences more so than will the parent. Be thinking of ways to avoid triangulation. This is not a time to "choose up sides," regardless of your personal feelings or beliefs. Appealing to a lack of information (as a reason to not agree or disagree) can provide the counselor/consultant some needed "wiggle room."

Frame this situation as being a "crisis" for the parent and student. In doing so, you can more easily remain open to understanding and responding rather than judging, agreeing, and reacting.

The Action Phase

1. Remain calm. This is an emotionally charged situation for *all* involved.

2. Slow the process down by using your facilitative skills. Clarifications can be especially useful. Feeling-focused responses can be used early on in the conversation to help build quick rapport and ease the tension. Understanding on your part is needed.

3. Buy time. If the parent has already escalated to the point where he or she is not able to "hear" you, attempt to reschedule the phone call once you have heard some of the parent's concerns. Even a half-hour "break" can go along way in diffusing the situation. Be sure to tell the parent that you appreciate his or her concern, you would like to talk more, and ask if it would be possible to call them back shortly when you have the "undivided" time to devote to this "important" concern now facing everyone involved.

4. Focus on "teamwork." Parents may have many unpleasant things to say about the teacher, the school, and/or the administration. It is important to hear about these feelings and observations and to assure the parents that they have been heard. However, what often gets lost in this type of situation is the focus on the student. Assure the parent that everyone involved wants the best for their child, and inform them that is your major focus of concern. The parent has the right, and responsibility, to question decisions made at school. Express appreciation for him or her as a concerned parent. This can help relieve parental guilt.

5. Encourage the parent to talk with the teacher directly. If this has already occurred, help the parent process that exchange. It may well be that the parent knows and agrees their child has a problem, but the parent may be reacting to an unsatisfactory interaction with the teacher. Your facilitative skills can be of great help in this situation.

6. Contact the teacher. Mention the parent called you. Use discretion when discussing the conversation with the teacher. It might be helpful to disclose some information to the teacher because it will demonstrate that you are attempting to see their side of the issue. However, it is important to remember that you are also an advocate of the child and his

or her parents. Ask the teacher how you might be of some assistance and help brainstorm solutions. If needed, you might plan and coordinate a parent conference. At the conference, be certain your role is understood to be that of gathering information in order to be able to help the child and that you are there to help facilitate that process.

7. Follow-up with both parent and teacher. Coordinating the parent conference in this example is reflective of the importance of the school counselor's coordinating activities. In the following section, the school counselor as coordinator is presented.

Promoting the Guidance Program through Coordinating Activities

Coordination is a counselor initiated leadership process in which the counselor helps organize and manage the comprehensive guidance program and related services. As noted throughout the previous, and later chapters in this book, it is an important counselor intervention aimed at managing various indirect services which benefit students. Some examples include coordinating career development programs, student appraisal, child study teams, peer helper programs, teacher-as-advisor programs, academic/educational guidance programs, and many others.

Theoretically, the central thrust of coordinating efforts is aimed at "*institutionalizing*" the comprehensive guidance program. In other words, the goal is to have the school personnel "own" the counseling program (the guidance curriculum) so that there is routine infusion of such important concepts as self-esteem and career development issues into regular classroom activities and in other activities throughout the school.

The coordinating role will likely be the least visible role played by counselors if the program/activity is successful, while paradoxically being their most far-reaching and broad-based function. However, this can lead to a pitfall. The "invisible" nature of coordinating the program can influence counselors not interested in providing direct counseling services to prefer this role. This is made possible by the sheer time that can be involved in coordinating inappropriate, non-counseling type activities. However, as Myrick (1997) pointed out, this preference for behind-the-scenes-work can be at the expense of performing other necessary counselor functions such as responsive services (counseling) individual student planning, and so forth. Therefore, awareness of this potential pitfall is crucial for school counselors. As noted in section two of this book, coordination is only one aspect of the role of the developmental school counselor.

Myrick (1997) also pointed out that, similar to a consulting role, effective coordination of the program requires good *leadership skills, expertise in individual and group process*, and *effective listening skills*. In addition to this list there are other behaviors such as: an ability to diagnose student and program needs, awareness of how system change takes time, willingness to thoroughly plan and prepare for the activity, patience, persistence, time-management, "structural integrity" as explained earlier in this chapter, a commitment to the coordinating role, and foresight and forethought.

"Foresight and forethought" is a subtle skill, yet one that is most helpful. One's ability to attempt to "see into the future" allows the counselor to move from a *reactive stance* to a *proactive stance* and a more creative posture. A proactive stance helps the counselor maintain more control over his or her valuable time. Without this creative posture, the school counselor can quickly become absorbed into a coordinating role that becomes less productive to the overall counseling program goals and objectives.

Some school counselors take on the coordination of inappropriate activities because they believe the job will not get done unless they themselves do it. This tradition of over-extending serves some counselors well, but inappropriately, by providing them a non-counseling, "administrator driven" role and function. However, coordinating a comprehensive guidance program requires that counselors guard their time and determine which activities are appropriate to coordinate and which are not a function of the job. It is best to avoid inappropriate and untimely requests if possible.

Parents, teachers, and students rely on the counselor's leadership in planning and coordinating numerous special services and programs. And, as noted, the effectiveness of such programs and/or services often depends on the skills of the counselor/coordinator. In fact, poor coordination can ruin an otherwise excellent counseling program. In addition to those listed above, some other examples of appropriate coordinating activities a school counselor may be required to spearhead in a typical year are:

1. New student orientation/registration,

2. Career interest surveys,

3. Career Day,

4. Standardized testing program,

5. Student recognition programs,

6. Referrals for community services,

7. Referrals for psychological testing,

8. Peer facilitator program and special projects, and

9. Student records—maintenance and transfer.

It is important to begin early in the school year when planning a program or activity under your coordination. Involve others in the planning. Get their input on how to make it better than "last year." Keep everyone, including parents, fully informed about the program goals, objectives, and procedures for implementation. And, always evaluate the activity or program immediately following its conclusion so that you can improve it "next year."

Summary

Consulting and coordinating activities in the schools can be challenging and rewarding for school counselors. Both of these interventions require counselor knowledge and skill. The key to successful consulting/coordinating in the schools, however, lies in the counselor's ability to establish good working relationships with school personnel and parents. Through commitment, interpersonal skills, patience, and knowledge, the school counselor can address these challenges and find much reward through consulting and coordinating roles.

References

Brown, D., Pryzwansky, W.B., & Schulte, A.C. (1998). *Psychological consultation.* Boston: Allyn & Bacon.

Caplan, G., & Caplan, R.B. (1993). *Mental health consultation and collaboration.* San Francisco: Jossey-Bass.

Dettmer, P., Dyck, N., & Thurston, L.P. (1999). *Consultation, collaboration, and teamwork for students with special needs.* Boston: Allyn & Bacon.

Myrick, R.D. (1997). *Developmental guidance and counseling: A practical approach* (3rd ed.). Minneapolis, MN: Educational Media Corporation.

Schein, E. (1988). *Process consultation* (2nd ed.). Reading, MA: Addison-Wesley.

Schmidt, J. (1999). *Counseling in schools* (2nd ed.). Boston: Allyn & Bacon.

Chapter 17
The Counselor and the Family: An Ecosystemic Approach

by
Ellen S. Amatea and
Barbara E. Brown

Ellen S. Amatea, PhD, is a Professor of Counselor Education at the University of Florida. Dr. Amatea has developed a practical approach for school counselor's use in working with students with behavior problems. This approach is described in her book, Brief Strategic intervention for School Behavior Problems.

Barbara E. Brown, MEd.; EdS., is a school counselor in the Leon County School System, Tallahassee, Florida. Prior to becoming a school counselor, Ms. Brown taught both elementary and secondary aged students for several years. She received specialized training in school and family counseling and consultation at the University of Florida.

A third-grade teacher desperately consults the school counselor for help. One of her students, a little boy of eight named Andrew, has been stealing items from his classmates and from her. Not only has Andrew stolen pencils and apparel belonging to other children, he had recently urinated on all the toilet paper rolls in the boys' bathrooms. The teacher reports that her efforts to resolve Andrew's problems by using questioning, behavioral rewards, punishments, or scolding have been fruitless. Her efforts to have the Andrew's grandmother, with whom he lives, take action to correct the child have been equally unsuccessful as the grandmother has admitted that she is unable to make the child behave.

● ●

An angry parent calls the school principal complaining that an eighth-grade teacher has been too punitive and demanding with her daughter, Robin, in terms of homework and academic expectations. This has resulted in Robin being so anxious about going to school that she vomits every day before school. The principal refers this case to the school counselor. When the counselor meets with the teacher and tells her of the parents' call, the teacher is indignant and counters that the parents are overly accommodating to Robin, allowing her to avoid work at school. The teacher refuses to decrease Robin's homework. When the counselor calls the parents, they report that Robin has continued to vomit every day before school, and insist that she is too upset to attend school.

● ●

Melissa, a tenth-grader, writes an essay describing a violent fight she has had with her father. The teacher is concerned and consults the counselor. She reports to the counselor that Melissa appears withdrawn from peers, and that there has been a gradual drop off in her academic performance during the past few weeks (she is now getting Cs and Ds, although she was a solid B student earlier in the term). However, in her phone call home to Melissa's mother, the teacher reports the mother has minimized the girl's behavior stating that Melissa was "just going through a phase that will soon pass".

● ●

The above vignettes are typical of the encounters between teachers and student families in which the school counselor is invited to participate. Not only is each student described above demonstrating serious problems, but significant difficulties are also evident in the relations between the student's family and his or her teacher(s). In such situations, teachers frequently feel that students' caregivers are not following their recommendations or supporting their efforts to teach or correct their child. Families, in turn, often feel blamed or unheard. School counselors not involved in the initial exchanges about a student's problem are often "caught in the middle," expected to validate a position taken by the teacher or to use their authority to make the case for a teacher's recommendation to a student's caregiver (Power & Bartholomew, 1985). How can the school counselor effectively intervene to resolve these difficulties?

Two very different courses of action are being taken by today's school counselors to address these difficulties. One course of action taken by counselors is to deal with the immediate crisis at hand by deliberately inserting themselves into and influencing the pattern of family school relations in which adults at school and at home are often embroiled (Amatea & Sherrard, 1992; Fine, 1997; Johnston & Zemitzsch, 1997; Peeks, 1992). A second, long-range, more preventative course of action is to work with other school staff to change the nature of the relations school staff *routinely* build with their students' families (Christenson & Hirsch, 1998; Weiss & Edwards, 1992). In this way problems between adults at home and at school do not develop when they attempt to resolve student difficulties. Each of these courses of action requires the school counselor to use a way of thinking and intervening which moves beyond the traditional view of the individual student or the student's family as their primary unit of intervention. Instead, the counselor sees the larger school/family *ecosystem*—the relationship system formed when the family and school come together to create ways of relating that either facilitate or impede students' learning and development— as their appropriate target for intervention.

In this chapter we examine these ways of thinking and working by describing: (a) the common relationship patterns in which adults at school and at home often become engaged, (b) a problem-focused model that school counselors can use to intervene in the family-school ecosystem when a student demonstrates learning or behavior problems, (c) a report of its use in an actual case with which we have been involved, and (d) the prevention-centered efforts now being implemented by many school counselors to change the nature of family-school relations before student problems develop.

Families and Schools as Interconnected Systems

Both schools and families can be defined as *relationship systems* in that each has its own distinctive memberships and activities, predictable ways of interacting, shared values and beliefs, and coherent identity as separate units. However, when a student enters school these two distinctive human systems join forces to carry out the aims of educating and socializing the student and thus become interconnected. If a student develops difficulties at school, additional persons such as the school counselor as well as other helping professionals both in and outside of the school may become members of this ecosystem as they join in the effort to assist the student or assist members of the school staff or student's family in resolving the student's difficulty. Thus a variety of persons at school (e.g., teachers, classmates, counselors, principals, etc.), at home, and in related helping positions who are communicating about a student and attempting to resolve the student's difficulties comprise the student's *ecosystem*. That is, that system of persons constructing meaning about the student's behavior (See Figure 17.1).

For adults at home and at school to interact competently, it is important that a cooperative and mutually respectful relationship be developed between them with each party achieving coequal status. In addition, clear agreements need to be developed between adults at home and school in order for teachers and parents/caregivers to know which activities and responsibilities belong to whom. However, how responsibilities are defined depends on the beliefs and preferences of members of the particular school, the families whose children attend that school, and the community the school serves. For example, while one school (or teacher) may believe that homework is exclusively the student's responsibility, another school or teacher may believe that each homework assignment turned in by a student should have a parent's signature. Furthermore, teachers' views may differ considerably from students' caregivers' beliefs regarding their appropriate role in the student's homework. Consequently, explicit agreements often need to be developed as to what role the family might have in helping students with homework.

In addition, explicit agreements often need to be developed about how the family and school might work together to resolve a student's learning or behavior difficulties. Because there are often significant differences in beliefs and expectations held by adults at home and school concerning (a) whether a particular student behavior is problematic, (b) who is responsible for causing the behavior and responsible for its resolution, and (c) what methods of problem resolution are acceptable and how the family is to be involved in these problem resolution efforts; discussion of these expectations needs to be made explicit.

Regrettably, many times school staff and students' families come together without much conscious thought or discussion about how they expect to work together. Using the concepts of boundary and hierarchy to describe how school staff and parents often position themselves, Power and Bartholomew (1987) describe five common family/school interaction patterns that can result: avoidance, competitive, merged, one-way or collaborative. *Avoidant relations* are defined by no contact or communication between home and school. This is a common pattern found in many schools today. Often, when a child is not defined as demonstrating serious problematic behavior at school, the two authority systems of the home and school operate separately and independently from the other. Any problem the child displays at school is usually handled "in house" by the school staff, and no effort is made to form collaborative or conjoint efforts with the home. There is usually little exchange of information about problem definition or problem resolution efforts concerning the child. However in some schools, even when students' problems grow more serious, teachers may continue to attempt to handle the student problems completely on their own fearing that efforts to involve the family will create even more difficulties. Families may also avoid contact with the school staff and decide to handle student problems separately from the school and not to share relevant information about a student's past or current difficulties with school staff for fear their child might be stigmatized. Thus, a strict, rigid boundary may characterize relations between teacher and family with little information or contact between the two parties.

When a child's difficulties escalate and school staff believe that the responsibility for the child's school behavior should be returned to the parents, school staff may decide to shift from a pattern of avoidance to one of engagement with a student's family. Usually, at this point, parents may be brought in to the conversation about the child's problematic school behavior with the expectation on the part of the school staff that the parents should get the child to behave or perform at school. There may be notes and calls to parents about the problems at school, conferences at school, demands for increased homework supervision or tutoring by parents, behavioral contracts about school behaviors with the parents dispensing rewards and punishments, or suspension to the home.

If the school is successful in joining with parents, they may solve the child's school problems. However, if the school is unable to gain the parents' backing in developing a joint agreement as to how the student's problem is to be resolved, three other patterns of home-school relations may develop. One is a pattern of *competitive relations* between home and school in which both home and school try to exert influence over the other's domain. For example, in the case of Robin given above, both teacher and parent have strong ideas about how to respond to her with each attempting to dominate the other by having the other party act in accordance with their preferences. In such relations, conflicts often escalate to the point where the child is placed in a no-win position; neither party is willing to back down from their position and the relationships between home and school become increasingly competitive and hostile. The youngster's school problems begin to be defined as very serious and chronic by the school. Often the child is labeled and stigmatized as a "troublemaker," an "emotionally disturbed student," or an "underachiever." Adults at home or at school are also labeled and stigmatized. A parent may be stigmatized by the school staff as "irresponsible," "ineffective," or "dysfunctional"; while a teacher may be labeled by the family as "rigid," "biased," or "uncaring." The interaction between persons at home and school often becomes laced with feelings of mutual blame and anxiety, as each party seeks to determine who is responsible for the problem and how best to solve it. Each adult blames the other for the child's problem and argues with the other regarding what should be the appropriate way to solve the child's difficulty. For example in the case of Robin, the more the teacher feels attacked and dictated to, the more entrenched he or she becomes in her original position, triggering the parent to feel more strongly that if only the teacher would change, the child's problem might be resolved. The teacher in turn feels likewise. Thus these patterns of interaction often escalate in a "vicious circle," in that each side is prompted to elicit more of a particular behavior when they perceive the other as having elicited more of that behavior. Such competitive struggles can extend beyond the adults at home and at school, to include a bevy of other helpers (e.g., outside therapists, welfare workers) lined up on each side to continue the original battle. At this point, the child's problems at school are often exacerbated by the confused expectations and failure experienced by adults at home and at school and the overt conflict emerging between them.

In the *merged relationship* teacher and caregiver may agree that a problem exists and agree on a joint plan of action. However such agreements are often made by one party "giving in" to the perspective of the other. For example, parents may find themselves attempting to assist a student in completing homework which is not appropriate for the child's level of comprehension. Rather than question the appropriateness of the assignment with the school, they spend inordinate amounts of time and effort with their child to complete the assignments. One hazard of both systems merging is that the student can feel that an alliance against them has been created, feel more and more isolated, and increase their problematic behavior.

The *one-way relationship* occurs when the attempts of an individual in one system to direct the other person to act are ignored by individuals in the other system. For example, in the first case of Andrew given above, the more the school attempts to call attention to the situation and demand the family take charge, the more the grandmother defines herself as helpless, triggering the school to push harder to have something be done by the grandmother. Such actions result in the grandmother feeling even more discouraged and hopeless and ineffective in her management of the child. Feeling overwhelmed with the care of three young children, the grandmother ignores the school's requests that she manage Andrew. The more responsible action the school presses the grandmother to take charge, the less action Andrew's grandmother takes to control him. The above-mentioned case of Melissa reveals a similar pattern of relations—the mother seemed to avoid acknowledging any of the teacher's concern for Melissa's performance. Consequently, it can be very frustrating for the teacher, and we might predict that the teacher will eventually become frustrated and either attack the caregiver or withdraw altogether.

The fifth pattern of interaction, *collaborative,* involves adults at home and at school having regular contact and communication and working together in a reciprocal and complementary fashion. That is, where parents and educators do not need to perform the same task or behavior to assist the child's school productivity. What is important is that the partners reach some agreement as to what each party's role will be and complement each other's efforts by working toward similar goals. For example, consider the case of Tyrone, a fifth- grade student with a learning disability who had been in a full-day special education classroom since first grade. His teachers believed his math skills were strong enough to have him begin to attend a regular education math class. A team meeting was held that included Tyrone's parents. The school staff was in favor of Tyrone transitioning to the regular math class, but his parents were hesitant. They were concerned about Tyrone's ability to function in a less supportive setting and were afraid they were setting Tyrone up for failure. His parents were afraid that Tyrone, who is easily frustrated, would give up too easily in the new setting. After a long discussion, it was decided that Tyrone would be supported at school with a teaching aide in the math class until he felt comfortable on his own. At home, Tyrone would be supported by his parents, who would discuss with Tyrone his concerns and fears and encourage him not to give up. The team decided they would try the plan on a trial basis; the plan would be discontinued if either the team or Tyrone did not consider it effective. In this case, teachers and parents held common goals for Tyrone and collaborated on a solution to the problem. Each party felt comfortable sharing concerns, and neither dictated what the other should/would do.

Applying the Ecosystemic Model to Resolve an Existing Problem

One may choose to use an ecosystemic approach to resolve an existing family-school problem or to prevent the development of problems between the family and the school. In using this approach to address an existing problem it is important to keep in mind that this approach represents a major departure from traditional parent education or family therapy approaches. Most available methods for working with parents/families in the schools have assumed that either the parent's or the family's interaction is the exclusive target for one's intervention efforts. A variety of intervention approaches used by school counseling practitioners, such as family intervention (Kral, 1986; Steele & Raider, 1991), parent education (Fine & Gardner, 1997), or parent consultation and referral (Walsh & Williams, 1997) take this perspective by assuming that there is some causal relation between problems at school and in the child's family (i.e., that some 'flaw" in the family is causing a child's school difficulty). What is often overlooked in these ways of working, are the resources for change that exist in the school or in the relations between the school and the family. By including these various persons in the child's world in addition to the family, the boundaries of "the system of interest" can be drawn differently and greater resources for change can be accessed (Anderson, Goolishian & Winderman, 1987).

The language-determined systems model (Anderson, Goolishian & Winderman, 1987) and the strategic therapy model of the Mental Research Institute (Fisch, Weakland & Segal, 1982), provide the theoretical bases for the assessment of an intervention in the school/family ecosystem described in the following case. A number of premises concerning formation and problem resolution undergird this way of working. First, by *ecosystem* we mean the social context for the presenting problem which evolves out of the recurrent exchanges of messages about the child and his/her problem among participating individuals. In the school setting, this context may include parents, teachers, and the school principal; classmates and teachers; or family members, school staff, peers, and outside therapists. Second, it is assumed that while a child's problem can originate in any number of communication exchanges in a particular life arena (e.g., at school or at home), a student's "problem" behavior is often maintained by the responses to that behavior by other members of the "problem-determined ecosystem." Third, these responses often persist because the people involved feel their efforts are the only right and logical ways to respond to the problem. In effect, then, the problem is not the identified symptom but the solution efforts enacted around the

problem (Amatea, 1989). Fourth, it is assumed that change can be effected by interrupting these problem-maintaining solution cycles and allowing the patterning to reorganize so that the symptom can no longer be maintained. To alter these problem-maintaining patterns, a change in action quite different from the original solution efforts is usually required. A key to such a change in action is the use of language. Often different meanings must be attributed to a change in action in order for the persons involved to be moved to attempt it. These meanings must be close enough to fit "the facts" of the situation but different enough to provide an opportunity for different solution efforts to evolve. Thus the role of the school counselor in such a change effort becomes that of a co-participant who interjects new meanings and a new reality into the larger system to bring about change.

Identifying and Assessing the Ecosystem

Deciding who in the ecosystem should be included in the change effort in order to interrupt the current solution efforts and how to involve them are the first steps. The counselor should concentrate his or her efforts on the persons who are most concerned about the problem and therefore most strongly motivated to take action toward change. This person may or may not be the child demonstrating problems. In addition, but secondarily, it is useful to consider who has the most power to change things. For example, in the case of the eighth grader vomiting before school each day, while the child is clearly suffering, it is the parents (specifically the mother), and secondarily, the child's teacher who seem most involved in the problem. Since these are warring parties (i.e., involved in a competitive struggle with one another), having several meetings in which they are both involved will probably only result in putting the counselor in the position of referee. An easier and more productive alternative would be to see one or both of the warring parties alone at which time the counselor can readily take a commiserating position of agreeing that the other party is indeed difficult. Such a position of alliance relaxes the teacher/parent's defensive posture and sets the stage for acceptance of suggestions for changes in behavior in dealing with the other party— which can be defined as necessary, precisely because such a difficult person requires special handling.

A sampling of the types of questions that a counselor may use to elicit information as to the membership of the "ecosystem" and the nature of their solution efforts appears below. These questions can be phrased to include both family members, classroom members (i.e., teachers and students) or other school staff (e.g., the principal, special resource teachers or aides), outside helpers (e.g. therapists in private or public agencies, child welfare workers, probation officers, etc.), and friends. The questions can be addressed either to the individual identified as having the problem or individuals seeking help for the identified client.

1. **Who else has been involved in helping with this problem?** This question immediately expands the frame of the problem from one belonging to the student demonstrating the problem to one that has interactional connections. The resulting answers provide information for determining who talks to whom about this problem and how they talk about it.

2. **What is the nature of the problem and what solutions have been tried to solve this problem?** The counselor begins to gather data on the problem-maintaining interactional cycle. Each involved persons' responses need to be addressed separately to gain clarity about the solution efforts they employ, the value positions these signify, the possible conflicts in advice given by the various persons involved, and the existence of escalating relationship patterns between adults at home and at school.

3. **If you were to bring in anyone to help with this problem whom would you invite?** The answer to this question can be used to identify how people may be aligned around the problem and problem person and what potential resources may be available. The answer may or may not be a reflection of whose solutions are actually most helpful. Phrasing this question as a hypothetical one, suggests in a nonthreatening and nondemanding way that intervention for the child's problem may best be conducted by involving others beside the child.

4. **Who would be the last person(s) you would bring in to help with this problem?** The answer to this question provides information about the pattern of interaction among adults at home and at school which has developed, possible secrets among members, peripheral members of the larger system, or coalitions of protectiveness toward other members. Whether or not these identified individuals are worked with in the intervention is a secondary issue. What is important is that the answer to this question provides the counselor with clues as to whom to include in conceptualizing the membership of the ecosystem.

5. **If this present problem is solved, how would things be different? What, for example, would happen between (a specific family member) and (a specific school staff person/helper)?** Answers to these questions reveal the degree of hope that members of the system have for change, and the expectations various members hold for the change effort.

Intervening in the Ecosystem

The following case illustration demonstrates how the relations between the school staff and the family around the resolution of a student's problem can be targeted for change. Andrew was one of the first cases referred to the new school counselor in the fall of the year. A third grader who lived with his 78-year-old grandmother and a younger brother and sister (ages 7 and 5), Andrew was a teacher's worse nightmare—he stole, he lied, and when provoked by his peers, he did the most outlandish things he could think of—like urinating on all the rolls of toilet paper in the boy's bathrooms at the school. He and his siblings had been placed with their paternal grandmother a year earlier due to the fact that their father, who struggled with chronic alcoholism, and their mother, who was addicted to cocaine, had physically and emotionally abused all three children. The family was considered "no-good" by members of the small community in which they lived with the father often returning to town between jail terms, becoming drunk, and beating up his wife in public. Andrew and his younger brother had already developed a negative reputation among the teaching staff who had little hope that the children would turn out any differently from their parents. In considering who was involved with Andrew and how were they defining and responding to his problem (Questions 1 & 2), the counselor learned from his teachers that despite his placement in a class for emotionally handicapped children, Andrew constantly created problems in this as well as the larger school facility, had many confrontations with teachers and the other children, and exhibited considerable difficulty with learning. The teachers perceived that Andrew was "severely disturbed" and that he had not mastered even the most basic interpersonal skills. They had attempted to manage Andrew's outbursts by sending him to the principal's office (where he often spent the majority of the school day), calling his grandmother and insisting that she make him behave, or temporarily suspending him from school. It was quite evident that many of the teaching staff felt that Andrew was a "hopeless case" and that the family was at fault for his behavior.

Meeting with Andrew individually, the counselor observed that Andrew was quite guarded and had few skills for expressing how he felt. It took a great deal of gentle nudging for him to talk about himself. Over a few weeks, however, using play media, Andrew began to reveal how upset he was that his family, and his father, in particular, were made fun of by the other students. He described a number of situations in which he had initiated a number of serious fights after being teased by a group of boys about "his daddy being a no-good drunk." He now seemed to go out of his way to keep his classmates and teachers in an uproar, and had managed to get himself completely ostracized by his peers because of his behavior.

Dropping by to chat with Andrew's grandmother (since she had no phone) to see how she was aligned with the others involved with Andrew (Questions 3 & 4) , the counselor said "I'm worried about your grandson, and I'll bet you are too. I am new to the school and I know you know your grandson better than I do. Would you help me understand what has happened and how we might be able to get him on track at school? " The counselor learned that the grandmother seemed overwhelmed as to where to start to deal with him. She complained angrily about Andrew's problems at schools, which she described as "his being bad," yet acknowledged that she felt completely helpless as to how to manage him. The school had called her numerous times and was now threatening to expel Andrew permanently , her health was fragile, and she was completely exhausted from trying to manage him and the other two children who were very much like him. Although outside therapy had been recommended by the school several earlier times, the grandmother felt that it was useless to try to deal with him.

It was obvious that the school and home were caught in a one-sided relationship pattern. The more desperate the school became that something be done with Andrew and the more they indicated to his grandmother that he was seriously disturbed, the more powerless the grandmother felt at having any impact on his behavior, and the less she did to control him, triggering the school to grow even more concerned, and press her even harder. To alter this vicious cycle the counselor decided to frame Andrew's behavior differently so that the grandmother might be more hopeful that she could have some impact on him and the counselor could build an alliance with her in which the grandmother felt she had some power. In addition, it would be important to interdict the negative feedback cycle so that the grandmother would not constantly be told how hopeless things were. Volunteering to serve as a conduit for information about Andrew from the school to the grandmother could serve this purpose. Thus the counselor asked the grandmother if she knew exactly what the fights that Andrew had gotten into at school seemed to involve. The grandmother admitted that she did not. The counselor then indicated that she had learned from Andrew that most of his fighting seemed to involve protecting the family's, and particularly his father's, honor. The counselor stated that: "It's as if Andrew feels he has to be the family's champion." As the counselor described a number of the situations in which Andrew had initiated serious fights after being teased about his family, the grandmother seemed to visibly soften. She admitted that

although she often scolded him when he got into trouble, she did not question him about the circumstances surrounding the fights. The counselor acknowledged how difficult it was for her too to get Andrew to describe how he felt. She then proposed that she would like to drop by and chat with the grandmother every so often, since maybe between the two of them they could get some idea where Andrew was coming from and how they might work together to help him.

Over the next several weeks, the counselor met with Andrew on an individual basis several times. Andrew slowly began to develop some language for describing his feelings and shared more and more about his anger and disappointment with school. He began to see the counselor as someone who did not treat him like a "bad kid," but instead was nurturing and playful with him. At the same time, the counselor consulted with Andrew's teachers at school and indicated that she agreed with them that Andrew did not know how to behave in school and that that she would be willing to work with him if and when he behaved disruptively. During this same time the counselor dropped by the grandmother's house on a regular basis, and rather than sharing Andrew's school mishaps with the grandmother, she shared things that Andrew had said that showed his soft, nurturing side and asked for the grandmother's help in trying to understand what he meant.

As the grandmother began to be treated like a coequal by the counselor, she became less defensive and discouraged and began to ask how to handle certain situations with the children. She disclosed in response to the counselor's inquiry as to what she would like to have be different (Question 5), that when her husband had died recently, each of the three children "went nuts, tearing up the house, and everything in it" rather than acting sad. She was confused and upset by their response and unsure what to do. The counselor suggested that the grandmother was probably the first person in these children's lives who cared about how they felt and who would take time to talk to them about their feelings. She encouraged the grandmother to talk with the children about how they felt about the situation with their father and mother. As the grandmother became more confident in being nurturing, she admitted that she probably needed to be firmer with the children. The counselor stated that she knew that these children had been through a lot, and that both she and the grandmother might need some help figuring out what to do. The counselor then suggested that one of the family counselors in the local mental health clinic might be able to help them. With the grandmother agreeing, the counselor then arranged a meeting with an agency counselor whom she knew in the community. In this initial meeting, which both the family and school counselor attended, they all decided that the grandmother and the children would meet with the agency counselor and deal with family matters and that the school counselor would continue to drop by for a chat with the grandmother every so often and fill her in on school matters. In addition, the school counselor would continue to meet with Andrew on a regular basis. The grandmother and her family followed this arrangement conscientiously, meeting with the agency counselor regularly for the next several months. They experienced considerable success in developing a clearer routine and structure for the children at home, and in building in more opportunities to talk to the children about emotional issues. The counselor worked with Andrew and his teachers to reinforce his behavior in the classroom and with other students. By the spring, Andrew had developed a much more cooperative attitude with his teachers, was working up to grade level in all his subjects, and had begun to develop workable relationships with some of his peers.

Applying the Ecosystemic Model to Develop More Collaborative Family-School Relations

Many school counselors are now working collectively with other members of their school staff to rethink how they might structure the ecosystem of relations they have with students and their families. Rather than involve parents only when there is a crisis or problem to be solved, school faculties are thinking about how to create opportunities to collaborate with families on a regular basis before problems occur (Christenson & Hirsch, 1998; Weiss & Edwards, 1992).

But what exactly is collaboration and how does it differ from our typical family-school patterns of relating? Seeley (1985) offers an elegantly simple definition: "Collaboration is a common effort toward a common goal by participants who share power "(p. 65). Because most school staffs have been trained to follow an "authority-client" approach to relating to families in which the authority (e.g., the teacher or counselor) identifies the concern or problem that merits attention, decides what type of solution is necessary, and decides how the client (i.e., the student and/or his or her family) should be involved with a philosophy of "doing to" or "doing for" the client, collaborative patterns of relating to families are quite different. In contrast to the "authority-client" model of practice, counselors and teachers using a collaborative model interact with students and their families to identify *together* those resources existing in the family and school for taking action to solve children's problems or to celebrate their learning. These differences are significant and have to do with the focus of the relationship; the roles of the teacher, the counselor, the student, and parents; the nature of the relationship, including the goal toward which it is directed; the nature of the activities; and the expected outcome.

How are schools translating this collaborative model into practice? One set of principles, developed by the staff at Ackerman Institute's Family School Collaboration Project (Weiss & Edwards, 1992), illustrates the distinctly different ways of thinking and working to consciously build a collaborative family-school ecosystem. Successfully tested in schools in the United States and Canada over a fifteen year period, this set of principles helps school faculties successfully transform their current family-school activities in order to "connect the two key systems in a child's life—the home and the school—in ways which create a shared commitment to children's learning" (Weiss, 1992, p. 215)

The first principle is that the school commits to building relationships with all parents whether the parents can come to school or not. To do this, the school must make clear to parents how their active participation in their children's educational experience will directly enhance their subsequent academic achievement and development. In addition, the school must look for ways to communicate a genuine interest in connecting with the parents of all of its students to insure these outcomes. Consequently, if some parents are not able to come to the school because of work or family demands, the school staff signals their belief that these parents still care deeply about their child's learning by providing them with the means to understand and keep up with what is happening in school (e.g., through use of summary letters describing an event they missed, regular newsletters, and homework assignments).

A second principle is that all family-school activities are planned to maximize student learning. Rather than simply trying to "get parents involved," school staff use the family-school relationship to meet specific educational goals, solve problems, and celebrate the children and their achievements. Rather than be organized only around discussion of problems, the school maintains a dialogue about learning and about the school's interest in each child. Consequently, the school staff look for opportunities for parents, students and school staff to interact with one another in ways which emphasize family involvement in children's planning, decision making, problem solving and learning. To do this, staff examine the various aspects of the school experience (curriculum, administrative and communication procedures, special programs, after school activities, assessment and evaluation programs, health programs, etc.) to design opportunities for families and school staff to experience each other differently.

In keeping with this emphasis on maximizing student learning, the third principle is that the child is included as an active participant in virtually all family-school interactions. To do this, school children of all ages are taught to function as active participants in "family-teacher" (i.e., the old parent-teacher) conferences. Since it is their life at school which is to be discussed, they come to such meetings as "experts on themselves" who are present so as to describe their own experience, thoughts and feelings. As the children contribute to the solution of their problems and the improvement of their own school experience, they gain confidence and a sense of efficacy. Family-school interactions involving the children are embedded in orientations, classroom instruction, homework routines, cel-

ebrations, and presentations of new curriculum, transitions to new grade levels and programs, procedures for home-school communication and for resolving difficulties. (See Figure 17.2 for an illustration of one parent's account of how a routine school orientation was redesigned with these principles in mind.)

A fourth principle is that parents should be actively involved in all family-school events, not as an audience but as full participants. Rather than unnecessarily restrict the role of parents to that of classroom volunteer or of instructional support person; family-school events are designed to underscore the role of parent as co-decision-makers and illustrate the belief that everyone—parents, teachers and students has a job to do to insure the student's educational success.

Such collaborative interactions transform the ecosystem in which families and schools experience each other. As parents learn they can make a difference in their child's learning, they invest in the school. As staff learn to build on the strengths of children and their families and to block blaming from undermining the collaborative process, they create a shared vested interest in the child which brings the family and school much closer together. When each person feels known, understood, and cared about by the other parties, a sense of community and common purpose unites the classroom and school with the families of school-age children.

Conclusion

There are numerous pitfalls involved for the school counselor working with adults at school and at home, not the least of which is the tendency for him/her to be drawn into a destructive cycle of blame and discouragement. There is a need to think proactively about how effective relationships between adults at home and school might be developed. The authors' experience indicates that an ecosystemic orientation can not only be used to effectively resolve the more entrenched problems which children demonstrate at school, it can be useful in developing more constructive relations between students' families and school staffs before problems develop. Central to each situation is the belief that if student families are approached as coequals, the resources and strengths inherent in any given school system to educate children can be enhanced and a broader array of resources can be accessed to support student learning and development.

Figure 17.1
The Child's Ecosystem

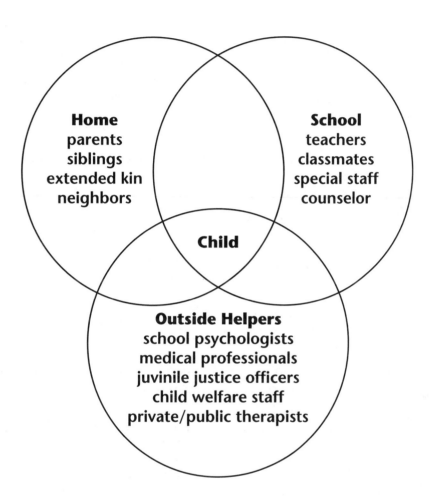

Home
parents
siblings
extended kin
neighbors

School
teachers
classmates
special staff
counselor

Child

Outside Helpers
school psychologists
medical professionals
juvinile justice officers
child welfare staff
private/public therapists

Figure 17.2
A Parent's View of a "Collaborative" Fall Orientation

Below is one parent's reaction to a fall orientation designed in terms of the collaborative principles described.

Dear Sir:

Do I have news for you! After years of dutifully attending school "open house" events at Tim and Stephen's schools, I thought I had them all figured out. Was I ever surprised by the "back to school" night put on by Stephen's teacher and school! I had expected for this fall orientation to be like every other one I had attended. I would sit in a large auditorium, listen to a parade of speakers talk to a huge audience of parents and a few wiggly children (whose parents had not been able to get babysitters), and hen "race" to each teacher's classroom in which I had a child. My purpose for going was to, at least, "show my face" and let these teachers know that I was interested in meeting them.

This orientation night was far different. First, Stephen was invited to come with me (as a matter of fact, he invited me to accompany him to the orientation.) Second, Stephen and I spent the evening just with his teacher, classmates, and their parents. (The school had organized a schedule in which the grade levels met on different evenings so that parents would not feel rushed to get to every child's room in the same evening!) Third, his teacher had organized an activity in which, after greeting us and giving us a preview of the evening's activities, she asked each parent and child to talk together privately for a few minutes about what their goals were for the student's learning this year, and what the parents might do to help their child accomplish these goals. After Stephen and I talked we had a chance to share our ideas, and to hear the ideas of his classmates and their parents. The teacher listed all these ideas on the board and then talked about how our ideas fit with her goals and plans for the year. It was obvious, when all those ideas got written on the board, that we shared many of the same goals and concerns about the new school year!

Not only was this activity useful for showing us as parents what we have in common, it also provided me with an experience of interacting with my child at school which I had never had before. Usually parents expect to come to these types of events and be quiet and listen; if a parent had to bring their child (due to not getting babysitting) he/she is expected to be quiet and entertain himself or herself. This time it was different; we were asked to talk with each other during a school event. I was surprised by how seriously Stephen took what I had to say to heart about him doing his homework without me having to nag him to get down to work. (Of course, we'll have to see just how much he follows through on this!) I think that he liked being treated and talked to as a grown-up. I certainly liked my opinion being asked for too!

More importantly, this activity gave me an opportunity to see "up close" how Stephen's teacher relates to him and to the other children . It is obvious that she cares about each one of them. It showed in the way she solicited their participation in the discussion, and took their answers seriously. So I'm relieved that he's got such a caring teacher.

What's more, I'm amazed that with just this one orientation night, I've gotten a very different view of what this year may have in store for me as well as Stephen!

Sincerely,

Anne

References

Amatea, E., & Sherrard, P. (1997). When students cannot or will not change their behavior: Using brief strategic intervention in the schools. (pp. 59-68) In W.W. Walsh & G.R. Williams (Eds.) *Schools and family therapy: Using systems theory and family therapy in the resolution of school problems.* Springfield, IL: Charles C. Thomas.

Amatea, E. (1989). *Brief strategic intervention for school behavior problems.* San Francisco, CA: Jossey Bass.

Anderson, H., Goolishian, H., & Winderman, L. (1987). Problem-determined systems: Toward transformation in family therapy. *Journal of Strategic and Systemic Therapies, 5*,1-13.

Christenson, S.L., & Hirsch, J.A. (1998). Facilitating partnerships and conflict resolution between families and schools. In K.C. Staibler & T.R. Kratochwill (Eds.) *Handbook of group intervention for children and families.* Boston: Allyn & Bacon.

Fisch, R., Weakland, J.H., & Segal, L. (1982). *The tactics of change: Doing therapy briefly.* San Francisco, CA: Jossey Bass.

Fine, M.J. (1992). A systems-ecological perspective on home-school intervention. (pp. 1-17) In M.J. Fine & C.I. Carlson (Eds) *Family-School Intervention: A Systems Perspective.* Boston: Allyn & Bacon.

Johnston, J.C., & Zemitzsch, A. (1997). Family power: An intervention beyond the classroom. (pp. 23-37). In W. W. Walsh & G.R. Williams (Eds.) *Schools and family therapy: Using systems theory and family therapy in the resolution of school problems.* Springfield, IL: Charles C. Thomas.

Kral, R. (1986). Indirect therapy in the schools. In S. deShazer (Ed.) *Indirect approaches in therapy.* Family Therapy Collection (Vol. 19). Rockville, MD: Aspen.

Peeks, B. (1992). Protection and social context: Understanding a child's problem behavior. *Elementary School Guidance and Counseling, 26,* 295-304.

Power, T.J., & Bartholomew, K.L. (1985). Getting uncaught in the middle: A case study in family-school system consultation. *School Psychology Review. 14(2),* 222-229.

Power, T.J. & Bartholomew, K.L. (1987). Family-school relationship patterns: An ecological assessment. *School Psychology Review, 16(4),*498-512.

Seeley, D.S. (1985). *Education through partnership.* Washington, DC: American Enterprise Institute for Public Policy Research.

Steele, W., & Raider, M. (1991). *Working with families in crisis: School-based intervention.* New York: Guilford.

Walsh, W.M., & Williams, G.R. (1997). *Schools and family therapy.* Springfield, IL: Charles C. Thomas.

Weiss, H., & Edwards, M. (1992). The family-school collaboration project: Systemic interventions for school improvement. In S. Christenson & J.C. Conoley (Eds.) *Home-school collaboration: Enhancing children's academic and social competence,* (pp. 215-243). Silver Spring, MD: National Association for School Psychologists.

Chapter 18
The K-12 Developmental School Counselor and Appraisal

by
**Larry C. Loesch and
William J. Goodman**

Larry C. Loesch, PhD, NCC, is a Professor in the Department of Counselor Education at the University of Florida. Prior to receiving his doctorate he taught in a secondary school and later was a school counselor in a K-12 school in Kent, Ohio.

William J. Goodman, EdS, LMHC, has been a school counselor at Hawthorne, Florida Junior-Senior High School since 1982. He also is a licensed mental health counselor who specializes in counseling children and youth.

Introduction

Almost all school personnel receive some pre-service training in appraisal methods ("tests and measurements"), the primary focus usually being on construction of classroom tests. However, *only* school counselors and school psychologists *routinely* receive advanced, graduate-level training in appraisal. School psychologists typically use specialized appraisal techniques (e.g., individual intelligence or personality assessments), and therefore the scope of their appraisal activities is relatively small. In contrast, school counselors are involved with tests and other appraisal techniques applicable to and used by a wide variety of people. Thus, school counselors in K-12 settings should, can, and do fulfill important appraisal functions in schools.

It is not possible to separate completely the appraisal functions school counselors fulfill because the natures of the activities as well as the persons affected by them are complex and interrelated. However, sets of roles can be clustered for discussion purposes. Shown in Figure 18.1 are three primary school counselor appraisal functions and some of the major focal points within them.

Coordination

The coordination function capitalizes upon school counselors' training and expertise in appraisal techniques because it calls for use of relatively specialized knowledge and skills. The selection of appraisal techniques is a good example.

Selection

The primary uses of appraisal techniques include: (a) gathering information not easily obtained through other methods (e.g., when students are hesitant to self disclose the information), (b) confirming subjective impressions of students (e.g., when a school counselor has a "hunch" about some characteristic of a student), (c) collecting large amounts of data (e.g., when information about an entire class is desired), and (d) evaluating change (e.g., when empirical evidence of the effectiveness of a counseling activity is needed). The information derived from appraisals is useful only to the extent that the appraisal methods from which the information is derived are *appropriate, reliable,* and *valid.* Indeed, the *1995 Code of Ethics and Standards of Practice of the American Counseling Association* stipulate in subsection E6a that, "Counselors carefully consider the validity, reliability, psychometric limitations, and appropriateness of instruments when selecting tests for use in a given situation or with a particular client." Although these terms are commonly used in casual conversation, they have specific meanings within the context of appraisal. School counselors are aware of the technical meanings and use them in evaluating appraisal methods.

In selecting an appraisal potentially suitable for use with students, the school counselor first determines whether the appraisal is *appropriate*. For example, if the students have limited reading abilities, visual impairments, or physical disabilities, the use of a "paper-and-pencil" appraisal instruments may be inappropriate. The psychosocial development levels of students also is an important consideration (i.e., some students may not be emotionally ready to respond to certain types of appraisals). Similarly, depending upon whether the school counselor wishes to use an appraisal on a single or two or more occasions, the appraisal's *reliability* information is an important consideration. *Validity* is the primary selection criterion because without it the other criteria are meaningless. Further, school counselors are aware that validity is a situation-specific construct. A test is not valid in general, but rather is valid only for use with particular persons in specified situations. Much of the information needed for these evaluations can be obtained from careful reading of the technical manuals for appraisal instruments. Additional information can be obtained from critiques in professional journals and books. Thus school counselors' specialized preparation in appraisal allows them to evaluate the evidence supporting use of an appraisal for the particular context in which the appraisal is to be used.

Effective appraisal selection requires that school counselors have comprehensive and accurate knowledge of appraisal techniques, the students to whom appraisals will be applied, and the persons who will use the appraisal results. School counselors are uniquely suited for this task because of their specialized training in appraisal and their comprehensive understandings of students, parents, and other professionals.

Administration

Effective administration of appraisal techniques also capitalizes on school counselors' specialized appraisal and counseling skills and knowledge. The conditions under which an appraisal is conducted must be conducive to students' responding and the students must be in "the right frame of mind" in order for the appraisal to yield meaningful and useful information, and for students to respond or perform effectively on appraisals. Excessive anxiety (including feelings of pressure to respond in the "right" ways) or excessive complacency (including not understanding the importance) invalidates the results of appraisals. Therefore, providing "orientation" to forthcoming appraisal is always professionally appropriate. It is also ethically appropriate. For example, the 1998 (ASCA) *Ethical Standards for School Counselors* stipulate in subsection A9.b that:

> *The professional school counselor provides explanation of the nature, purposes, and results of assessments/evaluation measures in a language that can be understood by the student client(s).*

Similarly, the *ACA Code of Ethics and Standards of Practice* stipulate in subsection E7.d that:

> *Prior to administration, conditions that produce most favorable results are made known to the examinee.*

School counselors use large group, small group, and individual activities to facilitate students' appropriate responding to appraisals. For example, the junior author conducts regularly scheduled classroom guidance activities to help senior high school students be prepared for participation in various state (e.g., high school competency) or national (e.g., Armed Services Vocational Aptitude Battery) tests. Other times, commercial materials (e.g., films, videotapes, or print media) and/or structured activities available from publishers and testing companies are used. In either case the purposes are to enable students to *understand* the purposes and uses of the appraisal and to *motivate* students to respond accurately, honestly, and to the best of their abilities.

Small group activities are used for similar purposes. However, often this modality is preferred when several students have a commonality (i.e., are a "target" group) that distinguishes them from a class-size group of students. For example, each February the junior author conducts a three-session group counseling activity for groups of 15 or less students who are experiencing relatively high levels of test anxiety.

Individual pre-appraisal counseling/orientation activities are appropriate when a student will benefit most from specific, individually-tailored activities. For example, some college-bound students experience relatively severe test anxiety when confronted with having to take the Scholastic Assessment Test (SAT) or the American College Test (ACT). For these students the school counselor can use individual anxiety reduction interventions such as desensitization and/or relaxation training.

Development

The development component of school counselors' appraisal functions involves creation of appraisal instruments and/or techniques for local (i.e., within the school or district) purposes. Successful fulfillment of this function necessitates that school counselors directly *apply* their knowledge and skills to create appraisals which will yield information uniquely useful to their settings. In particular, it requires that school counselors have good skills in item or technique, response format, and scoring procedure development. Applications of these skills differ for different school and/or grade levels, and therefore they must be applied within the context of good understanding of respondent groups. Appraisal development functions are closely related to evaluation functions because school counselors typically develop locally-appropriate instruments or techniques to fulfill their evaluation functions.

Evaluation

Appraisal evaluation functions conducted by school counselors usually are implemented either before or after other school counseling activities. As a prelude to activities, a comprehensively useful function in which school counselors typically engage is "needs assessment." Many school counseling experts suggest that a needs assessment should serve as the foundation for a school counseling program. In general, a needs assessment is a process which identifies the counseling-program-related needs of any of a variety of persons who may benefit from the program, including students, parents, teachers and other school personnel, and even professionals in agencies associated with schools. For example, the junior author administers personally developed needs assessment surveys to students, teachers, and parents in the Fall of each academic year. Some of the items on the surveys are parallel to allow comparisons across respondent groups while others are specific to the needs of the respective respondent groups. The results then serve as the basis for the year's program planning.

The usual form of a needs assessment is a survey that includes items reflecting elements and/or services that could be included in a school counseling program and a response scale that allows respondents to indicate the extent to which they believe each element would be of particular use to them. The results of the survey can be prioritized by total respondent group mean per element and/or by element group mean for selected subgroups (e.g., males and females or parents, teachers, and students). In either case, school counselors derive information from needs assessments that serve as the basis for establishing counseling program priorities. These priorities are established most effectively when considered by school counselors in collaboration with others such as a Guidance Committee, an Educational Planning Team, teachers, parents, or administrators. Because programs can not encompass all potentially appropriate services all the time, needs assessments are the best way to develop school counseling program priorities.

Another important evaluation method being used with increasing frequency by school counselors is behavioral observation, which typically includes use of a behavior checklist or rating scale. This technique involves a school counselor identifying specific, carefully defined behaviors and then observing and noting or rating the frequency with which a student engages in the "targeted" behaviors within a defined time period. The targeted behaviors observed usually are ones for which change is desired through a counseling intervention. Often the targeted behaviors are academic in nature and observed in classrooms. However, behavioral observations also may yield information about social behaviors. For example, the junior author uses a classroom observation record form developed for use in the Alachua County, Florida schools to assess students' classroom/academic behaviors and several locally developed behavior rating forms to appraise students' social, assertiveness, learning, time management, decision making, or relationship skills.

Sociometry is another evaluation method useful for school counselors at the local level and as a prelude to specific counseling interventions. A sociometric technique is one in which students are provided questions (e.g., With which students in your class would you most like to play?) or a context (If you owned a company, which three students in your class would you make the managers?) to which they respond. The results are useful for identifying peer perceptions of students having, or not having, targeted characteristics such as friendliness, leadership skills, compassion, and so on. School counselors then use the results to help selected students develop in beneficial ways through a variety of possible counseling activities.

Appraisal methods are commonly used after counseling activities as a means of determining the effectiveness of those activities. One simple tactic useful in both large and small group and individual contexts is to readminister the same appraisal instrument after counseling as was used before counseling to determine what, if anything, has changed in the dynamics or behaviors addressed. Even more common is the similar use of appraisals for program evaluation. For example, the junior author developed several surveys (presented at the end of this chapter), based in part on items from his needs assessment surveys, to obtain students, parents, and teachers' evaluations of various school counseling services provided throughout each academic year.

The four coordination functions within the context of appraisal evolve directly from the more technical aspects of the school counselor's appraisal expertise. However, effective completion of those functions is not possible unless the resultant information can be understood effectively, and that involves use of school counselors' interpersonal skills.

Interpretation

Good professional practice, as well as legal standards, require that participants in appraisals (or their legal guardians) be informed of the results of the appraisals in ways that are understandable to them. For example, both the AERA/APA/NCME *Standards for Educational and Psychological Testing* and the laws derived from the *Family Educational Rights and Privacy Act of 1974* stipulate that it is the appraisal user's responsibility to insure that participants understand the results. This requirements necessitates skills beyond understanding item discrimination and difficulty indices, reliability coefficients, and the like. It necessitates appraisal users having good *communication* skills— what effective developmental school counselors have!

For large scale appraisal programs, such as district-wide achievement or aptitude testing, in which commercial tests are used, the test publishers routinely provide extensive interpretive materials for respondents and/or their parents or legal guardians. To the credit of the test publishers, most of these materials are very well-developed, nicely packaged, and most importantly, relatively self-explanatory. They do much to help people understand appraisal results and school counselors are well-advised to use them to supplement interpretations if they determine that such materials are potentially helpful. However, rarely are they fully sufficient for fully effective interpretations because most people simply *do not understand* normal distributions, deviation scores, stanines, and so on by just reading about them or looking at even well-conceived diagrams or graphs. Students, parents, teachers, and others who receive appraisal information have all kinds of questions about appraisal results, and usually face-to-face interactions are needed to provide effective answers to those questions.

Students

School counselors often use *large-group* (i.e., classroom) appraisal interpretation activities for students in middle or secondary schools when the appraisals are in regard to "nonthreatening" topics such as achievement, aptitudes, or vocational interests. For example, each December the junior author conducts classroom-group activities to help students understand the results of the Preliminary Scholastic Assessment Test they took earlier in the year. Large-group interpretation activities also may be appropriate when an entire class has participated in a specific type of appraisal, such as of career maturity or attitudes toward drug use and abuse. Some of these activities are intended to supplement information provided in test publishers' interpretive materials. More importantly, however, even large-group interpretation activities allow students to ask questions about their results and what they mean in personal ways. Perhaps most importantly, they allow students opportunity to request further, perhaps individualized, interpretation assistance or for school counselors to identify students in need of such assistance.

Small-group (counseling) interpretation activities are particularly appropriate for use in elementary schools and/or when students can gain from learning about their similarities or dissimilarities to others. In the latter context the primary benefit is most likely from the discussions which follow from the interpretations rather than from simply understanding the appraisal results. If students have been appraised in regard to social attitudes or behaviors, study habits, familial values, or career plans, the appraisal results provide effective stimuli for discussions in which students can come to understand one another better. For example, the junior author uses a survey of family relationships when conducting small-group counseling sessions for students experiencing difficulties in family life; some of the items serve to stimulate group discussions.

The small group context also provides a forum in which students can support one another so that appraisal results are not personalized in inappropriate ways. That is, students can encourage one another to "accept" the results as simply descriptive rather than as reflecting personal deficiencies. Again, the school counselor's expertise in both appraisal and counseling are essential to facilitate appropriate interpretations.

Students should be provided *individual* interpretations when there is likelihood that they will personalize appraisal results in ways that will not facilitate their positive developments. This potential exists most commonly for appraisals of personal characteristics such as self-concept, personality traits, or interpersonal behaviors. Appraisal results are almost always simply descriptive; typically there are no value judgments inherent in them. However, people make value judgments about the results, and therefore some students may interpret some appraisal results to mean there is something "wrong" with them. Through counseling in conjunction with interpretation, school counselors can help students individually to foster students' self understanding in ways that will facilitate students' self-improvement.

Parents

Appraisal interpretations for parents usually are made through large group or individual activities. Large group sessions for parents are routinely conducted to explain the results of system-wide achievement, aptitude, or competency testing. These sessions have essentially the same purposes and functions as those for students: to facilitate understanding of appraisal results and to allow for questions. However, parents usually have greater interest than students in the *long-term* implications of the results. For example, they often are interested in what the results mean in particular for their children's class placements, psychosocial developments, or vocational possibilities. They also may be interested in the curricular implications of the results—how well are their children doing in comparison to other children in the area, state, or nation? School counselors can use information provided by testing companies, school districts, and/or their own surveys, tests, or questionnaires to respond effectively to their questions.

Individual meetings with parents to discuss appraisal results are appropriate when either the parents do not understand appraisal results as explained through other means or when they have particular concerns about implications for their child. The former is simply a substitute for other means of explanation. However, the latter requires that school counselors use their counseling skills to present information so that the best interests of the child can be fostered. For example, a school counselor may have to explore family dynamics and behaviors to determine appropriate ways and means for a child to improve studying practices, interpersonal relationships with peers or adults, or academic and career planning decisions.

Teachers and Other Professionals

Some of the most valuable appraisal interpretation assistance school counselors provide is that for teachers and other professionals in schools. Given that the primary purpose of schools is to educate children, appraisal results frequently can be used to enhance educational processes. When school counselors help school personnel understand appraisal results effectively, those school personnel can then provide the best educational services to students. When a teacher understands the differences in a child's various abilities, the teacher can instruct the child in ways that capitalize on the child's strengths as well as improve on the child's limitations. In effect, appraisal results can be used to individualize instruction. Similarly, competent understanding of the results of appraisal of a child's non-academic characteristics will enhance school personnel's abilities to interact with the child in ways that will improve the child's personal and social developments.

The school counselor's role in interpreting appraisal results is crucial to helping students and others gain maximum benefit from appraisals. However, there is another context in which school counselors can use their combined appraisal and counseling expertise to assist students without direct provision of interpretation services.

Consultation

School counselors frequently serve in consultation roles as they work with other professionals to help students. Each professional in any consultation scenario contributes information, and school counselors often have access to appraisal information that can be useful. In such situations, school counselors do not necessarily need to provide (technical) interpretations of appraisal data; they need only be able to communicate the meanings and implications of those data pertinent to the purposes of the consultee's activities.

Teachers

In consulting with a student's teacher about how the teacher can modify a student's classroom behaviors, a school counselor who has appraisal information about the child's personality characteristics may not need to provide a complete interpretation of the appraisal data. Rather, the school counselor may relate only the implications of the appraisal results for the teacher's future interactions with the student (e.g., appropriate "positive behavior" reinforcers). Conversely, the school counselor may determine from the consultation that an appraisal is appropriate, conduct it with the student, and then provide implications within a consultation relationship.

Parents

Similar procedures may be used by school counselors in consultation activities with parents. However, in this context, activities recommended should probably be more specific and instructive; school counselors may have to provide direct, explicit instruction. For example, if the goal is to have parents help to improve a child's self-concept, the school counselor may have to provide detailed descriptions of desired parental behaviors such as when and how to reinforce positive self-concept behaviors or what words to use to encourage a positive self-concept.

Trainees

On-site supervision of school counselor trainees is an important professional function fulfilled by many school counselors. As aspiring school counselors, trainees need to become familiar with and adept at use of appraisals in school counseling activities. It is not the school counselor's responsibility to teach trainees about the technical aspects of appraisal; that responsibility is inherent in counselor education programs. It is appropriate for practicing school counselors to engage trainees in the various appraisal functions and to provide feedback, assistance, and consultation whenever trainees need them. Thus practicing school counselors should involve school counselor trainees in coordination, interpretation, and consultation appraisal functions in ways that reflect their own activities in fulfilling each of these functions.

Other Professionals

An increasing number of students are receiving mental health counseling services from professionals not officially connected with schools (e.g., counselors in community agency or private practice settings). Those professionals usually are called upon to provide services not frequently available in schools (e.g., long-term counseling or family counseling), but their efforts can be enhanced by information from and consultation with school counselors. In particular, school counselors often have access to appraisal information which could be obtained by counselors in other settings only through greater effort (and possibly expense). For example, the junior author sometimes uses a measure of family cohesion to appraise students' perceptions of their family dynamics and provides the results (with permission) to other counselors in a professional consultation context for students and their families who enter into family counseling. Thus school counselors can provide useful information and foster better interprofessional relationships through appraisal-related consultation activities.

School counselors' appraisal activities also may serve as the basis for initiating consultation activities with counseling professionals not in the schools. In consultation with other professionals, school counselors can rely to some extent on the other professional's expertise for determination of appropriate behaviors. For example, school counselors often use children's drawings as a form of appraisal with elementary-age school children. Sometimes revealed in those drawings are indicators of need for counseling services beyond those which can be provided by school counselors. Children's drawings in which child abuse and/or neglect are indicated are good examples because school counselors are required by law to report those indicators to "outside" authorities. In such situations school counselors' appraisal activities lead directly to consultation activities with professionals outside the schools.

Summary

School counselors' successful fulfillment of their appraisal coordination, interpretation, and consultation functions is crucial to their effective provision of school counseling services. Fortunately, by virtue of their training, knowledge, and skills in both appraisal and counseling, they are well-suited to fulfill these functions effectively. The most effective school counselors are those who routinely integrate appraisal activities into their functioning, and who therefore derive the most benefit from appraisals.

Figure 18.1
School Counselor Appraisal Functions

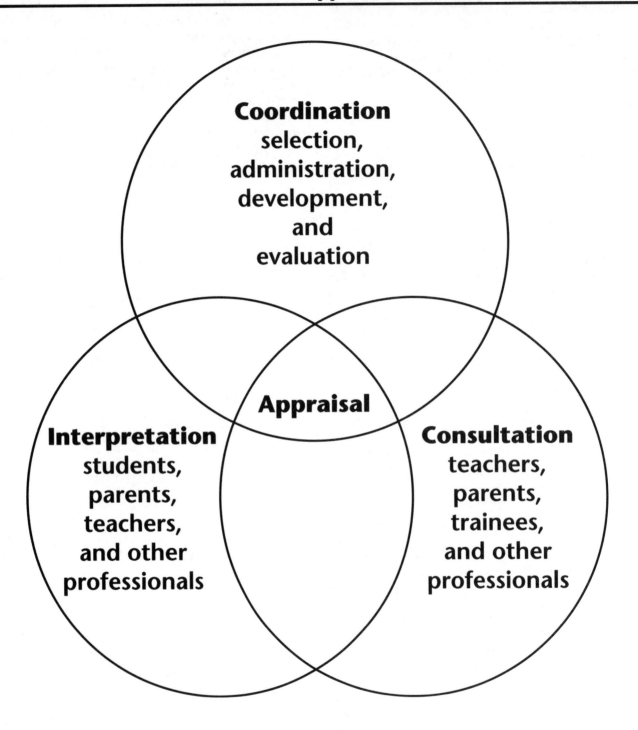

Coordination
selection,
administration,
development,
and
evaluation

Appraisal

Interpretation
students,
parents,
teachers,
and other
professionals

Consultation
teachers,
parents,
trainees,
and other
professionals

Chapter 19

Career Development: The Counselor's Role in Preparing K-12 Students for the 21st Century

by
**Pat Schwallie-Giddis and
Linda Kobylarz**

Pat Schwallie-Giddis, PhD, is an Assistant Professor at George Washington University in Counseling/Human and Organizational Studies. She is also serves as a consultant to the American School Counselor Association (ASCA) and the Center for Occupational Research and Development (CORD). Dr. Schwallie-Giddis was formerly an elementary counselor, district-level administrator, school board member and the program director for Career Education in the Florida Department of Education. Most recently she served on the executive staff at the American Counseling Association (ACA) and the Association for Career and Technical Education (formerly AVA).

Linda Kobylarz, MEd, is President of Kobylarz & Associates, a consulting group specializing in the broad area of life-long career development. She has been a junior high school teacher, a counselor, program director, business manager, and college professor. She serves as a consultant to numerous school districts, federal and state government agencies, and organizations.

Introduction

During the past several decades our nation has experienced extensive psychological, sociological, and economic changes. Numerous reports indicate that we are no longer first in the global market and that our education system is not producing students who will be able to compete effectively in the work world of the 21st Century. In addition, surveys of adults and students themselves reveal a concern about their future careers and their role in a rapidly changing workplace. What role can schools play in dealing with this issue? More specifically, what role do K-12 school counselors play? A discussion of these questions, including effective counselor strategies, is the focus of this chapter.

In an attempt to address this important issue, the National Career Development Association (NCDA) and the National Occupational Information Coordinating Committee (NOICC) commissioned the Gallup Organization to conduct several surveys (1989 and 1993) designed to provide data for career development professionals, including school counselors. Work in America reported the results of the 1989 survey. According to the survey, only 41% of working Americans followed a definite plan in mapping out their careers. Of those surveyed, 64% said that if they had the opportunity to do it over again, they would get more information about potential career choices. (The Gallup Organization, Work in America, 1989.) A majority of the respondents (at least 58%) in the 1993 Gallup Poll indicated that high schools do not pay enough attention to helping students choose careers, develop job skills, and find jobs after they leave school. This finding suggests that a majority of Americans feel that our students need assistance in making successful transitions from school to work and that schools have a large role to play in providing such help (The Gallup Organization, *Learning to Work: The NCDA Gallup Survey* (1995).

To meet the challenges of the new millennium, all educators, but especially K-12 school counselors, need to seek to improve and extend existing career development programs and create new methods and strategies within the school's guidance programs. Career development is a lifelong process in which individuals come to understand themselves and how they relate to the world of work. Through the career development process individuals gain self-knowledge, explore educational and occupational options, acquire work related skills, and develop decision-making and planning skills. This process should be an essential component of any comprehensive K-12 guidance and counseling program (Herr & Cramer, 1995).

Generally speaking, experts have defined four broad competency areas involved in an individual's career development process; 1) self-knowledge, 2) educational and occupational exploration, 3) career planning, and 4) aca-

Who Needs a Career Development Program?

demic and vocational skill development. In the self-knowledge area individuals increase in awareness of their interests, aspirations, aptitudes, abilities, and values. They move toward becoming more self-directed individuals, accepting responsibility for their own behavior, and developing positive interpersonal skills.

As individuals become more skilled in the career development area of educational and occupational exploration they acquire a deeper understanding of the interrelatedness of the various roles they will (or do currently) play as family members, citizens, friends, and workers. Students become more aware of the nature and structure of the world of work and the major trends impacting our economy. Information about self and the world of work are combined to focus on career options. Skills required for seeking, obtaining, keeping, and advancing in a job are learned.

The development of career planning and decision making also takes place over time. Students gain experience in relating their personal values and priorities to potential career plans. They recognize the impact of career decisions on their lifestyle and on those near to them. They come to understand that career planning is a lifelong process and to accept responsibility for their own choices, for managing their own resources, and for directing their own lives.

The career development process also involves academic and occupational skill development. Such skills should be marketable and of realistic value in the work place. Students also learn that education and work are closely related and that lifelong learning is a necessity. The four competency areas listed above should be at the center of any K-12 career development program.

Career development programs are appropriate for all people and at all educational levels; kindergarten through adult. We are all in various stages of the career development process. Children in the elementary grades are gaining new awareness of themselves as they interact with others. They should be systematically introduced to workers in the community and begin to relate education and work. As a school counselor, your role is to help them come to know that good work habits and personal responsibility are expected of them and that decisions they make have consequences for themselves and others (Wittmer, Thompson, & Loesch, 1997).

Counselors help youth in middle/junior high school to fine tune the interpersonal and social skills required for positive interaction with others. Students should, as a result of your middle school counseling program, grow in self-confidence and become aware of their interests and abilities. They need to see clearly the relationship between educational achievements and career opportunities and to express positive attitudes towards work and learning. The ability to locate and use information in their educational and career planning is also important. They must have knowledge of job seeking and survival skills and begin to develop work competencies.

High school students are at a pivotal time in their lives where decisions about staying in school, entering work directly after graduation, joining the armed forces, or continuing with some form of post-secondary education will have a significant impact on their lives for years to come. School counselors must ensure that their career development programs respond to the individual needs of students while helping all students prepare for transition into the adult world. The following are key to the successful career development of high school students: 1) clarification of individual interests, 2) an understanding of personal strengths and skills, 3) well developed interpersonal skills, 4) a wealth of knowledge about occupations and how the self relates to them, 5) good work attitudes, and 6) sound decision-making and planning skills.

Who Delivers the Career Development Programs?

As noted, career development programs are essential to any quality K-12 developmental counseling program that seeks to offer comprehensive, systematic, and sequential services to all students. The delivery of career development programming is a team effort with counselors, teachers, administrators, parents, and the community-at-large all playing a part. However, school counselors have a leadership role in designing the program and identifying student outcome standards; assuring coordination with other programs and articulation across levels; supporting the professional development of staff; and conducting ongoing program evaluation and improvement. School counselors must also be proactive in public relations and advocating the allocation of necessary resources and budget.

The National Career Development Guidelines

Under the leadership of the National Occupational Information Coordinating Committee (NOICC), numerous counseling associations and organizations collaborated to produce the National Career Development Guidelines. The Guidelines project has gone far to operationalize career development theory into practical application. For this reason, it is important that school counselors become familiar with the Guidelines (Zunker, 1998).

The Guidelines are intended to provide a basis for improving career guidance and counseling programs that are integrated within the total guidance and counseling program. The Guidelines serve as a catalyst for the adoption, at the local school level, of student outcome standards that will lead to stronger career guidance and counseling programs. The Guidelines address three major components: *student competencies and indicators for career development, personnel requirements and counselor competencies,* and *organizational capabilities.* The Guidelines also outline a process to help school counselors at all levels to *plan, design,* and *implement* a developmental approach to career guidance and counseling.

As is noted in detail below, the NOICC Guidelines complement the ASCA National Standards for School Counseling Program.

The student *competencies* and *indicators* offer a framework for identifying student outcomes of career guidance and counseling programs and thus become the basis for program development. It is best to think of the *competencies* as broad goals. In contrast, the *indicators* describe specific attitudes, knowledge, and skills related to career development. The Guidelines provide recommended career development competencies and indicators for students at the elementary, middle/junior high school, and high school levels. There are twelve competencies at each level organized around the areas of self-knowledge, educational and occupational exploration, and career planning.

The *personnel* requirements and *counselor competencies* discussed in the Guidelines give school counselors insight into the roles of various staff members as well as the specific skills they need to deliver career guidance and counseling programs effectively (Zunker, 1998).

The Guidelines also describe the organizational capabilities; the commitments, structure, and support required for effective career guidance and counseling programs. Important information for school counselors is included regarding administrative commitments, physical facilities, in-service training, and materials and equipment (NOICC, *National Career Development Guidelines Handbook K-Adult,* 1996).

Career Development Implementation: Activities, Methods, and Strategies

The effective delivery of a career guidance and counseling program requires a team approach involving school administrators, counselors, teachers, support staff, parents, and the business community. Presented below is a strategy to assist counseling professionals initiate or revise career guidance and counseling programs at the elementary, middle/junior high school, and high school levels. The strategy suggested by the National Guidelines has three phases: *planning, development,* and *implementation* (NOICC, *National Career Development Guidelines Handbook K-Adult,* 1996).

During the *planning* phase, steering and advisory committees are formed under the direction of the school counselor, commitments are gained, program benefits are identified, and a needs assessment is conducted. Decisions are made regarding the selection of local standards for student outcomes and a scope and sequence of activities is developed. Plan evaluation issues are discussed.

The *development* phase moves the advisory and steering committees into action to review current school career development programs, develop a career guidance and counseling plan, write staff role descriptions, identify staff development needs, and design evaluation methods.

Implementation focuses on the counselor/coordinator conducting staff development, launching the revised career guidance and counseling program, conducting ongoing monitoring and evaluation, and using the evaluation results to revise and improve the program. The advisory and steering committees remain intact and continue to provide leadership for the program (Zunker, 1998).

Counselor Delivery Methods

A variety of processes are used by K-12 counselors to deliver the career guidance and counseling program content to students. They include: *outreach, classroom instruction, counseling, assessment, career information, work experience, placement, consultation, referral,* and *follow-up.* These eleven processes are described (briefly) below.

1. **Outreach.** A proactive approach to alerting students to the career guidance and counseling services available from the school helps ensure that the program reaches all students.

2. **Classroom Instruction.** Planned and sequential career-related curriculum activities, delivered by teachers and counselors through classroom instruction or large group guidance activities, can be used as one vehicle to reach all students in your school. The classroom instruction process couples academic curriculum objectives with career development competencies. For each subject, the existing curriculum is reviewed and areas that can be used to deliver career development concepts are identified. Lesson plans are refocused to include both academic and career development objectives. For instance, a short story might be used to help students clarify their own goals, or math problems could be written to reinforce the use of math in various occupations. Integrating career development concepts into academic instruction helps make instruction meaningful to students and actively engages them in the learning process.

3. **Counseling.** Counseling focuses on helping students explore personal issues related to career development, examine how to apply information and skills learned to their personal plans, and develop individualized career plans. This includes both individual and small group counseling approaches.

4. **Assessment.** Assessment includes the administration and interpretation of a variety of formal and informal measures to provide students with a clearer understanding of their skills, abilities, interests, achievements, and needs (see Chapter 14).

5. **Career Information.** Resources are available to provide current and unbiased information to students about occupations, educational programs, post secondary training, the military, and employment opportunities.

6. **Career Information Delivery System (CIDS).** In many states, a computer-based career information delivery system brings comprehensive, accurate, and up-to-date information about occupations and education/training opportunities to students, usually through the school counselor's office. Some CIDS target high school to adult audiences while others offer versions of the system suitable for upper elementary to middle/junior high school students. The State Occupational Information Coordinating Committee (SOICC) is usually affiliated with the CIDS and can answer any questions you might have as a counselor regarding the system in your state. The foundation of a CIDS is the quality of its data. Most CIDS provide descriptions of hundreds of occupations including duties, requirements, earnings, and employment out-

look for the respective state. Some also contain national information. Information about related education and training in your state is generally part of the CIDS as well as information about financial aid resources available at the state level. The information is easily accessed and printed copies can be generated. The primary delivery vehicles for a CIDS are computers; stand alone micros, networked micros, or large mainframe computers serving many sites. However, some CIDS also have a microfiche component. Staff supporting the CIDS might offer statewide training workshops or a hot-line to assist counselors. We urge you to check into the CIDS in your state. You will find the system extremely helpful to your career development program.

7. **Work Experience.** Opportunities for students in actual work settings facilitate the testing of career decisions and develop effective work abilities and behaviors.

8. **Placement.** Placement resources and assistance help students make a successful transition from high school to employment, postsecondary education, military service, or other options.

9. **Consultation.** Through consultation, counselors provide direct assistance to teachers, administrators, parents, and others who interact with students that will help them to better understand the nature of career development and effective strategies for supporting career development.

10. **Referral.** For some students, physical or psychological problems may inhibit career development. Professional school counselors who coordinate career guidance and counseling programs will recognize such problems and make appropriate referrals.

11. **Follow-up.** Maintaining long-term contact with students as they progress through their school years and beyond has benefits for both the students and the career guidance and counseling program (NOICC, *National Career Development Guidelines Handbook K-Adult,* 1996).

School/Community Connections

It is evident from the above information that the array of career development competencies that students must acquire cannot be addressed by schools alone. To be successful, the school counselor's career development efforts require the involvement of the entire community; the home, business and industry, labor, and government. Very important resources are available close at hand; usually only a phone call away. Parents, senior citizens,

employers and employees, civic organizations and youth groups can make major contributions to the development of students by offering a dimension not normally available in the classroom. Employers, especially, have a vested interest in the youth who will eventually staff their enterprises. Local employers realize they have a valuable resource that can extend the learning environment of students beyond the school walls. A counselor's public awareness and public relations are both keys to developing community connections. It is important to know what you want from the community and to be able to clearly articulate your needs and wishes. It is important that a school district's approach to the community be coordinated throughout all of the schools. A school counselor's time spent developing concrete ways to coordinate the use of community resources is time well spent. Some ideas follow:

1. Local chambers of commerce might help in disseminating materials about your school's career development program; provide speakers, identify interesting field trip sites, work shadow sites, and/or work experience sites. The Chamber member may also serve as a point of general coordination with the business community.

2. The Boy Scouts, Girl Scouts, 4-H Clubs, and Junior Achievement offer a wealth of resources such as career-related booklets, career awareness programs, interest surveys, field visits, and even experience in running a small business. Contact them. They are usually "help" oriented people who will be invaluable to you and your career development program.

3. Parents and senior citizens, if asked, will willingly serve as volunteers in the guidance office and career resource center as well as serve as the role models so critical to a youth's career development.

4. Local businesses have traditionally been supportive of field trips to their respective businesses, in providing career speakers, work-experience sites, and work shadowing experiences. They might also consider supplying some career related materials or equipment to your school. Local businesses can also provide teachers and counselors with new insights by offering them summer employment. However, again, you will have to actively seek their involvement in your program.

5. Colleges, universities, and vocational-technical schools also make excellent field trip sites and will provide guest speakers as well if requested.

6. The military has a great deal of free career information available to schools and the ASVAB aptitude

test is a resource used effectively by many high school counselors.

7. Many labor organizations have an educational unit that will be happy to work with schools in a variety of ways.

Remember, the resources are out there but you must ask for help. Be sure to coordinate (district-wide when possible) your efforts. Keep your community informed about what you and your school are doing in the career area and how they can participate. If you ask them they will be there.

Career Resource Center

The school career resource center serves as a focal point for many different kinds of career development activities and is central to any developmental guidance program. Students at all levels can use the center's materials to research information about occupations and postsecondary education/training options. The center is also a great place for high school counselors to hold meetings with college recruiters, military recruiters, or local business people.

Counselors might also use the center for meetings with small groups of students to discuss career development issues, to administer an interest inventory to student and/or to conduct a mini course on various career related topics.

School career resource centers, coordinated by counselors, come in all sizes and shapes. They fit into guidance areas, corners of the media center or library, sprout wheels and move into the cafeteria during study halls and lunch periods, or take up temporary residence in classrooms for special projects, and/or spill over to bulletin boards in the hallways. More than simply a place, the career resource center is a concept that fosters easy access to a variety of career information and related activities. Effective K-12 developmental school counselors make full use of such a center.

Just as the location of a career resource center will vary from school to school, so do staffing arrangements. Many schools use community volunteers quite successfully in their career center. Using student aides or peer helpers is a very important method of providing coverage in the resource center, especially if the center has a computer-based career information delivery system as previously described. You might also take advantage of existing staff such as media specialists, librarians, or teacher aides to oversee the operation of the center. However, as noted, the center should be under the coordination of the guidance department.

Career resource centers house a variety of information and are usually organized around interest areas. Typically, they contain information about occupations, postsecondary education and training opportunities, financial aid, the military, job seeking and job survival skills, and perhaps part-time and full-time jobs available in the local community.

Information about occupations is delivered through print publications, media (films, film strips, video), the computer, and microfiche available in the center. Numerous low-cost, career information materials are also available from government agencies. *The Occupational Outlook Handbook*, the *Guide for Occupational Exploration*, and the *Dictionary of Occupational Titles* are three excellent resources available from the federal government. Your State Occupational Information Coordinating Committee (SOICC) office probably produces a variety of materials such as a career information tabloid, a job hunter's guide, an apprenticeship directory, state employment outlook, wage rates, and more.

Many commercial companies also produce career information books, kits, films, film strips, and videos for use by school counselors. There are several career magazines that provide timely and inexpensive career information. When selecting commercially produced materials the school counselor should ensure that they are bias free, accurate, and up-to-date. The *Occupational Outlook Handbook* has a section that provides addresses for more information about specific occupations. This is often a good source of free brochures.

Technology adds another dimension to information delivery. Computer-based career information delivery systems (CIDS) and microfiche are examples. As noted, many states have a CIDS that contains state and national information regarding many occupations, postsecondary educational opportunities, and financial aid. Some states also offer career information on microfiche. Check with your State Occupational Information Coordinating Committee (SOICC) Director for more information about what is available in your state.

Computers certainly provide an exciting vehicle for the dissemination of career information, but, counselors are encouraged not to overlook some more traditional and very cost effective methods for sharing information. Career posters are a lively way to provide information and brighten the school's career center. Bulletin board displays scattered throughout the school and within the career center can be used to stimulate student thinking about the many decisions facing them and to present concepts such as career clustering and career ladders. In addition, using bulletin boards (and, do change them frequently) is good public relations for the counseling department. Some bulletin board ideas are:

1. "Math—Who Needs It:" (features occupations that require math skills).

2. Personal Values "Coat of Arms" (students draw a large shield and express on it personal values and priorities by completing sentences such as: A word that describes me _____, I am proud of _____, It's important to _____, Someone I admire is_____).

3. Life Style Collage (students express various aspects of a desired lifestyle through a collage which might include interests, hobbies, family, occupation, etc.).

4. Educational Level/Occupations (highlights post secondary education/training routes and shows sample occupations for each).

5. Interests Collage (nice follow-up to interest inventories and can be done as a student group project).

Many students are planning some sort of education or training following high school graduation. Catalogs from vocational technical schools, community colleges, two and four year colleges and universities should be included in the career resource center (see Chapter 10). Information about apprenticeships is available from the State Labor Department. Scholarship and financial aid information is also very important. A telephone call to your state Labor Department can get you a wealth of free materials.

As a high school counselor, you will find many students exploring the military as an option for additional education and training and/or as a career. Abundant free information is available from each of the branches of the armed services. The *Military Career Guide* contains descriptions of over 200 military occupations with related information about civilian occupations. The military will also provide, administer, and interpret an aptitude test for military occupations: the Armed Service Vocational Aptitude Battery (ASVAB). The ASVAB also includes the Self Directed Search (SDS), a popular interest inventory provided free to every student who takes the ASVAB.

Many school counselors have a section of the career center devoted to materials about job seeking skills; finding your first job, filling out applications, resumes, and interviewing. Others have "job boards" with part-time job openings in the community listed as well as full-time employment opportunities for graduating seniors.

A Working Career Preparation Model

The Florida Department of Education's approach to career development in schools embraces the concepts presented in the NOICCC guidelines described above and uses many of the methods described above. The Florida K-12, statewide plan, the Florida Blueprint for Career Preparation, addresses the need to prepare students for the global market place. Career Development has been the backbone of this statewide initiative that has impacted thousands of Florida's K-12 students. The Blueprint for Career Preparation provides the framework for educators to prepare youth and adults to successfully enter and remain in their chosen fields of work. It requires that every Florida school district provide a comprehensive education program including self-awareness, career awareness, academic and vocational preparation and job placement for each student.

The Blueprint touches all levels of education, taking the core curriculum of basic skills and making it relevant to today's workplace. Schools, through the coordination of their counselors integrate academic and vocational education making both meaningful for students' career development. The Blueprint stresses that curriculum should relate to careers and vice versa. The integration of the two approaches means that students gain both career and academic training. Six steps are emphasized in the Blueprint as essential to career preparation. In our opinion, these steps summarize an effective career development component for a K-12 program. The six steps are:

1. Begin by developing an awareness of self, the value of work and exposure to careers and technology in grades K-5.

2. By grade six, students (with the help of their counselors, teachers and parents should assess personal aptitudes, abilities and interests and relate them to future careers. They should also learn the role of technology in the world of work.

3. In grades seven and eight, students should set career oriented goals and develop a four –year program of study for grades nine through twelve that supports their goals. Since plans may change, they are reviewed annually by students, parents, and educators. Such individualized plans set students on a viable course and provide a basis for curriculum selection.

4. During high school, a new "applied curriculum" makes academic concepts relevant to the workplace, especially in communications, math and science. Vocational courses and academic instruction are integrated to enhance student competencies in academic skills.

5. Students choosing post-secondary education programs should be able to successfully gain employment, advance within their fields or change occupations. Vocational-technical centers community colleges and universities deliver these programs.

6. Educators should intensify efforts to share information and to involve parents, business and the entire community in this very important process. Partnerships and the involvement of people beyond educators are critically important.

The American School Counselor Association (ASCA) has long been a strong advocate of K-12 career development programs and in 1997, the association developed the National Standards for School Counseling Programs of which one-third concern K-12 career development standards. In Chapter Two of this book, Wittmer presented an overview of ASCA's National Standards for School Counseling Programs.

The ASCA Standards provide the foundation for skill, attitude and knowledge acquisition that enable students (K-12) to make a successful transition from school to the world of work, and from job to job across the life career span. Career development, according to the ASCA Standards, includes using strategies that enhance future career success and job satisfaction as well as assisting understanding of the association between personal qualities, education and training, and a career choice. The recommendations of the Secretary's Commission on Achieving Necessary Skills (SCANS) and the content of the National Career Development Guidelines are also reflected in the career content area standards and competencies found in the ASCA Standards. The three Standards are: 1). Students will acquire the skills to investigate the world of work in relation to knowledge of self and to make appropriate career decisions; 2). Students will employ strategies to achieve future career goals with success and satisfaction, and 3). Students will understand the relationship between personal qualities, education, training and the world of work.

As students progress through school and into adulthood, ASCA believes they need to acquire a firm foundation for career development. ASCA urges school counselors to implement activities and strategies related to the content standards for career development provide K-12 students with the foundation for future career success (Dahir, Sheldon & Valiga, 1998).

Summary

It is clear that the workplace of tomorrow will be very different from the workplace of today. The emphasis in the new millennium will, as in the decade of the 90's, continue to be on change, flexibility, multiple career paths and lifelong learning. Numerous reports detail for us what will be required of our students, suggest strategies for school reform and challenge Americans to re-dedicate themselves to attaining new standards of quality and productivity.

The career development concepts and practices described above support the call to re-energize our schools and help our students succeed in a dynamic and demanding workplace. Research affirms that comprehensive career guidance and counseling programs, coupled with other interventions, can provide students with the means to develop the career survival competencies they need. School counselors are uniquely positioned to promote movement toward a truly comprehensive approach to career development. As a school counselor and/or future school counselor, you have an exciting opportunity to make a difference, not only for your students, but also for the very future of our country.

References

Dahir, C., Sheldon, B., & Valiga, M. (1998). *Vision into action: Implementing the national standards for school counseling programs.* Alexandria, VA: ASCA Press.

Gallup Organization. (1989). *Work in America: A survey of U.S. adults on jobs, careers, and the workplace.* Washington, DC: Author.

Gallup Organization. (1995). *Learning to work: the NCDA Gallup survey.* Washington, DC: Author.

Herr, E., & Cramer, S. (1995). *Career guidance through the lifespan* (5th ed.). Boston, MA: Little Brown.

Holland, J.L. (1997). *Making vocational choices: A theory of vocational personalities and work environments* (3rd ed.). Englewood Cliffs, NJ: Prentice-Hall.

National Occupational Information Coordinating Committee. (1996). The *national career development guidelines handbook k- adult.* Washington, DC: Author.

Osipow, S.J. (1996). *Theories of career development* (4th ed.). New York: Appleton-Century-Crofts.

Wittmer, J., & Thompson, D. (1995) *Large group counseling: A k-12* sourcebook. Minneapolis, MN: Educational Media Corporation.

Wittmer, J., Thompson, D., & Loesch, L. (1997). *Classroom guidance activities: A sourcebook for elementary school counselors.* Minneapolis, MN: Educational Media Corporation.

Zunker, G. (1998). *Career counseling: Applied concepts of life planning.* Pacific Grove, CA: Brooks/Cole.

Chapter 20
Educational Guidance and Counseling

by

James H. Pitts

James H. Pitts, PhD, is a counselor educator at the University of Florida. His career in education has included public school teaching, college counseling, and teaching both undergraduate and graduate students at the university level. Among his interests are college student development and conflict resolution in educational settings.

Introduction

The main goal of educational guidance and counseling, a vital function of a developmental school counselor's job, is to help students keep their educational options open. As with many situations school counselors encounter, there is "good news" and "bad news" concerning this goal. The good news is that many young people have families that provide them with positive role models and encouragement to do their best in school and make the most of their abilities. The bad news is that many other young people are not so fortunate. In these cases counselors need to help students realize that they *do* have options, that elementary schools, middle schools, and high schools provide them with opportunities to become more productive and successful than they might imagine possible.

In this chapter, I focus on educational *counseling* and educational *guidance*. Educational counseling refers to counselors' efforts to help students develop self concepts which keep their educational options open. Educational guidance refers to counselors' interventions aimed at assisting students to make the best use of the options available.

The chapter is divided into three sections: elementary school, middle school, and high school. At the elementary school level the focus is on counseling. At the middle school level the need to maintain positive self concepts and to make appropriate course selections are reflected in a blend of counseling and guidance activities. High school students' choices of courses have even more impact on educational outcomes, but their individual self concepts still play a vital role. The high school section of this chapter is devoted primarily to helping school counselors assist their student clients in making the transition from secondary to post secondary education. The material relating to self concept, motivation, and career development in other chapters of this book should be considered as an integral part of educational guidance and counseling. Each of these components is interwoven in effective educational counseling at any level.

Elementary School

A basic developmental need of elementary school children is described by Erik Erikson (1963) as developing the capacity for industry and overcoming feelings of inferiority. "To bring a productive situation to completion is an aim which gradually supersedes the whims and wishes of play" (Erikson, 1963, p. 259). An aspect of this gradual developmental process can be understood in terms of helping elementary school students begin to develop a self-concept which includes seeing themselves as future workers. Helping students develop a vocational self concept (Super, 1992) contributed to the accomplishment of this developmental task. Obviously, an elementary school child would not be expected to have a highly refined concept of his or her future vocation, although many have ideas of becoming a firefighter, nurse, astronaut, or whatever. Even at a young age, however, a few children have already begun to pick up ideas contrary to a positive vocational self concept. An example that a colleague heard expressed by a four year old rural southern boy at a nursery school illustrates this problem: "I ain't gonna work; it's dumb to work." His "vocational" self-concept was beginning to form at an early age, undoubtedly influenced by a role model of questionable merit.

Middle School

Many children have positive role models; many don't. An effective way for an elementary school counselor to combine vocational information with self-concept formation in a developmental guidance program is to enlist the help of community volunteers who can serve as role models. Persons of varying backgrounds and occupations can relate their "life stories" to elementary school children via school assemblies, closed circuit TV, and so forth. A key to the effectiveness of this approach is to be certain the volunteers maximize the ways in which the children can identify with them. Having volunteers from a variety of racial, ethnic, and social backgrounds is important. Social learning theory (Bandura, 1997) suggested that models whom observers see as similar to themselves are far more effective than those who are perceived as too different. The volunteers can enhance their perceived similarity to the children by talking about their lives when they were young, describing how they grew up, entered their present careers, and so forth. Teachers, perhaps following a structure put forward by the counselor, might follow up these sessions with stories, videos, or news items concerning other people in careers similar to those of the volunteers.

Elementary school counselors will want to remember that the development of a positive vocational self concept is highly important to the child's future receptiveness to educational guidance and counseling. Without such a view of self, a student may find goal-directed behavior involving learning and, later on, the selection of courses which are not the "path of least resistance" an unappealing prospect. Schwallie-Giddes' chapter on vocational development (Chapter 11 of this book) provides useful information concerning this aspect of educational counseling.

Vocational self-concept is only one part of an elementary school child's view of self and the world. Other considerations influence his or her future educational options as well. All aspects of a well-rounded developmental guidance program are designed to help elementary school students acquire the skills and attitudes needed to succeed in school. Success tends to be cumulative and becomes increasingly important as students enter middle school and have increasing options concerning the courses they select in preparation for high school.

Educational counseling and guidance should be a major aspect of any comprehensive guidance program at the middle school level, and educational counseling continues to be closely associated with self concept issues at this level. A major effort of middle school counselors is to help students develop and maintain positive self concepts, including vocational self concepts. Students' vocational self concepts have a more tangible effect on educational decisions at this age than during the elementary years because students now have more choices concerning the courses they will take. Hitchner and Tifft-Hitchner (1996) recommended that counselors begin working with students on post secondary school preparation by seventh grade because the courses taken in eighth and ninth grades are vitally important to college preparation. Whatever the students' post high school plans may be, taking courses that keep their options open for some form of post secondary education is desirable.

An example of a program designed to help middle school students develop their ideas about personal interests and career choices is the Program of Advisement with Teachers Helping Students (PATHS) at Milwee Middle School in Longwood, Florida. (This program is an example of a TAP program as described by Gonzalez and Myrick in Chapter 19 of this book.) Students are assigned to small groups by grade level with a teacher who continues with the group for the three years the students are in middle school. The program combines homeroom activities with a program which emphasizes career exploration, thinking skills, study skills, and efforts to develop students' self esteem. Eighth grade students are administered career interest and aptitude inventories by a guidance counselor. The PATH students then develop a four year plan which helps assure that they will continue to think about their career goals as they progress through high school (Mason, 1992).

In addition to programs such as PATHS and other Teachers as Advisors Programs (TAP), many middle school counselors have initiated successful large group guidance activities designed to assist students with career choice and personal interests. Some "target" students would also benefit from a small group approach.

High School

Developmental Considerations

Developmental activities aimed at positive self-concept remain important to high school students. They continue the trend begun in middle school of needing to be reflected more and more in students' concrete decisions concerning course selection. Many students whose self-perception does not include continuing in school beyond what is required by law drop out after the tenth grade. Having a concrete goal for continuing becomes increasingly important. Fortunately, in many high schools a sizable number of students have the goal of attending college and have no intention of dropping out. Other students have goals which include vocational-technical education and also intend to graduate from high school. Some students, however, have little in the way of plans for the future and seem not to want to think about what lies ahead. This is where the skill of the school counselor comes into play. Finding programs which capture these students' imaginations and guiding them into courses which keep their options open require a combination of developmental counseling and practical guidance. For some of these unmotivated students, information about vocational-technical education may provide a spark of interest that will lead to their remaining in school through high school and beyond. Materials, videos, or guest speakers from a local vocational-technical school or community college may prove useful to high school counselors in their approach to effective educational counseling.

Tech Prep Career Programs

Many counselors and teachers may not be as familiar with tech prep (also known as vocational-technical education) as they are with "traditional" college education and might, therefore, be unaware of some of the opportunities that exist for students for whom this track is viable. In the Bureau of Labor Statistics' list of 20 occupations with the fastest growth in total employment, by percent, 12 of these occupations fall into tech prep fields:

Rank   Occupation

1. Database administrators, computer support specialists and all other computer scientists

4. Personal home care aides

5. Physical and corrective therapy assistants and aides

6. Home health aides

7. Medical assistants

8. Desktop publishing specialists

10. Occupational therapy assistants and aides

11. Paralegals

15. Data processing equipment repairers

16. Medical records technicians

18. Dental hygienists

20. Physician assistants (Hettinger, 1998, p. 37)

Tech prep provides a seamless transition between high school and postsecondary educational experiences. In order to have a tech prep program, a high school must belong to a consortium, consisting of at least one high school one post secondary institution. The addition of other high schools, as well as representatives from business and industry, is highly desirable. (Fagan & Lumley, 1997).

Tech prep programs that allow students to combine high school work and postsecondary training in an articulated program are cited by the American Vocational Association as a highly promising way to meet the needs of students for whom they are appropriate. According to Fagan and Lumley (1997), tech prep practitioners list the following desirable results which arise, at least in part, from tech prep programs:

1. Better levels of performance of students in math, English, technology, and science.

2. Increased student motivation to learn.

3. High school connected with college by a coordinated sequence of courses.

4. Decreased dropout rates of high school students.

5. Increased student preparedness to enter college programs.

6. Increased skill levels of high school graduates.

7. Age-appropriate school-to-work transition activities.

8. Availability of career opportunity information for community college graduates (pp. 14-16).

If a tech prep consortium is not available in a given area, creating one may help open educational opportunities for students who, for whatever reason, will not attend a four year college and pursue a bachelor's degree. The following reference provides practical guidance for counselors and others who are interested in developing a tech prep program and forming a consortium with other institutions and with business and industrial employers.

Fagan, Carol, & Lumley, Dan. (1997). *Tech prep career programs: A practical guide to preparing students for high-tech, high-skill, high-wage opportunities.* Thousand Oaks, CA: Corwin Press.

Tech prep programs will continue to exist for the foreseeable future. The Carl D. Perkins Vocational-Technical Education Act of 1998 provides continued federal support for tech prep. "The new law strengthens tech prep programs by asking consortia to develop longer-range plans, to use technology more in classroom instruction and to communicate among tech prep partners" (Hettinger, 1999, p. 41).

In settings where tech prep type programs are not feasible, students can still make plans to pursue vocational-technical education following high school graduation. Visits to community colleges and vocational-technical schools that have programs in students' areas of interest may help stimulate students to make post secondary educational plans. Representatives from schools with vo-tech programs can be invited by the counselor to visit the high school to meet with interested students.

Helping Students Select and Apply to Post Secondary Institutions

Note: *Much of the information presented in this section is most useful for orientation meetings for eleventh grade students and their parents.*

Selecting and applying to post-secondary institutions can be a bewildering experience for students. Even those students who are certain that their post high school plans include college can become frustrated if they do not understand how the process works and when to do what. Students who are less determined to go to college or to pursue other training may become disenchanted enough with the process to give up. Helping students through the "maze" of selection and application is an important task for counselors and for students' parents alike.

Involvement of Parents

Counselors are well advised to acknowledge and encourage parents' roles in the selection and application process by including them in orientation meetings, as well as other meetings where students' college plans are discussed. Parent involvement is an important part of educational planning (Hitchner & Tifft-Hitchner, 1996). Many parents want to be involved; all should be highly encouraged to participate in this important step in their children's educational development, whether the student intends to go to a two- or four-year college, a university, or a vocational-technical school. For convenience, the term "college" will often be used in this section to refer to all post-secondary institutions, although another term might be more technically correct in some instances. Some counselors may wish to include students (and their parents) planning to attend vocational-technical institutions in the general college orientation meetings; others may choose to hold separate meetings for this group.

Financial Aid

A good way to gain credibility with parents in an orientation meeting is to begin by addressing their interest in the financial aspects of their children's attending college. For many parents, the question of how to pay for college is a major consideration. An overview of when and how to make application for financial aid is an effective way to acknowledge their concerns in this area and to remove some of the uncertainty concerning the process. The following description of the financial aid application process has been summarized from the *College Costs & Financial Aid Handbook, 1999.* Since financial aid procedures and regulations are subject to frequent change, school counselors should update their financial aid information on a regular basis.

During the winter of the twelfth grade, the student should file a Free Application for Federal Student Aid (FAFSA) form and all other financial aid forms required by the college(s) to which application(s) is/are being made. The FAFSA contains information about family finances and is used to determine financial aid eligibility, including eligibility for a Pell Grant or Federal Stafford Loan. The FAFSA should be submitted as soon after January 1 of the senior year as possible. After the FAFSA is processed, the Department of Education will send a Student Aid Report to the student. The student then needs to send the Student Aid Report to the financial aid office of the college or university to which he or she is applying.

Many colleges and universities require the CSS/Financial Aid Profile for purposes of awarding private aid funds. This form is different from the FAFSA and requires the payment of a fee. Students should be advised not to confuse the FAFSA, required for all federal aid, with the Financial Aid Profile. When the FAFSA, and the Financial Aid Profile if it is used, have been processed by the college's financial aid office, that office will construct a financial aid package and send the student an award letter describing the financial aid the student has been awarded. The student must respond to the award letter, indicating acceptance of all, part, or none of the financial aid package that has been offered. Additional information concerning the financial aid process may be obtained from the financial aid offices of colleges or universities and from the following source:

College Costs & Financial Aid Handbook. College Scholarship Service, The College Board.

To order this book, contact The College Board in one of the following ways:

College Board Publications, Two College Way, Forrester Center, WV 25438

Fax: (800) 525-5562

Online: *www.collegeboard.org*

Types of Colleges and Universities

A wide variety of colleges and universities exists in the United States. They may be divided into two-year colleges, most of which are community colleges, and four-year colleges and universities. Students typically commute to and from community colleges; many students live on or near campus while attending four year institutions. Another way of sorting these institutions is by ownership: public or private. Public universities are typically less expensive than private. The following breakdown of average costs gives some indication of what students and their families should expect. Information broken down by region of the country will give a more accurate estimate, and individual institutions can provide more precise cost data. Public institutions charge out of state tuition rates, not shown in the chart, for non-residents.

	Residential	**Commuter**
2 year public	-----------	$6,196
2 year private	$13,697	$11,466
4 year public	$10,069	$8,133
4 year private	$21,424	$18,623

College Costs & Financial Aid Handbook 1999, p. 33.

Colleges and universities also can be separated on the basis of selectivity—the high school grade average and test scores required for admission. The institution's catalog will describe the criteria used for admissions decisions. Many of the more selective institutions require that the applicant submit an essay as part of the application materials.

Another basis on which institutions of higher education may be separated is by the ethnicity of students traditionally attending. Some colleges and universities are traditionally African American, with a high majority of African-American students in attendance. African-American students may wish to attend such an institution or may prefer to attend a college or university with a more diverse student population.

Community Colleges

Community colleges are usually public, although some are private, and offer two year associate of arts programs which are designed to allow students to transfer to a four year college to complete a bachelor's degree. They also offer associate of science degrees in vocational-technical areas. Associate of science programs are not designed specifically to meet transfer requirements, so additional courses are typically needed before a student can transfer to a four year college as a junior. Advantages of community colleges include relatively open admission policies and low tuition costs. They often offer programs in remedial education for students whose academic skills are not sufficient to begin college level academic work, although many students who attend such colleges do not need remedial courses.

Community colleges are typically commuter colleges; students do not ordinarily live in residence halls on campus. This arrangement allows students whose parents live near a community college to live at home and thereby save the cost of room and board at a residential college. While living at home provides economic benefit, it makes more difficult becoming involved in campus life and activities. That is, the major "trade-off" in attending a non-residential college is often the relatively minimal involvement that students have in out of class activities associated with the college.

Four-Year Colleges

Four year-colleges and universities vary in admissions requirements, size, and mission. An institution which is a "college," rather than a "university," is generally smaller than most universities and has a mission which emphasizes *teaching* more than *research* as a major responsibility of its faculty. Since college faculty are primarily responsible for teaching, students may find that individual attention in classes is more readily available than it may be at a university. While the quality of courses may be quite high, the quantity and variety of classes available at a college is not likely to be as great as at a larger university. A student's intended major will help dictate whether or not a college is a desirable choice. Many liberal arts majors are available at such institutions, as are a number of others, depending on the individual college. Opportunities for involvement in out of class activities are often readily available at colleges, and living in a residence hall provides many experiences that will be remembered fondly for years to come. Colleges vary widely in cost and admissions requirements; many are private, but a number of public colleges are also available.

Universities

Universities have an appeal for many students. Some of the attraction is the wide range of academic offerings; some is associated with the appeal of "big time" football and other athletic events. As is the case with colleges, there is a wide range of cost and admissions requirements. Public universities are typically much less expensive than private

ones, especially if the student attends a public university in his or her state of residence. Universities typically offer opportunities to live in residence halls with a diverse group of students and to participate in a large selection of out of class activities. Since a major responsibility of faculty is conducting research, classes are sometimes quite large and are sometimes taught by graduate assistants rather than regular faculty. Counselors may wish to advise students to find out who will be teaching the majority of the classes they will be taking, especially the first two years, and weigh this aspect of the universities they are considering. This is a fair question for a student applicant to ask university authorities before agreeing to enroll at a specific institution.

In general, if financial resources and academic ability permit, there are some real benefits to attending a college or university which provides an opportunity to live on campus and become involved in campus life. Organized student activities can add a dimension to the college experience that is difficult to achieve any other way. Research (Astin, 1993) has shown that students who become involved in campus activities are more likely to persist in college and graduate than are those who do not become involved. It is, of course, quite possible for students to succeed in college without extensive involvement in campus life, but it is a desirable aspect of the college experience when conditions permit. School counselors have an obligation to share such information with their aspiring college or university clientele.

The following publications contain extensive information concerning colleges and universities and the application process:

- *Barron's Profiles of American Colleges.* Barron's Educational Series, Inc., 250 Wireless Blvd., Hauppauge, NY 11788.

- *The College Handbook 1999.* College Board Publications, Two College Way, Forrester Center, WV 25438.

  Fax: (800) 525-5562

  Online: *www.collegeboard.org*

- Websites:

  College Board Online

  http://www.collegeboard.org

  Minority On-Line Information Service

  web.fie.com/web/mol

  U. S. Government Sites

  www.ed.gov/prog_info/SFA/FYE/

  www.fafsa.ed.gov/

Advanced Placement and CLEP Credit

Some students are interested in opportunities to receive college credit or to be placed in higher level courses through taking advanced placement (AP) courses in high school and taking an AP exam. Individual colleges vary in their policies concerning AP credit, so counselors should assist students in finding out whether an acceptable score (usually in the 3 to 5 range) will enable them to obtain credit for the course or will simply permit them to skip an introductory course and begin at a higher level.

Other avenues exist for students to earn college credit through testing at some colleges (i.e., the College Level Examination Program—CLEP) offers exams in a number of courses, generally those taken in the first two years of college. Some colleges accept CLEP credit, some do not. The use of AP or CLEP credit can be useful to some students, but it is sometimes a mixed blessing. If an inexperienced college freshman obtains CLEP credit to replace a number of introductory courses and begins college in a number of advanced courses, with "seasoned" college students as classmates, he or she may feel overwhelmed by the experience. Careful planning is advisable in the use of AP or CLEP; students may need your counsel when making this important decision.

Overview of Timeline for the College Application Process

The following timeline is suggested as a guide for students and their parents as a way to organize the college application process. It is intended only as a guide and should be modified if conditions warrant.

Eleventh Grade

Fall:

Orientation meeting for students and parents.

- Students planning to attend 2 or 4 year colleges/ universities.
- Students planning to attend vocational-technical schools/colleges.

Students begin gathering information on colleges.

Take Preliminary Scholastic Aptitude Test/National Merit Scholarship Qualifying Test (PSAT/NMSQT). Take Preliminary

American College Test (PACT) if planning to attend a college that uses the ACT.

Meet with college representatives when they visit your school.

Begin visits to colleges being considered.

Spring:

May: Take SAT/ACT.

June: Take some achievement tests if required by colleges being considered.

Summer between eleventh and twelfth grades:

Preparation for second SAT/ACT if student's scores on first try suggest it is advisable. Again, many will need the counselors assistance when making this decision.

Twelfth Grade

Fall:

Submit applications to colleges.

- Be aware of lead-time for essay if required.
- Be aware of lead-time for recommendation letters and secondary school reports.

Winter:

Take any remaining achievement tests necessary.

Submit financial aid forms.

- Be aware of lead-time for financial information needed by parents.

Spring:

Make final decision concerning the college or university to attend.

Some Administrative Considerations for Counselors

In addition to the orientation meetings for eleventh grade students and their parents, high school counselors have a number of other responsibilities concerning educational counseling and guidance. Individual meetings with students and their parents may be indicated as the college selection process moves along. Hosting college representatives is a matter that is worthy of planning and preparation. If the representatives feel welcome, are given adequate facilities in which to meet with students, and have reasonable access to students who are genuinely interested in talking with them, they are likely to be cooperative with the high school in scheduling future visits. Counselors sitting in on group meetings conducted by college representatives can become informed about what is being discussed and, by their presence, communicate the counseling department's interest in the college selection process. The information gathered through this process will improve the counselors' educational counseling and guidance sessions with students.

High school counselors are asked by college and university admissions people to complete secondary school report forms concerning applicants. The importance of these written evaluations varies greatly, depending on the selectivity of the college or university. Highly selective institutions often make careful use of the counselor's evaluation; less selective institutions typically make little or no use of them. Hitchner and Tifft-Hitchner (1996) offered specific advice about writing a counselor evaluation for students applying to colleges and universities, as well as a number of other practical suggestions for high school counselors.

- Hitchner, K. W., & Tifft-Hitchner, A. (1996). *Counseling Today's Secondary Students.* Prentice Hall Career and Personal Development, Englewood Cliffs, NJ 07632. On the web: *http://www.phdirect.com*

Summary

Helping students realize that they have options, helping them keep their options open, and assisting them to make the best use of those options are important school counselor tasks. Counselors can make a difference in students' lives by finding ways to do these things effectively. Effective educational counseling and guidance is highly important and should be a high priority for all developmental K-12 school counselors. This chapter, the other chapters in this book, and the additional materials cited can assist counselors in making a difference with their student clients.

References

Astin, A.W. (1993). *What matters in college: Four critical years revisited.* San Francisco: Jossey Bass.

Bandura, A. (1997). *Self-efficacy: The exercise of control.* New York: W.H. Freeman.

Erikson, E.H. (1963). *Childhood and society* (2nd ed.). New York: W.W. Norton.

Fagan, C., & Lumley, D. (1997). *Tech prep career programs: A practical guide to preparing students for high-tech, high-skill, high-wage opportunities.* Thousand Oaks, CA: Corwin Press.

Hettinger, J. (1998). Where the BLS numbers *really* come from. *Techniques, 73*(6),36-39.

Hettinger, J. (1999). The new Perkins... finally. *Techniques, 74*(1), 40-42.

Hitchner, K.W., & Tifft-Hitchner, A. (1996). *Counseling today's secondary students.* Englewood Cliffs, NJ: Prentice Hall.

Mason, N.K. (1992). Career guidance: The teacher's role. *Vocational Education Journal, 67*(2), 22-23, 55.

Super, D.E. (1992). Toward a comprehensive theory of career development. In D.H. Montross, C. J. Shinkman, & Associates, *Career development: Theory and practice* (pp. 35-64).

The College Board. (1998). *College costs & financial aid handbook 1999* (19th ed.). New York: Author.

Joe Wittmer, Ph.D.

Section VI

Strategies for Involving Others in the School Counseling Program: Peer Helpers, Parents, Community Members, Teachers, and Other Professionals

The notion of using students to help other students is not a new idea. However, structured peer helper programs where school counselors specifically train student peers in helping techniques is a relatively recent idea in schools. And, as Dr. Chari Campbell indicates (Chapter 21): *Peer helper programs proliferated during the 1970s and '80s and will continue to grow in numbers into the new century.* Dr. Campbell continues: *Everyone benefits from a peer helper program. Research reveals that the student helper benefits as much, if not more than does the student helpee. Teachers and parents benefit from the program because the guidance services in the school are expanded. The counselor also benefits in numerous ways.* She highlights these benefits and then presents some unique strategies for getting a peer helper program started, training the peer helpers, the needed supervision, peer projects (at all three school levels), and so forth. There are many other helpful suggestions and strategies given for the school counselor who wishes to initiate a peer helper program or who desires to improve an existing one.

In Chapter 22, Drs. Gerardo Gonzalez and Robert Myrick describe the Teachers as Advisors Program (TAP) and the value of such a program to the developmental school counseling program. In addition, they describe a unit for drug education and how such an approach can be effectively delivered via TAP as coordinated by the school counselor. Gonzalez and Myrick write: *There is an obvious need for teachers and other school staff to be more directly involved in the personal development of their students. The single, most innovative approach to meeting this need has been through programs where teachers are trained and then designated as student advisors and assigned a group of 15 to 20 students who become their advisees.* They also discuss how the counselor can build support for TAP, the management/coordination of TAP, the necessary teacher training involved, how to evaluate the program, and so forth.

In Chapter 23, Drs. Vacc, Bloss, and Martin Rainey write regarding multidisciplinary teams in schools and the coordinating role played by school counselors. They indicate that to assure that pupils, especially those with unique needs, are provided appropriate assistance that encourages their personal, social, and educational development, counselors and other specialists, teachers, and administrators, must work together as a team to offer an effective educational delivery system. They write: *Thus, rather than working alone, school counselors have a major role in "teams" which involve a variety of educational professionals who plan, coordinate, evaluate, and provide direct services concerning students, parents, and staff.*

The writers also examine the role of the school counselor as a member of a multidisciplinary school team, as well as the roles of various other members of the team. In addition, they present suggestions and strategies for avoiding "turf" issues, the most effective organizational approaches, the coordinating role of the counselor, how to evaluate the work of the multidisciplinary team, and so forth.

In the final chapter of this section, Ms. Nancy Perry, a long-time school counselor, State Supervisor of Guidance, and ASCA leader, addresses school counselor interactions with parents and families. She suggests management strategies to effectively involve the parents and community in the comprehensive, developmental school counseling program.

Ms. Perry writes: *The effective school counselor realizes that he/she must understand the entire system if the whole child is to be best served. Since developmental school counselors are dedicated to the development of the whole child, they must reach beyond the walls of the school building and actively involve and interact with the families and community.* She indicates that school counselors need to involve parents, educators, and community members in their developmental guidance program if it is to be truly responsive to the needs of all students. Several "hands on" ideas for such involvement are presented for K-12 counselors.

Joe Wittmer

Chapter 21
K-12 Peer Helper Programs

by
Chari Campbell

Dr. Chari Campbell, PhD, LPC, NCC, is an Associate Professor of Counselor Education at Florida Atlantic University. Dr. Campbell was an elementary school counselor for twelve years and then moved to the junior-senior high level where she implemented a developmental counseling program. She coordinated peer helper programs each of her 16 years as a school counselor.

History and Current Status of Peer Helping Programs

The notion of using students to help other students is not a new idea. Peer helping was a natural occurrence in the one-room schoolhouses during the 1930s. Teachers who were responsible for teaching basic academic skills to children in eight or more grade levels turned automatically to an older, more skilled student to assist with the learning of younger, less accomplished students. These early teaching pioneers were simply applying a common sense solution to the problem of the lack of enough teacher time for each student. They also realized how much the experience of teaching younger students reinforced skills in the older student. Wouldn't they have been surprised to discover that their practical solution would be considered an innovation in the late twentieth century?

In the 1960s peer helper programs once again became very popular. As drugs became more of a problem in our society, counselors and educators searched for ways for reaching students before they developed problems with drug addiction. Surveys from this decade revealed that students with problems turned to other kids first, then to their counselors, and to coaches last. Peer helper programs proliferated, especially at the high school level. However, many of these programs did not last due to lack of planning and commitment by the adults coordinating the programs. According to Myrick (1997), those peer programs which flourished concentrated on training the peer helpers in the areas of interpersonal and communication skills. The variety of projects expanded, and high school peer helpers were trained to lead preventive guidance with elementary students, to help with cancer projects in hospitals, and to work with incarcerated youth, and so forth.

Peer helping spread to elementary schools in the 1970s. Counselors trained fourth and fifth grade students to work with primary grade students in a variety of projects including: orientation programs for students new to the school ("Meeters and Greeters"), Study Buddies, small and large Group Leaders, Special Friends, and Teachers' Assistants.

Current Status

As the peer helping movement grew, school counselors and other educators interested in peer helping began to network informally, sharing training techniques and successful projects. In 1983, Dr. Bob Bowman, an early contributor in this area became the first editor of the *Peer Facilitator Quarterly*, a journal devoted entirely to the interests and needs of student peer helpers and their trainers. The National Peer Helper Association (NPHA), grew from sixty members to over a thousand in a period of about four years. The Association has sponsored a national conference each summer since 1987 which is well attended by school counselors, school psychologists, teachers, and other mental health workers. These are professionals devoted to assisting others learn about and remain abreast of this rapidly growing, and unique, care delivery approach.

Hundreds of articles have been written in professional journals and popular magazines since the early 1970s describing successful programs and substantiating the effectiveness of peer programs aimed at reducing the school drop-out rate, increasing appropriate school behaviors and positive attitudes towards school. Today, numerous books are available outlining curriculum for K-12 school peer helper programs, the type of training required, who should be a peer facilitator, how to select the helpers, and so forth.

Many school counselors at both the elementary and secondary level, devoted to implementing a comprehensive, developmental guidance and counseling program, include peer helper coordination as one of the six major roles of today's developmentally oriented school counselor (Myrick, 1997).

Rationale for a Peer Program

Everyone benefits from a peer helper program. Research reveals that the student helper benefits as much, if not more, than does the student helpee. Teachers and parents benefit from the program because the guidance services in the school are expanded. The counselor benefits in numerous ways. Some of the benefits occurring to the peer helpers, the counselor, and others are highlighted below.

Benefits to Students

It is difficult to discern who benefits the most, the helper or the helpee. Ample research shows gains in productive behavior, attitudes towards school, self-esteem, and report card grades for both the helper and the helpee.

Students generally apply for and are selected into the peer helper program on the basis of their application and teacher recommendations. The position of peer helper appears to carry status among students and places considerable responsibility on the helpers selected. The students take pride in the trust that has been placed upon them by their teachers and counselors. Helping a younger student brings out the best in them. It is explained from the beginning that only students who are positive role models for other students are chosen for the program and that it is their responsibility to maintain their grades and to make up any assignment missed in their own class as a result of a peer project away from school, and so forth. Many peer helpers have discovered that having extra responsibilities in school fosters excellent time management skills. Many student helpers also indicate they are able to complete their own classroom and homework assignments more efficiently after they receive training in the peer helping preparation program.

The peer helper program essentially provides leadership training for students. Feedback given by business and industry about our public school graduates is that many of our "elite" students don't know how "to get along" or "relate to" those they work with, sell to, and

so forth. Sometimes our "good kids" are so isolated in top academic classes that they lack the people skills required in many real life work positions. The training experience and helping projects that follow provide student peer helpers with excellent leadership training.

Benefits to the Counselor

Why implement a peer helper program in your school? Many school counselors, whether their counselor-to-student ratio is 1 to 700 or whether they are one of the fortunate few who serve closer to 250 students, have learned that (as did the teachers in the one room schoolhouses of the 1930s) they don't have time to meet all of the (counseling) needs of all of their students. Many times a student simply needs someone who will listen and care as they solve minor social, family problems, and so forth. Counselors all across the nation—literally in all 50 states—have learned how to expand their counseling program through the use of well trained peer helpers. These skillful listeners "become the eyes and the ears" for the guidance department. Counselors report that their counseling load sometimes increases significantly due to referrals by teenage peer helpers of students who need professional help, but probably would not have turned to an adult on their own. Even elementary students will frequently "tell a secret" to a same aged friend before they would tell an adult. Frequently, kids don't turn to adults for help because they think the adults "wouldn't understand." Thus, counselors can spread their positive influence throughout the entire school with trained peer helpers.

Another part of the rationale for training students to help other students is that kids of all ages are influenced by peer pressure. This is particularly true of upper elementary and junior and senior high school students, although their is evidence of peer pressure existing even in kindergarten. The pressure is so powerful that many parents cave in and purchase $50 to $150 tennis shoes for a middle schooler who will outgrow them in a few months. Peer pressure influences the way kids dress, wear their hair, carry their books, complete or don't complete homework assignments, experiment with drugs and sex, and so forth. While I was a practicing middle school counselor, a seventh grade girl told me that "everyone who is anyone in the seventh grade has French kissed." When asked if she had tried it and what did she think of the experience, it was apparent that having a seventh grade boy stick his tongue in her mouth had not been very rewarding. However, in her relating her experience to me, it was obvious that she felt it was worth it to feel that she was part of the "in-crowd."

Many other examples of how peer pressure influences the behavior and attitudes of students in a negative way could be given. The challenge for counselors and teachers is to somehow harness this powerful peer pressure existing in the hallways and the school parking lot and turn it into a positive force within the school. This is what peer helper programs can do. Many counselors deliberately solicit volunteers for the program from different cliques and groups that reflect the population of the school (i.e., some "preppie", some student athletes, maybe a cheerleader, some "new-age" types, and students from differing racial and socioeconomic groups. In this manner, hopefully, every student in the school can find a trained peer helper that they can relate to and view as a positive model for themselves.

Another major reason, or part of the rationale for establishing a peer helper program, is that it serves as a good public relations campaign for the school counselor. The peer program enhances the reputation of the counselor in the eyes of the teachers as well as the students. Teachers are favorably impressed because it puts the counselor's skills on display. When teachers observe a well trained peer helper leading a small or large group discussion with obvious polish and self-confidence, they recognize that the counselor can teach as well as counsel. Students see that the counselor who has a peer program works with the "good kids," and there is no longer the stigma that attaches so quickly when the counselor is only seen with the kids "who have problems." Thus, the counselor's image in the school is greatly enhanced.

Another benefit of the peer helper program is what it will do for professional development and morale as a counselor. Both beginning and veteran counselors recognize that when they share their facilitative communication skills with students, they often refine and reinforce their own effective listening skills. In addition to polishing their own counseling skills, counselors benefit from the peer helpers through the enjoyment that comes from having the opportunity to work with delightful, happy, well-adjusted kids. Counselors must so often work with the students who drain and strain them. Suicidal, disruptive, alienated kids who are hurting are rewarding to work with when you can see some improvement in the coping skills of the youngster, but they will also drain your "emotional cup." The peer helpers will have the opposite effect on you. They will help to relieve the symptoms of burnout often felt by educators who work only with very troubled students.

A Rose is a Rose, is a Rose, is a Rose...

Most counselors involved with peer helper programs today avoid the use of the term "peer counseling." The term "Counselor," in the school setting, is a professional role which requires extensive graduate level training. The title of "peer counselor" concerns some people who believe this title gives the impression that the students are doing more than they are capable of doing. Thus, terms such as *peer helpers, peer facilitators, peer mentors,* and *teen aiders* are preferred. Some students give their groups a catchy name which identifies them with their schools such as the "Bishop Buddies," or the "Fairfield Friends." Tee shirts with such names on them are the norm in schools where peer programs exist.

It is important for administrators, teachers and parents to understand that the guidance department does not view the peer helpers as low budget, junior counselors. On the other hand, kids are "counseling" kids in every school, at all grade levels, across the nation without any training in communication skills or, for that matter, referral skills. By giving at least some of the students in the school special training to enable them to be more effective listeners and to know when and how to refer friends for professional help results in more students (who are in need) actually finding their way to the counselor's door. Legal issues such as liability become a non-issue when peer helpers are students trained to be special friends. These are students who have explored with a professionally trained adult the difference between "squealing" on a friend, and making a referral or consulting with a mental health professional about a friend who is in trouble.

How to Get Started

Getting started is easier than you might imagine, especially if you begin small and build on your success. There are four issues to consider when initiating a peer helper program: (1) building support, (2) selection, (3) training, and (4) projects.

Building Support

Tailoring the program to the particular demands of the setting will help to ensure support for the program. It is helpful to solicit faculty and administrative input when developing the goals and objectives of the peer program.

Peer helper projects should reflect the guidance needs of the schools in which they are established. Hence, the needs, attitudes and values of the students, teachers and parents influence the types of projects in which the helpers will engage. After the needs of the school have been assessed, projects can be outlined which specifically address those needs. This process helps to build the teacher commitment essential to the program.

As noted, the best way to gain support for any program is to start small and then build on success. It seems trite, but in peer programs, success truly breeds more success. For example, if, as an elementary counselor you can identify just one fifth grade teacher who shows interest and enthusiasm in the program, then you can select six volunteers from that class for the peer program. If you train these six students for a highly visible role, such as assisting with classroom guidance activities with a second grade class, then the second grade teacher will have a chance to see the peer helpers perform. It's likely that the second grade teacher will say complimentary things about the fifth graders and their performance to other teachers and the "good word" spreads. Soon other teachers will want the peer helpers to work with their students and the fifth grade teachers will want their students to have an opportunity to be trained and to participate in a similar project, and on and on. Starting small, with a highly structured project which fits the needs of the school (with a high probability of success) helps to get the peer helper program off to a good start. In sum, start small, take your gains where you can, and build on your successes! It is easy and can be fun!

Selecting Peer Helpers

There is no one best way to select peer helpers in a school. Some counselors, at both the elementary and secondary levels, have selected from the highest grade level in their school. Others have been successful by selecting from the two highest grade levels. This allows them to have some previously trained peer helpers always ready to help with orientation and with classroom guidance projects at the beginning of the following school year.

Peer helpers are generally drawn from the pool of students who have good study habits and earn good grades. They need not be the "straight A" student, or the brightest kid in the class to be successful as a peer helper. Frequently, honor role students are more concerned with academic competition than they are with helping someone. On the other hand, you will want students who are succeeding in school and who can afford to take some time away from their routine academic activities and who are responsible enough to make up any assignments missed as a result of being in the peer program.

A major point central to an effective peer program is to look for the student who is consistent and dependable. It's essential to have students who will show up for training sessions and for appointments with their helpers on time and who will be well prepared for any project assigned. Consistent kids also seem to be viewed as more trustworthy, a prerequisite for successful peer helpers.

A good peer helper is also someone who is well liked by their classmates and teachers. This need not be the "most popular" kid in the class because kids who are experiencing problems at home or in school frequently have difficulty relating to the "local stars." Also, sometimes the "local stars" lack compassion for a kid who is having difficulty "fitting-in." Therefore, *seek out a student that other students are likely to choose as someone in whom they would be able to confide, rather than the first person they would think of to invite to a party.* You are looking for the "natural helpers," the kids who possess the core helping qualities of empathy, genuineness, caring, compassion, and respect for others. And, above all, look for personal commitment. The peer helpers will occasionally be torn between competing activities (i.e., working with targeted younger students or free time with their own-aged friends). Thus, commitment to the peer program is essential.

There are a variety of ways of identifying the natural helpers. Some counselors use sociograms, others depend on a combination of teacher referral and volunteers. It is best to first advertise the program through class presentations conducted by you. The peer program may be an elective course (Peer Helping I) at the high school level, or a club (The "Bishop Buddies" Club) at any level.

By asking potential helpers to reflect on the causes of stress in their lives or in the lives of their friends, to look carefully at the large percentage of students who never complete high school, and so forth, helps students become aware of the need to try to help peers who are "at risk" for school failure, and so forth. After this awareness is developed, you might describe a specific peer helper project designed to reduce the risk for a particular group of students. Then, describe the training experience needed to be a peer helper and ask for volunteers. Generally, a structured approach such as this will help you "weed out" those who won't become good helpers.

There are numerous checklists available to the counselor to facilitate a quick screening by teachers of the qualities previously described as desirable in a good helper (see Figure 21.1).

In addition to positive recommendations by teachers, a student may be asked to complete an application form (Figures 21.2 and 21.3) and to turn it into the counselor's office by a certain date. This process serves two purposes. First, it gives the student a chance to reflect on their skills and aptitude for helping other students. Usually they are requested in the application to tell what qualities they possess which would be helpful to another student and why they want to be in the program. You will learn a lot about the student and the student's insight about self and relationships through this structured selection process.

Secondly, the process of filling out the application form correctly and turning it in by a certain date is a good way to assess commitment and dependability. Students who care enough to get the application turned in on time, tend to be conscientious about the responsibility of showing up for training and project appointments later.

One counselor designed a creative approach to the application process with lower elementary students by requesting that a picture be drawn to represent friendship. Students were requested to put their pictures in a box by a certain date if they wanted to be a helper. Then the counselor interviewed the children as each explained their pictures and described their thoughts about friendship.

Other elementary and middle school counselors have incorporated peer helping into a career education program. The counselor serves in the role of a personnel specialist who screens and trains the helper for a given job. The teacher of the helpees "hires" the applicant, a contract is signed, and the teacher can "fire" the student for not fulfilling the contract. Students very seldom need to be fired from the program. The opportunity to help another student is usually so rewarding that it serves as a "carrot" for the peer helper to get his/her own work done and to stay out of trouble that might result in dismissal from the peer program.

Training

The most critical variable in a peer helper program appears to be systematic training . It is important to define the training program in detail and to select peer projects carefully tailored to the skills of your student helpers (Myrick, 1997).

The training naturally will reflect the theoretical orientation of the counselor/coordinator. The professional literature on peer helper programs provides examples of training programs which vary in theoretical basis from person centered, to Adlerian, to behavioral. In addition, the training usually reflects the professional strengths and personality of the trainer.

Wittmer, Thompson, and Sheperis (1999) suggested a training model that has two phases. Phase one focuses on basic relationship and communication skills, phase two concerns more advanced skills. Students are prepared to carry out some structured beginning projects following their initial training. Peer helpers are best trained in groups, even if their project involves working with students individually.

The emphasis in phase one is on experiential learning and skill development, rather than on didactic training. Therefore, the training of elementary peer helpers does not differ greatly from the training of secondary peer helpers. In fact, some young children seem to possess a natural empathy and easily pick up the active listening skills that graduate students in counseling sometimes labor to acquire.

The length and number of training sessions varies according to the nature and sophistication level of the peer project as well as the availability of counselor and student helper time. It is possible to train students successfully to handle some beginning projects (i.e., welcoming newcomers to the campus, in a few half hour sessions). A more advanced project, such as serving as a small group leader may require over twenty 45-minute training sessions. Some school counselors have found weekend marathon training sessions to be successful with all ages of students. In some school districts where peer helper programs are widespread throughout the district, senior high peer helpers are used to assist in training middle school and elementary peer helpers in phase one skills.

Following the initial training, focusing on interpersonal and communication skills, specific skills needed for the particular project are taught and practiced. As a general rule, the younger the peer helpers, the more structured the project should be. Regardless of the age of the helpers, however, care should be taken to break down the project into manageable steps and to be certain that the helpers have the necessary skills or can acquire them in the training sessions. Peer helpers have been trained to serve in various helping roles. Myrick (1997) categorized the helping roles as follows: (1) student assistants, (2) tutors, (3) special friends, and (4) small group leaders.

Student assistants require the least amount of training. They assist teachers, librarians, or office staff with clerical assignments such as answering the phone, checking books in or out, or putting up bulletin board materials. Tutors assist students to acquire or review academic skills. They are trained to clarify the speaker's content, to reflect feelings, and to use encouragement to motivate students who are reluctant to "try on their own" to succeed in school. A special friend is trained in interpersonal skills and is paired with a younger student needing extra personal attention. The special friend serves in a big brother or big sister role, taking interest in the younger child and their progress in school. Small or large group leaders usually receive extensive training on how to facilitate group discussions on topics such as friendship and safety at the elementary level, college applications, substance abuse prevention, or career exploration at the secondary level.

Peer Helper Projects

Projects can be viewed as beginning, intermediate, or advanced according to the amount of training required for the task and the degree of structure with characterizes the project (Myrick 1997). The following description of projects may help to illustrate the variety of activities at which peer helpers can excel and the extent to which they can add to your developmental school guidance program.

Elementary School Projects

An example of a beginning project at the *elementary* level is the Meeters and Greeters Club. These are usually children from the intermediate grade levels who have been taught how to ask open ended questions, summarize content, and to reflect feelings. They are given some suggestions of comments and questions they can use to help draw out a new student and make them feel welcome in their new school. For example, while taking a newcomer and perhaps their parents, on a tour to show them the cafeteria, the library, and the location of various classrooms, the peer helper might ask "where are you from?" After paraphrasing, the peer helper might share where they are from or how long they have been in the school, and then say "tell me about your previous school," or "what was something you liked about your previous school." They might also ask "was there something you didn't like about your old school" and share a gripe they have about school. They could end the conversation by saying "I bet you miss your friends from (Name of City, State), but we are glad to have you here. I think you're going to like it here. I'll look for you tomorrow." This is an example of a structured beginning project because, although the students can ad lib and just be their genuine selves, they also will want to try to use the facilitative skills practiced in the training sessions.

Another use of peers in elementary schools is that of mediators. Peer mediators have shown to be very effective at solving student conflicts (Wittmer, Thompson, & Sheperis, 1999).

Middle School Projects

An example of an *intermediate* project with elementary students which requires more training is a small group leader for the primary grades. In my school, six fifth grade students who had made the commitment to learn the skills and become group leaders for a unit on friendship, first participated in a small group on the same topic, led by myself, the counselor/trainer. I modeled the skills needed to lead a group discussion and stopped (froze) the conversation from time to time to talk about each skill as it is used so that the students could learn the skills of summarization and reflection of feelings. Gradually, I turned over control of the group, allowing students to share in the responsibility of leading or co-leading the group. Following sufficient practice, the group topics were put on cue cards and the students entered a primary grade classroom, each with their own small group to lead. The peer helpers returned to the same small group for six visits, until the unit was completed. Sometimes it is best to pair a strong, effective group leader with one who is less skilled and allow the peer helpers to co-lead the discussions. This is especially good when peers are "leading" their first group.

High School Projects

Junior and senior peer helper projects are frequently less structured than projects for younger helpers. An example, however, of a fairly structured *secondary* project is using peer helpers to lead college preparation seminars. Giving information about what tests to take, where to take them, how much they cost, how to find information about particular colleges, their specific admission requirements, costs, financial aid information, and how and when to apply for admission, are covered in such student led seminars. Such things generally take up a lot of a high school counselor's time, and, if properly coordinated, can be done by peer helpers. It is possible to give peer helpers enough preparation to not only help them find their own way through this maze of information, but to prepare them to answer most of the general questions that student colleagues have concerning this subject; plus orienting other students regarding how to find out more information. By using peer helpers to give college prep seminars to their own age-mates, as well as to interested freshman and sophomores, counselors have more time to work with potential drop-outs and students with personal problems.

Another example of a *high school* project is having the peers work with students at-risk for school drop-out. The counselor identifies freshman who have two or more failing grades (D or F) on the first report card of the year and arranges to pull out all such "targeted" freshman at a time when the peer helpers are available. The junior and senior helpers offer support during the "rough" times and invite the freshman to participate in motivational activities such as goal setting, values clarification, career education, and so forth. Research has shown that programs of this kind result in improved academic grades for student helpees.

The possibilities for high school projects are endless. In one high school peers are trained to use puppets to communicate with kindergarten children about abuse and safety issues, and, in another to coordinate orientation programs for entering freshman and to welcome new students during the year. One counselor trained her peers to lead large and small group discussions on a variety of topics ranging from teen sex, drugs, career exploration, to reducing test anxiety. They also assisted the counselor in leading small groups of students (five or six each) during large group guidance activities within classroom settings.

Supervision

Most peer projects require on-going supervision by the counselor. It is imperative that time for the supervision be scheduled into the program as this can become an ethical and legal issue. Supervision of peer helper projects is also a practical concern, because without proper supervision, peer helper programs will fail. Even the seemingly simply role of tutor needs timely supervision (weekly) to help the peer facilitator reflect on how things are going and solve small problems as they occur.

At the elementary level it is best to reserve the last 5 to 10 minutes of each "session" with a student, or group of students, for "de-briefing." This could occur informally in the hallway to save time. For example, you may want to ask each peer helper to share something fun or positive about their experience with the younger children that day. Then each child can describe an unexpected problem that came up that they didn't know how to solve or deal with. The fifth graders will occasionally be frustrated by a youngster's misbehavior and are ready and able to learn how to use positive reinforcement tactics to gain co-operation from their group.

At the high school level where more individual peer helping sessions occur, students need formal, confidential supervision sessions. In these sessions they can discuss concerns they might have about a friend's personal safety without breaking confidentiality, when its not necessary, or help decide when it is time to break confidentiality and to seek professional help for their friend. Sometimes, supervision simply focuses on a review of basic listening skills. Counselors realize that these basic, important counseling skills can atrophy when not monitored carefully.

Evaluation of the Peer Program

Everything that can be and has been said or written (in this book and others) concerning accountability for a developmental school counseling program applies equally as well to a peer helper program. Accountability can become a counselor's best friend. Administrators, parents, teachers, and others who influence the guidance program, and hence the peer helper program, have a right to know how it's working. Collecting written feedback from students and teachers served by the program is helpful. Taking the time to do a pre and a post test using a control group technique occasionally is helpful, productive and even enjoyable. If several schools in the same district have peer programs it is helpful to plan a project together (perhaps a "targeted" group of disruptive students) and pool the data. Presenting such effective outcomes data to the school board at the end of the year will bring about positive results.

Cautions and Problem Moments

At the *high school* level, perhaps the most controversial issue in peer helper programs is the notion of having teenagers "counseling" other teens who may have deeper problems than the teen aider is prepared or trained to deal with. The issue becomes even more controversial when the "counseling" takes place on school time. Some peer helpers actually maintain office hours during which any interested student may drop in for assistance and teacher referrals are accepted. Counselors who set up this kind of program argue that the "counseling" and advice given between teens occurs all the time anyway and that by doing it in a structured, supervised manner with trained peers, the likelihood that adult intervention will be sought when needed is increased.

A more cautious approach used by some counselors is to schedule any one-on-one sessions to take place in a large room where a group of peer helpers pair up with their respective helpees in semi-privacy. In this supervised approach, the professional counselor remains in the same room and is available for consultation as needed. Other counselors prefer to only schedule structured group projects and to allow the individual counseling to occur naturally (i.e., in the locker room, on the school bus, and/or after school). Most counselors have regular peer supervision on school time so that the teen aiders can review cases and obtain advice from their peer group or the counselor on how to proceed.

At the *elementary* level, one of the most controversial issues is whether or not parent permission is needed for a student to become a peer helper. Some counselors feel that to request parent permission insinuates that there is something potentially dangerous about the program. Of course, parent permission is required before a student goes off-campus (for any reason due to potential liability issues) and this includes off-campus peer projects. If permission is requested for training their child as a peer helper, the parents may wonder why, and question whether the program may be potentially harmful. Some counselors prefer to notify parents that their child has been *selected* to become a peer helper as opposed to requesting permission. The written notification implies clearly that it is an honor to have been chosen and that their child has been selected for a position of leadership in the school; they have earned the trust and respect of their peers, the teachers, and especially the counselor(s) (see Figure 21.4).

Most elementary counselors schedule a parent meeting to orient the parents about the goals and benefits of the peer program and to answer questions and address any concerns a parent might have. It is rare for a parent to ask that their child not participate in the peer program if it is appropriately explained.

Another problem that seems to be especially troublesome for elementary counselors is the issue of helping young children understand and respect confidentiality. Some counselors are concerned that its a mixed message to tell children to be wary of people who ask them to "keep secrets" and then ask them to keep confidential personal information that was shared in a group session. Experience working with younger children usually proves to counselors that children are frequently very wise. Fourth and fifth grade students are able to understand the difference between respecting a friend's privacy and withholding important safety information from adults. Confidentiality issues, and when and how to break it, are an important part of peer helper training.

A problem that sometimes occurs at the elementary and secondary level is that occasionally a peer helper will engage in behavior that is "unbecoming" of a peer helper (i.e., embarrassing to the school and reflects negatively on the counselor). The guidelines concerning peer helper behavior should always be made clear at the beginning of the program. Students are generally asked to sign a contract to formalize the agreement they are making with the other peer helpers and the counselor to serve as a "model student" (see Figure 21.5). These guidelines generally reflect "good citizenship" at both the elementary and secondary levels.

For high school and middle school peer helpers, counselor supervisors always make it clear that drug use, including cigarettes and alcohol, are prohibited. Breaking confidentiality is also grounds for dismissal from the peer program. When a student makes a mistake resulting in grounds for dismissal it is wise to allow the entire peer helper group to participate in a problem solving discussion. Sometimes these mistakes can be turned into very meaningful learning opportunities for the student peers. However, as the counselor in charge, you will be called on to use your best "facilitating" skills when such a problem occurs in your peer program.

Materials and Resources

Many counselors have trained peer helpers and have supervised very successful projects by teaching students the communication skills they learned while seeking their degrees in counselor education. It is not essential to have a large budget to initiate a peer helper program in your school. There are many helpful inexpensive books available to the school counselor that outline in detail excellent peer training programs. Most have been found successful and easy to use. You need not re-invent the wheel; simply purchase at least one of the numerous books available and get started! Commercial kits and packages on peer helping are also available and are helpful. Most counselors discover that just as in parent education, it is advantageous to have a book or a kit to lead your first group, but following an exposure to a sampling of materials, most professionals pick and choose what they like best from various programs and add some ideas of their own to meet the specific needs of their school. An excellent book with accompanying training manuals is *Peervention: Training Peer Facilitators for Prevention Education*, by R.D. Myrick and B.E. Folk (1991).

Summary

A word of warning to the school counselor implementing a peer helper program for the first time: be careful, peer helping programs may be addictive! Most school counselors who are involved in peer facilitation report that this is their favorite part of their entire school counseling program. The school counselors look forward to the training sessions and the project supervision as enthusiastically as do the student helpers. So, what may begin as an experiment in your school could easily turn into a career-long habit.

Figure 21.1
Teacher Recommendation: Teen-Aiders

Dear (Teacher),

_____ has applied to the Peer Facilitator/Teen-Aiders Class. Please take a few minutes to evaluate this student (your rating will remain confidential) according to the following qualities:

	Poor	Fair	Good	Excellent	Unknown
Respectful	❑	❑	❑	❑	❑
Friendliness	❑	❑	❑	❑	❑
Sense of Responsibility	❑	❑	❑	❑	❑
Reliability	❑	❑	❑	❑	❑
Self-Confidence	❑	❑	❑	❑	❑
Trustworthiness	❑	❑	❑	❑	❑
Concern for Others	❑	❑	❑	❑	❑
Leadership Potential	❑	❑	❑	❑	❑
Emotional Stability	❑	❑	❑	❑	❑
Sense of Humor	❑	❑	❑	❑	❑
Accepts Criticism	❑	❑	❑	❑	❑
Sense of Judgment	❑	❑	❑	❑	❑
Politeness	❑	❑	❑	❑	❑
Personal Energy	❑	❑	❑	❑	❑
Sensitivity	❑	❑	❑	❑	❑
Adaptability	❑	❑	❑	❑	❑

Comments: _____

Signed: _____

Please Return To: _____

Figure 21.2
Peer Helper Job Application (Elementary School Level)

Job Applied For:_____   Date: _____

Last Name_____ First _____ Middle_____

    Male ❑   Female ❑   Age _____ Grade _____

1. Write a short paragraph giving reasons for wanting this job.

    _____
    _____
    _____
    _____

2. What are your qualifications for this job?

    _____
    _____
    _____
    _____

3. If your best friend were recommending you for the job of Peer Helper, what would they write about your qualifications?

    _____
    _____
    _____
    _____

4. Write, in one sentence, why you should be "hired" as a peer helper.

    _____
    _____
    _____
    _____

Figure 21.3
Peer Facilitator Application (High School Level)

Last Name: _____   First Name _____

Date: _____   Grade: _____

1. List the names of 5 teachers who would recommend you for a Peer Facilitator Program.

   _____
   _____
   _____

2. Write a short paragraph telling why you would like to be a Peer Facilitator.

   _____
   _____
   _____

3. What personal qualifications do you have that would enable you to be a good Peer Facilitator.

   _____
   _____
   _____

4. Write what you would say and do in the following hypothetical situations:

   a. A friend tells you that she is afraid that she might be pregnant.

      _____
      _____

   b. A classmate of yours is visibly upset because his science grade was lower than he expected.
      His grade was a "B."

      _____
      _____

   c. You have noticed that your friend is getting into the habit of drinking—a lot.

      _____
      _____

5. What else would you like us to know about you as it concerns your being a Peer Facilitator:

   _____
   _____
   _____

Figure 21.4
Parent Notification
(Name of your school, address and phone number)

Dear :

    Your child, _____ , has been selected by the counselor(s) to be trained as a Peer Facilitator. Your child was chosen because he/she is perceived by teachers and others as someone who:

1. Is easy to get along with and is capable of helping others.
2. Has the personal traits of: acceptance, patience, consistency, a sense of humor, and caring about others.
3. Has positive attitudes towards peers, school, and adults.
4. Is a good student and overall good citizen.

    Peer Facilitators work with other students. They are guidance assistants. They are trained by the school counselor to be effective listeners. In addition, they are given systematic training in interpersonal skills, which they use to help other students talk about their ideas and feelings. They work through carefully organized and supervised guidance activities. As they help others learn, they learn about themselves.

    Peer Facilitators are regarded as positive leaders in our school. They are expected to keep up with their school work and their behavior should set a good example for others. Your child has made the commitment to make up any academic assignments missed while working on a guidance project. Please feel free to call me if you have any questions regarding this program.

Sincerely,

(School Counselor)

cc:

Figure 21.5
A Student Facilitator Contract

_____ has been selected to participate in the student facilitator program. Training sessions to become a Friendly Helper will begin shortly and upon completion of training, helping projects around the school will take place. It is understood that Friendly Helpers:

1. Attend school regularly

2. Complete class assignments

3. Serve as model students

4. Assist other students

5. Follow school rules

I, _____ hereby agree to conduct myself as a Friendly Helper and to take an active part in the student facilitator program.

_____

Reference Person #1

_____

Reference Person #2

_____

Student Signature

_____

Trainer or Coordinator Signature

_____

Parent Signature

References

Foster, E.S. (1992). *Tutoring: Learning by Helping.* Minneapolis, MN: Educational Media Corporation.

Hazouri, S.P., & Smith, M.F. (1991). *Peer listening in the middle school: Training activities for students.* Minneapolis, MN: Educational Media Corporation.

Myrick, R.D. (1997) *Developmental guidance and counseling: A practical approach* (3rd ed.). Minneapolis, MN: Educational Media Corporation.

Myrick, R.D., & Bowman, R.P. (1991). *Children helping children: Teaching students to become friendly helpers,* (rev. ed.). Minneapolis, MN: Educational Media Corporation. (Originally published in 1981)

Myrick, R.D., & Folk, B.E. (1991). *Peervention: Training peer facilitators for prevention education.* Minneapolis, MN: Educational Media Corporation.

Myrick, R.D., & Sorenson, D.L. (1997). *Peer helping: A practical guide* (2nd ed.). Minneapolis, MN: Educational Media Corporation.

Myrick, R.D., & Sorenson, D.L. (1992). *Teaching helping skills to middle school students*: *Program leaders guide.* Minneapolis, MN: Educational Media Corporation.

Sorenson, D.L. (1992). *Conflict resolution and mediation for peer helpers.* Minneapolis, MN: Educational Media Corporation.

Stone, D.J., & Keefauver, L. (1990). *Friend to friend: Helping your friends through problems.* Minneapolis, MN: Educational Media Corporation.

Sturkie, J., & Gibson, V. (1992). *The peer helper's pocketbook.* San Jose, CA: Resource Publications.

Tindall, J. (1994). *An in-depth look at peer helping* (4th ed.). Muncie, IN: Accelerated Development.

Tindall, J.A., & Salmon-, S. (1991). *Peers helping peers.* Muncie, IN: Accelerated Development.

Wittmer, J., Thompson, D., & Sheperis, C. (1999). *The peace train: A school-wide violence prevention program.* Minneapolis, MN: Educational Media Corporation.

Chapter 22

The Teachers as Student Advisors Program (TAP): An Effective Approach for Drug Education and Other Developmental Guidance Activities

by

Gerardo M. Gonzalez and Robert D. Myrick

Gerardo M. Gonzalez, PhD, is Interim Dean, College of Education, University of Florida. An authority on the prevention of substance abuse, Dr. Gonzalez has served on the National Advisory Board of the Alcohol, Drug Abuse and Mental Health Administration and is active in efforts to implement drug education programs internationally.

*Robert D. Myrick, PhD, Professor, Department of Counselor Education, University of Florida, is a nationally recognized authority regarding Teachers as Advisors Programs and as a pioneer in the movement toward developmental school counseling programs. He is the author of **Developmental Guidance and Counseling: A Practical Approach**.*

Introduction

There is an obvious need for teachers and other school staff to be more directly involved in the personal development of their students. The single, most innovative approach to meeting this need has been through programs where teachers are designated as student advisors and assigned a group of 15 to 20 students who become their advisees. This is often called an advisor program, a mentoring program, or a teacher as advisor program (TAP). In Hillsborough County Florida, TAP is known as "*Quality Time*" and has the endorsement and support of the superintendent of schools and the School Board; in Green Bay, Wisconsin the program is titled "*Our Time*"; in Orlando, the middle school TAP program is termed *"IM-PACT"* (Interdisciplinary Middle School Program for Advisement/Counseling/Teaming); and, in Sarasota, Florida it is titled, "*Prime Time*." Regardless of the title given the program, TAP is designed to provide effective, continuous adult guidance within a school where student-centered education is the main focus. And, the TAP concept coincides well with a comprehensive developmental guidance program (Myrick, 1997).

Teachers in such programs have regular academic assignments based on their interests and training, but each teacher also has a group of about 15 or 20 students assigned to him or her as advisees. The program works effectively when the advisors do not have their advisees in a classroom or any other situation where evaluation of the advisee by the advisor occurs. That is, where they are not in a situation to ever issue a "report card" on their advisees. It is also effective when the advisors have advisees assigned them whom they also have in a subject matter, classroom setting. Some schools have advisees choose their advisors and vise versa. One Florida High School has the Teacher Advisor select *some* of their advisees—from a group of those considered at risk (each advisor selects so many—their "fair share" of at risk students, if you will). However, it is important that an advisor not have too many "troublesome" students as advisees. There may be less or more advisees, depending upon the number of students and the number of faculty and staff who are available (and selected and willing to be trained) to become student advisors. The best ratio is about 15 to 20 students, but in practice it has been lower in a few cases and it has been as high as 25 when space and personnel were limited (Myrick, 1997).

It is assumed that each student needs a friendly adult, an "everyday advocate" (significant other) in the school setting who knows and cares about him or her in a personal way. The advisors are responsible for helping their advisees to deal with the problems of every day life stressors that face them. It is the advisor-advisee relationship that is the core of developmental guidance in a school setting. An effective TAP program helps to establish a school climate conducive to learning and is an excellent delivery mode for various components of the guidance curriculum.

A teacher-advisor is usually responsible for an advisee's cumulative folder, work folders, conducting teacher-student conferences, and follow-up academic and extra-curricular progress reports. Advisors also consult with other teachers and, especially school counselors about their advisees. TAP seems to work most effectively when coordinated through the school guidance department, the Guidance Steering Committee, and the teacher coordinating committee.

Teacher-advisors meet with their advisees regularly through a home base group. The "home base" period is a home within the school for students. It is here that they have an advisor and a supportive group of peers with whom they can explore their personal interests, goals, and concerns. It is here that issues which get in the way of effective learning or coping with life can be addressed. The teacher advisor is the facilitator of the group. In addition, the advisor encourages, and teaches, each group member to become a facilitator of others in their advisee group.

These home base periods are about 25 to 30 minutes in length and preferably happen at the beginning of every school day. At least two days of the week should be scheduled for developmental guidance unit and activities. A guidance unit focuses on a particular topic that is relevant to the advisees age, sex, and so forth. The topics often come from the advisees—economic pressures, male-female relationships, career concerns, problems with authority, AIDS, substance abuse, and so forth. In addition to these group activities, time is set aside for the advisor to meet individually with each advisee as needed.

The two or three day a week guidance lessons are typically built around structured activities which encourage students to be more responsible for themselves and to take an active part in developing positive working relationships with their peers and teachers. For example, here is a list of 13 units that were included in one Florida middle school.

- Getting Acquainted—Orientation to School
- Study Skills and Habits—Time Management
- Self-assessment
- Communication Skills
- Decision making and Problem solving
- Peer Relationships
- Motivation
- Conflict Resolution
- Wellness—Common Health Issues
- Career Development
- Educational Planning
- Community Pride and Involvement
- Substance Abuse Prevention

Each of these units consisted of about five or six 25-minute guidance oriented sessions (coordinated by the Guidance Department) presented during TAP periods, which enabled teacher-advisors to complete a unit in about two weeks. The other two days for TAP, which take place at the same time during the week, were given to individual conferences as most students used the time for quiet study, silent reading or writing, and tutoring sessions. If needed, additional sessions can be added to a unit for more in-depth treatment of a particular topic (Myrick, 1997).

Teachers are busy people and they often feel burdened with their responsibilities. Their time is limited and they cannot build close personal relationships with all their students. The reality of schedules and class arrangement in schools frequently forces teachers to be selective and to take a greater interest in some students than in others. The favored students receive teacher support and personal guidance while the others must turn elsewhere. A TAP program permits all students in the school such an opportunity (Schmidt, 1999).

Building Support for TAP

Despite the apparent value of TAP, there will be some teachers in your school reluctant to adopt it. According to Myrick (1997), in general, about 20% of most school faculties will quickly embrace the program. These teachers like the idea of a developmental guidance approach by a teacher or significant other and they have the skills and personality to put the program in practice without much preparation. They can make it work with a minimum of support, as they thoroughly enjoy the opportunity to form closer helping relationships with students.

There is another 20% of a school faculty, generally, who are clearly skeptical and resistant. They argue against it and see only an extra preparation for themselves. To them TAP is a waste of time. They try to discourage others, erroneously believing that guidance should be left to specialists, such as counselors and psychologists. This disinclined group needs special assistance or in-service training, if they are ever to be supportive and become involved in building a TAP program. Unfortunately, of this 20% probably half of them do not have the personality, skills, interests, or energy to make TAP work and they may need to be assigned other duties.

The middle 60% of the faculty can make the difference. This is the group you will want to sell on TAP. If this group is for TAP, then the program will make a positive contribution in your school and can become the core of your developmental guidance program. If the majority of this middle group is against it, then the program will have trouble surviving. It will be sabotaged. There will be a tremendous waste of time and energy. Student needs will not be met and, being disappointed with TAP, students will "add fuel to the fire" by their criticism and lack of interest. (Myrick, 1997).

What makes the difference whether or not the middle 60% moves toward supporting TAP and developmental guidance? The result, as Myrick (1997) indicated, seems to depend upon the following:

Teachers and staff need to understand the philosophy behind TAP and how it is related to developmental guidance for youth. This includes an understanding of student needs and awareness of student problems. It also includes a recognition of how guidance is directly related to helping students grow socially and personally.

The time commitment for TAP needs to be adequate. Time management or the organizational scheme of TAP is a critical factor. Sometimes, TAP programs suffer because there is not enough time for advisors to meet with their advisees. There is a very little chance that valuable helping relationships between teachers and their advisees will develop in such little time. Commitment is not evident. When meeting times are scheduled far apart, there is not much opportunity for continuity and consistency. TAP works best when it is scheduled every other day. This gives advisors an opportunity to know their advisees and to talk with them individually and in groups.

Scheduling TAP two days a week seems to be a minimum. Otherwise, there is a tendency for a teaching faculty to view TAP as an *unimportant* adjunct program instead of an integral one within an organized guidance curriculum. It is difficult to feel committed to a program that is not a part of the regular weekly schedule.

TAP must have a written, developmental guide with supporting materials and activities. Teachers are accustomed to having written guides and they often depend on learning activities that stimulate student thinking and participation. Therefore, teachers like to have organized handbooks which contain various activities that they might use in TAP. This handbook is usually developed by a TAP committee made up of advisors, administrators and students and coordinated by the Guidance Office. As a counselor, you will want to be highly involved in the development of the supporting materials and activities. Some counselors have found it particularly effective to involve the drama teacher in the development of student based video tapes for use through their school's close-circuit television system. When given the opportunity, students will become very creative when developing these TAP activities. And, it has been found that TAP activities

planned, developed, and delivered by students are among the most popular. Others have used peer groups to serve as panels, or as small group leaders, in selected TAP rooms, and so forth.

Teachers need preparation in facilitation and interpersonal skills. This is often ignored. And, if teachers do not receive the necessary training, the TAP will fail. Many teachers do not understand how a TAP program is developed to meet student needs and how their own guidance interventions can be used to help students. Some teachers have limited interpersonal and group facilitation skills and many have not had much preparation in how to manage groups. More specifically, far too many teachers rely on one group arrangement—all students facing the front of the room—and need more training in how to get students working cooperatively in small groups. The TAP seldom succeeds where the "teacher as lecturer" is the mode of delivery.

Most teachers talk too much at students. Many have not learned the skills needed to facilitate class discussion with group discussion skills. They need help in knowing more about group dynamics and how to facilitate a group. Also, many of them need assistance in learning how to help a student think about a personal problem and to take some steps in solving that problem. This does not mean that the advisor is always a problem-solver. Rather, the advisor helps students explore situations, alternatives and consequences, and possible plans of action. They also need help in knowing when to refer an advisee to the school counselor. In addition, they receive help from other students within their advisee group.

TAP needs administrative support. Most administrators try to accommodate their teachers and to make teaching an enjoyable endeavor. They are fully aware of how difficult teaching can be and how some students—teachers as well—can dampen the spirit of a school. Some students and teachers make everyone's work more difficult and the school environment unappealing.

Administrators set the tone of a school. Their personal style and commitment is the glue that holds the program together. If they are supportive, then the TAP teachers will try harder. If they are indifferent, then teachers find other places to invest their time and energy. Therefore, they must not only speak favorably about TAP, but they must take time to understand how TAP works and to find ways to show their support. We always suggest that administrators go through the TAP training program with the future advisors. And, in most effective TAP schools, the administrators also have an advisee group of their own.

Effective Drug Education Through TAP

Advisors need specific training. Interestingly enough, effective teachers have the same characteristics as effective advisors. Among these are the willingness and ability to:

- See the student's point of view without condoning or judging them.
- Personalize the education experience.
- Facilitate a discussion where students listen and share ideas in an atmosphere of trust.
- Develop a helping relationship with students.
- Be flexible.
- Be open to letting the student try new ideas.
- Model interpersonal and communication skills.
- Foster a positive environment where respect, understanding, kindness, concern, warmth, and genuineness are evident.
- Be an effective listener.
- Facilitate students to "tune in to other students;" to become a facilitator of others.

When students have problems, they turn to those who they think can be of most help. Surveys repeatedly show that adolescents and older youth turn first to peers and then to teachers. Generally, the first line of helpers are among those people who students see almost every day, especially if they have positive relationships with them. It has been our experience that approximately 80% of those teachers with the characteristics mentioned above can be trained as effective advisors.

TAP needs to be evaluated. In order for TAP to be an accountable part of the school's guidance program, it must be monitored and evaluated. Evaluations provide data upon which to make decisions and to decide what new directions, if any, might be taken. Student and teacher evaluations of TAP are essential if it is to develop progressively into an effective program.

Advisors must be carefully selected. It is obvious from previous comments that not all teachers should or can become effective advisors. Selection for training is very important. Those selected should have such personal qualities as a willingness to try new ideas, an enthusiasm for teaching and a favorable rapport with other teachers and each other. In addition, they should have the support of the administration and communicate well with the administrators (Myrick, 1997).

As mentioned previously, TAP is an excellent vehicle for various types of large group guidance activities. What follows is a TAP program shown effective for drug education at the middle school level.

Alcohol and other drug abuse problems have been recognized as one of the leading threats to the health and well-being of young people today. The 1991 National Household Survey on Drug Abuse (NIDA, 1991), based on a national sample of individuals 12 years old and over, reported substantial initiation of illicit drug and alcohol use by youth 12 to 17 years of age. For example, the survey showed that the percentage of 12- to 17-year-olds in 1991 who had used marijuana and alcohol was 13% and 46.4% respectively. In another study examining demographic and psychosocial factors associated with drug use among high school seniors, 26.5% reported using illicit drugs once a month or more during the previous year. More than 18% of the seniors surveyed indicated they had used an illicit drug weekly (Wisniewski & Miller, 1997). They also reported that junior high students use of marijuana rose more than 40% from 1994-95 to 1995-96. These findings are particularly troublesome in view of the research which indicates that early initiation of drug use is one of the strongest predictors of later drug abuse and dependence problems.

The emphasis of psychosocial drug education approaches on the development of social competence skills make them uniquely appropriate for implementation within the developmental guidance programs in the schools.

One effective program for such implementation is the Teachers as Advisors Program (TAP) described previously. The emphasis of the developmental guidance approach through TAP closely parallels the competence areas found to be important in psychosocial approaches to substance abuse prevention. Thus, it seems a natural extension of the developmental guidance program to organize and expand a specific TAP unit to form a drug education curriculum. School counselors could then implement the unit through TAP by training teachers to implement the unit, or train peers to do it. Such an application would make use of existing resources in the schools and would ensure involvement of teachers and peers in drug education efforts.

One very important goal for incorporating the drug education curriculum into the developmental guidance program through TAP is to provide more opportunities for student-teacher and student-counselor interaction on the subject of substance abuse. Although TAP emphasizes the developmental and preventive approach, it also provides a framework in which teachers can establish positive relationships with students who are at risk or who are having substance abuse problems. TAP teachers can work directly with students and at other times, acting as ombudsmen, they can refer them to school counselors for more assistance. Through TAP, teachers and school counselors can work together on the implementation of the drug education curriculum, as well as in leading group discussions, advising or confronting individual students, referring and using community resources, and so forth.

A TAP Drug Education Curriculum

A TAP drug education curriculum unit consisting of a core twelve sessions focusing on factors that influence the use of tobacco, alcohol, and marijuana was developed by the authors (Myrick & Gonzalez, 1990) under sponsorship of the U.S. Department of Education. An assessment session was also included. Each TAP session, regardless of the content, must be appropriately organized for delivery by the TAP teachers. Teachers are used to well-organized lesson plans and will appreciate structured, easy to follow TAP guidance activities.

The TAP drug education unit described here was based on a broad psychosocial approach to substance abuse prevention called Life Skills Training (LST). The LST program was developed by Botvin and Willis (1984) and has been used effectively to prevent the use of alcohol, tobacco and marijuana with junior high school and populations. The main thrust of the LST program is to facilitate the development of basic life skills and the improvement of personal competence, with particular emphasis on coping with pro-drug social influences. Presenting LST through TAP has the added advantage of enabling teachers as advisors to develop helping relationships with students, beyond those in the typical academic areas. Teachers become more trusted and valued personal resources to students as a consequence of TAP.

Although there are several drug education curriculums available which could conceivably be adapted for implementation through TAP, most of these are too extensive or lack the broad-based psychosocial focus of the LST program. Therefore, they are less comparable with traditional school guidance approaches.

The basic concepts covered in the TAP drug education curriculum developed by Myrick and Gonzalez (1990) are as follows:

Session	**Topic**	**Description***
1, 2	Drug Use: Myth, Realities, and Consequences	Common attitudes and beliefs about tobacco, alcohol, and marijuana use; current prevalence rates, the process of becoming a regular (habitual) user, and the difficulties of breaking these. Also the school policy on the use of substances and the consequences of use n school (i.e., suspension, expulsion, academic failure) are addressed.
3, 4	Social Influences	Routine decision making, a general decision-making strategy, social and media influences affecting decisions, recognizing persuasive tactics, and the importance of independent thinking on drug issues.
5,6	Resisting Influences	Formulating counter-arguments and Refusal Skills other cognitive strategies for resisting social and advertising pressures.
7	Self-Image and Self-Improvement	Discussion of self-image and how it is formed, the relationship between self-image and drug behavior. The importance of a positive self image, alternative methods of improving one's self and self image.
8	Coping with Anxiety and Problems	Discussion of common anxiety-inducing situations, demonstration and practice of drug-free cognitive-behavioral techniques for coping with problems, and instruction on the application of these techniques to everyday situations.
9,10	Communication Skills	Verbal and non-verbal communication, techniques and helping responses for avoiding misunderstanding, the value of asking questions. Overcoming shyness without the use of alcohol or other drugs, initiating social contacts, giving and receiving compliments, boy-girl relationships.
11	Helping Oneself or Others	Learning a problem-solving model and ways it can be used to deal with challenging situations or to help a student who has a concern or decision to make.
12	Evaluation	To evaluate the unit and identify next steps students can take to help make our society drug free.

* Modified from Botvin et al. (1984).

You may wish to add supplemental sessions to the above curriculum for use with special populations in your school who may be at high risk for drug involvement. These sessions might focus on getting help and dealing with family alcohol or other drug dependence. High risk students could be identified through TAP and assisted through guidance sessions or referred to other resources.

Training of Teachers and Counselors

As mentioned previously, the effective implementation of the TAP drug education curriculum depends upon well prepared and trained teachers. A practical and feasible training experience might consist of appropriately designed workshops presented as a preschool, or during school in-service program. The training would focus primarily on the etiological research on substance abuse, indicators of involvement in the use of psychoactive substances, community resources and referrals, and how to deliver the drug education unit to students during TAP or other development guidance programs.

Additional workshops could focus on building the TAP teacher's self-confidence in working with high risk students, forming helping relationships, leading group discussions, and timely interventions with students. School counselors can serve as consultants and trainers. With their support and encouragement developmental drug education programs can be implemented through TAP to reach all students within a school. Moreover, counselors can lead or co-lead some sessions when TAP teachers need assistance. When TAP teachers identify students who need extra attention they can refer them to counselors, who can be a link between a school and community agencies specializing in substance abuse.

Advantages of the TAP Approach to Drug Education and Other Guidance Units

One of the major advantages of using TAP as the method for the delivery of drug education in the schools is that it integrates teacher/counselor interventions within a school. It is a practical and feasible approach for reaching young adolescents. It is more direct than relying on teachers to integrate drug education within the regular curriculum. This does not preclude teachers from incorporating substance abuse education in their classes. However, through developmental guidance delivery modes such as TAP a more comprehensive, structured approach is obtained in which *all* students, the administration, and most, if not all, teachers in the school are involved. This provides an opportunity for such things as more drug education activities with minimum modifications of already existing school resources.

Homebase teacher-advisor programs are already in place in many schools. Some schools have extensive programs and will welcome the TAP drug education curriculum described herein. Other schools have less developed teacher-advisor programs and this curriculum could encourage teachers to give more time to guidance and substance abuse education. In either case, however, more helping resources would be mobilized for the prevention of substance abuse and more students could be positively affected at a crucial time in their development.

As stated at the beginning of this chapter, there is an obvious need for teachers do be more closely involved with students (to become their friend, and advocate) and with the guidance program. TAP provides these opportunities and can be an excellent and efficient delivery mode for various large group guidance activities.

Figure 22.1
Family and Student Development: The Role of Teacher as Advisor

Joe Wittmer and Paul Jeorge

Family and Student Development: The Role of the Teacher as Advisor is a new course recently approved by the College of Education faculty as a requirement in the revised preservice, middle school, teacher preparation curriculum at the University of Florida. The course will be taught by faculty in the Counselor Education Department. What follows is simply an overview of the course; one aspect of the syllabus.

Overview of the Course

In this course we explore the question, How can teachers establish appropriate and effective advisory relationships with all young adolescent students and their families? What role should middle school teachers play in the personal, social, and career development of their students?

Teachers, as well as other professionals in and outside of education, increasingly find themselves involved in relationships with persons who might be thought of as clients. At the middle school level, the teacher-student relationship is at the heart of how teachers achieve effective teaching and learning relationships with their students and students' families. When teachers must interact daily with as many as 150 or more students, however, establishing growth-producing relationships becomes problematic. In effective middle schools, therefore, teachers more often act as affective guides to, ombudsmen for, and school experts on small groups of students and their families.

Middle school educators often identify the teacher-student relationship as the starting point of the entire school program. Among the list of characteristics which determines the uniqueness of the young adolescent, the need for a particular kind of teacher-student relationship is almost always placed at the top. Written philosophies from middle schools consistently strive to highlight the student-centered nature of the program, implying a concern for each student and a commitment to firm teacher-student, and teacher-parent bonds.

This course is about that kind of relationship, one in which a teacher acts as advisor/facilitator to a group of students, and by extension, to their families. As such, participants in this course will be involved in the study of ways in which middle school teachers act out this important role. Students in the course will provide evidence of competence in a number of areas.

Of particular importance, in the area of advisement and teacher-student relationships, is the provision of these services for students in a time of dramatically increasing diversity in the middle school classroom. Students with disabilities or special needs, at-risk students, and students of color may require even more effective relationships with, and advisement from, their teachers. All middle school teachers must learn to provide such services and establish such relationships.

Transitions are at the heart of the middle school experience for young adolescents. Moving to middle school from the elementary school, and from the middle school to the high school, are powerful factors in shaping the success or failure of school experience. A powerful transition of another sort, from childhood to adolescence, also requires the attention and support of middle school educators. So, this course is about families, transitions, and how teacher/advisors can assist in these crucial developmental experiences.

Course Components:

1. The Theory and Philosophy of TAP (Teacher-Advisor-Program)

   Every student deserves a friendly adult in the school who will advocate for them as appropriate and do something to show that the student is known, respected and cared about.

   Every student deserves an opportunity to belong and take part in a small group in which student academic interests, as well as personal needs, and concerns are addressed.

   Every student needs to be involved in a developmental guidance curriculum which focuses on personal, social, academic, and career development.

   Every parent needs contact with an adult at school who knows and cares about their child's academic and personal progress.

2. Organization of TAP in the Schools

   TAP is an integrated, structured part of the school curriculum.

   - *When does it take place during the school day? Why?*

   - *How much school time is set aside for TAP?*

- *How many student advisees are appropriate for each TAP teacher?*

- *How are student advisees assigned to a particular TAP teacher?*

- *When is the best time to have TAP scheduled?*

- *What titles and names are sometimes given to TAP?*

- *How are students involved in determining TAP activities?*

3. The Roles Played by Teachers in a TAP Program

- *The teacher as academic expert on a group of students*

- *The teacher as a facilitator of academic, personal/ social and career development*

- *The teacher/advisor/facilitator and student relationships*

- *The teacher as liaison with the school*

- *The teacher as communicator with parents and family*

- *The teacher/advisor as student advocate*

- *The teacher/advisor as provider of social and emotional education and = support*

- *The teacher as liaison with the high school, community, and the world of work*

4. The Advisory Curriculum

   TAP can be organized around the following representative topics:

- *Transition to Middle School*

- *Orientation & Getting Acquainted*

- *Time Management*

- *Study Skills*

- *Stress Management*

- *Peer Relationships*

- *Health and Personal Development Issues*

- *Drug &Alcohol Abuse*

- *Violence Prevention*

- *Sexual Harassment*

- *Eating Disorders*

- *Sex-Related Problems*

- *Multicultural Awareness*

- *Personal Awareness and Assessment*

- *Career Development and Other Planning for the Future*

- *Conflict Resolution Education*

- *Communication Skills*

- *Group Leadership*

- *Educational Planning*

- *Cooperative Learning Skills*

- *Transition to High School*

5. Knowledge, Skills and Attitudes of Effective Teacher/ Advisors

- Knowledge of the characteristics and needs of young adolescents, especially those students with special needs

- *An attitude which predisposes the teacher to seek to establish positive teacher-student relationships with all students and their parents*

- The skills which enable a teacher to establish such relationships

- Knowledge of and skills related to designing and implementing an effective home base, teacher/advisor program

- Managing student information via TAP

- Being a member of a Multidisciplinary Team

- Skills for working effectively with parents

References

Bottvin, G., Baker, E., Renick, N., Filazzala, A., & Botvin, E. (1984). A cognitive-behavioral approach to substance abuse prevention. *Journal of Addictive Behaviors, 9*, 137-147.

Myrick, R.D. (1997). *Developmental guidance and counseling: A practical approach* (3rd ed.). Minneapolis, MN: Educational Media Corporation.

Myrick, R.D., & Gonzalez, G.M. (1990). *Alcohol and other drug prevention through teacher advisors* (Contract No. S184-A-90089). Washington, DC: U.S. Department of Education.

National Institute on Drug Abuse (1991). *Overview of the 1991 national household survey on drug abuse* (NIDA Capsules c-83-1a). Rockville, MD: Author.

Schmidt, J. (1999). *Counseling in schools: Essential services and comprehension programs* (3rd ed.). Needham, MA: Allyn & Bacon.

Wisniewski, S., & Miller, K. (1997). Character education: The importance of educating the heart. *ASCA Counselor, 35*, 16.

Chapter 23
Multidisciplinary Teams: The School Counselor and Other Professionals

by

Nicholas A. Vacc, Kim Bloss, and Leslie Martin Rainey

Nicholas A. Vacc, EdD, NCC, is the Joe Rosenthal Excellence Professor, Department of Counseling and Educational Development at the University of North Carolina at Greensboro. He has been a school counselor and a school psychologist.

Kim Bloss, PhD, is a counselor educator and chair of the Department of Curriculum and Instruction at Southern Kansas University. She has been a classroom teacher and school counselor.

Leslie Martin Rainey, PhD, NCC, is currently a student assistance program counselor, Buncombe County Schools, North Carolina. With more than 15 years of K-12 counseling experience, Dr. Rainey also teaches classes for teachers, counselors, and administrators at Asheville-Buncombe Technical Community College.

Introduction

To assure that pupils, especially those with unique needs, are provided appropriate assistance that encourages their personal, social, and educational development, counselors and other specialists, teachers, and administrators, must work together to offer an effective educational delivery system. Business, industry, and medical organizations view team work as essential to enhance service delivery in their settings, particularly those that are complex. For schools, however, the use of teams to provide service delivery for the increasingly diverse population of students is a relatively new phenomenon. In contrast to traditional education programs, school counselors are increasingly involved with other service providers in comprehensive efforts to meet the needs of students. Thus, rather than working alone, school counselors have a major role in "teams" which involve a variety of educational professionals who plan, coordinate, evaluate, and provide direct services concerning students, parents, and staff.

The overriding purpose of this school multidisciplinary team approach is to provide a framework for meeting the needs of students. The team concept assures the likelihood of having the expertise of many disciplines available to address the diversity of issues and needs presented by individual students.

This multidisciplinary approach is known by many names (e.g., child-study team, student-advisory system, student services management team, educational planning team, school-based committee, school-wide assistance team, crisis-intervention team, multi-professional team, interdisciplinary team, student advisory program, and pupil services team). Regardless of the name, however, the ultimate goal of such an approach is the coordination and effective delivery of the various school and community-based services available to students.

In this chapter the role of the school counselor as a member of a multidisciplinary school team is examined, as well as the roles of various other members of the team.

Rationale

School-based teams came about largely as a result of Public Law 94-142, the Education for All Handicapped Children Act of 1975, which requires a school-based team approach for the identification and placement of exceptional children. While a team structure for service delivery for all children is relatively new, the examples learned from providing services in special education have been a contributing factor in the realization of a team's potential.

The primary advantage for adopting the multi-disciplinary team approach to providing services for students in the schools is that professionals no longer inadvertently isolate themselves from each other. Consequently, they are able to provide high quality and perhaps more cost-effective services than is possible without this communication across disciplines. A secondary benefit is the explicit acknowledgment that educational specialists such as the school counselor, school nurse, school administrator, school social worker, school psychologist, and classroom teacher are intimately inter-related and reciprocally influential in shaping a child's development. "Working with the child" in isolation and separate from a multidisciplinary team approach significantly reduces the opportunity and likelihood for effective, positive, meaningful, and lasting change in a pupil's life.

An Illustrative Case

Mr. Bolick, a third-grade teacher, referred one of his students, Chris, to the school counselor for assistance with adjusting to school. Chris cries every morning upon arrival at school and has difficulty completing daily assignments. After meeting Chris and conducting an initial interview, the school counselor, with Mr. Bolick's support, presented the case of Chris to a multidisciplinary team at the school. The team included Mr. Bolick, the school counselor (who chaired the meeting), the school nurse, the school social worker, the school psychologist, one of the exceptional children teachers, and the assistant principal. Since Chris' family had recently moved into the community, no one on the team was familiar with the home environment. The initial plan developed by the team included the following: (a) the social worker would make a home visit to determine the family situation, (b) the school counselor would continue to provide supportive counseling to Chris, (c) the assistant principal would begin to meet him when his bus arrived at school each day as a way to demonstrate the school staff's interest in him, and (d) Mr. Bolick would continue to observe Chris in the classroom daily and conduct a complete review of Chris' records. Upon visiting the home, the social worker learned that Chris' family had recently moved to the area for the purpose of seeking employment, but no one in the family was presently working. The family consisted of the parents, Chris, and two younger siblings.

At the next team meeting, the social worker recommended that Chris be enrolled in the free breakfast and lunch program at school based on the level of family income. Also, after reviewing Chris's records from his previous school, Mr. Bolick and the school counselor agreed to refer Chris for initial screening for possible special educational services. The screening process included vision and hearing screening conducted by the nurse, a classroom observation conducted by the assistant principal, and a psycho-educational assessment conducted by the school psychologist.

The school-based multidisciplinary team assisted Chris not only in his initial adjustment to a new school, but also supported the family with financial assistance and referral for special educational services. Educational support for Chris was provided by placing him in a resource program for learning disabled students and modifying and individualizing his classroom assignments.

Organizational Perspective

The value of a multidisciplinary team approach is that it provides for the enhancement of educational services for individual students with special needs. Without a team perspective, key personnel often represent different constituencies and philosophies of service delivery and, as a result, generate mutually exclusive, and sometimes confusing, expectations for a student's welfare. As a consequence, school personnel operate in what has been termed as a loosely coupled system; there is relative lack of control, influence, coordination, and interaction between events or parts of an organizational system.

Collaborative Relationships

Because a team approach involves professionals from many disciplines, "turf" issues can arise and strained relationships between team members could result in unproductive meetings. Beder (1984) identified four dominant themes that are important for successful collaborative relationships. These include (a) reciprocity, which is defined as a balance in receiving information and in relinquishing some domain and power, (b) system openness or a receptiveness to outside perspectives, (c) trust and commitment, and (d) an adjustable structure to help team members adapt to one another and create a climate of openness and receptivity. The effectiveness of the team will depend upon the extent to which these themes are in place and maintained. One way of achieving this is to have school counselors, as permanent staff members in their schools, assume the function of a leader and coordinator for their respective multidisciplinary team. This is especially appropriate given their background in communication skills, group work, and overall understanding of the school environment (Keys, Benmark, Carpenter, & King-Sears, 1998). This type of school counselor role is a becoming more and more common in school districts across the United States.

Case Consultation Approach

It also is recommended that within the organization of the multidisciplinary team, a "case consultation" approach be used. In such an approach one member of the multidisciplinary team is assigned to share with the classroom teacher the responsibilities for overseeing and maintaining an individual child's program as was illustrated above with the care of Chris. The case consultant may be the only adult who maintains sustained contact with the student and family throughout the delivery of multiple services. The case consultant may be another teacher or an educational specialist whose role is to synthesize the relevant information that the team members have provided about a child and help operationalize the recom-

mendations. Such follow-through is of vital importance. For example, recommending changes in a student's instruction as an intervention is not helpful unless teachers involved with the child's instructional program understand the nature and scope of the intervention and how to adapt the recommendation to best meet the child's needs. The shared responsibility aspect of the case-consultant approach implies a more active commitment than typically occurs with many multidisciplinary teams. In essence, it appears that the most effective approach to implementing a multidisciplinary team is to assign a team member to work with the teacher, while the entire team serves as a resource for the team member. Thus, rather than only the school counselor consulting with a classroom teacher about a child who is exhibiting behavioral adjustment problems and educational learning difficulties, the school psychologist who observes the child within the classroom and the special education teacher who conducts an educational assessment work together with the teacher, counselor, and significant others. As a cautionary note, however, research has found school psychologists to be the most active and influential participants in such team meetings (Ysseldyke, Algozzine, & Allen, 1982). One possible reason for a school psychologist assuming this responsibility is the perceptions of others concerning their level of expertise. An assignment plan based on a case consultation approach is a means for addressing this concern. It also benefits everyone through the knowledge gained by association with other educational specialists from a variety of disciplines and brings a new perspective to members of the team. Strategies which the school counselor can employ as a team leader to foster a case-consultation climate include (a) carefully selecting team members, (b) clearly specifying the purpose of the team, (c) determining and collecting pertinent information about cases, (d) allowing adequate time for team members to fully understand the student issues they are being asked to staff, (e) monitoring the group dynamics of team meetings, (f) modeling appreciation for the contributions of all team members, (g) allowing adequate time during meetings for team members to brainstorm potential solutions to student problems, and (h) gaining closure on final decisions so that they will be more fully supported by team members during implementation.

Community Resources

Often it is helpful to include social service agency personnel as members of school-based teams. Thus, information and resources can be combined which helps reduce the duplication of services and avoids competition. A report by the National Association of State Boards of Education (Levy & Copple, 1989) supported involving community personnel on school-based teams by calling for comprehensive services and education. Levy and Copple (1989) stated that schools alone are unable to compensate for disadvantages created by troubled communities and troubled homes. Also, involvement of community personnel allows school staff, particularly school counselors, to become aware of and utilize community resources. Also, community professionals can gain insight about the challenges and issues of children and adolescents that schools address (Smaby, Peterson, Bergmann, Zentner-Bacig, & Swearingen, 1990).

Role of Team Participants

School based teams are composed of school personnel and on occasion social service personnel, depending on the structure of community resources where the school is located. As cited earlier, participants on the team usually include the school counselor, administrative personnel, the classroom teacher, school social worker, school nurse, school psychologist, and the school attendance officer where available and if appropriate to the case. Additionally, other specialists may be included in specific cases where warranted. Most teams vary in composition, but all tend to be multidisciplinary; they are comprised of professionals from diverse but related areas of training. Due to the confidential nature of information processed by a school based multidisciplinary team, parents and students are involved only in those cases specific to an individual student. Parents and students often become members of the team in situations which result in the development of an individualized discipline plan or recommended placement in an exceptional student's program. In the latter case, the student and parents are invited to participate in developing an Individualized Educational Plan (IEP) which addresses education goals and needs for the specific student.

Figure 23.1 is a conceptual illustration of a multidisciplinary school-based team which depicts the convergence of professionals focused on issues of concern to the school. The outer circle of social service agency personnel represents involvement "as needed." An understanding of the roles of each of the potential team participants and the services provided by each is essential to effective service delivery.

School Counselor

The school counselor, certified or licensed by the particular state educational agency, provides expertise and direction on understanding appropriate developmental issues, needs, and cultural considerations of students of

all ages. Based on these needs, the counselor implements effective counseling strategies in an individual, small group, or family setting. The counselor contributes knowledge of counseling theory and practice to the multidisciplinary team. As previously indicated, the counselor frequently serves as coordinator of the team (see Figure 23.1).

School Social Worker

The school social worker conducts home visits to determine the physical needs of students. Assistance is provided in furnishing clothing, food, and transportation for families. The social worker may also be responsible for monitoring attendance of students to ensure compliance with state attendance laws. In addition, the social worker provides knowledge of availability of community resources such as food banks, clothing closets, and volunteer support groups. State educational agencies also certify school social workers.

School Psychologist

The school psychologist conducts the testing and assessment program for students to determine individual educational needs and eligibility for placement in an exceptional children's program. The psychologist is available for interpreting assessment data and makes recommendations regarding the least restrictive placement to meet the needs of students. Leadership is provided in developing educational and behavioral intervention plans. In some cases, the psychologist may provide direct service to a student on a continuing basis. School psychologists are certified by state departments of education and, in some states, by state psychological licensure boards.

School Nurse

The school nurse assesses and monitors the physical health needs of students. Responsibilities of this position include providing direction for meeting physical needs such as vision and hearing, nutrition, and personal hygiene. The school nurse also coordinates referrals to county or city health agencies. Public school nurses are required to hold a nursing degree from an accredited training program.

Teacher

The classroom teacher contributes knowledge of academic policies and programs and appropriate modifications of curricula that may be employed in the classroom setting. The teacher provides direction in identifying the compatibility of learning styles of specific students with instructional styles of teachers. Adherence to state curriculum competencies and grade level expectations is also ensured by the classroom teacher. Teachers of exceptional children (special education) provide the assessment of specific exceptionalities and direct appropriate educational planning for students who meet the guidelines for placement in a specific program. These teachers assist in the development of individual educational plans (IEP's) for students with identified exceptionalities. These teachers are usually the professional with the responsibility to make families of exceptional students aware of community resources available to them. Exceptional children's teachers are certified or licensed in specific areas by respective state departments of education.

Administration (Principal, Assistant Principal, Dean of Students)

The administrator serving on the multidisciplinary team usually monitors student behavior and discipline areas throughout the school environment (e.g., classroom, bus, special services areas). Knowledge of legal and ethical guidelines, state and local school board policy, program planning, and staff development opportunities are contributed by the administrator. Local school administrators are specifically certified by state departments of education.

Jobs Training and Placement Act (JTPA) Coordinator

The JTPA coordinator provides knowledge and awareness of employment training and placement opportunities in the community. The coordinator conducts job training and work skills orientation and monitors students who are placed in jobs in local businesses.

Juvenile Court Counselor

The juvenile court counselor provides counseling and consultation to minors who have entered the legal system due to delinquent behavior. This person monitors probation restrictions and makes recommendations to the judiciary regarding adjudicated youth. Services are also provided to the families of delinquent youth.

Child Protection Service (CPS) Worker— Department of Social Services

The CPS worker is responsible for investigating reports of abuse or neglect of minors. CPS departments monitor families and homes in which abuse or neglect has been substantiated. Supervision of foster care placements and coordination of custody agreements with the legal system are provided by the CPS worker. A social work degree is generally required.

Coordinating a Multidisciplinary Team

As a team leader, the school counselor's responsibility includes facilitating the group dynamics and advancing the team's effectiveness by clarifying the purpose of the team and each member, facilitating conflict resolution, encouraging the participation of all team members, delegating tasks, fostering a positive environment, and providing a sense of closure to team meetings (Gysbers & Henderson, 1999). Some of the issues concerning a team's effectiveness are time allotment, referral process, case management, and evaluation.

Time Allotment

Myrick (1997) noted that the role of coordinating services is one that cannot be ignored. Of primary concern to the school staff is the amount of time available for the coordination and management of the multidisciplinary team. School staff members are responsible for a large number of services and time looms as a constraint. Accordingly, it is important that the existing school structure is accommodated. For example, meeting times could be before or after school hours or during lunch to accommodate teachers' and parents', where appropriate, schedules. Meeting times may need to be changed or varied on a systematic schedule. However, the important issue is to meet on a regular scheduled basis; perhaps every two weeks.

Referral Process

While multidisciplinary teams will vary in composition and purpose from school to school, a variety of documents and referral forms will provide information to involved persons and give direction to services. It is important to provide school staff with uncomplicated forms to refer students to the team. This form may include the name of the student and teacher, concerns that the teacher has regarding the student, support services currently being provided, and a section for team members to complete upon making intervention plans for the student. It is also important that students, parents, and faculty are aware of the team's services. Figure 23.2 presents a sample Student Service Information form.

Case Management

Once the multidisciplinary team is involved in staffing a case, appropriate documentation of services is imperative. Assignment of responsibility for gathering data on specific cases is within the role of team coordinator. Accurate data insure appropriate services and case management. Figure 23.3 illustrates a sample form that may be used in tracking referrals.

Evaluation

The evaluation of multidisciplinary teams, which is often overlooked, is a crucial component of effective service delivery. The process of evaluation becomes the vehicle for self-improvement of the multidisciplinary team. It is important to consider the evaluation process in the early stages of team formation. Two types of evaluation may be conducted. Formative evaluations become a part of the team process, are conducted throughout the school year, and provide ongoing feedback to the team to give direction to its work (e.g., individual/case impact). Summative evaluations are conducted at the end of the school year and provide data on the number of students served and the accomplishments of the team. One efficient approach might be to conduct informal evaluations throughout the school year and a comprehensive evaluation at the end of the year.

Evaluation information may be obtained from team members as well as students who receive services. Potential areas for team members to evaluate include (a) effectiveness of the referral procedures, (b) appropriateness of documentation procedures, (c) productivity of communication patterns within the team, (d) confidentiality of students, (e) conflict management, (f) timeliness of interventions, (g) efficiency and effectiveness of team meetings, (h) effectiveness of specific intervention plans, and (i) plans for improvement. Student evaluations are frequently omitted. Yet, they may provide another perspective on the team's effectiveness. Figure 23.4 provides a sample form that students may use to evaluate the effectiveness and efficiency of the multidisciplinary intervention.

Summary Illustrative Case

Presented below is an actual example of a complex issue which involved both school and community social service staff working together to effectively provide the necessary services needed.

Marsha, a 15-year-old eighth grade female, was referred to a multidisciplinary team because of her history of truancy, low grades, aggressive behavior, and grade retention the previous school year. The team consisted of a school counselor, classroom teacher, assistant principal, school psychologist, juvenile court counselor, Child Protective Services (CPS) worker, and mental health adolescent counselor. Marsha's continuing patterns of truancy, lack of grade improvement, and increasing aggression towards others were a source of concern to team members. Based on this concern, the team requested that the CPS team member meet with the family, and the school counselor scheduled a conference with Marsha to determine the degree of support she was receiving regarding her school program. During the conference, the school counselor learned that Marsha was responsible for her own care, including meals, clothing, and school attendance. Marsha's mother was determined by the CPS team member to be an alcoholic who was not providing adequate care for Marsha. The multidisciplinary team developed a four-point intervention plan for Marsha that included the following: family counseling through a mental health agency for Marsha and her mother, referral of the mother to Alcoholics Anonymous and referral of Marsha to Alateen, referral of Marsha to a school-based at-risk program, and continued monitoring of the home situation by the CPS team member. The team reviewed Marsha's progress on a monthly basis. Through this intervention, Marsha was able to stay in the home, began attending school regularly, showed improvement in grades, and exhibited a decrease in aggressive behavior. Marsha was promoted to the ninth grade at the end of the school year.

Summary

Serving on multidisciplinary teams is an integral part of the services that school counselors provide to students and school staff. The diversity of knowledge and perspectives among various professionals promotes the efficient and effective delivery of services. Developing and implementing a team approach to service delivery may be a time consuming task for the school counselor. However, the increased potential of holistic support for the student enhances the school counselor's ability to address the developmental needs of the student and to become more proactive in working with the staff.

Figure 23.1
Multidiciplinary School-based Team

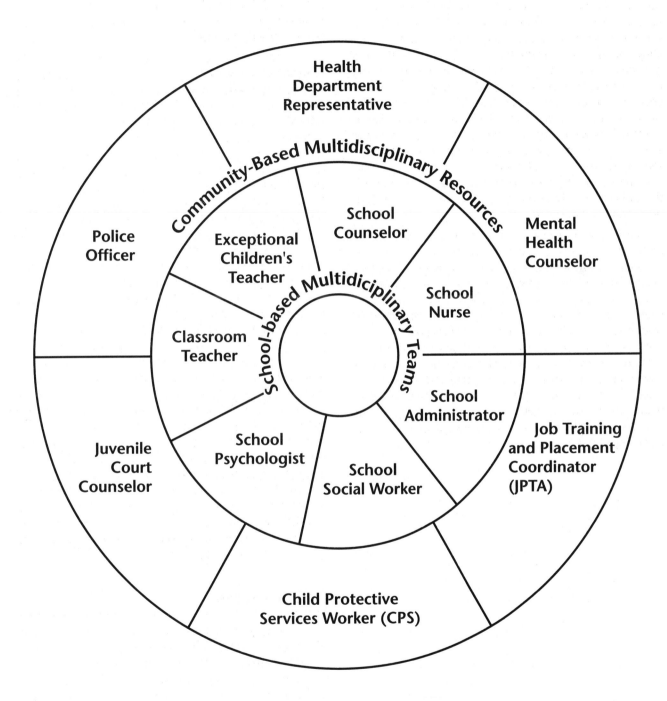

Figure 23.2
Example of a Student Services Information Form

Student Services Management Team:

The Student Services Management Team at (name of your school) _____

is composed of the school counselor, assistant principal, school psychologist, attendance officer, speech therapist, school nurse, exceptional student education teacher, school social worker, and teacher consultants from within the school. The goal of this team is to help all students maximize their abilities and find productive ways of coping with the daily concerns and problems they encounter. All of these professionals are available individually or as a team to assist you. The Student Services Management Team meets every other Monday after school. Some typical issues the team can focus on include students' problems at school, at home, at work, or with friends. We discuss options that are available to the student and develop action plans to assist the student in becoming more productive.

How Are Students Referred?

Students are referred by discussing the problem with any of the team members or by scheduling yourself for team time. Also, students may be referred by any teacher, administrator, counselor, parent, or any other school-based personnel.

What Happens in These Meetings?

The primary purpose of the Student Services Management Team is to develop a plan to assist students in managing problems. A problem-solving format is utilized that usually includes:

1. a concise statement of the problem

2. identification of the steps that have already been taken to manage the problem

3. options, resources, personnel, programs, or strategies that may be utilized to manage/cope with the problem more effectively

4. choosing the best course of action to be taken (action plan)

5. determining the team member who will be responsible for carrying out the action plan and reporting the results to the team at the next meeting

Other activities that take place during planning team time include:

1. inviting students to discuss their problem and develop a plan, contract, or agreement

2. inviting students in to congratulate them on a job well done, or for demonstrating responsible behavior by adhering to their agreement/commitment

Minutes are taken during each meeting and distributed to team members within two days of the meeting. These minutes include the action plans developed.

NOTE: These forms may be modified to adapt to services provided by individual schools and may be distributed to students, parents, and teachers at the beginning of the school year.

Adapted from a form used at Hawthorne High School, Hawthorne, Florida.

Figure 23.3
Sample Form for Monitoring Referrals Intervention Strategies Checklist

Student: _____

The following intervention techniques have been or are being implemented concerning this student.

Dates Action Taken

_____	Parent conference
_____	Conference with teacher
_____	Conference with school counselor
_____	Classroom/Instruction Modifications
_____	Individual counseling
_____	Group counseling
_____	Conference with principal
_____	Note(s), call(s) to parent
_____	Home visit
_____	Tutoring
_____	Point system
_____	Special jobs, privileges, recognition
_____	Classroom observation
_____	Support group referral
_____	Work program referral
_____	Public/private agency
_____	Conference with court counselor
_____	Community resources referral (list)
_____	Ongoing monitoring of performance
_____	Other (specify)_____
_____	_____

Adapted from: Division of Student Support Services, North Carolina Department of Public Instruction

Figure 23.4
Sample Evaluation Form to Assess a Team's Perceived Effectiveness
Student Evaluation of Student Services Management Team

Student Name: _____

Directions:

Please circle an "A" for each statement you **AGREE** with, and a "D" for each statement you **DISAGREE** with. Please add any comments that will help explain your answer.

The Student :Services Management Team assisted me as follows:

A   D   1. Encouraged me to develop confidence in myself.

A   D   2. Encouraged me to take more responsibility for my actions.

A   D   3. Encouraged me to learn to manage unpleasant feelings (anger, hurt, sadness, fear) more effectively.

A   D   4. Encouraged me to learn to manage problems more effectively.

A   D   5. Encouraged me to make more effective decisions.

A   D   6. Encouraged me to set realistic and achievable goals.

A   D   7. Encouraged me to get along better with my parents.

A   D   8. Encouraged me to get along better with friends.

A   D   9. Encouraged me to get along better with teachers.

A   D   10. Encouraged me to stay in school.

A   D   11. Encouraged me to improve my school attendance.

A   D   12. Encouraged me to improve my attitude toward school.

A   D   13. Encouraged me to improve my classroom behavior.

A   D   14. Encouraged me to improve my grades.

A   D   15. Encouraged me to complete more assignments

A   D   16. Enabled me to receive tutoring.

A   D   17. Encouraged me to organize my time better.

A   D   18. Encouraged me to develop better study habits.

A   D   19. Encouraged me to prepare for tests.

A   D   20. Enabled me to obtain necessary medical/health care.

Comments:

Adapted from an evaluation used at Hawthorne High School, Hawthorne, Florida.

Joe Wittmer, PhD

References

Beder, H. (1984). Interorganizational cooperation: Why and how? *New Directions for Continuing Education, 23,* 3-22.

Gysbers, N.C., & Henderson, P. (1999). *Developing and managing your school guidance program.* Alexandria, VA: American Counseling Association.

Keys, S., Benmark, F., Carpenter, S., & King-Sears, M. (1998). Collaborative consultant: A new role for counselors serving at-risk youths. *Journal of Counseling & Development, 76,* 123-133.

Levy, J.E., & Copple, C. (1989). *Joining forces: A report from the first year.* Alexandria, VA: National Association of State Boards of Education. (ERIC Document Reproduction Service No. ED 308 609.)

Myrick, R.D. (1997). *Developmental guidance and counseling: A practical approach* (3rd ed.). Minneapolis, MN: Educational Media Corporation.

Smaby, M.H., Peterson, T.L., Bergmann, P.E., Zentner-Bacig, K.L., & Swearingen, S. (1990). School-based community intervention: The school counselor as lead consultant for suicide prevention and intervention programs. *The School Counselor, 37,* 370-377.

Ysseldyke, J., Algozzine, B., & Allen, D. (1982). Participation of regular education teachers in special education team decision making. *Exceptional Children, 48,* 365-366.

Chapter 24
Reaching Out: Involving Parents and Community Members in the School Counseling Program

by

Nancy S. Perry

Nancy S. Perry, MS, NCC, NCSC, is the Executive Director of the American School Counselor Association, Alexandria, Virgina. She has been a teacher, counselor, and state supervisor of guidance.

Introduction

School counselors serve a unique position in the education of our young people in that they are charged with serving both the individual student and the environment in which they function. That means, to be truly effective, counselors must reach beyond the school milieu to the families and community which shape the lives of children. Children, especially in their formative years, live within the powerful force of family and community influence. The child and his or her environment are interconnected. The effective school counselor realizes that he or she must understand the *entire* system if the whole child is to be best served. Since developmental school counselors are dedicated to the development of the whole child, they must reach beyond the walls of the school building and actively involve and interact with the families and community.

In this chapter, interactions with parents and families are addressed, and strategies to effectively involve the parents and community in the comprehensive, developmental school counseling program are suggested.

Involving Parents and Families

Without a doubt, parents are the strongest influence in a child's life. Researchers report that parental involvement in a child's education transmits the importance of education to the child, thus enhancing self-esteem and academic achievement. Therefore, it is imperative that parents be actively involved in the school in positive ways which will help them better understand the schooling process.

Every educator knows that the parents most actively involved in their children's education are those whose children are most actively involved in the educational process. Open Houses at school always bring out the parents whose children are doing well. These parents eagerly attend parent-teacher conferences, lead the parent/teacher groups, and volunteer to assist in many ways. This group of parents needs to be nurtured and provided with opportunities to show their support and to extend in-school learning at home. These parents thrive on outside speakers, literature on child development, and information about their children's in-school activities. It is especially important that school counselors explain the guidance curriculum to them in detail as most parents have not experienced such a program themselves. Unfortunately, in many schools parents are not actively involved in their child's education. And, many simply don't want to be involved. Ideas for involving the "resistant" parent are provided later in this chapter.

Orientation to the School Counseling Program

An orientation to the entire school counseling program should always be offered for parents whose children are new to the school. Such a program should include a rationale, objectives, and strategies for involving parents in the program. For example, at the orientation, parents may be requested to complete a short questionnaire to help the counselor in understanding the concerns parents may have with their children about the guidance program. Using the results of this needs assessment, the counselor may decide to form parent support groups around certain issues; invite experts to address major issues listed; provide reading lists or other resources on those issues; or take the issues to the Guidance Program Advisory Council to determine how the needs expressed by the parents can best be met. It is important to have materials used in the guidance curriculum available for parental review at all times. Invite participation and involvement in the program. Most complaints concerning the guidance curriculum come from lack of understanding or information on the part of the parents. Use the opportunity of an orientation meeting with new students' parents to open new avenues of communication.

Guidance Curriculum

Most parents have never experienced affective education. In fact, many may even be concerned about the word "affective." Consider your use of words carefully as unfamiliarity of their usage may trigger negative reactions. Even such terms as "Magic Circle" can bring out fears of voodoo or brain-washing. Some counselors have used terms such as "Learning for Life," or "Responsibility Curriculum" to describe their classroom efforts. These labels seem to be better understood by parents. It is important that parents be aware of each guidance unit, especially at the elementary level. A rule of thumb might be that the younger the child, the more parents need to be involved and informed. Do not assume that just because a program has been in place for five years that it will automatically be accepted. Keep in mind that a school's parental audience is constantly changing.

Parents can be valuable assets to a developmental guidance curriculum, especially when counselors "empower" them to extend the lessons into the home. For example, if one is teaching primary age children about the world of work, together, children and their parents might list the jobs in their home—cooking, cleaning, nurturing, and so forth—and who the particular workers are in the home performing these tasks. The activity will help children develop an appreciation of their home, an understanding of responsibility, and possibly an appreciation of gender equity issues. When teaching effective communication skills to early adolescents, ask for the cooperation of the parents in practicing the skills at home. Invite the parents to a session where they, too, can learn what their children are learning in large group guidance. Parental inclusion or involvement may produce benefits well beyond the teaching of a skill. For example, as eighth graders are beginning to think about educational decisions and careers, have them interview a parent about his or her career pathway from the earliest job up to the present one. Most children think that their parents are doing now what they have always done. In other words, look for opportunities to extend the learning at home in every guidance lesson taught. One middle school guidance department invites the parents of each eighth grader (written invitations) to sit in on an educational planning session regarding high school that a counselor plans to have with their child. This is a routine part of their guidance program and has come to be expected by the eighth graders and their parents alike.

Barriers to Parental Involvement

As noted above, the parents most likely to attend school functions are those least likely to need to be there. They are the parents who demonstrate, in other ways, involvement in their child's education. The parents of the neediest children are often the most difficult to involve in the school. Do not assume that this means that they do not care. Most parents want their children to succeed. However, some parents find it extremely difficult to actually enter the school for many different reasons. It may be due to their own negative experiences in school, or perhaps they are fearful of doing the wrong thing or embarrassing their children. School events might not be scheduled at convenient times when these parents are available and have access to transportation to and from the school. Additionally, their culture or lifestyle may not promote involvement in school activities. If faced with particularly resistant parents, the best strategy may be to practice empathy at the basic level—the counselor puts him/herself into their shoes and acts accordingly!

Some parents are uneasy in large groups. Therefore, opportunities for small group or individual interaction may be the most successful alternative. As a former junior high counselor, I invited every parent of a seventh grader to come to school for coffee in a small group, not to exceed the size needed to accommodate the parents of eight children. I talked about adolescent development, what to expect, and how the school counseling program could help them and their children to master and survive those developmental tasks. I used this opportunity to become acquainted with the parents, to help them know me, and to hear their concerns. It opened communication pathways that still exist sixteen years later as some now call me about their grandchildren! It also garnered the support needed for a comprehensive, developmental school counseling program.

Time spent with parents at this point will pay future dividends. Sending a letter of invitation home may not be enough. Offer a variety of times—morning, afternoon, and evening—to meet, create a comfortable environment, offer light refreshments—food is a wonderful socializer, and provide baby-sitting if at all possible. The writer paid junior high aged students to baby-sit their younger siblings at the school. Follow up the letters of invitation with phone calls when a response is not received. It is wise to state within the letter that the counselor will be calling if no response is given. Receiving such a letter from their child's school counselor *motivates* parents to respond. Be careful not to forget the non-custodial parent in families of divorce. Unless the courts have stated otherwise, both parents should have equal access to and participation in their child's education (see Remley, Chapter 24). Let the parents decide if they want to attend together or separately, but encourage both to be in attendance.

High school counselors may invite parents by class (freshman, sophomore, junior, senior) or by homeroom (depending on class size) to spend an evening using the career resources of the Guidance Office. Have several "stations," such as the computer, video, career books and brochures, and interest surveys set up for parent use. Parents are especially impressed by computerized career information systems and will encourage their children to use the resources if they understand them through their own personal use. Use any method available to get them "hooked" into the guidance program. Small group gatherings for parents provide the foundation for future involvement. And, this writer has found that most are simply waiting for an "invitation" to get involved—ask and they'll show up!

Parenting Education

Many school counselors understand the importance of parenting education but feel overwhelmed at the thought of providing it. One of the most successful methods of offering parenting education is through the adult education program already offered within the school system. There are several excellent syllabi offered commercially or one may develop and construct his or her own program. Convince the school district to provide scholarships for parents unable to afford the small fee. It is especially important to encourage parents of "at-risk" children to attend as a way of working with the counselor and the school to help their child. A more subtle form of parenting education is forming support groups for parents of children who are involved in a counseling group in school. For example, if a target group of children has difficulty with conflict management, form a small group at school to teach conflict resolution skills and then ask their parents to form a group with the counselor to learn the same skills so that they may reinforce them at home. Many parents have difficulty with conflict at home and will welcome the opportunity to work on the issue. It may also give the child an opportunity to get positive attention at home.

Empowering the parents to help their child may be the most important role of a school counselor. And, any effort at parenting education should have the ultimate goal of *empowering* parents in their child-rearing roles. Thus, ample opportunity for open discussion and flexibility to meet emerging needs should be built into the program. Parenting education must be non-judgmental and built on enrichment of skills and growth rather than remediation for failures. It is not a time to "stamp out" their mistakes as parents. The needs of both the parent and the child need to be considered with the focus on the future. Parenting education, especially in families with young children, can truly make a difference in the child's life. It takes counselor time, but it is well worth the effort!

Parent Volunteers

School counselors, like teachers, can often use a helping hand. Parental volunteers may offer on-going assistance or respond to a "one-shot" appearance. Besides the usual field trip chaperons and cookie making duties, counselors may use such volunteers in more creative ways within the guidance program. However, a word of caution is in order since much of what school counselors do is in the realm of confidential information. Particular care must be taken with who gains access to student records. The Family Education Rights and Privacy Act (FERPA) is very clear about who may view and have access to student records (see Remley, Chapter 24). It may be better not to give such responsibilities to volunteers. However, under any circumstances, parent volunteers should understand that "What's says here, stays here." As the school counselor, one has an obligation to protect the privacy of his or her students.

Parents are particularly helpful in career development activities. They may share their expertise or experiences with classes or help facilitate the use of computer-assisted career or college exploration and information giving activities. You may call on a parent for expertise in designing a computer program to fit your needs, or to provide job shadowing experiences for a student. Many working parents want to assist but cannot obligate themselves to regular volunteerism. Solicit information early in the school year about special skills or talents that parents are willing to share. Give away as much of your job as is ethically possible and responsible. You will always have more than you can handle. Work yourself out of a job when and where appropriate by utilizing parents and others in your developmental counseling program.

Newsletters

Regular letters or notices to parents and the schools' community can build support for your school counseling program and bring about needed involvement in the program. At the high school level, a calendar of college and employer visits, important testing deadlines, and informative workshops can keep parents and community members informed. At the elementary level, information about guidance units in process will keep parents aware. However, the newsletter also offers opportunities to educate. Write articles about issues that concern parents such as "Signs of Substance Abuse," "Motivating the Under-achiever," "Understanding the Shy Child," "Communicating With Your Teenager," and so forth. Share resources such as magazine articles or books that provide effective hints for everyday problems—bibliotherapy works with parents! Present child-raising issues and ask for strategies to handle them from the parent readers. For example, many parents are concerned about the TV-watching habits of their children. One creative mother said that she allowed her children to watch anything they wanted. However, they had to write a short review of every program watched. This certainly led to more discriminating viewing on the part of the children and simultaneously enhanced their writing skills.

The written word is a powerful tool and an inexpensive way to involve parents in your school guidance program. Know the type of parents whose children attend your school—poor, wealthy, culturally different, and so forth, and develop the guidance newsletter accordingly. If your school has a large Hispanic population, for example, ask for a parent volunteer to translate the newsletter into Spanish. This will acknowledge the diversity of the school's population, reveal that you value diversity, and help you to reach *all* parents.

Advisory Council

As noted several times in this book, a Guidance Advisory Council is your official link to the needs and wishes of the community. This council usually consists of representatives of those populations which you serve. Typical membership might include teachers, administrators, special service providers (nurse, social worker, school psychologist, etc.), parents, community official, business/industry representatives, a law enforcement official, clergy, and a school board member. Middle and secondary levels may also want to include student members. The role of the Advisory Council is to make recommendations, in an advisory capacity, for guidance programming based on perceived student needs and available resources. Time and patience are required to educate the Advisory Council as

to the purposes and scope of a comprehensive school counseling program, but the political support, public relations, and procurement of resources that may result from such widespread community support provide the incentives to make it work.

School Board

You work for the School Board, School Committee, or whatever your governing body is within your specific school system. Ultimately, on the recommendations of administrators, they can make or break your program. Therefore, it is in your best interest to assure that they are well-informed and supportive of your school guidance program. Such communication should be on-going in the form of interesting newsletters delineating the activities of your program, minutes of Advisory Council meetings, and so forth. Keep administrators informed. However, most boards want hard data documenting that what counselors are doing is the best use of school time and available resources.

Accountability is important, both quantitative and qualitative. One strategy to deliver numbers is to keep a daily record of activities. This can be done easily by setting up a data-base on the computer and filling in the blanks at the end of each day. This might include the number of students seen in classroom guidance, small groups, individual counseling, peer advisors, consultation with parents, teachers, administrators, committee meetings, and so forth. At the end of a period, month or quarter, total the numbers and report them to your principal with copies to the superintendent and school board. Even you will probably be surprised at the number of student contacts you have made. Generally speaking, providing others in authority with such "head counts" pays off in the long run. However, we must also assure our public that we perform "quality" work through supplying the community with "hard," supportive data.

Qualitatively, one of the easiest and most effective strategies this writer has observed was by a practicing K-8 counselor who conducts classroom guidance at all grade levels. At the end of each guidance lesson, she asks the students to list three things they have learned that day and then she writes them on the board (and keeps them for later). Since this is done every time, even the five year olds know that they must listen to learn. This also allows the counselor time to reinforce any important learnings and to correct any misunderstandings. At the end of a unit, the counselor reports to the Board, and others via the newsletter, what the purpose of the unit was and what the children said they learned. It is very impressive to have the children's own words giving value to their learning experiences. These can also be shared with your principal, school board, and so forth.

School Board members often wonder aloud if the money spent to send educators to conferences or workshops is a good use of dwindling financial resources. Continuing professional development is important but counselors seldom convey that message to those who make the decisions. Therefore, it is important that counselors let them know what benefit they derive from participating in such activities. One sure-fire method is a simple thank-you note to the Board for allowing the counselor time and/or financial support to attend a conference. The counselor might include a reference to a session that was of particular value in helping him or her to be a better, more effective counselor. Let the Board know the professional impact this conference had and ultimately, it's value to the students in the school. Another strategy is to write an article for the school/guidance newsletter, or do an in-service for others sharing one's newly acquired knowledge. These are tangible benefits to an employer and future insurance that one will be able to continue his or her professional development.

Arrange to periodically update the School Board on the counseling program with numbers, stories, and future needs. As an example, you might talk about the number of teenage pregnancies you have dealt with in the past quarter, the resolution of issues involved, and the trend toward increasing numbers. Then, when presenting a proposal for a new program to meet this need, they will be better prepared to listen and support your request. Their approval is your job guarantee.

Community

Schools are generally community-based and community supported. People often make choices of where to live based on the reputation of schools. School budgets are the major topic of conversation every spring. Community members who do not have children in school are also often the most vocal and least informed. Therefore, it is important to let the public know what you are doing and why their support is valued. Service organizations such as the Kiwanis or Lion's Clubs, church fellowships, town councils, and others are usually eager to learn what is happening locally. Let them know you are available and plan to be on their program as a speaker at a time when you are *not* making a request for something. Then, when you do need their support, they will be more willing to listen. When provided the opportunity, talk about what the major issues

facing young people today are and relate the issues to your school counseling program. *Don't be afraid to blow your own horn.* If you're doing good things, don't be modest about them. How else will they learn about your accomplishments?

Such groups can also be a resource when needed for special programs in your school. Mentoring is a meaningful way to involve community members in your program. Intergenerational bonds can be formed when children adopt a grandparent from a nursing home or vice versa. Contacts for job shadowing and career days can also be found in such organizations. Don't be afraid to ask, or assume that someone is too busy to help the children in your school. People want to be proud of their schools and their community. Give them the opportunity to get involved.

School Counselors as Change Agents

It is generally accepted that school counselors serve as change agents for individual students, faculty and others. They work with students and others to bring about a desired or agreed upon outcome. This usually means some kind of behavior or performance change in the individual. Although school counselors interact with specific individuals to bring about internal change, they are also concerned with the environment in which their students operate. That environment may be defined as the collective perceptions of those who work and learn there. The environment can be described as good, poor, relaxed, restrictive, creative, or any variety of adjectives. A term often used to describe this set of perceptions is "school climate." Just as the system itself is affected by the external forces acting upon it, the members of the system—students, staff, parents community—are affected by what occurs around them in the internal environment. Counselors know that physical and psychological safety and comfort are important to the learning process. Therefore, the counselor's task to help students become better learners means that he or she must be as concerned with the school climate as with the other forces that impact on the individual. The motivation and behavior of students are directly related to the environment in which they operate. The question is not *whether* the school counselor should act as a change agent for the school climate, but *how* the school counselor can make a positive difference in the school's climate. Counselors serve as the "catalyst" for school climates more conducive to learning.

Some counselors may feel that they are not in a power position to effect change in the school environment. However, as a school counselor, you are uniquely positioned to "see the big picture." You hear from students, parents, teachers, members of the community, and administrators, and, not being a part of the authority hierarchy, you are more likely to hear honest feelings and perceptions. And, the more favorably this population perceives the climate in which they interact, the easier your job will be to effect change in the individual. For example, if the school staff feel that they are treated as professionals, they will be more willing to take that extra step to accomplish the goals of the individual student or the school. If parents feel that the school staff really cares about the welfare of their children, they will be more open to listening and cooperating with recommendations made on behalf of their children. The same can be said regarding other members of the community. A positive and healthy school climate is the key for individual change and improvement.

In a counseling relationship, the counselor usually assesses the problem, determines the desired change or outcome with the client, and then works on strategies/ interventions to effect the change. The same process is appropriate in effecting change in a system. The problem is identified, the desired outcome is determined and the strategies for effecting the change are considered. The principal difference for the school counselor is that the strategies may need to be delegated to those who have the *power* to make the change. For example, assigned seats in the junior high cafeteria during lunch may be an effective management technique but such a practice is depriving the emerging adolescents of one of the few opportunities to satisfy their need to socialize with friends of their choice. Therefore, as the human development specialist in the school, use your facilitative skills in bringing this concern to the attention of your principal.

Raising the awareness level of the administration and other staff as to the developmental needs of the students can be a valuable consideration in establishing a positive school climate. Effective counselors meet with the top administrator regularly to discuss climate issues and provide in-service for the staff on relevant topics affecting the school's climate (e.g., conducting a multicultural communication workshop). There are many other ways to effect change. One counselor, frustrated by the resistance of teachers in allowing students to participate in small group counseling, formed a support group for teachers. As the teachers recognized the value of the small growth group experience in their lives, they were more willing to support such involvement for their students. School counselors can be advocates for change by reaching out to parent groups,

service clubs, and businesses, and seeking their support for programs that will enhance the overall learning environment. Of course, as noted earlier, a knowledgeable school board may be the strongest ally for supporting and initiating change in a school.

School counselors are change agents, individually and systemically. Their knowledge of human development and relationships can be invaluable in garnering the support of others to create the kind of school climate that nurtures learning.

Summary

The current reform movements are centering more and more on the need to provide community services within the school and making the school the center of the community. The educational community is finally realizing that it cannot fragment a child's life by separating their physical, emotional/social, and cognitive development into small, convenient niches. As human development specialists, school counselors must reach out to "parents as partners." They must work together in the best interest of the child. School counselors need to involve parents, educators, and community members in their developmental guidance program if it is to be truly responsive to the needs of all students. Comprehensive, developmental school counseling programs lead the way for educational reform. It is up to the counselors to let others know what services they provide and how they positively affect students' growth and abilities to learn.

Figure 24.1
Tips for Parent Conferences

School counselors are frequently asked to participate in parent-teacher conferences. This list of helpful tips, which appeared in *The ASCA Counselor*, will enhance your work with parents.

Do....

- Arrange for an uninterrupted private session.
- Be as friendly and relaxed as possible.
- Explain that the child's behavior and school performance are the result of many variables.
- Describe the performance of students as precisely as possible.
- Emphasize the child's strengths and assets leading to realistic suggestions for improvements.
- Provide time to ask questions and encourage interruptions.
- Ask for parents' help and cooperation.
- Gain insights into parents' attitude toward child.
- Listen to what parents have to say without showing alarm, disgust, or disapproval.
- Encourage children to attend; Include them in the problem solving process.

Don't....

- Dwell on the inadequacies, such as intelligence, and so forth.
- Sit behind a desk.
- Answer questions in reference to administration or school policies unless you are absolutely accurate.
- Assume full responsibility for the child's education. Do stress the parents' role.
- Use misleading technical terms (parents will seldom ask for explanations).
- Discuss other teachers, students, or administration unless positive.
- Argue with parents.
- Criticize parents' effectiveness, even subtly.
- Assume parents want advice.
- Forget how you would feel as a parent. (Fox, R. *The ASCA Counselor*, ASCA, Alexandria, VA, December, 1991).

Figure 24.2
Food for Thought: PR for Parent Involvement

The following appeared in *The ASCA Counselor* (1992), and provided some excellent strategies for involving parents in school programs.

The recent dramatic increase in parent involvement and citizen interest in Maine's public schools puzzled some folks. But the statewide grocery chain was not surprised because they had recently tucked one of the brightly colored brochures called "Your schools won't make the grade without YOU," into every shopper's grocery bag. The brochure, developed by the Maine State Board of Education, was full of ideas for all to get involved in the schools. More than 200,000 brochures made their way into Maine homes and response was immediately gratifying.

Counselors in several Maine schools have had offers from brochure-inspired volunteers to assist with their work and requests from business and civic leaders offering career awareness activities. The following points to parents were taken from the Maine brochure:

To Parents: Your Schools Won't Make the Grade Without You

Get involved. If you believe that education is important, if you care about children, if you care about the future of Maine, get involved in your schools. You can make a difference.

In Schools

- Volunteer as a classroom assistant, as a tutor, as a library aide; share a hobby or skill; show slides from a trip; serve as a resource for local history
- Be an audience for children
- Attend school events
- Get to know a teacher or administrator
- Be a mentor or a special friend to a child
- Attend parent conferences
- Request parenting classes and discussion groups

At Home

- Show your children that you care about their education
- Provide books and a place for studying
- Make reading a family activity
- Establish high expectations for children
- Show an interest in your child's progress
- Discuss schoolwork with children
- Establish rules and let children know what they are
- Be consistent in discipline matters
- Monitor television time
- Observe routines for meals, bedtime, and homework
- Provide good nutrition and health care
- Continue your own education
- Learn about appropriate toys and activities for your child's age level
- Help children learn to make decisions
- Give children time to play
- Limit the number of hours your child can work in after school jobs

At Work

- Invite a class to visit the workplace
- Share information about your occupation with students
- Develop company policy encouraging parents to attend school conferences and activities
- Release employees to volunteer in the schools
- Talk with educators about the curriculum needed for success in your job
- Give a child his or her first job
- Stay in touch with student employee needs
- Limit the number of hours students can work in after school jobs
- Be a mentor
- Donate toward scholarships, books, equipment, class trips
- Offer internships to teachers and students

In the Community

- Join PTA/PTO or get one started
- Serve on an advisory council or a study committee
- Attend School Board meetings
- Run for the School Board
- Vote on school related issues
- Learn more about the schools in your town

You Want to Help but You Don't Have Much Time

- Get your service club or organization to make supporting schools a priority
- Take a teacher to lunch
- Make a donation
- Write a thank you note to a teacher or school administrator
- Vote in federal, state, local elections

You can make a world of difference and a difference in our world by becoming actively involved in your schools. (Adapted from *The ASCA Counselor*, December, 1992).

Section VII

Accountability, Public Relations, Ethical and Legal Issues, Technology, and School Counselor Professionalism

Being accountable within the developmental counseling program has been a central theme throughout this book. In Chapter 25, Dr. John Schmidt advocates that school counselors *must* assume the leadership role in designing and conducting evaluation procedures as it concerns the counseling program. He writes: *As a school counselor, you have responsibility for evaluating your program, reporting the results, and suggesting changes to address the findings of the evaluation process. Without an accountability process, you run the risk of failing to address the needs and expectations of the students, parents, and teachers you serve. In doing so, you threaten the program's value and jeopardize your reputation as a significant and essential member of the school team. Comprehensive school counseling programs are essential to today's schools, and adequate program accountability and accurate counselor performance appraisal verify the importance of these services.*

Dr. Schmidt presents several easy to understand and use evaluation procedures, techniques, and processes that contribute to a counselor's ability to be accountable.

In Chapter 26, Dr. Harry Daniels and Ms. Diane Daniels, present a step-by-step process that school counselors can use to document their counseling services. They address the importance of documenting service delivery and provide examples of strategies for doing so.

Selling, promoting, and marketing the developmental counseling program is essential to its survival and a deliberate, planned public relations program is needed. In Chapter 27, I present such a structured PR approach along with the strategies and techniques to ensure the successful promotion of a K-12 counseling program. Several unique, "workable" PR ideas and concepts suggested by others are also presented at the end of the chapter.

Dr. Theodore Remley and Ms. Mary Herman (Chapter 28) address the ethical and legal issues facing school counselors today. They indicate that professional counselors in all settings increasingly are finding the legal and ethical issues they face to be complex and challenging. Although problems related to the law and ethical standards may be difficult for counselors in various agencies, school counselors are regularly confronted with the most difficult issues on a daily basis.

Remley and Herman state: *There are two basic reasons why school counselors have substantial problems addressing legal and ethical issues. First, K-12 school counselors offer services most often to minors and the law and professional ethical standards are inadequate regarding a practical resolution of the competing interests of children and the adults who are responsible for their welfare. In addition, despite the fact that dual relationships are prohibited in counseling, counselors in schools have multiple roles and interact with a variety of individuals who demand their professional services.*

They also address minors as clients, custody cases, nonlegal parents, child abuse laws, and so forth. He also provides some excellent guidelines for the school counselor facing an ethical or legal problem.

In the next chapter, Dr. Tom Clawson, in writing about the school counselor and the importance of appropriate credentialing, states: *As school counseling continues to strengthen, the profession has created ways to symbolize our professionalism and show our public that we care to meet higher and higher standards. The best way to show your publics that you are indeed a professional is to seek the appropriate state and national credentialing. It is a major part of being a "professional" in the true sense of the word.*

Dr. Clawson aptly defines several, sometimes confusing, credentialing terms, discusses the importance of appropriate credentialing for school counselors, and discusses several credentialing concerns facing the school counselor.

Dr. Russell Sabella (Chapter 30) does an excellent job in writing about the impact that technology will play in the role of the school counselor in the next millennium.

Section VII concludes with a brief chapter (31) concerning the school counselor and professionalism as developed by Dr. Beverly O'Bryant. Drs. O'Bryant, a longtime proponent of school counselor professionalism, offers some excellent tips (and a "quiz") to school counselors desiring to enhance their professional images.

Joe Wittmer

Chapter 25
Counselor Accountability: Justifying Your Time and Measuring Your Worth
by
John J. Schmidt

John J. Schmidt, EdD, is Professor and Chair of the Counselor and Adult Education Department at East Carolina University, Greenville, NC. His career includes experience as a teacher, counselor, director of counseling services, and state coordinator of school counseling programs.

Introduction

In a comprehensive program, school counselors offer a wide range of services and activities to students, parents, and teachers. One challenge that counselors face in determining which services to provide and how much time to devote to specific activities is in designing procedures for assessing priorities, monitoring the use of time, and evaluating the effects of their services. These are processes that contribute to a counselor's ability to be accountable. In this chapter you will learn about accountability processes and how they help you as a school counselor set program goals, link these goals to specific services, and measure how well you meet objectives.

The importance of accountability in school counseling emerged in the 1970s and 1980s, and continues today as an essential element of comprehensive school counseling programs (Aubrey, 1982; Schmidt, 1991, 1999). The same national events and legislative actions that encouraged the identification and evaluation of effective schools have fueled discussion about how important it is for counselors "to demonstrate clearly *what* they do and *how well* they do it" (Schmidt, 1999, p. 256). Some counselors are hesitant to design and implement accountability processes. In part, this is because they are so busy performing important functions, that so little time is available to evaluate how effectively they deliver services. Also, school counseling relationships and services are so varied, and at times so personal, that it is difficult to assess counselor's effectiveness or measure the broad impact of a comprehensive program of services. Nevertheless, school counselors must accept responsibility for identifying the important services of their programs and evaluating the effectiveness of those services. This stance is imperative if we expect school counseling to continue as a credible profession and as an essential component of educational programs.

As a practicing school counselor, you share this responsibility. Your willingness to identify your role in the school, account for the time you allot to specific activities, and measure whether or not these services make a difference in the lives of students, parents, and teachers adds to the efficacy of the profession.

Accountability Processes

A counselor's accountability begins with an assessment of needs of students, parents, and teachers who are being served by the school counseling program. The importance of needs' assessment was addressed earlier in this book (Chapter 2). It is from this assessment that school counselors, administrators, and advisory committees make decisions about program goals, learning objectives, and specific services. At the same time, they assign responsibilities for delivering these services. As seen in the descriptions of comprehensive school counseling programs throughout this book, many people—counselors, teachers, and others—have a variety of responsibilities to fulfill for a comprehensive, developmental program to be successful. In addition to needs' assessment, accountability includes the assessment of activities, surveys of students, parents, and teachers, self-rating scales by counselors, performance appraisal of counselors by supervisors and principals, and time management procedures (Schmidt, 1990, 1999). In this chapter you will learn about these procedures by focusing on two aspects of accountability: program evaluation and counselor effectiveness. Each of these has specific purpose within the broad arena of counselor accountability.

Purpose of Evaluation

The processes that you create to evaluate your school counseling program and to measure your effectiveness as a counselor have three major purposes. First, they are used to gather evidence to support your position as a counselor in the school and make a case for comprehensive school counseling services. Second, adequate evaluations enable you to participate in research that advances the counseling profession. Lastly, when you develop and implement reasonable methods of accountability, you gather data about your performance with which to enhance your professional development.

There are countless methods of evaluation to create, adopt, and adapt. The methods you choose can focus on either a single purpose or address several. Before you decide which evaluative methods to adopt in your program, some general guidelines are worth considering.

Evaluation Guidelines

1. Everyone involved in a school counseling program has a role in the evaluation process. In comprehensive, developmental programs, students, parents, and teachers, should all partake and contribute to the evaluation process. It may be that the evaluation methods you design would not include all these groups for every service you assess, but generally you seek participation from everyone who uses services in the program. In addition, you want to receive information and feedback from your principal, counseling supervisor, and yourself about the progress of your program and the success of particular services.

2. The goals and objectives of your school counseling program must be clearly defined with consensus among those who participate in and benefit from the program. As noted in previous chapters, a clear description of your program goals and objectives helps students, parents, teachers, and administrators understand your unique role in the school. In addition, it enables them (your publics) to assess accurately the effectiveness with which you implement services to reach those goals and objectives.

3. Program evaluation is most beneficial when the methods and procedures used to gather data emphasize positive aspects of your services. In other words, you want to plan methods of evaluation that focus on the benefits of counseling and consulting services. While it is helpful to discover weaknesses and deficiencies and to correct these defects, it is more important to determine whether or not the services you provide have met program goals and satisfied the populations you serve.

4. The instruments and processes you develop to gather data about the counseling and consulting services you deliver should generate valid measures of what you do and how well you meet program goals and objectives. It serves little purpose to develop instruments and processes that do not reliably show how you spend your time and whether or not your services effectively help others. That is, such instruments and processes should be locally appropriate.

5. Guard your time carefully, and be cautious about creating accountability procedures and methods of assessment that consume too much time to administer, or an inordinate amount of time to score. Because time is such a precious commodity for counselors, teachers, and others who work in school

settings, it should not be squandered needlessly. You want to design clear and efficient procedures because "accountability methods that are cumbersome, time-consuming, and confusing overwhelm us and detract from the primary services for which we are responsible" (Schmidt, 1991, p. 7). Streamline your evaluation procedures to use as little time as possible, while simultaneously generating useful results.

6. Program evaluation is a continuous process developed and executed throughout the year to illustrate the importance of comprehensive counseling services and to identify your role as a school counselor. For this reason, evaluation processes are an ongoing aspect of a comprehensive program and not simply a temporary response to administrative requests or public outcries for accountability.

7. Evaluation of school counselors, by definition, enables the school to demonstrate that the services of a comprehensive school counseling program advance the mission of the school to educate all students and to provide them equal opportunity to learn. In this sense, evaluation of counselors should be more than simply noting the strength and weaknesses of performance or gathering data to take personnel action. Counselor performance appraisal should be an additional avenue within which to explore the relationship between program goals and the services offered. In sum, your annual evaluation is another means of examining whether or not you have achieved program goals that help the school towards its ultimate mission. For this reason, it is essential that you accept responsibility for gathering some of the data and information used in your performance appraisal each year.

8. All evaluation is predicated on the belief that action is forthcoming. Planning, developing, and implementing accountability procedures without hope of follow-through and appropriate action is a senseless and needless waste of time. Part of your responsibility as a counselor is to decide how to use the results of your program evaluation and the assessment of your own effectiveness. What program changes are indicated? What services should receive more emphasis? Which aspects of your program should be adjusted to satisfy needs of students, parents, and teachers? Questions such as these are addressed and appropriate action is taken as an integral part of the evaluation process.

The preceding guidelines, generated and adapted from various sources (Atkinson, Furlong, & Janoff, 1979; Fairchild, 1986; Krumboltz, 1974; Schmidt, 1991, 1999; Stronge & Helm, 1991), illustrate the importance of developing a clear plan and purpose for accountability processes. They are a framework to guide you in this planning process. In the remaining sections of this chapter you will learn about specific procedures to use in program evaluation and for measuring your own effectiveness as a school counselor. I begin with aspects of program evaluation.

Program Evaluation

There are countless ways that counselors and their supervisors design and carry out program evaluation. In this section, you will read about strategies to help you, the school counselor, focus on what you do, whether or not you reach identified goals, and the degrees to which students, parents, and teachers are satisfied with the services you deliver. As noted in earlier chapters, program planning and organizing consist of the identification of specific goals to address various aspects of student development. These goals include personal adjustment, academic achievement, career development, and social skills learning, among others. As a counselor who guides the school in the selection of these goals, you have responsibility to assess whether or not these objectives are achieved during the year.

Goal Achievement

The goals you set for your school counseling program evolve from an analysis of the annual needs assessment done with students, parents, and teachers. They also reflect local school system objectives established by the administration and state initiatives planned by state boards of education, state departments of education, and state legislatures. In most instances, the procedures for evaluating whether or not these goals are met rests with the individual school counselor.

Some goals relate to specific information, skills, or tasks to be learned by students. For example, a goal in a middle school might indicate: *all eighth grade students will learn about the requirements for high school graduation*. Evaluation of this type of goal requires that you design particular processes and instruments that will indicate whether or not students know and understand what courses they need to take in high school and other requirements related to graduation. Such processes might include a survey of students asking them about high school requirements or an assessment of how efficient these students are in responding to preregistration for ninth grade classes. Figure 25.1 illustrates a survey used by a middle school counselor to follow up presentations conducted regarding high school graduation requirements. Analysis of students' responses to this questionnaire enables the counselor to report how well this learning goal was met by students after hearing the presentation (Figure 25.1).

Sometimes the goals you select for your counseling program relate to specific services. As an example, if several parents express an interest in learning more about preadolescent behavior and development, you might set a goal to plan and present educational programs for parents of middle school students. To meet this goal you might design and implement parent education seminars throughout the year. Evaluation of this goal could consist simply of counting the number of sessions held and the number of parents who attended these meetings. While this type of evaluation does not reflect the *quality* of your presentation, it does indicate how you spent your time meeting this goal and the number of people who attended. These kinds of assessments are important to show people where and how you allot your time, the types of services you deliver to address identified goals, and the number of students, parents, and teachers (a head count) you served in the process of meeting these goals; all aspects of being accountable. Without these types of quantitative summaries, people may not understand the multitude of services you offer in a comprehensive school counseling program, the time you spend in delivering these services, and the proportion of the school population that benefits from these helping relationships. By offering these types of data, you demonstrate the breadth of your program and the range of issues addressed by your services. At the same time, you analyze your use of time, and assess where to make adjustments so that your efficiency increases. Many school systems ask counselors to complete a monthly report of activities they use in their programs. If this is true in your school system, a monthly report form is probably available. If not, you may want to design a form of your own so that you can assess and report on the services you deliver. Figure 25.2 illustrates a sample monthly report form for an elementary school counselor. You can adapt this form to fit your particular situation (Figure 25.2).

While processes and reports that account for time and assess broad program goals are essential in establishing your identity and monitoring efficient use of your time, they do not adequately speak to the issue of counselor effectiveness. In planning accountability processes, it is equally important to examine how well particular services meet intended goals. To do so, you will want to assess the outcome of the services and activities in your school counseling program. It is especially important to assess student outcomes of the counseling services and other activities you design and deliver.

Student Outcomes

Throughout this book, you have read that a comprehensive school counseling program assists students with a myriad of learning problems, developmental issues, career concerns, academic concerns, information gathering, behavioral adjustment, and other goals. When you as the school counselor plan and deliver services to help particular students reach specific goals, it is imperative to evaluate whether or not these students succeed. For example, if you organize group counseling sessions to assist students with peer relationships, it is important that you establish some evaluative process to determine whether the students have improved their interactions with others and enhanced their peer relationships. Without such assessment, no one can say that this service has been beneficial to the students.

There are several methods of measuring student outcomes, and some methods are more practical for school counselors to use than others. Here I will briefly describe four procedures for measuring student outcomes. The first method uses prepared standards issued by the local school, district-wide school system, or state board of education. For example, a predetermined standard might state: *Over half of all the students will achieve an attendance rate of 95% for the school year.* If a school counselor planned services to address students' attendance during the year, the counselor could measure success by compiling the absentee rates of participating students and comparing the results to this prearranged standard.

Another method of measuring student outcomes uses a "control group" or "waiting group" procedure. In this procedure, the counselor establishes one group of students who will receive services first while a second group waits to receive the same services later. Data are collected on both groups at the beginning of the program and then again after the first group finishes. The counselor examines the results to determine if there are any changes in the first group and if any differences exist between the first group and the second group. If differences are found, the counselor then provides the same service to the second group and again measures any changes after the students participate in the program. When you design this type of evaluation and find that changes do occur, you establish a reasonable level of certainty that the service has had a beneficial impact on students. By evaluating activities in this way, you make a stronger claim regarding the value of counseling and consulting services in the school program.

A third type of outcome evaluation asks students to assess their participation in particular services or activities, or requests parents and teachers to provide feedback about changes they have observed among students who have participated in a specific program. This method often employs the use of checklists, rating scales, and surveys to gather data from students, parents, and teachers. As with other types of self-assessment instruments and processes, reliability and validity are essential conditions for drawing accurate conclusions (Schmidt, 1999). You can design your own school appropriate instruments or use ones designed and validated by others. In either case, you want to be comfortable with the reliability of the forms you choose to use. Figure 25.3 illustrates a sample questionnaire designed by a counselor to assess students' reactions to participation in group counseling sessions (Figure 25.3).

One type of outcome assessment that is useful to school counselors is to conduct a study using a pretest and post-test comparison. This type of evaluation can be used with individual cases or with groups of students. To begin, you gather data about the individual student or group regarding the specific problem or concern to be addressed. For example, if you were beginning to work with a student who was fighting much of the time at school, you might first ask the teacher to collect baseline data to assess the frequency of fighting. Once these data were collected, you would begin an intervention such as individual counseling. After several counseling sessions in which you and the student focused on the use of fighting to solve differences, and also explored alternative forms of problem solving, you would again ask the teacher to gather data for the same length of time that the baseline data were collected. A comparison of the "before counseling" data with "post counseling" data would enable you, the student, and the teacher to note any improvement in behavior and any use of alternative strategies for resolving differences.

Sometimes, counselors demonstrate sufficient success with student outcomes, yet struggle to prove themselves to their teaching colleagues, administrators, parents, or the community at large. In part, this lack of approval may come from the uncertainty people have about the counselor's role in the school, and this, in turn, results in indecision about the value of counseling services. For this reason, it is important that, in addition to goal attainment, and student outcomes, counselors also seek input from students, parents, teachers, and administrators about their satisfaction with services.

Consumer Satisfaction

Comprehensive school counseling programs include a wide range of services for students, parents, and teachers. In a sense, as noted throughout this book, these three groups are the primary consumers served in a school counseling program. As such, another method of accountability is to gather information from these three groups and summarize their opinions about the services they have received. In contrast to some of the *empirical* measures proposed earlier for assessing goal achievement and student outcomes, consumer satisfaction consists in large part of *perceptual* measures gathered through informal interviews or more formal surveys with students, parents, and teachers (Myrick, 1997; Schmidt, 1999).

Given the diverse and expanded services counselors offer in a comprehensive school counseling program, it is unrealistic to conceive evaluative procedures that empirically assess the level of attainment for all program goals or the degree of effectiveness for every service provided. Some measures of goal achievement and student outcomes are necessary to demonstrate the value of particular counseling and consulting processes. However, if you spend all your time designing and implementing these types of evaluations, you will find little time to actually offer the services of your comprehensive program. Therefore, the methods you choose for assessing consumer perceptions about your program complement the empirical measures you use.

When you design surveys for students, parents, and teachers, it is important to make them clear, understandable, and easy to complete. Think of questionnaires you have received in the past and recall your reactions to them. If they seemed too intimidating or too long, you probably ignored them. In most instances, people discard surveys that appear threatening or are time-consuming to answer. For this reason, it is essential to design surveys that are brief and "user friendly."

The first step in developing questionnaires to evaluate your counseling services is to decide *what* you want to know. In a comprehensive school counseling program it may be impossible for you to assess every aspect each year. Therefore, you might focus on different components of the program each year, and design different instruments depending on the focus you choose. For example, you might decide to assess student, parent, and teachers' opinions about group counseling services. If so, the instruments you create would contain similar items about group counseling to which all three groups would respond. Figures 25.4, 25.5, and 25.6 illustrate sample questionnaires for students, parents, and teachers with an emphasis on group counseling services.

Reporting Results

You will notice from these sample surveys for students, parents, and teachers that they contain some parallel items. By designing surveys in this way, you are able to check perceptions across all three populations about similar issues related to student development. For example, on the sample surveys illustrated here, the counselor assesses how the students, parents, and teachers perceive adherence to confidentiality. (See items 7, 11, and 5 on the respective questionnaires.)

Differences in levels of satisfaction across these three groups will help the counselor plan strategies to explain the importance of maintaining confidences in counselor-student relationships. At the same time, this information will help the school counselor identify groups that may need to have more feedback about ongoing counseling services than they are currently receiving. Of course, sharing of information must be done in a way that maintains confidentiality when appropriate to do so.

One final note about designing and using survey questionnaires in program accountability is appropriate here. Depending on the size of your school populations, it may not be necessary to have every student, parent, or teacher complete a questionnaire. Sample groups of students and parents may be sufficient to give you an overall picture of consumer satisfaction and program effectiveness. In sampling your populations be careful to randomly select participants, thereby avoiding a biased and inaccurate view of your program. For most school counseling programs, I advise selecting a sample of students and parents, but recommend including *all teachers* in these types of surveys. The exact size of your sample will be influenced in part by the methods available to you for tallying the results. If you have access to electronic or computer scoring systems, larger samples are more feasible.

In this section I have offered different methods of program evaluation for your consideration. Assessing program goals, measuring student outcomes, and evaluating consumer satisfaction are ways of gathering data to enable you, the counselor, to take stock of your program, account for your time, and determine whether the direction you have chosen meets the needs and expectations of the groups you serve. How you *use* these results is as important as the processes you design for collecting data. Program evaluation is incomplete if the results obtained are not shared with the people who benefit from the program, and with the administrators who make decisions about hiring counselors and expanding school counseling services. In addition, the evaluation is incomplete if changes are indicated by the results, but not incorporated into the program. In being accountable, part of your responsibility is to use these results in an appropriate manner.

To determine how you will use the *results* of various program evaluation procedures it is best to begin with the *purposes* for which you designed and implemented the evaluation. Earlier in this chapter I identified three major purposes for evaluation: (1) to support your position as counselor in a comprehensive school counseling program; (2) to provide research about effective services that advances the school counseling profession; and (3) to examine areas of skill development, knowledge, and understanding that will expand and enhance your professional development. The methods you choose to report the findings of your ongoing and annual evaluations can support each of these goals. For example, by posting the summary of each monthly report (see Figure 25.2) in the front office near the teachers' mail boxes or in the faculty lounge on the bulletin board, you show your colleagues where your time is being spent; who is doing what and how effectively! By sharing this information with teachers, non-teaching staff and administrators you remove all mystery about what goes on in the counseling program, and you verify that the services being offered are ones that address the *important* goals set by the school. This will assist you and your program's reputation, both in and outside the teachers' lounge.

By the same token, a summary of students and parents' evaluations demonstrates how they perceive the counseling program and what services they believe to be most important. These reports allow you, the counselor, to take control of your program by making decisions that reflect the needs and desires of students, parents, and teachers whom you serve. In this way, you avoid the pitfall of serving only a single group, or restricting your program to a narrowly defined mission. By sharing these types of evaluation reports, "counselors take control of *who* they are and *what* services they should offer in helping students reach their educational, personal, and career goals" (Schmidt, 1999, p. 266). At the same time, when you share these results, you inform others of the perceptions of all the groups who are being served by the school counseling program.

Sometimes the results you report will not show a positive reaction to services in the program. Sharing these negative findings can be as powerful as reporting positive results, particularly when you demonstrate an acceptance of these perceptions and illustrate plans for change. Counselors who demonstrate a willingness to listen to other points of view and make appropriate adjustments in their programs win many allies and cultivate strong support for their services.

Evaluations that demonstrate the effectiveness of particular counseling and consulting services contribute to the identification and authenticity of the school counseling profession. Avenues by which you can share these types of results include columns in your school and town newspapers, a counselor's website, articles in your state counselor's newsletter, research publications in state and national journals, and reports for your local school board about effective services. All of these reporting processes help to identify and clarify the counselor's role in school and demonstrate the efficacy of comprehensive counseling services.

Lastly, the types of evaluation procedures encouraged in this chapter enable you to examine skills and areas of knowledge in which you excel in addition to ones for which you need additional training or other technical assistance. School counseling, as with many other professions, is an emerging field of study. The issues that students, parents, teachers and administrators face today may not be the same issues they will confront in the future. For this reason, effective counselors continuously assess their knowledge and skills, and seek avenues to enhance their professional development. By sharing evaluation results with your principal and supervisor, you gather ammunition to make a case for assistance and support from the school or school system. This support might come in the form of financial assistance to pay for graduate course work or registration at a counselor's workshop. Similarly, it might come in the form of paid leave to attend classes or participate in a national symposium. However, unless you can demonstrate this need with hard data, the chances of obtaining such assistance are probably remote.

In some instances, your annual evaluations may provide support for an external assessment of your school counseling program (Schmidt, 1999; Vacc, Rhyne-Winkler, & Poidevant, 1993). An external assessment would provide the funds and technical assistance to bring outside experts to your school to evaluate the counseling program. An external assessment offers the opportunity for a broader perspective that reflects statewide, national, and international trends and issues. It also guards against a parochial posture that limits your internal "evaluations to restricted and repetitious views of *what should be*" (Schmidt, 1999, p. 267). When financial assistance for an external view is not feasible, developing a peer auditing model is another option. In this process, you would ask a fellow counselor (or counselors) from another school to visit your program, assess its scope and effectiveness, and write a report of the findings. If a number of counselors expressed inter-

est in this type of evaluative process, the outcome could provide an excellent avenue for sharing successful ideas and strategies for all involved.

All the evaluation procedures advocated here have the potential to strengthen your role and position in the school as a professional counselor. In addition to these procedures there is one other aspect of accountability that needs to be addressed, and it is counselor evaluation, which is sometimes referred to as counselor performance appraisal (Schmidt, 1990; Stronge & Helm, 1991).

Counselor Performance Appraisal

Public attention on accountability in schools has included an additional focus on the performance appraisal and evaluation of professional staff. School counselors have been included in this process, but only in the last few years have we seen a distinction between the evaluation processes used with teachers and those designed especially for counselors (Schmidt, 1990, 1999). When planning your own performance appraisal as a school counselor, you might consider the following guidelines:

1. Instruments used to rate a school counselor's performance should reflect the functions for which counselors are hired, and the goals for which programs are designed. Instruments designed to evaluate teacher or administrator performance, therefore, are probably not suitable for counselor evaluation.

2. An instrument that is used to rate a school counselor's performance should reflect the major functions outlined in the literature of the counseling profession. Generally, these functions, as noted in previous chapters, include descriptions of individual and group counseling services, consulting services with parents, teachers, and other professionals, group consultation and instructional services (e.g., classroom guidance, parent education, and teacher inservice), student appraisal and assessment, ethical and legal practices, and program development and coordination. Good standards and fair practices prescribe that you be evaluated according to the actual assignment and expectations of your school counseling position.

3. The person who gathers and interprets data by which a rating is determined for any given practice or function should be highly trained and competent in that particular skill area. The purpose of a perfor-

mance appraisal system is defeated if the person responsible for assessment does not have adequate knowledge and competence in the areas being evaluated. Since most school principals are not trained counselors, this raises a significant dilemma. The challenge for you, your principal, and your school system is to identify methods and procedures for you to receive appropriate supervision and accurate performance appraisal for the job you do in the school.

4. The major purpose for performance appraisal is to help counselors identify strengths and weaknesses in order to make sound decisions about professional development and program improvement. The least important reason to evaluate a counselor is for personnel action, but sometimes this is unavoidable. For this reason, you want to become familiar with the evaluation guidelines and procedures of your school system, and be aware of your rights and responsibilities as outlined in personnel policies.

5. The methods used to gather data for performance appraisal with counselors should be determined at the beginning of the evaluation cycle. Counseling services offer a unique challenge in performance appraisal processes. Due to the confidential nature of many relationships formed by counselors, direct observation may not be an option for the evaluator. As a counselor, you can take charge of this decision by suggesting alternative methods of evaluation for you and your supervisor to use. Such alternatives might include interviews, audio or video taping, simulations, or results of surveys with students, parents, and teachers (Schmidt, 1990,1999). Observations are appropriate for some services, such as classroom guidance, but you want to have a range of methods available due to the diverse nature of services offered in a comprehensive school counseling program.

The preceding guidelines set the stage for developing an appropriate, fair and accurate performance appraisal system. If your school system has a clear performance appraisal process, you will want to become familiar with the policies and procedures that are involved. If your school does not have a clear process you may want to establish one with your principal and supervisor. The following steps are offered as suggestions for establishing a clear process.

Performance Appraisal Process

One of the first goals to accomplish in setting up a performance appraisal process is for you, your supervisor, and principal to agree on the purpose of evaluation. As stated earlier, this purpose is primarily to assist you in your professional development. A second goal is to establish a collaborative relationship with your evaluator (either the principal or supervisor) in which you both accept responsibility for gathering data to use in the performance appraisal process. Following an agreement on these two points, you proceed to design steps for the evaluation. Briefly, these steps might include:

1. An initial conference in the beginning of the year to discuss the major functions and practices to be evaluated during the year. Because school counselors provide such a wide array of services, it may not be realistic to assess all these functions equally in a single year. In which case, you and the evaluator might agree to focus on particular functions one year and save other functions for the next evaluation cycle. In this conference, you would also agree on how data would be gathered and who would be responsible for the different types of data needed in the evaluation. Next, a schedule for gathering data and holding formative conferences during the year would be established.

2. Formative conferences would be held between you and your evaluator periodically during the year. At these conferences, data on particular functions would be shared and an assessment would result. If weaknesses are noted, the evaluator offers suggestions about ways to address these deficiencies. At this time, discussion about technical and financial support to take courses, attend seminars, or participate in professional conferences takes place.

3. At the end of the year, you and the evaluator would meet in a summative conference to review the evaluations performed, assess the progress made, and discuss an annual performance appraisal. As noted earlier, the instrument used for this process should reflect the expectations of a comprehensive school counseling program as presented in professional literature. With your annual performance appraisal complete, you can then begin to formulate professional goals and a plan of action for your further professional development.

A related aspect of performance appraisal is self-assessment by the counselor. The counselor's perspective adds another dimension to the evaluation process. By creating a self-assessment process and tying it to your annual evaluation, the goals and plans you make for professional development become personalized and thereby more attainable.

Self-Assessment

When you perform a self-assessment, you are the first to identify and recognize your own strengths and weaknesses. In this way, you identify skills and knowledge to share with colleagues, while at the same time you note areas for further development and improvement. An accurate self-assessment is an appropriate initial step to your annual performance appraisal because it enables you to gather evidence of competent practices to share with your principal or supervisor. In this manner, you become a collaborator in the performance appraisal process, advocating a credible and valid relationship that will assist you in your own professional development.

A starting point in your self-assessment is to write your professional goals for the year. By writing down your objectives, you make a personal commitment to see that these goals are targeted during the school year. To help you determine what goals are most important, it is useful to design a self-assessment instrument about you and your school counseling program. Figure 25.7 illustrates a sample assessment form designed by a counselor who is preparing for a new school year. This sample form attempts to evaluate the balance of services in the school counseling program and examine aspects of the program the counselor may want to adjust. An assessment form such as this one is easy to create, or you can use forms published by counseling associations and other organizations.

A final way that you can be actively involved in your self-assessment and annual performance appraisal is to document your work and achievements by compiling a counselor's portfolio (Rhyne-Winkler & Wooten, 1996). By gathering evidence to place in a portfolio under each of the major functions expected of you, each year you take control and responsibility for your annual evaluation.

Summary

In this chapter, I have explored various issues and ideas related to counselor accountability. The position taken here advocates that school counselors assume a leadership role in designing and conducting evaluation procedures. As a school counselor, you have responsibility for evaluating your program, reporting the results, and suggesting changes to address the findings of the evaluation process. Without an accountability process, you run the risk of failing to address the needs and expectations of the students, parents, teachers, and administrators you serve. In doing so, you threaten the program's value and jeopardize your reputation as a significant member of the school team. Comprehensive school counseling programs are essential to today's schools, and adequate program accountability and accurate counselor performance appraisal verify the importance of these services.

Figure 25.1
Middle School Survey of a High School Presentation

Students: Please answer the following questions about the presentation you just heard regarding high school graduation requirements. Your responses will help the counseling department and teachers plan future programs to help students prepare for high school. Thank you for your help.

1. How many total credits are required for high school graduation in this state? _____

2. Write down the number of credits that are required in each subject area for high school graduation:

   English   _____

   Mathematics   _____

   Social Studies   _____

   Science   _____

   Vocational Educ.   _____

   Physical Educ.   _____

   Foreign Lang.   _____

   Electives   _____

3. What are the exams you have to pass to qualify for a high school diploma in this state? _____
   _____

4. What science classes are required for high school graduation? _____
   _____

5. What mathematics courses are required? _____
   _____

6. For which ninth grade classes do you plan to preregister? _____
   _____

Figure 25.2
Elementary Counselor's Monthly Report Form

Month:_____

1. Number of individual counseling sessions   _____

2. Number of group counseling sessions   _____

3. Number of students served in group counseling sessions   _____

4. Number of group guidance sessions   _____

5. Number of consultations with parents   _____

6. Number of consultations with teachers   _____

7. Number of parent education presentations   _____

8. Number of teacher in-service presentations   _____

9. Number of referrals to in-school programs   _____

10. Number of referrals to outside agencies   _____

11. Number of meetings attended   _____

12. Hours spent coordinating special events   _____
    (listed below)

_____

_____

_____

Figure 25.3
Student Evaluation of Group Counseling

Students: Thank you for participating in our group. Please give your responses to the following items so that I can plan other groups in the future. Do not put your name on the form. Return the form to the counselor's mail box in the office. Thank you.

Circle your response for each statement.

1. I enjoyed being in this group.	Yes	No	Unsure
2. This group helped me learn new things about myself.	Yes	No	Unsure
3. I have changed some behaviors as a result of being in this group.	Yes	No	Unsure
4. I feel better about myself since being in this group.	Yes	No	Unsure
5. The counselor was helpful in this group.	Yes	No	Unsure
6. This counselor listened to me in this group.	Yes	No	Unsure
7. I want to be in another group sometime.	Yes	No	Unsure
8. I would recommend this type of group to my friends.	Yes	No	Unsure

Figure 25.4
Student Evaluation of a High School Counseling Program

Instructions: Please help your counselor(s) evaluate services of the school counseling program for this school year. Your answers will help the counselor(s) plan services for the coming year. Thank you for your assistance.

Circle your responses for each question.

1. Have you met with your counselor this year?   Yes   No   Unsure

2. Did you meet with your counselor individually?   Yes   No   Unsure

3. Did the counselor invite you to participate in group counseling this year?   Yes   No   Unsure

4. Was the counselor helpful in any way this year?   Yes   No   Unsure

5. Would you recommend the counselor to your friends if they needed to talk to someone? Yes   No   Unsure

6. Did you participate in a group led by your counselor this year?   Yes   No   Unsure

If you participated in group counseling this year, please answer the remaining questions.

7. Was the group helpful to you?   Yes   No   Unsure

8. Did the counselor keep information shared in group confidential?   Yes   No   Unsure

9. Did the counselor effectively lead the group?   Yes   No   Unsure

10. Do you believe the group was helpful to other students?   Yes   No   Unsure

11. Would you recommend this type of group to other students?   Yes   No   Unsure

Figure 25.5
Parent Evaluation of a School Counseling Program

Instructions: Please complete this survey to help the counseling department plan future services in the school counseling program. Return the questionnaire to the school counseling office in the self-addressed envelope. Thank you for your help.

Circle your response to each question.

1. Do you know the counselor at your child's school?	Yes	No	Unsure
2. Has the counselor met with your child this year?	Yes	No	Unsure
3. In your opinion, has the counselor been helpful to your child at school?	Yes	No	Unsure
4. Have you talked with your child's counselor?	Yes	No	Unsure
5. Did the counselor help you in any way this year?	Yes	No	Unsure
6. Would your recommend the counselor to other parents who needed assistance?	Yes	No	Unsure
7. Was your child in a group with the counselor this year?	Yes	No	Unsure

If your child was in a group with the counselor this year, please answer the following questions.

8. Did your child talk with you about being in the group?	Yes	No	Unsure
9. Do you know the purpose of the group?	Yes	No	Unsure
10. Was the group helpful to your child?	Yes	No	Unsure
11. Did the counselor maintain confidentiality about information your child shared in group?	Yes	No	Unsure
12. Do you think groups such as these are important services for students?	Yes	No	Unsure

Figure 25.6
Teacher Evaluation of a School Counseling Program

Instructions: Please complete this survey to help the counseling office plan future services in the school counseling program. Return the questionnaire to the school counselor's mail box in the office. Thank you for your help.

Circle your response to each question.

1. Has the counselor met with any of your students this year?   Yes   No   Unsure

2. In your opinion, has the counselor been helpful to your students?   Yes   No   Unsure

3. Have you received feedback from the counselor?   Yes   No   Unsure

4. Does the counselor maintain confidences?   Yes   No   Unsure

5. Did the counselor help you in any way this year?   Yes   No   Unsure

6. Would your recommend the counselor to students or parents who needed assistance?   Yes   No   Unsure

7. Were any of your students in a group with the counselor this year?   Yes   No   Unsure

If any students were in a group with the counselor this year, please answer the following questions.

8. Do you know the purpose of the group?   Yes   No   Unsure

9. Did the group schedule interfere with class instruction?   Yes   No   Unsure

10. Was the group helpful to your student(s)?   Yes   No   Unsure

11. Do you think groups such as these are important services for students?   Yes   No   Unsure

Figure 25.7
Counselor Self-Assessment Form

	Met	Partially Met	Not Met
1. The counseling program consists of a wide range of services, including individual counseling, group counseling, parent consultations, teacher collaboration, referrals, large group guidance, parent education programs, and student appraisals.	❏	❏	❏
2. The counselor spends sufficient time in individual relationships with students.	❏	❏	❏
3. The counselor leads sufficient number of group counseling sessions with students.	❏	❏	❏
4. The counselor plans classroom guidance activities with teachers.	❏	❏	❏
5. The counselor develops a written plan for the program each year	❏	❏	❏
6. An Advisory Committee assists the counselor with program planning.	❏	❏	❏
7. The counselor spends limited time in clerical tasks, and these functions do not detract significantly from direct service to students, parents, and teachers.	❏	❏	❏
8. The counselor spends a majority of time in crisis intervention.	❏	❏	❏
9. The counselor is comfortable leading large group activities with students, parents, or teachers.	❏	❏	❏
10. The counselor uses appropriate assessment procedures to make decisions about professional services for students.	❏	❏	❏

References

Atkinson, D.R., Furlong, M., & Janoff, D.S. (1979). A four component model for proactive accountability in school counseling. *The School Counselor, 26,*222-228.

Aubrey, R.F. (1982). Program planning and evaluation: Road map of the 80s. *Elementary School Guidance and Counseling, 17,*52-50.

Fairchild, T.N. (1986). Time analysis: Accountability tool for counselors. *The School Counselor, 34,* 36-43.

Krumboltz, J. D. (1974). An accountability model for counselors. *Personnel and Guidance Journal, 52,* 639-646.

Myrick, R. D. (1997). *Developmental guidance and counseling. A practical approach* (3rd ed.). Minneapolis, MN: Educational Media Corporation.

Rhyne-Winkler, M.C., & Wooten, H.R. (1996). The school counselor portfolio: Professional development and accountability. *The School Counselor, 44,* 146-150.

Schmidt, J.J. (1990). Critical issues for school counselor performance appraisal and supervision. *The School Counselor, 38,* 86-94.

Schmidt, J.J. (1991). *A survival guide for the elementary/middle school counselor.* West Nyack, NY: The Center for Applied Research in Education.

Schmidt, J.J. (1999). *Counseling in schools. Essential services and comprehensive programs* (3rd ed.). Needham, MA. Allyn and Bacon.

Stronge, J.H., & Helm, V.M. (1991). *Evaluating professional support personnel in education.* Newbury Park, CA. SAGE Publications.

Vacc, N.A. Rhyne-Winkler, M.C., Poidevant, J.M. (1993). Evaluation and accountability of counseling services: Possible implications for a midsize school district. *The School Counselor, 40,* 260-266.

Chapter 26
Documenting Counseling Services: A Step-by-Step Method
by
Harry Daniels and Diane Daniels

Harry Daniels, PhD, is Professor and Chair of the Counselor Education Department at the University of Florida. He has devoted his professional career to public education, serving as a classroom teacher, a high school counselor and as a counselor educator. He also has ten years of experience as a school board member.

Diane Daniels, EdS., works as a school counselor at Glen Springs Elementary School in Gainesville, Florida. She also has experience as a high school counselor and as an elementary teacher.

When we began our careers in the 1970s, accountability was not a critical issue for school counselors. Back then, a counselor was primarily accountable to the building principal. The evaluation of accountability tended to be equated with whether we satisfied the particulars of our position descriptions. Of course, each position description included a variety of responsibilities, all of which we were expected to fulfill while conducting ourselves in an ethical and professional manner. Yet, we remained uncertain about how the different school principals for whom we worked assessed the quality of our efforts since we were not required to provide documentation of our efforts or effectiveness.

How times have changed, and we believe for the better! During the last two decades, the public demand for accountability has been a constant theme for all aspects of public education, including school counseling. More and more frequently, counselors have been expected to provide evidence of the effectiveness of both their programs and practices. Interestingly, the demands for evidence have come from a widening audience of stakeholders including parents, teachers, and school administrators as well as accrediting bodies, state legislatures, professional organizations, and the courts. Today counselors are expected to be accountable for the all of the programs they deliver as well as for the services they provide.

For many school counselors, the prospect of demonstrating accountability for one's programs can be, and, altogether too frequently, is both daunting and threatening. But it need not be, because demonstrating accountability involves only two essential components: evaluating counseling programs and documenting counseling services. In another chapter of this text, John J. Schmidt provides an excellent description of the basics of program evaluation. In this chapter, we address the importance of documenting service delivery and provide examples of strategies for doing so.

Our purpose here is to outline a step-by-step method for documenting the delivery of school counseling programs and services. The step-by-step method considers four issues that school counselors will want to consider, when they develop a system for documenting counseling services. These issues include the:

1. **Structure** for determining what needs to be documented;

2. **Techniques** for recording and storing information;

3. **Easy to use forms** that can be adopted for local use; and

4. **Procedures** for using the information to guide decision making.

Considered together, the first letter of each of these issues provides an acronym (**STEP**) that can be used to remember the critical issues to attend to in the process of documenting counseling services. We now turn our attention to a brief discussion of each issue.

Structure

During a school year a school counselor may be involved in literally hundreds of professional contacts that pertain to the students with whom they work. These contacts may be with the students themselves with their parents, teachers, administrators and/or friends. The contacts with students may be made directly in one-on-one sessions, or in small or large group counseling, or they may be made through more indirect means such as telephone calls or e-mail. Given the variety of ways that counselors connect with students, it is essential to determine what needs to be documented and by whom. We believe that the determination of what needs to be documented is informed by two primary factors: the counselor's position description and the local standards and expectations. Because local standards and expectations will vary widely from place to place, we will emphasize the counselor's position description.

According to the American School Counseling Association (1999), school counselors help create and organize comprehensive counseling programs at all educational levels. As described elsewhere in this text, comprehensive school counseling programs are developmental and systematic in nature, sequential, clearly defined, and integral to the educational program. These programs are, by definition, proactive and preventive in their focus. School counselors also provide a variety of services that are developmentally appropriate for the students whom they serve. Both counseling programs and services focus on the needs, interests, and issues related to the various stages of student growth. They are designed to help all students pursue their individual uniqueness in terms of academic, career, and personal/social development.

School counselors have a responsibility for documenting *all* of the programs and services that are part of their counseling program including, but not limited to, any assistance provided to students, parents, teachers and administrators, or contacts with appropriate state agencies or court officials. The prospect of documenting almost everything they do can be overwhelming for most counselors. Indeed, the task of documenting the delivery of counseling programs and services can be arduous and time consuming. Yet, as many experienced school counselors know, the benefits of providing documentation will far outweigh the costs of doing so, particularly in instances when a counselor's course of action is questioned by a third party. Moreover, we believe the task of documenting program and service delivery can be structured in such a way as to make the process almost second nature. One example of such a structure is presented in Figure 26.1.

Figure 26.1 provides a summary of the types of counseling interventions for which documentation is recommended. Identified in the summary are four different types of information, each of which is linked to a critical issue that counselors need to consider as they begin to organize their documentation efforts. Framed as questions, the critical issues are:

• Who is the client?

• What is the nature of the counseling intervention and/or contact?

• What information about the intervention/contact is critical and needs to be documented?

• Who is (are) the potential beneficiary (ies) of the documentation?

Column 1: Who is the client?

For purposes of this step-by-step model, the client is the recipient of the counselor's attention and energy. As noted above, school counselors are employed to create and organize comprehensive, developmental counseling programs that are designed to help students pursue their individual uniqueness in terms of academic, career, and personal/social development. From this perspective, one may assume that the client will always be a student. However, in order to operate an effective program, the counselor may have other clients including students' parents, school staff (e.g., teachers, administrators, support staff), community members (e.g., mental health agencies and/or providers, service groups, or social organizations), and the representatives of the judicial system.

Column 2: What is the nature of the counseling intervention and/or contact?

School counselors work with clients in a variety of settings using an assortment of different interventions. With student clients, counselors may see students individually, or they may work with them in small or large groups. Similarly, they may communicate with students by telephone, e-mail, or letter. Experienced counselors also know that students' parents want to know what is happening in the lives of their children. This means that counselors employ a number of different strategies to communicate with parents including individual contacts, telephone calls, e-mail, and personal letters as well as workshops and large group presentations. Experience also teaches that counselors communicate with teachers, administrators and other school staff in a variety of formats including individual consultations or conferences, workshops or training sessions, or in educational or disciplinary staffings. More and more frequently, school counselors are interacting with other health care providers in the communities in which they live by making appropriate referrals. Finally, the sad reality of child abuse and neglect and/or threats of violence to self or others on the part of students places the counselor in the position of a mandated reporter. In all such instances, counselors are required to work with the appropriate child welfare agencies and officers of the judicial system.

Column 3: What information about the intervention/contact is critical and needs to be documented?

Given the variety of interventions and/or contacts that school counselors engage in and the expectation to document all contacts, it is important to recognize that different contacts will require different types of documentation. In Column 3, we have identified the types of information that should be collected. Later in this chapter, we provide examples of the different types of forms that may be used to collect the data.

Column 4: Who benefits from the documentation?

As displayed in Column 4, we believe that many parties benefit because of the counselor's accurate documentation. Traditionally, it has been argued that counselors should keep records for the following three reasons: (1) to document the quality of service provided to clients (i.e., promote accountability); (2) to insure that current interventions are based on past services; (3) to have available a set of data which can be transferred to another professional should the need arise. All of these reasons provide benefits for the client and/or the counselor. But it is becoming increasingly clear that clients have a right to know what interventions are going to be used and what, if any, risks are involved. In this way, the record documents the client's informed consent. In short, a good record enables the counselor to reconstruct the services a student has received and demonstrates that the care provided was in accordance with accepted practice and reasonable under the circumstances.

Techniques

Hopefully, it is clear that documenting counseling interventions and/or contacts is an essential component of every school counselor's job. Despite its importance, there is no single best technique for counselors to use in fulfilling this responsibility. Most counselors' first experience in documenting their activities occurs during their supervised field experiences in their graduate programs. Then, with additional experience and experimentation with different strategies for keeping accurate records, counselors adopt a strategy that works for them. We encourage you to experiment with different ways to record your efforts, but we also provide some general guidelines that we think will be helpful.

1. Keep counseling records in such a way that they will both benefit clients and assist you in being a more effective practitioner. Good records enable counselors to reconstruct the student's participation in all aspects of the counseling program and to demonstrate that the services provided were consistent with accepted practice. Additionally, the retention of accurate and thorough client records will be the best counter to *any* assertion of professional negligence.

2. When writing your notes, use behavioral, objective language (ACA eNews, 1999; Mitchell, 1999). Your written words will be the only record of any contact you have with a client, and it is important that you emphasize clarity and precision in all that you write. Insofar as possible avoid using adjectives! It is vital that your notes are clear and precise—using adjectives adds to the subjectivity of the record.

3. Know what information is required to be included in client records by state statute and take pains to provide it. Although different states have different requirements about what is to be included in an intervention record, most will include the following elements:

   - Basic information such as the client's name, dates of contact, types of service provided;

   - A summary of the client's presenting concerns, what transpired in the session, any comments the client made regarding sensitive matters (i.e., abuse and/or neglect, threats of violence, etc.), and a record of the client's progress;

   - Records of contacts with significant others in the client's life, including telephone contacts, e-mail messages, and face-to-face conversations.

4. Document client participation whenever appropriate, perhaps including the client's signature.

5. Retain records for as long as there is a need for them. There is no general record retention rule, but know whether your school district has such a policy. Then, maintain as accurate and complete a client record as possible during the period of time established by the retention policy.

6. Assume any of your records may someday be read in open court with you and your client present along with newspaper, radio and television reporters.

(Readers interested in obtaining a more detailed description of this topic are encouraged to read *Documentation in Counseling Records*, Volume 2, of the *ACA Legal Series*)

Easy to Use Forms

We have discovered that it is easier to keep accurate and up-to-date records if we use pre-designed forms to record our contacts and activities. We have included a number of these forms here (see Figure 26.2 to Figure 26.7) including the following:

- Documentation of Individual Counseling—Elementary/Middle/High School

- Documentation of Small Group Counseling—Elementary/Middle/High School

- Documentation of Large Group Guidance—Elementary/Middle/High School

- Documentation of Individual Consultations

- Documentation of Inservice Activity/Presentation

- Documentation of Community Referrals

All of these forms were constructed for our own purposes and may not be appropriate for use in your school or district. We encourage you to use and/or modify the forms as needed to fit your own purposes. That is, redesign each as appropriate to make it locally relevant.

Procedures

The single most important factor to consider in terms of procedures for documenting counseling services is timeliness. The word *timely* is a directive to record information immediately! (ACA eNews, 1999) Notes about contact with clients should be made as soon as possible after the end of the session, presentation, or other contact. Waiting even one day can blur one's memory and thus, the accuracy of the record. Having a supply of the forms described above on hand – either on one's desktop or in a desk drawer – will allow school counselors to make a record of any session before going on to the next one. It only takes a few minutes, and it is good practice.

Increasingly, it is becoming possible to do record keeping on desktop computers. Many medical doctors as well as other health care providers are now recording and storing records of patients' visits on computer. School counselors are beginning to adopt this strategy for keeping records (Sabella, 1999). Recently, Sabella conducted a survey of school counselors to identify software programs they use for record keeping. Among the more popular ones were the following: FileMaker Pro 4.1, Therapist Helper, and Therascribe 3.5. Users of these programs indicated that they are user friendly and a valuable aide in keeping accurate records that can be used to prepare reports. (For more information about each of these programs, look at the following website: *http://www.schoolcounselor.com/software.htm*

Alternatively, school counselors may find it useful to adapt computer programs developed for school principals to document discipline cases. For example, Logger is a school discipline/contacts software for education professionals who want to keep track of discipline and other contacts with students, parents and teachers. See the following website for more information: *http://www.ctsports.com/8adminis.htm*

Another computer program counselors may find helpful is the Behavior Observation Assistant (BOA) by Bunger Solutions. BOA is an easy to use and completely user definable data collection software that was designed to assist teachers, counselors and other professionals with collecting and interpreting behavioral data. More information about the BOA is available at the following website: *http://www.bungersolutions.com*

Concluding Remarks

Keeping complete and accurate records of counseling programs delivered as well as services you provide as a school counselor might seem burdensome at first, but it will prove to be a benefit for you and your counseling program. Maintaining accurate records is basically a step-by-step procedure, one that is repeated again and again. Hopefully, the information that we have provided in this brief chapter will prove to be helpful for your purposes.

References

ACA eNews. (1999). Clarity in documentation (On-line). Available: *http://www.counseling.org/enews/volume2/0207a.htm*

American School Counseling Association (1999). *Role statement: The school counselor.* Author. Available: *http://www.schoolcounselor.org/General Info/role.html*

Mitchell, R.W. (1999). *Documentation in counseling records. ACA legal series. Volume 2.* Alexandria, VA: American Counseling Association.

Sabella, R.A. (1999) Software survey. *Schoolcounselor.com.* Available: *http://www.schoolcounselor.com/software.htm*

Figure 26.1
Summary of the Types of Counseling Interventions
for which Documentation is Recommended

Client	Intervention/Contact	Critical Information	Potential Beneficiaries
Students	Individual Counseling	Student's Name Date Purpose Summary Outcome	Client Counselor Parents School Staff Court
	Group counseling	Participants' names Date Purpose/Topic Summary Outcome	Clients Counselor Parents School Staff Court
	Classroom guidance	Class/Teacher's name Class list Date/Time Purpose/Topic Summary	Students Counselor Parents School Staff
	Telephone contact	Student's Name Date/Time Purpose/Topic Summary Outcome	Client Counselor Parents School Staff Court
	E-mail contact	Student's Name Date/Time Purpose/Topic Summary Outcome	Client Counselor Parents School Staff Court
	Letter	Contents of letter	Client Counselor Parents School Staff Court

Figure 26.1 (cont.)
Summary of the Types of Counseling Interventions
for which Documentation is Recommended

Client	Intervention/Contact	Critical Information	Potential Beneficiaries
Parents	Individual consultation	Parent's Name Date/Time Purpose/Topic Summary Outcome	Student Parents Counselor School Staff Court
	Telephone contact	Parent's Name Date/Time Purpose/Topic Summary Outcome	Student Parents Counselor School Staff Court
	E-mail contact	Parent's Name Date/Time Purpose/Topic Summary Outcome	Student Parents Counselor School Staff Court
	Workshops	Purpose/Topic Date/Time Participants Summary	Parents Students Counselor School Staff
	Large group presentations	Purpose/Topic Date/Time Organization Summary	Parents Students Counselor School Staff
	Letter		

Figure 26.1 (cont.)
Summary of the Types of Counseling Interventions
for which Documentation is Recommended

Client	Intervention/Contact	Critical Information	Potential Beneficiaries
School Staff	Individual consultation Teachers Administrators Resource officers Other	Contact's name Student's name Date/Time Purpose Summary	School Staff Students Counselor Parents
	Workshops/Inservice	Purpose/Topic Date/Time Participants Summary	School Staff Students Counselor Parents
	Staffings IEP Staffings Disciplinary Staffings	Student's name Participants' names Date Purpose Summary Outcome	Students School Staff Counselor Parents
Community	Referrals to other professionals Counselors Psychologists Physicians Other	Student's name Referral's name Date Purpose Summary Outcome	Students Parents Counselor
	Referrals to agencies	Student's name Referral's name Date Purpose Summary Outcome	Students Parents Counselor
	Presentations	Purpose/Topic Date/Time Organization Summary	Parents Students Counselor School Staff
Court	Mandated reporting Abuse/Neglect Violence/Suicide	Student's name Referral's name Date Purpose Summary Outcome	Students Counselor Community

Figure 26.2
Documentation of Individual Counseling—
Elementary/Middle/High School

Student's Name: _____

Counselor: _____

Date: _____

Grade Level (Circle):   K   1   2   3   4   5   6   7   8   9   10   11   12

Purpose (Check One):
_____Educational Concerns
_____Career Concerns
_____Personal/Social Concerns

Specific Topics Addressed:

Summary:

Outcome(s):

Joe Wittmer, PhD

Figure 26.3
Documentation of Small Group Counseling—
Elementary/Middle/High School

Counselor: _____

Date: _____

Students: _____   _____

_____   _____

_____   _____

_____   _____

Purpose (Check One):

_____Educational Concerns

_____Career Concerns

_____Personal/Social Concerns

Specific Topics Addressed:

Group Summary:

Individual Summaries (Students 1 – n):

Student 1:

Student 2:

Student 3:

Student n:

Outcome(s)

Figure 26.4
Documentation of Large Group Guidance—
Elementary/Middle/High School

Counselor: _____

Date: _____

Teacher: _____

Grade Level (Circle):   K   1   2   3   4   5   6   7   8   9   10   11   12

Number of Students:

Purpose (Check One):
_____Educational Concerns
_____Career Concerns
_____Personal/Social Concerns

Specific Topics Addressed:

Summary:

Figure 26.5
Documentation of Individual Consultations

Counselor: _____

Type: _____ Parent/Guardian _____ _____ School Staff
    _____Teacher   _____Administrator
    _____Other_____

Consultee: _____

Student: _____

Specific Topics Addressed:

Summary:

Figure 26.6
Documentation of Inservice Activity/Presentation

Counselor: _____

Date: _____

Group:

_____Teachers

_____Parents

_____Community Group

Number of Participants:

Specific Topics Addressed:

Summary:

Figure 26.7
Documentation of Community Referrals

Counselor: _____

Date: _____

Student: _____

Referred to:

_____ Health care professional

_____ Educational specialist

_____ Social service agency

_____ State agency/Court authorities

Mandated referral: _____No   _____Yes

Reason(s) for referral:

Chapter 27
Promoting a K-12 Developmental Guidance Program

by

Joe Wittmer*

---

* Appreciation is extended to Dr. Teresita Leeson for her helpful assistance with this chapter. Thanks also to the following for their help with this chapter: Darren Covar, Michelle McPeak, Robert Peeling, and Ron Vickery.

Introduction

Selling, promoting, and marketing a comprehensive, developmental counseling program to students, professional colleagues, and parents is not an easy task, nor one to be taken for granted. It is essential to the survival of the program and a structured, deliberate, and planned, public relations (*PR—performance recognized*) approach is needed. The strategies and techniques presented in this chapter have been used to help promote developmental guidance at all grade levels; they can be adapted to coincide with any school level (elementary, middle, high).

Cialdini (1996) outlined several stages that individuals attempting to successfully sell, promote, market, or otherwise persuade others to use a product, a service, or a program, should follow. Among these are:

Identification—To recognize what is being "sold" and promoted to whom and why. The program (product) is then promoted within the target population (students, teachers, administrators, and parents) through the use of newsletters, logos, slogans, success stories, and other types of appropriate promotional activities.

Legitimacy—A legitimate product (i.e., a developmental counseling program) has credibility which has been established. Several strategies can be employed including the testimony of experts and the visible participation of supporters and consumers of the product (program).

Participation—Cialdini defines this as that phase when even the previously uncommitted individuals begin to show support and begin participating in the program. In the case of school counseling, this means all publics—administrators, parents, teachers, students, and so forth.

Accountability—A program (i.e., the counseling program) that has been successfully sold will have lived up to promises previously made and produces tangible results. That is, who is delivering what services to whom and how effective is the specific service being provided?

These four stages are briefly presented below concerning each target population deemed important to "sell" on a comprehensive counseling program: *administrators, teachers, parents,* and *students*. Several ideas and suggestions are listed, but are not intended to be all inclusive. It is suggested that counselors select from among those most appropriate and applicable to their particular school and publics.

Administration

As stated in the beginning of this book, it is imperative that the school administration be sold on the need for a developmental school counseling program or the program will fail. And, as also noted, it is the job of the school counselor to "sell" the program to his or her administrators. If the school administration is not sold, the program will be nearly impossible to implement, even if the other target populations listed here are successfully sold on the program. It is a well-known fact that the administration sets the climate of the school. An administration sold on a "developmental" counseling program will ensure a developmental focus in the overall school.

Identification

First and foremost, it is important to describe (in writing) the comprehensive developmental counseling program to the school administration and gain their support for same. This can be best accomplished by informing the administration that you are/will:

- Develop and implement a school counseling curriculum for *everyone* in the school.

- Make individual, small and large group counseling available to all students in the school.

- Plan and organize a system of parental involvement in the program.

- Organize and implement a peer helper/peer mediation program.

- Provide consultation and coordination of direct and indirect guidance services to parents, faculty, and community agencies.

An important aspect of the identification of the program is for you to be visible: i.e, a school principal will not support nor appreciate a counselor they never see. Also, agree to write a regular press release for the principal's newsletter (monthly?) describing important components of the counseling program.

Legitimacy

Establish the genuine credibility of the counseling program to the administration. This cannot be accomplished through words alone; the administration must see action-oriented results. Assist them in understanding a developmental counseling program. Your credibility with the administration is best established if you:

- Recognize the movement away from reactive counseling to the preventive, proactive, developmental approach: work at the image of becoming a facilitator of affective education across the school's entire curriculum.

- Watch for increasing opportunities to serve as a consultant, working with individual groups of teachers concerning classroom management, dealing effectively with special problem students, behavioral techniques, motivation, and so forth.

- Demonstrate your effectiveness as a program planner. A legitimate, effective planner possesses three general planning skills: needs assessment, program design, and program evaluation/accountability.

- Work at continually convincing (gentle persuasion) the administration to the point that they sense that you are using your special skills to make *their* job easier as a school administrator; that you are a vital member of the educational team, not just an auxiliary service provider!

Participation

Administrative support will grow for a school developmental counseling program if you:

- Learn and use the art of positive influence and persuasion.

- Offer to help lead in-service teacher and other staff development programs (agree to serve on the in-service staff development committee for your school).

- Request time to make announcements or reports in faculty meetings, at PTA meetings, and so forth.

- Report back when you attend any in-service, professional development meetings. Make copies of your notes from these meetings for distribution to others in the school who might benefit. Write a memo to the administrators apprising them of what you learned and how you will apply it. Offer in-service training for others on what you learned at the meeting/convention.

- Keep a *regular, weekly* appointment time with your administrator. Listen! Your principal probably has very few people to confide in; as the counselor, become that person.

- Present an administrator(s) with a certificate or plaque recognizing his or her accomplishments and contributions to the guidance program when appropriate. Let them know they are appreciated.

- If your school does not currently have a developmental guidance program, talk with the principal about working into an authentic, developmental program "one step at a time." Do not ask for too much too soon. Take your gains where you can.

- At the beginning of the school year, ask your head administrator to help you set three priority goals for the academic year, then together, plan a program to meet these goals. And, let the administration periodically know of your progress toward meeting these goals.

- Remember that what happens in your counseling program is everybody's business, and the more sensitive the staff (especially administrators) become to the counseling related needs of students, the more successful the school counseling program will be.

Accountability

An ongoing, continuous evaluation system is imperative. Reveal, in writing, the results of your program. Gather "hard" data and present it to the administration periodically. This can best be accomplished by:

- Providing a weekly schedule of services—a weekly, semester-long, and yearly calendar for the administration and others in the school.

- Regularly advise the administration of program accomplishments through monthly reports. Don't burden them with long, drawn out reports—keep them brief and to the point; "just the facts."

- Invite your principal to sit in on a large group counseling unit in a classroom, or present it to him or her on video; show off some of your accomplishments.

- Place your program, goals, objectives, plans for implementation, materials, and accountability procedures on paper. Give copies to the administration and revise as often as necessary. And, request a personal evaluation periodically from your principal.

- Keeping your principal informed at all times (i.e., regarding any media coverage forthcoming, etc.). Keep them informed about everything you deem important. Your school principal won't appreciate being surprised, but will appreciate being kept informed.

Teachers

As noted throughout this book, teachers play a vital role in a developmental school counseling program. They are the ones who know students best, probably better than any other adult in the school. Thus, they are in a prime position to notice changes in students' behaviors and refer them for counseling, special assistance, and so forth. It is essential that open communication exist between counselors and teachers if the developmental guidance program is to be successful.

Identification

Inform the teachers of the types of services the counseling department has to offer to assist them as they work with students on a day to day basis. This can be accomplished best if you:

- Let them know you are available to them. Pencil in "flexible" or "teacher consultation" time on your calendar and share it with all teachers. And, "be there" for them when needed.

- Send them memos describing groups and other developmental services that can, or are, being provided to assist with target students (i.e., those who are disruptive, experienced a recent death in the family, are depressed, parents are divorced, etc.). Request they nominate students for certain "targeted" groups of students.

- Develop a structure for meeting substitute teachers and develop a short handout for their use that details services you can offer them.

- Form a list of possible in-service activities for teachers and then set up some programs for which they might volunteer (i.e., Teacher Effectiveness Training, Managing Diversity in the Classroom, Dealing With the Unmotivated Student). Also, order "Guidance Films" for their use.

Teachers will agree to refer students to the guidance office more frequently if they know of your services. However, be aware that you don't oversell, that somehow you have a magic wand!

Legitimacy

Establish the credibility of the guidance program to teachers. Some suggestions include:

- Work with the administration to give incentives to teachers to attend in-service training where you discuss your developmental program, the goals, objectives, and so forth.

- A teacher appreciation day might be held stressing the benefits of a developmental guidance and counseling program and how it benefits all students and teachers.

- Share with teachers student success stories that are non-confidential in nature.

Participation

Work at gaining the support of teachers who are not yet committed to the program. This can be best accomplished by:

- Having teachers fill out personal needs assessments and provide them with the results—what services do they "expect" and "desire" from the guidance department?

- Holding workshops to discuss the results of the needs assessments and ask teachers for ways to meet these needs.

- Getting teachers to utilize peer facilitators where appropriate.

- Ask reluctant teachers which "special" academically oriented large group classroom activities they would like to see implemented (i.e., study skills, note taking, paying attention in class, asking appropriate questions, etc.).

- Send "Thank-u-Grams" to teachers who have provided you with assistance, who have helped a student in a "special" way, and so forth.

- Hold annual orientation meetings with new teachers concerning the counseling program. Develop a structure to assign a "buddy" to each new teacher in your school.

Accountability

Demonstrate the value of your developmental counseling program through evaluative methods. Ask for the teachers' evaluation of you and the overall program at least once a year by having:

- Teachers complete evaluative forms that focus on the various specific components of the developmental counseling program of which they are aware.

- Teachers offer suggestions for changes in the program through a suggestion box in the guidance complex.

- Teachers evaluate your effectiveness as a counseling professional. Have the "teacher completed" evaluation forms given directly to a teacher colleague to tabulate who, in turn, gives the data directly to the principal.

Parents

As noted throughout this book, it is important and essential that parents become involved in the developmental counseling program. Parents play a vital role in effective developmental programs. Parental involvement is also vitally important to the success of their own child. Parents who understand the goals and objectives of the counseling department are more likely to become involved and to assist in meeting these goals in a variety of ways.

Identification

Increase the awareness of your developmental counseling program to the parents whose offspring are enrolled in your school. By doing this, parents learn who you are, what you do, and how this helps their own child, as well as others in the school. This can be accomplished by:

- Developing a brochure that describes you, your job, and your developmental program. This should include a brief written philosophy, goals, and objectives of your developmental counseling program. Then, send it home to the parents.

- Inviting parents to a parent-counselor pot luck dinner at the beginning of each year.

- Sending home a periodic calendar of events concerning the counseling program.

- Sending home a certificate of achievement/improvement when their child successfully completes a group, individual work project, and so forth.

- Developing assorted publicity items that can be sold or given to parents and students that are specifically counseling related and designed (i.e., key chains, tee shirts, etc.).

- Attending and participating in PTA meetings where you describe the counseling program in detail. You may want to do this two or three times during the year to describe current and upcoming counseling related activities.

- Make phone calls to the homes of each new student by the end of their first week at your school. A letter of welcome to the home of the new parents is always appreciated.

Legitimacy

Parents must be convinced that the counseling program is sound and helpful to their *own* child.

- Present a slide show or video of successful program activities at the PTA meeting or other meetings where parents are invited.

- Have students who have successfully used your services speak with parents at the beginning of the year, perhaps a panel of students at the PTA meeting.

Participation

As parents learn to know you better, what you do, and the successes you've had, they will be much more willing to participate in your counseling program. Some suggestions for increasing parental participation in the program are as follows:

- Conduct a needs assessment of parents.

- Provide each parent with a calendar that lists program activities for each month.

- Solicit parents as volunteers (i.e., for career week, college night, as tutors, helpers for special projects, etc.).

- Invite parents to sit in on an educational and/or career counseling/planning session with you and their child.

- Establish a counseling "hotline" for parents.

Accountability

Parents will want to see the results of your program.

- At the end of the year, send each parent a survey on the efficiency and effectiveness of the guidance department and its program. Also, on the same survey, ask for volunteers to serve on a special guidance committee to help decide goals for the following year and for their suggestions concerning the guidance program.

Students

Students need to know the goals and objectives of your program, what you do and can do for them. If they do not know the counselors, or what services are provided by the counseling office, the program will not be effective. Develop the program in such a manner so that each student in school knows who the counselors are and what services they have to offer. Students are your primary concern; your main *consumers*!

Identification

Use different methods to identify who you are and what you do. Give the students an opportunity to match a face with a name. Be creative!

- Visit each classroom early in the year, make a brief presentation, and distribute information (a student-oriented brochure) regarding the role and function of the counseling department.
- Begin a special Counseling Department section in the school newspaper (i.e,. perhaps a "Dear Abby" type column).
- Be visible: keep in touch with what students are doing; be in attendance at athletic events, and so forth.
- Use bulletin boards to provide information on what is offered to students through the counseling department, as well as upcoming events, appointment forms, groups that are being formed, and so forth.
- Involve students in publicity campaigns, especially the student council, peer helpers, and so forth.
- Have a *Counseling Services Week* at your school. Involve the students in planning the week.

Legitimacy

Continually demonstrate that the developmental counseling program is credible and is there for the basic purpose of meeting the *needs* and *concerns* of *all* students. Legitimacy can be gained and maintained by:

- Having students who have utilized your program's services tell other students about their experiences (i.e., at a student assembly, via closed circuit TV, written surveys, etc.).
- Advertising small groups such as "Peer Facilitators," "New To School Student Groups," "Your Changing Family," and so forth, by using available school media, bulletin boards, and so forth.

Participation

The primary goal is to get all students interested and involved in the developmental counseling program. This can best be accomplished by:

- Utilizing positive peer pressure.
- Distributing questionnaires in the classrooms, including needs assessment surveys, possible topics of interest to them, setting up a counseling department suggestion box, and so forth.
- Establish a positive atmosphere in the counseling department and make access easy for the students.
- Increase students awareness of current events and forthcoming counseling related activities. This will increase their involvement.

Accountability

Continually update and work on your image with the students by being accountable. Have them assist you in deciding whether what you are doing is effective, and make revisions where necessary.

- Have every student who has used your services fill out an evaluation form. The lower grades can do this also.

- Find out what students know about your guidance services through surveys.

- Publish results of evaluations in the school paper, through announcements, and so forth. Then, follow-up with articles in the school paper concerning *changes* that have, or will be made, as a result of the student evaluations.

- Keep a "real" open door policy.

- Be accessible to students. Develop a system as to how you can be reached when out of the office.

- Encourage self-referrals and referrals from concerned students regarding their friends who they think need to see you ("Care-Grams").

- Develop a "buddy system" for new students and provide them with a "You are Here" map of your school.

- Visit hospitalized students, send cards, and so forth.

Summary

A public relations program needs to be an ongoing part of the developmental counseling program. To gain the support from your publics it is imperative that you inform them of what you are doing, and how effectively. Basically, school counselors need to promote themselves and their program, or their importance in the academic, personal/social, and career successes of students will not become known. Good public relations are an excellent way to gain and strengthen the support and encouragement of everyone. Though it will take much time and creative energy, developing and implementing a good public relations program can help you and your counseling program immeasurably.

Dozens of additional creative PR ideas are presented in Figure 27.1 (Ayes & Buchan, 1992). As a practicing counselor, review the list given and check off those you think appropriate for you and your school. Then, ask the question; how does my PR program rate? Does it measure up? Answering the questions provided in Figure 27.2 in the affirmative would be a good indication of just how good your current PR program is and may suggest some needed changes.

References

Ayes, Z., & Buchan, B.A. (1992). School counselors exploring human potential: Set sail with PR. *The ASCA Counselor*, p. 7.

Cialdini, R.B. (11996). Influence science and practice. Glenview, IL Scott Foresman.

Figure 27.1
School Counselors Exploring Human Potential: Set Sail with PR

Publicity

- Posters
- Flyers
- Awards
- Public service announcements
- Information about scholarships
- Booths at school fair
- Radio and television announcements
- Newspaper articles
- Brochures
- Community events
- Invite legislators to speak
- Cable TV programs

Professional Services

- Advisory committees
- Advisor for school clubs
- PTA/PTO presentations
- Conduct workshops
- Institute a teacher swap shop within district and neighbor districts
- Participation in telethons
- Coordination of school activities or events
- Newsletter
- Public speaking
- Consultation with parents, teachers, administrators, and community agencies
- Fund-raising

Student Activities and Events

- Celebrate National School Counseling Week
- Assemblies
- Career fair contests (essay, art, song writing, poetry, brainstorming, and so forth.)
- Peer helper program
- College Fair Step-up Day
- Initiate International Pen-Pal Club
- Create a Holiday (i.e., Crazy Hat Day, Stress Reduction Day)
- Student involvement in National Career Development Month activities
- Incorporate student ideas into professional services
- Orientation programs
- Career Inventions project

Visual Displays

- Bulletin boards
- Calendars
- T-shirts
- Bumper stickers
- Mugs
- Buttons
- Videos
- Banners
- Wall signs
- Lapel pins
- Calling cards
- Tote bags with school counselor message
- Displays in the hall
- Wallet-size cards with emergency numbers on them
- Order specialty logo items through ASCA
- Posters
- Bookmarks

(Adapted from Ayes, Z. & Buchan, B.A., *The School Counselor*, February, 1992).

Figure 27.2
Self-Evaluation Inventory for a School Guidance Public Relations Program

	YES	NO
1. Have you worked with the sponsor of your school newspaper and discussed *regular* coverage of guidance news?	❑	❑
2. Do you know the person at your local newspaper/radio/TV station you should contact for a story? Have you recently developed a Public Service Announcement (PSA)?	❑	❑
3. Do you have an orientation program for incoming kindergarten, sixth or seventh, ninth or tenth graders? Did you evaluate it and share the findings?	❑	❑
4. Do you have an orientation program for new students? (Ones who transfer in after school begins.) Did you evaluate it and show the results?	❑	❑
5. Have you developed a brochure to explain your guidance program to students, parents, teachers, administrators and others?	❑	❑
6. Do you make a presentation concerning the guidance program at one school board meeting each year?	❑	❑
7. Do you have a minimum of three articles or feature stories about the guidance program in the local newspaper each year?	❑	❑
8. Do you have written plans or guides for a public relations plan for your program?	❑	❑
9. Do you have news from the guidance department in each issue of the school newspaper?	❑	❑
10. Do you give a minimum of three speeches each year to local, civic, and service organizations?	❑	❑
11. Do you make a minimum of three annual presentations concerning guidance programs at your school faculty meetings?	❑	❑
12. Do you make reports about the guidance program at one or more administrative staff meetings annually?	❑	❑
13. Do you talk to a minimum of four school clubs/organizations each year about the guidance program?	❑	❑

Chapter 28
Legal and Ethical Issues in School Counseling

by

Theodore P. Remley, Jr.
and Mary Herman

Theodore P. Remley, Jr., JD, PhD, is Professor and Coordinator of the Counseling Graduate Program at the University of New Orleans. He has served as a school counselor and a university counselor educator. In addition, he has maintained private practices in both counseling and law.

Mary Herman, JD, MEd, is a teacher at Mount Carmel Academy in New Orleans, Louisiana. She is both an attorney and counselor and teaches school law at the University of New Orleans.

Introduction

Professional counselors in all settings increasingly are finding the legal and ethical issues they face to be complex and challenging. Although problems related to the law and ethical standards may be difficult for counselors in community mental health agencies, rehabilitation facilities, universities, or private practices, school counselors are regularly confronted with the most difficult issues on a daily basis.

There are two basic reasons why school counselors have substantial problems addressing legal and ethical issues. First, K-12 school counselors offer services most often to minors and the law and professional ethical standards are inadequate regarding a practical resolution of the competing interests of children and the adults who are responsible for their welfare. In addition, despite the fact that dual relationships are prohibited in counseling (Herlihy & Corey, 1992), counselors in schools have multiple roles (counselor, educator, colleague, and parent substitute) and interact with a variety of individuals who demand their professional services (students, parents, guardians, other interested adults, teachers, and administrators). Legal and ethical standards that prohibit dual relationships with clients cause continuing headaches and hardships for school counselors, as dual relationships seem almost unavoidable.

Minors as Clients

As a school counselor, you will primarily be counseling and otherwise serving children below the age of 18, the age of legal majority in the United States. Until individuals are 18, they are legally under the control and care of their parents or court appointed guardians. Minors have only in the last few decades been recognized as having a legal status that extends beyond the rights of their parents (Wrightsman, 1997).

While the ethical standards for counselors inform you that you have primary responsibilities to your clients, the law clearly implies that, until your clients reach the age of 18, parents are the individuals to whom you are *legally* responsible. As a result, even though you have personal counseling relationships with minors, their parents or guardians have legal authority and control over those relationships.

A good practice rule to follow when counseling students is to assume that your professional responsibilities are to your minor clients. On the other hand, if parents or legal guardians become involved in the counseling process, you must acknowledge that they have authority over minors. They, therefore, are legally in charge of the counseling relationship and you must defer to their rights.

Because counseling is a part of the general educational experience in schools, parental permission for students to receive counseling services is not required by law. Many school principals or school districts have enacted policies that do require parental permission before counselors enter into counseling relationships with minors. Such policies are based on the preference of administrators or board members and are not legally required. Thus, it is extremely important that you become familiar with the policies in your specific school system.

In the event, however, parents insist that counseling or guidance services within a school environment be discontinued, they *probably* have a legal right to have their wishes followed because such services are not a required part of the school curriculum. If you ever plan to ignore the demands of parents requesting that you stop counseling their child, it is strongly suggested that you obtain the support of your direct supervisor before doing so, since you may violate the parents' legal rights. That is, the legal rights, in this case, belong with the parents.

Our legal system is based on a strong belief that individual and family privacy should not be violated by others, particularly those who are public employees. Generally, parents have complete control and authority over their children, unless it is determined by formal means that parents are harming their children in some way. As a school counselor, it is important that you remember the legal rights of parents and guardians concerning their children, even when it may seem to you that the interests of children are not being best served. Simply stated, poor or inappropriate judgment (in your opinion) on the part of parents does not diminish their legal rights over their minor offspring.

Consultation with Attorneys

For some yet inapparent reason, school counselors seem to be reluctant to seek the advice of attorneys when they are faced with a legal problem. All schools have attorneys available to advise them. The best way to access your school's attorney is to ask your supervisor to arrange for you to consult with your school's lawyer. You may be required to submit your question in writing, but school officials generally are willing to supply you with legal advice when it is requested. Don't hesitate, seek legal advice when needed.

In the event you ask for legal advice, and your school does not comply, it is suggested that you document your request in writing. A written document will protect you later if it turns out legal advice could have prevented a problem. In this litigious day and age, you must also protect yourself.

Confidentiality

Graduate school professors in counselor education programs always emphasize to their students that they *must* keep "secret" that information they learn in counseling relationships. And, most students have little or no problem grasping the importance of such a requirement. What graduate counselor education professors may fail to tell you, however, is that there are many *exceptions* to this confidentiality requirement and that most of the problems that occur when you begin practicing school counseling center around the *exceptions*, not the rule itself. Confidentiality issues are particularly troublesome for school counselors because most of their clients are minors. While the attitudes of counselors have a significant impact on the respect they have for the privacy of minors (Varhely & Cowles, 1991), there are many legal aspects of confidentiality related to counseling minors. Issues such as teen pregnancy, drug abuse, and suicide are causing school counselors to become more vulnerable to legal action. (Davis & Ritchie, 1993). The student on student violence that is prevalent in our schools is also complicating the confidential relationship between student and counselor and increasing the legal vulnerability of school counselors.

A major exception to the rule that counselors must keep secret what is told to them by clients occurs when counselors determine that their clients are a "*danger to themselves or others.*" If you arrive at the professional judgment that a client is a danger to self or others, you *must* take whatever steps are necessary to prevent harm. Often, the prohibition against telling others information you have learned in a counseling session must be compromised when you are taking steps to prevent harm. Counselors can be held accountable for an ethical violation or legal malpractice if clients they are serving harm themselves or others and it can be shown that the counselors *knew*, or *should have known*, that the clients were a danger to themselves or others.

For example, if a school counselor knew or should have known that a student was at risk for suicide and the child commits suicide, the counselor can be held legally liable. In recent years, school counselors have been sued and found negligent for not responding to suicidal threats made by students. Courts have found that even if the risk of the student actually committing suicide is remote, the possibility may be enough to establish a duty to contact the student's parents.

A counselor could be held liable if the counselor knew or should have known that a student was a danger to others and didn't take steps to prevent the harm. The Fifth Circuit Court of Appeals has stated that the "epidemic of violence in American public schools is a relatively new phenomenon, but one which has already generated considerable caselaw." *Johnson v. Dallas Independent School District,* 38 F.3d 198 (5th Cir. 1994). Counselors and other school personnel have a legal obligation to exercise reasonable care to protect students from foreseeable harm. *Eisel v. Board of Education,* 597 A.2d 447 (Md. 1991). In 1999, the United States Supreme Court noted that state courts routinely uphold claims alleging that schools have been negligent in failing to protect their students from the violent acts of their peers. *Davis v. Monroe County Board of Education,* 119 S.Ct. 1661 (1999).

Yet, counselors are only required to act like reasonable professionals. In determining what is reasonable, courts have found that school counselors are accountable for the degree of care that would be utilized by other professionals with similar education and experience. *Wyke v. Polk County School Board,* 129 F.3d 560 (11th Cir. 1997). You cannot anticipate acts of random violence and are not required by law to do so. Only failure to exercise reasonable care exposes counselors to liability.

When clients request that you give information obtained in a counseling session to a third party, you may do so, and in most circumstances, it would be inappropriate not to comply. In the case of minors, parents or guardians should grant permission to transfer confidential information to another individual.

A major exception to the confidentiality requirement occurs when a parent or legal guardian demands to know the contents of counseling sessions that have transpired with their children (Zingaro, 1983). If parents inquire about your sessions with their child, *always* ask the child if he/she they would object to your relating the contents of your sessions to the parents. Children are often less concerned about their privacy than are adults.

In the event children object, or you feel it would not be in the best interests of children you are counseling for their parents to be informed of the contents of counseling sessions, you certainly should try to convince the parents that hopefully, they are willing to trust you to tell them anything they need to know. You should explain to the parents why confidentiality is important in a counseling relationship and assure them you will involve them to the fullest possible extent in their children's lives. Conducting a joint session with parents and their children might satisfy the parents' concerns. However, always clear this with your client prior to conducting such joint sessions.

As a school counselor, it is doubtful you would be held in violation of any ethical or legal standards if you told parents information you obtained from counseling sessions with their children. However, there may be instances in which you might decide that you should not give parents the information they are demanding. You should realize that you could be violating the legal rights of the parents. Historically, the courts have protected parental rights (Isaacs & Stone, 1999).

A legal and ethical exception to confidentiality exists when a *court* formally *orders* you to disclose information obtained in a counseling relationship. A subpoena, however, is *not a court order* to disclose information and an attorney's advice must be sought when you are presented with a subpoena. That is, do not produce any records simply because you receive a subpoena until you have been advised to do so by an attorney. However, you must comply with court orders and you cannot be held legally or ethically accountable for breaching confidentiality if you are following the formal instructions of a judge.

Some of the other exceptions to confidentiality include the following situations: 1) you are receiving clinical supervision of your work as a counselor; 2) your secretary has access to confidential information; 3) you are consulting with a colleague or expert regarding a difficult case; and/or 4) you are consulting your employer or an attorney regarding a questionable circumstance.

As a school counselor, you may often be asked by a teacher or administrator to reveal personal information about the students or families you are counseling. An important question to consider in deciding whether the person asking has an "educational" need to know. In other words, does he or she need to know the information in order to provide appropriate educational services for the student. Will providing such information enhance the student's learning? Certainly, students and parents have a right to know if a counselor relates personal information about them to another school professional.

Confidentiality is an *ethical* obligation that you owe to clients. You can be held *legally* accountable, however, for any harm that occurs to clients because you *did not* keep information confidential (see Figure 28.1).

Privileged Communication

A different, but similar, concept is privileged communication. Communication between two individuals is legally privileged if a statute exists in your state that specifically grants it. If privilege exists, a judge *cannot* require that confidential information be disclosed. If legal privilege does not exist, judges *always* can order counselors to disclose information obtained in counseling relationships.

In order for school counselors to have privilege with their clients, a state statute must specify that privilege exists between school counselors and students. Approximately 20 states have such statutes (Sheeley & Herlihy, 1987). If a school counselor is a licensed, certified, or registered professional counselor, it is possible that privilege may exist based on that credential. An excellent reason for school counselors to become licensed, certified, or registered professional counselors is to qualify for "privilege" with their clients. Certification by a state department of education or by a national credentialing board (i.e., NBCC) does not extend privilege to the clients of school counselors.

Counseling Records

School counselors must be concerned about two types of records—*administrative* and *clinical*. Administrative records include cumulative folders and other records concerning students that are available to other school personnel. Clinical records are case notes that are kept to refresh the counselor's memory and to document important events regarding a counseling relationship with a student.

As a school counselor, it is important that you read and understand the provisions of the Family Educational Rights and Privacy Act of 1974, commonly known as the Buckley Amendment (Walker & Larrabee, 1985). Essentially this federal law requires that schools receiving federal funds provide access to all school records to parents of students under the age of 18 and to students themselves once they reach 18. In addition, the amendment requires that *no student records* be released to third parties without the express written consent of parents of minor students or the written consent of adult students.

One exception to the requirement that students or their parents have access to school records is that records kept in the *sole* possession of the maker do not have to be shown to students or parents. Counselor clinical records, or case notes, would come under this exception if you do not show them to anyone else. You should be cautioned, however, that just because students or parents do not have access to your clinical records under the Buckley Amendment, they might gain access through a court ordered or subpoena or the records might be obtained through other legal processes.

You should keep any administrative or clinical records you need as a counselor in order to do a good job. It is important that you record enough information to refresh or jog your memory, and to document events that take place that demonstrate you have performed your responsibilities in an appropriate and professional manner based on "standards of practice." In court, experts might be asked to review your records and make a judgment concerning whether you followed "standards of practice." You should not be concerned that students or parents may eventually see the records you are keeping. In fact, it is recommended that you *write each record as if it might someday be given out in court as public information with you, TV cameras, your student client, his or her parents, and others present!*

The same principles that apply to confidentiality and privileged communication apply to student records as well. Even if the relationship between you and the students you counsel is privileged by state or federal statute, there are circumstances under which you might be forced to reveal clinical records you have kept. For example, students *themselves* may subpoena records you have kept regarding sessions with them.

Keeping secret records does not protect them from a subpoena. Most subpoenas that seek records ask for *all* records kept under *all* circumstances in any location. You could be asked, following the taking of an oath, if there are any records related to the case being litigated. Records must be kept in secure locations, but there is no reason to keep records in secret places.

If you receive a subpoena requesting your records, tell your supervisor and consult the school's attorney as soon as possible. Do not automatically comply with the subpoena and do not panic. You could violate your client's legal rights if you turn over records in response to a non-court ordered subpoena without first protesting the subpoena in court.

Never destroy records you think might be subpoenaed at a later date. You could be guilty of a serious crime if you destroy evidence. In a school setting, you should destroy your clinical records on a regular schedule. For example, it might be wise to destroy clinical records at the beginning of each school year for students who are not presently attending the school. Inform your supervisor of your plan and procedure for destroying records and then act accordingly. In addition, check to see if your school system or state has a policy concerning records. It is *unwise* to keep records forever because they could be accidentally seen by others. However, if you regularly destroy most records, you should keep particular records for extended periods of time if the records document actions you took that would prove you acted responsibly in difficult situations. Check your local and or state regulations concerning the length of time (if any) that records should be kept.

Interaction with Families

School counselors must face many difficult legal and ethical problems related to family situations due to the fact that family life has become more complex (Sprinthall, Hall, & Gerler, 1992). As noted, most school students are minors, they are under the control of either parents or legal guardians. And, as mentioned previously, you must acknowledge the rights of parents and guardians and you have a legal obligation to interact with them.

Custody Cases

One of the more difficult areas is divorce and child custody. Parents who are going through the divorce process often seek to involve school counselors to assist them in obtaining custody of their children. That is, parents might ask you agree to testify on their behalf at custody hearings. However, you should *never* agree to take sides in a custody struggle, no matter how strongly you may feel that one parent is "superior" to the other (Remley, 1991).

There are several things that occur if you become involved as a witness at a child custody hearing. First, you lose your objectivity and effectiveness as the child's counselor and second, you run the risk of the accusation of being a biased expert witness by the opposing attorney. In addition, you become an advocate rather than an impartial helper and you will probably have difficulty responding to your other job responsibilities because of the time and energy such involvement demands.

It is recommended that you refuse to testify willingly in custody hearings. Of course, you may be subpoenaed and forced to participate. If you receive a subpoena, immediately ask your supervisor to arrange for you to speak with your school's attorney. It would be in your best interest to inform the attorney that you would rather not be involved in custody hearings and then follow the attorney's advice. In the event you do appear as a witness at a custody hearing, it is strongly recommended that you *never* give an opinion (unless ordered to do so by the judge) and that you restrict your testimony to *factual* information only regarding the parents and the child in question.

Once a court order has been issued involving custody, it is important to realize that most legal rights regarding the child have not been compromised for the noncustodial parent. In most states, noncustodial parents are entitled to many of the same rights that the custodial parent has, except that the custodial parent has the right to the physical possession of the child. Check with your supervisor concerning the existing policies regarding noncustodial parents in your state or school. Obtain a copy, if available, and become familiar with it.

When noncustodial parents demand records, visits, or even the right to remove their children from the school, the matter should be *referred* to school administrators. As a school counselor, you generally should not have to make decisions regarding the rights of noncustodial parents without administrative or legal assistance.

Non-Legal Parents, Guardians, and so forth

Stepparents, grandparents, and non-married partners of parents cause problems for school counselors. Legally, these individuals have no control over children you counsel, unless there are specific court orders giving them these rights. On the other hand, such people often are intimately involved with children and perform many parenting functions. You should be aware that individuals who are not parents or legal guardians *cannot waive* the rights of children or families of the children you serve. Obtaining written consent of a parent or legal guardian to interact with an adult who is in a child's life is one possible way to involve a non-parent or non-guardian without risking violation of another person's rights. Administrators *should* be consulted and their directions should be followed when questions arise concerning the involvement of stepparents, grandparents, and non-married partners of parents.

Laws and Child Abuse

Almost all political jurisdictions in the United States (all states, the District of Columbia, and territories) require that school counselors report to authorities cases of *suspected* child abuse. If child abuse is suspected and a report is not made, in most situations, you can be found guilty of committing a crime. In addition, statutes protect those who make reports from being sued by individuals who are suspected of child abuse.

Laws requiring that reports of suspected child abuse be made were passed because legislators were concerned that children were being harmed by those who were supposed to be taking care of them. And additionally, because these abused children had no recourse. Our society has decided that it is better to make a report of a *suspicion* of abuse that later proves to be false, than it is to hesitate in reporting simply because you are not absolutely certain that abuse has taken place.

Although the ethical standards of counselors prohibit you from revealing information you receive as a result of a counseling relationship, statutes that require reporting of suspected child abuse are an exception to this requirement.

Statutes in Your Jurisdiction

As a school counselor, you *must* read the exact words of the statute in your jurisdiction that controls the reporting of suspected child abuse cases. Become *completely* familiar with all the details of the statute. It will pay off in the long run. You can find the statute in the state code books in most local public libraries or in college or university libraries. Obtain a copy for your files. The exact words of the statute are very important because they vary so much from jurisdiction to jurisdiction. In some statutes, reports must be made directly by the person who suspects the abuse; in others, those who suspect abuse have fulfilled their legal obligations if a report is made to their *direct* supervisor in their work setting. In some laws, reports of abuse inflicted by *anyone* must be made; while in others, only abuse inflicted by a parent or guardian must be reported (and the person making the report is only protected if the report is made against a parent or guardian). In most statutes, the length of time that has passed since the abuse occurred is not mentioned (Smith, 1990); while in others, the language specifically states that abuse that occurred at any point in time must be reported. Some laws have defined "emotional abuse," but the wording varies. As mentioned, the wording of statutes varies greatly and each word can be important as you attempt to comply with legal requirements as to when and how you report suspected child abuse situations. Again, it will be in your best interest to obtain a copy of your states's statutes and that you become familiar with the "reporting" policies in your school or district.

Professional Judgment and Suspected Abuse

The first difficult tasks regarding suspected child abuse cases is to make a professional judgment whether abuse might have occurred. Ferris and Linville (1985) have offered some guidelines regarding abuse determinations. You do not have to be certain, you only must, in your professional judgment, have a legitimate suspicion. Exercising professional judgment means that you have to take into account all of the facts concerning this particular case and make an evaluation based on the knowledge and experience you have had as a counselor. From an ethical perspective, it is wise to consult with colleagues and experts when you are unsure. However, consultation is not required under child abuse reporting statutes. After you have carefully reviewed a situation, if you have any indication at all that child abuse might have occurred, you must make a report in the manner that is required by statute.

You may be tempted to not make a report even when you do suspect that a child has been abused. You may feel that it would cause more harm than good for a report to be made. If you do not understand the process that occurs after a report is made or are frustrated with the response of social services agencies, you should schedule a meeting with case workers who investigate reports of suspected child abuse cases (Wilder, 1991). If you *fail* to make a report and abuse is later discovered, along with the fact that you knew about it, you could be found guilty of a crime.

It is important that you remain involved in child abuse investigations, to the extent possible (and if it does not violate school policy), so that you can continue to be of help to students and their parents. Filing a report of suspected child abuse fulfills your legal obligations, but your ethical responsibilities require that you continue to offer the best professional services available to the students and families you serve (Horton, Johnson, Roundy, & Williams, 1990). However, again, become familiar with your school and/or school system's policy. Some school administrations forbid counselors' continued involvement in a case if that counselor was the individual reporting the suspected abuse. If the latter is the case, ethically you *must* refer your former client.

Supervision

School counselors have ethical and legal obligations related to supervising others. Individuals you might supervise include graduate program practicum students or interns, other full-time counselors who are employed in your department, clerical employees, and peer helpers in your school.

Since supervision implies control over the person being supervised, it is possible that you could be held ethically or legally responsible for the improper acts of others. A supervisor generally must ensure that people being supervised are performing their duties in an appropriate manner. You need to train those you supervise and check their work. Of course, you cannot observe or direct everything completed by those under your supervision. You are expected to maintain the amount of control over your supervisee that a *reasonable* counselor would exercise in a similar situation.

In the event you learn that someone you are supervising is involved in any activities that violate school policies or procedures, ethical standards of the counseling profession, or laws, you must take whatever steps are necessary to correct the situation. If you look the other way or ignore the situation, you personally could be held accountable for harm that results.

Requiring a graduate student or employee you are supervising to buy professional liability insurance for themselves does not protect you from being sued if they harm someone. Although professional liability insurance is a good idea for any person who renders professional services, it protects the individual who purchases the insurance, not the supervisor. Generally, professional liability insurance will cover you, however, if you are sued for the act or omission of a supervisee.

School counselors sometimes are given responsibility for supervising an employee, but are not given evaluation or dismissal power over the individual. If you find that an employee under your supervision is acting inappropriately, but you do not have the authority to correct the person, it is vital that you put your supervisor on notice of the problem and request that he or she take whatever action is necessary to ensure that the employee is acting ethically and legally.

Counselors as Employees

Employers have the right to demand that employees do what they are told. If an employee refuses to follow an employer's directive, the employee can be accused of insubordination, which is legal cause for dismissal. As long as the demands of your employer or supervisor are legal, you are required to comply.

School counselors have the responsibility of knowing all rules and regulations within the environment in which they work. It is important for you to follow the policies of your school, district, and state. If you find rules, regulations, or policies that are objectionable, you should work toward getting them changed, but must adhere to them in the interim.

A Written Job Description

For your own protection, you should have an accurate and complete job description that you and your employer have agreed constitutes your responsibilities. *Written* job descriptions signed by both you and your supervisor are preferable. You can ask for a written job description if one does not exist. Job descriptions developed within your school must conform to district or state job descriptions, which generally are rather broad.

A good job description lists all duties you regularly perform and does not include any activities for which you are not responsible. It is detailed enough that an outsider could understand your job, but does not include so many specifics that you are given little or no flexibility in accomplishing your objectives.

Ethical Violations and Employment

School counselors may find that they are being forced by their employers to do things that they feel violate the *Ethical Standards* (1995) of the American Counseling Association (ACA) or the *Ethical Standards for School Counselors* (1998) promulgated by the American School Counselor Association (Figure 28.2). If you find yourself in such a situation and refuse to follow your employer's directives, you could find yourself being fired for insubordination. If you challenged your dismissal, you would have to prove that what you were being asked to do violated the standards of your profession and that your employer's demands were therefore unreasonable. Because the burden would be on you to prove your employer's unreasonableness, and that would be difficult, you have a better chance of correcting a situation if you use *persuasion* and *education*, rather than confrontation. You might offer to your employer the professional literature which supports your position that whatever you are being asked to do is unethical. You also could ask the American Counseling Association or the American School Counselor Association ethics committees (assuming you are a member) to provide you formal rulings related to the questionable activity. Most employers are respectful of professional ethical standards and will yield if they can be convinced that a particular activity or act constitutes a violation of those standards.

Private Practice and the School Counselor

School counselors sometimes open part-time private practices. It is important that any private practice activities in which you become involved are within legal and ethical standards.

In many states, you must have a state license as a professional mental health counselor in order to open a private practice. Licenses are issued by state regulatory boards.

A private practice is a business, and you must have a business license to operate in most political jurisdictions. Business licenses are available in town halls, city halls, or county court houses. Local political entities issue business licenses to collect local taxes on the income of businesses. If you fail to purchase a business license, you could be found guilty of a crime and perhaps even tax evasion.

Ethical standards require that you not accept clients in your private practice who have a relationship to your school. You must use your own judgment, given your particular circumstances, but it is possible that you should not accept private practice clients who are connected to your school district in any way. Some school districts have policies concerning private practice on the part of their counselor employees. It would be in your best interest to know about and adhere to such an existing policy. For example, one Florida school board does not permit its school counselor employees to conduct private practice within the boundaries of their particular county.

Personal Liability

All professionals should purchase professional liability insurance, and school counselors are no exception. Although the chance of school counselors being sued for negligence or malpractice still is quite low, as counselors become more visible and accepted as mental health professionals in our society, the number of cases is increasing dramatically.

School counselors sometimes are under the mistaken impression that if their school is covered by professional liability insurance, then they are protected as well. Policies that cover schools will defend the *school* and pay off any judgments against the school related to malpractice cases. In defending a school, attorneys for the school often work closely with individuals who are also named in a suit and give the appearance that they are attorneys for the individuals as well. In reality, the best interests of the *school* and the *counselor* in question may not be the same. Anytime you are individually named in a lawsuit (which usually is the case if a counselor is involved), you need to have your own professional liability insurance which will provide you with your own personal lawyer who has only *your* best interests in mind.

Professional liability insurance sometimes is an automatic benefit for school counselors who belong to unions. It can be purchased from the American Counseling Association, but is available only to members.

Facing Ethical and Legal Problems: Some Guidelines

Listed below are some general guidelines for dealing with ethical and legal dilemmas as they arise:

- Know and follow the ethical standards of the American Counseling Association and the American School Counselor Association. The ethical practice recommendations given in Figure 28.3 will also prove helpful.
- Always consult with colleagues and experts when you are unsure. Since the standards for ethics and law relate to generally accepted practices, consultation that leads to a consensus of opinion can be very important if decisions you make are later challenged.
- Always ask for a legal opinion or a personal consultation with the school's attorney when you are facing a difficult legal problem.
- Document any actions you take that can prove that you have acted in a professional and appropriate manner.
- Turn over to administrators difficult situations that are not within your power to resolve.
- Read the current professional literature related to law and ethics to ensure that you understand the issues and have the latest advice.
- Attend professional seminars and programs related to legal and ethical issues in counseling.
- Be sure you have your own professional liability insurance policy.

Figure 28.1
Exceptions to Confidentiality and Privileged Communication

1. Client is a danger to self or others.
2. Client requests release of information.
3. A court orders release of information.
4. Systematic clinical supervision of the counselor.
5. Clerical assistants who process information and papers.
6. Client care team members.
7. Legal and clinical consultation.
8. Clinical supervision.
9. Clients raise the issue of their mental health in a lawsuit.
10. A third party is present in the room.
11. Group counseling.
12. Family counseling.
13. Clients are below the age of 18.
14. Counselors must defend themselves against a complaint regarding their services.

Joe Wittmer, PhD

Figure 28.2
Ethical Practice Recommendations

School counselors should:

- Act in the best interests of their clients at all times. Act in good faith and in the absence of malice.

- Inform clients of possible limitations on the counseling relationship prior to beginning the relationship.

- Increase awareness of personal values, attitudes, and beliefs; and refer when personal characteristics hinder effectiveness.

- Function within the boundaries of personal competence. Be aware of personal skill levels and limitations.

- Be able to fully explain why they did what they did. A theoretical rationale should undergird counseling strategies and interventions.

- Encourage family involvement, where possible, when working with minors in sensitive areas which might be controversial.

- Follow written job descriptions. Be sure that what they are doing is defined as an appropriate function in their setting.

- Read and adhere to the ethical standards of their profession. Keep copies of the ethical standards on hand, review them periodically and act accordingly.

- Consult with other professionals (colleagues, supervisors, counselor educators, ethics committees, etc.). Have a readily accessible support network of professionals.

- Join appropriate professional associations. Read association publications and participate in professional development opportunities.

- Stay up-to-date with laws and current court rulings, particularly those pertaining to counseling with minors.

- Consult with a knowledgeable attorney, when necessary. In questionable cases, seek legal advice prior to initiating actions (*The ASCA Counselor*, December, 1991).

Figure 28.3

American School Counselor Association
Ethical Standards For School Counselors

(Revised June 25, 1998)

Preamble

The American School Counselor Association (ASCA) is a professional organization whose members have a unique and distinctive preparation grounded in the behavioral sciences, with training in clinical skills adapted to the school setting. The counselor assists in the growth and development of each individual and uses his/her highly specialized skills to protect the interests of the counselee within the structure of the school system. School counselors subscribe to the following basic tenets of the counseling process from which professional responsibilities are derived:

1. Each person has the right to respect and dignity as a human being and to counseling services without prejudice as to person, character, belief or practice, regardless of age color, disability, ethnic group, gender, race, religion, sexual orientation, marital status or socioeconomic status.

2. Each person has the right to self-direction and self-development.

3. Each person has the right of choice and the responsibility for goals reached.

4. Each person has the right to privacy and thereby the right to expect the counselor-counselee relationship to comply with all laws, policies, and ethical standards pertaining to confidentiality.

In this document the American School Counselor Association has specified the principles of ethical behavior necessary to maintain and regulate the high standards of integrity, leadership, and professionalism among its members. The Ethical Standards for School Counselors were developed to clarify the nature of ethical responsibilities held in common by its members. As the code of ethics of the association, this document establishes principles that define the ethical behavior of its members. The purposes of this document are to:

1. Serve as a guide for the ethical practices of all professional school counselors, regardless of level, area, population served, or membership in this professional association.

2. Provide benchmarks for both self-appraisal and peer evaluations regarding counselor responsibilities to counselees, parents, colleagues and professional associates, schools and community, self and, the counseling profession.

3. Inform those served by the school counselor of acceptable counselor practices and expected professional behavior.

A. Responsibilities to Students

The professional school counselor:

a. Has a primary obligation to the counselee who is to be treated with respect as a unique individual.

b. Is concerned with the educational, career, emotional, and behavior needs and encourages the maximum development of each counselee.

c. Refrains from consciously encouraging the counselee's acceptance of values, lifestyles, plans, decisions, and beliefs that represent the counselor's personal orientation.

d. Is responsible for keeping informed of laws, regulations or policies relating to counselees and strives to ensure that the rights of counselees are adequately provided for and protected.

A2. Confidentiality

The professional school counselor:

a. Informs the counselee of the purposes, goals, techniques and rules of procedure under which she/he may receive counseling at or before the time when the counseling relationship is entered. Notice includes confidentiality issues such as the possible necessity for consulting with other professionals, privileged communication, and legal or authoritative restraints. The meaning and limits of confidentiality are clearly defined to counselees through a written and shared statement of disclosure.

b. Keeps information confidential unless disclosure is required to prevent clear and imminent danger to the counselee or others or when legal requirements demand that confidential information be revealed. Counselors will consult with other professionals when in doubt as to the validity of an exception.

c. Discloses information to an identified third party, who by his or her relationship with the counselee is at a high risk of contracting a disease that is commonly known to be both communicable and fatal. Prior to disclosure, the counselor will ascertain that the counselee has not already informed the third party about his or her disease and that he/she is not intending to inform the third party in the immediate future.

d. Requests from the court that disclosure not be required when the release of confidential information without a counselee's permission may lead to potential harm to the counselee.

e. Protects the confidentiality of counselee's records and releases personal data only according to prescribed laws and school policies. Student information maintained in computers is treated with the same care as traditional student records.

f. Protects the confidentiality of information received in the counseling relationship as specified by federal and state laws, written policies and applicable ethical standards. Such information is only to be revealed to others with the informed consent of the counselee, consistent with the obligation of the counselor as a professional person. In a group setting, the counselor sets a norm of confidentiality and stresses its importance, yet clearly states that confidentiality in group counseling cannot be guaranteed.

A3. Counseling Plans

The professional school counselor:

• works jointly with the counselee in developing integrated and effective counseling plans, consistent with both the abilities and circumstances of the counselee and counselor. Such plans will be regularly reviewed to ensure continued viability and effectiveness, respecting the counselee's freedom of choice.

A4. Dual Relationships

The professional school counselor:

• avoids dual relationships which might impair his/her objectivity and increase the risk of harm to the client (e.g., counseling one's family members, close friends or associates). If a dual relationship is unavoidable, the counselor is responsible for taking action to eliminate or reduce the potential for harm. Such safeguards might include informed consent, consultation, supervision and documentation.

A5. Appropriate Referrals

The professional school counselor:

• makes referrals when necessary or appropriate to outside resources. Appropriate referral necessitates knowledge of available resources, and making appropriate plans for transitions with minimal interruption of services. Counselees retain the right to discontinue the counseling relationship at any time.

A6. Group Work

The professional school counselor:

• screens prospective group members and maintains an awareness of participants' needs and goals in relation to the goals of the group. The counselor takes reasonable precautions to protect members from physical and psychological harm resulting from interaction within the group.

A7. Danger to Self or Others

The professional school counselor:

• informs appropriate authorities when the counselee's condition indicates a clear and imminent danger to the counselee or others. This is to be done after careful deliberation and, where possible, after consultation with other counseling professionals. The counselor informs the counselee of actions to be taken so as to minimize his or her confusion and clarify counselee and counselor expectations.

A8. Student records

The professional school counselor:

• maintains and secures records necessary for rendering professional services to the counselee as required by laws, regulations, institutional procedures, and confidentiality guidelines.

A9. Evaluation, Assessment and Interpretation

The professional school counselor:

a. Adheres to all professional standards regarding selection, administration, and interpretation of assessment measures. The counselor recognizes that computer-based testing programs require specific training in administration, scoring and interpretation which may differ from that required in more traditional assessments.

b. Provides explanations of the nature, purposes, and results of assessment/evaluation measures in language that can be understood by counselee(s).

c. Does not misuse assessment results and interpretations and takes reasonable steps to prevent others from misusing the information.

d. Utilizes caution when using assessment techniques, making evaluations, and interpreting the performance of populations not represented in the norm group on which an instrument was standardized.

A10. Computer Technology

The professional school counselor:

a. Promotes the benefits of appropriate computer applications and clarifies the limitations of computer technology. The counselor ensures that (1) computer applications are appropriate for the individual needs of the counselee, (2) the counselee understands how to use the application, and (3) follow-up counseling assistance is provided. Members of under-represented groups are assured equal access to computer technologies and the absence of discriminatory information and values within computer applications.

b. Counselors who communicate with counselees via internet should follow the NBCC Standards for WebCounseling.

A11. Peer Helper Programs

The professional school counselor:

- has unique responsibilities when working with peer helper programs. The school counselor is responsible for the welfare of counselees participating in peer helper programs under his/her direction. School counselors who function in training and supervisory capacities are referred to the preparation and supervision standards of professional counselor associations.

B. Responsibilities to Parents

B1. Parent Rights and Responsibilities

The professional school counselor:

a. Respects the inherent rights and responsibilities of parents for their children and endeavors to establish as appropriate, a collaborative relationship with parents to facilitate the maximum development of the counselee.

b. Adheres to laws and local guidelines when assisting parents experiencing family difficulties which interfere with the counselee's effectiveness and welfare.

c. Sensitive to the cultural and social diversity among families and recognizes that all parents, custodial and noncustodial, are vested with certain rights and responsibilities for the welfare of their children by virtue of their position and according to law.

B.2 Parents and Confidentiality

The professional school counselor:

a. Informs parents of the counselor's role with emphasis on the confidential nature of the counseling relationship between the counselor and counselee.

b. Provides parents with accurate, comprehensive and relevant information in an objective and caring manner, as appropriate and consistent with ethical responsibilities to the counselee.

c. Makes reasonable efforts to honor the wishes of parents and guardians concerning information that he/she may share regarding the counselee.

C. Responsibilities to Colleagues and Professional Associates

C1. Professional Relationships

The professional school counselor:

a. Establishes and maintains a professional relationship with faculty, staff and administration to facilitate the provision of optimum counseling services. The relationship is based on the counselor's definition and description of the parameters and levels of his/her professional roles.

b. Treats colleagues with respect, courtesy, fairness and in a professional manner. The qualifications, views, and findings, of colleagues are represented to accurately reflect the image of competent professionals.

c. Is aware of and optimally utilizes related professionals and organizations to whom the counselee may be referred.

C2. Sharing Information with Other Professionals

The professional school counselor:

a. Promotes awareness and adherence to appropriate guidelines regarding confidentiality, the distinction between public and private information, and staff consultation.

b. Provides professional personnel with accurate, objective, concise and meaningful data necessary to adequately evaluate, counsel, and assist the counselee.

c. If a counselee is receiving services from another counselor or other mental health professional, the counselor, with client consent will inform the other professional and develop clear agreements to avoid confusion and conflict for the counselee.

D. Responsibilities to the School and Community

D1. Responsibilities to the School

The professional school counselor:

a. Supports and protects the educational program against any infringement not in the best interests of counselees.

b. Informs appropriate officials of conditions that may be potentially disruptive or damaging to the school's mission, personnel and property, while honoring the confidentiality between the counselee and the counselor.

c. Delineates and promotes the counselor's role and function in meeting the needs of those served. The counselor will notify appropriate officials of conditions which may limit or curtail his/her effectiveness in providing programs and services.

d. Accepts employment only for positions for which he/she is qualified by education, training, supervised experience, state and national professional credentials, and appropriate professional experience. Counselors recommend that administrators hire for professional counseling positions only individuals who are qualified and competent.

e. Assists in the development of (1) curricular and environmental conditions appropriate for the school and community, (2) educational procedures and programs to meet the counselee's developmental needs and (3) a systematic evaluation process for comprehensive school counseling programs, services and personnel. The counselor is guided by the findings of the evaluation data in planning programs and services.

D2. Responsibility to the Community

The professional school counselor:

- collaborates with agencies, organizations, and individuals in the school and community in the best interest of counselees and without regard to personal reward or remuneration.

E. Responsibilities to Self

E1. Professional Competence

The professional school counselor:

a. Functions within the boundaries of individual professional competence and accepts responsibility for the consequences of his/her actions.

b. Monitors personal functioning and effectiveness and does not participate in any activity which may lead to inadequate professional services or harm to a counselee.

c. Strives through personal initiative to maintain professional competence and keep abreast of scientific and professional information. Professional and personal growth is continuous and ongoing throughout the counselor's career.

E2. Multicultural Skills

The professional school counselor:

- understands the diverse cultural backgrounds of the counselees with whom he/she works. This includes, but is not limited to, learning how the school counselor's own cultural/ethnic/racial identity impacts his/her values and beliefs about the counseling process.

F. Responsibilities to the Profession

F1. Professionalism

The professional school counselor:

a. Accepts the policies and processes for handling ethical violations as a result of maintaining membership in the American School Counselor Association.

b. Conducts himself/herself in such a manner as to advance individual, ethical practice and the profession.

c. Conducts appropriate research and reports findings in a manner consistent with acceptable educational and psychological research practices. When using client data for research, statistical, or program planning purposes, the counselor ensures protection of the identity of the individual counselees.

d. Adheres to ethical standards of the profession, other official policy statements pertaining to counseling, and relevant statutes established by federal, state and local governments.

e. Clearly distinguishes between statements and actions made as a private individual and as a representative of the school counseling profession.

f. Does not use his/her professional position to recruit or gain clients, consultees for his/her private practice, seek and receive unjustified personal gains, unfair advantage, sexual favors, or unearned goods or services.

F2. Contribution to the Profession

The professional school counselor:

a. Actively participates in local, state and national associations which foster the development and improvement of school counseling.

b. Contributes to the development of the professional through the sharing of skills, ideas, and expertise with colleagues.

References

G. Maintenance of Standards

Ethical behavior among professional school counselors, Association members and non members, is expected at all times. When there exists serious doubt as to the ethical behavior of colleagues, or if counselors are forced to work in situations or abide by policies which do not reflect the standards as outlined in the Ethical Standards for School Counselors, the counselor is obligated to take appropriate action to rectify the condition. The following procedure may serve as a guide.

1. The counselor should consult with a professional colleague to confidentially discuss the nature of the complaint to see if he/she views the situation as an ethical violation.

2. When feasible, the counselor should directly approach the colleague whose behavior is in question to discuss the complaint and seek appropriate resolution.

3. If resolution is not forthcoming at the personal level, the counselor shall utilize the channels established within the school, school district, the state SCA and ASCA Ethics Committee.

4. If the matter still remains unresolved, referral for review and appropriate action should be made to the Ethics Committees in the following sequence:

   • State school counselor association

   • American School Counselor Association

5. The ASCA Ethics Committee is responsible for educating and consulting with the membership regarding the ethical standards. The Committee periodically reviews and recommends changes in the code as well as the Policies and Procedures for Processing Complaints of Ethical Violations. The Committee will also receive and process questions to clarify the application of such standards. Questions must be submitted in writing to the ASCA Ethics Chair. Finally, the Committee will handle complaints of alleged violations of our ethical standards. Therefore, at the national level, complaints should be submitted in writing to the ASCA Ethics Committee, c/o The Executive Director, American School Counselor Association, 801 North Fairfax Street, Suite 310, Alexandria, Va 22314.

American Counseling Association. (1995). *Ethical standards.* Alexandria, VA: Author.

American School Counselor Association. (1998). *Ethical standards for school counselors,* Alexandria, VA. ASCA Press.

Corey, G., Corey, M.S., & Callahan, P. (1998). *Issues and ethics in the helping professions* (5th ed.). Pacific Grove, CA: Brooks/Cole.

Davis, T., & Ritchie, M. (1993). Confidentiality and the school counselor: A challenge for the 1990s. *The School Counselor, 41,* 23-30.

Ferris, PA, & Linville, M.E. (1985). The child's rights: Whose responsibility? *Elementary School Guidance & Counseling, 19,* 172-180.

Herlihy, B., & Corey, G. (1992). *Dual relationships in counseling.* Alexandria, VA: American Counseling Association.

Horton, A.L., Johnson, B.L., Roundy, L. M., & Williams, D. (1990). *The incest perpetrator A family member no one wants to treat.* Newbury Park, CA: Sage Publications.

Isaacs, M.L., & Stone, C. (1999). School counselors and confidentiality: Factors affecting professional choices. *Professional School Counseling, 2,* 258-266.

Remley, T. P., Jr. (1991). *Preparing for court appearances.* Alexandria, VA. American Counseling Association.

Sheeley, V.L., & Herlihy, B. (1987). Privileged communication in school counseling: Status update. *The School counselor, 34,* 268-272.

Smith, K.M. (1990). A counselor goes to court. In B. Herlihy & L.B. Golden, *AACD ethical standards casebook* (4th ed.). Alexandria, VA. American Counseling Association.

Sprinthall, N. A., Hall, J.S., & Gerler, E.R., Jr. (1992). Peer counseling for middle school students experiencing family divorce: A deliberate psychological education model. *Elementary School Guidance and Counseling, 26,* 279-294.

Varhely, S.C., & Cowles, J. (1991). Counselor self-awareness and client confidentiality: A relationship revisited. *Elementary School Guidance and Counseling, 25,* 269-276.

Walker, M.M., & Larrabee, M.J.). (1985). Ethics and school records. *Elementary School Guidance and Counseling, 19,* 210-216.

Wilder, P. (1991). A counselor's contribution to the child abuse referral network. *The School Counselor, 38,* 203-214.

Wrightsman, L.W. (1997). *Psychology and the legal system.* Pacific Grove, CA: Brooks/Cole.

Zingaro, J.C. (1983). Confidentiality: To tell or not to tell. *Elementary School Guidance and Counseling, 17,* 261 - 267.

Chapter 29
The School Counselor and Credentialing

by

Thomas Clawson

Thomas W. Clawson, EdD., NCC, NCSC, is the Executive Director of the National Board for Certified Counselors, Inc. (NBCC®). Dr. Clawson has been a school counselor, private practitioner, and counselor educator. He is a past chair of the National Commission for Certifying Agencies and a past president of the National Organization for Competency Assurance. He currently is a board member of The Center for Quality Assurance in International Education.

Introduction

During the decade of the '90s, most of the focus of counselor credentialing centered on the movement toward licensure of counselors, state by state. In fact, the term "counselor licensure" has come to be often substituted for any state legislation that regulates the private practice of counselors. It should be acknowledged that as a profession, school counselors have played an important, vital, and often decisive role in the chronology of state counselor regulation. The professional school counseling movement has given tremendous support to the "appropriately credentialed" practicing counselor through the years. The first credentialed counselors were school counselors, then regulated as guidance counselors or guidance teachers by individual state departments of education. Since school counselors functioned in a milieu of teachers and other educators, they were originally required to have teaching certificates in a cognitive subject area, as well as an additional endorsement in school counseling. In the early 1970s, some states began to remove the requirement of teaching experience and teaching certificates for counselors; thus began formal recognition by the field of education that school counselors, like school nurses and school psychologists, for example, need not also be experienced or credentialed as teachers. Many states, however, continue to require teacher certification prior to one being permitted to seek certification as a school counselor.

The professional school counselors have been instrumental in helping the private practice clinical counselors gain statutory recognition. Almost all of the original committees in states seeking counselor licensure legislation, for example, have included school counselors. In some cases, particularly in the early '80s, school counselors have chaired and made up the majority of such committees. School counselors have always represented a significant percentage of the current 55,000 licensed, private practice counselors. Their motivation for appropriately credentialed counselors has been, and remains exemplary.

Motivation for school counselors to help seek state regulation for private practitioners falls into four categories:

First, school counselors rarely practice privately, but often have opportunities to do so. They see private license as a means of second income, retirement income or as a possible career move. Second, school counselors accept and understand credentialing as they have a history of familiarity with such state regulation. In addition, referral of "troubled" students to private practitioners is a routine activity of school counselors.

Since credentialing is newer to most in professional counseling (e.g., mental health counselors or substance abuse counselors), the purpose of licenses and certifications is often a foreign concept. Graduates of most counselor education programs have little practical knowledge about the next step in their professional careers. School counselors, on the other hand, have familiarity with state department of education regulations because of likely past teaching experience and the fact of knowing they must become state licensed or certified to practice in a school.

The American School Counselor Association (ASCA) actively promotes professionalization through credentialing. Leadership speeches, journal and newsletter articles, and workshops continue to promote professionalism. ASCA presidents from the late '80s through today have vigorously espoused the role of the school counselor as a professional member of our educational and mental health teams, as well as the need for individual credentialing. Professionalism is a theme of the current ACA movement; credentialing is one of the essential avenues to reach its goals.

Third, school counselors are active in professionalization movements and understand that private practice credentialing elevates all professional counselors with more public recognition. Any enhancement of the whole profession also enhances the specialty practices of the profession, especially school counselors.

In addition to the three points made above, school counselors have a long history of political and social activism in support of credentialing. The fact is, many of the school counselor supporters of private practice simply do so because it is the best thing for the profession and their individual colleagues. And, as noted, they often make referrals to these professionals whom they have supported.

A real "maze" exists today in the credentialing realm and some brief definitions might be helpful.

Definition of Terms

License: Permission granted by a state government allowing practice of a trade by an individual meeting professional criteria. While most states designate teaching and school counseling as a *certificate or endorsement,* that educational credential is probably a *license* in the strictest of terms.

Certification: Usually a voluntary credential granted by a private agency or government to denote professional status. Again, the use of the term "certification" in education is confusing. National certifications (discussed later) are voluntary, while state educational certificates are mandatory to hold school counselor positions.

Registration: Of the three types of credentials for individuals, registry is the least restrictive. Registry can range from formal submission of a portfolio including training, experience and examination to simple listing of names, addresses and areas of expertise.

Endorsement: Many state boards of education require a school counselor to hold a teaching license (or certificate) and then go on to endorse specific areas of competence. Endorsements vary from state to state. Some endorse a teaching certificate for K-12 or K-6/6-12 or as a Guidance Counselor, School Counselor or Pupil Personnel Specialist. Training required for endorsements varies widely across states.

Accreditation: Official agency approval of an academic institution's degree program. In counseling, the Council for the Accreditation of Counseling and Related Educational Programs (CACREP) has approved 133 (CACREP 1999) institutions with counselor education programs meeting high standards of quality, length, supervision, and curriculum.

School Counseling programs existing in institutions of higher education can receive CACREP recognition and often are the most comprehensive master's degree programs within counselor preparation programs. They definitely have the longest history of any other counseling degree programs within the profession.

Importance of State Credentialing

Professionals in any field sometimes use credentialing as a means of personal/professional enhancement and prestige instead of recognizing that obtaining a credential is primarily designed for the protection of the public, their consumers. Legislation and regulation dealing with professional school counselors is meant to assure parents, teachers and students (their publics) that counselors dealing with children meet minimum requirements of education, experience, character, and adhere to a code of ethics. Counselors are often frustrated with state regulatory agencies' inability to deal with individual differences in the training of counselors. The state board of education, in turn, responds that their mission is not to protect or enhance the practice of counseling, but conversely, to protect clients from malpractice. As minimum standards have increased for school counselors over the years, so has the quality of practice in the field. The public is protected by the regulation of school counselors, especially since minimum standards for practice have risen steadily over the past three decades.

Professional school counselors are not only regulated but also protected by state credential regulations in various ways. Their title is clear to the public which allows school counselors the opportunity to practice their trade. School systems which hire unqualified school counselors risk the loss of accreditation and open themselves to scrutiny by the public and counselors, as well as to legal action against such hiring practice. The practice of hiring unqualified counselors is, unfortunately, common (O'Rourke, 1991).

Professional protection also is useful when salary negotiations in school systems ignore special services. Role definition is more easily argued when a strong tradition of credentialing is evident; hence, the school counselor can make a strong case for salary equity in the teaching profession. Their being appropriately credentialed adds greatly to their professionalism.

Closely aligned with title protection, as well as public protection, is the often overlooked security that ethical standards provide professional school counselors. While ethical standards delineate the code of conduct for practice, they also give school counselors a method of defending themselves from baseless or false charges. In the majority of ethics charges brought against National Certified Counselors (NCC) over a 17-year period (1982-1999), NCCs were able to have professional validation of their proper practice. In short, the ethical codes that protect the public can also protect the school counselor's reputation. Of note is that school counselors have a very low rate of ethics charges.

Most state school counselor credentials require continuing education. The field of education has long held that current training is necessary to keep up with developments in the field. School counselors have a wealth of options to continue their learning. Most school districts provide in-service training and/or support to attend workshops and seminars. An additional advantage to school counselors is the fact that, with an estimated 80,000 school counselors in the United States (*Occupational Outlook Handbook,* 1998-1999), state and national credentialing mandate hundreds of thousands of hours of training each year. Professional school counselors are the primary source of training delivery, so the profession has created another source of employment, that of peer training.

Importance of National Credentialing

School counseling as a specialty of the counseling profession is still emerging. While our roots go back to the beginning of the century, as Wittmer noted in Chapter 1 of this book, the years since 1958 have been the most dynamic in fashioning the field; thus, school counseling is still young enough to be considered at the end of the "first generation" of the counseling profession. The development of research, systems and literature has enabled us to define school counseling and proffer supportive, public statements. National standards are created and refined to ensure that individual states do not redefine present practice. National certification remains an important ingredient, not only in maintaining the status quo, but in continually upgrading minimum requirements. A "first generation" of any profession cannot continue without such guidance. National standards, not state edicts, are the heart of school counseling's continuance as a viable professional specialty. There was a time when administrators solely defined the role of counselors. That relic remains, but for the most part, counselors define their new roles—not as clerical help for administration—but as developmental experts serving as the primary coordinators of a professional team.

School counselors now have available a national certificate; the *National Certified School Counselor* (NCSC). Those holding this important credential have signified their willingness to voluntarily challenge themselves with an examination, peer assessment, and continuing education requirements. It adds greatly to individual self-esteem and to the personal feeling of professionalism. The NCSC credential is an advanced specialty of the National Certified Counselor (NCC) general practice credential created by the National Board for Certified Counselors (NBCC). It is a result of the joint efforts of NBCC, the American Counseling Association (ACA), and ACA's school counseling division, the American School Counselor Association. The NCSC specialty credential attests to the educational background, knowledge, skills and competencies of the specialist in school counseling.

The purposes of national certification are to:

- **Promote** school counselors' professional identity, visibility and accountability on a national level.

- **Identify** to the counseling profession and the public those counselors who have met national professional school counseling standards.

- **Advance** cooperation between school systems, professional organizations and other credentialing and professional development agencies.

- **Encourage** professional growth and development of school counselors (NBCC, 1992).

National Certified School Counselors must first meet the general practice requirements for the NCC certification: a minimum of a master's degree in counseling or a closely related field, two years post-master's professional counseling experience, skills assessment by a supervisor and colleague and pass the National Counselor Examination (NCE). The NCE is also the industry standard examination in counselor licensure for private practice.

Requirements for the NCSC specialty include additional experience (specific to school counseling), specialized coursework and competency assessments. Certified School Counselors must meet the following areas of competence:

1. Assessing student needs.
2. Individual counseling.
3. Group counseling.
4. Consultation with staff, students and parents.
5. Coordination of programs; e.g., testing career development, substance abuse.
6. Career counseling.
7. Educational counseling.
8. Pre-college counseling.
9. Identifying and making appropriate referrals.
10. Administering and interpreting achievement tests, interest surveys, aptitude tests and personality inventories.
11. Cultural diversity in counseling.
12. Ethical decision making.
13. Building supportive climates for students and staff.
14. Removing or decreasing race and gender bias in school policy and curriculum.
15. Explaining to the staff, community and parents the scope of practice and functions of a school counselor.
16. Planing and conducting in-service for staff.
17. Identifying resources and information relating to students.
18. Evaluating the effectiveness of counseling programs.

Besides setting minimum standards of training and experience for school counselors, NBCC requires continuing education and adherence to formal ethical standards. At the conclusion of each five-year certification period, all National Certified Counselors must have completed 100 hours of continuing education, and National Certified School Counselors must have completed an additional 25 clock hours in the school counseling field.

The ethical standards set forth by NBCC and the American Counseling Association (ACA) contribute to client protection, as well as providing needed answers to complicated questions of ethical practice. As stated earlier, ethical standards are helpful to the client as well as the profession.

National certification is also a help in establishing *reciprocal agreements* between states. We have seen interstate reciprocity be possible in state licensing because so many state private practice laws are modeled after national certificates such as NBCC's. There are many stated education department reciprocal agreements, but they vary from year to year as individual states continue to upgrade requirements. Some states have laws that forbid any reciprocity agreements. It is the hope of NBCC that the NCSC credential will serve as the first viable avenue of cross-state certification. New Mexico, Nevada and Oklahoma currently use the NCSC as an alternative entry for state school counseling credentialing. It is a part of NBCC's long-range plan to propose to state boards of education that the NCSC be adopted in each state as an "alternative" method to gain state school counselor endorsement. Under such a proposal, each state's unique requirements would remain the same, but for those holding the NCSC, the state requirements would be considered to have been met. If all states could adopt such a plan, a de facto reciprocity would be created. Thus, as noted, the NCSC has added greatly to school counseling as a whole and, hopefully, will be considered essential to current and aspiring school counselors.

Hollis (2000) listed around 450 educational institutions offering master's degrees in counseling. Certification, in conjunction with accreditation, establishes commonality for these 450 divergent programs. A national certificate creates a benchmark to be met by counselor education programs and students planning their programs of study. Since national boards solicit experts from academia to help formulate requirements, master's degree programs are well served by noting their standards and later modifications.

Accreditation agencies of counselor education programs are: the Council for Accreditation of Counseling and Related Educational Programs (CACREP) and the Commission on Rehabilitation Education (CORE). Both groups are made up primarily of counselor educators who set standards of training based upon extensive experience in the field. Even unaccredited programs tend to subscribe to the common core of training required of recognized schools. Accreditation of programs, like certification of individuals, is another way to ensure continuing and recognized standards. CACREP is the only accreditation agency that recognizes school counseling as an individual program of study.

Legislatures and state agencies depend upon professions to define themselves. A profession such as school counseling must monitor legislation from a national perspective and continue to "redefine" itself as a profession. Leaving decisions regarding professional definition up to multiple state legislatures will erode the fabric of the profession and could eventually mean that professional school counseling would be weakened, if not eliminated. National certification and accreditation supported by counselors, academic institutions and professional counseling organizations like ACA are two of the cornerstones of the legal definition of school counseling as a professional specialty of counseling.

A New Credential

As this book goes to press, the National Board for Professional Teaching Standards (NBPTS) is debating whether to proceed with a planned certification for school counselors. Since the first mention of this plan in 1990, NBCC, ASCA, and ACA have closely monitored and kept open communications with NBPTS. Because NBCC interacts continually in the credentialing community, they have most closely interacted with NBPTS to assure that any future NBPTS certification will involve NBCC/ASCA standards.

Hopefully, by 2002, school counselors will be able to take part in a combined certification that will end in NBCC and NBPTS certification.

In 1999, the Mississippi legislature passed a law entitling all Mississippi school counselors who are National Certified School Counselors (NCSCs) to a $6,000.00 yearly pay supplement. This figure matches the original award offered NBPTS credentialed teachers. As more states pass NBPTS legislation, the stakes of the negotiations between NBCC/ASCA and NBPTS rise. To explore this issue check the NBCC web site. *www.nbcc.org*

Other Credentialing Concerns Facing the School Counselor

There are a variety of concerns regarding the credentialing of school counselors. Test anxiety probably is a factor in many of the personal decisions made not to be nationally certified. In reality, national certification examinations are meant to assess minimum knowledge gained in master's degree programs. Most counselors should pass such examinations with little reviewing of material. But, as in all professions, the examination itself is a major psychological obstacle. A help to many counselors has been packaged study guides. The Center for Credentialing and Education, Inc. (CCE) offers the official study guide. *www.cce-global.org*

Some school counselors see voluntary certification as superfluous, as these individuals are required to meet state board of education requirements and hold the state certification. Voluntary certification is a matter of professional pride and belief in continuing the profession. The fact that counselors choose to present proof of professionalism through certification is a continuing strength for all of us.

As noted, there are around 80,000 school counselors in the United States. Over 12,000 are members of the American School Counselor Association, and many are members of their respective state school counselor associations. The members and leaders of these organizations are the driving force behind progress and change. Those who do not participate in their professional associations and do not choose to be nationally certified are slowing the process of the professionalization of counseling. Apathy is a hindrance for any movement. It is my opinion that all 80,000 should be appropriately credentialed! There is strength in numbers.

All too often, school counselors identify with the teaching profession first: contracts, resources, salary negotiations, school assignments—all the realm of education—constitute the daily routine for counselors. In reality, school counselors are a specialty of the profession of counseling. They are members of comprehensive educational teams which include teachers, administrators, school psychologists, school attorneys, school nurses, school social workers and a host of other team members. A look at the list above shows a variety of nonteaching professionals who make up the system of education. School counselors can retain their unique identity and continue to be an integral part of education without being teachers. As noted, the teaching requirement is still, in several states, a prerequisite for gaining state certification as a counselor. Thus, school counseling is one of the few, if not the only professional group in which someone aspiring to be a member of one profession must first be trained to work in another profession; one they plan not to pursue! This requirement impedes the movement of school counselors as "professionals." Teaching experience is one of *many* skill areas from which a school counselor can draw.

Presently, there is no vehicle in place permitting school counselors to regulate their job titles and functions. And, school systems employ personnel to counsel or either they contract with outside agencies (often with unqualified personnel) to counsel. So long as tight financial budgets remain in education, we will hear of these abuses.

Summary

Credentialing for school counselors is now a permanent part of our lives. We now have alternatives from which to select: whether to work in public schools (and be state credentialed), whether to voluntarily become nationally certified for general practice and whether to become a National Certified School Counselor. In 1980, we had no such options, aside from state board of education mandates. Now, as counseling continues to strengthen as a profession, the profession itself has created ways to symbolize our professionalism and show our public that we care to meet higher and higher standards. It is suggested here that the best way to "show your publics" that you are indeed a professional is to seek the appropriate state and national credentialing. It is a major part of being a "professional" in the true sense of the word.

References

Hollis, J. (2000). *Counselor Preparation 2000-02: Programs, personnel trends.* Muncie, IN: Accelerated Development.

CACREP (1999). Newsletter *The CACREP Connection,* Summer, 1999.

U.S. Bureau of Labor Statistics (1998-1999). Occupational *outlook handbook.* Chicago, U.S. Government Printing Office.

Figure 29.1
National Certified School Counselor (NCSC)

The National Certified School Counselor (NCSC) credential was created as a result of the joint efforts of the American Counseling Association (ACA), the American School Counselor Association (ASCA), and the National Board for Certified Counselors (NBCC). The NCSC specialty credential attests to the educational background, knowledge, skills, and competencies of the specialist in school counseling. A requirement for the NCSC credential is the National Certified Counselor (NCC) credential.

NBCC offers a combination application process where candidates can apply for both the NCC and the NCSC at the same time. Information on deadlines and fees is available on NBCC's web site at *www.nbcc.org.* An application can be printed from the web site at *www.nbcc.org/documents.htm.*

Applicants must still meet the requirements for both credentials:

- Master's degree with a major study in counseling with 48 semester hours of graduate-level counseling courses.

- Specific coursework requirements (one course each in Growth and Human Development, Social/Cultural Foundations, Helping Relationships, Group Work, Career and Lifestyle Development, Appraisal, Research and Program Evaluation, Professional Orientation, Fundamentals of School Counseling, and two academic terms of field experience, one of which must be in a school setting).

- Minimum of two years full-time experience as a school counselor.

- 100 hours of face-to-face supervision over a two-year period (the supervisor must be someone with a master's degree or higher in counseling or a closely related field; education, curriculum, and administration are not considered closely related fields).

- Two endorsements, one from a counseling supervisor and one from a counseling colleague.

- Completion of a Self-Assessment.

- Achieve a passing score on the National Counselor Examination for Licensure and Certification (NCE). There is no separate exam for the NCSC credential.

**National Board
for Certified Counselors (NBCC®)
3 Terrace Way Suite D
Greensboro NC 27403-3660**

Chapter 30
School Counseling and Technology*

by
Russell A Sabella

Russell A. Sabella, PhD, is an Assistant Proffessor in the Department of Counselor Education at Florida Gulf Coast University in Ft. Myers, FL. He has worked as a school counselor and currently serves as the Interactive Technology Committee Chair for the American School Counselor Association.

Dr. Sabella specializes in comprehensive school counseling programs, sexual harassment risk reduction, peer helper programs and technology applications in counseling. He may be reached via email at rsabella@fgcu.edu.

* Parts of this chapter were adapted from Sabella, R.A. (1999). SchoolCounselor.com: A Friendly and Practical Guide to the World Wide Web. Minneapolis, MN: Educational Media Corporation by permission.

Technology underpins our fastest growing industries and high-wage jobs, provides the tools needed to compete in every business today, and drives growth in every major industrialized nation. In the 21st century, our ability to harness the power and promise of leading-edge advances in technology will determine, in large measure, our national prosperity, security, and global influence, and with them the standard of living and quality of life for all. President Bill Clinton, recognizing this trend, stated in an early October speech in 1998 that students must have a basic grasp of computers and the Internet (also known as the Net) and called on states to make technological literacy a requirement for leaving middle school. Speaking to 2,400 students graduating from the Massachusetts Institute of Technology (MIT), he said that, "All students should feel as comfortable with a keyboard as a chalkboard; as comfortable with a laptop as a textbook ... The rest of society would fall behind if it is did not get a grounding in the rudiments of computers at a early age (McQuillan, 1998)." To effectively work with students and other stakeholders while avoiding "falling behind," counselors too must maintain basic levels of technological literacy.

Indeed, progressively powerful computers, software, and expanding networks are rapidly changing traditional school counseling approaches and standards of performance. Although no one is truly certain if or when the exponential growth of technology will taper, it is well recognized that we are immersed in a new age of information, communication, and collaboration. For better or worse, computers are changing the ways in which we conduct our work, interact, and especially make decisions. Counseling professionals must adapt to new ways of interfacing with machines and the people that use them in a way that promotes the goals and objectives of their work (Sabella, 1998). According to McClure (1996), no aspect of society or economy can function effectively and completely without such tools. School counselors that decide to "opt out" of information technology would be working with students who perceive them to live in a world that no longer exists. Information and networking technologies are now essential tools for manipulating ideas and images and for communicating effectively with others—an important component of the counselor's job. This chapter introduces school counselors to a number of practical computer and networking technologies with special attention to the Internet.

Counselors whom have used computers to assist them in their work have done so in many areas such as computer-assisted live supervision (Froehle, 1984; Neukrug, 1991); discussions of counseling issues with other counselors (Rust, 1995); supervision (Myrick & Sabella, 1995); counselor training (Cairo & Kanner, 1984); as part of counselor interventions with children (D'Andrea, 1995; Glover, 1995; Shulman, Sweeney, & Gerler, 1995) and counseling simulations (Sharf & Lucas, 1993). Probably the most extensive use of computers in counseling so far has been in the area of career development (e.g., Chapman & Katz, 1983; Haring-Hidore, 1984; Harris, 1972; Katz & Shatkin, 1983; Kivlighan, Johnston, Hogan, & Mauer, 1994; Pyle, 1984). Career counselors need to amass and process a great deal of information about various careers, the career decision-making process, and a diversity of client personal and professional characteristics. Computers do a splendid job of compiling such data and helping individuals select the best fit among working environments, required aptitudes, interests, values, and other human qualities.

Many counselors, however, have avoided or only very recently began using computers in their work. One reason for relatively late entry into computing is that some see computer technology as an evil force to be circumvented at all costs. Such counselors hold computers in contempt because they see them as replacing people in jobs such as telephone operators, professional desktop publishers, and even perhaps as "teachers." This belief is sometimes true for people in more product oriented professions or those in human service professions that involve simple and repetitive tasks. For counselors however, no technology has ever come close to providing quality and appropriate counseling services. Computers have merely changed the shape of the work force by introducing new vocations and changing the methods for how we accomplish our work tasks.

Some counselors say they can still effectively perform their jobs "the old fashioned way" — keeping index cards instead of a database; using a typewriter rather than a word processor; using overheads in lieu of multimedia presentations; and relying on perhaps a handful of periodicals rather than accessing the highly expansive menu of online full-text resources. They justify avoiding computer technology by reminding us that their already familiar low-tech solutions are still effective. On the other hand, critics of this excuse say that such thinking is shortsighted because the world of technology is the world in which our children live and will be more an integral part of their society than even ours.

And, while other counselors might acknowledge the usefulness and need for keeping up with the rapidly changing times, they are frozen in the fear generated by an unknown frontier. "I feel intimidated by computers," has been a common comment by counselors, who even after training, frequently revert to more traditional procedures. The customary statements, "My kids know more about computers than I do" and "I'm not a technical person" suggest that although counselors may be interested or even intrigued, they frequently feel awkward and uneasy with computers and their operations (Myrick & Sabella, 1995). Ironically, it's the same fear that, when attempting to become computer literate, makes the learning curve significantly more steep. Joyce L. Winterton, Ph.D., national education advisor for USA Today couldn't have said it better during a presentation I attended when she

quipped that, "Computers are like horses, if they know you're scared of them, they'll try to throw you off."

Although computers and related technologies are rapidly changing, one fact remains constant — counselors who resist the new tools of this and future centuries will find it increasingly more difficult to do so. One tool in particular that is changing the fabric of how we interact, work, and conduct business is the Internet. Consider that the Internet, which connected 2,000 computers in 1985, now connects 30 million computers, and is continuing to double in size every year. By the end of 1997, it was estimated that more than 100 million people worldwide were using the Internet. The number of users could surpass one billion as early as 2005. And, in addition to growing in terms of people accessing the Internet, it is growing in terms of the types of services provided over the network. Satellite and wireless systems will soon provide users with "anytime, anywhere" communications. Directory and search services help users locate important resources on the Internet. Electronic mail servers manage and store critical information. Authentication and electronic payment services handle more and more of the Nation's commerce. Building blocks for new applications are being developed such as digital signatures, secure transactions, modeling and simulations software, shared virtual environments for collaboration, tools for discovering and retrieving information, and speech recognition (President's Information Technology Advisory Committee, 1998). Computers and the Internet provide access to a wealth of information on countless topics contributed by people throughout the world. On the Net, counselors have access to a wide variety of services: electronic mail, file transfer, vast information resources, interest group membership, interactive collaboration, multimedia displays, and more.

If not for professional competency, then perhaps more personal reasons for becoming proficient in information technologies might make the case for counselor technological literacy. Within the next two decades, computer networks will have penetrated more deeply into our society than any previous network, including telephone, radio, television, transportation, and electric power distribution networks. Soon we will depend on the information infrastructure for delivery of routine services such as banking and financial transactions, purchases of goods and services, entertainment, communications with friends, family, and businesses, as well as for vital services, such as government and medical services. As users come to depend on the Internet each and every day, and as billions of dollars are transacted using electronic commerce, the information infrastructure becomes more critical to each counselor's and our Nation's well being. A counseling profession literate in information technology will be critical for ensuring that it is prepared to meet the challenges and opportunities of the Information Age (President's Information Technology Advisory Committee, 1998). Therefore, be it by necessity or interest, the time is now for exploring contemporary methods for accomplishing our work using computer and networking technologies such as the Internet.

According to Sabella (1998), counselors who took an early interest and continued to gradually follow technology's progression have probably accumulated relatively high levels of technological literacy at a manageable pace. Veterans to computer and Internet technology may find themselves only having to keep pace with incremental changes, new additions, and creative ways for harnessing their power to more effectively and efficiently do their jobs. For those whom have more recently taken an interest, or force themselves to be exposed to technology because of trends or new standards, becoming technologically literate may be a burdensome venture. The good news, however, is that you can effectively start today. The road to technological literacy does not necessarily have a beginning and an end, but like an intricate system of highways and sideroads, can be accessed from many on-ramps. Today's software is more user-friendly and more highly automated than ever before. Beginning a course of self-study and formal training will better assure more enjoyable travel for the road ahead. Before you know it, you will be traveling along side others whom have laid many more miles behind them on the information superhighway. And sooner, rather than later, you will be staking and claiming your property on this vast electronic terrain.

Effective use of current and emerging communication and information technologies allow counselors to take advantage of new conveniences and opportunities not before available. For instance:

- Using computer conferencing, electronic mail, and voice mail applications, counselors can communicate with each other and other stake holders at any time and any place. This allows a new freedom of discussion, collaboration, and professional development no matter the size or location of one's work place.

- Interactive multimedia instructional software allow counselors to better control learning segments and explore new segments at a depth and pace appropriate to their students' own learning needs during psychoeducational groups.

- Electronic links can help extend the counselor and school to community partners such as health centers, community counseling centers, business and industry, government and non-profit agencies, cultural facilities and vast library resources.

- Information databases that are available for counselors and others to access and update, as authorized, allow for more convenient and efficient services such as off-site college registration; financial aid and admissions processing; student career counseling profiles; full-text databases of scholarly publications; student progress data, and more.

- Networking technologies and software tools affect the way decisions are made by expediting the availability and distribution of data throughout a counselor's school. Cross-institutional work groups and an appropriate balance between distributed and centralized technical support will make possible collaborative planning and resource management.

Additionally, others have already discovered uses of computers and the Internet in particular to augment various school counseling goals. Consider the following examples of how these technologies are enhancing the work of school counselors:

- In late 1996, The Georgia Board of Regents Office of Information and Instructional Technology (OIIT) in collaboration with the Georgia Department of Education (DOE) Office of Technology Services announced that an electronic account will be provided to middle school and high school buildings as part of an ongoing project called "Connecting Students and Services." The account is intended for use by middle school and high school counselors only and provides schools with a single point of access to various Internet resources including e-mail addresses. The goal is to enhance the guidance counselor's utilization of resources available on the Internet's World Wide Web (WWW). School counselors are able to access admission's information for institutions in the University System of Georgia through the institution's web pages, exchange information via e-mail, access the "Georgia Career Information System" and do electronic transcript transfers between high school and colleges and universities.

- Similar to traditional penpals that maintain a relationship via correspondence using letters sent through the mail, KeyPals send electronic mail to establish and maintain a friendly peer relationship. One such site (*www.teaching.com/*) contains the following introduction:

Mighty Media presents the KeyPals Club , a place for young people, teachers and students to locate and correspond with other youth and students around the world. The service provides an incredibly easy-to-use interface and database to quickly locate and contact a student or a class from around the world. Start a project with another class, or just create a new friendship with someone on the other side of the globe. KeyPals Club is another free educational service from Mighty Media, creators of the Youth in Action Network and Teacher Talk (Mighty Media, 1997).

Counselors might think about the following example of how KeyPals was used as a way to create, implement, and evaluate more expanded peer helper programs using the Internet: One high school teacher wanted to improve student activity, participation, and outlook toward physical education. His alternative class of special education students became "KeyPals" with university kinesiology majors. Through e-mail communication, the students established rapport with older students who value physical activity. A bond developed between the high school and college students, which helped the younger students improve their attitude about positive active participation. A research study to help determine whether this KeyPal relationship between high school alternative Physical Education (PE) students and university kinesiology majors could positively influence their participation and attitude toward gym class was conducted. Results suggested that attitudes, motivation, and relationships positively influenced the KeyPal relationships. Complaints about participating in PE class had been replaced by enthusiastic participation in basketball and volleyball games with the university KeyPals. Most of the KeyPals demonstrated a sense of belonging and connectedness, perhaps for the first time since their elementary school PE experience. And, most important, the essential ingredient of fun in gym class had reappeared (Fargen, 1996).

- Hewlett Packard (HP), a well-known computer and printer company, created an e-mail mentor program. This program creates one-to-one mentor relationships between HP employees (worldwide) and 5-12th grade students and teachers throughout the United States. HP employees motivate students to excel in math and science and improve communication and problem-solving skills. In addition, students are encouraged by their mentors to pursue their unique interests and link these interests with their daily school experience. The program created 1654 mentor relationships with participation from 1546 HP mentors, 1508 students, and 146 teachers (HP, 1997).

- D'Andrea (1995), wrote about how peer helpers can consult the WWW and provide teachers with educational resources and information related to people from diverse cultural, ethnic, and racial groups, which might be helpful when planning class discussions and activities. This might include sharing materials that describe the unique traditions, values, foods, clothing, and lifestyles associated with people from various cultures. Also, peer helpers may gather information

about the ways in which children are raised in other cultures and the roles they are likely to play within their communities, families, or tribes. This sort of information may be of particular interest to elementary school students who enjoy making comparisons between their own lifestyles and other youngsters from different cultural, ethnic, or racial groups. The author also suggested methods for using telecommunications such as the Net to promote multicultural awareness among elementary school age students. Students can exchange photos, text, sound (e.g., music), and language from various cultures to gain a better appreciation of self and others.

- School counselors can help students with disabilities by learning how computers and the Internet can serve as assistive technologies. For instance, once counselor downloaded a text-to-speech converter (from *www.readplease.com*) to have children's stories read to a group of children without site. Another counselor used a website (*where.com/scott.net/asl/*) to help teach the siblings of a hearing impaired child American sign language (ASL). The site has an ASL dictionary, interactive quiz, and text to ASL converter.

- An elementary school counselor uses "HIV and AIDS: What Kids Want to Know" and "Lets Talk About HIV and AIDS," two interactive, multimedia, computer-based training programs for children ages 9-12 and children ages 6-9 (see *http://www2.uta.edu/cussn/kidshiv/kidsaids.html*). The most innovative part of the software is the use of children who are affected by HIV/AIDS to guide development and narrate the programs. The programs contain voice, sounds, animation, and video to keep children involved in the learning. The use of sound is an important feature in the software. Using children affected by HIV/AIDS as narrators creates a powerful experience while hearing the children talk openly and honestly about HIV/AIDS.

- A software program called Therascribe assists school counselors in developing Individual Educational Programs (IEPs) and conducting functional assessments. The treatment planning program helps you choose from thousands of pre-written treatment statements to help you create comprehensive treatment plans and detailed progress notes. The program recommends appropriate combinations of behavioral definitions, long-term goals, short-term objectives, and therapeutic interventions for all major DSM-IV diagnoses. It tracks client demographic data, mental status and prognosis, treatment modality, discharge criteria, and provider credentials; it also provides treatment outcome tracking with 3-D graphing (see *http://www.parinc.com/profess/THERASCRIBE150a.html*).

- Some counselors have provided websites with links to colleges, financial aid sources, GPA calculators, planning checklists, after school homework centers, and resources for parents to name a few (for an annotated directory of over 700 counseling related websites, see Sabella, 1999).

In general, computers and the Internet can be especially helpful in a variety of ways including as technologies for information retrieval, communication, collaboration, accountability, and intervention delivery.

Technologies for Information Retrieval

The Internet could be described as the world's largest library and the availability of psychology-related bibliographies, abstracts, full-text journal articles, lectures, research projects, and funding sources is currently a "mouse click" away from your desktop. Mental health organizations, associations and individual professionals are creating web sites every day and access to authoritative information on specialized topics is current, convenient, and almost limitless (Jackson & Davidson, 1998). Following are descriptions of various information resources.

The World Wide Web

The World Wide Web (also known as the WWW or the Web) is the multimedia part of the Internet. Once accessed, a counselor can view information in the form of text, graphics, sounds, video, and animated icons. A distinctive feature of the Web is the breadth and depth of culturally rich information that one can instantaneously access from anywhere around the globe. Also, rapidly changing data can be updated within minutes thus allowing counselors to retrieve information that is highly current. The Web has, until recently, mostly been found useful among academicians, scientists and businesses as a way to share and coordinate information, communicate, and conduct transactions. However, the current proliferation of Web content in the areas of human resource, psychology, counseling, and mental health (for example, see Grohol, 1997), has now rendered the Web as a valuable resource for counselors. School counselors can be better informed about knowledge and practical techniques via the repertoire of materials in the form of scholarly journals, resource information, program descriptions, and articles to name a few. And, as the cost of getting on-line becomes more affordable, counselors may find that gaining Web access is steadily more realistic.

Web sites are dynamic documents which usually contain links to other related documents in the form of selected words or symbols (called hypertext links). For example, when a new word or concept is introduced in a document, hypertext makes it possible for a user to point to that word or symbol and retrieve another related document which gives more details about the original reference. The second document may also contain links to other documents providing further details, and so on. The user need not know where the referenced document is, and there is no need to type a command to display it, browse it, or to find the right paragraph. Hypertext links may also lead a user to graphics, photos, data, maps, movie clips, sound clips, or any kind of information that can be digitized. Viewing this rich array of information can occur from any computer in the world that has the requisite hardware, software, and Internet connection (Sabella, 1998).

To view a Web resource, a computer user must have at least four things: A computer with a modem or similar hardware; a telephone or similar connection; the proper software; and an Internet service provider (ISP). Computers can be either IBM or Macintosh compatible and must include a modem - a device that allows one's computer to communicate with other computers over telephone lines. The software needed to properly view the Web is known as a browser. The most popular browsers are Netscape Navigator® and Microsoft Explorer®, which are both free to educators and available for both Windows and Macintosh compatible computers. Finally, to view the Web, a user must have Internet access, which is a service available either nationally (e.g., America Online or Compuserv) or locally (visit *www.thelist.com* to locate an ISP by area code). Often, an Internet service provider will provide a user with software tailored to gaining access to the Web once the user subscribes to the service. In this case, a separate browser would not be necessary.

Once you access the Web using your browser, you can find specific sites or home pages by using one or more of four methods:

1. Each site on the Web has its own unique, case-sensitive, electronic address called a Universal Resource Locator (URL) that points a computer to the Web page's location. Users who discover a useful site might communicate to others, probably via electronic mail, the page's URL. Once known, a user can simply enter the URL into his or her Web browser and go directly to the intended site. Once at the site, a counselor can then place an electronic "bookmark" that will allow him or her to point and click on a description of the site without ever again

having to recall the URL. This form of finding information on the Web is quickest and easiest.

2. A second method for finding information is to rely on the hypertext feature of the Web and "jump" from page to page using related links. Moving from one link to another is affectionately known as "surfing the Web." As a counselor surfs the Web, he or she might bookmark and essentially create his or her own compilation of valuable Web sites. The advantage of surfing the Web is that it gives the user control over what sites are deemed valuable. The disadvantage is that such a search is less than systematic and can be very time consuming and costly in the form of on-line charges.

3. Third, you might consult an Internet directory such as Yahoo! (*www.yahoo.com*) which categorizes websites into various hierarchies of information: a vast collection of categories and sub-categories created by people, not computer programs. By browsing the directory, you can have in front of you a good, perhaps complete listing of all the sites that cover a particular subject.

4. One tool that has evolved for conducting research over the Web is the search engine (McMurdo, 1995; Symons, 1996). A search engine is a computer program designed to surf the Web and index pages from available sites (Courtois, 1995). Also, a computer user who creates a new Web page can submit the page's description and URL to a particular search engine (Scales & Felt, 1995). Much like electronic databases found in libraries, a search engine on the Web can find a page's location based on various key words and search conditions. Searching for information becomes more systematic, focused, and rapid using a search engine. Using unique search terms and search conditions can narrow the results from thousands of possible sites to a more manageable number in a matter of seconds. One disadvantage of using a search engine, however, is that the vast number of Web pages are apt to contain various forms of any keyword. Even the best of search words and conditions will sometimes produce a superfluous set of relatively inconsequential Web page references. Search engine results still require the user to scan a list of Web pages and judge them against relevance and usefulness. Examples of search engines include *www.yahoo.com, www.excite.com, www.lycos.com, www.snap.com, www.alltheweb.com,* and *www.av.com.*

Full-Text Electronic Databases

The number of journal, magazine, and newspaper titles available online has grown rapidly in recent years (Tenopir, 1999). Many databases are only accessible by paying a fee although, often, schools and local universities provide free access to anyone while on campus. Some databases are designed for individual users and are more reasonably priced. Finally, other full-text databases have been provided for free as a government service or by the incredible generosity of individuals and organizations. Following are examples:

Larger and More Expensive Databases Typically Subscribed to by Institutions

1. **CollegeSource® Online** features over 10,900 College Catalogs in complete cover-to-cover original page format including 2-year, 4-year, graduate, and professional schools. Also available are close to 11,000 college catalogs in PDF format and full-text information about: assessment testing; career information; college application services; college guides; college planning sites; counseling; education related search engines; financial aid information. *www.college-source.com*

2. **CIS® Congressional Universe** is the world's most comprehensive access to U.S. legislative information from Congressional Information Service, Inc. The service offers access to a variety of information by and about the United States Congress. With Congressional Universe, you can: search an index of congressional publications from 1970 to the present; retrieve CIS legislative histories for public laws going back to 1970; find testimony from congressional hearings; track bills as they move through the house and senate; search the congressional record and federal register; locate information about members and committees; and search the national journal. *web.lexis-nexis.com/congcomp*

3. **EBSCOhost** is an index covering a wide range of academic areas with selective full-text for over 1,000 journals. *www.ebscohost.com/*

4. **Online Computer Library Center (OCLC)** is a nonprofit, membership, library computer service and research organization dedicated to the public purposes of furthering access to the world's information and reducing information costs. *www.oclc.org*

5. **Ovid** is a Platform-independent access to bibliographic and live full text databases for academic, biomedical and scientific research. *www.ovid.com/*

6. **ProQuest®** is Bell & Howell Information and Learning's premier online information service. We

provide powerful, convenient search and retrieval, right from your desktop, to one of the world's largest collections of information, including summaries of articles from over 8,000 publications, with many in full text, full image format. *www.umi.com/*

7. **ReferenceUSA**- Online access to a database of 10.5 million business in US. Search for a company provides contact information, single point mapping, credit rating codes, lines of business and executive names. Possible to search by selecting one criteria or a combination of multiple criteria like geography, type of business, business size, and SIC codes etc. Allows downloading of Customized reports. *http://reference.infousa.com/*

8. **Northern Light Search.** This unique search service combines web searching and full-text databases. Search for free, read abstracts, and purchase items if you wish. Purchase price is $1-$4 per item, money back guaranteed if the item is not useful. By selecting Special Collection, you may limit your search to full-text periodicals, including excellent titles in the social sciences dating back to 1995. *www.northern-light.com/power.html*

9. **UnCover.** UnCover is a document delivery and table of contents service with over 17,500 periodicals in all academic disciplines. Anyone may search the database for references to articles from journals and magazines. People who enter a user profile may order fax copies of articles, charged to a credit card. A growing number of articles are available to be downloaded. *http://uncweb.carl.org*

Inexpensive Full-Text

For those that do not have access to expensive full-text databases provided by schools or other institutions, the Electric Library (*www.elibrary.com*) is a comprehensive general reference product which contains content from a wide variety of sources, including more than 150 full-text newspapers; hundreds of full-text magazines; national and international news wires; 2,000 complete works of literature; over 28,000 photos, images and maps; television, radio and government transcripts; book, movie and software reviews; complete encyclopedia, dictionary, thesaurus, almanac, and fact books; and more. For convenience, this database service also provides a unique service, Elibrary Tracker, that searches the database each day, week, or month for any topic you want and e-mails you the latest articles automatically. A monthly subscription is $9.95 and $59.95 for an annual subscription.

Another example of an inexpensive full-text database ($5 per month) is the Encyclopedia Brittanica (EB) online which includes the complete encyclopedia, as well as Merriam-Webster's Collegiate Dictionary and the Britannica Book of the Year. You can also use EB Online to search an Internet directory that includes more than 130,000 links to Web sites selected, rated, and reviewed by Britannica editors. Through this service, you can find more than 72,000 articles, updated and revised by EB editors and contributors; over 10,000 illustrations, including photographs, drawings, maps, and flags; and more than 75,000 definitions—including pronunciation guides and word histories—from Merriam-Webster's Collegiate Dictionary. Advanced search and navigation capabilities and the power of the Internet make the Encyclopedia Britannica an invaluable reference and research tool. *www.eb.com.*

Free full-text

Following are examples of various full-text resources which are available online:

1. National Center for Research in Vocational Education (NCRVE) is the nation's largest center engaged in research, development, dissemination and outreach in work-related education, and is funded by the Office of Vocational and Adult Education of the U.S. Department of Education. Headquartered at the University of California, Berkeley since 1988, NCRVE has played a key role in developing a new concept of workforce development. The Center's mission is to strengthen school-based and work-based learning to prepare all individuals for lasting and rewarding employment, further education, and lifelong learning. *http://vocserve.berkeley.edu/fulltext.html*

2. Maintained by an individual, this page seeks to link to sites containing full-text state constitutions, statutes (called codes or compiled laws in some states), legislation (bills, amendments and similar documents) and session laws (bills that have become laws). *www.prairienet.org/~scruffy/f.htm*

3. The ERIC® Clearinghouse on Assessment and Evaluation full text internet library contains full-text books, reports, journal articles, newsletter articles and papers on the Internet that address educational measurement, evaluation and learning theory. We have selected these documents based upon criteria that are widely accepted in the library and information science community and we have provided a frame-

work so that you can easily browse these resources. *http://ericae.net/ftlib.htm*

4. A list of free (29 titles at the time of this writing) free full-text journals on the Web and maintained by the Lesley College Library are located at *www.lesley.edu/faculty/kholmes/libguides/cpfulltext.html*

5. The Journal of Technology Education provides a forum for scholarly discussion on topics relating to technology education. Manuscripts should focus on technology education research, philosophy, and theory. In addition, the Journal publishes book reviews, editorials, guest articles, comprehensive literature reviews, and reactions to previously published articles. *http://borg.lib.vt.edu/ejournals/JTE/jte.html*

6. The Journal of Technology in Counseling publishes articles on all aspects of practice, theory, research and professionalism related to the use of technology in counselor training and counseling practice. The Journal accepts manuscripts that respond to the full scope of technology interests of its readers. The Journal recognizes that modern technology has surpassed traditional ways of presenting information to readers by encompassing learning methods that go beyond the two-dimensional page. Authors are encouraged to use the full range of available web resources when submitting manuscripts including hyperlinks to other web resources, audio, graphics, video clips and video-streaming. *http://jtc.colstate.edu/*

7. The RECORD is an online journal and news periodical with articles published, written, and submitted by Psychwatch.com readers and website visitors whose credentials follow their articles. Some articles have been published in professional journals, and thus have been peer-reviewed. Others are not peer reviewed, and are submitted for by persons whose credentials follow the article, and are posted by Psychwatch for the interest of their readers. *http://psychwatch.com/*

Technologies for Communication

As agents of change, school counselors use communication techniques to build a therapeutic alliance with clients and to assist them in leading and managing a comprehensive school counseling program. Computer and networking technologies for communicating continues to witness exponential development and may be the most familiar for quickly communicating with others.

E-Mail

E-mail is like sending a letter or message through the post office, only it is much faster. In some respects, it is like talking on the telephone, except that you type out everything that you want to say. In general, it connects the message sender to one or more receivers at other computer stations. Each person has his or her own e-mail address in which messages can be sent and retrieved by a recipient. When an e-mail message is sent to another user via a network, it is posted until the recipient turns on his or her computer and pushes a few keys to tap into the Net. The computer's E-mail message board shows that a message is pending. At the recipient's convenience this message is retrieved and read. If desired, the message can be forwarded to others. Or, by pushing one or two keys, a reply can be sent directly back to the sender. The message can also be printed as a hard copy or saved to a floppy disk. One e-mail advantage to school counselors is the opportunity to participate in a network that enables participants to share professional ideas and information. It offers counselors a unique and valuable opportunity for collaboration, consultation, and supervision.

Because the Web is becoming a ubiquitous part of network activity, many recent versions of e-mail software allow you to click on a website addresses sent as part of e-mail text and automatically open your Web browser to go to that address. Many Web browsers such as Netscape Navigator® and Microsoft Explorer® have built-in e-mail, so it's easy to switch between applications within a single program. The advantage of dedicated non-browser e-mail programs is that they often have more mail features than Web-based systems. The disadvantage is that you have to switch back and forth between two programs—e-mail and your browser (Koufman-Frederick, Lillie, Pattison-Gordon, Watt, & Carter, 1999).

As personal computers become available in more counselors' offices and as more schools come on-line with the Internet, there will be new opportunities for e-mail applications such as in consultation and coordination. More specifically, e-mail offers counselors the same kind of advantage that it offers those involved with distance learning education. It forms the basis of a network that conveniently connects counselors and others (e.g., supervisors, community members, parents, and students) individually and in groups (Myrick & Sabella, 1995).

Advantages of using e-mail to communicate with others includes:

- the convenience of doing so at any time of the day or night

- being able to think through a communication before making it

- not having to rely on a mutual time to communicate as one would with a phone conversation

- saving money in long distance charges when having to make only brief comments

- instantaneously communicating the same message to multiple people on a distribution list;

- diminished inhibitions that face-to-face conversation may present;

- that, whereas spoken words must remain in memory and are sometimes lost in a quick exchange, written e-mail messages can be reviewed;

- large files, especially documents, can be instantly sent to others via e-mail which can save precious time and money as compared to printing and shipping the document via traditional postal carriers.

Disadvantages of e-mail communication include:

- for some, typing can be slow and tedious;

- the absence of nonverbal communication such as gestures, facial expression, or tone of voice can sometimes lead to mistaken interpretations of an e-mail message;

- although relatively very secure, sending an e-mail over the Net is sometimes like sending a postcard through the mail - others whom desire to do so might intercept and read an e- mail. Therefore, issues of confidentiality and privacy are central to communicating sensitive information;

- if not careful, counselors can receive too many e-mail messages which may lead to time and organizational management challenges. In this sense, counselors must be smart consumers of information and determine how much one reads, digests, and to which messages one should respond.

Many school counselors take the opportunity to participate in an electronic network that enables participants to share professional ideas and information. It offers counselors a unique and valuable opportunity for supervision and consultation. For example, Myrick & Sabella (1995)

write about how they used e-mail as a supplement to practicum and internship supervision.

The student counselors, during group supervision, first learned how to access the Internet through computers in their schools or with their own personal computers and modems at home. They could also access the system through computer stations at various locations on campus. Each person had his or her own e-mail address, which was known to the supervisor and other group supervision members. Using e-mail, a student-counselor could send written messages to a supervisor asking for information or describing a case. When appropriate, the case was forwarded to other group members for their interest and reactions.

The group supervision members discussed the best way to send an e-mail case. It would include (a) a brief description of the counselee; (b) the presenting problem, including the referral source; (c) the observed behaviors related to the problem or concern; (d) the counselor interventions to that point; and (e) any concerns or questions that were evolving. The authors concluded that e-mail supervision supplements the traditional modes office-to-face meetings, telephone conferences, and fax transmissions. An on-going group experience, it can take place in remote and diverse locations. Although the common once-a-week group meeting has its own value, group members felt that they were always within reach of assistance or encouragement. They felt closer to one another, and E-mail created a special bond that also enabled them to be more open about their situations.

List Servers

List servers are programs that allow an administrator to create lists of e-mail addresses and attach them to a single e-mail address. All messages that are e-mailed to the list are distributed, again via e-mail, to all subscribers, sometimes by a "moderator" who reads them first (in a "moderated list") and sometimes automatically (in an "unmoderated list"). Some mailing list servers require an administrator to add people to the list. In others, anyone who wishes can automatically subscribe (or un-subscribe) by sending an e-mail message to the program, which resides on a server. Mailing list server programs can provide some security by allowing only authorized users to post to the list or by using a moderator to approve messages before they are posted to the list. This kind of list server acts more like a mailing list for those who simply want to receive reminders, newsletters, or announcements. The creators of these publications are usually the only people who can send an e-mail via the list server. Any one else who tries is humbly and automatically rejected.

Try subscribing to one - The Scout Report is the flagship publication of the Internet Scout Project. Published every Friday both on the web and by e-mail, it provides a fast, convenient way to stay informed of valuable resources on the Internet. Go to *http://scout18.cs.wisc.edu/cgi-bin/lwgate/listsavail.html* to view various mailing lists and instructions for subscribing.

Mailing list servers are an efficient way of sending e-mail to large and/or specific groups and are ideal for disseminating timely information, such as announcements of conferences, pointers to new Web sites of interest, and descriptions of print resources. Anyone on the list can be a source of information. Mailing list servers are well-suited to groups of users who regularly use e-mail and who need to receive information in a timely way. They are less effective for extended or lengthy discussions, because participants may not be able to remember all the previous entries when they respond to a particular item. Another disadvantage is that mailing list servers can be inconvenient for recipients, filling their e-mail in-boxes when they're busy with other things. Two of the most commonly used mailing list server programs are Majordomo (*www.greatcircle.com/majordomo/*) and list server (*www.lsoft.com*) (Koufman-Frederick, Lillie, Pattison-Gordon, Watt, & Carter, 1999).

One list server, the International Counselor Network (ICN) has been a highly active medium for transmitting ideas and opinions related to counseling throughout the world. Scores of counselors have participated in or listened to heated discussions on controversial issues. Many more have responded quickly to requests for information or resources (Rust, 1995). According to it's founder, Ellen Rust, one of the most useful features of the ICN is in its giving counselors the ability to be instantly in touch with, at the time of this writing, more than 1000 counselors from all over the world. It is no longer necessary to wait for a conference or hope that the next issue of the journal addresses a particular question. An e-mail message to the network can result in a reply, if not many replies, within a few hours - sometimes minutes. Being on the ICN is like attending a conference with colleagues without leaving home (Rust, 1995). To learn more about the ICN, including directions for subscribing, visit *http://members-.home.com/ruste/icn.html.*

There are primarily two methods for learning about available list servers of interest. First, you might learn about a specific list server as it is announced in professional or other publications such as journals, newsletters, or newspapers. Second, you may seek list servers of interest by querying a database of list servers maintained on some Internet sites. Several of the most comprehensive databases of list servers can be found at *www.liszt.com.* Once at this site, you can conduct a search using keywords or phrases and receive a "list of lists" that contain your keywords in the title of the list or in the body of the list's description. Moreover, this site makes it especially easy to then subscribe to the list server by providing simple directions and a convenient link that automatically calls on your e-mail software and inserts the proper address for the list server. To create your own list servers of interest, you should check out Listbot (*www.listbot.com*) or Egroups (*www.egroups.com/*), both of which provide free list server services.

Chat Room

E-mail is a great way to communicate electronically although this method suffers from the lack of real-time interaction between one person and with others whom he/she would like to communicate. Historically, real-time communication has occurred either in face-to-face conversation or over the telephone. The use of chat software, especially over the Internet, makes it possible to electronically converse in real time. Following the metaphor for which this technology is named, imagine yourself entering a room in which you can converse with other users you will find there. You can see on screen what each user is typing into the conversation, and when you type something, the other users in the room can see your message as well (Hofstetter, 1998).

Chat environments have progressed from simple text-based interactions to full blown graphical user interfaces (GUIs). Today's chatrooms allow users to personalize their communications by posting their photos or a close facsimile (sometimes a computer generated likeness) next to their text communications. Other programs also allow for sending to members of the chatroom audio files that contain music, sound effects, or the users own recorded voice. One of the most popular chat clients is a program called mIRC available for download at most shareware sites. However, many chats are now conducted over the Web which eliminates the need to download any software. Simply visit the site, choose your chat community, log in, and begin chatting (e.g., see *http://communities.msn.com/chat/*). You should know that, like anything else on the Net, some chatrooms are not for the easily offended. Not all, but many of the rooms are "R" to "X" rated because they contain highly graphical communications including text, sound, and sometimes graphics. Also, users of chatroom can easily maintain anonymity and, even worse, pose as someone they are not. Consider the following quote from a story printed across many newspapers on October 20, 1997.

A man dubbed the "Internet Romeo" warned parents to supervise their children's use of the network after he was sentenced to more than five years in prison Monday for using an on-line chat room to solicit sex with a teen-ager. Keir Fiore, 21, of Manchester, N.H., pleaded guilty to two federal counts of interstate transportation of a minor for illegal sex after using an on-line chat room to solicit sex from a 13-year-old girl in Salem, New Hampshire. U.S. District Judge Joseph DiClerico sentenced him to five years and three months in prison. Fiore, who faces sentencing in New Hampshire and Massachusetts Tuesday on state charges of sexual assault and soliciting, read a statement to the court apologizing to the teen-ager and her family. "The Internet is dangerous for young children who use it without parental supervision," the statement read in part. Prosecutors said Fiore flirted with the teen-ager in an on-line chat room last summer and convinced her to run away with him. Police eventually found the pair in New Hampshire after a national search.

ICQ

According to the ICQ website (*www.icq.com*), ICQ can be described as a user-friendly Internet tool that informs you who's on-line at any time and enables you to contact them at will. No longer will you search in vain for friends or associates on the Net. ICQ does the searching for you, alerting you in real time when they log on. The need to conduct a directory search each time you want to communicate with a specific person is eliminated. With ICQ, you can chat, send messages, files and URL's, play games, or just interact with your friends and colleagues while still surfing the Net.

ICQ lets you choose the mode of communication you wish to employ. Regardless of the application, be it chat, voice, message board, data conferencing, file transfer or Internet games, ICQ will get your entire message across in real time. ICQ supports a variety of popular Internet applications and can also be used in a multiple-user mode, so groups can conduct conferences or just convene on-line. The program runs in the background, taking up minimal memory and Internet resources. While you work with other applications, ICQ alerts you when friends and associates log in, allowing you to work efficiently while maintaining a wide range of Internet functions at your fingertips. Among the functions available are: chat, message, e-mail, and URL and file transfer. All these functions are consolidated into one program that integrates smoothly into desktop systems.

WebBoards

One drawback of e-mail and mailing list server discussions is that they organize discussions chronologically. This type of organization is fine for many short discussions or written materials, but most discussions aren't linear and well-organized. One comment can generate ideas on many different tangents. In this case, you may want to organize the discussion by topic. But that doesn't always work well; what if one message in a discussion has ideas that relate to several different parts of the discussion? Topic-oriented and threaded discussion systems, oftentimes called Bulletin Board Systems or WebBoards, attempt to respond to this problem by keeping an archive and allowing different ways of organizing the discussion. Because of the creative, inventive, and nonlinear nature of human conversation, it's difficult to develop an ideal method of organizing records of conversation. The information in a threaded discussion system is organized and displayed hierarchically, so you can see how the messages are related. Each posting (or "article") in a threaded discussion has a topic or subject. Users can comment on the topic, see what others have to say about it, and reply to questions or other people's comments. All of the comments, replies, and discussions on a single topic are collectively called a "thread." The difference between topic oriented and threaded discussions is a matter of format and organization. Usually messages in topic oriented discussions are listed chronologically on a single topic page, messages in threaded discussions are organized in an outline format with replies indented and listed directly under the message to which they are a reply (Koufman-Frederick, et al., 1999). Check out *www.school-counselor.com/bbs* for an example of a WebBoard medium for school counselors.

Technologies for Collaboration

Collaboration is a process by which people work together on an intellectual, academic, or practical endeavor. In the past, that has meant in person, by letter, or on the telephone. Electronic collaboration, on the other hand, connects individuals electronically via the Internet using tools such as e-mail, or through access to sites on the World Wide Web. This Internet-based work allows collaborators to communicate anytime, from anywhere to any place. People from different parts of a building, state, country, or continent can exchange information, collaborate on shared documents and ideas, study together, or reflect on their own practices.

Most counselors are used to short-term professional development seminars and workshops that provide finite information. Electronic collaboration —because it can be done at any time, from anywhere—allows for a sustained effort where participants can propose, try out, refine, and shape ideas themselves. The potential to communicate with others from all over the world provides a pool of resources and professional companions that counselors might not find within their own school walls. It can also provide them with a sense of belonging, a sense of identity within a larger community.

Collaborating electronically can take many different forms. Some of the more common activities include the following (Koufman-Frederick, et al. 1999):

- Discussion groups are focused around a topic or a specific activity, goal, or project. Some groups are open-ended and unmoderated, allowing users to solicit information from each other. Other, more structured, groups may use a moderator to guide the discussion by filtering and posing questions and/or making comments, suggestions, and connections.

- Data collection and organization activities use databases and search engines to organize and retrieve data. Users contribute data individually to a shared database and retrieve data from it as needed. Data can be in the form of references (such as pointers to related work and Web sites), information (such as weather conditions or whale sightings), curriculum projects, research papers, and contact information for colleagues.

- Some projects involve sharing documents—from simply displaying them to having several people work on them simultaneously. Collaborators can display documents online and discuss the contents via e-mail, video conference, or chat. They can use annotation systems to comment on shared documents and editing tools to co-edit documents online.

- Synchronous communication activities such as Internet "chat" and videoconferencing—differ from the other types of activities in that they happen in real time, over a short period. In text based "chat" environments participants see what the other person is typing on the screen in real time. Videoconferencing is like a conference call with pictures. These technologies allow users to discuss ideas, debate problems, and share information electronically when face-to- face interaction is desired but not possible.

- Some counselors might participate in online courses or workshops to learn something new. They are like traditional courses and workshops, but without face to face meetings. The electronic component allows people to participate whenever and from wherever they want. Such activities involve an instructor who distributes assignments, guides the conversation, and responds to participants' questions. The material for discussion, as well as the discussions themselves, can take place via a discussion group or through an integrated distance learning tool. An added benefit is that participants learn about using an electronic medium.

According to Koufman-Frederick et. al, (1999), advantages of online collaboration include:

- Electronic collaboration brings people out of isolation. Unfortunately, opportunities for collaboration don't always exist within a single school. Electronic collaboration allows counselors to connect to a new set of colleagues. Participants can communicate with people who share the same interests and experience the same challenges. Because it allows for the inclusion of many people, electronic collaboration promotes the exchange of a larger range of opinions and resources.

- Electronic collaboration provides time for reflection. Typically, during the school day counselors are pressed for time and lack opportunities to stop and reflect on their work experiences or move beyond on-the-fly brainstorming that may happen by chance in the hallway. The asynchronous nature of electronic collaboration allows participants to contribute to the conversation when it's convenient and to reflect on what others have said before responding. In addition, having to articulate in writing professional struggles and suggestions forces writers to take time to be thoughtful and reflect carefully about new ideas and pathways.

- One of the most common uses of the Internet is gathering (or "surfing" for) information. Electronic collaboration adds a different dimension — participants don't just surf for resources on the Internet, but actively and interactively contribute to exploring innovative ideas. With electronic collaboration, the adage "two heads are better than one" could just as well be "two hundred heads are better than one." One person's provocative question can lead to many creative, exciting solutions. By sharing what they know with others, participants advance their own knowledge and the collaborative community's knowledge.

Several free collaboration tools available on the Web now exist. Examples of these include:

1. **NetMeeting** is a product that provides a conferencing solution for the Internet and corporate intranet. Powerful features let you communicate with both audio and video, collaborate on virtually any Windows-based application, exchange graphics on an electronic whiteboard, transfer files, use the text-based chat program, and much more. Using your PC and the Internet, you can now hold face-to-face conversations with friends and family around the world, and it won't cost a fortune to do so! Because NetMeeting works with any video capture card or camera that supports Video for Windows®, you can choose from a wide range of video equipment. *http://www.microsoft-.com/windows/netmeeting/* Similar to NetMeeting is Cu-SeeMe from White Pine software (*www.wpine-.com/*).

2. **Visto** (*www.visto.com*) is a website which allows you free services to collaborate with others. Specifically, the site allows you to:

   a. Stay in touch via an e-mail account to send and receive messages.

   b. Set up a group message board to communicate with fellow group members.

   c. Stay organized with a web based calendar which provides e-mail reminders for important appointments. Choose to share your schedule with others, or print it out and take it with you.

   d. Share information by creating a photo album with your favorite pictures to share with friends; share documents and files; and schedule group activities and events.

Technologies for Accountability

School counselors are increasingly being held responsible for knowing and keeping track of all sorts of information such as student records, student contacts, parent conferences, case notes, counseling schedules, accountability data, list of tasks, and sometimes grades. Without the help of technology, counselors may feel overwhelmed, unorganized, or lost as a result of the sheer quantity of information. Consequently, effectiveness and motivation could suffer. Yet, measuring outcomes or using the current research to help inform school counselors of the nature of their efforts is an important task for ensuring the viability of a school counseling program. Technology can make the process more efficient, accurate, and automated.

Database/Spreadsheet

Database and spreadsheet programs are designed and intended to help users store, organize, and retrieve data. This function can be especially helpful as counselors feel the effects of the "information age." In addition to managing information, database programs can also be used to facilitate decision making. For instance, Sabella (1996) wrote about how school counselors can use a database program to use existing data collected by his/her school to identify and assign students to small groups for counseling. Using a database program for small group assignment is especially helpful when group membership is contingent on traits such as age, race, and sex (e.g., balancing groups by race and sex while perhaps keeping age uniform). The key to this procedure lies in how the data are identified, sorted (also known as indexed), and processed.

Current database and spreadsheet programs allow counselors to collect and conduct basic analyses to their data such as monitoring changes in client test scores or attendance rates throughout the year. Once a data query is initially set up and run, all a counselor needs to do next time is press a button which conducts the same procedure over any data set. The savings in time over the long run can be quite significant. Relatedly, database/spreadsheet programs do a very good job of seamlessly integrating with word processors and other programs so that a counselor can then glean any data from a spreadsheet, for instance, and insert it in appropriate places in a counseling report. Sabella (1996) gave several examples of how school counselors use the integration of database and word processing programs to collect, process, and use data in various documents:

- In consultation with the dean of students and the county database person, a counselor obtained a file containing a list of students who had not been referred for discipline problems that year. It was requested that the list be sorted by home room teachers, who were also included in the data file. The Dean and the counselor created an award on the computer and merged the names of each student on the award. The certificates printed in the same order that they appeared in the file—by home room teacher. After each certificate printed, all that had to be done was deposit them in the home room teachers' mailboxes, which were also in alphabetical order. This process required 30 minutes to set up and 90 minutes to print the approximately 600 awards. A nearby student assistant was responsible for refilling the printer with paper when it ran out.

- A counselor who conducted an outdoor adventure field trip at the beginning of each semester asked her county office to put on computer disk the names, lunch numbers, last semester grade point averages (GPAs), and home room teachers for all students at her school. She also asked that the list be sorted by GPA, race, and sex. The counselor was then able to identify students with the lowest GPAs and print out a list balanced by race and sex. Then, she merged a list of names with lunch numbers to give to the cafeteria staff who provided lunches for the trip. Using the disk of data and her word processor, the counselor was also able to generate certificates, permission letters, and a list of participants that would be used for gathering post intervention data. At the end of the year, she had the county office provide GPAs for the same students so that she could compare them against beginning of the year GPAs.

- For an annual career day, an elementary school counselor maintained a database of speakers and other participants. He merged this information into standard invitations, confirmations, brochures, and thank-you letters.

- Another counselor used the merge capability of her word processor while working closely with a program designed for students who were not successful in the regular classroom environment. These students were self-contained with only 15 other students and a teacher with advanced training. The counselor worked with the students, their parents or guardians, and juvenile case workers. She maintained information about each student in a database file to help her manage each case. She then used these files to complete already formatted reports for the juvenile justice department, drop-out prevention office, county office, and parents. All she had to do was indicate to the computer which report she wanted to complete and for which child or group of children. The computer and printer did the rest.

- Using a spreadsheet program, a counselor maintained an activity log which included time spent in various categories of activities (e.g., consulting with parents, individual counseling, large group guidance, peer helper training, and professional development to name a few). With one click of the mouse each quarter, he could print out a report which he provided to his principal compete with textual descriptions and bar graphs.

Personal Information Managers

Personal information managers (PIMs) are a type of software application designed to help users organize random bits of information. Although the category is fuzzy, most PIMs enable you to enter various kinds of textual notes - reminders, lists, dates - and to link these bits of information together in useful ways. Many PIMs also include calendar, scheduling, and calculator programs. The usefulness of this type of software lies in it's ability to integrate data and provide feedback in the form of potential scheduling conflicts and event reminders. Several online PIM's such as *www.visto.com* and *www.jump.com* also allow you to automatically import events that others manage (e.g., educational programming on television) as well as coordinate mutual times of availability for meeting with important others.

Accounting for Your Time

Because, unlike others who work in a school setting, school counselors have flexible time throughout their day, they are usually expected to be accountable for how they spend it. Some counselors simply try to maintain a respectable level of productivity in the face of seemingly insurmountable counselor-to-student ratios and mounting obligations. There are available a growing number of available electronic tools that can help. Many tools in the form of interactive software have become available for free over the Internet and therefore tend to be highly cost effective as well as contribute to overall counselor effectiveness. For instance, various websites offer free maps and driving directions by simply typing in an address. Some map generators are so sophisticated that they may also allow you to click on a street address and learn of all listed residents on that street (*www.anywho.com*). Others will allow you to learn of other attractions such as hotels or restaurants close to a designated address (*www.maps-.yahoo.com*). With Fax4Free (*www.fax4free.com*), you can send faxes to and within the United States, Canada, and Australia for free, and more countries are on the way. If your organization qualifies for nonprofit status, Fax4Free.com allows you to broadcast faxes to your members in the U.S., Canada, & Australia for free. This site obviously will save you money although can also save you the time needed to print a document, feed it into a fax machine, and wait for a successful outcome. Another example of a time saving utility is AltaVista's online language translator (*http://babelfish.altavista.com/cgi-bin/translate?*) which performs two types of tasks. Once a user visits the site, he/she can type or past text from another application into a window, choose a certain translation (e..g, English to Spanish), and have the text rapidly converted. The other function of the translator is for typing in a website address and having an entire web page translated into the designated language. AltaVista also hosts other tools (*www.altavista.com/av/content/tools/*) such as in the areas of business, finance, careers (e.g., finding a school, salary calculator, relocation wizard, and job ads), government information, health and reference.

Technologies for Intervention Delivery

As schools acquire new computers and other related technologies, counselors are increasing using new equipment and software which assist them in catching the interest of clients in ways never before imagined. For instance:

1. Some counselors use computers to access the Internet, locate, and print out appropriate puppet patterns to later personalize and animate with their clients (e.g., *http://www.kn.pacbell.com/wired/fil/pages/webpuppetsjo.html*).

2. Many counselors have discovered desktop publishing, paint, and animation software to help clients use the computer screen as a three dimensional palette on which to "draw" or create a virtual world (e.g., *http://www.connectedcounseling.com/*).

3. In addition to puppets and art, computers can help counselors and their clients develop many variations of creative dramas complete with set design, wardrobe, scripts, and actual delivery of the scripts in different chosen voices (e.g., The American Girls Premiere—2nd Edition by The Learning Company, see *www.learningco.com*)

4. Many counselors are uncovering the advantages of using multimedia presentation software such as Microsoft PowerPoint to embellish their small group counseling and large group guidance interventions.

5. Others are supplementing their counseling efforts in the area of mentoring by including professionals and students from around the world via the Net. For instance Epals (*www.epals.com*) considers itself the world's largest K-12 Educational electronic penpal network with over 16,318 classrooms from 108 countries, representing over 1 million students.

6. A growing number of interactive software titles designed especially with counselors in mind in areas such as grief counseling, conflict resolution, anger management, and confronting sexual harassment allow counselors to increasingly deliver highly visual and interactive lessons with one client or with groups of clients. NickJr, the website for the television channel for children provides many games and other tools which can easily be applied in a school counselor's work (*www.nickjr.com*). For example, a Blues Clues game, Blue 214—Everyone has feelings, helps users find out how our friends feel by matching the expressions on the cards with the expressions on their faces. *www.nickjr.com/blue_archive/archive_page5.html*

Perhaps the most talked about and controversial technology for intervention delivery is web counseling or cybercounseling. When you think of conducting counseling with your students, you probably envision you and your client(s) in your office, in the classroom, or perhaps even on a "walk and talk." However, others may also have a mental image of a counselor who sits in front of the computer and conducts counseling over the Internet. Webcounseling is the attempt to provide counseling services in an Internet environment. The environment may include e-mail, chatrooms, or Internet video conferencing. For example, one site (*www.psychology.com/holmes.htm*) allows visitors to ask a psychologist for help with a personal problem, and he responds with a few paragraphs of advice. Clients pay for the service only if they are satisfied with the advice (Stern, 1996). The practice of webcounseling began slowly although is rapidly finding popularity among both counselors and cyberclients. Among counseling professionals, webcounseling has created somewhat of a debate about the utility and effectiveness of this new medium. Moreover, those involved in traditional counseling ethical and legal issues are wondering how such matters relate to the Internet environment.

In an attempt to determine the pervasiveness of counseling related activity on the Internet, Sampson, Kolodinsky, and Greeno, (1997) conducted an analysis in April 1996, using the WebCrawler search engine. Results of the analysis revealed that two thirds of the counseling-related home pages examined were group home pages, and fully 50% were groups advertising some type of counseling-related service. Only 15% were home pages placed by individuals. Of particular note were on-line services offered by groups or individuals for a fee, either as a reply to questions posed via e-mail or for interactive chat sessions. The credentials for practitioners involved a wide range, including M.D., Ph.D., M.A., and L.P.C. Many "counselors" identified no professional credentials at all. In fact, most home pages provided little information about the nature of qualifications of those providing services other than degree-level designation. For example, an individual with "M.A." listed after his or her name frequently did not disclose the subject area of the degree. In a separate nonrandom analysis of 401 sites from the same 3,764 home pages, 15 home pages were identified that offered direct on-line services. Offerings ranged from $15 charged for answering a question via E-mail to $65 for a 60-minute chat session. These on-line offerings ranged from single treatment interventions to an individual offering services in 35 different specialty areas.

The authors concluded that the results of their search can be used to encourage debate about counseling over the Internet. Based on the percentage of home pages offering direct on-line services, there are at least 275 practitioners currently offering direct counseling services across the Internet. Given that 275 practitioners are offering services to clients, it is impossible to ignore that counseling (at some level) is being conducted on the Internet. Instead of being a "potential" future event, counseling and counseling-related activities are a "present" reality. Although these numbers are relatively small in comparison with the tens of thousands of counselors currently offering services through more traditional means, the annualized growth rate indicates that increases in Internet counseling will occur. Future enhancements in technology are likely to only accelerate the availability of counseling services through networking.

The evolution of the Internet into the information highway offers many future possibilities and potential problems in the delivery of counseling services. Following is an overview of each:

Possibilities

❖ Delivery of counseling services: Walz (1996) noted that the information highway "allows counselors to overcome problems of distance and time to offer opportunities for networking and interacting not otherwise available" (p. 417). In addition, counseling over the Net may be a useful medium for those with physical disabilities whom may find even a short distance a significant obstacle. And yet for others whom are reticent in meeting with a counselor and/or self-disclosing, the Net may prove to be an interactive lubricant which may very well foster the counseling process.

❖ Delivery of information resources: The Internet is a convenient and quick way to deliver important information. In cybercounseling, information might be in the form of homework assignment between sessions or bibliocounseling. Also, electronic file transfer of client records, including intake data, case notes (Casey, Bloom, & Moan, 1994), assessment reports, and selected key audio and video recordings of client sessions, could be used as preparation for individual supervision, group supervision, case conferences, and research (Sampson, et al., 1997).

❖ Assessment and evaluation: Access to a wide variety of assessment, instructional, and information resources, in formats appropriate in a wide variety of ethnic, gender, and age contexts (Sampson, 1990; Sampson & Krumboltz, 1991), could be accomplished via WWW and FTP sites.

❖ Communications: Especially via e-mail, counselors and clients can exchange messages throughout the counseling process. Messages may inform both counselor and client of pertinent changes or progress. E-mail can provide an excellent forum for answering simple questions, providing social support, or to schedule actual or virtual meeting times.

❖ Marriage and family counseling: If face-to-face interaction is not possible on a regular basis, marriage counseling might be delivered via video conferencing, in which each couple and the counselor (or counselors) are in different geographic locations. After independent use of multimedia based computer-assisted instruction on communication skills, spouses could use video conferencing to complete assigned homework (e.g., communication exercises) (Sampson, et al., 1997).

❖ Supervision: Anecdotal evidence has shown that e-mail is an enhancing tool in the process of counselor supervision and consultation, It provides an immediate and ongoing channel of communication between and among as many people as chosen (Myrick & Sabella, 1995).

Potential Problems

❖ Confidentiality: Although encryption and security methods have become highly sophisticated, unauthorized access to online communications remains a possibility without attention to security measures. Counselors whom practice on the Net must ethically and legally protect their clients, their profession, and themselves by using all known and reasonable security measures.

❖ Computer competency: Both the counselor and client must be adequately computer literate for the computer/network environment to be a viable interactive medium. From typing skills to electronic data transfer, both the counselor and client must be able to effectively harness the power and function of both hardware and software. Similar to face-to-face counseling, counselors must not attempt to perform services outside the limitations of their competence.

❖ Location-specific factors: A potential lack of appreciation on the part of geographically remote counselors of location-specific conditions, events, and cultural issues that affect clients may limit counselor credibility or lead to inappropriate counseling interventions. For example, a geographically remote counselor may be unaware of traumatic recent local events that are exacerbating a client's reaction to work and family stressors. It may also be possible that differences in local or regional cultural norms between the client's and counselor's community could lead a counselor to misinterpret the thoughts, feelings, or behavior of the client. Counselors need to prepare for counseling a client in a remote location by becoming familiar with recent local events and local cultural norms. If a counselor encounters an unanticipated reaction on the part of the client, the counselor needs to proceed slowly, clarifying client perceptions of their thoughts, feelings, and behavior (Sampson, et al., 1997).

❖ Equity: Does the cost of Internet access introduce yet another obstacle for obtaining counseling? Does cybercounseling further alienate potential clients whom might have the greatest need for counseling? Even when given access to the Net, could a client competently engage cybercounseling without possibly having ever had a computer experience? Webcounseling seems to exacerbate equity issues already confronting live counseling.

❖ Credentialing: How will certification and licensure laws apply to the Internet as state and national borders are crossed electronically? Will counselors be required to be credentialed in all states and countries where clients are located? Could cybercounseling actually be the impetus for a national credential recognized by all states? Will we need to move towards global credentialing? Who will monitor service complaints out-of-state or internationally?

❖ High Tech v. High Touch: How can counselors foster the development of trusting, caring, and genuine working relationships in cyberspace? Until video transmission over the Web makes telecounseling a reality, cybercounseling relies on a process devoid of nonverbal or extraverbal behavior. Even if we were able to conduct real-time counseling over the Net via video, can this medium help us to communicate so as to foster the counseling core conditions? Further, Lago (1996) poses a key question: "Do the existing theories of psychotherapy continue to apply, or do we need a new theory of e-mail therapy? (p. 289)" He then takes Rogers' (1957) work on the necessary and sufficient conditions for therapeutic change as his starting-point and lists the computer-mediated therapist competencies as: the ability to establish contact, the ability to establish relationship, the ability to communicate accurately with minimal loss or distortion, the ability to demonstrate understanding and frame empathic responses, and the capacity and resources to provide appropriate and supportive information. This proposal begs the question as to whether such relationship conditions as outlined by Rogers can be successfully transmitted and received via contemporary computer-mediated telecommunications media.

❖ Impersonation: A famous cartoon circulated over the Net depicts a dog sitting in front of a computer. The caption says, "The nice thing about the Internet is that nobody knows you're a dog." Experienced Internet users can relate to the humor in this cartoon because they know that there are many people who hide behind the Net's veil of anonymity to communicate messages they ordinarily would not communicate in real life. Messages that convey unpopular sentiments and would ordinarily be met with castigation. Others rely on anonymity provided by the Net to play out fantasies or practical jokes. Who is your cyberclient, really? Does your client depict himself/herself as an adult and is actually a minor? Has the client disguised their gender, race, or other personal distinctions that may threaten the validity or integrity of your efforts.

❖ Ethics: How do current ethical statements for counselors apply or adapt to situations encountered online? For the most part, counselors can make the leap into cyberspace and use current ethical guidelines to conduct themselves in an ethical fashion. However, problems exist. The future will inevitably see a change in what it means to be ethical as we learn the exact nature of counseling online.

The Ethics of WebCounseling

In 1995, the NBCC Board of Directors appointed a webcounseling Task Force to examine the practice of online counseling and to assess the possible existence of any regulatory issues NBCC might need to address. The task force established a listserv composed of more than 20 individuals who had specific knowledge, expertise, skills and opinions regarding the practice of what is herein referred to as webcounseling. Soon it became apparent that counseling had a diverse presence on the Internet, from websites that simply promoted a counselor's home or office practice, to sites that provided information about counseling and others which actually claimed to offer therapeutic interventions either as an adjunct to face-to-face counseling or as a stand alone service. Some sites were poorly constructed, poorly edited and poorly presented. Others were run by anonymous individuals, individuals with no credentials or fraudulent credentials, and some sites were operated by individuals with appropriate credentials and years of professional experience. However these credentials were all based on education and experience gained in face-to-face counseling, and the relevance of these credentials to the practice of webcounseling is unknown. No one knew if the lack of visual input made a difference in the outcome of the counseling process. No one knew about the legality of counseling across state or national boundaries. No one knew if there was any relevant research in any field of communication which could shed light on these questions (Bloom, 1997). As a result of the Task Force's work, a set of standards, the Standards for

the Ethical Practice of Webcounseling, were developed and are included in Figure 30:1.

Ethical and Legal Use of Technology

Computer and networking technologies such as the Internet provide vast power, especially as a medium for communication, collaboration, and as an intervention delivery. Internet users enjoy the freedom of conducting all kinds of transactions, including counseling, over the Net. With this freedom, however, comes an important responsibility to use computers, and especially the Internet, in a manner which is safe, secure, ethical, and contributes to the overall welfare of all involved. Counselors should dedicate themselves to becoming aware of the dangers involved in using computers and traveling the information superhighway. For instance, Sabella (1999) wrote about counseling related issues that computer and Internet technology have spawned and includes: Internet addiction, equitable access, pornography, online sexual harassment, security, and safety. With increased awareness, counselors can more effectively make decisions about their computing and online behavior.

Confidentiality

One essential focus of ethical computer use is on the issue of confidentiality. The counselor-client relationship is a private one and requires compliance with laws, policies, and ethical standards pertaining to confidentiality (American School Counselor Association, 1998). Mudore (1988) provided several recommendations for counselors for protecting the confidentiality of student records and ensuring that only authorized persons would have access to the information. Recommendations include the following:

1. Keep the computer in a private area so that student data can be entered privately.

2. Put student data, particularly counseling records, on a second (backup) disk.

3. Mark counseling disks in code rather than titling them "Student Data."

4. Protect against unauthorized duplication of disks by removing disk tabs, locking up disks, and not allowing disks to be removed from their location.

5. Place a password on your computer's opening screen to avoid unauthorized access to your hard drive.

6. Talk to other staff to share your concerns about confidentiality; inform the school community about the challenges posted by computer technology.

Sampson and Pyle (1983) also recommended that (a) only essential data are maintained; (b) the data are accurate; (c) they are destroyed once they are no longer needed to provide services; (d) no individually identifiable data be maintained to which there is access through a computer network; and (e) individually identifiable data are not used for research purposes without the consent of those who provided the data.

Many software programs (e.g., word processing and database programs) now come with the ability to assign a file a password. The advantage is that without the password the file is encrypted in code and rendered illegible. Although it is possible to "crack" the code, doing so would take relatively extensive computer programming knowledge and access to the files. The disadvantage of using this feature is that if the counselor fails to remember the password, it is also difficult for him or her to retrieve the file. Therefore, it is suggested that passwords be written down in safe and secure places. It is also good practice to periodically change one's password to further discourage a breach of confidentiality in the event a file is stolen or inappropriately accessed. Finally, passwords should not be created using names or adjectives that might be easily deciphered by others. Safe passwords do not constitute personal names, birthdays, anniversaries, or popular names. Rather, they should be a combination of letters and numbers that are less obvious (e.g., ROBO212, LUNCH442, PET655; Sabella, 1996).

Technology and the Future of School Counseling

Computers, like any new tools, can be either an opportunity or a threat to the development of our work as school counselors and to our profession. Focusing on the parts that are helpful and avoiding those which are not can be a difficult task because of the vastness and morphological nature of technology. Compromising issues of psychological health and overall well-being while using computer and networking technologies may be mitigated knowledge and skills which promote robust discovery. As part of ongoing professional development, school counselors should stay informed of new technological developments and how they are being applied to our work, especially in the highly sensitive area of counseling intervention delivery. Technologies currently under development and becoming more pervasive (and thus usually less expensive) merit special attention:

1. Digital cameras allow for counselors to take pictures and instantly use them in a variety of ways. Some are posting photos of evidence of their work on counseling websites or electronic portfolios as a matter of public relations and accountability. Others are using digital cameras, both video and still, to help clients capture "their world" and expressed in an electronic

collage or journal which is then used in the counseling process.

2. Voice recognition software allows for humans and machines to interact in more meaningful ways than ever before considered. Counselors can dictate their words into various applications as well as issue computer voice commands that will further increase efficiency and effectiveness.

3. WebTV is an appliance and service which uses a television and cable connection to access the Internet. Because most homes have televisions and purchase cable services, counselors can better interface with difficult to reach clients who cannot afford a computer. And because WebTV integrates with television programming, counselors will be able to supplement short films or television programs with interactive exercises and activities.

4. As bandwidth (the capacity of copper and fiberoptic wires to move data) increases, we will see the proliferation of Internet videoconferencing and online full-length videos which will further enhance efforts in communication, collaboration, consultation, distance education, and intervention delivery. Websites will become more dynamic, offering virtual three dimensional worlds.

5. Computer scientists are making rapid gains in developing what is known as natural language so that computers can better "understand" human questions or commands and more appropriately respond.

6. Computers are breaking capacity and speed barriers every day. As they become faster, smaller, and are able to store more data, computers will help us to perform and manage tasks with unprecedented proficiency.

The experience and world views of our clients and stake holders have been profoundly impacted by the rapid evolution of computer technologies. We sit at the edge of an electronic frontier without knowing for certain what lies ahead. The journey, with its extraordinary potentials and realistic pitfalls, is exciting and oftentimes frightening. Careful and purposeful practice, however, can help us to stay connected and competent amidst chaotic transition. This chapter sought to provide readers with an introduction and overview of technology and its special meaning to school counselors. As an agent of change and advocacy, it is your job now to explore how technology best works for you so that you may work best for your clients.

References

American School Counselor Association. (1998). Ethical standards for school counselors. Alexandria, VA. ASCA Press.

Bloom, J.W. (November, 1997). NBCC Webcounseling Standards. Alexandria, VA. Counseling Today. Available online: [http://www.nbcc.org/ethics/ wcstandards.htm]

Cairo, P. C., & Kanner, M. S. (1984). Investigating the effects of computerized approaches to counselor training. Counselor Education and Supervision, 24, 212-221.

Casey, J. A., Bloom, J. W., & Moan, E. R. (1994). Use of technology in counselor supervision. In L. D. Borders (Ed.), Counseling supervision. Greensboro: University of North Carolina, ERIC Clearinghouse on Counseling and Student Services. (ERIC Document Reproduction Service No. ED 372 357)

Chapman, W., & Katz, M. R. (1983). Career information systems in the secondary schools: A survey and assessment. Vocational Guidance Quarterly, 32, 165-177.

Courtois, M. P. (1995). Cool tools for searching the Web: A performance evaluation. Online, 19(6), 14-32.

D'Andrea, M. (1995). Using computer technology to promote multicultural awareness among elementary school-age students. Elementary School Guidance & Counseling, 30(1), p. 45-55.

Fargen, T. (1996). Surfing the Internet in gym class: Physical education E-mail. KeyPals. Teaching & Change, 3(3), 272- 281.

Froehle, T. C. (1984). Computer-assisted feedback in counseling supervision. Counselor Education and Supervision, 24, 168-175.

Glover, B. L. (1995). DINOS (drinking is not our solution): Using computer programs in middle school drug education. Elementary School Guidance & Counseling, 30, 55-62.

Grohol, J.M. (1997). The insider's guide to mental health resources online. New York, NY: The Guilford Press. (Also see www.mentalhelp.net).

Haring-Hidore, M. (1984). In pursuit of students who do not use computers for career guidance. Journal of Counseling and Development, 63, 139-140.

Harris, J. (1972). Computer-assisted guidance systems. Washington, DC: National Vocational Guidance Association.

Hofstetter, F.T. (1998). Internet literacy. Boston, MA. Irwin/ McGraw Hill.

HP E-mail Mentor Program - Largest Telementoring Program HP E-mail Mentor Program - One on One Telementoring, (1997). Available online: [www.telementor.org/hp/]

Jackson, M.L., & Davidson, C.T. (1998). The web we weave: Using the Internet for counseling research; Part 1. Counseling Today, 39(2).

Katz, M. R., & Shatkin, L. (1983). Characteristics of computer-assisted guidance. The Counseling Psychologist, 11(4), 15-31.

Kivilghan, D. M., Jr., Johnston, J.A., Hogan, R. S., & Mauer, E. (1994). Who benefits from computerized career counseling? Journal of Counseling Development, 72, 289-292.

Koufman-Frederick, A., Lillie, M., Pattison-Gordon, L., Watt, D.L., & Carter, R. (1999). Electronic Collaboration: A Practical Guide for Educators. Providence, RI: The LAB at Brown University. Available online [www.lab.brown.edu].

Lago, C. (1996). Computer therapeutics. Counseling, 7, 287-289.

McClure, P.A. (1996, May/June). Technology plans and measurable outcomes. Edcom Review, 31(3).

McMurdo, G. (1995). How the Internet was indexed. Journal of Information Science, 21(6), 479-489.

McQuillan, L. (06/05/98). Clinton, at MIT, says all must grasp computers. Reuters.

Mighty Media, Inc., (1997). Available on-line [www.mightymedia.com/KeyPals/]

Mudore, C. (1988). Computers, ethics, and the school counselor. Clearing House, 61(6), 283-284.

Myrick, R.D, & Sabella, R.A. (1995). Cyberspace: New place for counselor supervision. Elementary School Guidance & Counseling. 30(1), p. 35

Neukrug, E. S. (1991). Computer-assisted live supervision in counselor skills training. Counselor Education and Supervision, 31, 132-138.

President's Information Technology Advisory Committee Interim Report to the President (August, 1998). National Coordination Office for computing, Information, and Communications, 4201 Wilson Blvd., Suite 690, Arlington, VA 22230, 703-306-4722.

Pyle, K. R. (1984). Career counseling and computers: Where is the creativity? *Journal of Counseling and Development, 63,* 141-144.

Rogers, C.R., (1957). The necessary and sufficient conditions of therapeutic personality change. *Journal of Consulting Psychology, 21,* 95-103.

Rust, E. B. (1995). Applications of the international Counselor Network for elementary and middle school counseling. Elementary School Guidance & Counseling, 30,16-25.

Sabella, R.A. (1996). School counselors and computers: Specific time-saving tips. *Elementary School Guidance & Counseling,* 31(2), p. 83-96.

Sabella, R.A. (1998). Practical technology applications for peer helper programs and training. *Peer Facilitator Quarterly,* 15(2), 4-13.

Sabella, R.A. (1999). *SchoolCounselor.com: A friendly and practical guide to the World Wide Web.* (Including over 700 counseling related websites). Minneapolis, MN: Educational Media Corporation.

Sampson, J.P., Kolodinsky, R.W., & Greeno, B.P. (1997). Counseling on the information highway: Future possibilities and potential problems. *Journal of Counseling and Development,* 75(3), p. 203-214.

Sampson, J.P., Jr., & Krumboltz, J.D. (1991). Computer assisted instruction: A missing link in counseling. *Journal of Counseling & Development, 69,* 395-397.

Sampson, J.P., & Pyle, K.R. (1983). Ethical issues involved with the use of computer-assisted counseling, testing, and guidance systems. *The Personnel and Guidance Journal, 61,* 283-287.

Sampson, J. P., Jr. (1990). Computer-assisted testing and the goals of counseling psychology. *The Counseling Psychologist, 18,* 227-239.

Scales, B. J., & Felt, E. C. (1995). Diversity on the World Wide Web: Using robots to search the Web. *Library Software Review,* 14(3),132-136.

Sharf, R. S., &.Lucas, M. (1993). An assessment of a computerized simulation of counseling skills. Counselor *Education and Supervision, 32,* 254-266.

Shulman, H. A., Sweeney, B., & Gerler, E. R. (1995). A computer-assisted approach to preventing alcohol abuse: Implications for the middle school. *Elementary School Guidance & Counseling, 30,* 63-77.

Stern, E. (1996). High-tech help on the Internet. *Psychology Today,* 29(5).

Symons, A. K. (1996). Intelligent life on the Web and how to find it. *School Library Journal,* 42(3), 106-109.

Tenopir, C. (1999). Should We Cancel Print? *Library Journal,* 124(14), p. 138-140.

Walz, G. R. (1996). *Using the I-Way for career development.* In R. Feller & G. Walz (Eds.), Optimizing life transitions in turbulent times: Exploring work, learning and careers. Greensboro: University of North Carolina, ERIC Clearinghouse on Counseling and Student Services. p. 415-427.

Figure 30:1
Standards for the Ethical Practice of Webcounseling

The relative newness of the use of the Internet for service and product delivery leaves authors of standards at a loss when beginning to create ethical practices on the Internet. This document, like all codes of conduct, will change as information and circumstances not yet foreseen evolve. However, each version of this code of ethics is the current best standard of conduct passed by the NBCC Board of Directors (see *www.nbcc.org/ethics/home.htm*; reprinted by permission). As with any code, and especially with a code such as this, created for an evolving field of work, NBCC and CCE welcome comments and ideas for further discussion and inclusion.

The development of these webcounseling standards has been guided by the following principles:

- These standards are intended to address practices which are unique to webcounseling and WebCounselors.

- These standards are not to duplicate non-Internet-based standards adopted in other codes of ethics.

- Recognizing that significant new technology emerges continuously, these standards should be reviewed frequently.

- webcounseling ethics cases should be reviewed in light of delivery systems existing at the moment rather than at the time the standards were adopted.

- WebCounselors who are not National Certified Counselors may indicate at their website their adherence to these standards, but may not publish these standards in their entirety without written permission of the National Board for Certified Counselors.

- The Practice of webcounseling shall be defined as "the practice of professional counseling and information delivery that occurs when client(s) and counselor are in separate or remote locations and utilize electronic means to communicate over the Internet."

In addition to following the NBCC Code of Ethics pertaining to the practice of professional counseling, Web Counselors shall:

1. Review pertinent legal and ethical codes for possible violations emanating from the practice of Web Counseling and supervision. Liability insurance policies should also be reviewed to determine if the practice of webcounseling is a covered activity. Local, state, provincial and national statutes as well as the codes of professional membership organizations, professional certifying bodies and state or provincial licensing boards need to be reviewed. Also, as no definitive answers are known to questions pertaining to whether webcounseling takes place in the WebCounselor's location or the WebClient's location, WebCounselors should consider carefully local customs regarding age of consent and child abuse reporting.

2. Inform WebClients of encryption methods being used to help insure the security of client/counselor/supervisor communications. Encryption methods should be used whenever possible. If encryption is not made available to clients, clients must be informed of the potential hazards of unsecured communication on the Internet. Hazards may include authorized or unauthorized monitoring of transmissions and/or records of webcounseling sessions.

3. Inform clients if, how and how long session data are being preserved. Session data may include WebCounselor/WebClient e-mail, test results, audio/video session recordings, session notes, and counselor/supervisor communications. The likelihood of electronic sessions being preserved is greater because of the ease and decreased costs involved in recording. Thus, its potential use in supervision, research and legal proceedings increases.

4. In situations where it is difficult to verify the identity of WebCounselor or WebClient, take steps to address impostor concerns, such as by using code words, numbers or graphics.

5. When parent/guardian consent is required to provide Webcounseling to minors, verify the identity of the consenting person.

6. Follow appropriate procedures regarding the release of information for sharing WebClient information with other electronic sources. Because of the relative ease with which e-mail messages can be forwarded to formal and casual referral sources, WebCounselors must work to insure the confidentiality of the Webcounseling relationship.

7. Carefully consider the extent of self disclosure presented to the WebClient and provide rationale for WebCounselor's level of disclosure. WebCounselors may wish to ensure that, minimally, the WebClient has the same data available about his/her service provider as would be available if the counseling were to take place face to face (i.e., possibly ethnicity, gender, etc.). Compelling reasons for limiting disclosure should be presented. WebCounselors will remember to protect themselves from unscrupulous users of the Internet by limiting potentially harmful disclosure about self and family.

8. Provide links to websites of all appropriate certification bodies and licensure boards to facilitate consumer protection.

9. Contact NBCC/CEE or the WebClient's state or provincial licensing board to obtain the name of at least one Counselor-On-Call within the WebClient's geographical region. WebCounselors who have contacted an individual to determine his or her willingness to serve as a Counselor-On-Call (either in person, over the phone or via e-mail) should also ensure that the WebClient is provided with local crisis intervention hot line numbers, 911 and similar numbers in the event that the Counselor-On-Call is unavailable.

10. Discuss with their WebClients procedures for contacting the WebCounselor when he or she is off-line. This means explaining exactly how often e-mail messages are to be checked by the WebCounselor.

11. Mention at their websites those presenting problems they believe to be inappropriate for Webcounseling. While no conclusive research has been conducted to date, those topics might include: sexual abuse as a primary issue, violent relationships, eating disorders, and psychiatric disorders that involve distortions of reality.

12. Explain to clients the possibility of technology failure. The WebCounselor gives instructions to WebClients about calling if problems arise, discusses the appropriateness of the client calling collect when the call might be originating from around the world, mentions differences in time zones, talks about dealing with response delays in sending and receiving e-mail messages

13. Explain to clients how to cope with potential misunderstandings arising from the lack of visual cues from WebCounselor or WebClient. For example, suggesting the other person simply say, "Because I couldn't see your face or hear your tone of voice in your e-mail message, I'm not sure how to interpret that last message."

Chapter 31
Maintaining Your Professional Image: A Report Card
by
Beverly O'Bryant

Beverly J. O'Bryant, PhD, NCC, NCSC, LPC, is a nationally certified school counselor and counselor educator serving as Director of Community Service and Service Learning Programs for the District of Columbia Public Schools, Washington D.C. She has been a teacher, a school counselor at all levels (elementary, junior high, senior high, and with at-risk K-12 youth), and an educational administrator. She is a Past President of the American Counseling Association, a Past President of the American School Counselor Association (ASCA) and the current President of Counseling and Training Systems, Inc.

Introduction

A primary issue in our profession is the role of the counselor-as-person. Counseling professionals have long felt that this may be the most important aspect in effective counseling outcome. We ask our clients to face the truth about themselves; to look honestly at what they are and to choose how they want to change and grow. Should we as counselors not be willing to do the same? Should we not be willing to focus on counselor-as-person as well as on counselor-as-professional?

Growing personally and professionally contributes significantly to our success with student clients and others with whom we work. Keeping abreast of new and innovative changes in our profession enables us to serve our "publics" better; and, provides our student clients with a measure of confidence that their welfare is most important. Being ever mindful of our "professional image" provides indices of competence and professionalism. And, the individual commitment to attend to each of these areas provides a fairly good indicator of the overall well being of the discipline, and a prognostication of longevity relative to the profession's acceptance by its constituents.

How would you fair? Are you growing professionally and personally? Do you keep abreast of new and innovative changes? Are you attentive to your professional image among your various publics? Do you know who your many publics are? Are you committed to your own professional development? And, are you the type of counselor from whom you would seek help?

Our graduate counselor preparation programs require grounding in both theory and practice. Use of theory provides the framework and direction for the most effective practice. However, because the profession of counseling is constantly in a state of flux, it becomes incumbent of each professional counselor to remain conversant with the best and latest information.

Continued self-enhancement and professional growth is made easy today through the myriad of professional opportunities available. Professional school counselors will want to take advantage of them. Professional growth necessitates keeping in touch with other professionals and professional organizations, and with new concepts and new materials. Membership in ACA and ASCA provides a relationship with other counselors and information about what is happening nationwide. Maintaining current facts from the counseling journals keeps the proactive, developmental counselor abreast of the trends. Attending local, state, and national conferences opens doors to new ideas and exciting personal and professional contacts.

It is our duty (ethically) as professional school counselors to maintain and enhance our "professional image." And, staying in touch with developing, growing, innovative people in our profession can be fun and very rewarding. It can sometimes be a little disconcerting to learn how little we may know in comparison to some others in our profession, but it can also be very rewarding to learn that we know enough to contribute to the professional growth of others.

Throughout this book reference has been made to the counselor as a professional. There are chapters concerning your appropriate role and function, legal and ethical issues, effectively promoting your school counseling program, and so forth. All of these are topics of concern to the professional school counselor. However, none may be more important than the preceding chapter (29) by Dr. Tom Clawson concerning credentialing and the school counselor. Are you appropriately credentialed? Are you a Nationally Certified Counselor (NCC)? A Nationally Certified School Counselor (NCSC)? If not, are you interested in becoming one? If yes, see Figure 29.1 and then write: *NBCC, 3-D Terrace Way, Greensboro, NC 27403* for an application. The appropriate credential identifies to our "publics" that we have met specific professional standards and most importantly, that we "cared" enough about them and ourselves to meet such standards.

What kind of a "professional image" report card would you issue concerning yourself at this time in your career? Would it be "Satisfactory" or "Unsatisfactory"? If you are a practicing school counselor, respond honestly to the following items as they pertain to you. If you are a school counselor-to-be, respond to the items as to how you would like to "grade" yourself two years following your graduation from a graduate level program in counselor education.

Counselor's Report Card

Use one of the following as your response to each item: below:

    S = Satisfactory Progress
    N = Needs Improvement
    U = Unsatisfactory Progress

As a professional school counselor, I:

S N U 1. conduct appropriate school counselor functions.

S N U 2. follow a written job description.

S N U 3. am a member and involved in ASCA.

S N U 4. attend and participate in my annual state counseling association meetings.

S N U 5. made a presentation (or submitted a proposal for consideration) at my state or national ASCA Conference this past year.

S N U 6. attended an in-service workshop, a conference, or took a non-required graduate course for my own personal growth during the past year (other than 4 above).

S N U 7. am familiar with the ASCA Ethical Standards and adhere to them.

S N U 8. conduct individual and group counseling only within my level of expertise.

S N U 9. subscribe to and read all ASCA and state school related journals, newsletters, and so forth.

S N U 10. am up-to-date on State and Federal laws effecting my work as a school counselor.

S N U 11. read professional books.

S N U 12. am a member of ACA and attend the annual ACA conference.

S N U 13. have published a journal article (or have recently submitted one for publication).

S N U 14. have an attractive and inviting office.

S N U 15. have a pleasant yet efficient and professional, personal demeanor.

S N U 16. use my many talents to create a positive atmosphere in my school.

S N U 17. am a voluntary participating committee member as requested by others at my school and/or by state, regional, or national counseling organization representatives.

S N U 18. am actively involved in determining my own schedule as well as goals and directions for the school counseling program.

S N U 19. model mental and physical health.

S N U 20. hold membership and participate in local service clubs.

S N U 21. promote the image of the counseling profession.

S N U 22. take a stand as an advocate for my students.

S N U 23. carry professional liability insurance.

S N U 24. attend a conference and then share what I learned with colleagues.

S N U 25. exhibit pride in myself as a counselor.

S N U 26. speak with assurance, even when saying "I'm not sure about that, but I'll be glad to investigate it for you."

S N U 27. appear, in dress, and mannerisms revealing professionalism.

S N U 28. have the appropriate professional accessories: briefcase, business cards, and so forth.

S N U 29. take advantage of the home study (video/cassette tapes) programs offered by ACA and other reputable agencies.

S N U 30. network with counselors from other schools and school systems as often as possible.

S N U 31. am a National Certified Counselor (NCC)—a National Certified School Counselor (NCSC).

S N U 32. display my degrees, certifications, plagues and honors prominently on my office walls.

S N U 33. articulate the positive.

S N U 34. "write-up" some of the innovative in-the-field things I do for publication.

S N U 35. attend legislative hearings.

S N U 36. know my local, state, and national legislators.

S N U 37. am accountable.

S N U 38. participate in locally relevant research.

S N U 39. have written an article for a counseling journal or newsletter (very few writers to our journals are school counselors).

S N U 40. know and understand the six National Educational Goals (If not, re-read Chapter Two of this book).

S N U 41. am doing what I was trained to do (you probably were not trained in "lunchroom duty" or "class scheduling").

S N U 42. do things to avoid "burning out" professionally.

S N U 43. believe my "publics" perceive me as a "professional" in the truest sense of the word.

S N U 44. perceive myself as an up-to-date, growing "professional".

S N U 45. respect the confidentiality of the counseling relationship (and never "talk too much" in the teachers lounge).

S N U 46. make a clear distinction between my personal views and opinions and those I make as a representative of the school counseling profession (if different).

S N U 47. view my professional development as a continuing *must*.

S N U 48. strive to impact legislation and decisions affecting my profession: locally, statewide, and nationally.

S N U 49. am working at changing the perception, attitudes and systems that are working against our young people?

S N U 50. am an advocate of the school counseling profession.

What sort of a "report card" did you issue yourself? Do you "need improvement" in several areas? If yes, the best way to strengthen your weak areas, to "remain abreast," is to get involved professionally. The "involved" school counselor seldom burns out.

Now that you've finished reading this book you have been exposed to many, many excellent strategies and plans for use in effectively managing your school counseling program. How well do you manage your own personal and professional growth? As a counselor, developing a plan to effectively manage your own personal and professional growth may be more important than managing your school counseling program. Develop a plan and stay with it! However, it is true, the best laid plans will forever be "best laid" if not put into action. As you've read throughout this book, there is a lot (to say the least) going on in our profession! "Buy in!" Its your profession and your future.

A school counselor's continued professional development is not really a choice, it is imperative.

Figure 31.1
My Professional Development:
A Self-Assessment Inventory By Joe Wittmer

Directions: Below are several current professional issues, questions, etc. which should be of concern to you as a professional school counselor or school counselor to be. Answer each item by checking "Met," "Partially Met", or "Not Met". A "Met" answer means you are convinced that you possess the skills and knowledge to fully meet the statement as written. Of course, if you are a student preparing to become a professional school counselor, you may not be able to respond appropriately to each item given below.

1. I am a member of the American Counseling Association, the American School Counseling Association, a national certified counselor (NCC) and a national certified school counselor (NCSC).

    Met _____   Partially Met _____   Not Met _____

2. I am prepared to work as a counselor in a diverse, multicultural school setting:

    I have obtained formal instructions, practice and supervision on providing multicultural counseling to school aged student clients.

    Met _____   Partially Met _____   Not Met _____

3. Technology is/will be an integral part of my overall developmental school counseling program:

    I am able to construct a web page, make power point presentations, etc. in support of my personal counseling and school counseling program activities.

    Met _____   Partially Met _____   Not Met _____

4. I remain updated (and have obtained the necessary skills) regarding current social issues that do, and/or will, impact my student clients, i.e. drug use, school violence, etc.:

    I have obtained knowledge and skills regarding the current social issues facing my student clients.

    Met _____   Partially Met _____   Not Met _____

5. I remain abreast and understand the changes in careers and the labor market and how these currently affect my student clients/future student clients:

    I have obtained knowledge about the impact of technology, diversity, and globalization on work/workers and apply (will apply) it as appropriate thorough out my school counseling program.

    Met _____   Partially Met _____   Not Met _____

6. I am competent in mental health (Clinical) counseling skills: both individual and group skills.

I have obtained training and supervision regarding my individual and group counseling skills during the previous 5 years.

Met _____   Partially Met _____   Not Met _____

7. I have knowledge and skills in the latest assessment and diagnosis tools available to me as a school counselor:

I have the knowledge and skills in the latest assessment tools used in my school district as well as the skills to use with individual student clients to formulate a diagnosis as needed.

Met _____   Partially Met _____   Not Met _____

8. I have a copy of the ACA, ASCA and NBCC Ethical Standards and conduct myself accordingly:

I have obtained formal instruction in ethical decision making and have a working knowledge of the current ASCA, NBC, and ACA Ethical Standards.

Met _____   Partially Met _____   Not Met _____

9. I am aware of the referral sources in my community and know when to refer my student clients as needed.

Met _____   Partially Met _____   Not Met _____

During the next year I will seek professional development in the following area(s):

_____

_____

_____

Some Concluding Thoughts

In these 31 chapters the contributing writers and I have described a developmental K-12 school counseling program and have raised some important problems, concerns and issues that school counselors of today and the future will most surely encounter. Additionally, we've provided the school counselor with effective strategies to assist in managing a K-12 developmental school counseling program.

If there is one fundamental theme that serves to tie together the wide array of issues, approaches, and challenges discussed in this book, it is that a school counseling program should serve *all* students in the school as well as *all* teachers, *all* administrators, and *all* parents; the school's entire public. With this theme in mind, in summary, we've written concerning the developmental school counselor's: 1) *goals and objectives* (What are you trying to accomplish? Are your goals in written form and shared with others?) 2) *role and function* (what are you doing to accomplish your goals? Have you "sold" your principal on developmental counseling? Is your role and function statement written and approved by the administration? How are you managing your time? Have you established priorities? Is your "calendar" available to everyone?) 3) *procedures, activities, and tasks needed to carry out your role* (How have you organized your time? Are you conducting individual and small group counseling? Large group guidance? Consulting? Coordinating appropriate programs? Do you have a peer program?) 4) *Are you being accountable?* (Are you "proving" your worth or just 'doing good?" What results are you getting? With whom have you shared these results?) and, 5) *Are you effectively managing your personal and professional growth?* (What contributions are you making to the profession? Do you know, understand and adhere to ASCA's Ethical Standards? Do you stay abreast and updated through continuing education, reading, attending conventions, etc.?)

In a nutshell, these are the important aspects covered in this book. However, whether you use the strategies and advance and achieve the goals and objectives put forth in this book, will be up to you. That is, it does not depend on textbook writers, but on you; school counselors of the present and of the future.

I close this volume with the conviction that those school counselors and others committed to the "developmental" approach to school counseling will welcome the challenges raised, the approaches discussed, and the strategies provided within this book. I appreciate your interest in the book and wish you well!

Joe Wittmer

Index

A

Abuse
    child, 16, 50-53, 68, 116, 149-151, 153-154, 209, 274, 294, 319-320, 358
    emotional, 112, 152, 319
    physical, 151, 153, 166
    prevention, 16, 112, 149, 152, 154, 156, 159, 234, 244, 246-247
    remediation, 156
    sexual, 57, 112, 124, 127, 150, 153-154, 156, 359
    suspected, 320
    victims of child, 149
Accountability
    processes, 273, 275-278, 283
Accreditation
    of counseling, 4, 11-12, 331-332, 334
    CACREP, 1, 4, 9, 11-12, 20, 331, 334
Action Plan, 33-34, 63, 94, 260
Administrative
    functions, 39, 42, 46
    understanding
Administrator, 14, 30-31, 33, 43, 51, 72, 75, 168-169, 178, 183-187, 191, 211, 254, 257, 260, 269, 271-272, 281, 303, 307, 316, 345, 360
Adolescence
    adolescent development, 18, 265
Adult Education, 41, 266, 275, 343
Advanced Placement, 24-25, 79, 90, 166, 225, 352
Advisement, 7, 24, 220, 243, 250
Advisor-Advisee, 51, 243
Advisors
    advisors program, 24, 227, 243, 246
Advisory
    committee, 14-15, 19, 25, 61, 71, 76, 214, 276, 290, 312, 338-339
    council, 7, 264, 267, 272
    program, 24, 46, 51, 77, 127, 220, 227, 243, 246, 251, 253
AIDS, 16, 50, 124, 169, 244, 340
Alcoholics Anonymous, 258
All Handicapped Children Act, 254
AltaVista, 351
American College Testing Program, 21
Annual Guidance Plan, 43
Anti-harassment, 164
Anxiety, 27, 90, 108, 113, 115, 156, 162, 185, 194, 205, 235, 248, 335
AOL, 163
Appreciating Cultural Differences, 39
Aptitude Test, 60, 215, 217, 225

Armed Services Vocational Aptitude Battery, 205
Asian American(s), 137
Asian Pacific Islander, 137, 147
Assessment, 6, 8, 11, 15, 24, 26, 28, 42-43, 47, 49, 57, 76-78, 90, 114, 151, 162, 184, 186, 189, 196, 200, 205-207, 214, 247, 251, 254-256, 264, 276-279, 281-283, 290, 307, 309-310, 325, 332-333, 342-343, 352, 364
Associations
    AACD, 2
    ACA
        ethical standards, 50, 150, 321, 333, 364
    American Counseling Association, 12, 64, 80, 111, 113, 136, 150, 163, 204, 211, 321-322, 333, 336, 360, 363
    ACES, 4, 58, 136
    AERA, 207
    APA, 2, 162-163, 207
    American Psychological Association, 2, 68, 163
    APGA, 2
    ASCA
        conference, 361
        counselor, 29, 270-272, 323
        ethical standards, 205, 361
        ethics committee, 328
        position statement, 150-151
        president, 331
    American School Counseling Association, 7-8, 10-12, 19-20, 24, 29, 56, 58, 62, 70, 80, 150, 165, 176-177, 211, 218, 264, 293, 321-322, 324, 327-328, 331, 333, 335-337, 354, 360, 363
    ASGW, 112-113
    AVA, 211
    American Vocational Association, 221
    CACREP
        manual, 12
        standards, 1, 9, 11-12
    National Education Association, 9, 166
    National Peer Helper Association, 229
    household survey, 17, 246
    merit scholarship, 225
    occupational information, 211, 213-214, 216
    peer helpers association, 229, 337, 340
    school counseling week, 50, 312
    school counselors, 2, 4, 7-12, 19-20, 24, 29, 40, 49, 54, 56, 58, 62, 70, 76, 80, 136, 150, 165, 172, 176-177, 183, 211, 218, 220, 229, 264, 293, 321-322, 324, 326-328, 331, 333, 335-337, 354, 360, 363
    state boards of education, 255, 277, 331, 333
Asynchronous, 348

Joe Wittmer, PhD